Law of Evidence

Combining straightforward explanation with scholarly analysis, *Law of Evidence* introduces students to the full range of topics covered in law of evidence courses, with clarity and depth. Highlighting the context within which the law operates, the textbook maintains an engaging narrative with a strong practical focus. Integrated extracts from key judgments and statutes, as well as academic articles and books, lead students to develop a deeper understanding of the subject, and detailed commentary on these extracts helps students develop the ability to read and analyse case law effectively. Student learning is further supported by numerous visual aids, including diagrams, flowcharts and tables, which illustrate the relationships between principles and provisions and clarify the complex aspects of the law. A companion website with regular updates to the text ensures that students always have the most up-to-date coverage of the law at their fingertips.

NICOLA MONAGHAN is Principal Lecturer in Law at GSM London.

Law of Evidence

NICOLA MONAGHAN

CAMBRIDGE
UNIVERSITY PRESS

University Printing House, Cambridge CB2 8BS, United Kingdom

Cambridge University Press is part of the University of Cambridge.

It furthers the University's mission by disseminating knowledge in the pursuit of
education, learning and research at the highest international levels of excellence.

www.cambridge.org
Information on this title: www.cambridge.org/9781107604612

First published 2015

Printed in the United Kingdom by TJ International Ltd. Padstow Cornwall

A catalogue record for this publication is available from the British Library

Library of Congress Cataloging in Publication data
Monaghan, Nicola (Lawyer) author.
Law of evidence / Nicola Monaghan.
    pages   cm
ISBN 978-1-107-02033-7 (hardback)
1. Evidence (Law) – England.   I. Title.
KD7499.M66   2015
347.42′06–dc23
2014036874

ISBN 978-1-107-02033-7 Hardback
ISBN 978-1-107-60461-2 Paperback

Contents

Figures and tables

TABLES

Table of cases

Table of legislation

UK Statutory Instruments

Preface

The law of evidence is a fascinating subject which covers a range of controversial and complex topics, from the admissibility of confessions and other evidence obtained as a result of police brutality or trickery, to the dangers presented by mistaken visual identification evidence, and the impact of a defendant's refusal to answer questions or the admissibility of his previous convictions on the verdict. Much of the study of the law of evidence focuses on the admissibility of certain types of evidence: the law seeks to control the admissibility of evidence to ensure that the tribunal of fact has access to evidence that is relevant and reliable. The rules governing admissibility are often complicated and nuanced, requiring a solid understanding of more general principles relating to the purpose of the trial process, due process, justice, fairness and legitimacy.

The first two chapters of the book provide an introduction to the subject and to these preliminary principles. Chapter 3 explores matters concerning proof, including the burden and standard of proof in criminal and civil proceedings. Chapters 4 to 6 cover the investigative stage of evidence gathering and focus on the impact of the defendant's silence in the police station on the trial and the admissibility of illegally or improperly obtained evidence, including confession evidence. Chapters 7 and 8 deal with the admissibility of hearsay evidence and character evidence respectively. Chapters 9 and 10 cover the rules relating to the competence and compellability of different categories of witnesses and the testimony given by witnesses, such as the different types of questioning permitted in examination-in-chief and cross-examination. They also deal with the rules relating to the cross-examination of a complainant regarding their sexual history and the measures which may be used to assist an intimidated or vulnerable witness to improve the quality of the evidence that they give. Chapter 11 examines the safeguards provided by the law where the prosecution seeks to rely on hazardous evidence. Chapter 12 considers the admissibility of opinion and expert evidence, and Chapters 13 and 14 explore the rules of disclosure, public interest immunity and privilege.

This book is predominantly written for students studying a module on Evidence at under-graduate level, but it would also serve as an introduction to the subject for students studying Evidence at postgraduate level. The chapters in this book could have been ordered in a variety of different ways and the order in which the chapters are presented here should not deter students or lecturers from approaching the substantive content in a different order. It is certainly not necessary to take these chapters in the order in which I have placed them: the chapters can be taken in any order and where appropriate I have used cross-referencing to assist the reader in identifying areas of overlap and in linking the topics together.

While it is an interesting subject academically, the law of evidence is also of crucial importance for practitioners who must have a precise and detailed understanding of the rules of procedure and evidence, and be able to draw upon this quickly at any moment in court. The law of evidence is in constant development: important legislative reforms take place on an almost annual basis, and the appeal courts regularly interpret these and existing statutory provisions.

The book takes a practical approach to the law of evidence and aims to present the subject in an accessible and engaging manner. Students are sometimes deterred from studying evidence because the subject has a reputation for being technical and difficult. In writing this book, I have sought to make the subject more accessible. I have endeavoured to break down the subject in a structured way and present the legal principles clearly and concisely, setting out the context within which the relevant legal principles operate and explaining how the law works in practice. Where appropriate, I have used visual aids, such as diagrams, flowcharts and tables, to assist the reader by presenting an overview of topics and demonstrating how principles and provisions fit together. I hope that I have achieved my aims and that this approach appeals to students, with the ultimate aim of attracting students to study Evidence modules.

One of the distinguishing features of this book is the incorporation of a range of important extracts from key cases, statute and academic literature to introduce the reader to both original sources and academic commentary. I hope that readers will use these extracts along with the annotated further reading lists at the end of each chapter to delve further into the legal arguments and academic opinions surrounding the subject.

I am grateful to my editor, Valerie Appleby, for her support and guidance throughout the writing process. My thanks are also due to Helen Francis, Marta Walkowiak, Charles Howell, Bethany Gaunt and all at Cambridge University Press who have been involved in the editorial process, design and production of the textbook. I would like to express my sincere thanks to Sinead Moloney, who persuaded me to write this textbook and commissioned it initially, for encouraging me throughout the writing process. Finally, I am also grateful to Chris, for his support and for tolerating me devoting countless weekends to writing.

Any errors are my own. I have endeavoured to state the law as at 1 June 2014.

This book is dedicated to my grandmother, Dee.

Nicola Monaghan
London, June 2014

1 Introduction to the law of evidence

1.1 INTRODUCTION

This book is concerned with the law of evidence which governs the presentation of evidence in criminal and civil proceedings. Rules of evidence transcend all aspects of the trial stage of proceedings. They govern who has to prove what in a trial (the burden of proof) and the level to which those facts have to be proved (the standard of proof). They govern what evidence can go before the court (by the rules relating to relevance and admissibility), the format in which it is presented to the tribunal of fact and the reasons why it may be adduced (i.e. what the evidence goes towards proving or disproving). They ensure that members of the tribunal of fact are provided with guidance (usually by way of a direction from the judge) as to how they should approach their deliberations and what certain evidence may go to prove or disprove. The law of evidence provides rules as to who can be called as a witness (and by which party in proceedings) to give evidence (competence) and who must give evidence if called to do so (compellability). The rules of evidence also dictate the type of questions which may be asked of a particular witness depending upon the party calling them. The law provides safeguards for the protection of vulnerable witnesses in order to maximise the quality of their evidence. The law safeguards against miscarriages of justice by providing rules of evidence and discretionary powers to exclude certain types of evidence or evidence which has been improperly obtained.

1.2 WHAT IS EVIDENCE?

Evidence is information which may be used to prove the existence of a fact in issue or a collateral fact or to disprove a fact in issue or collateral fact. These terms will be explored in paragraphs 1.3.1 and 1.3.3 below.

There are many different types of evidence including the testimony from a witness given in the witness box, forensic evidence, the evidence of identification, evidence in documentary form, and objects (e.g. a weapon). These are merely examples of types of evidence and they do not provide a definition of what evidence is or its purpose.

Before evidence is relied upon by the tribunal of fact (the jury), that evidence must pass three hurdles:

- the evidence must be relevant
- the evidence must be admissible
- the tribunal of fact must consider the evidence to have weight.

These issues of relevance, admissibility and weight will be considered in more detail in Chapter 2. For now it suffices to state that relevance is a question of law for the judge to determine. In order to be admissible, the evidence must be relevant to a fact in issue or collateral issue. Irrelevant evidence will never be admissible. However, just because evidence is relevant, it does not mean that it is automatically admissible. Admissibility is also a question of law for the judge to determine. The rules of evidence largely govern the admissibility of evidence and the bulk of this book is about the admissibility of certain types of evidence. If evidence is ruled inadmissible by an exclusionary rule of law or judicial discretion to exclude evidence, the jury will not see or hear about the evidence. If evidence is ruled admissible, it will then be placed before the jury. The jury will then consider the weight (or cogency) of the evidence (see Figure 1.1).

1.3 TERMINOLOGY

This paragraph explains some of the key terms that will appear throughout the book and with which you need to become familiar.

1.3.1 Facts in issue

A fact in issue (or material fact or *factum propandum*) in a case is a fact which it is necessary for the prosecution (in criminal proceedings) or claimant (in civil proceedings) to prove if it is to succeed with its case. In a criminal trial, the burden of proof is usually on the prosecution, so the prosecution must prove the elements of the offence that the defendant is accused of as well as disprove the defence that he raises. Thus, the facts in issue in a criminal case are all of the elements of the offence and defence that are in dispute as well as the identity of the defendant (i.e. that the defendant in the dock was the person to commit the crime). If the defendant was charged with criminal damage, the prosecution would need to prove that the defendant

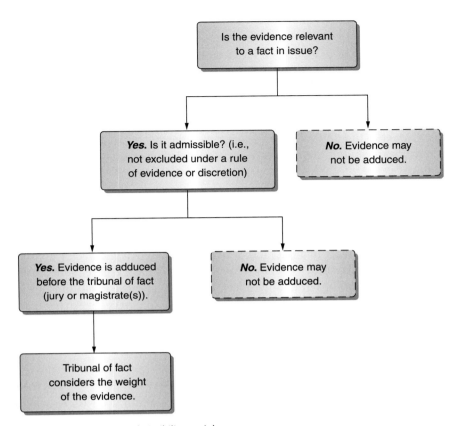

Figure 1.1 Relevance, admissibility, weight

intentionally or recklessly destroyed or damaged property belonging to another without lawful excuse.[1] If the defendant raised the defence of lawful excuse, then the facts in issue would be:

- that the defendant destroyed or damaged property belonging to another;
- that the defendant had no lawful excuse;
- that the defendant intended to destroy or damage the property or was reckless about such destruction or damage.

The prosecution might rely on direct evidence to prove the facts in issue (e.g. witness testimony to the effect that the witness saw the defendant strike the property in question with a hammer).

In a civil action for negligence, the facts in issue would essentially be the disputed factual elements of negligence:

- that the defendant breached the duty of care that he owed the injured party;[2]
- that the breach caused the injury.

---

1 s. 1(1), Criminal Damage Act 1971.
2 The question of whether he owed that duty of care is a question of law rather than fact and thus not a fact in issue.

1.3.2 Relevant facts

A relevant fact (or *factum probans*) is a fact which is not a fact in issue, but is a fact which tends to prove or disprove a fact in issue. For instance, in a criminal case a relevant fact would be the existence or (non-existence) of a motive of the defendant. The existence of a motive is not a fact in issue because it is not a requisite element of any criminal offence (i.e. it does not form part of the *actus reus* or *mens rea* elements of a criminal offence), but it is a relevant fact because motive tends to prove a fact in issue (i.e. that the defendant performed the *actus reus* of the offence charged with the necessary *mens rea*). Evidence of a relevant fact is circumstantial evidence.

1.3.3 Collateral facts

A collateral fact is a fact which is not a fact in issue but is ancillary to a fact in issue. Examples of collateral facts include facts which affect the competence or credibility of a witness or facts which affect the cogency of a piece of evidence. Where there are conditions precedent to the admissibility of another piece of evidence, those conditions are collateral facts. For example, under the 'best' evidence rule[3] a condition precedent to adducing a copy of a document in evidence is proof of the (collateral) fact that the original document is not available.

1.3.4 Formal admissions

Where the parties in criminal or civil proceedings agree about the existence of a fact in issue, they may make formal admissions[4] regarding that fact. A fact which is formally admitted in evidence becomes conclusively proved and ceases to be a fact in issue. Thus, the party who would otherwise bear the burden of proving that fact is relieved from doing so.

1.3.5 Judicial notice

Judicial notice[5] may be taken with respect to a fact which means that the fact is deemed by the judge to have been conclusively established, such that no proof of that fact is required. A judge may judicially note a fact which is of common knowledge without enquiry or he may conduct an enquiry into the matter before doing so by consulting authoritative texts. One example of a fact judicially noted is the ruling that a fortnight is too short a period for human gestation.[6]

---

3 See documentary evidence at paragraph 1.4.4 below.
4 Formal admissions are covered in more detail in Chapter 3.
5 This is covered in more detail in Chapter 3.
6 *R* v. *Luffe* (1807) 8 East 193.

1.4 CATEGORIES OF EVIDENCE

The different categories of evidence that you will come across in your study of the law of evidence are outlined below. It is important to note that there is a degree of overlap between them, so they are not mutually exclusive.

1.4.1 Direct evidence

Direct evidence is evidence which directly proves or disproves a fact in issue. An obvious example of direct evidence might be the oral testimony of a witness given under oath. A witness is only permitted to give evidence as to what they directly perceived (saw, heard, smelt, etc.); the opinion of a witness is not admissible evidence.[7] Thus, in a murder case if a witness gives evidence to the effect that he saw the defendant stab the victim, this constitutes direct evidence of a fact in issue (whether the defendant caused the death of the victim).

1.4.2 Circumstantial evidence

By contrast, circumstantial evidence does not directly prove or disprove a fact in issue. Circumstantial evidence is evidence of a relevant fact from which the existence or non-existence of a fact in issue can be inferred. Examples of circumstantial evidence include: evidence of the defendant's motive, evidence of opportunity (i.e. the defendant's presence at a place at a particular time), evidence of forensic identification (i.e. forensic evidence of a bodily sample or fingerprints found at the scene of the crime that matches similar samples from the defendant), evidence of the possession of incriminating objects (such as a jemmy or paraphernalia associated with the supply of drugs), evidence of the defendant's silence in interview or at trial, evidence of the defendant's preparation to perform a particular act, evidence of the defendant's bad character (such as his propensity to commit certain types of offences), etc.

From each of these examples of circumstantial evidence a relevant fact can be inferred. Thus, from evidence that the defendant was present at a particular place at a particular time, it can be inferred that the defendant had the opportunity to commit the offence. This, of course, is not direct evidence that the defendant did in fact commit the offence and in that sense one piece of circumstantial evidence does not carry as much weight as direct evidence. However, the cumulative effect of a number of separate pieces of circumstantial evidence is to increase the weight of that evidence. This is often expressed through the use of the 'rope analogy': imagine each piece of circumstantial evidence as a strand of a rope. One strand on its own is weak and insufficient to carry a weight, but several strands together increase the strength of the rope which may then carry more weight. In *R* v. *Exall and others*,[8] Pollock CB approves the rope analogy.

---

7 See Chapters 9 and 10 on witnesses and witness testimony and Chapter 12 on opinion evidence.
8 (1866) 176 ER 850 at 853.

R V. EXALL AND OTHERS (1866) 176 ER 850
Pollock CB

[at 853]

It has been said that circumstantial evidence is to be considered as a chain, and each piece of evidence as a link in the chain, but that is not so, for then, if any one link broke, the chain would fall. It is more like the case of a rope composed of several cords. One strand of the cord might be insufficient to sustain the weight, but three stranded together may be quite of sufficient strength.

Thus it may be in circumstantial evidence – there may be a combination of circumstances, no one of which would raise a reasonable conviction, or more than a mere suspicion; but the whole, taken together, may create a strong conclusion of guilt, that is, with as much certainty as human affairs can require or admit of.

1.4.3 Real evidence

Real evidence is evidence which is adduced in court for the tribunal of fact to physically inspect or evidence that the tribunal of fact has directly perceived. Thus, where a witness gives evidence in the witness box, any evidence as to the appearance or demeanour of a witness is real evidence. Similarly, where the jury are shown photographs of the victim's injuries or are played CCTV footage of the offence in court, these are forms of real evidence perceived by the jury. Where a physical object is adduced in court as evidence which tends to prove or disprove a fact in issue, that object is real evidence. Examples of real evidence include a weapon alleged to have been used in committing an offence or the clothing that the victim was to have been wearing at the time of the offence. In a criminal trial on indictment, such objects would be passed to the jury for inspection and they would be asked to draw inferences from that visual inspection. For instance, they might be asked to infer from the weight and shape of the weapon that the defendant intended serious injury or that the tears in a victim's clothing were due to a struggle. A document shown to the jury may be real evidence, but it is also documentary evidence and will be subject to the rules of hearsay (see below).

1.4.4 Documentary evidence

Any written document which is adduced in court as evidence which tends to prove or disprove a fact in issue is documentary evidence. A witness statement is a form of documentary evidence, as are a police officer's notes in his notebook. Other examples of documentary evidence might include documents such as bank statements, receipts, a written contract or a letter. Where documentary evidence is being adduced to prove the truth of its contents, it is technically hearsay evidence and thus is inadmissible. The provisions governing the admissibility of documentary evidence are found under ss. 114(1)(a) and 117, Criminal Justice Act 2003. The admissibility of documentary hearsay will be considered in Chapter 7.

The 'best' evidence rule once provided that only the best evidence was admissible in court. Primary evidence is the 'best' or the highest kind of evidence which can be adduced, such as the original of a document. By contrast, secondary evidence is an inferior kind of evidence, such as the copy of a document. Thus, if documentary evidence was to be adduced, the original had to be used. However, this rule is of limited significance today; in *Garton* v. *Hunter*, Lord Denning MR stated that:

> That old rule has gone by the board long ago. The only remaining instance of it that I know is that if an original document is available in your hands, you must produce it. You cannot give secondary evidence by producing a copy. Nowadays we do not confine ourselves to the best evidence. We admit all relevant evidence. The goodness or badness of it goes only to weight, and not to admissibility.[9]

1.4.5 Testimony

Testimony refers to the evidence given by a witness from the witness box in court or in a witness statement which is read to the court. The subject of witnesses and witness testimony will be explored in Chapters 9 and 10.

1.4.6 Hearsay evidence

Hearsay is an out-of-court statement which is adduced to prove truth of its contents. In criminal proceedings, hearsay is generally inadmissible unless it falls under a paragraph within s. 114(1), Criminal Justice Act 2003. In civil proceedings, hearsay is generally admissible: s. 1(1), Civil Evidence Act 1995. Hearsay evidence will be covered in Chapter 7.

1.4.7 Original evidence

Original evidence is really the direct opposite to hearsay evidence in the sense that it is an out-of-court statement which is adduced not to prove its truth, but to prove that the statement was made. Original evidence is not subject to the rules relating to hearsay evidence, and thus is admissible.

1.5 ISSUES OF CRIMINAL PROCEDURE

Since the study of evidence is inherently linked to the trial,[10] it is useful at this stage to consider briefly some issues of criminal procedure. The subject of civil procedure is not considered here because the rules of evidence are generally more complicated within the criminal justice system. Civil evidence is largely admissible because the tribunal of law and tribunal of fact in a civil trial are the same and usually is a professionally trained lawyer. However, the law of criminal evidence contains more rules regarding the admissibility of certain types of evidence; this is

---

9 [1969] 2 QB 37 at 44.
10 The adversarial nature of the criminal trial will be considered in Chapter 2.

because the tribunal of fact in a criminal case is often a lay tribunal (the jury in the Crown Court or a lay bench of three justices of the peace in the magistrates' court).[11]

All criminal cases begin life with a first appearance in the magistrates' court. At an early stage in proceedings, cases will be allocated to a court based upon the classification of the offence that the defendant has been charged with. All indictable only offences will be sent to the Crown Court under s. 51, Crime and Disorder Act 1998. Summary only offences will remain in the magistrates' court for trial and mode of trial proceedings will take place to determine the venue for trial for either way offences.

The prosecution is subject to duties of pre-trial disclosure of evidence. The concept of pre-trial disclosure supports the defendant's right to a fair trial under Article 6, European Convention on Human Rights by ensuring that the defendant is aware of the evidence against him before trial. The prosecution is subject to duties of disclosure according to which they must disclose to the defence all material which they intend to rely on at court[12] as well as any unused material which might reasonably be considered capable of undermining the prosecution case or assisting the defence.[13] The defence will[14] then serve a defence statement on the prosecution and the prosecution will then serve any further unused material on the defence under its continuing duty of disclosure.[15] (See Figure 1.2.)

Potential applications regarding the admissibility of evidence at trial should be identified early and these applications will be made prior to trial. Examples of potential applications might include applications as to the admissibility of the bad character of the defendant or a non-defendant, the admissibility of hearsay evidence, or for the use of special measures when a vulnerable witness is giving evidence.

When the trial begins[16] the prosecutor will open the case with a speech to the jury and will then call its first witness, who is usually the victim. The prosecution will conduct an examination-in-chief of the witness before tendering the witness to the defence for cross-examination. This will be repeated for each prosecution witness until the prosecution has called all of its witnesses. This is the end of the prosecution case and the 'half-time' period in a trial. At this stage, the defence may choose to make a submission of no case to answer. If successful, the judge will direct the jury to acquit the defendant and the case is over. If this submission fails, the case will continue with the defence case. In a Crown Court trial the defence is only allowed to deliver an opening speech if it is calling a witness as to fact other than the defendant. The defence will then call its witnesses, starting with the defendant. The defence will conduct an examination-in-chief of the witness before tendering the witness to the prosecution for cross-examination. This will be repeated for each defence witness until the defence has called all of its witnesses. This signifies the end of the defence case and by this stage all of the evidence that will be relied upon in the trial has been adduced. The prosecution will then deliver a closing speech and then the defence will do the same. Finally, the judge will sum up the evidence to the

---

11 The exception here is the district judge who also sits alone in the magistrates' court.
12 Advance Information (disclosure of 'used' material) under Part 21, Criminal Procedure Rules.
13 Initial disclosure of 'unused' material under s. 3, Criminal Procedure and Investigations Act 1996 (CPIA 1996).
14 The defence must serve a defence statement if the trial is taking place in the Crown Court (s. 5, CPIA 1996). However, service of a defence statement is optional for a summary trial (s. 6, CPIA 1996).
15 See s. 7A, CPIA 1996.
16 This paragraph focuses on the procedure in a Crown Court trial.

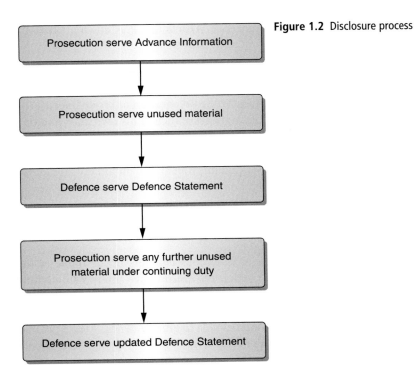

Figure 1.2 Disclosure process

members of the jury and direct them on matters of law before they retire to consider their verdict.

1.6 IMPACT OF THE HUMAN RIGHTS ACT 1998

When the Human Rights Act 1998 came into force on 2 October 2000, the Articles under the European Convention on Human Rights became directly enforceable in our domestic courts. This meant that a defendant could now challenge proceedings on the grounds that the police, prosecution or the courts were in violation of his human rights. Under s. 3(1), HRA 1998 the courts are required to interpret legislation 'so far as it is possible to do so . . . in a way which is compatible with the Convention rights'. The courts have stretched this obligation of interpretation in relation to the compatibility of reverse onuses with Article 6(2). Where the court decides that a 'provision is incompatible with a Convention right, it may make a declaration of that incompatibility' under s. 4(2).

The Convention rights are now invoked daily in the criminal courts. They have had a significant impact upon the rules of criminal procedure and evidence. The most relevant Convention right for the purposes of the law of evidence is Article 6, loosely known as the right to a fair trial. Article 6 is actually made up of a number of different rights that are concerned with providing the defendant with a fair trial. Article 6(1) provides for the right to 'a fair and public hearing within a reasonable time by an independent and impartial tribunal'.

Article 6(2) governs the presumption of innocence. Article 6(3) lays down a number of minimum rights, namely:

(a) to be informed promptly, in a language which he understands and in detail, of the nature and cause of the accusation against him;

(b) to have adequate time and the facilities for the preparation of his defence;

(c) to defend himself in person or through legal assistance of his own choosing or, if he has not sufficient means to pay for legal assistance, to be given it free when the interests of justice so require;

(d) to examine or have examined witnesses against him and to obtain the attendance and examination of witnesses on his behalf under the same conditions as witnesses against him;

(e) to have the free assistance of an interpreter if he cannot understand or speak the language used in court.

You will come across references to Article 6 in various chapters in the book. In Chapter 3, consideration will be given to the way in which the courts have interpreted statutes which appear to place the burden of proof on the defendant in order to ensure compatibility with the Convention right under Article 6(2). Issues relating to Article 6 also arise in relation to the admissibility of hearsay where a witness is unavailable to give evidence,[17] the right to silence[18] and illegally or improperly obtained evidence.[19]

1.7 REFORMS

The law of evidence has been subject to significant reforms over the past 25 years. In 1986 the Police and Criminal Evidence Act 1984 ('PACE Act 1984') came into force. Not only did this Act reform police practices and provide guidance on all aspects of police conduct during the investigative stages of proceedings in the form of Codes of Practice, but the Act provided important provisions governing the exclusion of confession and other improperly obtained evidence.[20]

The Criminal Justice and Public Order Act 1994 had a great impact on the right to silence at the police station or at trial, providing that 'such inferences as appear proper' can be drawn against a defendant in certain circumstances.[21] The Youth Justice and Criminal Evidence Act 1999 provided a new statutory framework to improve the quality of the evidence of vulnerable or intimidated witnesses. The 1999 Act provides for special measures (such as the use of a screen, live link or the removal of wigs and gowns) to be used where eligible witnesses give evidence.

---

17 See Chapter 7 on hearsay.

18 See Chapter 4 on silence.

19 See Chapter 6 on illegally and improperly obtained evidence.

20 Sections 76 and 78. See Chapter 5 on confession evidence and Chapter 6 on illegally and improperly obtained evidence.

21 See Chapter 4.

The changes to the law of evidence have been just as significant in the last decade. In 2001, Auld LJ conducted a review into the criminal courts[22] in which he made numerous recommendations about criminal procedure. In respect of the admissibility of evidence, Auld LJ recommended that there was:

> an urgent need for a comprehensive review of the whole law of criminal evidence to make it a simple and an efficient agent for ensuring that all criminal courts are told all and only what they need to know. I believe that an important part of this exercise should be an examination of the justice and feasibility of a general move away from rules of inadmissibility to trusting fact finders to give relevant evidence the weight it deserves.[23]

Auld LJ's recommendation was essentially that the law of evidence should take an inclusionary approach to the admissibility of evidence, rather than an exclusionary approach, which existed in 2001. His Lordship took the view that the justice system ought to trust juries to 'give relevant evidence the weight it deserves', thus shifting the traditional focus of the law of evidence from questions of admissibility to questions of weight. The Auld review led to the enactment of the Criminal Justice Act 2003 in which Parliament adopted some of the recommendations made by Auld LJ. The 2003 Act radically reformed the law relating to disclosure, the admissibility of character evidence and hearsay. The Act did adopt a more inclusionary approach to the admissibility of both evidence of character and hearsay. We will consider these reforms in Chapter 13 (disclosure), Chapter 8 (character) and Chapter 7 (hearsay).

More recently, Parliament's focus has returned to the law relating to witness testimony with provisions for the delivery of evidence by an anonymous witness with witness anonymity orders under ss. 86–97, Coroners and Justice Act 2009 (repealing most of the provisions of the short-lived Criminal Evidence (Witness Anonymity) Act 2008). The most current topic of reform within the law of evidence is that relating to expert evidence. In light of a number of miscarriages of justice involving unreliable expert evidence, the Law Commission published its Report on *Expert Evidence in Criminal Proceedings*[24] in March 2011. In the Report, the Commission recommends a new test of reliability for the admissibility of expert opinion evidence and produces a draft Bill. At the time of writing, Parliament has not yet responded to these recommendations.

Further reading

C. Allen, *Practical Guide to Evidence* (Routledge Cavendish, 2008), ch. 1.
This chapter provides a Wigmorean analysis of Dr Crippen's case, explores the concepts of relevance, admissibility and weight, and considers the terminology used within the law of evidence.

---

22 *A Review of the Criminal Courts of England and Wales* (2001) accessible at www.criminal-courts-review.org.uk (accessed on 18 July 2014).
23 Ibid. at para. 77.
24 Law Commission Report, *Expert Evidence in Criminal Proceedings* (Law Com. No. 325, HC 829, HMSO, 2011). This report will be considered in Chapter 12 on opinion and expert evidence.

Blackstone's Criminal Practice 2015 (Oxford University Press), Section F1.

This is a comprehensive practitioners' text. Section F1 of the text explores the general principles of evidence in criminal cases.

R. Pattenden, 'Authenticating "things" in English law: principles for adducing tangible evidence in common law jury trials' [2008] E&P 273.

This article explores the nature and general principles of authentication of tangible evidence. It identifies the roles of the judge and jury in authenticating tangible evidence and examines principles of authentication in relation to different types of evidence.

S. Phipson, '"Real" evidence' (1920) 29 *Yale Law Journal* 705.

This article considers the definitions given to the term 'real evidence' by other academics and questions whether the term is worth preserving in light of the fact that it is not used in practice.

C. Tapper, *Cross and Tapper on Evidence*, 12th edn (2010), pp. 1–64.

These pages explore the development of the law of evidence, different types of proceedings and the objects and means of proof.

2 Preliminary issues

2.1 INTRODUCTION

Television programmes featuring court proceedings often portray the trial process as pompous, overly dramatic, aggressively adversarial and dominated by an heroic counsel who elicits vital and previously unrealised evidence from a shaken witness while gasps of shock echo around the public gallery. The reality of court proceedings is very different. Proceedings are generally slow-moving and drama-free; the principle of open justice requires that evidence is disclosed during pre-trial stages, so shocks involving the admission of new evidence of the magnitude displayed on television dramas are rare. This chapter explores some of the fundamental principles of the law of evidence. We will begin by looking at the adversarial nature of the criminal trial and we will compare the key features of both adversarial and inquisitorial systems. We will explore the role of the judge and the jury in the trial process. We will briefly consider some of the fundamental aspects of the law of evidence, including the models of criminal justice systems, the concepts of truth, due process, justice and fairness in the proceedings, and the legitimacy principle. The final paragraph of this chapter will be devoted to a consideration of the crucial principles of relevance, admissibility and weight, with a particular focus on the meaning of relevance.

2.2 THE ADVERSARIAL NATURE OF THE CRIMINAL TRIAL

This paragraph of the chapter looks at the nature of the criminal trial. The criminal justice system in England and Wales operates on the basis of an adversarial system. By contrast, the Continental system is generally inquisitorial. In the adversarial system, the prosecution and defence act as opposing parties in a battle. The prosecution will call evidence to prove that the defendant is guilty of the offence charged, and this means that witnesses will be called to give oral evidence in front of the judge and jury. The oral evidence of a witness is required in accordance with the principle of orality. Counsel for the defence will often make an emotive closing speech, urging the jury to acquit the defendant. It is easy to see why adversarial trials feature in so many television programmes: the courtroom is a great stage setting. In the extract below, John Jackson explores the procedures and rituals of the adversarial trial.

J. JACKSON, 'MANAGING UNCERTAINTY AND FINALITY: THE FUNCTION OF THE CRIMINAL TRIAL IN LEGAL INQUIRY' IN A. DUFF, L. FARMER, S. MARSHALL AND V. TADROS (EDS.), *THE TRIAL ON TRIAL VOLUME 1: TRUTH AND DUE PROCESS* (HART PUBLISHING, 2004)

[at p. 134]

Critics of the modern adversarial trial and the exclusionary rules associated with it have viewed it as an aberration from a rationalist theory of proof whereby triers of fact are given free rein to make inquiries as to the facts and draw their own conclusions as to guilt . . . the modern adversarial trial has retained a number of key irrational vestiges from its past . . . the oral tradition whereby witnesses swear to the truth of the facts at a public hearing has been retained. The oath continues to play an important ritualistic role in the modern trial . . . The lay jury has also been retained as the body responsible for handing down the verdict and a number of rituals associated with the jury have been retained in many jurisdictions, such as the public summation by the judge to the jury of the law and the facts, the secrecy of the deliberation process that follows upon the summation, and the sphinx-verdict that emerges from this deliberation without any indication of the reasons behind it. The adversary trial itself has also assumed a number of ritualistic formalities as battle lines are drawn up between the two sides, each with their own respective teams of witnesses who give evidence in a courtroom which is laid out in a highly formalised manner, the witness box representing the central stage but with other equally significant props such as the elevated bench from which the judge presides on high and the much more lowly 'dock' where the prisoner sits. The symbols communicated by the bible placed beside the witness box, the raised dais for the judge and the lowly position of the dock are further reinforced by the red ermine traditionally worn by the judge and the wigs and gowns of the learned counsel.

The judge's role in an adversarial trial is largely one of an umpire. The judge is permitted to ask questions but will generally do so only to clarify matters; he does not take on the role of investigator or inquirer, as he would under an inquisitorial system. The jury (in a Crown Court trial) is the tribunal of fact and will decide whether the defendant is guilty or not.

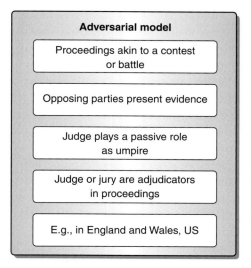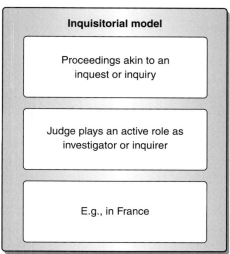

Figure 2.1 Comparing adversarial and inquisitorial models of the criminal justice system

J. JACKSON AND S. DORAN, 'THE UMPIREAL ROLE OF THE JUDGE' IN *JUDGE WITHOUT JURY* (OXFORD UNIVERSITY PRESS, 1995)

[at p. 58]

The heart of the contrast between adversarial and inquisitorial models of proof is that while one is essentially a contest, the other is essentially an inquiry or inquest. The adversarial model emphasises the role of contestants and regulates what contestants may or may not do, with much less attention being given to the activities of inquirers.

In an inquisitorial system, the judge is more of an inquisitor or investigator and the proceedings are more akin to an inquest or inquiry. The focus of the inquisitorial system is on finding out the truth of what happened. The judge plays an active role in gathering evidence before the court. The judge controls the investigation and prepares a written report of the evidence to put before another judge for trial. Figure 2.1 above summarises some of the main features in adversarial and inquisitorial models of the criminal justice system.

2.3 THE ROLES OF JUDGES AND THE JURY

In civil proceedings, a professional judge is the arbiter of fact and law. In criminal proceedings, the tribunals of fact and law vary according to the mode of trial. The most serious cases are tried in the Crown Court where the tribunals of fact and law are separate bodies: a lay jury acts as the tribunal of fact while a professional judge presides over the trial as the tribunal of law. The judge and the jury are both key institutions of the criminal trial but they have very different roles in the trial process. Questions of law are for the judge to determine and include issues relating to the admissibility of evidence, such as the admissibility of evidence of the defendant's bad character, hearsay evidence, illegally or improperly obtained evidence, or whether it is necessary to direct the jury in relation to adverse inferences from silence. Questions of fact are for the jury to decide upon, so it is for the jury to decide what the facts of the case are and whether the defendant is guilty of the offence charged or not. They will reach their decisions on the facts based upon the evidence they have heard and the directions on the law given to them by the judge. The least serious cases are tried in the magistrates' court in front of a bench of three lay magistrates or one professional district judge. The magistrates (or district judge) act as both the tribunal of law and the tribunal of fact, thus, since there is no jury in the magistrates' court, the tribunals of fact and law are mixed. This becomes significant in trials in which the magistrates are required to decide upon the admissibility of evidence which is potentially prejudicial to the defendant (a question of law) prior to deciding upon whether the defendant is guilty or not (a question of fact). For instance, if the magistrates decide to exclude evidence of the defendant's previous convictions under the Criminal Justice Act 2003, or if they decide that evidence should be inadmissible under s. 78 of the Police and Criminal Evidence Act 1984 on the basis that its admission would have an adverse effect on the fairness of the proceedings, they will then require themselves to disregard the evidence when they come to make their decision as to whether the defendant is guilty or not. This provides magistrates with a potentially difficult task where the evidence that has been excluded was highly prejudicial.

2.3.1 Role of the judge

As stated above, questions of law are for the judge in a Crown Court or the magistrates in a magistrates' court.[1] The judge (or magistrates) will decide upon questions such as the competence and compellability of witnesses, the extent to which any special measures might be used in relation to the evidence of a vulnerable or intimidated witness, the admissibility of evidence and, in the case of a Crown Court trial, the directions which should be given to the jury. At the end of the trial in a Crown Court, the trial judge will deliver a summing up speech to the jury.

Summing up to the jury

In summing up the case, the judge will summarise the evidence that was given in the trial before directing the jury on the law. In summarising the evidence to the jury, the judge is permitted to comment on the evidence in the case and express confident views on the evidence. However, if the judge's comments go too far such that he effectively invites the jury to share his view and taken as a whole the summing up is fundamentally unbalanced and unfair, the defendant's conviction should be quashed.[2] The trial judge will go too far if he usurps the functions of the jury.[3]

---

1 On the role of the judge in a criminal trial, see P. Otton, 'The role of the judge in criminal cases' in M. McConville and G. Wilson, *The Handbook of The Criminal Justice Process* (Oxford University Press, 2002); D. Pannick, *Judges* (Oxford University Press, 1988).
2 *Winn-Pope* [1996] Crim LR 521, CA.
3 *Mears* v. *R* (1993) 97 Cr App R 239.

In directing the jury on the law, the judge must inform the jury of the respective functions of the judge and jury, direct them on the burden and standard of proof and address any legal issues which have arisen during the course of the trial. In *Jackson*[4] the Court of Appeal provided a suggested direction on the respective functions of the judge and jury in a criminal trial.

JACKSON [1992] CRIM LR 214, CA

[Suggested direction on the respective functions of the judge and jury, at p. 214]

It is my job to tell you what the law is and how to apply it to the issues of fact that you have to decide and to remind you of the important evidence on these issues. As to the law, you must accept what I tell you. As to the facts, you alone are the judges. It is for you to decide what evidence you accept and what evidence you reject or of which you are unsure. If I appear to have a view of the evidence or of the facts with which you do not agree, reject my view. If I mention or emphasise evidence that you regard as unimportant disregard that evidence. If I do not mention what you regard as important, follow your own view and take that evidence into account.

Until 2010, trial judges relied upon specimen directions published by the Judicial Studies Board to direct the jury on the law. However, the specimen directions were replaced by the *Crown Court Bench Book: Directing the Jury*,[5] which aimed to 'move away from the perceived rigidity of specimen directions towards a fresh emphasis on the responsibility of the individual judge, in an individual case, to craft directions appropriate to that case'.[6]

The judge as a fact-finder

In some circumstances a trial judge may also be required to make decisions on questions of fact in a Crown Court trial. For example, where the defence makes a submission of no case to answer, the judge may be required to consider the weight of the evidence that has been adduced by the prosecution, including the credibility of prosecution witnesses.[7] Another example would be where a *voir dire* ('a trial within a trial') takes place to determine matters such as the admissibility of confession evidence which the defence claims was obtained by oppression. In deciding whether or not to exclude the evidence under s. 76(2)(a) of the Police and Criminal Evidence Act 1984, the judge will hear evidence from witnesses as to the circumstances of the confession before deciding on the facts whether the confession was obtained by oppression or not.

---

4 [1992] Crim LR 214, CA.

5 Judicial Studies Board, *Crown Court Bench Book: Directing the Jury* (March 2010). The Bench Book can be found at www.judiciary.gov.uk/publications-and-reports/judicial-college/Pre%202011/crown-court-bench-book-directing-the-jury (accessed on 18 July 2014).

6 Ibid. in the foreword by Sir Igor Judge (former LCJ) at p. v.

7 There are two limbs to the test in *Galbraith* [1981] 1 WLR 1039 which requires the trial judge to stop the case if (i) there is no evidence, or (ii) the evidence is so tenuous that taken at its highest no jury could properly convict on it.

Judges as umpires

Judges are often said to act as umpires in the contested battle of an adversarial trial. The notion of an umpire implies a relatively passive role whereby the judge merely ensures that the proceedings are fair and that the parties act within the rules of the battle. By contrast, a trial judge in an inquisitorial system would act more like an investigator or inquirer, asking questions of witnesses in order to establish the evidence. In the criminal justice system of England and Wales, the trial judge certainly plays an important role in ensuring that the defendant has a fair trial and that the rules of evidence and procedure are followed, but a judge is also permitted to ask questions of witnesses, albeit he must exercise restraint in intervening.[8]

The extent to which judges should have a passive or an active role in trial proceedings is considered by John Jackson and Sean Doran in the extract below from *Judge without Jury*.

J. JACKSON AND S. DORAN, 'THE UMPIREAL ROLE OF THE JUDGE' IN *JUDGE WITHOUT JURY* (OXFORD UNIVERSITY PRESS, 1995)

[at pp. 99–100]

On one view, the judge's role should be kept essentially flexible in criminal trials because although the umpireal ideal should be aspired to, judges ... have specific responsibilities in criminal trials which may require greater judicial intervention. The one judicial statement which is frequently quoted as encompassing the umpireal ideal is indeed to be found in the context of a civil and not a criminal case:

> The judge's part in all this is to hearken to the evidence, only himself asking questions of witnesses when it is necessary to clear up any point that has been overlooked or left obscure; to see that the advocates behave themselves seemly and keep to the rules laid down by law; to exclude irrelevancies and discourage repetition; to make sure by wise intervention that he follows the points the advocates are making and can assess their worth; and at the end to make up his mind where the truth lies. [Footnote: *Jones* v. *National Coal Board* [1957] 2 QB 55, 64.]

Lord Denning's statement of the trial judge's function can be viewed as approaching the adversary ideal, stressing that, while not a passive observer, the judge should intervene only to keep the proceedings orderly and to ensure that the rules of evidence and procedure are observed by the parties. It has been generally accepted as applying also to the criminal trial judge. Of course, the closing reference to the ultimate decision on the 'truth' is inapposite as regards the judge's role in a jury trial but adherence to the umpireal role is, if anything, more important in jury trials because of the clear risk that juries may become unduly influenced by judicial intervention.

---

8 See *Archbold Criminal Pleading Evidence and Practice 2013*, para. 8–300. Also see *R* v. *Marsh, The Times*, 6 July 1993, in which the trial judge interrupted the witness more than ninety times. The Court of Appeal held that the trial judge should not interrupt a witness while they are giving evidence because it might prevent the witness from presenting his case. In *Jahree* v. *State of Mauritius* [2005] 1 WLR 1952, the Privy Council emphasised the particular importance of the judge refraining from interrupting a witness in a jury trial because the jury might be unfairly influenced by the judge's questioning.

2.3.2 Role of the jury

A jury[9] is made up of 12 lay people who are:

- aged between 18 and 70,[10]
- ordinarily resident in the UK for at least 5 years since the age of 18,[11]
- not disqualified for jury service,[12] and
- on the electoral role.[13]

In a criminal trial in the Crown Court, the jury is the tribunal of fact, responsible for deciding upon questions of fact. The ultimate question of fact, namely whether the defendant is guilty or not guilty of the offence charged, is left for the jury to decide. Jurors take an oath or affirm when they are empanelled to 'faithfully try the defendant and give a true verdict according to the evidence'.[14] Thus, their role is to listen to the evidence given during the trial and to decide whether the defendant is guilty or not of the offences charged based upon that evidence.

The right to jury trial

The 'right to trial by jury' is a very limited one. A defendant will only be tried by a jury if he is charged with an indictable offence[15] and is to be tried in the Crown Court. Where the defendant is charged with an indictable only offence, the case will be sent to the Crown Court after a first appearance in the magistrates' court under s. 51, Crime and Disorder Act 1998. If the defendant is charged with an either way offence, the magistrates may reject jurisdiction of the case if they deem it to be too serious to be tried in the magistrates' court. In such circumstances, the defendant will have no choice but to be tried in the Crown Court. Where the magistrates accept jurisdiction of the case, the defendant may invoke his right to be tried by a jury and elect to be tried in the Crown Court. Consequently, only a very small percentage of criminal cases are tried in the Crown Court; the vast majority of criminal cases (over 95 per cent) are dealt with in the magistrates' courts.[16] The right to trial by jury has been threatened repeatedly over the past few decades. In 1999, the government proposed to limit the right to trial by jury by reclassifying the

---

9 On the role of the jury in the criminal trial, see J. Baldwin and M. McConville, *Jury Trials* (Oxford University Press, 1979); W. R. Cornish, *The Jury* (Allen Lane/The Penguin Press, 1968); Lord Devlin, *Trial by Jury* (Stevens, 1956); S. Enright and J. Morton, *Taking Liberties: The Criminal Jury in the 1990s* (Weidenfield & Nicolson, 1990); P. Ferguson, 'The criminal jury in England and Scotland: the confidentiality principle and the investigation of impropriety' (2006) 10 E & P 180; M. Findlay and P. Duff, *The Jury Under Attack* (Butterworths, 1988); J. Gastill, E. P. Deess, P. J. Weiser and C. Simmons, *The Jury and Democracy: How Jury Deliberation Promotes Civil Engagement and Political Participation* (Oxford University Press, 2010); V. P. Hans and N. Vidmar, *Judging the Jury* (Perseus Publishing, 1986); J. Jackson and S. Doran, *Judge without Jury* (Oxford University Press, 1995); L. McGowan, 'Trial by jury: still a lamp in the dark?' (2005) 69 JCL 518; N. Vidmar (ed), *World Jury Systems* (Oxford University Press, 2000).
10 Section 1(1)(a), Juries Act 1974. The upper limit will be changed to 75 by the Criminal Justice and Courts Bill 2014.
11 Section 1(1)(b), Juries Act 1974.
12 Section 1(1)(d), Juries Act 1974.
13 Section 3, Juries Act 1974.
14 *Consolidated Criminal Practice Direction* at para. IV.42.4.
15 Note that this phrase refers to both indictable only offences and either way offences.
16 See A. Ashworth and M. Redmayne, *The Criminal Process*, 4th edn (Oxford University Press, 2010) at p. 323 and A. Sanders, R. Young and M. Burton, ibid. at p. 554.

either way offences with the Criminal Justice (Mode of Trial) Bill. The Bill failed to win approval in the House of Lords and the government tried again with the Criminal Justice (Mode of Trial) (No. 2) Bill in 2000. However, this also failed to win approval in the House of Lords. Despite these unsuccessful attempts, Parliament did enact two provisions in the Criminal Justice Act 2003 under which the prosecution could apply for a judge-only trial for complex fraud trials (s. 43, Criminal Justice Act 2003) or where there is a real and present danger of jury tampering (s. 44, Criminal Justice Act 2003). Section 43 of the Criminal Justice Act 2003 was never brought into force and was repealed by the Protection of Freedoms Act 2012. Section 44 of the Criminal Justice Act 2003 was brought into force and the first judge-only trial to take place under this provision was *R* v. *Twomey (John)*.[17]

Protecting the jury: the secrecy rule and juror misconduct

The jury has generally been celebrated as a 'hallowed institution' of the criminal justice system.[18] Sir William Blackstone described the jury as the 'sacred bulwark of the nation',[19] while Baldwin and McConville have stated that the jury is 'the corner-stone of the criminal trial'.[20] Lay participation in the administration of justice is effected through the civic duty of jury service and thus the jury is representative of the freedom of the citizens of England and Wales: Lord Devlin famously described the jury as 'the lamp that shows that freedom lives'.[21] The deliberations of the jury are a closely guarded secret protected from disclosure by common law and s. 8 of the Contempt of Court Act 1981.[22] Investigating into the deliberations of the jury is prohibited for three reasons:

1. in order to encourage jurors to speak freely in the jury room, without fear of reprisals (promotion of candour),
2. to protect the finality of the verdict by ensuring that the decision-making process is not subject to scrutiny, and
3. to protect the privacy of jurors.[23]

There have always been cases of juror misconduct,[24] but while it is recognised that individual jurors sometimes misbehave and fail to discharge their duty in the way that they should, the

---

17   [2011] 1 WLR 1681.

18   Auld LJ, *A Review of the Criminal Courts of England and Wales* (2001), ch. 5, para. 1.

19   Sir William Blackstone, *Commentaries on the Laws of England* (1765–1769), Book IV, Chapter 27, 'Public Wrongs', p. 344.

20   J. Baldwin and M. McConville, *Jury Trials* (Oxford University Press, 1979), p. 1.

21   Lord Devlin, *Trial by Jury* (Stevens, 1956), p. 164.

22   See *Ellis* v. *Deheer* [1922] 2 KB 113 and *R* v. *Mirza*; *R* v. *Connor and Rollock* [2004] 1 AC 1118, HL.

23   See N. Haralambous, 'Investigating impropriety in jury deliberations: a recipe for disaster?' 68 *Journal of Criminal Law* 411 at 414 and N. Monaghan, 'Protecting the secret deliberations of the jury in the interests of efficiency – has the law "lost its moral underpinning"?' in C. Monaghan and N. Geach (eds.), *Dissenting Judgments in Law* (Wildy, Simmonds & Hill, 2012).

24   For example, see *Vaise* v. *Delaval* (1785) 1 TR 11 in which the jurors tossed a coin to decide upon guilt; *R* v. *Young* [1995] QB 324 in which the jurors used a Ouija board to ask the spirits if the defendant was guilty or not; *R* v. *Qureshi* [2002] 1 WLR 518, CA and *R* v. *Mirza*; *R* v. *Connor & Rollock* [2004] 1 AC 1118, HL in which some jurors expressed racist views and based their decision to convict upon these prejudices and some jurors bullied other jurors; *Attorney General* v. *Scotcher* [2003] EWHC 1380 (Admin) in which jurors neglected their duties by changing their vote in order to be able to get out of the jury room and go home; *R* v. *Cadman* [2008]

integrity of the system is safeguarded by having twelve jurors on a jury. Thus, even where one juror does misbehave, there are eleven other jurors to put him straight and ensure that a true verdict is reached according to the evidence. However, in recent years there have been several reported cases of jurors using the internet to conduct research online or social networking websites to disclose or share jury deliberations.[25] It is submitted that these cases threaten to undermine the integrity of the jury system.[26] In light of the recent attention on jury misconduct, a Practice Direction on 'jury irregularities' was handed down by Sir John Thomas, then the President of the Queen's Bench Division of High Court,[27] and this has since been consolidated in Criminal Practice Direction of the Senior Courts.[28] More recently, the Criminal Justice and Courts Bill 2014 proposes to create four new criminal offences of jury misconduct, including research by jurors, sharing research with other jurors, jurors engaging in other prohibited conduct and disclosing jury deliberations. In their current form, each of the offences is indictable only and carries a maximum sentence of imprisonment of two years.

2.4 FUNDAMENTAL ASPECTS OF THE LAW OF EVIDENCE

This paragraph of the chapter briefly considers some of the fundamental aspects of the law of evidence. We will explore Packer's famous models of the criminal justice system, the concept of truth, due process, justice and fairness in the proceedings, before examining the legitimacy principle and the principle of open justice.

2.4.1 Models of the criminal justice system

Herbert Packer famously espoused two models of the criminal justice system: a 'crime control' model and a 'due process' model.[29] The main objective of the 'crime control' model is the repression of criminal behaviour through the apprehension and conviction of offenders. The focus in this model is on the abilities of the police and prosecuting authorities to achieve a high

---

EWCA Crim 1418 in which the jury conducted their own handwriting comparisons in the jury room; and *R* v. *Boseley (Paul)*, unreported, Worcester Crown Court, 31 July 2008 in which the jury carried out experiments in the jury room by trying to tear underwear they had bought in order to test the truth of a witness's evidence.

25 For example, see *R* v. *Karakaya* [2005] 2 Cr App R 77 in which at least one juror used the internet to conduct research on the case; *Attorney General* v. *Fraill and others* [2011] EWHC 1629 (Admin) in which a juror was convicted of contempt of court after she contacted a defendant on Facebook, struck up a friendship with her and revealed details of jury deliberations; and *Attorney General* v. *Dallas* [2012] EWHC 156 (Admin) in which a juror was also convicted of contempt of court after she conducted research into the defendant on the internet.

26 For further discussion on jury misconduct and this point, see N. Haralambous, 'Investigating impropriety in jury deliberations: a recipe for disaster?' (2004) 68 *Journal of Criminal Law* 411, N. Haralambous, 'Educating jurors: technology, the internet and the jury system' (2010) 19(3) *Information and Communications Technology Law* 255 and N. Monaghan, 'The problem of jury misbehaviour in an internet age: recent cases and the Law Commission's consultation' (2013) 18(1) *Coventry Law Journal* 69.

27 *Practice Direction (Crown Court: Jury Irregularities)* [2013] 1 WLR 486.

28 *Practice Direction (Criminal Proceedings)* [2013] 1 WLR 3164.

29 H. L. Packer, 'Two models of the criminal process' (1964) 113 *Pennsylvania Law Review* 1–68. Also see D. McBarnet, *Conviction* (1981), Macmillan on the distinction between ideological theory and substantive law.

apprehension and conviction rate speedily and with finality. By contrast, while the 'due process' model does not deny 'the social desirability of repressing crime', it questions the reliability of human fact-finding and has as its main objective the removal of the possibility of error in conviction. As such, the 'due process' model focuses on the protection of citizens from wrongful conviction through the use of safeguards and checks in procedures. Packer likened the 'crime control' model to a conveyor belt, while the 'due process' model was like an obstacle course.[30] These two models are not polar opposites and it is difficult to label the English criminal justice system as wholly 'crime control' or 'due process'; rather, our system draws on elements of each of the models in its operation.

2.4.2 Truth

While the inquisitorial system of trial is clearly truth-centred with the trial judge acting as an investigator to determine the facts, the adversarial system is less truth-centred.[31] We have already seen how the adversarial trial is more like a contest or a battle between two parties: the prosecutor, whose objective is to discharge the burden of proof to the high criminal standard of beyond reasonable doubt; and defence counsel, whose objective is to raise a doubt in the minds of the fact-finders. To put it another way, the prosecutor's job is to make the fact-finders sure that the defendant is guilty, while defence counsel will hope to inject doubt into their minds such that they cannot be sure of his guilt.

> **Cross-reference**
> Refer to Chapter 3 for a more detailed discussion of the burden and standard of proof in both criminal and civil proceedings.

However, this is not to say that an adversarial trial is not concerned with the truth. As we have seen above, jurors take an oath or affirm to 'give a true verdict according to the evidence' and witnesses called to give evidence take an oath or affirm to 'tell the truth, the whole truth and nothing but the truth'. Having heard the evidence in a trial, fact-finders are asked to decide what happened. They must ultimately decide whether the defendant is guilty of the offence charged or not, and this may involve them making decisions as to what the facts were, what happened in the minutes leading up to the crime and during the commission of the offence itself, i.e. what the truth was. Truth, justice and due process go hand in hand: in determining what the truth is, the fact-finder is trying to ensure that justice is done, that due process is observed. However, as Ho observes, 'it is not only the case that truth is needed to do justice; the court must do justice *in* finding the truth'.[32]

---

30 Packer (n. 29) at 11 and 13.

31 See H. Jung, 'Nothing but the truth? Some facts, impressions and confessions about truth in criminal procedure' in A. Duff, L. Farmer, S. Marshall and V. Tadros (eds.), *The Trial on Trial Volume 1: Truth and Due Process* (Hart Publishing, 2004), pp. 147–56 and H. L. Ho, *A Philosophy of Evidence Law: Justice in the Search for Truth* (Oxford University Press, 2008), pp. 51–84.

32 H. L. Ho, *A Philosophy of Evidence Law: Justice in the Search for Truth* (Oxford University Press, 2008), p. 51.

2.4.3 Due process, justice and fairness in the proceedings

The law of evidence provides for rules and discretion that govern the admissibility of evidence in a trial. The rules and discretion that provide for the exclusion of evidence do so in order to ensure due process in the trial and fairness to the proceedings. For example, s. 76(2)(a), Police and Criminal Evidence Act 1984 provides a rule of law which requires the exclusion of confession evidence that has been obtained by oppression. Due process is concerned with error-free verdicts and the exclusion of such evidence works as a safeguard against error. It could be said that the evidence is excluded because of the risk that it is unreliable (or untrue) or out of the protection of the defendant's rights which have been violated, or in order to protect the integrity of the system. Whatever the reason, the exclusion of the evidence ensures that the proceedings are fair. Similarly, there is a discretion to exclude evidence at common law where its prejudicial effect outweighs its probative value[33] and there is a statutory discretion to exclude evidence if its admission would have such an adverse effect on the fairness of proceedings that it ought not to be admitted.[34] This discretion is concerned with ensuring that the trial (or proceedings) is/are fair.

> **Cross-reference**
> Refer to Chapter 6 for a more detailed discussion on the exclusionary rules and discretion to exclude at common law and under statute.

2.4.4 Legitimacy principle

Espoused by Professor Dennis, the legitimacy principle holds that the overriding objective in the criminal trial is the promotion of the legitimacy of the decision. Dennis states that while accuracy of the verdict is a major part of this principle, other notions of integrity and acceptability are also important: '[t]he aims will be to promote legitimacy of decision-making in adjudication through law designed to ensure that verdicts and judgments are factually accurate and morally authoritative'.[35] Thus, the rules and discretion to exclude evidence operate to ensure the legitimacy of the verdict. Dennis states that unreliable evidence could need to be excluded in order to protect the moral authority of the verdict.[36]

2.4.5 Open justice

The courts operate on the principle of open justice. In *R (Guardian News and Media Ltd)* v. *City of Westminster Magistrates' Court*, Toulson LJ stated that open justice is a 'principle at the heart of our system of justice and vital to the rule of law'.[37] Most court proceedings are open to the

---

33 *R* v. *Sang* [1980] AC 402, HL.
34 Section 78, Police and Criminal Evidence Act 1984.
35 I. H. Dennis, *The Law of Evidence*, 5th edn (Sweet & Maxwell, 2013) at pp. 51–62.
36 Ibid. at p. 55.
37 [2013] QB 618 at 630.

public and courtrooms include a public gallery in which anyone can sit to watch the workings of the court. Controversially, since 2013 cameras have been allowed into the Supreme Court and the Court of Appeal, and court proceedings are now streamed live.[38] To date, permitting cameras into the courtroom has had a mixed response,[39] but at the time of writing there is a suggestion that this will soon be extended to Crown Courts such that criminal trials might be streamed live. Toulson LJ further stated that an exception to the principle of open justice can only be accepted if it is 'justified by some even more important principle'.[40] Sections 6 to 14 of the Justice and Security Act 2013 provide for a new and highly controversial 'closed material procedure' under which courts may sit secretly in civil cases which would otherwise involve the disclosure of sensitive material that it would not be in the public interest to disclose.

Cross-reference

Refer to Chapter 13 on disclosure and Chapter 14 on privilege.

2.5   RELEVANCE, ADMISSIBILITY AND WEIGHT

Most of the chapters in this book deal with questions of the admissibility of evidence. However, before the question of the admissibility of evidence is considered, the evidence must first be relevant to a fact in issue in the case. Evidence which is irrelevant is inadmissible. Evidence must be relevant to a fact in issue if it is to be deemed to be admissible. This does not mean that all relevant evidence is admissible; relevant evidence may be deemed to be inadmissible for a number of reasons, such as if it was illegally obtained and its admission would have an adverse effect on the fairness of proceedings under s. 78, Police and Criminal Evidence Act 1984. The questions of whether evidence is relevant and admissible are questions of law for the judge to decide in a Crown Court trial (or for the magistrates in a magistrates' court trial). If the evidence is deemed to be relevant and admissible, then its weight is to be determined next. This is a question of fact for the tribunal of fact, the jury in a Crown Court trial (or the magistrates in a magistrates' court trial). Figure 2.2 provides a summary of these three hurdles (relevance, admissibility and weight) which apply to a piece of evidence.

In *DPP* v. *Kilbourne*, Lord Simon considered the concepts of relevance, admissibility and weight and stated the following:

---

38 Sections 31 and 32, Crime and Courts Act 2013.

39 See M. Hyde, 'Hot telly it's not. But nor are the cameras in court the slippery slope of cliché', *The Guardian*, 1 November 2013 (accessed at www.theguardian.com/commentisfree/2013/nov/01/cameras-in-court-not-hot-legal-telly on 18 July 2014); H. Kennedy, 'Cameras in court are a threat to justice', *The Guardian*, 3 November 2013 (accessed at www.theguardian.com/commentisfree/2013/nov/03/cameras-in-court-threat-justice on 18 July 2014); and N. Morris, 'Courtroom cameras "risk turning trials into a circus"', *The Independent*, 29 March 2013 (accessed at www.independent.co.uk/news/uk/home-news/courtroom-cameras-risk-turning-trials-into-a-circus-7595013.html on 18 July 2014).

40 Above (n. 37).

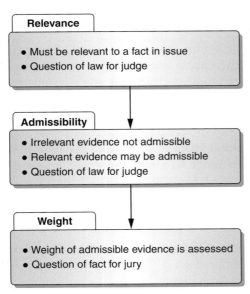

Figure 2.2 The three hurdles: relevance, admissibility, weight

DPP V. *KILBOURNE* [1973] AC 729
Lord Simon of Glaisdale

[at 756–7]

Your Lordships have been concerned with four concepts in the law of evidence: (i) relevance; (ii) admissibility; (iii) corroboration; (iv) weight. The first two terms are frequently, and in many circumstances legitimately, used interchangeably; but I think it makes for clarity if they are kept separate, since some relevant evidence is inadmissible and some admissible evidence is irrelevant (in the senses that I shall shortly submit). Evidence is relevant if it is logically probative or disprobative of some matter which requires proof. I do not pause to analyse what is involved in 'logical proba-tiveness', except to note that the term does not of itself express the element of experience which is so significant of its operation in law, and possibly elsewhere. It is sufficient to say, even at the risk of etymological tautology, that relevant (i.e., logically probative or disprobative) evidence is evidence which makes the matter which requires proof more or less probable . . . Evidence is admissible if it may be lawfully adduced at a trial. 'Weight' of evidence is the degree of probability (both intrinsically and inferentially) which is attached to it by the tribunal of fact once it is established to be relevant and admissible in law (though its relevance may exceptionally, as will appear, be dependent on its evaluation by the tribunal of fact).

Exceptionally evidence which is irrelevant to a fact which is in issue is admitted to lay the foundation for other, relevant, evidence (e.g., evidence of an unsuccessful search for a missing relevant document, in order to lay the foundation for secondary evidence of the document). Apart from such exceptional cases no evidence which is irrelevant to a fact in issue is admissible. But some relevant evidence is nevertheless inadmissible . . .

. . . All relevant evidence is prima facie admissible.

2.5.1 Relevance

Evidence must be relevant to a fact in issue before its admissibility will be considered. In *DPP* v. *Kilbourne*, Lord Simon stated that 'Evidence is relevant if it is logically probative or disprobative of some matter which requires proof ...'.[41] Evidence is relevant if it 'makes the matter which requires proof more or less probable'.[42] Professor Ian Dennis refers to this as 'the theory of bare or minimum logical relevance' which he says 'does not require that the evidence of fact A should make the existence of fact B (the object of proof) probable or improbable; it requires only that fact A should increase or decrease the probability of the existence of fact B'.[43] In *R* v. *Guney*, Lord Judge CJ stated that '[t]he question whether evidence is relevant depends not on abstract legal theory but on the individual circumstances of each particular case'.[44]

The issue of relevance arose in the leading case of *Blastland*.[45] The defendant in this case was charged with the buggery and murder of a 12-year-old boy. The prosecution case was that the defendant forcibly buggered the boy before strangling him with a scarf. The defendant pleaded not guilty but he made admissions to the effect that he had met the boy and had attempted to have sexual intercourse with the boy, but that he had stopped when the boy complained that he was in pain. The defendant claimed that he then saw another man, Mark, nearby, and, worried that the man might have seen him committing a serious offence, the defendant panicked and ran off. The defendant's case was that it was the other man, Mark, who had committed the offences. There was evidence that Mark had been investigated by the police in respect of the murder and that Mark had previously had homosexual relationships with adults. The defendant sought to call witnesses to give evidence that, before the boy's body was found, Mark had told them that a young boy had been murdered. The trial judge ruled that the evidence was inadmissible hearsay. The defendant was convicted and the Court of Appeal dismissed his appeal. He appealed to the House of Lords. The House considered the operation of the rule against hearsay and held accordingly that the evidence of the statements made by Mark would be inadmissible hearsay if they were tendered to prove the truth of their contents, namely that a young boy had been murdered, but they would be admissible as original evidence if tendered to prove Mark's state of mind, namely that he knew about the murder before the body had been found. While the defendant had sought to adduce the statements to show Mark's knowledge of the murder before the body was found, the House held that the evidence was rightly held to be inadmissible by the trial judge because it was not relevant. Lord Bridge stated that original evidence was only admissible if it was relevant to a fact in issue. The issue in the trial (the *ultimate probandum*) was whether the defendant was guilty of the offences charged. Mark's knowledge of the murder was not relevant to that issue, although how Mark had come by that knowledge

---

41 [1973] AC 729 at 756.
42 Ibid.
43 Above (n. 35) at p. 69.
44 [1998] 2 Cr App R 242 at 265.
45 [1986] AC 41, HL.

would have been relevant. However, Lord Bridge observed that Mark might have come by that knowledge in a number of different ways: for example, he may have witnessed the defendant murder the victim or he may have committed the murder himself. Lord Bridge stated that the evidence was inadmissible as irrelevant evidence since the statements provided no rational basis on which the jury could infer the source of the knowledge, and hence, they could not use that evidence to reach a conclusion that Mark rather than the defendant was the murderer. The reasoning in this case has been criticised. As Professor Dennis comments:

I. H. DENNIS, *THE LAW OF EVIDENCE*, 5TH EDN (SWEET & MAXWELL, 2013)

[at p. 78]

Suppose . . . that the prosecution had been seeking to adduce the evidence of Mark's knowledge in support of a charge that *he* was the murderer. There can be no question but that it would have been admitted in proof of his guilt. It would not by itself make his guilt certain, or even probable, but it would increase the apparent probability of his guilt. The murderer had to be a member, possibly the only member, of a class of persons with knowledge of the murder before the body was discovered, and the evidence placed Mark as a member of that class. If the evidence of Mark's knowledge increased the probability of his guilt, it must tend therefore to decrease the probability of Blastland's guilt, given that there was nothing to suggest that he and Mark had been acting in concert.

At this point it is clear that a major collision between logic and policy is taking place. The prosecution may use circumstantial evidence of special knowledge to prove the identity of the defendant as the murderer, but the defendant may not, apparently, use such evidence to weaken the prosecution case by throwing suspicion on to another. Why should this be so?

Later cases of significance concerned the question of what evidence of a 'drugs lifestyle' was relevant to charges of possession of a controlled drug with intent to supply. In *R* v. *Kearley*,[46] the prosecution sought to adduce evidence of a number of telephone calls made to the defendant's house in which the callers requested to speak to the defendant and asked to be supplied with drugs and a number of visitors who called at the defendant's house asking to be supplied with drugs. At trial, the judge allowed the evidence to be given by police officers. The defendant was convicted of possession of a controlled drug with intent to supply and appealed. The Court of Appeal dismissed the appeal and the defendant appealed to the House of Lords. The House allowed the appeal and, by a majority of 3:2 (Lord Griffiths and Lord Browne-Wilkinson dissenting), held that the evidence was inadmissible as it was merely evidence as to the state of minds of the callers, which was irrelevant. The House held that the evidence was irrelevant to the issue of whether the defendant actually intended to supply drugs.

---

46 [1992] 2 AC 228.

R V. KEARLEY [1992] 2 AC 228

Lord Bridge of Harwich

[at 243]

The first question, then, is whether the fact of the request for drugs having been made is in itself relevant to the issue whether the defendant was a supplier. The fact that words were spoken may be relevant for various purposes, but most commonly they will be so when they reveal the state of mind of either the speaker or the person to whom the words were spoken when that state of mind is itself in issue or is relevant to a matter in issue. The state of mind of the person making the request for drugs is of no relevance at all to the question whether the defendant is a supplier. The sole possible relevance of the words spoken is that by manifesting the speaker's belief that the defendant is a supplier they impliedly assert that fact.

Lord Oliver

[at 263–4]

The first inquiry must be, 'Is it relevant evidence?', for nothing that is not relevant is admissible. 'Relevant' cannot, I think, be better defined than in article 1 of *Stephen's Digest of the Law of Evidence*, 12th ed. (1936), p. 3 that is to say, that the word means that: 'any two facts to which it is applied are so related to each other that according to the common course of events one either taken by itself or in connection with other facts proves or renders probable the past, present, or future existence or non-existence of the other'.

   To put it, perhaps, more succinctly, a fact to be relevant must be probative, and if one asks whether the fact that a large number of persons called at the premises seeking to purchase from 'Chippie' renders probable the existence of a person at the premises called 'Chippie' who is willing to supply drugs, the answer can, I think, only be in the affirmative. But the difficulty here is that it is only the combination of the facts (a) that persons called, (b) that they asked for 'Chippie' and (c) that they requested drugs, which renders the evidence relevant. The mere fact that people telephoned or called, in itself, is irrelevant for it neither proves nor renders probable any other fact. In order to render evidence of the calls relevant and therefore admissible there has to be added the additional element of what the callers said, and it is here that the difficulty arises. What was said – in each case a request for drugs – is, of course, probative of the state of mind of the caller. But the state of mind of the caller is not the fact in issue and is, in itself, irrelevant, for it is not probative of anything other than its own existence. It becomes relevant only if and so far as the existence of other facts can be inferred from it. So far as concerns anything in issue at the trial, what the caller said and the state of mind which that fact evinces, become relevant and probative of the fact in issue (namely, the intent of the appellant) only if, or because, (i) what was said amounts to a statement, by necessary implication, that the appellant has in the past supplied drugs to the speaker (as in two cases in which requests were made for 'the usual') or (ii) it imports the belief or opinion of the speaker that the appellant has drugs and is willing to supply them. And here, as it seems to me, we are directly up against the hearsay rule which forms one of the major established exceptions to the admissibility of relevant evidence. Clearly if, at the trial, the prosecution had sought to adduce evidence from a witness to the effect that the appellant had, in the past, supplied him with quantities of drugs, that evidence would have been both relevant and admissible; but equally clearly, if it had been sought to introduce the evidence of a police constable to the effect that a person not called as a witness had told him, in a conversation in a public house, that the appellant had supplied drugs, that would have been inadmissible hearsay evidence and so objectionable. It cannot, it is cogently argued, make any difference that exactly the same evidence is introduced in an indirect way by way of evidence from a witness D that he has overheard a request by some other person for 'the usual', from which the jury is to be asked to infer that which cannot be proved by evidence of that other person's direct assertion. Equally if, at the trial, the prosecution had sought to adduce evidence from a witness not that drugs had been supplied but that it was his opinion or belief that drugs had been or would be supplied, that evidence would be inadmissible as amounting to no more than a statement of belief or opinion unsupported by facts upon which the belief is grounded. A fortiori, it is argued, that same inadmissible belief or opinion cannot be introduced by inference from the reported statement of someone who is not even called as a witness. Thus, it is said, in seeking to introduce the evidence of the police officers of what callers said, the Crown faces the difficulty that it has to contend that by combining two inadmissible items of evidence – that is to say, the evidence of the calls (which are, standing alone, inadmissible because irrelevant) and the evidence of what was said by the callers (which might be relevant but is inadmissible because hearsay) – it can produce a single item of admissible evidence.

In *R* v. *Guney*,[47] the defendant was charged with possession of a class A drug with intent to supply and other offences. The police found a cardboard box containing £25,000 in cash and plastic bags containing heroin with a street value of £750,000. The defendant claimed that the heroin in his room had been 'planted', and thus the issue on appeal was the admissibility of evidence relating to cash and lifestyle. The prosecution argued that the evidence of £25,000 in cash in the defendant's room in close proximity to the drugs was relevant evidence which went to the defendant's knowledge of the drugs, which was in turn evidence of possession. Lord Judge CJ stated that:

> Relevance and admissibility are distinct questions. Provided evidence is sufficiently relevant to the issues in any particular case it is normally admissible provided 'the evidence tendered does not infringe any of the exclusionary rules that may be applicable to it' (Cross & Tapper on Evidence (8th ed., 1995), p. 66). The question whether evidence is relevant depends not on abstract legal theory but on the individual circumstances of each particular case.[48]

The Court of Appeal held that where a defendant was charged with possession of a drug with intent to supply, evidence of possession of large sums of cash and an affluent lifestyle might be relevant and admissible to the issue of the possession of drugs. This case is notable for the appeal court's refusal to follow earlier authorities, such as *R* v. *Kearley*, on this point.[49]

2.5.2 Admissibility

As we have seen above, only evidence that is relevant to a fact in issue in the case may be admissible in court. However, this does not mean that all relevant evidence is admissible; in fact, not all relevant evidence is admissible. The question of whether evidence is admissible or not is a question of law for the judge to decide; thus, evidence may only be adduced in court if it is admissible as a matter of law. Most of this book is about determining the admissibility of evidence; this book explores the rules of law regarding the admissibility of evidence and the

---

47 [1998] 2 Cr App R 242.
48 Ibid. at 265.
49 For a commentary on the case of *R* v. *Guney*, see M. Redmayne, 'Drugs, money and relevance' (1999) 3(2) E&P 128.

judicial discretion to exclude or admit evidence into court. The main rules of admissibility of evidence covered in this book relate to:

- the admissibility of unreliable confession evidence or confessions obtained by oppression (see Chapter 5),
- the admissibility of hearsay evidence (see Chapter 7),
- the admissibility of evidence of a defendant's or non-defendant's bad character (see Chapter 8),
- the competence and compellability of witnesses (see Chapter 9),
- the admissibility of evidence of previous consistent statements (see Chapter 10),
- the admissibility of evidence of a complainant's previous sexual history (see Chapter 10),
- the admissibility of hazardous or unreliable evidence (see Chapter 11),
- the admissibility of non-expert opinion evidence and expert evidence (see Chapter 12),
- the admissibility of evidence which is subject to public interest immunity or other privileged evidence (see Chapters 13 and 14).

In addition to these rules of admissibility, a trial judge also has a common law discretion to exclude any evidence where its prejudicial effect outweighs its probative value[50] and a statutory discretion to exclude evidence if its admission would have such an adverse effect on the fairness of proceedings that it ought not to be admitted[51] (see Chapter 6).

2.5.3 Weight

The weight of a piece of evidence refers to the cogency, probative value or quality of the evidence. The weight of evidence is a question for the tribunal of fact to determine. In a Crown Court trial, the jury will determine the weight of the evidence adduced in court. However, there are some circumstances in which a judge may be required to decide upon the weight of the evidence, such as when he is determining the relevance of evidence to a fact in issue, commenting upon evidence in his summing up to the jury, during a *voir dire*, when he decides whether to withdraw an issue from the jury or whether to uphold a submission of no case to answer, or when deciding whether preliminary facts have been established in deciding on questions of the admissibility of evidence (e.g. in deciding whether a confession was obtained by oppression in considering whether he must exclude the confession evidence under s. 76(2)(a), Police and Criminal Evidence Act 1984).

2.6 CONCLUSION

Both the criminal and civil justice systems in England and Wales operate on the basis of an adversarial system; the trial process is akin to a contest or battle. Civil cases are tried by a judge who is both the fact-finder and the tribunal of law. The least serious criminal offences are tried by lay magistrates or a district judge, who will act as both the fact-finder and the tribunal of law. Serious cases in the criminal courts are tried by a jury with a judge presiding over the trial, in a role similar to that of an umpire. While the questions of fact are for the jury to determine, matters of law are for

---

50 *R* v. *Sang* [1980] AC 402.
51 Section 78, Police and Criminal Evidence Act 1984.

the judge, and the judge will direct the jury on the law as part of his summing up at the end of a trial. By contrast, the continental inquisitorial system operates more like an inquest or inquiry, with the judge taking more of an investigatory role. Our criminal justice system borrows elements of both of Packer's models of the criminal justice system: there are elements of crime control and due process throughout our system. Concepts such as truth, justice and fairness are prevalent throughout the system and there should be a focus on Professor Dennis's legitimacy principle under which the moral authority of the verdict must be protected. While a large proportion of this book deals with issues of admissibility of evidence, there are three fundamental principles which are applied to every piece of evidence in a trial: the evidence must be *relevant* before it may be deemed to be admissible, it must be *admissible* in law, and its *weight* must be considered by the fact-finder.

Summary

- The criminal trial in England and Wales is adversarial in nature. This means that the trial is like a contest or a battle. The adversarial trial should be contrasted with the inquisitorial system followed in countries such as France. The inquisitorial trial is more like an inquest or inquiry.
- In a criminal trial in the Crown Court, the trial judge is the tribunal of law and the jury is the tribunal of fact. In a magistrates' court trial, the magistrates act as both the tribunal of law and the tribunal of fact.
- The role of the judge in a criminal trial is to decide upon questions of law, deliver a summing up speech to the jury and to act as an umpire in the trial.
- The role of the jury in a criminal trial is to decide upon questions of fact, including whether the defendant is guilty or not of the offences charged. The 'right to trial by jury' is limited to cases in which the defendant is tried with an either way offence and the magistrates accept jurisdiction of the case. Jury deliberations are protected by the common law secrecy rule and s. 8, Contempt of Court Act 1981.
- Packer's 'crime control' model of the criminal justice system aims to repress crime through the apprehension and conviction of offenders speedily and with finality. The 'due process' model aims to ensure that convictions are not wrongful through the use of procedural safeguards.
- The inquisitorial system is truth-centred, while the adversarial system is concerned with due process and ensuring the fairness of the proceedings.
- Evidence must be relevant to a fact in issue before its admissibility will be considered. 'Evidence is relevant if it is logically probative or disprobative of some matter which requires proof . . .' (per Lord Simon in *DPP* v. *Kilbourne*).
- The admissibility of evidence is a question of law for the judge to determine in a criminal case. Evidence must be relevant to a fact in issue before it is admissible, but not all relevant evidence is admissible. There are many rules relating to the admissibility of evidence, including rules on the admissibility of hearsay evidence, character evidence, confession evidence and the competence and compellability of witnesses. Judges also have a discretion to exclude evidence at common law and under statute.
- The weight of the evidence refers to the cogency or probative value of the evidence. The weight of the evidence is a question for the tribunal of fact to determine.

For discussion . . .

1. Compare and contrast the adversarial process and the inquisitorial process. Critically evaluate the adversarial nature of the criminal trial process in light of the concepts of truth and due process.
2. Explain the roles of the judge and the jury in a criminal trial.
3. Which of Herbert Packer's models of the criminal justice system is most akin to the English criminal justice system? Explain your answer with reference to specific aspects of the English criminal justice system.
4. To what extent does the justice system abide by the principle of open justice? Make reference to recent reforms in your answer.
5. What is relevance in the context of the law of evidence? Is evidence of lifestyle or drugs paraphernalia relevant to a charge of possession of a controlled drug with intent to supply? Explain why with reference to case law.

Further reading

P. Darbyshire, *Sitting in Judgment: The Working Lives of Judges* (Hart Publishing, 2011).
This book is the result of seven years of research by Professor Darbyshire into the working lives of the English judiciary. The book explores matters including where judges come from, the education and training they receive and the work that they do in all courts from the magistrates' courts, Crown Court, county courts through to the Court of Appeal and Supreme Court. Professor Darbyshire dispels the myths of the stereotypical views of judges and their backgrounds and argues that judges are more representative of society.

A. Duff, L. Farmer, S. Marshall and V. Tadros (eds.), *The Trial on Trial Volume 1: Truth and Due Process* (Hart Publishing, 2004).
This is the first in a series of three volumes on the nature of the trial. The volumes seek to develop a normative theory of the criminal trial. This volume explores specifically the themes of truth and due process. Through a collection of essays by different authors, the book questions the extent to which the discovery of truth can be said to be the central aim of the rules of procedure and evidence during the investigation and trial of a criminal offence. There are several essays of significance in the volume, but one of particular relevance to this chapter is the essay by J. McEwan, 'Ritual, fairness and truth: the adversarial and inquisitorial models of criminal trial'.

H. L. Ho, *A Philosophy of Evidence Law: Justice in the Search for Truth* (Oxford University Press, 2008).
This monograph explores the function and purpose of the rules of evidence in the criminal trial. The first three chapters of the book analyse the task of fact-finding, the connection between truth and justice in the context of the value and purposes of a trial and the epistemology of fact-finding. The remaining three chapters then evaluate three different substantive areas of the law of evidence in light of the theoretical approach.

J. Hodgson, 'Conceptions of the trial in inquisitorial and adversarial procedure' in A. Duff, L. Farmer, S. Marshall and V. Tadros (eds.), *The Trial on Trial Volume 2: Judgments and Calling to Account* (Hart Publishing, 2006).
This essay in the second volume of The Trial on Trial series of monographs compares and contrasts the procedures and rituals which occur in adversarial trials in England and Wales and inquisitorial trials in France.

P. Otton, 'The role of the judge in criminal cases' in M. McConville and G. Wilson, *The Handbook of The Criminal Justice Process* (Oxford University Press, 2002).
This essay sets out the role of the trial judge in criminal cases. It considers the role of the judge in both pre-trial and trial proceedings. Matters that a judge is required to deal with are explored, such as 'Newton' hearings, plea bargaining, the protection of witnesses and jurors, the admissibility of evidence, oversight of the examination and cross-examination of witnesses and the summing up of evidence.

D. Pannick, *Judges* (Oxford University Press, 1988).
This book explores all aspects of the judiciary, from their appointment and training, the discipline of judges whose behaviour affects the fair administration of justice, the criticism launched at judges, the mysticism surrounding them and the publicity surrounding the work of judges.

J. McEwan, 'From adversarialism to managerialism: criminal justice in transition' (2011) *Legal Studies* 1.
This article considers the implications of recent reforms which have the effect that the criminal justice system is moving away from its traditional adversarial heritage towards a more managerialistic approach.

3 Burden of proof

3.1 INTRODUCTION

This chapter is chiefly concerned with the principle known as the 'golden thread' which runs 'throughout the web of English criminal law' (otherwise known as the burden of proof) and the meaning of the famous phrase 'beyond reasonable doubt' (the standard of proof). The burden and standard of proof are fundamental aspects of the law of evidence. The legal system lays down rules about which party bears the burden of proof and the standard to which facts in issue must be proved. The general principle is that it is the party who brings the case who must prove the facts in issue. The relevant party must adduce evidence in an attempt to prove the facts in issue, and ultimately, in order to discharge its burden of proof and win the case. In criminal proceedings, the burden of proof is on the prosecution (the state) to prove that the defendant is guilty of the offence charged. The prosecution bears the burden of proof because it brings the case to court, and, compared to the defendant, the prosecution has a wealth of resources with which it can prove the facts in issue. That the prosecution carries this burden of proving an accusation against the defendant is the most fundamental principle of criminal law; as stated above, it has famously been described as the 'golden thread' which runs throughout the web of English criminal law.

This chapter will also consider the distinction between the legal burden and the evidential burden in legal proceedings, explore the operation of the general rule relating to the burden of proof in criminal proceedings and the exceptional situations in which the onus of proof is reversed. We will evaluate the two standards of proof (the criminal standard and the civil standard) and their application in proceedings. The standard of proof in criminal proceedings is 'beyond reasonable doubt' (this is a phrase which you have no doubt heard before), and the standard of proof in civil proceedings is 'on a balance of probabilities'. Finally we will consider matters that do not require proof and the use of presumptions in legal proceedings.

3.2 LEGAL BURDEN VERSUS EVIDENTIAL BURDEN?

Before delving into the more technical aspects of the burden of proof, it is vital that you have a clear understanding of the difference between the legal burden (or persuasive burden) and the evidential burden.

The legal burden (or 'persuasive burden') is more familiarly known as the burden of proof. This is an obligation that is placed on one party in proceedings to prove the facts in issue in a case. In order to discharge the legal burden, the relevant party must adduce evidence to prove the facts in issue. A standard of proof is attached to the legal burden (see paragraph 3.4) and the relevant party must adduce sufficiently probative evidence to meet the standard of proof. If the party bearing the legal burden does adduce sufficient evidence to meet the standard of proof, they are deemed to have discharged the burden of proof.

By contrast, the evidential burden is not a burden of proof. It does not require the party in question to prove facts in issue, but it is an obligation on a party to adduce some relevant evidence in order to make an issue a 'live' one. In other words, the party bearing the evidential burden must adduce some relevant evidence in order to persuade the judge that the issue should be left for the tribunal of fact to consider. This is sometimes referred to as 'the duty of passing the judge'. In contrast to the legal burden, there is no standard of proof attached to the evidential burden. This is because the evidential burden is not a burden of *proof*; thus, the party who bears the evidential burden does not have to prove the facts in issue to a particular standard.

> **Cross-reference**
> See paragraph 3.5 below for a more detailed discussion of the operation and significance of the evidential burden.

Figure 3.1 provides a summary of the key differences between the legal burden and the evidential burden, but each of these concepts will be discussed in more detail in paragraphs 3.3 and 3.5 respectively.

3.3 BURDEN OF PROOF

The legal (or persuasive) burden generally rests with the party bringing the case to court. In civil proceedings, the party asserting an issue bears the burden of proving that issue. Thus, as the claimant brings the case, he bears the legal burden of proving the facts in issue in his case

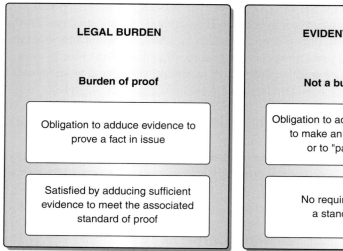
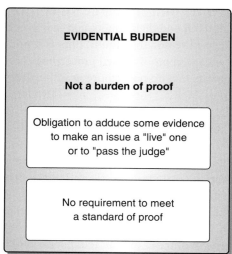

Figure 3.1 Differentiating legal and evidential burdens

against the defendant, and the defendant bears the legal burden of proving anything that he raises in his defence. In criminal proceedings, the prosecution brings the case to court on behalf of the Crown; thus, in criminal proceedings, the burden of proof is on the prosecution. In accordance with the presumption of innocence, the defendant is presumed to be innocent until he is proved guilty of the crimes charged and the prosecution has the obligation of proving the defendant's guilt. However, there are some circumstances in which the burden of proof in criminal proceedings will shift to the defence; this is called a 'reverse onus'. The circumstances in which the burden of proof is placed on the defence are necessarily limited and will be considered later, as will the extent to which a reverse onus conflicts with the presumption of innocence. In the paragraphs below, we will focus on the burden of proof in criminal cases; we will consider the general rule before exploring the exceptions to this rule.

3.3.1 Criminal proceedings: general rule

It has long been established in criminal proceedings that the prosecution bears the burden of proving that the defendant is guilty of the offences charged. This means that the prosecution must prove all of the elements of the offence that the defendant has been charged with as well as disprove any defence raised by the defendant. This is the general rule, which was confirmed by the House of Lords in the case of *Woolmington* v. *DPP*.[1] In this case, the defendant appealed against his conviction for his wife's murder. The defendant, Reginald Woolmington, was married to Violet Woolmington. They split up and Violet moved in with her mother. In a bid to win his wife back, the defendant visited his mother in law's house in order to see his wife. He decided to take a loaded sawn-off shotgun with him in order to frighten his wife into coming back to him by threatening to kill himself; he hid the gun under his overcoat. He knocked on the door and when

---

1 [1935] AC 462.

Violet answered the door he asked her, 'Are you coming back or not, Vi?' Violet told Reginald that she would not go back to him, at which point Reginald threatened to shoot himself. He unbuttoned his coat to show her the gun, but it went off accidentally, killing his wife. He was charged with murder. At trial, the judge directed the jury that the prosecution must prove that the defendant killed the victim, and, if that is proved, then it is for the defendant to show that there are circumstances that absolve him of liability for murder so that he is instead convicted of man-slaughter. Thus, the trial judge effectively directed the jury that once the prosecution has proved that the defendant caused the death of the victim, he was presumed to be guilty of murder unless he proved that the killing was accidental. The defendant appealed against his conviction for murder on the ground that the trial judge had misdirected the jury. The Court of Criminal Appeal dismissed the appeal and certified the case for consideration by the House of Lords. The House quashed the defendant's conviction and held that the trial judge had misdirected the jury on the burden of proof. The House held that there was no onus on the defendant to prove that the killing was accidental; rather, the burden of proof was on the prosecution to prove that the defendant carried out the killing and that the killing was not accidental.

WOOLMINGTON V. *DPP* [1935] AC 462
Viscount Sankey LC

[at 481–2]

Throughout the web of English Criminal Law one golden thread is always to be seen, that it is the duty of the prosecution to prove the prisoner's guilt subject to . . . the defence of insanity and subject also to any statutory exception. If, at the end of and on the whole of the case, there is a reasonable doubt, created by the evidence given by either the prosecution or the prisoner, as to whether the prisoner killed the deceased with a malicious intention, the prosecution has not made out the case and the prisoner is entitled to an acquittal. No matter what the charge or where the trial, the principle that the prosecution must prove the guilt of the prisoner is part of the common law of England and no attempt to whittle it down can be entertained. When dealing with a murder case the Crown must prove (a) death as a result of a voluntary act of the accused and (b) malice of the accused.

In summary, where the prosecution brings criminal proceedings against a defendant, the prosecution must prove that the defendant is guilty. This means that the prosecution must prove all of the elements of the offence and disprove the defendant's defence. This is so irrespective of whether the defendant's defence is a denial of one of the elements of the offence or a separate defence altogether. For instance, where a defendant is charged with murder and raises the defence of accident (as in *Woolmington* v. *DPP*), the prosecution will be required to prove that the defendant performed the *actus reus* of murder (he unlawfully killed a person within the Queen's Peace) with the requisite *mens rea* (he intended to kill or to cause grievous bodily harm). The defence of accident is in effect a denial of the *mens rea* and it is for the prosecution to satisfy the jury that the defendant did indeed intend to kill or cause grievous bodily harm to the victim, which is the same as showing that his conduct was not accidental. Similarly, take a defendant who is charged with the summary offence of battery, contrary to s. 39, Criminal Justice Act 1988, who raises the common law defence of consent. The defence of consent is really a denial

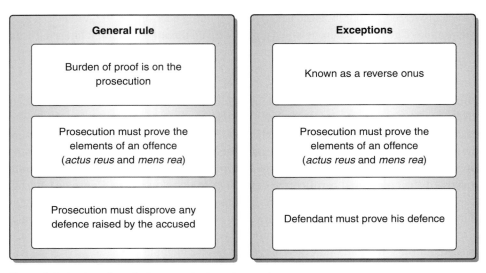

Figure 3.2 Burden of proof: the general rule and exceptions

of the 'unlawful' element of the infliction of force and can be regarded as a negative element of the *actus reus*: it will be for the prosecution to prove that the complainant did not consent to the infliction of force, as well as the other elements of the offence.

3.3.2 Criminal proceedings: exceptions

There are a number of exceptions to the general rule that the burden of proof in criminal proceedings is on the prosecution. Where the defendant raises a defence which carries a reverse onus, the legal burden in respect of the defence rests with the defendant. Thus, it will be for the prosecution to prove that the elements of the offence are present, but for the defendant to prove the elements of the defence (see Figure 3.2).

If the defendant is able to prove the defence and discharge this reverse onus, then he will be acquitted of the offence charged. The very nature of a reverse onus appears to conflict with the presumption of innocence which is protected by Article 6(2) of the European Convention on Human Rights. The presumption of innocence inherently holds that a defendant is presumed to be innocent unless the contrary is proved by the prosecution. It is not for the defendant to prove that he is innocent. The existence and operation of reverse burdens raises two important questions: (1) when does a reverse onus arise? and (2) how is a reverse onus justified? The first of these questions will be addressed in this paragraph. The second will be addressed in paragraph 3.3.3.

When does a reverse onus arise?
According to Viscount Sankey LC in *Woolmington* v. *DPP*, there are two categories of exceptions to the general rule that the burden of proof in criminal proceedings is on the prosecution, namely in cases in which the defendant pleads insanity and where there is a statutory exception

which reverses the burden of proof. In the case of *Hunt*,[2] the House of Lords held that Viscount Sankey LC's reference to 'any statutory exception' in *Woolmington* v. *DPP* was a reference to both statutory provisions which *expressly* place the burden of proving the defence on the defendant and those which do so by *implication*.[3]

Insanity

In *M'Naghten's Case*,[4] it was held that the burden of proving the defence of insanity falls on the defendant. There is a presumption of sanity: 'every man is presumed to be sane, and to possess a sufficient degree of reason to be responsible for his crimes, until the contrary be proved'.[5] Consequently, if a defendant wishes to defend himself on the basis that he was legally insane at the time of the offence, then he bears the burden of proving the elements of the defence of insanity. We will see from the leading case of *R* v. *Lambert*; *R* v. *Ali*; *R* v. *Jordan*[6] (discussed below) that the courts justify placing the legal burden on the defendant in cases in which the defendant has far greater knowledge about the matter to be proved. Where the defendant pleads insanity (or indeed diminished responsibility), the defence team is in a far better position to prove the elements of the defence since they relate to the defendant's state of mind.

Express statutory exceptions

A statutory provision may expressly place the legal burden on the defendant. One example of an express statutory exception which reverses the burden of proof is s. 1(1), Prevention of Crime Act 1953 which provides that it is an offence to have an offensive weapon in a public place without lawful authority or reasonable excuse. The provision uses the words '*the proof whereof shall lie on him*' and this phrase is an express statement that the burden of proving the defence of lawful authority or reasonable excuse is on the defendant.[7]

Another example is that of the defence of diminished responsibility under s. 2(1), Homicide Act 1957, a partial defence to murder. Section 2(2), Homicide Act 1957 provides an express statutory exception to the golden thread in respect of this defence. Thus, where the defendant is charged with murder and raises the defence of diminished responsibility,

---

2 [1987] AC 352, HL.
3 Ibid., see Lord Griffiths at 369–70 and Lord Ackner at 379–80: 'It is, of course, axiomatic that a statute may impose upon the accused the burden of proof of a particular defence to a statutory offence and may do so either expressly or by necessary implication. Whichever method Parliament uses it has created a 'statutory exception' and there is no difference in the quality or status of such an exception. As at the date of the decision in *Woolmington's* case, there were numerous examples of statutes in which the onus of proof of a particular defence had been placed upon the accused, either expressly or, on a proper construction of the Act, by necessary implication. There is no warrant to be found either in the words used by the Lord Chancellor quoted above or in their context for suggesting that 'statutory exception' is limited to express statutory exception.'
4 (1843) 10 Cl & F 200, HL.
5 Ibid. per Lord Tindal CJ at 210.
6 [2000] EWCA Crim 3542.
7 Section 1(1) of the Prevention of Crime Act 1953 provides that 'Any person who without lawful authority or reasonable excuse, *the proof whereof shall lie on him*, has with him in any public place any offensive weapon shall be guilty of an offence . . .' (author's emphasis).

the defendant bears the burden of proving the elements of the defence. The rationale for this express statutory exception lies in the similarity between the defences of diminished responsibility and insanity. Diminished responsibility requires proof that the defendant was suffering from an 'abnormality of mental functioning',[8] contrary to the presumption that every man is sane. Thus, it is for the defendant to prove that he suffered that abnormality. As stated above in respect of insanity, the defence team is in a better position to be able to prove the defence since it relates to the defendant's state of mind, a matter about which the defence has far greater knowledge.

The leading case on express reverse onuses is *R* v. *Lambert*; *R* v. *Ali*; *R* v. *Jordan*.[9] This case concerned three separate appeals to the Court of Appeal. In the first case, *R* v. *Lambert*, the defendant was charged with possession of a controlled class A drug with intent to supply, contrary to s. 5(3), Misuse of Drugs Act 1971. The defendant in this case admitted being in possession of the bag which contained the drugs, but he claimed that he had not known nor suspected that the bag contained a controlled drug. In doing so, he raised a defence under s. 28 of the Act. He was convicted of the offence after the trial judge directed the jury that in order to establish possession of a controlled drug, the prosecution had to prove that (1) the defendant had a package in his control and he knew this, and (2) the package contained a controlled drug. The trial judge then directed the jury that once those matters had been proved by the prosecution, it was for the defendant to prove on a balance of probabilities that he did not believe or suspect, and that he had no reason to suspect that the substance in question was a controlled drug; thus, it was for the defendant to prove his defence. The second and third cases in the appeal, *R* v. *Ali* and *R* v. *Jordan*, involved defendants who were each charged with murder. They raised the defence of diminished responsibility under s. 2(1), Homicide Act 1957 and the trial judge in each case directed the jury that the legal burden was on the defendant to prove the defence on a balance of probabilities. The defendant in each case was convicted and appealed. The defendants argued on appeal that the burden of proving the defence should not have been placed on the defendants in each case and that these reverse onuses conflicted with the presumption of innocence under Article 6(2) of the European Convention on Human Rights. The defendants claimed that the statutory provisions should be interpreted as placing an evidential burden on the defendants rather than a legal burden. The timing of the case was significant because judgment was handed down approximately two months before the enactment of the Human Rights Act 1998, which incorporated the Convention Rights into our domestic law, but the Court of Appeal decided to proceed on the basis that the Human Rights Act 1998 was in force.

Lord Woolf CJ gave the judgment and dismissed all of the appeals. His Lordship began by setting out each of the relevant statutory provisions and stating that these clearly place the burden of proof on the defendant to establish the defence on a balance of probabilities. His Lordship then considered the approach taken by the courts to the legal burden being placed on a

8 See s. 2(1), Homicide Act 1957 (as amended by s. 52, Coroners and Justice Act 2009).
9 [2000] EWCA Crim 3542.

defendant to prove his defence. He highlighted the reluctance of the courts to depart from the 'golden thread' but acknowledged the exception of insanity. Lord Woolf CJ stated that where Parliament wished to depart from the general rule, it must use 'clear language' to do so, as it did in these cases.

R V. LAMBERT; R V. ALI; R V. JORDAN [2000] EWCA CRIM 3542
Lord Woolf CJ

The attitude of the common law to the burden of proof being placed on a defendant

[8] The common law is fiercely resistant to a burden of proof being placed on a defendant. This is the 'golden thread' of English law identified by Viscount Sankey LC in his classic statement in *Woolmington v Director of Public Prosecutions* [1935] AC 462, 481. There is, however, what has been regarded as a well established exception in the case of insanity. It is an exception because of what is another equally glittering thread of English law. This is that the proof of the commission of any offence requires the existence of a guilty mind and the ability to prove this depends on courts being able to rely on the presumption of mental capacity in the absence of evidence to the contrary (see Viscount Kilmuir LC in *Bratty v Attorney General for Northern Ireland* [1963] AC 386, 407).

[9] Parliament has created many exceptions to the general rules. When it does so it must use clear language if it is to successfully achieve its purpose. The sections involved in the present appeals are examples of it successfully achieving this objective. A statute can require a defendant to do no more than satisfy an evidential burden. (When this is so, the issue will be required to be left for the jury to determine. Then it will be determined in the defendant's favour unless the prosecution satisfy the jury to the contrary.) The other approach which a statute can adopt is that the defendant has to satisfy a persuasive burden. (That is to satisfy the jury on the balance of possibilities that he is entitled to succeed on the issue). A variation of the first alternative, not only requiring the defendant to raise an issue but to raise a doubt, has not been adopted in legislation, as far as we are aware, although this could produce practical benefits.

The Court of Appeal considered that the Human Rights Act 1998 could have a 'significant effect' on statutory provisions which purport to depart from Article 6(2) of the European Convention on Human Rights by placing the burden of proof on the defendant. This is because s. 3 of the Human Rights Act 1998 requires statutory provisions to be 'read and given effect in a way which is compatible with the Convention rights'. The Court considered that the Convention is 'an instrument for the protection of fundamental rights' and that 'a broad and purposive approach not a rigid approach' could be given to its language in order to protect the fundamental rights of both individuals and of society as a whole.

Lord Woolf CJ considered the structure of the offences and distinguished between cases in which the defendant is being required to prove an element of the offence and cases in which he is required to prove a defence. His Lordship stated that, in the former case, it would be more difficult to justify a reverse onus, while in the latter case this would be 'less objectionable'.

R V. *LAMBERT*; *R* V. *ALI*; *R* V. *JORDAN* [2000] EWCA CRIM 3542
Lord Woolf CJ

[16] . . . it is important to start with the structure of the offences. If the defendant is being required to prove an essential element of the offence this will be more difficult to justify. If, however, what the defendant is required to do is establish a special defence or exception this will be less objectionable. The extent of the inroad on the general principle is also important. Here it is important to have in mind that article 6(2) is specifically directed to the application of the presumption of innocence of the 'criminal offence' charged. It is also important to have in mind that legislation is passed by a democratically elected Parliament and therefore the courts under the Convention are entitled to and should, as a matter of constitutional principle, pay a degree of deference to the view of Parliament as to what is in the interest of the public generally when upholding the rights of the individual under the Convention. The courts are required to balance the competing interests involved.

Thus, in *R* v. *Ali* and *R* v. *Jordan*, the Court rejected the suggestion that the defence of diminished responsibility under s. 2(1), Homicide Act 1957 was part of the offence. The Court confidently held that diminished responsibility was a special defence and was not an ingredient of the offence of murder: '[i]f the defendant does not seek to rely on the section he will not be required to prove anything. The count in the indictment does not refer to section 2'.[10] A reverse onus which requires a defendant to prove something which is entirely separate to the elements of the offence is clearly much less objectionable than a reverse onus which requires the defendant to disprove a constituent element of the offence itself. The Court further justified the reverse onus by considering the problems raised by the alternative of placing the burden of disproving diminished responsibility on the prosecution. For instance, the Court also pointed out that there might be situations in which a defendant was 'unco-operative' and refused to submit to medical assessment for the prosecution. This would make it very difficult for the prosecution to disprove diminished responsibility. The defendant is clearly in a far better position to be able to establish the defence as he has knowledge of the circumstances relating to the defence which the prosecution could not know and could be obstructed from obtaining. Placing the legal burden on the defendant here provides the defendant with an incentive to co-operate with a medical assessment. His Lordship also noted that in cases involving reverse onuses, the courts should bear in mind the fact that the statutory provisions which they are interpreting were created by a democratically elected Parliament. The role of the courts here is to give effect to the will of Parliament and Lord Woolf CJ considers that the courts should 'pay a degree of deference to the view of Parliament' here. Thus, the Court held that placing the legal burden on a defendant to prove diminished responsibility did not violate the presumption of innocence under Article 6(2) of the European Convention on Human Rights, and s. 2(2), Homicide Act 1957 was not incompatible with Article 6(2).

Considering *R* v. *Lambert*, the Court of Appeal held that '[t]he position is not as clear'.[11] The Court considered the domestic case law relating to the meaning of 'possession' of a controlled

---

10 Ibid. at [17].
11 Ibid. at [20].

drug. Where a defendant is accused of being in possession of a drug which is inside a container, case law previous to the Misuse of Drugs Act 1971 clearly states that in order to be in possession of that drug, the defendant must have knowledge that the container contains something even if he does not know what it contains.[12] The Court of Appeal stated that the intention of Parliament in drafting the Misuse of Drugs Act 1971 was to follow the route already established by the previous case law and 'to restrict the extent of the knowledge required for the commission of the offence'. Parliament then sought to establish a separate defence which a defendant could invoke if he had no suspicion as to the nature of the contents of the container. Nevertheless, the Court held that s. 28, Misuse of Drugs Act 1971 did 'not impose additional ingredients which have to be proved to complete the offence but a way of avoiding liability for what would otherwise be an offence'.[13] The Court stated that:

> It is commonplace for a defendant to seek to avoid his guilt by saying that he thought he had pornography or gold and not drugs in the box. Such a defence is difficult to rebut. What the offence does is to make the defendant responsible for ensuring that he does not take into his possession containers which in fact contain drugs ... there is a clear social objective in discouraging trading both in hard drugs and the softer drugs.[14]

Thus, the Court held that the legal burden was rightly placed on the defendant to prove the elements of his defence, and that the standard of proof imposed upon the defendant to establish his defence on a balance of probabilities was also justified on policy grounds and proportionate.

Lambert further appealed to the House of Lords against this decision. By a majority of 4:1 (with Lord Steyn dissenting), the House of Lords dismissed the appeal on the basis that the Human Rights Act 1998 did not apply retrospectively, and, thus, that the appellant could not rely on the Human Rights Act 1998 in his appeal.[15] Despite this, the House did in fact go on to consider the effect that the Human Rights Act 1998 would have in any event.

R V. *LAMBERT* [2001] UKHL 37
Lord Slynn

[16] The first question asks whether it is an essential element of the offence of possession of a controlled drug under section 5 of the Misuse of Drugs Act 1971 that the accused knows that he has a controlled drug in his possession. Bearing fully in mind the importance of the principle that the onus is on the prosecution to prove the elements of an offence and that the provisions of an Act which transfer or limit that burden of proof should be carefully scrutinised, it seems to me that the Court of Appeal in *R v McNamara* (1988) 87 Cr App R 246 rightly identified the elements of the offence which the prosecution must prove. I refer in particular to the judgment of Lord Lane CJ, at pp. 251–252. This means in a case like the present that the prosecution must prove that the accused had a bag with something in it in his custody or control; and that the something in the bag was a controlled drug. It is not necessary for the prosecution to prove that the accused knew that the thing was a controlled drug let alone a particular

---

12 See *R* v. *Warner* [1969] 2 AC 256.
13 Above (n. 9) at [23].
14 Ibid. at [24] and [25].
15 [2001] UKHL 37.

controlled drug. The defendant may then seek to establish one of the defences provided in section 5(4) or section 28 of the 1971 Act.

[17] The second question in effect asks whether, if the prosecution has proved the three elements to which I have referred, it is contrary to article 6(2) of the Convention rights for a judge to direct a jury that 'the defendant is guilty as charged unless he discharges a legal, rather than an evidential, burden of proof to the effect that he neither believed nor suspected nor had reason to suspect that the substance in question was a controlled drug'. If read in isolation there is obviously much force in the contention that section 28(2) imposes the legal burden of proof on the accused, in which case serious arguments arise as to whether this is justified or so disproportionate that there is a violation of article 6(2) of the Convention rights . . . In balancing the interests of the individual in achieving justice against the needs of society to protect against abuse of drugs this seems to me a very difficult question but I incline to the view that this burden would not be justified under article 6(2) of the Convention rights. For my part I do not think it is necessary to come to a conclusion on these arguments since even if section 28(2) read alone were thought prima facie to violate article 6(2) the House must still go on to consider section 3(1) of the 1998 Act. That section provides: 'So far as it is possible to do so, primary legislation and subordinate legislation must be read and given effect in a way which is compatible with the Convention rights.' This obligation applies to primary legislation 'whenever enacted'. *Even if the most obvious way to read section 28(2) is that it imposes a legal burden of proof I have no doubt that it is 'possible', without doing violence to the language or to the objective of that section, to read the words as imposing only the evidential burden of proof. Such a reading would in my view be compatible with Convention rights since, even if this may create evidential difficulties for the prose- cution as I accept, it ensures that the defendant does not have the legal onus of proving the matters referred to in section 28(2) which whether they are regarded as part of the offence or as a riposte to the offence prima facie established are of crucial importance. It is not enough that the defendant in seeking to establish the evidential burden should merely mouth the words of the section. The defendant must still establish that the evidential burden has been satisfied. It seems to me that given that that reading is 'possible' courts must give effect to it in cases where Convention rights can be relied on.* [author's emphasis]

[18] In the present case, however, I would dismiss the appeal on the ground that the appellant cannot rely on Convention rights in a national court in respect of a conviction before the 1998 Act came into force. I am also of the view that even if the trial judge had given a direction on the basis that the burden on the accused was only an evidential burden the jury would have reached the same result and that it cannot be said that the conviction of this appellant was unsafe.

Lord Slynn held that if the Human Rights Act 1998 were to apply, s. 3(1) of the Act should be used to interpret the statutory provision which provides for the defence. Section 3(1) requires that the courts read and give effect to legislation in a way which is compatible with the Convention rights. Thus, reading s. 28(2) of the Misuse of Drugs Act 1971, Lord Slynn stated that the most obvious way to read this section is that it imposes a legal burden on the defendant. However, his Lordship went on to say that it was 'possible' to read the section as imposing only an evidential burden, and that such a reading was possible 'without doing violence to the language or to the objective' of the section. His Lordship held that reading the section in this way would ensure that it would be compatible with Convention rights because it ensures that the defendant does not bear the legal burden in respect of matters of crucial importance.

Implied statutory exceptions

A statutory provision may impliedly place the legal burden on the defendant. In summary proceedings, s. 101 of the Magistrates' Court Act 1980 is used to determine whether or not a statutory provision impliedly places the legal burden on the defendant.[16]

S. 101, MAGISTRATES' COURT ACT 1981

Where the defendant to an information or complaint relies for his defence on any exception, exemption, proviso, excuse or qualification, whether or not it accompanies the description of the offence or matter of complaint in the enactment creating the offence or on which the complaint is founded, the burden of proving the exception, exemption, proviso, excuse or qualification shall be on him; and this notwithstanding that the information or complaint contains an allegation negativing the exception, exemption, proviso, excuse or qualification.

Section 101 provides that where the defendant is charged with a criminal offence which is proscribed by a statutory provision and he relies on a defence which is an exception, exemption, proviso, excuse or qualification, then the burden of proving that exception, exemption, proviso, excuse or qualification falls on the defendant. According to s. 101, whether or not the exception, exemption, proviso, excuse or qualification accompanies the description of the offence is not relevant. Thus, it does not matter whether the exception is contained within the general definition of the offence or in a separate provision. It is the task of the courts to interpret the relevant statutory provision to determine whether on its true construction the defendant is relying on an exception, exemption, proviso, excuse or qualification. In analysing the construction of the statute, the courts will be looking to see if the parts of the statute containing the offence and exceptions can be easily identified. Where there is clearly a part of the statute which creates the offence and another part which provides for an exception (a defence), then s. 101, Magistrates' Court Act 1980 can be used to place the legal burden of proving the defence on the defendant. It is said that the statute impliedly places the legal burden of proving the defence on the defendant. Thus, the legal burden will remain on the prosecution to prove the offence, and the legal burden of proving the defence will be on the defendant.

In respect of trials on indictment the same approach is adopted, although this is set down in common law rather than in statute. The leading authorities on implied statutory exceptions in trials on indictment are *R* v. *Edwards*[17] and *R* v. *Hunt*.[18] The defendant in *R* v. *Edwards* was convicted of selling intoxicating liquor without a justices' licence, contrary to s. 160(1)(a), Licensing Act 1964. The defendant was the lessee of premises in Brixton. He visited the police station in order to report that someone had smashed the windows to his premises. Consequently, the police kept watch over the premises for 3 days, during which they observed 323 people enter the premises between 8 pm and 4 am each day. Most people arrived late at night after the pubs had closed. The police raided the premises and found 70 people in the basement drinking beer.

---

16 This provision was previously to be found in s. 81 of the Magistrates' Court Act 1952 in substantially the same language, and before that it was contained in s. 39(2) of the Summary Jurisdiction Act 1879.
17 [1975] QB 27, CA.
18 [1987] AC 352, HL.

The basement had been set up as a bar. The defendant was not present at the time of the raid. He was tried for selling intoxicating liquor without a justices' licence. The prosecution did not call any evidence to prove that the defendant did not have a licence. The defendant represented himself. He did not give evidence and he did not make any submission at trial to the effect that the prosecution had failed to call any evidence to prove that the defendant did not have a justices' licence. The defendant was convicted and appealed on the ground that the prosecution had failed to prove that the defendant did not have a justices' licence. Thus, the first issue for the Court of Appeal to decide was who bears the legal burden in respect of the existence of a justices' licence. The Court of Appeal drew on precedent which demonstrated that the courts 'have long thought that the burden of proving that a licence has been granted to authorise the doing of an act which is prohibited by statute unless a licence to do it is held rests upon the defendant'.[19]

R V. *EDWARDS* [1975] QB 27, CA
Lawton LJ

[at 39–40]

... over the centuries the common law, as a result of experience and the need to ensure that justice is done both to the community and to defendants, has evolved an exception to the fundamental rule of our criminal law that the prosecution must prove every element of the offence charged ... It is limited to offences arising under enactments which prohibit the doing of an act save in specified circumstances or by persons of specified classes or with specified qualifications or with the licence or permission of specified authorities. Whenever the prosecution seeks to rely on this exception, the court must construe the enactment under which the charge is laid. If the true construction is that the enactment prohibits the doing of acts, subject to provisoes, exemptions and the like, then the prosecution can rely upon the exception.

In our judgment its application does not depend upon either the fact, or the presumption, that the defendant has peculiar knowledge enabling him to prove the positive of any negative averment. As Wigmore pointed out in his great *Treatise on Evidence* (1905), vol. 4, p. 3525, this concept of peculiar knowledge furnishes no working rule. If it did, defendants would have to prove lack of intent. What does provide a working rule is what the common law evolved from a rule of pleading. We have striven to identify it in this judgment. Like nearly all rules it could be applied oppressively; but the courts have ample powers to curb and discourage oppressive prosecutors and do not hesitate to use them.

Two consequences follow from the view we have taken as to the evolution and nature of this exception. First, as it comes into operation upon an enactment being construed in a particular way, there is no need for the prosecution to prove a prima facie case of lack of excuse, qualification or the like; and secondly, what shifts is the onus: it is for the defendant to prove that he was entitled to do the prohibited act. What rests on him is the legal or, as it is sometimes called, the persuasive burden of proof. It is not the evidential burden.

Thus, Lawton LJ held that the burden of proof could only be reversed in respect of statutory offences which prohibit an act save in specified circumstances or by specified classes of person

---

19 Per Lawton LJ, above (n. 17) at 31.

or those with specified qualifications or with the licence or permission of specified authorities. The Court held that where the provision was constructed in such as way as to prohibit an act, subject to provisos, exemptions, etc., then the burden of proving the provisos, etc. would be on the defendant. Applying this to the facts of *R* v. *Edwards*, the Court of Appeal held that the act prohibited by the statute was selling intoxicating liquor and that 'it was for the defendant to prove that he was the holder of a justices' licence, not the prosecution'.[20] Consequently, the defendant's appeal was dismissed and his conviction upheld. While the Court of Appeal in *R* v. *Edwards* did not expressly apply s. 101, Magistrates' Court Act 1980 to the facts of the case, the decision in the case has the same effect as s. 101.

In *R* v. *Hunt*, the defendant was charged with the unlawful possession of a controlled drug, morphine, contrary to s. 5(2), Misuse of Drugs Act 1971. The police discovered a substance which contained a mixture of morphine mixed with caffeine and atropine.[21] According to regulation 4 and Schedule 1, Misuse of Drugs Regulations 1973, there was no offence if the substance contained 'not more than 0.2 per cent of morphine'. Thus, the defendant would not be guilty of the offence if he fell within this exception. At trial, the prosecution did not adduce any evidence as to the proportion of morphine in the substance. The defendant made a submission of no case to answer, but when this was rejected by the trial judge, the defendant pleaded guilty and appealed against his conviction. The issue which arose on appeal was whether the burden of proving that the substance contained less than 0.2 per cent morphine fell on the defence. The Court of Appeal dismissed the appeal and held that the legal burden was on the defendant to prove on a balance of probabilities that the substance fell within the exception contained within the Regulations. The defendant appealed to the House of Lords.

Rather surprisingly, the House of Lords allowed the appeal and held that rather than dealing with exceptions to the offence under s. 5 of the Misuse of Drugs Act 1971, regulation 4 of the Misuse of Drugs Regulations 1973 actually dealt with the essential elements of the offence. Consequently, the legal burden was on the prosecution to prove that the defendant was in possession of the morphine in the prohibited form.

R V. *HUNT* [1987] AC 352, HL
Lord Griffiths

[at 374]

... *Woolmington* did not lay down a rule that the burden of proving a statutory defence only lay upon the defendant if the statute specifically so provided: that a statute can, on its true construction, place a burden of proof on the defendant although it does not do so expressly: that if a burden of proof is placed on the defendant it is the same burden whether the case be tried summarily or on indictment, namely, a burden that has to be discharged on the balance of probabilities.

The real difficulty in these cases lies in determining upon whom Parliament intended to place the burden of proof when the statute has not expressly so provided. It presents particularly difficult problems of construction when what might be regarded as a matter of defence appears in a clause

---

20 Ibid. at 40.
21 Caffeine and atropine are not controlled drugs under Schedule 2 to the Misuse of Drugs Act 1971.

creating the offence rather than in some subsequent proviso from which it may more readily be inferred that it was intended to provide for a separate defence which a defendant must set up and prove if he wishes to avail himself of it. This difficulty was acutely demonstrated in *Nimmo v. Alexander Cowan & Sons Ltd. [1968] A.C. 107*. Section 29(1) of the Factories Act 1961 provides:

> There shall, so far as is reasonably practicable, be provided and maintained safe means of access to every place at which any person has at any time to work, and every such place shall, so far as is reasonably practicable, be made and kept safe for any person working there.

The question before the House was whether the burden of proving that it was not reasonably practicable to make the working place safe lay upon the defendant or the plaintiff in a civil action. However, as the section also created a summary offence the same question would have arisen in a prosecution. In the event, the House divided three to two on the construction of the section, Lord Reid and Lord Wilberforce holding that the section required the plaintiff or prosecution to prove that it was reasonably practicable to make the working place safe, the majority, Lord Guest, Lord Upjohn and Lord Pearson, holding that if the plaintiff or prosecution proved that the working place was not safe it was for the defendant to excuse himself by proving that it was not reasonably practicable to make it safe. However, their Lordships were in agreement that if the linguistic construction of the statute did not clearly indicate upon whom the burden should lie the court should look to other considerations to determine the intention of Parliament such as the mischief at which the Act was aimed and practical considerations affecting the burden of proof and, in particular, the ease or difficulty that the respective parties would encounter in discharging the burden. I regard this last consideration as one of great importance for surely Parliament can never lightly be taken to have intended to impose an onerous duty on a defendant to prove his innocence in a criminal case and a court should be very slow to draw any such inference from the language of a statute.

When all the cases are analysed, those in which the courts have held that the burden lies on the defendant are cases in which the burden can be easily discharged.

The decision in *R* v. *Hunt* appears to conflict directly with that in *R* v. *Edwards* and the decision of the House of Lords suffered much criticism at the hands of many esteemed academics.[22] As can be seen from the extract of Lord Griffiths' opinion in *R* v. *Hunt* (reproduced

---

22 See generally P. Healy, 'Proof and policy: no golden threads' [1987] Crim LR 355; P. Mirfield, 'The legacy of *Hunt*' [1988] Crim LR 19; J. C. Smith, 'The presumption of innocence' (1987) 38 NILQ 223; A. Zuckerman, 'No third exception to the *Woolmington* rule' (1987) 103 LQR 170. For a particularly passionate critique of the decision, see G. Williams, 'The logic of exceptions' (1988) 47(2) *Cambridge Law Journal* 261–95, who begins his article (at 261) with: 'Every so often the Appeal Committee of the House of Lords produces a decision that sets back the rational development of the criminal law for several years or decades. Other courts do this too. But when the lords are at fault it is particularly disappointing: because they should be the elite of the judiciary; because they have the time to consider their decisions properly; because counsel who argue cases before them (having thrashed them out in two lower courts) should be unusually well-prepared; because the lords have the authority to overrule ill-considered decisions of the lower courts; and because their own pronouncements are (if things go wrong) especially hard to overturn. What makes these aberrational decisions particularly disconcerting is that the lords commonly show no appreciation of, and make no attempt to answer, the powerful arguments in the existing literature against the position they adopt. Now, in *Hunt*, they have done it again, despite a full argument addressed to them by Mr. Zucker which should have kept them on the right track.' Williams points out that the only academics who do not disagree with the House of Lords' decision are F. Bennion in 'Statutory exceptions: a third knot in the golden thread' [1988] Crim LR

above), policy considerations were important in the House of Lords' decision in the case of *Nimmo* v. *Alexander Cowan & Sons Ltd*[23] (which was decided before *R* v. *Hunt*). This was a civil case which involved s. 29(1), Factories Act 1961.[24] The section provided that 'There shall, so far as is reasonably practicable, be provided and maintained safe means of access to every place at which any person has at any time to work, and every such place shall, so far as is reasonably practicable, be made and kept safe for any person working there.' The claimant was a workman at a factory who was injured in the course of his work. He sued his employers for damages arguing that his place of work was not kept safe as required by s. 29(1) of the Act. However, he did not adduce any evidence to prove that it was reasonably practicable to make his place of work safe. The House of Lords held (by a majority of 3:2) that the legal burden to prove that it was not reasonably practicable to make the place of work safe was on the defendant employers, and, thus, the defendant was held to be liable. In *R* v. *Hunt*, Lord Griffiths explained that the majority in the House of Lords in *Nimmo* v. *Alexander Cowan & Sons Ltd* relied on certain policy factors, such as 'the mischief at which the Act was aimed' and 'practical considerations'. In terms of practical considerations, Lord Griffiths emphasised the importance of considering how easy or difficult it would be for each of the parties to discharge the burden. In the case of *R* v. *Hunt*, it is clear that due to the inequality of arms between the prosecution and the defence it would have been much easier for the prosecution (with the wealth of resources at its disposal) to prove the consistency of the morphine than it would for the defence to do so. Contrast this with the case of *R* v. *Edwards*, in which case it was much easier for the defendant to prove that he had the necessary licence than it would have been for the prosecution to prove that he did not have such a licence. Lord Griffiths also considered that Parliament would never lightly take the decision to intend to impose an onerous duty on a defendant to prove his innocence. His Lordship also took into account the seriousness of the offence and held that this was a further reason for placing the burden of proof on the prosecution: 'it seems to me right to resolve any ambiguity in favour of the defendant and to place the burden of proving the nature of the substance involved in so serious an offence upon the prosecution'.[25]

Unfortunately, the cases on implied statutory exceptions to the general rule in *Woolmington* v. *DPP* do highlight an inconsistent approach, which makes it rather difficult to predict what the decision of the courts will be in future cases. One example of such inconsistency involves two cases which dealt with different statutory provisions under the Highways Act 1959. In *Gatland* v. *Metropolitan Police Commissioner*[26] the defendant was charged with the offence of depositing something on the highway contrary to s. 140, Highways Act 1959. This provision stated that, 'If a person without lawful authority or

---

31 and D. Birch in 'Hunting the snark: the elusive statutory exception' [1988] Crim LR 221, whose view he describes as 'ambivalent'.
23 [1968] AC 107.
24 In *R* v. *Hunt*, Lord Griffiths states that while the action under s. 29(1) of the Factories Act 1961 in *Nimmo* v. *Alexander Cowan & Sons Ltd* was a civil one, the section also created a summary offence, so the same issue would have arisen in a criminal prosecution.
25 Above (n. 18) at 378.
26 [1968] 2 QB 279.

excuse, deposits anything whatever on a highway ... is an offence'. In *Nagy* v. *Weston*[27] the defendant was charged with wilfully obstructing the highway contrary to s. 121, Highways Act 1959. This provision stated that, 'If a person without lawful authority or excuse in any way wilfully obstructs ... it will be an offence'. A quick comparison of the wording of the sections reveals that they are almost identical in construction. Nevertheless, the courts in each case reached opposing conclusions. In *Gatland* v. *Metropolitan Police Commissioner*, it was held that the provision was constructed so as to provide a separate offence and defence. Consequently, applying the principle of implied exceptions to the general rule, the legal burden of proving the defence of lawful authority or excuse was on the defendant. By contrast, in *Nagy* v. *Weston*, it was held that the legal burden was on the prosecution to prove both the offence and that there was no lawful authority or excuse. It is difficult to justify the difference between these two decisions.

3.3.3 Reverse burdens and the presumption of innocence

This paragraph considers the conflict between the notion of reverse burdens which require a defendant to prove his defence on a balance of probabilities and the presumption of innocence and the authorities which have developed since the enactment of the Human Rights Act 1998.[28] This issue has already been explored above to some extent in our examination of the Court of Appeal decision of *R* v. *Lambert*; *R* v. *Ali*; *R* v. *Jordan*; and the House of Lords' decision in *R* v. *Lambert*.

> **Cross-reference**
> Refer back to paragraph 3.3.2 for the discussion of *R* v. *Lambert*; *R* v. *Ali*; *R* v. *Jordan* [2000] EWCA Crim 3542 and *R* v. *Lambert* [2001] UKHL 37.

In his article, 'Taking the burden of proof seriously',[29] Paul Roberts is highly critical of the use of reverse burdens of proof, arguing that they should not be used in any legal system which values the liberty of its citizens.[30] Roberts suggests that the general rule in *Woolmington* v. *DPP* which places the burden of proof on the prosecution acts as a check on the powers of the state and places a limit on the ability of the state to interfere in the lives of individuals. He outlines three practical reasons why the liberty of individuals is protected by placing the burden of proof on the prosecution and our freedom is threatened by reverse onuses which require a defendant to prove his defence and he states that these three arguments are 'mutually reinforcing':

---

27 [1965] 1 All ER 78.
28 For a more detailed analysis of the relationship between reverse onuses and the presumption of innocence, see I. Dennis, 'Reverse onuses and the presumption of innocence: in search of principle' [2005] Crim LR 901; G. Dingwall, 'Statutory exceptions, burdens of proof and the Human Rights Act 1998' (2002) 65(3) MLR 450–63; and V. Tadros and S. Tierney, 'The presumption of innocence and the Human Rights Act' (2004) 67(3) MLR 402–34.
29 P. Roberts, 'Taking the burden of proof seriously' [1995] Crim LR 783.
30 Ibid. at 788.

P. ROBERTS, 'TAKING THE BURDEN OF PROOF SERIOUSLY' [1995] CRIM LR 783

[at 785–7]

The first argument is straightforward and easily stated. Whenever the burden of proof on a particular issue rests with the defendant it follows that the jury or magistrates must convict in cases in which they remain undecided about facts material to that issue. A presumption of guilt is employed to fill the void of doubt, in place of the presumption of innocence which usually awards the benefit of any reasonable doubt to the defendant . . .

[The second reason is that the] prosecution has the dual advantage of dictating the nature of the proceedings and of being well prepared to participate in them. The state employs professional investigators to detect crime and to gather evidence, utilising offence definitions to structure the shape and direction of their inquiries. As proceedings develop, the facts to be proved by the prosecution are specified by the charges, which the prosecutor selects after reviewing the evidence. On the other hand, in contrast to the prosecutor who is both forewarned and forearmed, the defendant must respond to a procedural agenda that is already more or less fixed by the time that he is called on to explain himself. A moment's introspection reveals, at least to most of us, that we could not guarantee to be able to account for our past movements and motives in order to answer any charge that might, without warning, be brought against us. Guilty people may well invest time and effort in covering their tracks or in setting up false alibis, but innocent people are not generally concerned with being able to prove their innocence, unless and until they are called upon to do so; and then it might be too late.

The third reason [focuses] on the fact that the prosecution has access to investigative resources which are vastly superior to those available to most defendants in criminal cases . . .

A policy of reversing the burden of proof in criminal proceedings might commend itself to a totalitarian regime which, for reasons of domestic order or foreign diplomacy, wished to retain the bare window-dressing of legality, but it is not the badge of an administration which values and respects its citizens' freedom.

The presumption of innocence is found under Article 6(2) of the European Convention on Human Rights. Since the enactment of the Human Rights Act 1998, a defendant may rely upon the Convention rights in our domestic courts and the courts have an obligation under s. 3 to read and give effect to domestic legislation in a way which is compatible with the Convention rights. Consequently, the jurisprudence of the European Court of Human Rights relating to the presumption of innocence under Article 6(2) is significant. The Court has acknowledged that Article 6(2) is not an absolute right: it can be restricted.[31] While in principle, Article 6(2) does not prohibit presumptions of fact or law within a legal system, Contracting States must confine presumptions within certain 'reasonable limits which take into account the importance of what is at stake and maintain the rights of the defence'.[32] The Court has also held that reverse onuses of proof do not automatically violate the presumption of innocence.[33]

31 *Salabiaku* v. *France* (1991) 13 EHRR 379.
32 Ibid. at [28].
33 *Lingens* v. *Austria* (1981) 26 DR 171.

In *R* v. *DPP ex parte Kebilene and others*,[34] the House of Lords held that where a statute places a burden on the defendant, the court should examine:

- 'whether the legislative technique which has been adopted imposes a persuasive or merely an evidential burden',
- 'whether it is mandatory or discretionary', and
- 'whether it relates to an essential element of the offence or merely to an exception or proviso'.[35]

The House held that there would be no violation of the presumption of innocence where an evidential burden was placed on the defendant. Where a statutory provision contains a mandatory presumption of guilt and imposes the legal burden on the defendant to prove his innocence, this will prima facie violate the presumption of innocence. However, this will not necessarily mean that the provision is incompatible with Article 6(2). Lord Hope states that the courts will need to take into account the need to strike the right balance between the rights of the individual against the interests of society and the problems which the legislation was designed to address.[36] In considering how to balance these interests, Lord Hope adopted the questions suggested by counsel in argument, namely:

1. What does the prosecution have to prove in order to transfer the onus to the defence?
2. What is the burden on the accused – does it relate to something which is likely to be difficult for him to prove, or does it relate to something which is likely to be within his knowledge or to which he readily has access?
3. What is the nature of the threat faced by society which the provision is designed to combat?[37]

This approach was followed by the Court of Appeal in *R* v. *Lambert*; *R* v. *Ali*; *R* v. *Jordan*. The Court stated that where the defendant was required to prove an essential element of the offence, the reverse onus would be more difficult to justify, but it would be less objectionable to require a defendant to prove a special defence.[38] Thus, on the facts of the cases, s. 2(1), Homicide Act 1957 which expressly placed the burden of proving diminished responsibility on the defendant did not violate Article 6(2) because the defence under s. 2(1) was not an essential element of the offence of murder, but provided a special and distinct defence to murder. The defendant would not be required to prove anything if he chose not to rely on this special defence. In relation to the case under the Misuse of Drugs Act 1971, the Court held that s. 28 of the Act did 'not impose additional ingredients which have to be proved to complete the offence but a way of avoiding liability for what would otherwise be an offence'. In this case, the defendant objected to the standard of proof that he was required to attain to discharge his legal burden in respect of the defence. However, the Court held that the standard of proof was justified by policy reasons and was not disproportionate. When the case of *R* v. *Lambert* reached the House of Lords on appeal, the House held that while the Human Rights Act 1998 should not have been applied retrospectively by the Court of Appeal, it was possible to read the words of s. 28(2), Misuse of Drugs Act 1971 down so as to impose only an evidential burden on

---

34 [2000] 2 AC 326, HL.
35 Ibid. per Lord Hope at 380.
36 Ibid. at 384.
37 Ibid. at 386.
38 Above (n. 9) at [15].

the defendant. This would ensure that the statute was compatible with Article 6(2). Lord Steyn noted that any statutory interference with the presumption of innocence under Article 6(2) must be proportionate: '[t]he principle of proportionality must be observed'.[39]

The decision of the House of Lords in *R* v. *Lambert* was distinguished by the Court of Appeal in *Lynch* v. *DPP*[40] and *R* v. *Drummond*.[41] In *Lynch* v. *DPP*, the defendant was charged with possession of an article with a blade or point in a public place contrary to s. 139, Criminal Justice Act 1988. The Court of Appeal held that the defence under s. 139(4), Criminal Justice Act 1988 which provides that it is a defence for a person charged under this section to prove that he had good reason or lawful authority for having the article with him in a public place, imposed a legal burden on the defendant. The Court held that this did not violate Article 6(2) and drew a distinction between s. 139 of the Criminal Justice Act 1988 in this case and s. 28 of the Misuse of Drugs Act 1971 in *R* v. *Lambert*. The Court held that there was no violation of the Convention right under Article 6(2) because in this case the burden was on the prosecution to prove that the defendant knowingly had the article in his possession under s. 139(1), there was a strong public interest in bladed articles not being carried in public without good reason, and this requirement only required him to prove something that was within his own knowledge. Furthermore, the Court held that in the vast majority of cases the tribunal of fact makes a judgment as to whether there was a good reason without the decision depending on whether it has to be proved that there is a good reason. The Court also acknowledged the fact that there was a much more restricted power of sentence for an offence under s. 139 of the Criminal Justice Act 1988 than for an offence under s. 28 of the Misuse of Drugs Act 1971. In *R* v. *Drummond*, it was held that s. 15 of the Road Traffic Offenders Act 1988 imposed a legal burden on the defendant to prove that he had consumed alcohol in the time between the commission of the relevant offence and before providing a specimen to the police. Longmore LJ stated that: '... not all apparently persuasive burdens have to be "read down" to be evidential burdens; we think it necessary to look at the legislation as a whole in order to determine whether Parliament intended to impose a persuasive burden and whether such burden is justifiable'. This legal burden did not violate Article 6(2) as the interference with the presumption of innocence was justified and no more than necessary. In this case, the interference was proportionate because conviction for driving whilst over the prescribed limit followed from an exact scientific test and there was no requirement that the court assess the intention of the defendant. In such circumstances, it is the conduct of the defendant in drinking after the offence and before the specimen is provided which could render the test unreliable and there is a danger that the defendant might deliberately sabotage the test in this way in order to take advantage of this defence. Furthermore, the Court also stated that relevant scientific evidence was within the knowledge or means of access of the defendant.

The House of Lords considered the issue of reverse onuses again in 2003 in the case of *R* v. *Johnstone*.[42] This case involved the unauthorised use of a trade mark, an offence under s. 92, Trade Marks Act 1994 in relation to 500 'bootleg' CDs and cassettes comprising of performances by well-known music artists. The Court of Appeal held that it was for the prosecution to prove

---

39 Above (n. 15) at [34].
40 [2003] QB 137.
41 [2002] 2 Cr App R 352.
42 [2003] 1 WLR 1736, HL.

that the defendant used a sign on the CDs and cassettes as a trade mark (as an indication of trade origin). The defendant sought to rely on a defence under s. 92(5) and the Court held that, under this provision, the legal burden was on the defence to prove that he had reasonable grounds to believe that using the sign in question did not constitute the infringement of a trade mark and that this reverse onus did not violate Article 6(2) of the European Convention on Human Rights. The policy justification for this reverse onus was said to be the public interest in ensuring that trade marks were protected and the protection of both artists and genuine music manufacturers and the end consumer. The Court also relied upon the fact that those who trade in such goods are in the best position to know the sources they use and, thus, the matters in the defence under s. 92(5) are within the defendant's knowledge. By contrast, consumers who buy the end product from the trader are not in a position to have such knowledge of the source of the goods. In *Sheldrake* v. *DPP; Attorney General's Reference (No. 4 of 2002)*,[43] Lord Bingham stated that the House of Lords in *R* v. *Johnstone* did not intend to depart from or modify the decision in *R* v. *Lambert* and explained the differences in emphasis by the difference in the subject matter of the cases.[44]

In *Sheldrake* v. *DPP; Attorney General's Reference (No. 4 of 2002)*, the House of Lords heard several cases together which all raised the issue of reverse onuses. *Sheldrake* v. *DPP* concerned two appeals by the DPP relating to s. 11(1) and (2), Terrorism Act 2000, and s. 5(2), Road Traffic Act 1988; and *Attorney General's Reference (No. 4 of 2002)* concerned five conjoined appeals from the Court of Appeal relating to s. 353(1) of the Insolvency Act 1986, s. 1(2) of the Protection from Eviction Act 1977, s. 51(7) of the Criminal Justice and Public Order Act 1994 and s. 4(2) of the Homicide Act 1957. After exploring the previous authorities in this area, Lord Bingham outlined the principles which are derived from the body of case law:

SHELDRAKE V. DPP; ATTORNEY GENERAL'S REFERENCE (NO. 4 OF 2002) [2004] UKHL 43
Lord Bingham

[21] From this body of authority certain principles may be derived. The overriding concern is that a trial should be fair, and the presumption of innocence is a fundamental right directed to that end. The Convention does not outlaw presumptions of fact or law but requires that these should be kept within reasonable limits and should not be arbitrary. It is open to states to define the constituent elements of a criminal offence, excluding the requirement of mens rea. But the substance and effect of any presumption adverse to a defendant must be examined, and must be reasonable. Relevant to any judgment on reasonableness or proportionality will be the opportunity given to the defendant to rebut the presumption, maintenance of the rights of the defence, flexibility in application of the presumption, retention by the court of a power to assess the evidence, the importance of what is at stake and the difficulty which a prosecutor may face in the absence of a presumption. Security concerns do not absolve member states from their duty to observe basic standards of fairness. The justifiability of any infringement of the presumption of innocence cannot be resolved by any rule of thumb, but on examination of all the facts and circumstances of the particular provision as applied in the particular case.

---

43 [2004] UKHL 43.
44 Ibid. at [30].

Thus, Lord Bingham stated that the overriding objective is always that the trial should be fair, and this objective requires consideration of the presumption of innocence. His Lordship emphasised that it is Parliament's job to decide whether or not a reverse onus should be placed on a defendant, and this is never a task of the court. However, it is the courts' task 'to assess whether a burden enacted by Parliament unjustifiably infringes the presumption of innocence'.[45] In performing this role, the court must consider whether the interference with the presumption of innocence is reasonable or proportionate, and factors which will need to be taken into account include:

- the opportunity given to the defendant to rebut the presumption,
- maintenance of the rights of the defence,
- flexibility in application of the presumption,
- retention by the court of a power to assess the evidence,
- the importance of what is at stake, and
- the difficulty which a prosecutor may face in the absence of a presumption.

The court must reach its decision by examining all of the facts and circumstances of the provision as applied in the case.

3.3.4 Civil proceedings

In civil proceedings, the burden of proof falls on the party asserting the issue. Thus, the claimant bears the legal burden of proving the facts in issue in his case against the defendant. If the defendant raises and asserts a specific defence then he will bear the legal burden of proving the elements of that defence. However, where the defendant's defence merely constituted a denial of the action brought by the claimant, it will be for the claimant to prove what he asserts on a balance of probabilities. For example, if the claimant brings an action for breach of contract against the defendant, the claimant bears the legal burden of proving that there was a contract between the claimant and the defendant and that the defendant breached the contract. Similarly, where the claimant brings an action for negligence against the defendant, the claimant bears the legal burden of proving that the defendant owed the claimant a duty of care, that he breached that duty, that the breach caused loss to the claimant and that the loss was not too remote. In either example, the defendant might deny breach of contract or breach of a duty of care, but the onus is on the claimant to prove that element of his claim. However, if the defendant were to raise a specific defence which does not form part of the elements of the claim – for example, by asserting that the claimant was contributorily negligent – then it will be for the defendant to prove on a balance of probabilities that the claimant was contributorily negligent.

3.4 STANDARD OF PROOF

The standard of proof represents the degree to which the party bearing the legal burden must discharge that burden. If the standard of proof is met, then that party has discharged its burden

---

45 Ibid at [31].

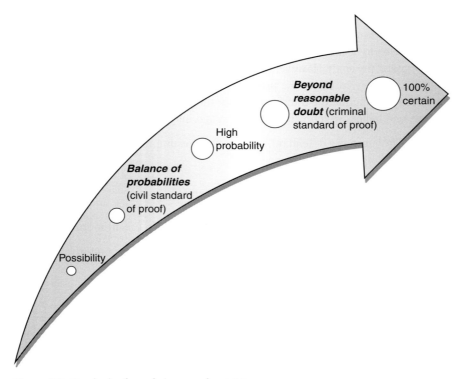

Figure 3.3 Standards of proof: degrees of certainty

of proof. It is for the tribunal of fact in a case to determine whether the party bringing the case has met the standard of proof. The range of possible degrees of certainty that a fact-finder might have in the prosecution's or claimant's case raises the necessary question of *how sure* the tribunal of fact must be in any given case before they may reach a guilty verdict in criminal proceedings or find that the defendant is liable in civil proceedings (see Figure 3.3).

There are different standards of proof for criminal and civil proceedings. The criminal standard of proof is 'beyond reasonable doubt'; in order for a defendant to be convicted, the jury must be satisfied that he is guilty 'beyond reasonable doubt'. This is a much higher standard of proof than the civil standard, which is a 'balance of probabilities'. In a civil case, the defendant will be held to be liable if the judge is satisfied on a balance of probabilities that the claimant's version of events is correct. The rationale for the different standards of proof in criminal and civil proceedings and a higher standard of proof being applied in criminal cases is based upon the different interests that the defendants in each system risk losing. A defendant in criminal proceedings needs to be protected against wrongful conviction by a higher standard of proof being imposed upon the prosecution. This is because the stakes are high in a criminal trial: he risks losing his liberty should he be convicted. The most obvious risk to liberty is through a sentence of imprisonment, but even where a non-custodial sentence is likely, a defendant risks losing his liberty through the imposition of some form of community sentence which may require him to perform unpaid work or some other activity or attend a specified programme, it may prohibit him from performing a specified activity, impose a curfew, a requirement of residence or exclude him from a particular area, require him to undertake treatment for his mental health or drug or alcohol addiction, to attend supervision sessions or an attendance centre, or to be electronically monitored with a 'tag'.[46] With so much at stake in a criminal trial, it is crucial that only the guilty are convicted; as Blackstone commented in the nineteenth century, 'it is better that ten guilty persons escape, than that one innocent suffer'.[47] The wrongful conviction of an innocent defendant is seen as far more serious than the wrongful acquittal of a guilty defendant. It is for the same reason that where the legal burden is placed upon the defendant in criminal proceedings to prove his defence, the standard that the defendant must meet is the lower, civil standard of a balance of probabilities. By contrast, a defendant in civil proceedings needs less protection against a wrongful verdict because the risk to him upon a finding of liability is financial, rather than a risk to his liberty. Of course, a finding of liability against a defendant in civil proceedings might result in the defendant being required to pay a substantial sum of money in compensation to the claimant; this may even result in bankruptcy for the defendant, but the law places a far greater weight on the liberty of a defendant.

3.4.1 Criminal standard

As stated above, in criminal proceedings, the burden of proof usually rests with the prosecution. The general rule is that the prosecution must prove that the defendant is guilty of the offence charged. The standard of proof is 'beyond reasonable doubt'. While one jury has come under fire recently for asking the trial judge for further explanation as to the meaning of 'beyond reasonable doubt',[48] this is actually a very difficult expression to define and one which can be difficult for juries to understand.[49] It is difficult to explain what makes a doubt a 'reasonable doubt' and how far 'beyond' this the jury must be sure before they can convict the defendant. One reason for the difficulty in defining this expression is that it is not easy to attach a numerical value to the degree of proof that it represents. While the civil standard of proof, 'balance of probabilities', is very easy to express in terms of numerical value (one has to be more certain than not, which equates to being 51 per cent sure), the same is not true of 'beyond reasonable doubt' and the courts have completely avoided trying to do so. In *Miller* v.

---

46 See s. 177 of the Criminal Justice Act 2003 for a full list of the various community order requirements which may be imposed on an offender sentenced to a community sentence.

47 W. Blackstone, *Commentaries on the Laws of England* (1765–69), Book IV, Chapter XXVII, 'Of trial, and conviction'.

48 In the trial of Vicky Pryce for perverting the course of justice, the jury asked the trial judge ten questions after they had retired to deliberate upon their verdict. One of these questions was 'Can you define what is reasonable doubt?': see 'Vicky Pryce trial: 10 questions jury asked the judge', *The Guardian*, 20 February 2013. The BBC reported that the trial judge, Sweeney J, replied, 'A reasonable doubt is a doubt which is reasonable. These are ordinary English words that the law doesn't allow me to help you with beyond the written directions that I have already given': see 'Ten questions posed by Vicky Pryce jury', *BBC News*, 20 February 2013. For the criticisms levelled at the Pryce jury for asking these questions, see S. Jones, 'Senior lawyers defend jury system after judge orders Vick Pryce retrial', *The Guardian*, 21 February 2013.

49 See *R* v. *Stephens* [2002] EWCA Crim 1529 and *R* v. *Majid* [2009] EWCA Crim 2563.

Minister of Pensions,[50] Denning J gave an explanation of the meaning of 'beyond reasonable doubt':

MILLER V. MINISTER OF PENSIONS [1947] 2 ALL ER 372
Denning J

[at 373]

It need not reach certainty, but it must carry a high degree of probability. Proof beyond reasonable doubt does not mean proof beyond a shadow of a doubt . . . If the evidence is so strong as to leave only a remote possibility in the defendant's favour, which can be dismissed with the sentence, 'Of course it is possible, but not in the least probable', the case is proved beyond reasonable doubt. But nothing short of that will suffice.

A few years later, in the case of *R* v. *Summers*,[51] Lord Goddard CJ expressed his dissatisfaction with explanations of the phrase 'beyond reasonable doubt' given by the courts: 'I have never yet heard a court give a satisfactory definition of what is a reasonable doubt, and it would be very much better if summings-up did not use that expression'.[52] His Lordship went on to state that such explanations of 'beyond reasonable doubt' are 'likely to cause more confusion than clarity'. His Lordship preferred the word 'sure' in place of 'beyond reasonable doubt'. Thus, it is said that the criminal standard of proof requires the prosecution to persuade the tribunal of fact that they are 'sure' that the defendant is guilty. In a Crown Court, the usual direction given to the jury is that they can only convict the defendant if they are 'sure that the defendant is guilty'.[53] If the jury is not sure, then they are directed that they must acquit the defendant.

SIR ANTHONY HOOPER LJ, 'FAIR TRIAL: "ONE GOLDEN THREAD" IN L. BLOM-COOPER, B. DICKSON AND G. DREWRY (EDS.), *THE JUDICIAL HOUSE OF LORDS 1976–2009* (OXFORD UNIVERSITY PRESS, 2009)
The modernisation of the reasonable doubt test

[at pp. 618–19]

Although the popular view is that the prosecution must prove the case beyond a reasonable doubt, difficulties with the meaning of 'reasonable doubt' (or perceived difficulties in explaining to a jury what is or is not a reasonable doubt) have led to the abandonment, in practice, of the reasonable doubt test. Juries are now told, in the words of the current Judicial Studies Board Specimen Directions[54]:

---

50 [1947] 2 All ER 372.
51 (1952) 36 Cr App R 14.
52 Ibid. at 15.
53 See the Judicial Studies Board *Crown Court Benchbook* at p. 16.
54 In 2010, the Specimen Directions were replaced with the *Crown Court Benchbook*. The *Benchbook* states that 'The prosecution proves its case if the jury, having considered all the evidence relevant to the charge they are considering, are sure that the defendant is guilty. Further explanation is unwise. If the jury are not sure they must find the defendant not guilty. Note: Being sure is the same as entertaining no reasonable doubt' (p. 16).

> How does the prosecution succeed in proving the defendant's guilt? The answer is – by making you sure of it. Nothing less than that will do. If after considering all the evidence you are sure that the defendant is guilty, you must return a verdict of 'Guilty'. If you are not sure, your verdict must be 'Not Guilty'.

According to the Specimen Directions:

> Normally, when directing a jury on the standard of proof, it is not necessary to use the phrase 'beyond reasonable doubt'. But where it has been used in the trial, e.g. by counsel in the speeches, it is desirable to give the following direction: 'The prosecution must make you sure of guilt, which is the same as proving the case beyond reasonable doubt' . . .

> I do not believe that Viscount Sankey would object to the change, although I am unaware of any decision in the House of Lords that has considered the change and approved it.

Difficulties arise where judges do not follow the advice of Lord Goddard CJ either in summing up to a jury on the standard of proof or when answering a jury's question on the meaning of 'beyond reasonable doubt'. In *R* v. *Majid*,[55] the Court of Appeal was asked to consider a trial judge's summing up on the standard of proof. The trial judge directed the jury that the standard that they must apply before convicting the defendant was: 'you must be satisfied of guilt beyond all reasonable doubt'. The Court of Appeal criticised the trial judge's direction, stating that it: 'not only does not comply with the Judicial Studies Board standard direction but led to the very problem that the Judicial Studies Board direction is designed to avoid. Judges are advised by the Judicial Studies Board, as they have been for many years, to direct the jury that before they can return a verdict of guilty, they must be sure that the defendant is guilty'.[56] As a result of that direction, the jury sent a question to the judge asking, 'If the evidence supports possible but very unlikely scenarios, which themselves would lead to a "not guilty" verdict, does this exclude a "beyond reasonable doubt" conclusion. There are concerns over how to interpret "beyond reasonable doubt" – does this need to exclude all possible scenarios associated with "not guilty"?' The trial judge answered the jury's question by reference to the Judicial Studies Board Specimen Direction that the jury should be directed that they should be 'sure' before they convict the defendant. The trial judge equated the phrases 'satisfied beyond any reasonable doubt' and 'sure', but he then went on to say: 'The prosecution do not have to prove the case so that you are certain of guilt and the reason I do not usually at all direct juries that they have to be sure of guilt is because, to my mind, juries can then become confused and think that "sure" is the same as "certain".' The Court of Appeal considered the judge's first use of the phrase 'beyond reasonable doubt' in his summing up and then his answer to the jury's question and held that the trial judge should not have drawn the distinction that he drew between 'sure' and 'certain', and stated that it is 'likely only to confuse' the jury.

---

55 [2009] EWCA Crim 2563.
56 Ibid. at [11].

R V. MAJID [2009] EWCA CRIM 2563
Moses LJ

12. ... Any question from the jury dealing with the standard of proof is one that most judges dread. To have to define what is meant by 'reasonable doubt' or what is meant by 'being sure' requires an answer difficult to articulate and likely to confuse. No doubt that is why the Judicial Studies Board seeks to avoid it in the direction they give to judges. The judge on receiving that question and debating it with counsel, said that he did not understand altogether what the jury meant. It seems to us that it is plain that the jury were asking what type of possibilities might be excluded from the road to their conclusion. The question, we suggest, could have been answered simply by telling the jury to exclude any fanciful possibility and act only on those which were realistic. But the judge chose not to do so and entered into a debate with Mr Tomlinson, as to the propriety, on the one hand, of a direction that the jury should be sure, as opposed as to a direction that they should be satisfied beyond a reasonable doubt.

13. The discussion continued, by reference to what the editors say in Archbold and led to the judge finally agreeing that he would tell the jury that 'satisfied beyond a reasonable doubt' meant the same as 'sure'.

. . .

16. There is, however, more merit in the challenge to the distinction that the judge drew between being sure and being certain. This is not a direction that a judge should give to the jury. It is likely only to confuse and it is difficult for anyone to articulate, in a clear and helpful manner, the difference between being sure and the difference between being certain. The distinction should therefore be avoided.

The Court of Appeal in *R* v. *Majid* relied upon the decision of the Court in *R* v. *Stephens*.[57] At first instance in *R* v. *Stephens*, the trial judge had directed the jury drawing a distinction between the words 'certain' and 'sure'. On appeal, the Court of Appeal held that it was not helpful to draw such a distinction and stated that 'judges should avoid doing so'. The Court further advised that should a trial judge be asked to explain the phrase 'beyond reasonable doubt', he should 'simply remind the jury that they had to be sure of guilt before they could convict, indicating, if he felt it necessary, that that was the limit of the help which he could give them'.[58] In *R* v. *Smith (Scott)*,[59] the Court of Appeal held that '[t]he standard of proof in a criminal case requires the jury to be sure of guilt, which is the same (but no more than) the proof of guilt beyond reasonable doubt'.[60]

In the rare circumstances that the burden of proof falls on the defendant in criminal proceedings, the lower civil standard of proof is used; the defendant must prove his defence 'on a balance of probabilities'. Expressed another way, the defendant must prove that his defence was 'more probable than not'.[61] This means that the jury must be 51 per cent sure that the elements of the defence are satisfied. As stated above, the rationale for applying the lower standard of proof where the burden of proof falls on the defendant is the protection

---

57 [2002] EWCA Crim 1529.
58 Ibid. at [15].
59 [2012] EWCA Crim 702.
60 Ibid. at [21].
61 *Miller* v. *Minister of Pensions* [1947] 2 All ER 372 at 374.

against wrongful conviction. The wrongful conviction of an innocent defendant is far more serious than the wrongful acquittal of a guilty defendant. The protection offered by the presumption of innocence would be more greatly offended by a requirement that the defendant not only bear the legal burden of proving his defence, but that he must reach the high standard imposed upon the prosecution. It is also worth mentioning here the inequality of arms: the lower standard of proof reflects the limited resources at the defendant's disposal to satisfy the standard of proof, especially when compared to the wealth of resources available to the prosecution.

3.4.2 Civil standard

In civil proceedings, the burden of proof is on the claimant to prove the facts in issue in the case that they bring against the defendant. The lower standard of proof is applied in civil proceedings: the claimant must prove the facts in issue 'on a balance of probabilities' so that it is 'more probable than not'. In *Miller* v. *Minister of Pensions*,[62] Denning J gave an explanation of the meaning of a 'balance of probabilities':

> ## *MILLER* V. *MINISTER OF PENSIONS* [1947] 2 ALL ER 372
> ### Denning J
>
> [at 373]
>
> . . . the case must be decided according to the preponderance of probability. If at the end of the case the evidence turns the scale definitely one way or the other, the tribunal must decide accordingly, but if the evidence is so evenly balanced that the tribunal is unable to come to a determined conclusion one way or the other, then the man must be given the benefit of the doubt. This means that the case must be decided in favour of the man unless the evidence against him reaches the same degree of cogency as is required to discharge a burden in a civil case. That degree is well settled. It must carry a reasonable degree of probability, but not so high as is required in a criminal case. If the evidence is such that the tribunal can say: 'We think it more probable than not,' the burden is discharged, but, if the probabilities are equal, it is not.

After a few cases which suggested that a higher standard of proof applied in more serious civil proceedings, the House of Lords has confirmed that there is only one civil standard of proof, namely a 'balance of probabilities'. In *Re B (Children)*,[63] Lord Hoffmann stated: 'I think that the time has come to say, once and for all, that there is only one civil standard of proof and that is proof that the fact in issue more probably occurred than not.'[64]

Table 3.1 summarises the allocation of the burden of proof and the different standards of proof associated with criminal and civil proceedings.

---

62 Ibid.
63 [2008] UKHL 35.
64 Ibid. at [13].

Table 3.1 Allocation of burden of proof and associated standards of proof

| | Criminal proceedings | | Civil proceedings |
	General rule	Exception	General rule
Burden of proof	On the prosecution	On the defence	On the claimant
Standard of proof	Beyond reasonable doubt	Balance of probabilities	Balance of probabilities

3.5 EVIDENTIAL BURDEN

The evidential burden is completely different to the legal (or persuasive burden). The evidential burden is not a burden of proof, but is an obligation on one of the parties in the case to raise some evidence to make an issue a 'live' one, or to persuade the judge that the issue is one which should be left for the tribunal of fact to consider (known as 'passing the judge'). Usually, the party who will bear the legal burden in respect of an issue will first have to discharge the evidential burden in respect of that issue; the evidential burden must be discharged before the legal burden is triggered. For example, if the defendant is charged with theft, some relevant evidence that the offence did indeed take place must be adduced by the prosecution to discharge the evidential burden before the legal burden of proving the offence is triggered. Once the evidential burden has been discharged and the judge is persuaded to leave the offence to the tribunal of fact to consider, then it falls to the prosecution to discharge the legal burden in accordance with the relevant standard of proof, namely to persuade the tribunal of fact that the defendant did commit the theft beyond reasonable doubt. In practice, discharging the evidential burden is not usually an onerous task for the prosecution. Since it is not a burden to prove a matter, there is no standard attached to the evidential burden. It is simply an obligation to raise some evidence, but that evidence need not actually prove anything. Thus, the evidential burden does not usually raise any complicated issues in practice.

In order to discharge the evidential burden, the defendant must be able to point to some relevant evidence in support of the fact in issue. In *R* v. *Lambert*, the House of Lords held that, '[i]t is not enough that the defendant in seeking to establish the evidential burden should merely mouth the words of the section'.[65] Rather, the evidential burden must be,

> ... [demonstrated] from the evidence. As I see it, the evidence can be given by the prosecution or by the defence. It might take the form of something said to the police at the scene, or something said in interview or something said by the defendant or anyone else in the witness box, provided in each case that it is put in evidence. I am not sure whether the question whether the accused has raised an arguable case is a matter for the judge or jury, although I would have thought that it was a matter for the judge, as with, for example, provocation or self-defence; ... in a case before the justices it is for them to decide both the question whether the accused has raised an arguable case and, if so, the question whether the prosecution has discharged the burden on it.[66]

---

65 [2002] 2 AC 545, HL at 563.
66 *Sheldrake* v. *DPP* [2003] EWHC 273 (Admin): ibid. at [52].

Thus, the evidential burden can be discharged simply by demonstrating the presence of some evidence, whether it is given by the prosecution or the defence. The evidence might be given in the form of a comment made in police interview or in witness testimony. The rationale for requiring the evidential burden is that it acts as a filter to prevent unsubstantiated issues from reaching the tribunal of fact. This serves at least two purposes: (1) it ensures that jurors only hear about issues which arise from the evidence – this in turn ensures that they decide the case on the evidence in accordance with their oaths and avoids the potential for speculation; and (2) it saves court time and costs as cases in which the allegation is completely unsubstantiated do not reach the jury. As stated above, in most situations, the party who bears the legal burden in respect of a particular fact in issue also bears the evidential burden in respect of that fact. Thus, in a criminal case, the prosecution usually bears the evidential burden as well as the legal burden in respect of every element of the offence and every element of the defence.

However, there are some situations in which the prosecution bears the legal burden to disprove the defendant's defence, but the defence bears the evidential burden in relation to the defence. This arises where the defence raises one of a number of defences relating to an issue which the prosecution is not required to raise as part of their task in proving that the elements of the offence are satisfied. These include self-defence,[67] duress,[68] non-insane automatism,[69] loss of control (the partial defence to murder)[70] and alibi. Where one of these defences is raised, the evidential burden must be discharged by the defence before the legal burden is placed on the prosecution to disprove the defence. The rationale for this is that the prosecution should not be expected to pre-empt every possible defence that the defendant might raise where his defence falls outside the scope of the matters which the prosecution has to prove in order to establish the elements of the offence. By requiring the defendant to discharge an evidential burden in respect of such a defence, this then alerts the prosecution to a further legal burden which will fall on them to disprove the defence in question.

For example, take a case in which a defendant is accused of assaulting a victim. Let's say that the prosecution charges the defendant with a non-fatal offence against the person, such as assault occasioning actual bodily harm contrary to s. 47, Offences Against the Person Act 1861. Imagine that the defendant claims that he acted in self-defence. Who bears the legal burden in respect of the elements of the offence and the defence? Who bears the evidential burden in respect of each? Starting with the offence, according to the general rule in *Woolmington* v. *DPP*, the prosecution bears the burden of proving (legal burden) that the elements of the offence are satisfied. Breaking the offence of assault occasioning actual bodily harm down into its constituent elements, this means that the prosecution must prove that the defendant committed an assault or battery on the victim and that that caused actual bodily harm. The prosecution must prove these elements to the higher criminal standard of proof, beyond reasonable doubt (as per *Miller* v. *Minister of Pensions* and *R* v. *Summers*). In addition to carrying the legal burden here, the prosecution also bears the evidential burden in respect of the elements of the offence. As stated above, this means that they must raise some evidence of the offence in order to make the issue a

---

67 *Lobell* [1957] 1 QB 547.
68 *Gill* (1963) 47 Cr App R 166.
69 *AG for Northern Ireland* v. *Bratty* [1963] AC 386, HL.
70 Section 54, Coroners and Justice Act 2009.

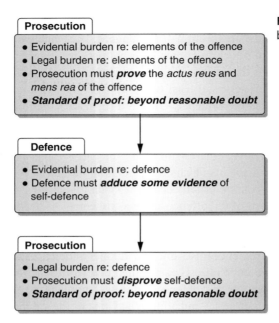

Figure 3.4 Operation of the evidential burden

'live' one. In practical terms, this evidential burden is of little significance and is rarely mentioned because it is effectively subsumed by the greater, legal burden of actually proving the elements of the offence to a high standard. We know that the legal burden usually also rests with the prosecution to disprove the defendant's defence. This is also true in respect of the defence of self-defence. Thus, the legal burden here rests with the prosecution so that it must disprove the defence (i.e. the prosecution must prove that the defendant did not act in self-defence). As the burden of proof remains with the prosecution, the standard of proof is beyond reasonable doubt. However, before it falls to the prosecution to disprove self-defence, the defendant must discharge the evidential burden in respect of this defence. This means that the defence must adduce some evidence of self-defence in order to raise the defence and place the legal burden here on the prosecution. The operation of the evidential burden in this example is illustrated in Figure 3.4.

Where a defendant is charged with a sexual offence under the Sexual Offences Act 2003,[71] and the evidential presumptions under s. 75(1), Sexual Offences Act 2003 apply, two rebuttable presumptions are triggered in respect of the element of consent in sexual offences. First, it is presumed that the complainant did not consent to the sexual activity, and, secondly, it is presumed that the defendant did not reasonably believe that the complainant was consenting to the sexual activity. In such circumstances, provided that the prosecution can discharge their burden in respect of the other elements of the offence, the defendant will be convicted unless he discharges his evidential burden in respect of consent. Suggestions that s. 75(1), Sexual

---

71 Such as rape (s. 1), assault by penetration (s. 2), sexual assault (s. 3) or causing a person to engage in sexual activity without consent (s. 4).

Offences Act 2003 does any more than impose an evidential burden on the defendant were rejected by the Court of Appeal in *R* v. *Ciccarelli*.[72] In this case, Lord Judge CJ stated that:

> It was suggested that section 75 of the 2003 Act reverses the ordinary principles relating to the burden of proof in criminal cases. We do not agree. Section 75 is an evidential provision. It relates to matters of evidence, and in particular evidential presumptions about consent in circumstances where, as we have already indicated, as a matter of reality and common sense, the strong likelihood is that the complainant will not, in fact, be consenting. If, however, in those circumstances there is sufficient evidence for the jury to consider, then the burden of disproving them remains on the prosecution. Therefore, before the question of the appellant's reasonable belief in the complainant's consent could be left to the jury, some evidence beyond the fanciful or speculative had to be adduced to support the reasonableness of his belief in her consent.[73]

Thus, the Court of Appeal has been very keen to emphasise that the presumptions under s. 75(1), Sexual Offences Act 2003 only impose an evidential burden on the defendant, and there is no legal burden on the defendant to prove the absence of consent or that he had a reasonable belief in consent.

3.6 MATTERS NOT REQUIRING PROOF

Finally, there are some further matters which are said not to require proof at trial. These are matters which therefore do not carry a legal burden. They include: formal admissions, facts on judicial notice, the findings of previous court hearings and presumptions of fact and law.

3.6.1 Formal admissions

Under s. 10, Criminal Justice Act 1967, a fact may be proved by formal admission in criminal proceedings. A formal admission is made by both parties where they agree that a fact is not in issue. Where a fact is formally admitted, the formal admission is regarded as conclusive evidence of the fact. In civil proceedings, a fact may be formally admitted under rule 14.1 of the Civil Procedure Rules 1998 by giving notice of the admission in writing to the other party.

3.6.2 Judicial notice

Certain facts are said to be 'judicially noted'. This means that the judge accepts that the fact is true. No evidence is required to prove these facts. There are two categories of judicial notice: judicial notice without enquiry and judicial notice after enquiry. Facts which are judicially noted without enquiry are facts which are common knowledge. Examples include taking judicial notice of the status of any foreign Government,[74] of the days in the calendar

---

72 See Lord Judge CJ in *R* v. *Ciccarelli* [2011] EWCA Crim 2665 at [18].
73 Ibid.
74 *Duff Development Co. Ltd* v. *Kelantan Government* [1924] AC 797.

(but not of the hours of sunset),[75] of boys' habits of being mischievous,[76] of the fact that the country is in a state of war,[77] of the history of the IRA,[78] of the Iraqi war,[79] of the global economic collapse,[80] of the difficulties in obtaining a mortgage in the current market,[81] that local authorities are financially hard pressed,[82] that the University of Oxford is a national institution, the purposes of which are the advancement of religion and learning,[83] that a camel is not a wild animal in any part of the world, and that a camel is a domestic animal,[84] that the life of a criminal was not a happy one,[85] of the fact that, in the ordinary course of gestation, the birth of a child occurs in or about nine months after fruitful intercourse,[86] and the House of Lords has taken judicial notice of the law of Scotland.[87] Facts which are judicially noted after enquiry are facts which are noted after the judge has undertaken some research into the matter. The judge may refer to sources such as dictionaries or other works of reference. Once the fact is judicially noted, it is then treated as a binding authority for future cases.

3.6.3 Previous court findings

At common law, any previous convictions of the defendant and any previous civil judgments were inadmissible in later proceedings to prove the matter stated. In *Hollington* v. *Hewthorn*,[88] the defendant's conviction for careless driving could not be adduced in the civil trial for negligence in order to prove that the defendant was negligent. The evidence of the previous conviction was inadmissible because it merely went to prove that another court was of the opinion that the defendant had been guilty of careless driving, and the opinion of that court was irrelevant to the current proceedings. This rule has now been overruled in respect of civil and criminal proceedings.

Sections 11 to 13 of the Civil Evidence Act 1968 deal with the admissibility of previous convictions in civil proceedings. According to s. 11(1), previous convictions are now admissible in civil proceedings to prove that the defendant committed that criminal offence. Section 11(2)(a) provides that proof of the conviction creates a rebuttable presumption that the defendant committed the offence, and the burden rests with the defendant to prove that he did not. Section 12(1), Civil Evidence Act 1968 provides that findings of adultery or paternity are admissible in civil proceedings to prove the matter stated. Section 13(1) provides that evidence

---

75 *Collier* v. *Nokes* (1849) 2 Car & Kir 1012.
76 *Clayton* v. *Hardwick Colliery Co. Ltd* (1915) 85 LJKB 292.
77 *Re X's Petition of Right* [1915] 3 KB 649.
78 *R* v. *Z* [2005] 3 All ER 95.
79 *Amin* v. *Brown* [2005] All ER (D) 380 (Jul).
80 *Myerson* v. *Myerson* [2009] 2 FCR 1.
81 *Milton* v. *Milton* [2008] EWCA Civ 926.
82 *Re T (Children)* [2012] 5 Costs LR 914.
83 *R* v. *Vice-Chancellor of Oxford University sub nom. Re Oxford Poor Rate Case* (1857) 21 JP 644.
84 *McQuaker* v. *Goddard* [1940] 1 KB 687.
85 *Burns* v. *Edman* [1970] 2 QB 541.
86 *Preston-Jones* v. *Preston-Jones* [1951] AC 391.
87 *Elliot* v. *Joicey* [1935] All ER Rep 578.
88 [1943] KB 587.

of a criminal conviction is admissible in a defamation action to prove that the defendant committed the offence.

Section 74(1), Police and Criminal Evidence Act 1984 deals with the admissibility of previous convictions in criminal proceedings and provides that previous convictions are admissible in criminal proceedings to prove that the defendant committed the offence. Section 74(2) also creates a rebuttable presumption that the defendant committed the offence, and the burden rests with the defendant to prove that he did not.

3.7 PRESUMPTIONS

There are a number of presumptions of law and of fact which may apply in certain circumstances. Where a presumption does apply, the matter which is the subject of the presumption does not need any further proof.

3.7.1 Presumptions of fact

There is a presumption of fact in criminal law that a defendant intends the natural consequences of his actions, but s. 8, Criminal Justice Act 1967 provides that a jury is not bound to infer that a defendant intended the consequence just because it was a natural and probable consequence of the defendant's actions. Instead, the jury should decide whether the defendant intended the consequences of his actions by looking at all of the evidence and drawing such inferences as appear proper in the circumstances. Another presumption of fact of significance is the presumption of guilty knowledge in respect of cases of handling stolen goods or theft. If a defendant is found in possession of goods which have recently been stolen and the defendant fails to give an adequate explanation for his possession of the goods, the jury are entitled to infer that the defendant is guilty of handling stolen goods or theft.[89]

3.7.2 Presumptions of law

There are several significant presumptions in law, including the presumption of innocence, the presumption of sanity, a presumption of infancy, a presumption of marriage, the presumption of death, presumption of legitimacy and *res ipsa loquitur*.

The most important presumption of law for the purposes of this chapter is the presumption of innocence, according to which everybody is presumed to be innocent. This is a rebuttable presumption, which can be displaced by evidence to the contrary. This presumption has been examined in detail above. Also mentioned above is the presumption of sanity from *M'Naghten's Case*. This presumption is also a rebuttable one. Since everybody is presumed to be sane in law, it is for a defendant who raises a defence such as insanity or diminished responsibility to prove that defence. Under s. 50, Children and Young Persons Act 1933, there is a conclusive presumption in law that a child under the age of 10 is *doli incapax*

---

[89] *R* v. *Schama* (1916) 11 Cr App R 45 and *R* v. *Garth* [1949] 1 All ER 773.

(i.e. incapable of committing a criminal offence), and thus, a child under 10 cannot be criminally liable.[90] Where two people have gone through a marriage ceremony and they then cohabit, there is a presumption that they are legally married. This comprises of a presumption that the marriage ceremony was a valid one and that both parties had the capacity to marry. There is a presumption of death in respect of a person who has not been heard from for seven years by people who would have been expected to have heard from him in that time and all due inquiries have been made. The death is presumed to have occurred at some point within the seven years rather than on a specific date.[91] There is a rebuttable presumption of legitimacy according to which, where it is shown that a married woman has given birth to a child during wedlock, the child is presumed to be the legitimate offspring of the married couple unless the contrary is proved.[92] Finally, the Latin maxim *res ipsa loquitur* ('the thing speaks for itself') applies in cases of negligence. While the burden of proving the elements of negligence will usually fall on the claimant, where there is no proof of how the incident occurred, the claimant might rely on this maxim which permits the tribunal of fact to infer liability from the very nature of the incident.

3.8 CONCLUSION

The presumption of innocence and the 'golden thread' from *Woolmington* v. *DPP* are fundamental aspects of the criminal justice process. The burden of proof in criminal proceedings necessarily rests on the prosecution since it brings the case to court on behalf of the state. This provides protection to a defendant accused of a criminal offence from the power of the state by requiring the prosecution to use its wealth of resources to justify the accusation it makes. Since there is much at stake for a person who is accused of committing a criminal offence, the prosecution is also required to reach a very high standard of proof: it must persuade the tribunal of fact that the defendant is guilty beyond reasonable doubt. The rationale for such a high standard of proof is the protection of the defendant's liberty and the desire to ensure that only those who are guilty are convicted of criminal offences. The legal system prioritises the protection of the innocent from wrongful conviction over the wrongful acquittal of a guilty defendant. Reverse onuses which place the legal burden of proving a defence on the defendant in exceptional circumstances do interfere with the presumption of innocence, but, provided that the interference is proportionate, it will be compatible with Convention rights. However, the defendant is not subject to the same standard of proof required of the prosecution; he must only prove the defence on a balance of probabilities. This lower standard of proof is also applied in civil proceedings in which the burden of proof rests upon the party asserting the issue. The lower standard of proof is justifiable in civil proceedings since it is usually only the financial interests of the parties at stake and their liberty is not at risk.

---

90 England and Wales has one of the lowest ages of criminal responsibility in Europe.
91 *Chard* v. *Chard* [1956] P 259.
92 Section 26 of the Family Law Reform Act 1969.

Summary

- In criminal proceedings, the general rule is that the burden of proof is on the prosecution: *Woolmington* v. *DPP*. The prosecution must prove the elements of the offence and disprove the defence.
- The standard of proof applicable is beyond reasonable doubt: *Miller* v. *Minister of Pensions* and *R* v. *Summers*. The jury should be directed that they should only convict if they are satisfied so that they are 'sure' that the defendant is guilty: *R* v. *Majid*.
- There are some exceptions to this general rule, in which the legal burden to prove the defence is on the defendant. These exceptions arise where the defendant raises the defence of insanity or where there is an express statutory provision which places the legal burden of proving the defence on the defendant: *Woolmington* v. *DPP*.
- Alternatively, a statutory provision might impliedly place the legal burden on the defendant: see s. 101, Magistrates' Court Act 1980 and *R* v. *Hunt*.
- Where the burden of proof is on the defendant to prove his defence, the applicable standard of proof is on a balance of probabilities.
- A reverse onus will not necessarily violate the presumption of innocence under Article 6(2), European Convention on Human Rights: *R* v. *Lambert*.
- In civil proceedings, the party asserting an issue must prove that issue. Thus, the claimant bears the legal burden in respect of the claim and the defendant will bear the legal burden in respect of any defence that he raises. The standard of proof in civil proceedings is on a balance of probabilities: *Miller* v. *Minister of Pensions*.
- The evidential burden is a burden to adduce some evidence to make an issue a 'live' one. This is known as 'passing the judge'. The party who bears the legal burden also bears the evidential burden in respect of an issue. However, there are some occasions in criminal proceedings in which the prosecution bears the legal burden of disproving a defence, but the defendant bears the evidential burden in respect of that defence, namely where the defendant raises defences such as loss of control, self-defence, duress and automatism.
- There are a number of matters which do not require proof, including formal admissions and matters on judicial notice. There are also a number of presumptions of law and of fact that may apply in certain circumstances. Where a presumption does apply, the fact that is the subject of the presumption does not need any further proof.

For discussion . . .

1. Explain the difference between a legal burden and an evidential burden.
2. How do the courts determine when a legal burden of proof falls on a defendant? To what extent is this approach satisfactory?
3. Critically evaluate the standards of proof in criminal and civil proceedings.
   Why is there a difference between the standards of proof required in each type of proceedings?

4. Explain when an evidential burden is placed on the defendant and the rationale for this?
5. To what extent does a reverse onus interfere with the presumption of innocence? When will this constitute a violation of Article 6(2) of the European Convention on Human Rights?

Further reading

A. Ashworth and M. Blake, 'The presumption of innocence in English criminal law' [1996] Crim LR 314.
This article is about derogations from the presumption of innocence and the presumption of *mens rea* in criminal cases. The authors explore the prevalence of cases in which either a legal burden is placed on the defendant or strict liability is imposed in the Crown Court. The authors conclude that 40 per cent of cases in the Crown Court appear to violate the presumption of innocence and argue that this fundamental presumption should be given more respect in the criminal courts.

D. Birch, 'Hunting the snark: the elusive statutory exception' [1988] Crim LR 221.
In this article, the author examines the House of Lords' decision in *R* v. *Hunt*. In contrast to other academic views, Birch argues that the decision in *R* v. *Hunt* is not unhelpful, but that rather it 'makes the best out of a bad job'. She states that the case has created workable guidelines which encourage the courts to interpret statutes so as to apply the intentions of Parliament in a consistent way.

I. Dennis, 'Reverse onuses and the presumption of innocence: in search of principle' [2005] Crim LR 901.
In this article, the author argues that the courts should follow general principles when determining whether a reverse onus is compatible with Article 6(2), European Convention on Human Rights in order to ensure certainty and consistency in judicial decision-making.

G. Dingwall, 'Statutory exceptions, burdens of proof and the Human Rights Act 1998' (2002) 65(3) MLR 450–63.
This article focuses on the decision of the House of Lords in *R* v. *Lambert* and explores the opinions handed down by the House. The author highlights the significance of the case in testing Parliament's right to determine whether a defendant should prove his innocence in light of the Human Rights Act 1998 and argues that the decision still leaves some practical issues unresolved.

V. Tadros and S. Tierney, 'The presumption of innocence and the Human Rights Act' (2004) 67(3) MLR 402–34.
This article is about state interference with the presumption of innocence. The authors raise two questions: (1) how such interference is to be measured; and (2) which principles should guide the courts in determining whether any such interference is proportionate.

G. Williams, 'The logic of exceptions' (1988) 47(2) *Cambridge Law Journal* 261–95.
In this article, the author provides a lively and passionate criticism of the decision of the House of Lords in *R* v. *Hunt*. This is a comprehensive article in which the author outlines the decision in *Woolmington* v. *DPP* and explores the development of further exceptions to the general rule by the courts through the peculiar-knowledge rule and statutory exceptions to statutory offences.

4 Silence

4.1 INTRODUCTION

Anyone who has watched an English[1] crime drama on television will have heard the words of the police caution recited when the suspect in the programme is arrested or interviewed by the police, but how many people pause to consider what the caution actually means? The police caution does in fact serve a very important purpose in notifying an accused about a fundamental right that he has to remain silent and not to contribute to the case against him by saying anything which might incriminate himself. The first part of the caution informs an accused that he does not have to say anything. This is a clear reference to the accused's right to silence, and viewers might even see a suspect exercising that right to silence by giving a 'no comment' interview. The meaning of the next part of the caution is, perhaps, less commonly appreciated by the lay television viewer. This part of the caution serves as a warning to the accused that there may be consequences at trial if he does elect to invoke his right to silence in interview but then relies on a fact in his defence at trial which he reasonably could have been expected to have mentioned when he was questioned by the police. These consequences are known amongst lawyers as 'adverse inferences'. The Criminal Justice and Public Order Act 1994 (hereafter

---

1 Or Welsh. All references to English law are also intended to cover the law of Wales. England or English law is referred to only for the sake of convenience.

referred to as 'CJPOA 1994') provides that there are circumstances in which a court or jury may draw adverse inferences against the accused from their silence.

This chapter is concerned with the right of the accused to remain silent and with its ally, the privilege against self-incrimination. The first part of this chapter will explore these principles and will consider the common law consequences (pre-CJPOA 1994) of exercising the right to silence. The latter part of the chapter will then consider in detail ss. 34 to 37 of the CJPOA 1994 which provide that adverse inferences may be drawn against an accused in certain circumstances.

4.2   PRIVILEGE AGAINST SELF-INCRIMINATION

The privilege against self-incrimination[2] derives from the Latin maxim *nemo debet prodere se ipsum* which is translated to mean that 'no one can be, or ought to be, compelled or required to betray himself'. It is also known as the *nemo debet* principle. In criminal proceedings, the privilege against self-incrimination means that the accused has a right not to answer questions which are put to him in relation to an offence which the police allege that he has been involved with during a police interview and a corresponding right not to testify in criminal proceedings against himself or not to answer questions put to him in cross-examination. Langbein claims that the right in its modern form stems from the late eighteenth and early nineteenth centuries when an accused was more frequently permitted to have a defence lawyer to speak on his behalf.[3] The privilege against self-incrimination is very closely linked to the defendant's right to silence.[4]

In civil proceedings, the privilege against self-incrimination means that a witness may refuse to answer questions which are put to him in cross-examination during a trial. In *Blunt* v. *Park Land Hotel Ltd*, Goddard LJ explained the privilege against self-incrimination by stating that 'no one is bound to answer any question if the answer thereto would, in the opinion of the judge, have a tendency to expose the deponent to any criminal charge, penalty, or forfeiture which the judge regards as reasonably likely to be preferred or sued for'.[5] This has been put onto a statutory footing in civil proceedings by s. 14(1), Civil Evidence Act 1968 which provides that a person has a right to 'refuse to answer any question or produce any document or thing if to do so would tend to expose that person to proceedings for an offence or for the recovery of a penalty'. This right is limited only to matters which would expose the person to proceedings for

---

2 See A. L.-T. Choo, '"Give us what you have" – information, compulsion and the privilege against self-incrimination as a human right' in P. Roberts and J. Hunter (eds.), *Criminal Evidence and Human Rights* (Hart Publishing, 2012).

3 See J. Langbein, 'The historical origins of the privilege against self-incrimination at common law' (1994) 95(5) *Michigan Law Review* 1047–85.

4 See I. H. Dennis, *The Law of Evidence*, 5th edn (Sweet & Maxwell, 2013) at pp. 152–5 for a detailed discussion of the difference between the privilege against self-incrimination and the right to silence. Dennis states that 'Broadly speaking, the difference between them is that the privilege against self-incrimination deals with questions of direct compulsion of an accused person to provide evidence against himself, whereas the right to silence covers certain situations of indirect compulsion' (see p. 151).

5 [1942] 2 KB 253 at 257.

a criminal offence or penalties within the UK.[6] It also extends to the potential incrimination of the person's spouse or civil partner for a criminal offence or for the recovery of a penalty.[7]

> **Cross-reference**
>
> The privilege against self-incrimination is also mentioned briefly in Chapter 14 on Privilege. In this chapter we will consider the various forms of privilege available to a person in both criminal and civil proceedings.

4.3 LIMITING THE RIGHT TO SILENCE

Evidence that the defendant has elected to exercise his right to silence can be relevant to the guilt of the defendant in a number of ways. Where the defendant refuses to answer questions, an inference might be drawn that he remains silent because he has no answers to the questions put to him or no answer that would stand up to scrutiny, that he remains silent because he is guilty or because he accepts that the accusation is true. Where a defendant remains silent in interview but later raises a defence at trial, it might be inferred that he has fabricated his defence.[8]

Prior to 1994, the defendant's right to silence was absolute; however, this permitted defendants to fabricate defences and launch ambush defences[9] at trial without consequence. In order to mitigate this, Parliament chose to enact sections 34 to 37 of the Criminal Justice and Public Order Act 1994, which provide that adverse inferences can be drawn from the defendant's silence in the following circumstances:[10]

- s. 34 – where the defendant fails to mention a fact in interview which he relies on in his defence at trial,
- s. 35 – where the defendant refuses to testify at trial or refuses to answer questions in evidence having been sworn,
- s. 36 – where the defendant fails to account for any object, substance or mark which is found on the accused's person, in or on his clothing or footwear, in his possession, or in any place in which he is at the time of his arrest,
- s. 37 – where the defendant fails to account for his presence in a particular place at or about the time of the offence for which he was arrested was committed.

It is worth noting that s. 38(6), Criminal Justice Act 1994 preserves the power of the court to exclude evidence of silence at its discretion. Thus, a judge may exercise his discretion under s. 78(1), Police and Criminal Evidence Act 1984 to exclude evidence of silence on the basis that its admission would have an adverse effect on the fairness of the proceedings.

---

6 Section 14(1)(a), Civil Evidence Act 1968.
7 Section 14(1)(b), Civil Evidence Act 1968.
8 See Dennis, above (n. 4) at p. 169 and R. Emson, *Evidence*, 5th edn (Palgrave Macmillan, 2010) at p. 214.
9 An ambush defence is a defence raised at trial which the prosecution had no notice of and were not prepared for. It has the effect of catching the prosecution out and damaging the case against the defendant.
10 In the Criminal Procedure and Investigations Act 1996, Parliament also legislated for the drawing of adverse inferences where the defendant (*inter alia*) fails to serve a defence statement or runs a different defence at trial from the one disclosed on the defence statement. See Chapter 13 on Disclosure for further detail.

4.4   FAILURE TO MENTION FACTS WHEN QUESTIONED OR CHARGED

This paragraph covers the position under the Criminal Justice and Public Order Act 1994 where the accused remains silent in police interview or upon charge. The main provision to be considered is s. 34, CJPOA 1994, the object of which has been said to have been 'to encourage early disclosure of genuine defences and to deter late fabrication of false defences'.[11] In *R* v. *Brizzalari*,[12] the Court of Appeal held that 'the mischief at which the provision was primarily directed, was the positive defence following a "no comment" interview and/or the "ambush" defence . . . We would counsel against the further complicating of trials and summings up by invoking this statute unless the merits of the individual case require that that should be done.'[13]

Under s. 34(2), where the defendant fails to mention any fact during questioning under caution which he then later seeks to rely upon at trial as part of his defence, the jury or court may draw such inferences as appear proper from the defendant's silence in interview. This provision applies where the accused makes no comment in police interview (known as a 'no comment' interview) or where he does answer some questions but fails or refuses to answer other questions, provided that the defendant fails to mention any fact in interview which he later relies on at trial as part of his defence.

S. 34, CRIMINAL JUSTICE AND PUBLIC ORDER ACT 1994

(1) Where, in any proceedings against a person for an offence, evidence is given that the accused –

   (a) at any time before he was charged with the offence, on being questioned under caution by a constable trying to discover whether or by whom the offence had been committed, failed to mention any fact relied on in his defence in those proceedings; or

   (b) on being charged with the offence or officially informed that he might be prosecuted for it, failed to mention any such fact; or

   (c) at any time after being charged with the offence, on being questioned under section 22 of the Counter-Terrorism Act 2008 (post-charge questioning), failed to mention any such fact,

   being a fact which in the circumstances existing at the time the accused could reasonably have been expected to mention when so questioned, charged or informed, as the case may be, subsection (2) below applies.

(2) Where this subsection applies –

   [. . .]

   (b) a judge, in deciding whether to grant an application made by the accused under paragraph 2 of Schedule 3 to the Crime and Disorder Act 1998;

   (c) the court, in determining whether there is a case to answer; and

   (d) the court or jury, in determining whether the accused is guilty of the offence charged,

   may draw such inferences from the failure as appear proper.

---

11 Per Pitchford LJ in *R* v. *Webster* [2010] EWCA Crim 2819 at [24].
12 [2004] EWCA Crim 310.
13 Ibid. at [57]. This was endorsed by Toulson LJ in *R* v. *Smith* [2011] EWCA Crim 1098 at [10].

Where s. 34(2) does apply, such inferences as appear proper may be drawn by the court or jury in determining whether the accused is guilty of the offence charged, or the court in determining whether there is a case to answer or whether the case should be dismissed.

Under s. 34(2A), where the accused was not allowed the opportunity to consult with a solicitor prior to being questioned or charged, the court or jury cannot draw such inferences from the accused's silence.

S. 34, CRIMINAL JUSTICE AND PUBLIC ORDER ACT 1994

(2A) Where the accused was at an authorised place of detention at the time of the failure, subsections (1) and (2) above do not apply if he had not been allowed an opportunity to consult a solicitor prior to being questioned, charged or informed as mentioned in subsection (1) above.

Section 34(3) provides that evidence that the accused failed to mention the fact can be adduced before evidence of the fact itself is adduced, although this is subject to any direction by the court to the contrary.

S. 34, CRIMINAL JUSTICE AND PUBLIC ORDER ACT 1994

(3) Subject to any directions by the court, evidence tending to establish the failure may be given before or after evidence tending to establish the fact which the accused is alleged to have failed to mention.

It should be noted that s. 38(3) states that the jury or court may not convict the defendant solely upon the basis of an inference drawn under s. 34, Criminal Justice and Public Order Act 1994. Thus, where the jury has decided to draw adverse inferences from his silence in interview, in order to convict the defendant the jury must rely on other evidence in addition to those inferences. Section 38(3) applies to each of the provisions providing for the drawing of adverse inferences, namely ss. 34 to 37, Criminal Justice and Public Order Act 1994.

4.4.1 Directing the jury

In *R* v. *Cowan*,[14] the Court of Appeal set out the directions which should be given by the trial judge where s. 35, Criminal Justice and Public Order Act 1994 applies. While this case specifically concerned the drawing of adverse inferences from the defendant's refusal to testify, the principles here are also relevant to s. 34. The Court of Appeal in *R* v. *Condron and Condron*[15] confirmed that the principles in *R* v. *Cowan* should also be applied to s. 34, so it is prudent to explore the principles in *R* v. *Cowan*.

---

14 [1996] QB 373.
15 [1997] 1 WLR 827, CA.

R v. COWAN [1996] QB 373
Lord Taylor CJ

[Lord Taylor CJ stated (at 381) that the jury should be directed in accordance with the following principles:]

(1) The judge will have told the jury that the burden of proof remains upon the prosecution throughout and what the required standard is.

(2) It is necessary for the judge to make clear to the jury that the defendant is entitled to remain silent. That is his right and his choice. The right of silence remains.

(3) An inference from failure to give evidence cannot on its own prove guilt. That is expressly stated in section 38(3) of the Act.

(4) Therefore, the jury must be satisfied that the prosecution have established a case to answer before drawing any inferences from silence. Of course, the judge must have thought so or the question whether the defendant was to give evidence would not have arisen. But the jury may not believe the witnesses whose evidence the judge considered sufficient to raise a prima facie case. It must therefore be made clear to them that they must find there to be a case to answer on the prosecution evidence before drawing an adverse inference from the defendant's silence.

(5) If, despite any evidence relied upon to explain his silence or in the absence of any such evidence, the jury conclude the silence can only sensibly be attributed to the defendant's having no answer or none that would stand up to cross-examination, they may draw an adverse inference.

A year later, in *R* v. *Argent*,[16] the Court of Appeal specifically considered the circumstances in which the jury may be entitled to draw inferences from the accused's silence pre-trial under s. 34. Lord Bingham CJ stated that there are six formal conditions which must be met before the jury may draw such inferences as appear proper to them.

R v. ARGENT [1997] 2 CR APP R 27
Lord Bingham CJ

[at 32–3]

What then are the formal conditions to be met before the jury may draw such an inference? In our judgment there are six such conditions. The first is that there must be proceedings against a person for an offence; that condition must necessarily be satisfied before section 34(2)(d) can bite and plainly it was satisfied here. The second condition is that the alleged failure must occur before a defendant is charged. That condition also was satisfied here. The third condition is that the alleged failure must occur during questioning under caution by a constable. The requirement that the questioning should be by a constable is not strictly a condition, as is evident from section 34(4), but here the alleged failure did occur during questioning by a constable, Detective Constable Armstrong, and the appellant had been properly cautioned. The fourth condition is that the constable's questioning must be directed to trying to discover whether or by whom the alleged offence had been committed. Here it is not in doubt that Mr Sullivan was

16 [1997] 2 Cr App R 27.

killed by someone. The Detective Constable was trying to discover who inflicted the fatal wound and whether the killing was murder or manslaughter, it being fairly clear that the offence must have been one or the other (unless the killer struck the fatal blow in the course of defending himself). The fifth condition is that the alleged failure by the defendant must be to mention any fact relied on in his defence in those proceedings. That raises two questions of fact: first, is there some fact which the defendant has relied on in his defence; and secondly, did the defendant fail to mention it to the constable when he was being questioned in accordance with the section? Being questions of fact these questions are for the jury as the tribunal of fact to resolve. Here it would seem fairly clear that there were matters which the appellant relied on in his defence which he had not mentioned. These included the fact that he had had no quarrel with Mr Sullivan in the club; that he and his wife had left the club before the rest of the party; that he had not at any stage of the evening carried a knife; that he had not been involved in any altercation in the street in which Mr Sullivan was stabbed; that he saw and was a witness of no such altercation; that he saw Mr Lee in the street waiting for a cab; that he went to a restaurant for a meal but found that he was too late and that the restaurant was closed; and that he returned home and saw his baby-sitter. The sixth condition is that the appellant failed to mention a fact which in the circumstances existing at the time the accused could reasonably have been expected to mention when so questioned. The time referred to is the time of questioning, and account must be taken of all the relevant circumstances existing at that time. The courts should not construe the expression 'in the circumstances' restrictively: matters such as time of day, the defendant's age, experience, mental capacity, state of health, sobriety, tiredness, knowledge, personality and legal advice are all part of the relevant circumstances; and those are only examples of things which may be relevant. When reference is made to 'the accused' attention is directed not to some hypothetical, reasonable accused of ordinary phlegm and fortitude but to the actual accused with such qualities, apprehensions, knowledge and advice as he is shown to have had at the time. It is for the jury to decide whether the fact (or facts) which the defendant has relied on in his defence in the criminal trial, but which he had not mentioned when questioned under caution before charge by the constable investigating the alleged offence for which the defendant is being tried, is (or are) a fact (or facts) which in the circumstances as they actually existed the actual defendant could reasonably have been expected to mention.

Like so many other questions in criminal trials this is a question to be resolved by the jury in the exercise of their collective common-sense, experience and understanding of human nature. Sometimes they may conclude that it was reasonable for the defendant to have held his peace for a host of reasons, such as that he was tired, ill, frightened, drunk, drugged, unable to understand what was going on, suspicious of the police, afraid that his answer would not be fairly recorded, worried at committing himself without legal advice, acting on legal advice, or some other reason accepted by the jury.

In other cases the jury may conclude, after hearing all that the defendant and his witnesses may have to say about the reasons for failing to mention the fact or facts in issue, that he could reasonably have been expected to do so. This is an issue on which the judge may, and usually should, give appropriate directions. But he should ordinarily leave the issue to the jury to decide. Only rarely would it be right for the judge to direct the jury that they should, or should not, draw the appropriate inference.

Thus, the six conditions which much be satisfied before the jury may be directed that they can draw such inferences as appear proper from the accused's silence under s. 34 are:

(1) there must be proceedings against a person for an offence;
(2) the alleged failure to mention facts must occur before the defendant is charged;
(3) the alleged failure must occur during questioning under caution by a constable;

(4) the constable's questioning must be directed to trying to discover whether or by whom the alleged offence had been committed;

(5) the alleged failure by the defendant must be to mention any fact relied on in his defence in those proceedings (whether the defendant relied on some fact in his defence, and whether the defendant failed to mention this fact to the constable on questioning, are questions of fact for the jury to decide);

(6) the defendant failed to mention a fact which in the circumstances existing at the time he could reasonably have been expected to mention when so questioned (and 'in the circumstances' is not to be construed restrictively, but it covers circumstances related to the defendant, such as his age, experience, mental capacity, state of health, sobriety, tiredness, knowledge and personality, and circumstances related to the interview, such as the time of day and the availability of legal advice. This condition is also subjectively assessed, such that the fact must be one which the actual defendant could reasonably have been expected to mention taking into account his qualities, apprehensions, knowledge and any legal advice that he had at the time).

In *R v. Petkar and Farquhar*,[17] the Court of Appeal reviewed its previous guidance on directing the jury regarding the drawing of adverse inferences (see Figure 4.1) set out in the cases of *R v. Argent*, *R v. Condron* and *R v. Cowan*. The Court concluded that the following matters should be set before the jury in a direction:

R V. PETKAR AND FARQUHAR [2003] EWCA CRIM 2668
Rix LJ

[at para. [51]]

(i)   The facts which the accused failed to mention but which are relied on in his defence should be identified . . .

(ii) The inferences . . . which it is suggested might be drawn from failure to mention such facts should be identified, to the extent that they may go beyond the standard inference of late fabrication . . .

(iii) The jury should be told that, if an inference is drawn, they should not convict 'wholly or mainly on the strength of it' . . . . The first of those alternatives ('wholly') is a clear way of putting the need for the prosecution to be able to prove a case to answer, otherwise than by means of any inference drawn. The second alternative ('or mainly') buttresses that need.

(iv) The jury should be told that an inference should be drawn 'only if you think it is a fair and proper conclusion' . . .

(v)   An inference should be drawn 'only if . . . the only sensible explanation for his failure' is that he had no answer or none that would stand up to scrutiny . . . In other words the inference canvassed should only be drawn if there is no other sensible explanation for the failure . . .

(vi) An inference should only be drawn if, apart from the defendant's failure to mention facts later relied on in his defence, the prosecution case is 'so strong that it clearly calls for an answer by him' . . .[18]

---

17 [2003] EWCA Crim 2668.
18 Reiterated in *R v. Parchment* [2003] EWCA Crim 2428 at [12].

(vii)   The jury should be reminded of the evidence on the basis of which the jury are invited not to draw any conclusion from the defendant's silence … This goes with point (iv) above, because it is only after a jury has considered the defendant's explanation for his failure that they can conclude that there is no other sensible explanation for it.

(viii)   A special direction should be given where the explanation for silence of which evidence has been given is that the defendant was advised by his solicitor to remain silent …'[19]

4.4.2   Judicial direction against drawing adverse inferences

Where, at the start of the interview, the defendant provides the police with a prepared written statement setting out his defence but gives a 'no comment' interview, then provided he does not rely on any further facts at trial, s. 34, Criminal Justice and Public Order Act 1994 does not apply. This was confirmed by the Court of Appeal in *R* v. *McGarry*.[20] The defendant in this case was arrested on suspicion of assault and interviewed by the police twice. In the first interview he refused to answer questions on the basis of legal advice from his solicitor. At the start of the second interview the defendant handed the police a prepared written statement in which he admitted punching the victim but stated that he had done so in self-defence. He then refused to answer any questions in the interview, responding 'no comment' to all questions put to him. At trial, the defendant put forward the defence of self-defence. The prosecution accepted that the defendant's defence at trial was consistent with the prepared statement disclosed in interview and that the defendant had not relied on any new facts at trial which he had not mentioned in the prepared statement. The trial judge decided that he would not invite the jury to draw adverse inferences from the defendant's silence in interview, but he also decided not to direct the jury against doing so. The defendant appealed against his conviction on the basis that the judge should have directed the jury not to draw any such inferences. The Court of Appeal quashed the defendant's conviction and held that the trial judge had misdirected the jury. The Court took the view that where s. 34 does not apply, the trial judge has a duty to positively direct the jury not to draw adverse inferences from the defendant's silence in interview.

4.4.3   Questioning under caution

The precise wording of s. 34, Criminal Justice and Public Order Act 1994 has already been set out above. It can be seen that s. 34(1) sets out the three circumstances in which s. 34(2) applies. Subsection (1) provides that s. 34(2) applies where the accused fails to mention a fact, either:

- in interview under caution;
- on being charged with the offence; or
- after being charged with an offence and during post-charge questioning (under s. 22, Counter-Terrorism Act 2008), and

---

19   Ibid.
20   [1999] 1 WLR 1500, CA.

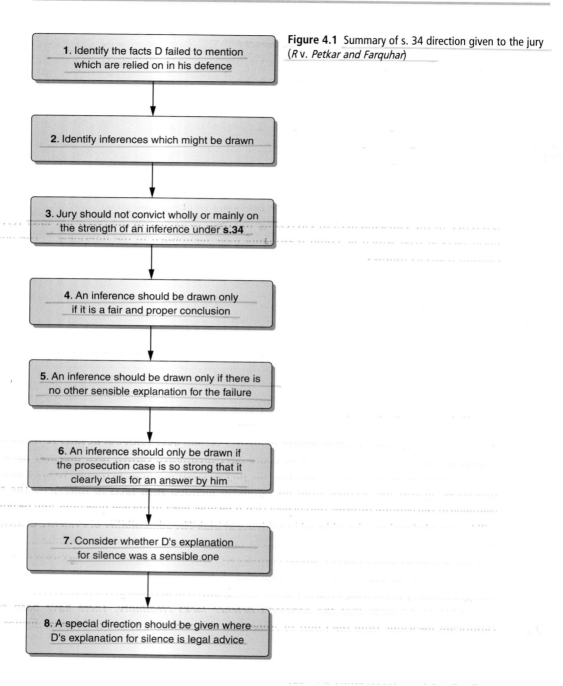

Figure 4.1 Summary of s. 34 direction given to the jury (*R* v. *Petkar and Farquhar*)

1. Identify the facts D failed to mention which are relied on in his defence

2. Identify inferences which might be drawn

3. Jury should not convict wholly or mainly on the strength of an inference under **s.34**

4. An inference should be drawn only if it is a fair and proper conclusion

5. An inference should be drawn only if there is no other sensible explanation for the failure

6. An inference should only be drawn if the prosecution case is so strong that it clearly calls for an answer by him

7. Consider whether D's explanation for silence was a sensible one

8. A special direction should be given where D's explanation for silence is legal advice

the suspect later relies on the fact in his defence, and the fact is one which in the circumstances existing at the time he could reasonably have been expected to mention. Questioning under caution is most likely to take place in the context of a formal police interview under caution. The Court of Appeal has held that a defendant's refusal to come out of his cell in order to be

interview in order 'to advise him on what served his interests best at that stage of the investigation, namely silence or co-operation'.[45]

BECKLES V. UNITED KINGDOM (2003) 36 EHRR 13
European Court of Human Rights

62. . . . the trial judge emphasised to the jury on two occasions in the course of his direction that there was 'no independent evidence' of what the solicitor said at the police station . . . without any reference to the fact that the applicant had been prepared to provide details of the exchanges which he had with his solicitor at the police station and that he had manifested his willingness to co-operate with the police on the way to the police station. It must be further observed that it was the trial judge who had first enquired of the applicant whether he was willing to reveal the content of his discussions with his solicitor. It cannot be overlooked either that the solicitor's advice appeared in the record of the police interview . . . and was entirely consistent with the applicant's own explanation for his silence. Moreover, the applicant remained steadfast at the trial as regards his initial, pre-interview explanation as to why Mr Mohamoud fell from the window. He did not seek at any stage to rely on new facts or circumstances which he might have been expected to reveal had he chosen to co-operate with the police at the interview in defiance of his solicitor's advice . . . For the Court, these are all matters which go to the plausibility of the applicant's explanation and which, as a matter of fairness, should have been built into the direction in order to allow the jury to consider fully whether the applicant's reason for his silence was a genuine one, or whether, on the contrary, his silence was in effect consistent only with guilt and his reliance on legal advice to stay silent merely a convenient self-serving excuse.

The Court held that the trial judge failed to give appropriate weight to the applicant's explanation for his silence at the police interview and he permitted the jury to draw adverse inferences from his silence despite the fact that the jury may have been satisfied with the applicant's explanation. The trial judge had also 'undermined the value of the applicant's explanation by referring to the lack of independent evidence as to what was said by the solicitor and by omitting to mention that the applicant was willing to give his version of the incident to the police before he spoke to his solicitor'.[46] The solicitor's advice had been recorded in the police interview and the applicant was willing to waive legal professional privilege in order to further explain his reasons for remaining silent. The Court also criticised the trial judge for failing to emphasise to the jury that they could only draw adverse inferences from the applicant's silence if his reason was consistent only with guilt.

4.4.8 Waiving legal professional privilege

In several decisions in the late 1990s, the Court of Appeal considered the admissibility of evidence of the privileged conversations between solicitor and client in which the solicitor

---

45 Ibid. at [60].
46 Ibid. at [64].

advised the defendant to give a 'no comment' interview, and the reasons for such legal advice being given.

Cross-reference

Privilege used in this context refers to the legal professional privilege afforded to a defendant and which protects communications between a legal adviser and his client. This will be discussed in more detail in Chapter 14 on Privilege.

In *R* v. *Roble*,[47] the Court of Appeal held that the crucial issue is not the legal advice given by the solicitor, but the question of whether or not the defendant's conduct in remaining silent is reasonable. The defendant in this case accepted that he had stabbed the victim. He was advised by his solicitor not to answer questions during the police interview and so he gave a 'no comment' interview. At his trial for wounding with intent under s. 18, Offences Against the Person Act 1861, the defendant raised the defence of self-defence. The trial judge directed the jury that they could draw such inferences as appear proper from the defendant's silence in interview in accordance with s. 34, Criminal Justice and Public Order Act 1994. The defendant was convicted and appealed on the basis that the judge's direction was defective. The Court of Appeal dismissed his appeal and held that the fact that the defendant had been advised by his solicitor to remain silent was not on its own enough to preclude the drawing of such inferences. The key issue when considering whether such inferences may properly be drawn is not whether or not the defendant was advised to remain silent by his legal representative, but is whether or not the defendant's conduct in doing so is reasonable. In this case, the defendant's solicitor was not called to give evidence as to the reasons for the legal advice that he gave. The Court of Appeal held that while the defendant did not waive legal professional privilege by adducing evidence that he remained silent in interview on legal advice, if the defendant adduced the details as to why the solicitor had so advised the defendant, this would amount to a waiver of legal professional privilege. Rose LJ acknowledged that a solicitor might properly advise the defendant to remain silent in interview where the police had made insufficient disclosure about the case such that the solicitor was unable to properly provide legal advice to his client, or where the case was particularly complex or the evidence in the case was complex, or where it related to matters alleged to have occurred so long ago that it was not feasible to expect an immediate answer from the defendant.[48]

In *R* v. *Daniel*,[49] the Court of Appeal held that evidence of a defendant's conversations with his solicitor pre-interview are admissible to rebut prosecution allegations that the defendant may have fabricated his defence after the interview. In this case, the defendant refused to answer questions in interview after being arrested on suspicion of being involved in the illegal importation of cocaine into England. The trial judge refused to allow the defendant to adduce evidence as to the conversations between him and his solicitor prior to

---

47 [1997] Crim LR 449, CA.
48 See ibid. at 449–50.
49 [1998] 2 Cr App R 373, CA.

interview and he directed the jury that they could draw such inferences as appear proper from the defendant's silence in interview. The Court of Appeal dismissed the defendant's appeal against his conviction. The Court held that the jury do not need to be satisfied that the prosecution have a prima facie case before drawing adverse inferences; in this respect, s. 34 differs from s. 35. The Court also held that where the prosecution alleges that the defendant has fabricated his defence post-interview, evidence of a defendant's conversations with his solicitor pre-interview should be admissible in order to rebut that allegation. The Court held that the jury need not conclude that the defendant's silence could only sensibly be attributed to his having fabricated his defence before drawing adverse inferences, but the Court provided a wider range of situations when the jury would be entitled to draw such inferences. Thus, the trial judge should have directed the jury that if the jury concluded that the defendant's reason for remaining silent could only sensibly be attributed to his 'unwillingness to be subjected to further questioning, or that he had not then thought out all the facts, or that he did not have an innocent explanation to give, they might then draw an adverse inference'.[50] Nevertheless, in this case, the Court took the view that the reason for the defendant's refusal to answer questions in interview was because he would have had to lie or incriminate himself.

The Court of Appeal has also held that where the defendant adduces evidence as to the reasons for the legal advice given by his solicitor, he waives his legal professional privilege and opens himself up to cross-examination on the details of conversations he has had with his solicitor. In *R* v. *Bowden*,[51] the defendant was arrested on suspicion of robbery. On the basis of legal advice from his solicitor, he refused to answer questions in interview. The solicitor gave a statement after the interview explaining his reasons for advising the defendant to remain silent. At trial, this statement was adduced by defence counsel and the trial judge ruled that this meant that the defendant had waived legal professional privilege. Therefore, the prosecution was permitted to cross-examine the defendant on the conversation that he had with his solicitor pre-interview and on the extent to which he disclosed to his solicitor facts which he later relied upon as part of his defence at trial. The defendant appealed against his conviction but the appeal was dismissed by the Court of Appeal. The Court held that a mere statement that the defendant's refusal to answer questions was based upon legal advice would not be enough to constitute a waiver of legal professional privilege, but where the defendant or his legal representative adduce evidence as to the grounds for that legal advice, this would be sufficient to constitute a waiver of the defendant's legal professional privilege. As such, the defendant had waived his privilege. In the Court of Appeal, Lord Bingham CJ stated, *obiter*, that where evidence of the reasons for the legal advice is adduced during a *voir dire*, legal professional privilege is waived whether the evidence is repeated in front of the jury or not: '[t]he defendant cannot at any stage have his cake and eat it; he either withdraws the veil and waives privilege or he does not withdraw the veil and his privilege remains intact. But he cannot have it both ways'.[52]

---

50 Ibid. at 382–3.
51 [1999] 1 WLR 823, CA.
52 Ibid. at 831.

More recently, in the case of *R* v. *Seaton*,[53] the Court of Appeal reviewed the authorities on the waiver of legal professional privilege and drew a number of conclusions which are set out in the extract below:

R V. *SEATON* [2010] EWCA CRIM 1980
Hughes LJ

[43]

(a) Legal professional privilege is of paramount importance. There is no question of balancing privilege against other considerations of public interest . . .

(b) Therefore, in the absence of waiver, no question can be asked which intrudes upon privilege. That means, inter alia, that if a suggestion of recent fabrication is being pursued at trial, a witness, including the defendant, cannot, unless he has waived privilege, be asked whether he told his counsel or solicitor what he now says is the truth. Such a question would require him either to waive his privilege or suffer criticism for not doing so. If any such question is asked by an opposing party (whether the Crown or a co-accused) the judge must stop it, tell the witness directly that he does not need to answer it, and explain to the jury that no one can be asked about things which pass confidentially between him and his lawyer. For the same reasons, in the absence of waiver, the witness cannot be asked whether he is willing to waive.

(c) However, the defendant is perfectly entitled to open up his communication with his lawyer, and it may sometimes be in his interest to do so. One example of when he may wish to do so is to rebut a suggestion of recent fabrication. Another may be to adduce in evidence the reasons he was advised not to answer questions. If he does so, there is no question of *breach* of privilege, because he cannot be in breach of his own privilege. What is happening is that he is waiving privilege.

(d) If the defendant does give evidence of what passed between him and his solicitor he is not thereby waiving privilege entirely and generally, that is to say he does not automatically make available to all other parties everything that he said to his solicitor, or his solicitor to him, on every occasion. He may well not even be opening up *everything* said on the occasion of which he gives evidence, and not on topics unrelated to that of which he gives evidence. The test is fairness and/or the avoidance of a misleading impression. It is that the defendant should not, as it has been put in some of the cases, be able both to 'have his cake and eat it'.

(e) If a defendant says that he gave his solicitor the account now offered at trial, that will ordinarily mean that he can be cross-examined about exactly what he told the solicitor on that topic, and if the comment is fair another party can comment upon the fact that the solicitor has not been called to confirm something which, if it is true, he easily could confirm. If it is intended to pursue cross-examination beyond what is evidently opened up, the proper extent of it can be discussed and the judge invited to rule.

(f) A defendant who adduces evidence that he was advised by his lawyer not to answer questions but goes no further than that does not thereby waive privilege. This is the ratio of *R v Bowden [1999] 1 WLR 823* and is well established. After all, the mere fact of the advice can equally well be made evident by the solicitor announcing at the interview that he gives it then and there, and there is then no revelation whatever of any private conversation between him and the defendant.

---

53 [2010] EWCA Crim 1980.

(g) But a defendant who adduces evidence of the content of, or reasons for, such advice, beyond the mere fact of it, does waive privilege at least to the extent of opening up questions which properly go to whether such reason can be the true explanation for his silence: *R v Bowden*. That will ordinarily include questions relating to recent fabrication, and thus to what he told his solicitor of the facts now relied upon at trial: *R v Bowden* and *R v Loizou [2006] EWCA Crim 1719*.

(h) The rules as to privilege and waiver, and thus as to cross-examination and comment, are the same whether it is the Crown or a co-accused who challenges the defendant.

4.4.9 Soundly based objective reasons for legal advice

In two further cases, *R* v. *Betts and Hall*[54] and *R* v. *Howell*,[55] the Court of Appeal considered the relevance of the defendant's reasons for following legal advice not to answer questions in interview. In *R* v. *Betts and Hall*, the defendant, Hall, was interviewed by the police regarding an attack on the victim. Hall refused to answer questions in the interview on the basis of legal advice because the police had not provided adequate disclosure of the facts of the offence. The Court of Appeal addressed the fact that the defendant failed to mention facts in interview on the basis of legal advice and held that the jury must be directed to consider whether the defendant's reason was a *genuine* one, rather than look at the quality of his decision (i.e. whether his decision not to answer questions was a good one). On this view, the jury could not draw adverse inferences if they believed that the defendant genuinely and innocently followed the advice of his solicitor, irrespective of whether that legal advice was based on good objective reasons. Adverse inferences could only be drawn if the defendant had a non-innocent reason for remaining silent (such as that he had no answer to the questions put to him in interview or none that would stand up to scrutiny) and he hid behind the convenient advice of his solicitor. This decision was not followed in *R* v. *Howell*, in which it was held that the *quality* of the defendant's decision to follow the legal advice is a relevant factor.[56] In this case, the defendant was convicted of wounding with intent contrary to s. 18, Offences Against the Person Act 1861 after he stabbed the victim with a knife. At the police station, the defendant told his solicitor that he had acted in self-defence after the victim had attacked him with a knife. The solicitor took a detailed statement to this effect from the defendant. The defendant gave a 'no comment' interview but signed a statement to the effect that he was making no comment in interview after legal advice and on the basis that there was no written statement from the alleged victim. At trial, the defendant's solicitor was not called to give evidence as to the basis for his advice and the statement signed by the defendant at the police station was not adduced in evidence. The trial judge directed the jury that they could draw adverse inferences under s. 34 if they were sure that there was no innocent explanation for his silence. The Court of Appeal dismissed the appeal against conviction and held in order to avoid adverse inferences there must be a soundly based objective reason for the defendant's silence. In this case there were no such circumstances

---

54 [2001] 2 Cr App R 16, CA.
55 [2005] 1 Cr App R 1, CA.
56 This approach was followed by the Court of Appeal in *R* v. *Knight* [2004] 1 WLR 340.

constituting a soundly based objective reason for the defendant's silence: the absence of the written statement from the alleged victim was not a good reason for remaining silent as there was adequate oral disclosure of the complaint, and it did not become a good reason by virtue of the legal advice given by the solicitor. The Court of Appeal gave examples of circumstances which might constitute an objective reason for remaining silent and these included: ill-health, mental disability, confusion, intoxication and shock.

R V. HOWELL [2005] 1 CR APP R 1
Laws LJ

24. ... the public interest that inheres in reasonable disclosure by a suspected person of what he has to say when faced with a set of facts which accuse him, is thwarted if currency is given to the belief that if a suspect remains silent on legal advice he may systematically avoid adverse comment at his trial. And it may encourage solicitors to advise silence for other than good objective reasons ... What is reasonable depends on all the circumstances. We venture to say, recalling the circumstances of this present case, that we do not consider the absence of a written statement from the complainant to be good reason for silence (if adequate oral disclosure of the complaint has been given), and it does not become good reason merely because a solicitor has so advised. Nor is the possibility that the complainant may not pursue his complaint good reason, nor a belief by the solicitor that the suspect will be charged in any event whatever he says. The kind of circumstance which may most likely justify silence will be such matters as the suspect's condition (ill-health, in particular mental disability; confusion; intoxication; shock, and so forth – of course we are not laying down an authoritative list), or his inability genuinely to recollect events without reference to documents which are not to hand, or communication with other persons who may be able to assist his recollection. There must always be soundly based objective reasons for silence, sufficiently cogent and telling to weigh in the balance against the clear public interest in an account being given by the suspect to the police. Solicitors bearing the important responsibility of giving advice to suspects at police stations must always have that in mind.

In a case commentary of *R* v. *Knight* in the *Criminal Law Review*, Professor Birch considers the inconsistency between *R* v. *Howell* and *R* v. *Betts and Hall* on the issue of silence following legal advice. Birch criticises the *obiter* comment expressed by Laws LJ in *R* v. *Howell*.

D. BIRCH, CASE COMMENT ON R V. KNIGHT [2003] CRIM LR 799

... Laws L.J. takes the opportunity to state that, in his view, there is no inconsistency between *Howell* ... and *Betts and Hall* ... although there may be a 'shift of emphasis' regarding what an accused can reasonably be expected to mention in the face of legal advice to say nothing (or, as in the instant case, nothing more).

With respect, however, there is more than a shift of emphasis involved. In *Betts* the court stated that no inference can be drawn where 'it is a plausible explanation that the reason for not mentioning facts is that the particular appellant acted on the advice of his solicitor and not because he had no, or no satisfactory answer to give'. Admittedly *Betts* does not create what Laws L.J.

describes as an immunity from inferences, because it remains open to the jury to decide that the accused has a separate, guilty reason for silence. Presumably the fact that the advice is self-evidently duff might be evidence to support the contention that the accused is merely hiding behind the advice, rather than relying on it. But *Howell* goes further, and says that even where the accused *is* simply and genuinely relying on the advice given, it is open to the jury to draw an inference. This is because they may think that silence on the accused's part is not what can 'reasonably be expected' in all the circumstances, and 'there must always be soundly based objective reasons for silence'. While there is nothing in this approach which does violence to the literal wording of the statute, the danger it creates is that the jury may see the role of an innocent person at interview as being to answer all the questions and spill all the beans. Any tactical withholding of facts (for instance, until there is better police disclosure) may thus be viewed as 'unreasonable'. Allowing the jury such licence effectively ties the hands of responsible legal advisers (although admittedly it also acts as a disincentive to solicitors to be unforthcoming without good reason, which was Laws L.J.'s concern in *Howell*). Even if *Howell* is only a shift of emphasis, it is submitted, it is not to be encouraged.

In *R* v. *Hoare and Pearce*,[57] the defendants remained silent during interview on the advice of their solicitor. The trial judge directed the jury that they could draw adverse inferences from the defendants' silence if they thought that the defendants had unreasonably relied upon the legal advice. The Court of Appeal followed the most recent line of cases[58] and held that reliance on legal advice provided no automatic immunity against the drawing of adverse inferences and that adverse inferences could be drawn even where the legal advice had been given in good faith and it had genuinely been relied upon by the defendants, provided that the jury were satisfied that the true reason for the silence was that the defendant had no explanation to give. The Court confirmed that the test to be applied is an objective one which also takes into account the circumstances, including the state of mind of the defendant at the time.

4.5 FAILURE OR REFUSAL TO ACCOUNT FOR OBJECTS, SUBSTANCES OR MARKS

This paragraph explores the implications of an accused failing to explain objects within his possession, or substances or marks found upon his person or clothing.[59] The main provision to be considered here is s. 36, Criminal Justice and Public Order Act 1994. Section 36 states that when determining whether the accused is guilty of the offence charged, the court or jury may draw such inferences as appear proper from the failure or refusal of the accused to account for any object, substance or mark which is found on the accused's person, in or on his

57 [2005] 1 WLR 1804, CA.
58 Following *R* v. *Howell* [2005] 1 Cr App R 1 and *R* v. *Knight* [2004] 1 WLR 340.
59 For an argument that the broad application of ss. 36 and 37 of the Criminal Justice and Public Order Act 1994 has increased the evidential significance of silence, see A. Owusu-Bempah, 'Silence in suspicious circumstances' [2014] Crim LR 126.

clothing or footwear, in his possession, or in any place in which he is at the time of his arrest. This provision also applies to the condition of the accused's clothing or footwear.[60] Thus, this provision might apply where, for example, the accused fails to explain why he has stolen property in his pocket, blood on his shoes or clothing, scratches or lacerations on his face or body, drug paraphernalia in his house, or why his clothing is torn. Section 36(1)(b) further requires that a police officer reasonably believes that the object, substance or mark may be attributable to the fact that the accused has committed an offence. Under s. 36(1)(c), the constable must inform the accused of his belief and must ask the accused to account for the object, substance or mark.

S. 36, CRIMINAL JUSTICE AND PUBLIC ORDER ACT 1994

(1) Where –
    (a) a person is arrested by a constable, and there is –
        (i) on his person; or
        (ii) in or on his clothing or footwear; or
        (iii) otherwise in his possession; or
        (iv) in any place in which he is at the time of his arrest,
        any object, substance or mark, or there is any mark on any such object; and
    (b) that or another constable investigating the case reasonably believes that the presence of the object, substance or mark may be attributable to the participation of the person arrested in the commission of an offence specified by the constable; and
    (c) the constable informs the person arrested that he so believes, and requests him to account for the presence of the object, substance or mark; and
    (d) the person fails or refuses to do so,
    then if, in any proceedings against the person for the offence so specified, evidence of those matters is given, subsection (2) below applies.
(2) Where this subsection applies –
    [. . .]
    (b) a judge, in deciding whether to grant an application made by the accused under paragraph 2 of Schedule 3 to the Crime and Disorder Act 1998;
    (c) the court, in determining whether there is a case to answer; and
    (d) the court or jury, in determining whether the accused is guilty of the offence charged,
    may draw such inferences from the failure or refusal as appear proper.
(3) Subsections (1) and (2) above apply to the condition of clothing or footwear as they apply to a substance or mark thereon.

No adverse inferences may be drawn against an accused unless the police officer who makes the request informed the accused in ordinary language of the effect of any failure to account for the object, substance or mark.[61] Similarly, no adverse inferences may be drawn against the

---

60 Section 36(3), Criminal Justice and Public Order Act 1994.
61 Section 36(4), Criminal Justice and Public Order Act 1994.

5.2.1 False confessions

The Runciman Commission concluded that there were 'four distinct categories of false confession':[9]

- a voluntarily made, false confession made out of a 'morbid desire for notoriety' or because due to mental instability they cannot distinguish between reality and fantasy;
- such a confession might be made in order to protect someone else from prosecution;
- a defendant might confess out of a belief that he will gain something from such a confession, for example, to get out of the police station (a 'coerced-compliant' confession); and
- a defendant might confess after being persuaded by the police in interview that they are guilty of the offence (a 'coerced-internalised' confession).

Judith Ward was a compulsive confessor who falsely confessed to carrying out three bombings, including the bombing of Euston train station in 1973 and that of the M62 in 1974. She was convicted at first instance, but in 1991 the Home Secretary referred the matter to the Court of Appeal over concerns about the validity of the scientific evidence put forward in the original trial. The defence also took this opportunity to adduce fresh evidence that the defendant had been suffering from a mental disorder in 1974, which was so severe that none of the confessions that she had made could be relied upon as being true. Ward's convictions were quashed by the Court of Appeal.

R V. *JUDITH WARD* [1993] 1 WLR 619, CA
Glidewell, Nolan and Steyn LJJ

[at 681–2]

It is trite law that when in a criminal trial the prosecution seek to rely upon a confession or admission, or a series of confessions or admissions, made by the accused person, it is necessary for the prosecution to prove (to the criminal standard of proof) the following matters: (1) that the accused spoke or wrote the words alleged; (2) that the confession was made voluntarily, not as the result of the use of force, or a threat or the holding out of an inducement; and (3) that the confession or admission was true.

Formerly the first of these matters was often in issue in criminal trials. Fortunately the tape recording of the great majority of interviews of suspects by the police has resulted in a lessening of allegations that the defendant did not say what he was alleged to have said, though of course this can still be an issue where it is alleged there was a verbal confession before arrival at the police station. As we have made clear, in the present case the appellant at her trial did not accept that she had said everything that she was alleged to have said, and sometimes said that she could not remember whether she had made a particular statement, but for the most part the fact that she had made the damaging confessions she was alleged to have made was not seriously in issue. Certainly the various written statements which were exhibited were not challenged in this respect.

Moreover, it was not suggested that any of the confessions which were made were the result of the use of force or of any threat, or of the holding out of any inducement ...

---

9 *Report of the Royal Commission on Criminal Justice* (Cm 2263, 1993) at para. 32. The Commission relied here on the research provided by G. H. Gudjonsson, *The Psychology of Interrogations, Confessions and Testimony* (Wiley, 1992).

While it is for the prosecution to prove that a confession was true, this is normally not a matter which creates any great difficulty for them. If they have succeeded in proving that the statement was made voluntarily, and the accused appears to be of normal intelligence, most juries will readily accept that an accused would be most unlikely to make a damaging series of confessions against his or her own interest unless they were true. This was no doubt in the mind of the judge when he said in his summing up to the jury (as reported in 'The Daily Telegraph' for 2 November 1974) that the jury were entitled to consider whether there was any possible reason for making the statements, other than to tell the truth and the weight of conscience after being in custody for nine or ten days. 'When people make very serious admissions you have to ask yourself if they are likely to do it, if they are not true.

When an accused person who is alleged to have made admissions or confessions asserts that he did so because of a threat or an inducement held out to him, he will normally also assert that the admissions or confessions were untrue. But the question of the truth or otherwise of the confessions is normally subsumed in the question whether they were made voluntarily. If the judge on the voire dire decides that the confessions were voluntary and thus are admissible, and the jury believe that they were not the result of threat or inducement, then normally there is no further challenge to the truth. In our experience, cases in which it is accepted that a confession was made and was made voluntarily but nevertheless it is asserted that the confession was wholly untrue are rare in the extreme. This of course is such a case . . .

[at 684–5]

. . . Dr. James MacKeith, a distinguished consultant psychiatrist . . . expressed the following views:

I think that Miss Ward probably suffered from personality disorder–hysterical type, long before her arrest in 1974. Moreover, I think it likely that she was suffering from mental illness as well . . . I believe her false claims, which she may have believed, served to reduce emotional distress and to enhance self-esteem. Her untrue claims related to romantic themes and her involvement with Ireland, Irish people and Irish causes. They were in a sense specific, not general as in an unprincipled compulsive liar . . . It is my opinion that Miss Ward was mentally disordered from the time of her arrest, on remand and during her trial. Her impaired functioning was both the product of her personality and mental illness. As explained in this report, this mental disorder had a profound effect on her capacity to give a reliable account of herself and her memories to anybody.

[at 691]

. . . we cannot now be satisfied that reliance can be placed upon the truth of any of the appellant's confessions or admissions.

Similarly, in *R* v. *Lattimore et al.*,[10] the appellants were three boys who were convicted of the murder of Maxwell Confait after two of them falsely confessed to the killing and all three falsely confessed to setting fire to the house that he lived in in order to destroy evidence. The boys had limited mental capacity and the admissions were made by the appellants during interviews which had been conducted with no appropriate adult present and in the absence of a solicitor. The interviews had not been tape recorded, so there was no independent record of the confessions. It also later transpired that Lattimore had an alibi for time of the killing. The Court of Appeal quashed the appellants' convictions and held that the fresh evidence was not

---

10 (1976) 62 Cr App R 53.

reconcilable with the admissions that had been made. As a result of this case, the Fisher Inquiry was set up in order to look at the circumstances leading to the trial of the appellants.[11] However, while commending some of the recommendations of the Fisher Report, Doreen McBarnet criticised the report for failing to provide an independent investigation into the case. McBarnet commented:

> The Fisher Inquiry was not a thorough and independent investigation into the police: it could not be in a situation where the police could refuse access to files, and where much of the reconstruction of events was based, ironically, given the doubts on their veracity, on police records. Sometimes, however, Fisher does seem over ready to accept the police version of events.[12]

The cases above serve as two examples in which the appellants' convictions had to be quashed as a result of unreliable confession evidence being admitted in evidence. In these cases, the confessions were unreliable because they were falsely made by the appellants. Another problem arises with the reliability of confession evidence where police officers alter notes made contemporaneously to an interview of the defendant or where police officers fabricate evidence of admissions made in interview in order to bolster the prosecution case and secure a conviction against the defendant.

5.2.2 Fabricated confessions

Traditionally, confession evidence was only admissible in criminal proceedings if the confession was freely or voluntarily given. In the early case of *R* v. *Jane Warickshall*, the court stated that:

> A free and voluntary confession is deserving of the highest credit, because it is presumed to flow from the strongest sense of guilt, and therefore it is admitted as proof of the crime to which it refers; but a confession forced from the mind by the flattery of hope, or by the torture of fear, comes in so questionable a shape when it is to be considered as the evidence of guilt, that no credit ought to be given to it; and therefore it is rejected.[13]

Some of the most damaging miscarriages of justice have involved the fabrication of confession evidence by the police in order to construct a case against the defendant or defendants whom the police believe are the perpetrators of the crime. One of the most notorious miscarriages of justice is the case of *R* v. *McIlkenny et al.*,[14] otherwise known as 'The Birmingham Six'. The six appellants in this case had been convicted in 1975 of twenty-one counts of murder after twenty-one people died in the IRA bombings of two pubs in Birmingham. Four of the appellants had admitted signing written confessions, but they argued that they were false confessions which had been elicited by force. The remaining two appellants were alleged to have made oral confessions, which they denied.

11 Report of an Inquiry by the Hon. Sir Henry Fisher into the circumstances leading to the trial of three persons on charges arising out of the death of Maxwell Confait and the fire at 27 Doggett Road, London SE6 (House of Commons Paper 90, 13 December 1977, HMSO).
12 D. McBarnet, 'The Fisher Report on the Confait Case: four issues' [1978] 41(4) MLR 455–63 at 457.
13 See *R* v. *Jane Warickshall* (1783) 1 Leach 263 CC at 263–4.
14 (1991) 93 Cr App R 287.

The prosecution case had been based on these confessions. One aspect of the appeal focused on the scientific analysis of the written account of a police interview with McIlkenny. Expert evidence cast doubt on the contemporaneity of the written account of the interview by demonstrating that four extra pages had been inserted into the interview at a later stage. The inference was that this (as well as other) evidence had been fabricated by the police in order to bolster the prosecution case against the defendants. The convictions were quashed in 1991 (some sixteen years after conviction) on the grounds that the scientific evidence in the case could no longer be regarded as reliable and the police witnesses had lied on oath.

Another notorious miscarriage of justice involving the fabrication of evidence was that of *R* v. *Silcott, Braithwaite and Raghip*,[15] otherwise known as 'The Tottenham Three'. The three appellants here had been convicted of the murder of a police officer, PC Blakelock, during the Broadwater Farm riots in Tottenham, London in 1985. Silcott supposedly made an oral confession admitting the murder but it was established on appeal that the notes of his interview were not taken contemporaneously and that the interviewing officer in the case has altered the interview notes. Thus, the oral admission was not reliable and Silcott's conviction was quashed.

Professor Gudjonsson, a leading Professor of Forensic Psychology, has conducted much research into the psychology of unreliable confessions. He states that:

> The recognition and acceptance by the judiciary that false confessions to serious crimes do occur on occasions, even in the absence of learning disability or mental illness, are fundamental to reducing the number of miscarriages of justice cases resulting from unreliable confessions. Once this principle is accepted then each case must be closely looked at on the basis of its own merit.[16]

The cases above demonstrate the potential unreliability of confession evidence which has been obtained by improper means, or admissions voluntarily given but false. These cases have led to some high-profile miscarriages of justice where innocent appellants have spent many years in prison on the basis of such confession evidence. In light of this, it is important to safeguard against unreliable confession evidence. Thus, the status of a confession within the law of evidence needs some consideration, as do the rules surrounding the admission of such evidence in criminal proceedings.

5.2.3 Safeguarding against unreliable confession evidence

Confession evidence does not constitute conclusive proof of the matters made in the confession. Evidence of a confession is not binding on a defendant in the same way that a formal admission under s. 10 of the Criminal Justice Act 1967 is binding. Instead, a confession is just one piece of evidence which may be used to support the case for the prosecution or which may be challenged by the defence. The defence might challenge the admissibility of confession evidence on the grounds that the confession was obtained through the use of oppressive conduct by the police,[17]

---

15 (1991) *The Times*, 6 December, CA.
16 G. Gudjonsson, 'Unreliable confessions and miscarriages of justice in Britain' (2002) 4(4) *International Journal of Police Science & Management* 332–43 at 338.
17 Section 76(2)(a), PACE Act 1984.

or through the use of other improper methods which was likely to render the confession unreliable,[18] or where the admission of the confession would have an adverse effect on the fairness of the proceedings.[19]

In light of the unreliability of confession evidence, an important question arises as to whether corroboration should be required before a defendant can be convicted on the basis of confession evidence. The law of England and Wales currently requires no corroboration in confession cases, such that the defendant can be convicted solely on the basis of confession evidence. In an article in the *Law Quarterly Review* called 'Should confessions be corroborated?',[20] Professor Rosemary Pattenden considered the current safeguards against unreliable confessions[21] and whether corroboration of confession evidence should be required before conviction is possible. Professor Pattenden compared the approaches taken in Scotland and America where corroboration is (generally speaking) required, and Australia where a warning is given where the reliability of the confession is called into doubt. She suggested that a warning should be given along the lines of the *Turnbull* warning given in cases involving unreliable identification evidence.

R. PATTENDEN, 'SHOULD CONFESSIONS BE CORROBORATED?' (1991) 107 LQR 317
The way forward: a *Turnbull*-style warning

[at 338]

A solution is needed which will reduce public concern about wrongful convictions without simultaneously allowing the patently guilty to go free or importing legal niceties which will encourage appeals. If it provides an incentive to the police to look further than a confession for evidence so much the better. The answer is a warning when conviction depends wholly or substantially on a disputed or retracted confession along the lines of the virtually mandatory *Turnbull* identification warning. Whenever a defendant denies making an admission or asserts that confessional evidence is untrue the judge should be required to

(1) tell the jury that in the past confessions have been found to be false for whatever reason the defendant alleges makes his confession untrustworthy;
(2) caution the jury about convicting on a bare confession;
(3) point out evidence, if any, which tends to show the confession is true, whether or not this amounts to corroboration in the strict sense;
(4) point out anything which tends to suggest the confession is false such as discrepancies between the known facts and the confession and any surprising omissions from it; and
(5) draw the jury's attention to the circumstances in which the confession was made.

---

18 Section 76(2)(b), PACE Act 1984.
19 Section 78(1), PACE Act 1984.
20 R. Pattenden, 'Should confessions be corroborated?' (1991) 107 LQR 317.
21 These include: the presence of an independent person, such as a solicitor (and where relevant an appropriate adult) at interview; the prohibition of oppressive interrogation; the tape recording of interviews or the preparation of a contemporaneous record of interview; the provisions excluding confession evidence under ss. 76 and 78 of the PACE Act 1984; and, finally, s. 77 of the PACE Act 1984, which requires a warning about the confessions of mentally handicapped persons.

Magistrates should caution themselves in similar terms. The warning would be additional to the court's discretion to exclude the confession under section 78 of the Police and Criminal Evidence Act. Where the impugned statement is exculpatory the decision-maker should be warned or warn himself not to act on the statement unless convinced from the circumstances in which it was made and any independent evidence that the only motive for the deception could have been to conceal the suspect's guilt.

A *Turnbull*-style warning would not eliminate completely the risk of a miscarriage of justice but it would counter any assumption that the police are always reliable and that the only explanation for the existence of an admission (to a material fact or the crime *in toto*) by a sane person is that it is true. If this is combined with a change in the law on the admissibility of expert evidence so that every defendant is allowed to adduce evidence on the effect of interrogation on him then considerable progress in preventing wrongful convictions will have been made.

5.3   WHAT IS A CONFESSION?

Under s. 76(1), evidence of a confession made by a defendant is admissible at trial as evidence against the defendant where it is relevant to any matter in issue in the proceedings and provided that it is not excluded under s. 76(2).[22] A partial definition of a confession is given in s. 82(1) of the PACE Act 1984 (see also Figure 5.1):

> 'confession', includes any statement wholly or partly adverse to the person who made it, whether made to a person in authority or not and whether made in words or otherwise.

5.3.1 'Wholly or partly adverse'

Confession evidence is evidence which contains a statement incriminating the defendant in relation to the offence charged. Thus, a statement may be a confession if any part of what the defendant says is adverse to him or incriminating. In the case of *R* v. *De Silva*,[23] the prosecution adduced evidence of recordings of controlled telephone calls which contained 'material which the jury might take to incriminate the appellant both in some of what he himself had said and in what had been said to him'.[24] The Court of Appeal held that the recordings contained evidence 'contrary to the interests of the appellant at the trial', and thus they were confessions within the definition in s. 82(1).

---

22 Note that s. 78(1), PACE Act 1984 also provides a judicial discretion to exclude evidence 'on which the prosecution proposes to rely to be given if it appears to the court that, having regard to all the circumstances, including the circumstances in which the evidence was obtained, the admission of the evidence would have such an adverse effect on the fairness of the proceedings that the court ought not to admit it'. This will be discussed further at paragraphs 5.6 to 5.6.2 and in Chapter 6.
23 [2002] EWCA Crim 2673.
24 Ibid. per Hughes J at [15].

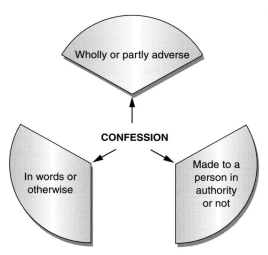

Figure 5.1 Definition of a confession

'Mixed' statements

The definition of a confession under s. 82(1) is widely construed in the sense that it includes statements which are either 'wholly or partly adverse' to the defendant. A 'mixed' statement is a statement which contains both exculpatory material (or self-serving statements), as well as incriminating admissions which are significant to a fact in issue in the case.[25]

J. C. SMITH, 'EXCULPATORY STATEMENTS AND CONFESSIONS' [1995] CRIM LR 280

[at 280]

... A mixed statement is one in which the defendant (hereafter, 'D') admits one or more of the elements of a particular offence but denies another or others. The statement, as a whole, is exculpatory – it amounts to a denial of guilt of the offence in question. D, being asked about a homicide, says, 'I killed him – but it was an unavoidable accident.' This a total denial of criminal responsibility; but, if D is charged with murder and sets up the defence of alibi, or simply denies or does not admit that he was the killer, the statement, subject to section 76 of PACE 1984, is admissible as evidence that he was present and was the killer. It is now clear that, when the inculpatory part of the statement is proved, the exculpatory part is also evidence, for what it is worth, that the killing was an accident. Where, however, the statement is wholly exculpatory of the offence charged, admitting no material fact, it is inadmissible as evidence of any fact asserted in it.

---

25 *R* v. *Garrod* [1997] Crim LR 445. The Court of Appeal in this case held that a 'mixed' statement should contain 'significant' admissions, thus basing the test upon the purpose for which the prosecution seek to adduce the statement. See D. J. Birch, 'The sharp end of the wedge: use of mixed statements by the defence' [1997] Crim LR 416–31 at 426–7 for criticism of the Court of Appeal decision in *R* v. *Garrod*. Professor Birch argues that *R* v. *Garrod* 'substitutes for the simple test of whether the prosecution relies on the statement a test which is more open to misunderstanding and needless complication'.

The question as to whether 'mixed' statements fall under the definition of a confession under s. 82(1) is important in order to ascertain whether they are admissible under the common law exception to the hearsay rule[26] and whether the exclusionary rules under s. 76(2) may be applicable. The House of Lords has held that where the defendant makes a 'mixed' statement, the exculpatory parts of the statement are admissible to prove the truth of their contents, just as the incriminating admissions are: *R* v. *Sharp.*[27] In this case, the appellant admitted presence at the scene of a burglary, but he denied participating in the offence and gave an innocent explanation for his presence in the area. The trial judge directed the jury to consider the incriminating statement as to the appellant's presence, but to disregard the evidence of his explanation for his presence. The House of Lords held that the whole statement should have been admissible. Lord Havers questioned:

> How can a jury fairly evaluate the facts in the admission unless they can evaluate the facts in the excuse or explanation? It is only if the jury think that the facts set out by way of excuse or explanation might be true that any doubt is cast on the admission, and it is surely only because the excuse or explanation might be true that it is thought fair that it should be considered by the jury ... a jury will make little of a direction that attempts to draw a distinction between evidence which is evidence of facts and evidence in the same statement which whilst not being evidence of facts is nevertheless evidentiary material of which they may make use in evaluating evidence which is evidence of the facts. One only has to write out the foregoing sentence to see the confusion it engenders.[28]

Exculpatory statements

Although the exculpatory parts of a mixed statement are admissible as part of a confession, a purely exculpatory statement (for example, 'I did not do it') does not fall under the definition of 'confession' under s. 82(1). In *Sat-Bhambra,*[29] the trial judge ruled admissible tape recordings of interviews with the appellant in which the appellant gave answers to questions put to him which were in fact exculpatory, but which later proved to be false or inconsistent with the defence case put forward at trial. On appeal, counsel for the appellant argued that the trial judge had been wrong to admit these statements and relied upon s. 76(2). The Court considered whether the exculpatory statements could fall under the meaning of 'confession' under s. 82(1) on the basis that they demonstrated that the defendant had been 'evasive and prevaricating', thus incriminating the defendant at trial. However, the Court of Appeal took the view that 'purely exculpatory statements are not [confessions] within the meaning of section 82(1)' and were not to be treated as such solely on the basis that they are adduced at trial as false or inconsistent statements.[30] The same approach was taken in *R* v. *Park.*[31] This approach was also approved recently by the House of

---

26 Under s. 114(1)(b) and s. 118, Criminal Justice Act 2003. The status of confession evidence as admissible hearsay is discussed at paragraph 5.3.4 below.
27 [1988] 1 WLR 7, HL.
28 Ibid. at 15.
29 (1989) 88 Cr App R 55.
30 Ibid. per Lord Lane CJ at 61.
31 (1994) 99 Cr App R 270.

Lords in *Hasan*[32] in which the House reconsidered the meaning of 'confession' under s. 82(1). Lord Steyn held[33] that there was no support for the argument that purely exculpatory statements could be classed as confessions under s. 82(1) and that it was 'wholly implausible that the draftsman would have made express reference only to wholly or partly adverse statement if he also had in mind covering under the definition of "confession" wholly exculpatory statements'.[34] Thus, wholly exculpatory statements were not protected by the exclusionary rule under s. 76(2), but they would nevertheless be protected by the discretion to exclude evidence under s. 78(1), PACE Act 1984. Consequently, Lord Steyn concluded that ss. 76(1) and 82(1) taken together were not inconsistent with Article 6(1) of the European Convention on Human Rights.

5.3.2 'Made to a person in authority or not'

A confession may be 'made to a person in authority or not'. Thus, it does not matter whether a confession is made to a police officer or to a civilian, as it will still fall within the definition of a confession under s. 82(1), PACE Act 1984. This ensures that confessions made to co-defendants, family members, friends or cellmates are all admissible as evidence against the defendant.

5.3.3 'In words or otherwise'

A confession may be made 'in words or otherwise'. This means that a confession may be made by a physical gesture. An example of a confession made by gesture can be found in the case of *Li Shu-Ling* v. *R*[35] in which, after confessing in interview to killing the deceased, the defendant then agreed to take part in a filmed re-enactment of the killing. The defendant was cautioned prior to the re-enactment, which was voluntarily performed. During the film he demonstrated how he had committed the murder by strangling the deceased both manually and with a ligature and he provided a commentary to explain his movements. The prosecution sought to adduce the evidence of the recording at the defendant's trial for the murder, but the defence objected. The Privy Council held that the trial judge had been right to admit the recording in evidence. Lord Griffiths stated (at 279) that:

> The truth is that if an accused has himself voluntarily agreed to demonstrate how he committed a crime it is very much more difficult for him to escape from the visual record of his confession than it is to challenge an oral confession with the familiar suggestions that he was misunderstood or misrecorded or had words put into his mouth. Provided an accused is given a proper warning that he need not take part in the video recording and agrees to do so voluntarily the video film is in principle admissible in evidence as a confession and will in some cases prove to be most valuable evidence of guilt.

---

32 [2005] UKHL 22; [2005] 2 AC 467.
33 With Lord Bingham, Lord Rodger, Baroness Hale and Lord Brown agreeing.
34 [2005] 2 AC 467 at 505.
35 [1989] AC 270, PC.

The definition of a confession is therefore quite widely construed, such that even physical gestures alone may constitute evidence of a confession.

5.3.4 Confession evidence as hearsay

Technically speaking, evidence of a confession made by a defendant is hearsay evidence because it is a statement made outside the courtroom, which the prosecution wishes to adduce in order to prove that the incriminating statements in the confession are true.[36] In the case of *R* v. *Sharp*, Lord Havers stated that:

> Evidence contained in a confession is however an exception to the hearsay rule and is admissible. The justification for the adoption of the exception was presumably that, provided the accused had not been subjected to any improper pressure, it was so unlikely that he would confess to a crime he had not committed that it was safe to rely upon the truth of what he said.[37]

According to s. 114(1)(b), Criminal Justice Act 2003, evidence of a confession is admissible under a common law rule relating specifically to confessions which has been preserved by s. 118(1), CJA 2003. Equally, confession evidence might be admissible under s. 114(1)(d), CJA 2003 in the interests of justice.[38]

5.4 EXCLUDING CONFESSION EVIDENCE

5.4.1 Applying to exclude confession evidence

Under s. 76(1), evidence of a confession made by a defendant is admissible at trial as evidence against the defendant where it is relevant to a matter in issue in the proceedings and provided that it is not excluded under s. 76(2), PACE Act 1984 (or by the exercise of judicial discretion under s. 78(1)). Evidence of a confession may therefore be excluded under a rule of law contained within s. 76(2), PACE Act 1984 or by the exercise of judicial discretion under s. 78(1), PACE Act 1984 or the common law (see Figure 5.2). An application to exclude a confession under s. 76(2) should be made where the confession was obtained by oppression (s. 76(2)(a)) or in consequence of anything said or done which was likely, in the circumstances, to render any confession unreliable (s. 76(2)(b)). Where the trial judge rules that there was oppression or the confession is unreliable under s. 76(2), then he must exclude the confession as he is bound by the rule of law under this provision to do so. Where the rule of law under s. 76(2) does not apply, an alternative application may be made appealing to the judge to exercise his discretion to exclude the evidence under s. 78(1) if its admission would have an adverse effect on the fairness of the proceedings, or under the common law

---

36 Refer to Chapter 7 for a fuller discussion on hearsay evidence.
37 [1988] 1 WLR 7 at 11.
38 Confirmed by the Court of Appeal in *R* v. *Y* [2008] 1 WLR 1683.

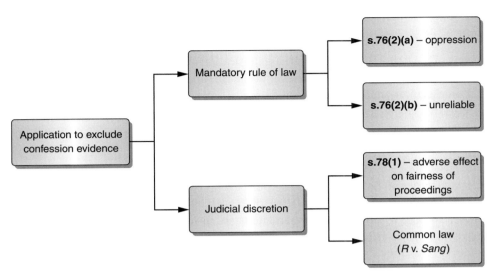

Figure 5.2 Applying to exclude confession evidence

discretion to exclude evidence which is found within *R* v. *Sang*[39] where the prejudicial effect of the evidence outweighs its probative value.

5.4.2 The *voir dire*

The question of whether a confession is admissible in court is a question for the tribunal of law to decide. In a trial on indictment (in the Crown Court) the judge will hear representations from counsel on the admissibility of such evidence in the absence of the jury. This hearing is known as a *voir dire* (or a 'trial within a trial').

Where responsible counsel makes a statement on the basis of documents that he has within his possession that the confession may have been obtained by oppression or in consequence of anything said or done which, in the circumstances at the time, was likely to render it unreliable, then that statement is a 'representation' for the purposes of s. 76(2) and the judge must hold a *voir dire* in order to require the prosecution to prove that the confession was not so obtained. The trial judge should have done this of his own motion in accordance with s. 76(3), even though neither counsel requested a *voir dire*: *R* v. *Bhavna Dhorajiwala*.[40]

During the *voir dire*, the judge may hear evidence from witnesses (such as police officers in the case or the defendant) as to the circumstances in which the confession was obtained. Where the defendant gives evidence in a *voir dire* that is relevant to the issue at the *voir dire* (for example, whether the confession was obtained by oppression, or in consequence of something said or done likely to render the confession unreliable, or its admission would have an adverse effect on the fairness of the proceedings) that evidence will not then be admissible at the substantive trial:

---

39 [1980] AC 402. This common law discretion to exclude has been preserved by s. 82(3), PACE Act 1984.
40 [2010] EWCA Crim 1237; [2010] 2 Cr App R 21, CA.

R v. *Brophy*.[41] In the House of Lords in *R* v. *Brophy*, Lord Fraser rationalised this principle on the basis that it was necessary so as to ensure that the defendant received a fair trial (at 481):

> It is of the first importance for the administration of justice that an accused person should feel completely free to give evidence at the *voir dire* of any improper methods by which a confession or admission has been extracted from him, for he can almost never make an effective challenge of its admissibility without giving evidence himself. He is thus virtually compelled to give evidence at the *voir dire*, and if his evidence were admissible at the substantive trial, the result might be a significant impairment of his so-called 'right of silence' at the trial.

In a summary trial (in the magistrates' court) the decision as to admissibility will be taken by the magistrates themselves who are both the tribunal of law and the tribunal of fact.[42] The magistrates must also hold a *voir dire* if representations are to be made to them under s. 76(2).[43] As the magistrates serve as both tribunals, where they decide that a confession should be inadmissible under s. 76(2), they should put it out of their minds.

5.4.3 Assessing the cogency of confession evidence

Where an application to exclude evidence of a confession is successful, the jury will not hear any evidence relating to the confession. However, where an application is not successful, the confession will be adduced in evidence before the jury. At this stage, it is open to defence counsel to attack the credibility of the confession in front of the jury in order to persuade the jury to disregard the confession during their deliberations or to place a lesser degree of weight or value on the confession. In doing so, the circumstances in which the confession was obtained may be aired again in court, this time in the presence of the jury. It is perfectly permissible for defence counsel to cross-examine prosecution witnesses, such as the police officers in the case, about the circumstances in which the confession was obtained.[44] In this sense, the defendant gets a 'second bite at the cherry'. In *R* v. *Mushtaq*, the majority in the House of Lords held that where a confession has been adduced in evidence before the jury, 'the logic of section 76(2) of PACE really requires that the jury should be directed that, if they consider that the confession was, or may have been, obtained by oppression or in consequence of anything said or done which was likely to render it unreliable, they should disregard it'.[45]

5.5 MANDATORY RULES OF EXCLUSION

Under s. 76(2), PACE Act 1984, there are two mandatory rules of law which provide for the exclusion of confession evidence.

---

41 [1982] AC 476.
42 Refer back to Chapter 2 on the function of the judge and jury.
43 *R* v. *Liverpool Juvenile Court, ex parte R* [1988] QB 1.
44 Per Lord Goddard in *R* v. *Murray* [1951] 1 KB 391.
45 Per Lord Roger [2005] UKHL 25; [2005] 1 WLR 1513 at 1531.

S. 76(2), PACE ACT 1984

If, in any proceedings where the prosecution proposes to give in evidence a confession made by an accused person, it is represented to the court that the confession was or may have been obtained –

(a) by oppression of the person who made it; or

(b) in consequence of anything said or done which was likely, in the circumstances existing at the time, to render unreliable any confession which might be made by him in consequence thereof,

the court shall not allow the confession to be given in evidence against him except in so far as the prosecution proves to the court beyond reasonable doubt that the confession (notwithstanding that it may be true) was not obtained as aforesaid.

Under s. 76(2)(a), confession evidence must be excluded where the confession has (or where it may have) been obtained by oppression. Under s. 76(2)(b), confession evidence must be excluded if the confession was (or may have been) obtained as a result of something said or done which was likely to render the confession unreliable. The defence may make an application (as a *voir dire*) to the judge to exclude any confession evidence under s. 76(2). Where such an application is made, the judge will make a finding of fact regarding whether or not the confession was obtained by oppression or whether or not something was said or done which was likely to render the confession unreliable. If the judge concludes that the confession was the result of oppression or was unreliable under s. 76(2), then he must rule that the confession is inadmissible for the purposes of trial. He may not exercise any discretion to admit the confession in such circumstances. Thus, s. 76(2) provides mandatory rules of exclusion.

There are broadly two justifications for the exclusion of confession evidence under s. 76(2). The first relates to the potential unreliability of the confession, whether obtained by oppression or by some other improper means. The second is based upon the premise that the defendant should not be compelled to incriminate himself. This rationale for exclusion was expressed by Lord Griffiths in *Lam Chi-ming* v. *The Queen*[46] and was restated more recently by Lord Hutton in the House of Lords in *R* v. *Mushtaq*:

> It is clear that there are two principal reasons underlying the rule that a confession obtained by oppression should not be admitted in evidence. One reason, which has long been stated by the judges, is that where a confession is made as a result of oppression it may well be unreliable, because the confession may have been given, not with the intention of telling the truth, but from a desire to escape the oppression imposed on, or the harm threatened to, the suspect. A further reason, stated in more recent years, is that in a civilised society a person should not be compelled to incriminate himself, and a person in custody should not be subjected by the police to ill treatment or improper pressure in order to extract a confession.[47]

Under the common law prior to the PACE Act 1984, confessions had to be voluntary and the burden was on the prosecution to prove beyond reasonable doubt that the confession was

---

46 [1991] 2 AC 212 at 220.
47 [2005] 1 WLR 1513 at 1518.

obtained voluntarily: *Ibrahim* v. *R.*[48] This common law position is now reflected in s. 76(2), PACE Act 1984 which also places the burden of proving that the confession was properly obtained on the prosecution. If the confession is to be adduced in evidence, the prosecution must prove this to the high criminal standard of proof, beyond reasonable doubt. In *Moss*,[49] a case involving a defendant who was of low intelligence and was interviewed without a solicitor, the defendant's conviction was quashed on appeal because the prosecution had failed to discharge the burden of proving that the confession was reliable.

Where the defence do not make representations about the admissibility of a confession under s. 76(2), the court may of its own motion require the prosecution to prove that the confession was not obtained improperly: s. 76(3), PACE Act 1984.

5.5.1 Oppression – s. 76(2)(a)

The first ground within s. 76(2) under which evidence of a confession might be excluded is on the basis that the confession was obtained by oppression: s. 76(2)(a). As the confession must be obtained *by* oppression, it must be established that there is a causative link between the oppressive conduct and the confession: the oppression must cause the confession.

Section 76(8), PACE Act 1984 provides a partial definition of 'oppression' which is comparable to and reflects the substance of Article 3, European Convention on Human Rights.

S. 76(8), PACE ACT 1984

In this section 'oppression' includes torture, inhuman or degrading treatment, and the use or threat of violence (whether or not amounting to torture).

In a number of cases, the courts have had cause to examine and interpret the definition of oppression. It has been given a narrow interpretation.

The leading case on oppression is *R* v. *Fulling*.[50] In this case, the defendant was arrested on suspicion of obtaining property by deception. She was interviewed twice by the police on the day of arrest, but she remained silent in interview. The following day she was interviewed again. The defendant was silent throughout the first part of the interview, but she then broke her silence after a break in interview. At this stage, the defendant made a number of admissions. At trial, the defence argued that the confessions should be excluded on the ground that they had been obtained by oppression. The defendant claimed that during the break in interview on the second day she had been informed by the police that her lover was having an affair with a woman who was in the cell next to the defendant's. The defendant claimed that she became distressed and confessed in order to get bail and get out of the police station. The trial judge held that the confession was admissible and that it had not been obtained by oppression. The defendant appealed, but the Court of Appeal dismissed the appeal and held that the PACE Act

---

48 [1914] AC 599, PC.
49 (1990) 91 Cr App R 371.
50 [1987] QB 426.

1984 was a codifying Act, thus the principles in *Bank of England* v. *Vagliano Brothers*[51] should apply and the word 'oppression' in s. 76(2)(a) should be given its natural meaning.

R V. *FULLING* [1987] QB 426
Lord Lane CJ

[at 432–3]

This in turn leads us to believe that 'oppression' in section 76(2)(a) should be given its ordinary dictionary meaning. The *Oxford English Dictionary* as its third definition of the word runs as follows: 'Exercise of authority or power in a burdensome, harsh, or wrongful manner; unjust or cruel treatment of subjects, inferiors, etc.; the imposition of unreasonable or unjust burdens.' One of the quotations given under that paragraph runs as follows: 'There is not a word in our language which expresses more detestable wickedness than oppression.'

We find it hard to envisage any circumstances in which such oppression would not entail some impropriety on the part of the interrogator. We do not think that the judge was wrong in using that test. What, however, is abundantly clear is that a confession may be invalidated under section 76(2)(b) where there is no suspicion of impropriety. No reliance was placed on the words of section 76(2)(b) either before the judge at trial or before this court. Even if there had been such reliance, we do not consider that the policeman's remark was likely to make unreliable any confession of the appellant's own criminal activities, and she expressly exonerated – or tried to exonerate – her unfaithful lover.

In those circumstances, in the judgment of this court, the judge was correct to reject the submission made to him under section 76 of the Act of 1984. The appeal is accordingly dismissed.

Notably, the Court of Appeal didn't apply the first meaning of oppression that was listed in the *Oxford English Dictionary*, but was rather selective in applying the third meaning listed. The Court envisaged that oppression would inevitably involve some impropriety on the part of the interrogator. Oppression was thus narrowly construed and there was held to be no oppression in this case.

One example of treatment which the Court of Appeal has held to be oppressive is found in the case of the 'Cardiff three': *R* v. *Miller*; *Paris*; *Abdullahi*.[52] The three defendants in this case and two other men were charged with the murder of a young prostitute, Lynette White. Miller had been living with the victim up until a few days before her death. Her body was found in the bedroom of her friend's (another prostitute's) flat. She had been stabbed over fifty times in the chest and her wrists and throat had been cut. Miller was one of five men arrested on suspicion of the victim's murder. He made three incriminating admissions, which the prosecution sought to rely on as part of its case against Miller, and the trial judge ruled the evidence admissible. On appeal to the Court of Appeal, the appellant argued that the evidence should have been excluded on the basis that the confessions were obtained by oppression. Expert evidence suggested that Miller was borderline mentally handicapped and that he had an IQ of 75, a mental age of 11, and a reading age of 8. There were 19 tapes of police interviews in which the police shouted at Miller for hours and rejected or ignored over 300 denials that he made. Finally, in tapes 18 and 19

---

51 [1891] AC 107 at 144.
52 (1993) 97 Cr App R 99.

Miller made the admissions. The defendant's solicitor was present for all but the first two tapes of interview but only intervened in tape 19. The Court of Appeal held that even in the absence of physical violence, the conduct of the police was oppressive. The Court expressed its horror at the way in which the defendant was bullied and hectored by the police in tape 7. The police had 'brainwashed' the defendant into accepting their words that he was present at the time of killing. The Court of Appeal held that Miller didn't contribute to the confession, but he merely repeated back to the officers the words that they had repeatedly asserted to him. This decision also demonstrates that the impropriety by the police need not involve physical injury in order to constitute oppression for the purposes of s. 76(2)(a).

At the opposite end of the spectrum, merely asking questions in interview in a raised voice, swearing at the defendant or asking questions more than once would not amount to oppression for the purposes of the exclusionary rule under s. 76(2)(a). An example of this is the case of *R* v. *Emmerson*[53] in which the interviewing officers became impatient with the defendant. The officer spoke with a raised voice and swore at the defendant in the interview. The Court of Appeal held that this did not amount to oppression. Similarly, in *R* v. *Heaton*,[54] the defendant appealed against his conviction for manslaughter on the basis that his confession to the crime had been obtained by oppression. The defendant had been interviewed for 75 minutes and in the presence of his solicitor. The police who questioned the defendant had raised their voices, but they were not shouting. There had been 'no oppressive hostility' in the interview and the questioning had proceeded at a reasonable pace with the defendant being given time to consider his replies. Some questions had been repeated by the police but the Court held that the police are not required to give up at the first denial or even after repeated denials. There was held to be no oppression and thus the confession was rightly admitted. The facts of *R* v. *Emmerson* and *R* v. *Heaton* are easy to distinguish from those in *R* v. *Miller*; *Paris*; *Abdullahi*. Although it is relatively easy to identify conduct at the extreme ends of the spectrum which is either definitely oppressive or conduct which is definitely not oppressive, there remains a grey area in the middle and it is difficult to know where the line between oppressive conduct and non-oppressive conduct is drawn.

Prior to the enactment of the PACE Act 1984, oppression was something that tended to sap the will of the suspect.[55] In assessing whether the confession had been obtained by oppression, the court would take into account the overall treatment of the suspect, such as how long he was questioned for, whether he was given rests and how long for, whether he was given refreshment, and the characteristics of the suspect. According to Sachs J in *R* v. *Priestly*, '[w]hat may be oppressive as regards a child, an invalid or an old man or somebody inexperienced in the ways of this world may turn out not to be oppressive when one finds that the accused person is of a tough character and an experienced man of the world.'[56] The Court of Appeal adopted this definition of oppression in *R* v. *Prager*.[57] In this case, there was held to be no oppression where the appellant, who was a suspected spy, was interrogated for roughly nine hours during one day, with a break after three-and-a-quarter hours and a further break for a short walk later on.

---

53 (1991) 92 Cr App R 284.
54 [1993] Crim LR 593, CA.
55 *R* v. *Priestley* (1967) 51 Cr App R 1.
56 Ibid. Similarly, in *R* v. *Gowan* [1982] Crim LR 821 it was held that less sympathy should be shown to professional criminals who could withstand more robust questioning.
57 [1972] 1 WLR 260.

However, by contrast, in the case of *R* v. *Hudson*,[58] the appellant was a planning officer who had never been in trouble with the police before and who was detained in the police station for five days and four nights, he was questioned for a total of twenty-five hours in two-and-a-quarter-hour sessions, he was in the presence of police officers for fifty hours, and he was asked 700 questions. His confession was held to be inadmissible because the prosecution failed to prove that there had been no oppression. The characteristics of the defendant are also taken into account post-PACE Act 1984. In the case of *R* v. *Seelig*; *R* v. *Spens*,[59] the appellants were intelligent and sophisticated merchant bankers who had been interviewed in relation to fraudulent share dealing. They were questioned by inspectors who had been appointed by the Secretary of State for the Department of Trade and Industry under the Companies Act 1985. They made confessions which were later admitted in evidence in criminal proceedings as against the appellants. The appellants appealed against their convictions on the basis that the trial judge had been wrong to admit such evidence at trial. The Court of Appeal dismissed the appeal and held that the trial judge was correct in taking into account the background of the appellants and the fact that they were 'extremely astute, professional men' who would have been used to answering questions of the sort posed to them by the investigators.

5.5.2 Unreliability – s. 76(2)(b)

The second ground within s. 76(2) under which evidence of a confession might be excluded is on the basis that the confession was obtained 'in consequence of anything said or done which was likely, in the circumstances existing at the time, to render unreliable any confession which might be made by him in consequence thereof': s. 76(2)(b). This ground for exclusion is wider than that under s. 76(2)(a). The test of unreliability is concerned not with whether the resultant confession is *actually* unreliable, but with whether the confession is *potentially* unreliable (i.e. the test is whether there was something said or done which was likely, in the circumstances, to render any resultant confession unreliable). Notably, it must be asked whether *any* confession which had been made in the circumstances existing at the time was likely to be rendered unreliable. Therefore, s. 76(2)(b) allows for the exclusion of confession evidence which is in fact true if it was obtained in consequence of anything said or done which was likely to render *any* confession given in those circumstances unreliable.

The Court of Appeal in *R* v. *Barry*[60] held that consideration of the application of s. 76(2)(b) requires a number of steps. According to Lloyd LJ:

1. The first step is to identify the thing said or done – a broad approach should be taken. In this case, '[e]verything said and done by the police should have been taken into account'.[61]
2. The second step is to ask whether what was said and done was likely in the circumstances to render unreliable a confession made in consequence – this test objective, '[b]ut all the

---

58 (1981) 72 Cr App R 163.
59 [1992] 1 WLR 148.
60 (1992) 95 Cr App R 384.
61 Note that in *R* v. *Wahab* [2002] EWCA Crim 1570, [2003] 1 Cr App R 15 it was held that the phrase 'by the police' here referred to the specific facts of the case in which the impropriety was in fact carried out by the police, but it was not the intention of the Court of Appeal in *R* v. *Barry* to restrict the application of s. 76(2)(b) to things said or done by the police.

circumstances had to be taken into account, including the circumstances affecting the appellant himself and in particular of course his urgent desire for bail. The test is also in a sense hypothetical since it relates not to *the* confession but to *any* confession'.

3. The last step is to question whether the prosecution has proved beyond reasonable doubt that *the* confession was not obtained in consequence of the things said or done – 'this is a question of fact to be approached in a commonsense way'.

Section 76(2)(b) does not require that the thing said or done must be said or done to the defendant by the police. There is also no requirement that the thing said or done is something illegal or improper. What must be present, though, is a causative link between the thing said or done and the confession; thus the prosecution must prove beyond reasonable doubt that there is no causation in order to be able to adduce the confession. The defendant in *R* v. *Harvey*[62] was a woman of low normal intelligence who suffered from a psychopathic disorder which was aggravated by alcohol abuse. She confessed to having committed a murder after she heard her lover confess. Psychiatric evidence was given that the defendant may have confessed in order to protect her lover and that due to her mental disorder at the time of the confession, her confession might not be true. The confession was excluded under s. 76(2)(b) because the trial judge was not satisfied beyond reasonable doubt that the confession was not obtained as a result of the defendant hearing her lover confess. The burden of proof was on the prosecution to disprove this possibility, and they had failed to do so. Thus, the confession was excluded here on the basis that the thing said or done came from the defendant's lover and there was no illegal conduct or bad faith on the part of the police.

The thing said or done must be external to the defendant and must be said or done *to* the defendant. Section 76(2)(b) does not cover things internal to the defendant or said or done *by* the defendant. Thus, in *R* v. *Goldenberg*[63] the appellant's drug addiction could not constitute a thing said or done under s. 76(2)(b). After being in police custody for some time, the appellant requested an interview with the police in which he confessed to an offence. The defence argued that the appellant was suffering from withdrawal symptoms from his heroin addiction whilst in custody and that the confession had been prompted by the hope of securing bail and getting access to drugs upon release. Therefore, the defence argued that the confession should be excluded under s. 76(2)(b) on the basis that it was made in consequence of something said or done likely, in the circumstances, to render any confession unreliable. This argument was rejected by the Court of Appeal which dismissed the appeal against conviction and held that the thing said or done must be said or done *to* the appellant and must be external to the appellant. Thus, the appellant's drug addiction, which came from within the appellant, was not sufficient. Although counsel for the appellant also put forward submissions on the basis that the judge should have exercised his discretion to exclude the confession under s. 78(1), PACE Act 1984, the Court of Appeal rejected this argument on the ground that trial counsel did not make any application to the trial judge under s. 78(1): 'it does not appear to us that it would be right for this Court to give effect to a submission which depends on the failure of a judge to exclude evidence by a discretion which at the trial he was not asked to exercise'.[64]

---

62 [1988] Crim LR 241, Central Criminal Court.
63 (1989) 88 Cr App R 285.
64 Ibid. at 289.

R V. *GOLDENBERG* (1989) 88 CR APP R 285
Neill LJ

[at 289–90]

It was submitted on behalf of the appellant that the words 'said or done' in the phrase 'in consequence of anything said or done' could include what was said or done by the appellant himself.

He had requested the interview and his motive, it was said, was to obtain bail or alternatively, as one of the police officers said in the course of the trial, to obtain credit for helping the police. It was also submitted, though without great force, that the confession was unreliable because of the words used by Detective Sergeant Leader at the outset of the interview which might have led the appellant to think that anything he said would be 'off the record,' or at any rate would not be used against him in the present proceedings. It is to be noted that this alternative submission was not advanced at the trial.

It is important to remember that in the present case there was an application on behalf of the appellant that the evidence should not be admitted. The case therefore fell within section 76(2) of the 1984 Act rather than within section 76(3), under which the court may, of its own motion, require the prosecution to prove the reliability of a confession.

It follows therefore that if criticism is now to be made of the judge's ruling, it is necessary to bear in mind the arguments addressed to him at the trial. Thus the obligation on the Court under section 76(2) arises where 'it is represented to the court that the confession was or may have been obtained in consequence of anything said or done which was likely, in the circumstances existing at the time, to render unreliable any confession which might be made by him in consequence thereof.'

In the present case it is clear that no reliance was placed at the trial on anything said or done by Detective Sergeant Leader at the start of the interview. The argument was based on what was said or done by the appellant himself and on his state of mind. It is in that context that the judge's ruling has to be considered. It is also to be noted that on the *voire dire* the appellant himself did not give evidence.

It was submitted on behalf of the appellant that in a case to which section 76(2)(*b*) of the 1984 Act applied, the Court was concerned with the objective reliability of the confession and not merely with the conduct of any police officer or other person to whom the confession was made. Accordingly the Court might have to look at what was said or done by the person making the confession, because the confession might have been made 'in consequence' of what he himself had said or done and his words or actions might indicate that this confession was or might be unreliable.

In our judgment the words 'said or done' in section 76(2)(*b*) of the 1984 Act do not extend so as to include anything said or done by the person making the confession. It is clear from the wording of the section and the use of the words 'in consequence' that a causal link must be shown between what was said or done and the subsequent confession.

In our view it necessarily follows that 'anything said or done' is limited to something external to the person making the confession and to something which is likely to have some influence on him.

In the circumstances of the present case we are satisfied that on the proper construction of section 76 (2)(*b*) the judge's ruling as to the admissibility of evidence relating to the June 16 interview was correct. We are also satisfied that the judge was right to rule against the submission that the prejudicial effect of this evidence outweighed its probative value. We therefore reject the second ground of appeal. Accordingly for these reasons the appeal against conviction must be dismissed.

R v. *Goldenberg* was considered more recently in the case of *R* v. *Wahab*,[65] in which the Court of Appeal reiterated the limitation on s. 76(2)(b) that the thing said or done must be external to the defendant. In this case, 'the appellant instructed his solicitor to see whether some convenient arrangement could be procured with the police, he was uninfluenced by anything said and done by anyone else. Everything thereafter originated from the appellant himself'.[66] The solicitor advised the appellant that if he made admissions the police would look at the whole picture and might release members of his family who had also been arrested. The appellant then made admissions to offences. The Court of Appeal stated that the advice of a solicitor properly given to the defendant will not usually constitute a thing said or done and will not therefore be sufficient to exclude a confession under s. 76(2)(b):

> One of the duties of a legal advisor, whether at a police station, or indeed at a pre-trial conference, or during the trial itself, is to give the client realistic advice. That emphatically does not mean that the advice must be directed to 'getting the client off', or simply making life difficult for the prosecution. The advice may, and sometimes ought to be robust, sensibly considering the advantages which the client may derive from evidence of remorse and a realistic acceptance of guilt, or the corresponding disadvantages of participating in a 'no comment' interview. The exercise of the professional judgment in circumstances like these is often very difficult, often dependent on less than precise instructions from the defendant.[67]

Provided that the thing said or done is external to the defendant and is done to the defendant, then the characteristics of the defendant, such as his mental condition, may be taken into account in determining admissibility under s. 76(2)(b). In the case of *R* v. *Everett*,[68] the appellant was 42 years old with the mental age of an 8-year-old. He had been interviewed without a legal adviser or an appropriate adult present and he made admissions in interview. The judge ruled that the confessions were admissible and so the defendant pleaded guilty and appealed to the Court of Appeal. The appeal was allowed and the court quashed the appellant's conviction on the basis that the trial judge erred in failing to take into account the mental condition of the appellant in determining the admissibility of the confession. The Court held that the test was an objective one, such that whether the police were unaware of the mental condition of the defendant or not was not relevant. What was relevant was the *actual* mental condition of the defendant. In the case commentary, Professor Diane Birch states (at 826) that the test under s. 76(2)(b) is both objective and hypothetical:

> Objective in the sense that the *actual* circumstances count, not (if they are different) the circumstances believed by the interrogator to exist. The provision does not judge the interrogator, but the reliability of the evidence he elicits. Hypothetical in the sense that the court is not asked to decide whether *this* confession *is* unreliable, but whether *any* confession the suspect might make is likely to be unreliable.

---

65 [2002] EWCA Crim 1570.
66 Per Judge LJ [2002] EWCA Crim 1570 at [41].
67 Ibid. at [42].
68 [1988] Crim LR 826.

Similarly, in *R* v. *Silcott, Braithwaite and Raghip*,[69] one of the appellants, Raghip, was 19 years old with an IQ of 73 and the reading age of a 6-year-old. On appeal against his conviction for murder it was argued that in considering the admissibility of admissions made by Raghip in interview, Raghip's mental condition at the time of interview, including his susceptibility and vulnerability, ought to have been taken into consideration. This new evidence relating to Raghip's mental condition had not been available to the trial judge at the time, and the Court of Appeal held that had the judge had the benefit of such medical evidence, he would have excluded the confession evidence. Where an application to exclude confession evidence is made on the basis of the mental condition of the defendant, this should be supported by medical evidence rather than the trial judge's own assessment of the appellant's mental condition at interview.

Another case in which the mental condition of the appellant should have been taken into account was *R* v. *Delaney*.[70] The appellant in this case was 17 years old and described as 'educationally subnormal' with an IQ of 80. He confessed to indecently assaulting a child after initially being interviewed for an hour and a half. Evidence from a psychologist was given that the appellant's emotional personality was such that when being interviewed he might have confessed in order to get the interview over with as quickly as possible. The Court of Appeal held that the confession should have been excluded by the trial judge under s. 76(2)(b), taking into account the mental characteristics of the appellant and the fact that the interviewing officers had come to the conclusion that the appellant had committed the offence and they played down the gravity of the offence when interviewing the appellant. The officers had also failed to maintain a contemporaneous record of precisely what was said to the appellant in 'flagrant breach' of the Codes of Practice. In a similar case, in *R* v. *Walker*,[71] the Court of Appeal held that any mental or personality abnormalities may be of relevance. There was expert psychiatric evidence that the appellant suffered from a personality disorder which might have led her to elaborate on her account of events without realising the consequences of what she was saying. The Court of Appeal quashed the appellant's conviction and held that the trial judge should have taken the characteristics of the appellant into account.

The case of *R* v. *McGovern*[72] is a further example of a case in which the characteristics of the appellant should have been taken into account by the trial judge in deciding whether to exclude the confession on the basis of potential unreliability under s. 76(2)(b). Upon arrest, the appellant requested a solicitor but was denied access, in breach of s. 58, PACE Act 1984 and Code C. She was then interviewed by the police, during which no contemporaneous notes were made, in breach of Code C. The appellant was 19 years old and of limited intelligence. She was 6 months pregnant and had been vomiting in her cell before the interview and she confessed in this first interview. A second interview was then held with a solicitor present, although the solicitor was unaware of the first confession. In this second interview, the appellant confessed again. The trial judge refused to exclude the confessions under s. 76(2)(b) and the appellant was convicted. On appeal, the Court of Appeal quashed her conviction and held that the appellant's characteristics, namely her

---

69 (1991) *The Times*, 6 December, CA.
70 (1989) 88 Cr App R 338.
71 [1998] 2 Cr App R (S) 245.
72 (1991) 92 Cr App R 228.

vulnerability and pregnancy, ought to have been taken into account by the trial judge. The breaches of s. 58, PACE and Code C in the first interview were things said or done likely to render any confession unreliable, and this had 'tainted' the second confession.[73]

R V. MCGOVERN (1991) 92 CR APP R 228
Farquharson LJ

[at 233]

. . . even if the confession given at the first interview was true, as it was later admitted to be, it was made in consequence of her being denied access to a solicitor and is for that reason in the circumstances likely to be unreliable. It follows that the prosecution has not in our judgment proved otherwise. We think . . . that if a solicitor had been present at the time this mentally backward and emotionally upset young woman was being questioned, the interview would have been halted on the very basis that her responses would be unreliable. It seems that the interview was held quickly and without the formalities prescribed by the Code of Conduct because the police were anxious to discover the missing girl, but this heightened the risk of the confession being unreliable.

[at 234]

In the circumstances of this case, it is difficult to determine what additional effect the breaches of the Code on their own may have had on the reliability of the confession that the girl made. The fact that the confession was in substance true is expressly excluded by the Act as being a relevant factor. In any case at the time he made his ruling the learned judge was not aware of whether the confession was admitted to be true or not. As already observed, the anxiety of the police at the time of the first interview was to establish the whereabouts of Helen, dead or alive, and whilst in no way wishing to detract from the importance of these rules being observed, it is not perhaps necessary for us to decide whether the breach of the rules in this case materially affected the reliability of the confession made by the appellant.

In our judgment, had a solicitor been called at the time the appellant requested one should be made available to her, the first interview would be most unlikely to have taken place – certainly in the form that it did. The girl was ill at the time, and it was apparent at the outset of the interview that she failed to understand the meaning of the caution. During the course of the interview questions were asked by the Detective Sergeant in the form which I have already described which would immediately, I would suggest, have caused protest on the part of a solicitor advising the girl. Certainly, when it was observed what condition she was in emotionally, it would, . . . inevitably have followed that the solicitor would have prevented the interview being continued further. In those circumstances, the learned judge should have found that the prosecution had failed to discharge the burden of proof which was laid upon it with regard to the admissibility of that interview.

The thing said or done to the defendant need not be illegal in the strict sense of the word and may constitute a technical breach of the Codes of Practice. In *DPP* v. *Blake*,[74] the defendant was a 16-year-old girl who was estranged from her parents. The police asked for her father's details

---

73 The effect of 'tainted confessions' will be considered at paragraph 5.8 below.
74 [1989] 1 WLR 432.

in order that they could secure the attendance of the defendant's father at interview as an 'appropriate adult'. The defendant refused to give her father's details and instead requested that a social worker be present during interview. However, the social worker refused to attend the interview unless the defendant's parents could not be contacted. In interview, the defendant confessed to criminal damage, but the confession was excluded at trial under s. 76(2)(b) on the basis that the defendant had not benefited from the presence of an appropriate adult in interview (although it was clear that the police had little choice but to interview the defendant with her father present), she should not have been left in the presence of male officers, and she should have been offered refreshments in accordance with Code C. These things done to the defendant meant that it was likely that any confession would be rendered unreliable. Where the police have acted improperly in breaching the provisions of the PACE Act 1984 or the Codes of Practice, such impropriety should be taken into account by the judge in considering the admissibility of any confession under s. 76(2)(b). In the Court of Appeal in *R* v. *Barry*,[75] Lloyd LJ stated that the trial judge 'gave ... much too little weight to the numerous breaches of Code C. It is now well established that a breach or breaches of the Code do not necessarily mean that evidence obtained in breach of the Code will be excluded. But it does not follow that breaches of the Code are therefore irrelevant'.

Case law clearly shows that a breach of the Codes of Practice or PACE may amount to something said or done for the purposes of s. 76(2)(b) and may therefore lead to the exclusion of a confession. Of course, this does not mean that any minor breach of the Codes of Practice will automatically justify exclusion of confession evidence. The question that must be asked is whether the breach renders the confession potentially unreliable; thus the causal link between the breach and the confession must be established. Consequently, the appellant's confession in *R* v. *Alladice*[76] could not be excluded under s. 76(2)(b). The appellant confessed to committing the robbery of a post office. The police had refused the appellant access to a solicitor in breach of s. 58, PACE Act 1984 and Code C; nevertheless, the appellant had been cautioned and he admitted that he understood the caution, that he could cope with interviews and that he knew his rights. While the breach of PACE and Code C was a thing done to the defendant, this did not *cause* the confession here. Similarly, in *R* v. *Law-Thompson*[77] the appellant was interviewed without an appropriate adult being present and confessed. The Court of Appeal held that there was no evidence that the confession made by the defendant was made as a result of the fact that there was no appropriate adult present.

5.6 DISCRETION TO EXCLUDE

Where a confession cannot be excluded by a mandatory rule of law under s. 76(2), there remains a judicial discretion to exclude[78] evidence under s. 78(1), PACE Act 1984 and at common law

75 (1992) 95 Cr App R 384.
76 (1988) 87 Cr App R 380.
77 [1997] Crim LR 674.
78 This chapter is concerned only with the admissibility of confession evidence. The judicial discretion to exclude evidence other than confession evidence under s. 78(1) and *R* v. *Sang* [1980] AC 402 will be considered in Chapter 6.

under *R* v. *Sang*.[79] The Court of Appeal has held that s. 78(1) does no more than restate the discretion at common law.[80]

The significant difference between s. 76(2) and s. 78(1) is that s. 76(2) sets out mandatory rules of exclusion under which the trial judge *must* exclude the confession if he decides that it was obtained by oppression or in consequence of anything said or done, likely, in the circumstances, to render the confession unreliable, while s. 78(1) provides for a discretion under which the judge *may* exclude the confession. Professor Diane Birch explains how the system works in an article published after the enactment of the PACE Act 1984.

D.J. BIRCH, 'THE PACE HOTS UP: CONFESSIONS AND CONFUSIONS UNDER THE 1984 ACT' [1989] CRIM LR 95
The system explained

From the point of view of a prosecutor seeking to adduce a confession, the system is best compared to a steeplechase in which each obstacle must be cleared in order to complete the race. The first hurdle is section 76 . . .

Section 76 . . . poses a double hurdle, both parts of which must be cleared. The confession must not be obtained by oppression, or in circumstances conducive to unreliability. Nothing prevents the defence from challenging the confession on both grounds . . .

Assuming that he succeeds, his next obstacle is section 78, which applies to all prosecution evidence including confessions, and which provides:

(1) In any proceedings the court may refuse to allow evidence on which the prosecution proposes to rely to be given if it appears to the court that, having regard to all the circumstances, including the circumstances in which the evidence was obtained, the admission of the evidence would have such an adverse effect on the fairness of the proceedings that the court ought not to admit it.

Here there is a difficulty in assessing the height and breadth of the fence to be cleared. Whereas section 76 involves proof of facts, section 78 involves the exercise of judgment by the court. In this sense section 78 embodies a discretionary power, but the words 'many refuse to allow' are not to be taken at face value, for once the court has decided that the evidence would have the required deleterious effect on the fairness of the proceedings it must exclude it. Nor is the apparent latitude allowed by the word 'such' necessarily all that it seems, for it would be a brave judge who declared, 'This evidence would have an adverse impact on the fairness of the proceedings, but not such a dire effect that I ought not to admit it.' This is not to say that such thoughts may not run through the mind of a judge trying a case in which an old lag was not cautioned before confessing, merely that it is wiser not to articulate them in argument and that debate in practical terms is more likely to revolve around whether it is at all unfair to admit the evidence in all the circumstances.

To add to the prosecutors' difficulties, section 78 is not, as section 76 is, explicit as to who bears the burden of proof. It has been suggested that it is for the defence to make good its objection but, even if this

---

79 [1980] AC 402.
80 *R* v. *Mason* [1988] 1 WLR 139. This will be discussed further in Chapter 6.

is so, the prosecutor needs to arm himself with arguments in rebuttal. And to cap it all, as we shall see, unfairness is susceptible of different meanings in different contexts, so that the prosecutor may have to defend on more than one front.

Again, let us assume that he succeeds. He is in possession of a confession which was not obtained by oppression or in a manner conducive to unreliability, and the circumstances are such that it will not be adverse to the fairness of the proceedings to use it. Surely he now has a clear run for home? Not necessarily, because a final obstacle presents itself in the form of section 82(3), which provides:

> (3) Nothing in this part of this Act shall prejudice any power of a court to exclude evidence (whether by preventing questions from being put or otherwise) at its discretion.

This preserves such power as the court may have had a common law to exclude evidence in its discretion. The full ambit of this power is unclear, but it extended at least to the exclusion of evidence the prejudicial effect of which outweighs its probative values. (In the context of confessions this would mean evidence the reliability of which is more apparent than real, for example the confession of an unusually suggestible defendant.)

Where the defendant appeals against the trial judge's decision under s. 76(2), the appeal is based upon the argument that the judge reached the wrong decision on the law. However, where the defendant appeals against the judge's exercise of his discretion, the test of 'Wednesbury unreasonableness' is applied.[81] Thus, the Court of Appeal will only overturn the trial judge's exercise of his discretion where the court is satisfied that the trial judge's conclusion was 'so unreasonable that no reasonable authority could ever have come to it'. The test to be applied is whether the judge's decision was perverse in the legal sense. The Court of Appeal is usually reluctant to overturn a judge's exercise of his discretion, even where the Court would not have reached the same decision as the judge.[82]

5.6.1 Discretion to exclude under s. 78(1)

Under s. 78(1), PACE Act 1984, an application may be made to the judge to exclude evidence of a confession made by the defendant. The judge may exercise his discretion to exclude such evidence if its admission would have such an adverse effect on the fairness of the proceedings that the court ought not to admit it. This provision applies to any types of evidence (including confession evidence) upon which the prosecution proposes to rely. An application under s. 78(1) is usually made as an alternative to an application under s. 76(2); thus, where the trial judge rejects an application under the rule of law under s. 76(2), counsel may appeal instead to the judge's discretion to exclude.

---

81 Per Lord Greene MR in *Associated Provincial Picture Houses Ltd* v. *Wednesbury Corporation* [1948] 1 KB 223 at 230.
82 Per May LJ in *R* v. *O'Leary* (1988) 87 Cr App R 387 at 391 and Hodgson J in *R* v. *Samuel* [1988] 1 QB 615 at 630.

S. 78(1), PACE ACT 1984

In any proceedings the court may refuse to allow evidence on which the prosecution proposes to rely to be given if it appears to the court that, having regard to all the circumstances, including the circumstances in which the evidence was obtained, the admission of the evidence would have such an adverse effect on the fairness of the proceedings that the court ought not to admit it.

Section 78(1) clearly states that the court may take into account the circumstances in which the confession was obtained. Thus, the court can take into account whether any improper pressure was placed on the defendant by the police, whether any inducements were offered to the defendant in exchange for confessing, the characteristics of the defendant, etc.

Contemporaneous record of interview

Evidence of a confession will not automatically be excluded under s. 78(1) just because the police have acted illegally or improperly in breach of the PACE Act 1984 or its Codes of Practice. The breaches will have to be 'significant and substantial' before they are likely to affect the fairness of the proceedings so adversely that the evidence of the confession ought not to be admitted. In *R* v. *Keenan*[83] the appellant was asked a series of questions which he answered, but no contemporaneous record was made of the conversation and the defendant was not shown a record of it in order that he could sign it to signify that it was an accurate record of what was said, or even to disagree with it. The Court of Appeal held that an informal discussion might be an interview and that Code C would apply to such an informal interview. The Court held that where there have been 'significant and substantial' breaches of the Codes, the evidence so obtained will frequently be excluded under s. 78(1). The Court stated that the Codes required an accurate record of interview to be taken, a record of the reason if the interview is not recorded contemporaneously, and that the interviewee be shown at the police station the record of interview with a view to signing it. Here there had been 'plain breaches' of Code C and the evidence of the interview should have been excluded under s. 78(1).

The appellant in *R* v. *Canale*[84] was interviewed at the police station on four separate occasions. He made admissions during interview, but they were not contemporaneously recorded as required by Code C. At trial, the judge allowed all of the interviews to be admitted in evidence. The Court of Appeal allowed the appeal against conviction and held that there had been 'flagrant breaches' and a 'cynical disregard of the rules'. Lord Lane CJ stated (at 5) that the object of Code C is two-fold: ' . . . to ensure, as far as is possible, that the suspect's remarks are accurately recorded and . . . (as) a protection for the police to ensure that, as far as is possible, it cannot be suggested that they induced the subject to confess by improper approaches or improper promises.'

---

83 [1990] 2 QB 54.
84 (1989) 91 Cr App R 1, CA.

Other impropriety in interview

Code C provides that a person suspected of committing an offence must be cautioned before interview. A confession obtained in interview without caution may be excluded under s. 78(1). In *R* v. *Nelson and Rose*[85] the Court of Appeal held that Nelson should have been cautioned before questioning where the officer had already formed the suspicion that she was committing an offence (possession of controlled drugs). She was not so cautioned, in breach of Code C. Consequently, the court held that Nelson's entire interview ought to have been excluded under s. 78(1). By contrast, the officer did not suspect Rose of committing an offence until after she was questioned, so there was no breach of Code C in relation to her interview, and it was admissible.

A suspect is entitled to know the level of offence that he is being interviewed in relation to. A failure to so inform the suspect may lead to the exclusion of any admissions given in interview under s. 78(1). In *R* v. *Kirk*,[86] the appellant was arrested in relation to burglaries and the theft of an elderly woman's handbag. However, when he was interviewed he was not informed that the woman had died and that he could be facing more serious charges of robbery or manslaughter. He confessed to involvement in the incident. The Court of Appeal allowed the appeal on the basis that when a suspect is interviewed the PACE Act 1984 and Codes of Practice require that the suspect is informed of the level of offence that he is suspected of. Where he is not so informed and gives answers in interview which he might not otherwise have given, those answers must be excluded because its admission will have an adverse effect on the fairness of the proceedings.

However, in *R* v. *Elleray*[87] where an appellant made admissions to a probation officer in an interview as part of the preparation of a pre-sentence report after pleading guilty to offences, these admissions were to be admissible at the defendant's trial for more serious charges relating to the same incidents. The trial judge ruled that the admissions were admissible despite a defence application under s. 78(1). The Court of Appeal upheld the trial judge's decision to admit the evidence.

Informed of right to legal advice

A further example of a breach which is significant and substantial is a failure to inform the defendant of his right to legal advice. In *R* v. *Absolam*[88] the appellant was arrested for using threatening behaviour. When he arrived at the police station, the custody officer asked him to empty his pockets onto the table. He did so and then the custody officer said 'And now put the drugs on the table'. The appellant then reached inside his trousers and produced some cannabis resin. The custody officer cautioned the appellant and then asked him some questions, such as 'Were these bags ones that you have left over from selling today?' to which the appellant replied 'yes'. No written record was made of the conversation at the time, although the custody officer did make a note of it later. The appellant was convicted of possession of the drugs with intention to supply and he appealed on the ground that the trial judge should have excluded the questions put to him by the custody officer under s. 78, PACE. The Court of Appeal allowed the appeal and

85 (1998) 1 Cr App R 399, CA.
86 [2000] 1 WLR 567.
87 [2003] 2 Cr App R 11.
88 (1989) 88 Cr App R 332.

held that failing to inform the appellant of his right to legal advice at the moment when the custody officer was aware that the offence had been committed was a serious breach. Further, failing to make a contemporaneous record of the interview and failing to show the record to the appellant were significant and substantial breaches of the Code. Bingham LJ stated that:

> It is of course plain that this was not in any formal sense a conventional interview, but equally in our judgment it is plain that it was an interview within the purview of the Code, in that it was a series of questions directed by the police to a suspect with a view to obtaining admissions on which proceedings could be founded. There was nothing in the nature of the questions and answers in this case which, in our judgment, makes the provisions relating to interviews in any way inapplicable. Indeed, this is just the sort of situation in which those provisions are most significant.[89]

Consequently, any admissions ought to have been excluded under s. 78.

Refusal of access to solicitor

Another breach significant enough to warrant the exercise of judicial discretion under s. 78(1) is the refusal of the defendant's access to legal advice. In *R* v. *Walsh*[90] the appellant was refused access to a solicitor in breach of s. 58, PACE Act 1984 and Code C. The Court of Appeal held that the trial judge should have excluded the evidence under s. 78(1) since the breaches of PACE and Code C meant that the admission of the confessions made by the defendant would have an adverse effect on the fairness of the proceedings. Saville J stated that there was no evidence in this case that the police had acted in bad faith, but this did not make any difference to the result: 'although bad faith may make substantial or significant that which might not otherwise be so, the contrary does not follow. Breaches which are in themselves significant and substantial are not rendered otherwise by the good faith of the officers concerned.'[91]

In *R* v. *Samuel*,[92] the appellant entered a Building Society to deposit money, where he was recognised by a cashier as a member of a gang that had previously robbed the Building Society. The appellant was arrested and questioned about the offence. He requested access to a solicitor but this was denied on grounds that there was a likelihood that other suspects would be inadvertently warned. After his second request to see a solicitor was denied, the appellant confessed to the robbery. He was convicted and appealed on the ground that the confession should have been excluded under s. 78(1), because there were no 'reasonable grounds for believing' that the appellant's solicitor would deliberately or intentionally alert other suspects or hinder the recovery of property. The Court of Appeal allowed the appeal and held that the confession ought to have been excluded under s. 78(1). The Court held that access to legal advice was one of the most fundamental rights of a citizen. Solicitors are officers of the court and intelligent, professional people. The circumstances in which the court would uphold a refusal of access to a solicitor would be rare. There would have to be evidence which related to a specific solicitor, rather than to solicitors generally.

---

89 Ibid. at 336.
90 (1990) 91 Cr App R 161.
91 Ibid. at 163.
92 [1988] 1 QB 615. *R* v. *Samuel* was applied by the Court of Appeal in *R* v. *Alladice* (1988) 87 Cr App R 380.

Trickery or deception

Where the police are guilty of trickery towards the defendant, this will not automatically justify the exclusion of evidence under s. 78(1). In *R* v. *Bailey and Smith*[93] the appellants were remanded in custody after being charged with robbery. They remained silent in interview, so in an attempt to obtain evidence against them the police placed them in the same cell, which had been bugged. They made damaging admissions about the offence which were recorded and adduced in evidence at trial. The defence application to exclude the admissions under s. 78(1) had been rejected. The Court of Appeal upheld the decision of the trial judge to admit the confession in evidence. The Court held that in light of the serious nature of the offences charged, the absence of oppression and the reliability of the evidence, the tape recordings were correctly admitted. Simon Brown LJ stated (at 375) that:

> . . . where, as here, very serious crimes have been committed – and committed by men who have not themselves shrunk from trickery and a good deal worse – and where there has never been the least suggestion that their covertly taped confessions were oppressively obtained or other than wholly reliable, it seems to us hardly surprising that the trial judge exercised his undoubted discretion in the manner he did.

However, where the deception is practised against a solicitor (an officer of the court), then the discretion under s. 78(1) should be applied to exclude evidence of any confession obtained in consequence of that deception. In *R* v. *Mason*,[94] the police falsely told the appellant and his solicitor that the appellant's fingerprints had been found on a piece of a glass bottle which had been used as a petrol bomb. On this basis, the solicitor advised the appellant to co-operate with the police and the appellant confessed to the offence. The Court of Appeal held that in admitting the confession evidence, the trial judge had failed to take into account the deception practised on the solicitor. By deceiving a solicitor, who is an officer of the court, the police had deceived the court itself and the confession should have been excluded under s. 78(1).

R V. *MASON* [1988] 1 WLR 139
Watkins LJ

[at 144]

It is obvious from the undisputed evidence that the police practised a deceit not only upon the appellant, which is bad enough, but also upon the solicitor whose duty it was to advise him. In effect, they hoodwinked both solicitor and client. That was a most reprehensible thing to do. It is not however because we regard as misbehaviour of a serious kind conduct of that nature that we have come to the decision soon to be made plain. This is not the place to discipline the police. That has been made clear here on a number of previous occasions. We are concerned with the application of the proper law. The law is, as I have already said, that a trial judge has a discretion to be exercised of course upon right principles to reject admissible evidence in the interests of a defendant having a fair trial. The judge in the present case appreciated that, as the quotation from his ruling shows. So the only question to be answered by this court

93 (1993) 97 Cr App R 365.
94 [1988] 1 WLR 139.

is whether, having regard to the way the police behaved, the judge exercised that discretion correctly. In our judgment he did not. He omitted a vital factor from his consideration, namely, the deceit practised upon the appellant's solicitor. If he had included that in his consideration of the matter we have not the slightest doubt that he would have been driven to an opposite conclusion, namely, that the confession be ruled out and the jury not permitted therefore to hear of it. If that had been done, an acquittal would have followed for there was no other evidence in the possession of the prosecution.

For those reasons we have no alternative but to quash this conviction.

Before parting with this case, despite what I have said about the role of the court in relation to disciplining the police, we think we ought to say that we hope never again to hear of deceit such as this being practised upon an accused person, and more particularly possibly on a solicitor whose duty it is to advise him unfettered by false information from the police.

5.6.2 Common law

Despite the enactment of a statutory discretion to exclude evidence under s. 78(1), PACE Act 1984, there also exists a discretion to exclude evidence at common law: the leading case on the common law discretion is the House of Lords decision in *R* v. *Sang*.[95] Under this case, a trial judge may exclude a confession where 'its prejudicial effect outweighs its probative value'[96] in order to ensure that the defendant receives a fair trial. The common law discretion to exclude evidence under *R* v. *Sang* was expressly preserved by s. 82(3), PACE Act 1984.

S. 82(3), PACE ACT 1984

Nothing in this Part of this Act shall prejudice any power of a court to exclude evidence (whether by preventing questions from being put or otherwise) at its discretion.

It has been argued[97] that in practice s. 78(1) has effectively superseded the common law in all but one situation. While ss. 76(2) and 78(1) can only be used to exclude evidence which has not yet been adduced before a jury, the common law discretion to exclude evidence under *R* v. *Sang* can be used to withdraw a confession from a jury which has already been adduced before that jury. Sections 76(2) and 78(1) both refer to evidence that the prosecution 'proposes' to give or rely on, thus an application under either provision must be made prior to the evidence being adduced in court.[98] No such restriction, however, applies to the common law discretion under *R* v. *Sang*. Where the common law discretion to exclude is relied upon in such circumstances, the judge would have to consider what steps to take 'to prevent injustice'.[99] The Court of Appeal in *R* v. *Sat-Bhambra*[100] took care to point out that the judge has options other than the discharge of the jury in these circumstances: he may decide either to direct the jury to disregard the confession that they have

---

95 [1980] AC 402.
96 Per Lord Diplock, [1980] AC 402 at 437.
97 See I. H. Dennis, *The Law of Evidence*, 5th edn (Sweet & Maxwell, 2013) at p. 93.
98 See also the *obiter dictum* to this effect in *R* v. *Sat-Bhambra* (1989) 88 Cr App R 55.
99 *R* v. *Sat-Bhambra* (1989) 88 Cr App R 55.
100 Ibid.

already heard; alternatively, he may decide to give a direction to the jury in which he points out to the jury matters which affect the weight of the confession, and then leave the matter in their hands; or he may choose to discharge the jury from the case. Despite the assurance by the Court of Appeal that the judge is not powerless where an application to exclude is made after confession evidence is adduced, these alternative options could indeed prove less than satisfactory in many cases.

5.7 WHY EXCLUDE CONFESSION EVIDENCE?

There is no single agreed rationale for the exclusion of confession evidence under s. 78(1), PACE Act 1984; however, four general principles relating to the exclusion of confession evidence have been identified: (1) the reliability of the confession evidence; (2) exclusion in order to discipline the police where they have acted improperly; (3) the protection of the rights of the defendant; and (4) the maintenance of the moral, judicial integrity of the criminal justice system.[101]

5.7.1 Reliability principle

Traditionally, confession evidence was excluded where the confession had been obtained by promises of favour made to the defendant: 'A free and voluntary confession is deserving of the highest credit ... but a confession forced from the mind ... comes in so questionable a shape that no credit ought to be given to it.'[102] It was thought that a voluntary confession was likely to be true, while an involuntary confession was likely to be false or unreliable. Professor Andrew Ashworth describes the reliability principle: 'determining the truth of the criminal charges is the sole purpose of the criminal trial, and evidence should be admitted or excluded solely on grounds of reliability'.[103] This principle of exclusion may apply in some individual cases, but it does not apply in all since some confession evidence which has been obtained improperly may very well be reliable, but may be nevertheless excluded.

5.7.2 Disciplinary principle

The disciplinary principle advocates that improperly obtained evidence should be excluded even if it has been reliably obtained, 'since the court should use its position to discourage improper practices in the investigation of crime'.[104] This principle purports to act as a deterrence to encourage the police to abide by lawful methods in accordance with PACE and the Codes of Practice. This principle has been rejected by the Court of Appeal, which has stated that it is not the function of the court to discipline the police.[105]

---

101 For a detailed discussion of these principles, see Dennis, *The Law of Evidence* at pp. 104–9; P. Mirfield, *Confessions* (Sweet & Maxwell, 1985), ch. 3; Mirfield, *Silence, Confessions and Improperly Obtained Evidence*; S. Sharpe, *Judicial Discretion and Criminal Investigation* (Sweet & Maxwell, 1998); and A. J. Ashworth, 'Excluding evidence as protecting rights' [1977] Crim LR 723.
102 *R* v. *Warickshall* (1783) 1 Leach 263 CC.
103 Ashworth, 'Excluding evidence as protecting rights' [1977] Crim LR 723 at 723.
104 Ibid.
105 *R* v. *Mason* [1988] 1 WLR 139 and *R* v. *Delaney* (1989) 88 Cr App R 338.

5.7.3 Protective principle

Professor Ashworth advocates the protective principle, which provides that 'If a legal system declares certain standards for the conduct of criminal investigation . . . it can be argued that citizens have corresponding rights to be accorded certain facilities and not to be treated in certain ways.'[106] Thus, this principle provides that evidence of a confession by the defendant should be excluded where the defendant has been mistreated by the police and his human rights have been infringed. It was thought that this human rights-based approach would become more popular after the enactment of the Human Rights Act 1998 in October 2000, but the courts do not appear to have adopted this rights-based approach.

5.7.4 Judicial integrity principle

The judicial integrity principle provides that evidence which has been improperly obtained should be excluded on the grounds that the state should lead by example and should not seek to obtain convictions on the basis of such evidence as this undermines the moral integrity of the justice system and the moral authority of the verdict.[107]

5.8 THE 'FRUIT' OF AN INADMISSIBLE CONFESSION

We have already seen from the case of *R* v. *McGovern* that where the defendant makes a series of confessions, the first of which is then ruled inadmissible under s. 76(2) or s. 78(1), PACE Act 1984, the evidence of the subsequent confessions is 'tainted' and those confessions are also rendered inadmissible.[108]

R V. *MCGOVERN* (1991) 92 CR APP R 228
Farquharson LJ

[at 234]

Mr. Clegg . . . argues, correctly in our view, that if the first interview is inadmissible where the appellant has made admissions she may not otherwise have done, then the subsequent confession was a direct consequence of the first. Moreover, the appellant's solicitor was not informed, as he tells us, that the appellant had been wrongfully denied access when she was brought to the police station. If the solicitor had known that she would have realised immediately that the first confession was suspect and in all probability would not have allowed the second interview to have taken place.

We are of the view that the earlier breaches of the Act and of the Code renders the contents of the second interview inadmissible also. One cannot refrain from emphasising that when an accused person

---

106 Above (n. 103) at 725.
107 See I. H. Dennis, 'Reconstructing the law of criminal evidence' (1989) 42 CLP 21 and Dennis, *The Law of Evidence* at pp. 108–9.
108 (1991) 92 Cr App R 228. See paragraph 5.5.2 above and P. Mirfield, 'Successive confessions and the poisonous tree' [1996] Crim LR 554.

has made a series of admissions as to his or her complicity in a crime at a first interview, the very fact that those admissions have been made are likely to have an effect upon her during the course of the second interview. If, accordingly, it be held, as it is held here, that the first interview was in breach of the rules and in breach of section 58, it seems to us that the subsequent interview must be similarly tainted.

Where the 'malign influence' which existed at the first interview ceases to exist, then any subsequent confessions may be admissible. However, the Court of Appeal quashed the defendant's conviction in *R* v. *Glaves*[109] since the defendant did not receive legal advice between the first inadmissible confessions made on 16 December and the subsequent confessions made 8 days later on 24 December, thus the trial judge could not have been sure that the malign influence was not still operating on the defendant. A simple change in the interviewing officers and the administration of a fresh caution was not sufficient.

A confession made by the defendant might also lead the police to other relevant evidence, such as stolen goods or a weapon, known as the 'fruit of the poisonous tree' (see Figure 5.3). Prior to the PACE Act 1984, evidence discovered as a result of an inadmissible confession could be adduced in evidence.[110] This rule has been preserved by s. 76(4)(a), PACE Act 1984 which states that the fact that a confession has been excluded under s. 76(2)[111] does not prevent any evidence discovered as a result of that confession from being admissible. Therefore, if the defendant confessed to the commission of a murder and also divulged the location of the murder weapon, but that confession was excluded under s. 76(2)(a) because it was obtained through the oppressive conduct of the police, the police could still adduce the murder weapon itself along with any forensic evidence which might link the defendant to the weapon. However, this is subject to the exercise of judicial discretion to exclude evidence under s. 78(1), which applies to any evidence that the prosecution proposes to rely on, not just confession evidence.

S. 76(4), PACE ACT 1984

The fact that a confession is wholly or partly excluded in pursuance of this section shall not affect the admissibility in evidence –

(a) of any facts discovered as a result of the confession; . . .

Despite the admissibility of evidence obtained as a result of a confession under s. 76(4)(a), s. 76(5) prevents the prosecution from explaining to the jury how they discovered these items. Thus, although the evidence discovered as a result of the confession is admissible, the jury could not be told that the evidence had been discovered as a result of the inadmissible confession. Thus, in *R* v. *Berriman*[112] where a woman concealed the birth of her child, while her confession

---

109 [1993] Crim LR 685.
110 *R* v. *Warickshall* (1783) 1 Leach 263.
111 Note that the operation of s. 76(4) only applies to confessions excluded under s. 76(2) and does not apply to confessions excluded under the exercise of judicial discretion under s. 78(1) or s. 82(3), PACE Act 1984.
112 (1854) 6 Cox CC 388.

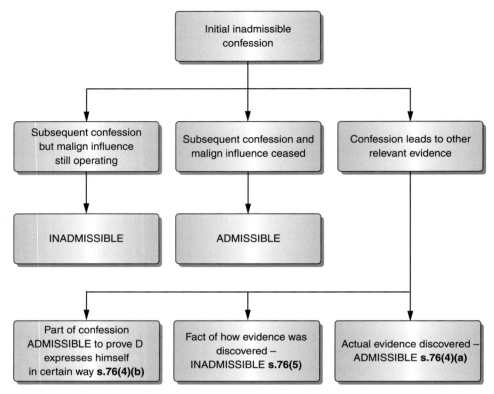

Figure 5.3 The 'fruit' of an inadmissible confession

was inadmissible, the prosecution could adduce evidence that they had searched a spot and found the bones of a child (which would today be admissible under s. 76(4)(a)), but they were prevented from explaining to the jury that they obtained that information from a confession. They were not permitted to link the discovery of the bones to the inadmissible confession. This common law rule has been preserved by s. 76(5), PACE Act 1984.

S. 76(5) – (6), PACE ACT 1984

(5) Evidence that a fact to which this subsection applies was discovered as a result of a statement made by an accused person shall not be admissible unless evidence of how it was discovered is given by him or on his behalf.

(6) Subsection (5) above applies –

  (a) to any fact discovered as a result of a confession which is wholly excluded in pursuance of this section; and

  (b) to any fact discovered as a result of a confession which is partly so excluded, if the fact is discovered as a result of the excluded part of the confession.

Under s. 76(4)(b), part of a confession excluded by virtue of s. 76(2) may be admissible in order to prove that the defendant speaks, writes or expresses himself in a certain way.

S. 76(4), PACE ACT 1984

The fact that a confession is wholly or partly excluded in pursuance of this section shall not affect the admissibility in evidence –

. . .

(b) where the confession is relevant as showing that the accused speaks, writes or expresses himself in a particular way, of so much of the confession as is necessary to show that he does so.

A pre-PACE Act 1984 example of this can be found in the case of *R* v. *Voisin*[113] in which the defendant was asked in interview to write on a piece of paper the words 'Bloody Belgian'. She wrote down 'Bladie Belgiam' and this was held to be admissible to demonstrate that the defendant spelt the words in that particular way. This was important because the defendant was charged with a murder and a piece of paper was discovered with the body with the words 'Bladie Belgiam' written on it.

5.9 CELL CONFESSIONS

Confessions made by one defendant to a fellow prisoner are known as cell confessions. These confessions are generally admissible in evidence in the same way that other confessions are admissible under s. 76(1), but they may be unreliable and the jury should be directed in relation to the 'dangers of placing reliance on alleged oral confessions to fellow prisoners'. In *R* v. *Stone*,[114] the Court of Appeal agreed with counsel for the appellant who argued that:

the courts have long recognised the dangers of cell confessions . . .:
(1) They are easily concocted and difficult to prove;
(2) Most prison informants are of bad character and willing to lie in their own interests;
(3) An informer, particularly if on remand, is likely to have an interest of his own, whether of benefit from the authorities or to gain kudos from his fellows in a case of this kind;
(4) These dangers may not be apparent to the jury.[115]

This is especially true in relation to high-profile cases where the fellow prisoner may feel that he has something to gain by fabricating a confession, or he may do so out of a hope of securing favour with the police or other prison officers. The safeguard against the admission of false cell confessions was identified by Rose LJ as a direction by the trial judge which should be tailored to the specific case. The Court of Appeal held that the trial judge would be

---

113 [1918] 1 KB 531.
114 [2005] EWCA Crim 105; [2005] Crim LR 569.
115 [2005] EWCA Crim 105 at [51].

best placed to decide upon the strength of that direction or warning and provided the following guidance.

R V. STONE [2005] CRIM LR 569
Rose LJ

83. . . . there will generally be a need for the judge to point out to the jury that such confessions are often easy to concoct and difficult to prove and that experience has shown that prisoners may have many motives to lie. If the prison informant has a significant criminal record or a history of lying then usually the judge should point this out to the jury and explain that it gives rise to a need for great care and why. The trial judge will be best placed to decide the strength of such warnings and the necessary extent of the accompanying analysis.

84. But not every case requires such a warning. This Court has said repeatedly that a summing-up should be tailored by the judge to the circumstances of the particular case. That principle bears repetition. If an alleged confession, for whatever reason, would not have been easy to invent, it would be absurd to require the judge to tell the jury that confessions are often easy to concoct. Similarly, for reasons which we shall explain later, in a case where the defence has deliberately not cross-examined the informant as to motive of hope of advantage, the law does not require the judge to tell the jury that, merely because the informant was a prisoner, there may have been such a motive.

Where the police use an informant to secure admissions from the defendant in the cells by persistent questioning, the evidence should be excluded under s. 78(1). In *Allan* v. *United Kingdom*[116] the European Court of Human Rights held that Article 6(1) of the ECHR was violated where the recordings of admissions made by the defendant to a police informant who had been tasked with channelling the conversations into discussions about the offence were adduced at trial. The admissions were made after persistent questioning in the cells and this was equated to a police interrogation without the necessary safeguards which would normally be present in a formal police interview. However, there was no violation of Article 6(1) where the tape recordings of admissions made by the defendant to another prisoner in the cells and a friend who visited him were admitted in evidence. These admissions were voluntarily made and the procedural safeguards had been in place to allow the appellant to challenge the reliability of the evidence.

5.10   CONFESSIONS BY 'MENTALLY HANDICAPPED' PEOPLE

Section 77(1), PACE Act 1984 provides a further safeguard where a mentally handicapped person confesses to the commission of a criminal offence. Where a substantial part of the case against the defendant depends upon the confession of a mentally handicapped person and the confession is not made in the presence of an independent person, then the judge must give the jury a warning pursuant to s. 77(1), PACE Act 1984.

---

116 (2003) 36 EHRR 12.

S. 77(1), PACE ACT 1984

Without prejudice to the general duty of the court at a trial on indictment to direct the jury on any matter on which it appears to the court appropriate to do so, where at such a trial –

(a) the case against the accused depends wholly or substantially on a confession by him; and

(b) the court is satisfied –

    (i) that he is mentally handicapped; and

    (ii) that the confession was not made in the presence of an independent person,

the court shall warn the jury that there is special need for caution before convicting the accused in reliance on the confession, and shall explain that the need arises because of the circumstances mentioned in paragraphs (a) and (b) above.

The Court of Appeal in *R* v. *Bailey*[117] noted that s. 77(1) does not provide for a rule of exclusion nor a discretion to exclude the confession, but rather it requires the judge to warn the jury of the special need for caution before convicting the defendant on the basis of the confession. The Court pointed to the notes to Annex E of Code C of the Codes of Practice under the 1984 Act for a statement of the rationale behind the provision:

> It is important to bear in mind that although persons who are mentally disordered or mentally handicapped are often capable of providing reliable evidence, they may, without knowing or wishing to do so, be particularly prone in certain circumstances to provide information which is unreliable, misleading or self-incriminating. Special care should therefore always be exercised in questioning such a person, and the appropriate adult involved, if there is any doubt about a person's mental state or capacity. Because of the risk of unreliable evidence, it is important to obtain corroboration of any facts admitted whenever possible.

Where such a warning would not be sufficient, the Court of Appeal has held that the trial judge should withdraw the case from the jury: see *R* v. *MacKenzie*,[118] in which the defendant's confessions were highly unreliable and there was no independent corroborating evidence.

Section 77(3) defines the term 'mentally handicapped' as 'a state of arrested or incomplete development of mind which includes significant impairment of intelligence and social functioning'. It appears from s. 77(1) that where a mentally handicapped person makes a confession in the presence of an independent person (who must be someone other than a police officer or person employed for or engaged on police purposes)[119] there is no need for the special caution to be given to the jury.

---

117 [1995] 2 Cr App R 262.
118 (1992) 96 Cr App R 98.
119 See s. 77(3), PACE Act 1984.

5.11   USE OF CO-DEFENDANT'S CONFESSION[120]

As against the maker

This paragraph deals with the question of whether a defendant (X) can rely on a confession made by a co-defendant (Y) where they are both jointly tried for an offence. The confession made by Y might be to the effect that Y committed the offence alone, in which case X would want to rely upon this as it assists his defence. If the prosecution does not adduce the confession, or if the prosecution is prevented from relying upon it under s. 76(2) or s. 78(1), can X seek to adduce the confession in evidence?

The problem of whether a defendant can adduce a co-defendant's confession in support of his own defence was considered by the House of Lords in *R* v. *Myers*.[121] The House held that the defendant can adduce the confession even if it would have been excluded under s. 78(1) if it was tendered by the prosecution, provided that:

1. it is relevant to the defendant's own defence; and
2. it was voluntarily made (i.e. there was no oppression and nothing said or done likely in the circumstances to render it unreliable).

The confession would be admissible as evidence of the truth of the matters stated. The House of Lords held that it may have been different had the confession been excluded under s. 76(2) (i.e. if it was not 'voluntary'). It is worth noting that, had the defendants been tried separately, the admissibility of the confession would have been subject to the hearsay provisions under s. 114(1), CJA 2003.

The situation in *R* v. *Myers* is now governed by s. 76A(1), PACE Act 1984 which was inserted into PACE by s. 128(1), CJA 2003. Under s. 76A(1), PACE Act 1984, the same rules apply to X adducing confession of Y as apply to the prosecution adducing evidence of such a confession.

S. 76A(1), PACE ACT 1984

In any proceedings a confession made by an accused person may be given in evidence for another person charged in the same proceedings (a co-accused) in so far as it is relevant to any matter in issue in the proceedings and is not excluded by the court in pursuance of this section.

Thus, under s. 76A(1), a confession made by one defendant (Y) may be relied upon by a co-defendant (X) and may be admitted as evidence in so far as it is relevant to a matter in issue (which may be the truth of X's defence). However, s. 76A(2) provides that X will not be able to use a confession by Y in order to undermine Y's case or to strengthen X's case if it was obtained in breach of s. 76(2) (i.e. if it was not voluntary). This reflects the decision

---

120 See J. Hartshorne, 'Defensive use of a co-accused's confession and the Criminal Justice Act 2003' (2004) 8(3) *International Journal of Evidence and Proof* 165 and M. Hirst, 'Confessions as proof of innocence' [1998] CLJ 146.
121 [1998] AC 124, HL.

of the House of Lords in *R* v. *Myers*. Where there are questions of oppression or involuntariness, the burden of proving that the confession was not obtained by oppression and was voluntary (i.e. negating the conditions of admissibility under s. 76(2)) would be on the co-defendant (X). However, X only needs to satisfy the lower, civil standard of proof, 'on a balance of probabilities'.

The meaning of 'person charged in the same proceedings' within s. 76A(1) has recently occupied the courts. Where a co-defendant pleads guilty, he is no longer 'charged in the same proceedings' as the defendant, and thus s. 76A(1) will not apply to any confession he has previously made.[122] However, in such a situation, the former 'co-defendant' can be called to give evidence because he becomes a compellable witness. A further possible avenue of admissibility might be an application to adduce the hearsay statements of admission in the interests of justice under s. 114(1)(d), CJA 2003.[123]

As against a non-maker

Where a co-defendant makes a confession which also implicates the defendant, can that confession be used as evidence against the defendant? Section 76A(1), PACE Act 1984 does not apply to this type of situation.[124] The general rule is that a confession is only relevant and admissible against its maker. Thus, a confession made by Y (which implicates both X and Y) is not evidence against X. Y's confession may only be used as evidence against Y. If it is adduced in a joint trial, the jury may be warned that it does not provide evidence against X: '[i]f no separate trial is ordered it is the duty of the judge to impress on the jury that the statement of one prisoner not made on oath in the course of the trial is not evidence against the other and must be entirely disregarded'.[125]

The issue of the admissibility of a co-defendant's confession as against another defendant fell to be considered by the House of Lords in *R* v. *Hayter*.[126] The facts were that three defendants were charged with murder. B wanted to hire a contract killer to kill her husband. H acted as the middle man and secured the services of R who carried out the killing. R later confessed to the murder and his confessions implicated H. In this case, the guilt of H and B as accessories to murder was dependent upon a finding that R was guilty of murder. The trial judge directed the jury to consider first the liability of R before H and B. In considering whether R was guilty, the jury were directed that R's confession was evidence against him. H argued that the effect of this direction violated the general rule that R's confession could not be used as evidence against H, unless H agreed with it. The House of Lords dismissed the appeal against conviction by a 3:2 majority and held that the trial judge was right to direct the jury as he did and that there had been no infringement of the general rule. The House stated that the trial judge was right to direct the jury not to take into account R's confession in the

---

122 See *R* v. *Finch* [2007] EWCA Crim 36; [2007] 1 WLR 1645.
123 See *R* v. *Y* [2008] EWCA Crim 10; [2008] 1 WLR 1683, although s. 114(1)(d) was held not to apply in *R* v. *Finch*.
124 Per Lord Steyn in *R* v. *Hayter* [2005] 1 WLR 605, HL at 609. Although s. 76A(1) was not in force at the time of the decision in *R* v. *Hayter*, Lord Steyn states that even if it had been it would not have applied to this situation.
125 Per Lord Goddard CJ in *R* v. *Gunewardene* [1951] 2 KB 600 at 610.
126 [2005] 1 WLR 605.

case against H, and to consider the guilt of H only if they were satisfied as to the guilt of B and R. They could then consider the guilt of H, taking into account their findings against B and R as well as other evidence. The House held that there was no good reason why R's guilt could not be used by the jury as a fact against H.[127]

5.12 CIVIL PROCEEDINGS – ADMISSIONS

In civil proceedings an informal admission is admissible in evidence under s. 1(1), Civil Evidence Act 1995 which states that hearsay evidence is admissible, provided that the maker of the statement would have been a competent witness at the time that the statement was made (s. 5(1)).

5.13 CONCLUSION

Confession evidence is generally admissible on the grounds that most people who confess to a criminal offence would only do so if they were guilty. However, a number of major miscarriages of justice illustrate that confession evidence is not always inherently reliable. The law has developed safeguards to permit the exclusion of confession evidence in certain circumstances; these safeguards are comprised of both rules of exclusion and judicial discretion to exclude confession evidence. Thus, where a confession has been obtained as a result of oppression or things said or done likely to render any confession unreliable, the confession must be excluded under s. 76(2)(a) or (b) of the Police and Criminal Evidence Act 1984 respectively. Alternatively, where these rules of exclusion do not apply, the trial judge may use his discretion to exclude confession evidence under the common law or s. 78(1) of the Police and Criminal Evidence Act 1984. While there is no single overarching rationale governing the exercise of judicial discretion to exclude confession evidence, an examination of case law illustrates that there are three main principles which the courts have employed in the past to justify the discretionary exclusion of confession evidence: the reliability principle, the protective principle and the judicial integrity principle. The disciplinary principle is generally not accepted by the courts as a reason justifying the exclusion of confession evidence.

Summary

- Evidence of a voluntary confession by the defendant is not necessarily reliable evidence. Traditionally, confession evidence was only admissible in criminal proceedings if the confession was freely or voluntarily given: *R* v. *Warickshall*. Under s. 76(1) of the PACE Act 1984, evidence of a confession made by a defendant is admissible at trial as evidence against the defendant where it is relevant to any matter in issue in the proceedings and provided that it is not excluded under s. 76(2).

---

127 See C. McGourlay, 'Is criminal practice impervious to logic? *R* v *Hayter*' (2006) 10(2) *International Journal of Evidence and Proof* 128.

- A partial definition of a confession is given in s. 82(1), PACE Act 1984: '"confession", includes any statement wholly or partly adverse to the person who made it, whether made to a person in authority or not and whether made in words or otherwise'.
- A 'mixed' statement is a statement which contains both exculpatory material (or self-serving statements), as well as incriminating admissions which are significant to a fact in issue in the case. The exculpatory parts of the statement are admissible to prove the truth of their contents, just as the incriminating admissions are: *R* v. *Sharp*.
- Evidence of a confession may therefore be excluded under a rule of law contained within s. 76(2), PACE Act 1984 or by the exercise of judicial discretion under s. 78(1), PACE Act 1984 or the common law under *R* v. *Sang*.
- Under s. 76(2)(a), confession evidence must be excluded where the confession has (or where it may have) been obtained by oppression. Section 76(8), PACE Act 1984 provides a partial definition of 'oppression'. 'Oppression' should be given its ordinary and natural meaning: *R* v. *Fulling*.
- Under s. 76(2)(b), confession evidence must be excluded if the confession was (or may have been) obtained as a result of something said or done which was likely to render the confession unreliable. The thing said or done must be external to the defendant and must be said or done *to* the defendant: *R* v. *Goldenberg*. The characteristics of the defendant, such as his mental condition, may be taken into account: *R* v. *Everett*.
- Where a confession cannot be excluded by a mandatory rule of law under s. 76(2), there remains a judicial discretion to exclude evidence under s. 78(1), PACE Act 1984 and at common law under *R* v. *Sang*. The breaches will have to be 'significant and substantial' before they are likely to affect the fairness of the proceedings so adversely that the evidence of the confession ought not to be admitted: *R* v. *Keenan*. Examples include: where there is a failure to inform the defendant of his right to legal advice, *R* v. *Absolam*; or where the defendant is refused access to legal advice, *R* v. *Samuel*.
- Where the defendant makes a series of confessions, the first of which is then ruled inadmissible, the evidence of the subsequent confessions is 'tainted' and those confessions are also rendered inadmissible: *R* v. *McGovern*.

For discussion . . .

1. Are there sufficient safeguards against the admission of false or unreliable confessions within ss. 76(2), 78(1) and 82(3), PACE Act 1984?
2. What justifications exist for the exclusion of confession evidence which might be highly reliable?
3. Should confession evidence be corroborated?
4. Was the Court of Appeal in *R* v. *Mason* right to distinguish the case on the basis that the trickery had been practised against a solicitor?
5. To what extent does the decision in *R* v. *Hayter* provide a means of circumventing the rule that a confession is only evidence against its maker?

Further reading

D. Birch, 'The pace hots up: confessions and confusions under the 1984 Act' [1989] Crim LR 95.
This article offers an analysis of the provisions under ss. 76(2) and 78(1), PACE Act 1984 and highlights the confusions within the statutory framework.

I. Dennis, 'Miscarriages of justice and the law of confessions: evidentiary issues and solutions' (1993) PL 291.
This article explores some of the key miscarriages of justice from the 1970s and 1980s as well as the importance of confession evidence to the criminal justice process as a whole. Professor Dennis makes a number of recommendations to safeguard against miscarriages of justice from false confessions.

M. Hirst, 'Confessions as proof of innocence' [1998] CLJ 146.
This article explores the House of Lords' decision in *R* v. *Myers* and criticises the House for failing to clarify the law and answer the certified question.

P. Mirfield, 'Successive confessions and the poisonous tree' [1996] Crim LR 554.
This article considers the law relating to the admissibility of 'tainted' confessions and the 'fruit of the poisoned tree' and the decision in *R* v. *McGovern*.

P. Mirfield, *Silence, Confessions and Improperly Obtained Evidence* (Oxford University Press, 1998).
This monograph provides a comprehensive analysis of confession evidence and the principles which underlie its exclusion. Mirfield also considers alternative approaches taken in other countries.

R. Pattenden, 'Should confessions be corroborated?' (1991) 107 LQR 317.
This article examines the causes of false confessions and the sufficiency of the safeguards against their admissibility before recommending the adoption of a judicial warning when conviction depends wholly or substantially on a disputed or retracted confession along the lines of a mandatory *Turnbull* identification warning.

6 Illegally and improperly obtained evidence

6.1 INTRODUCTION

Undercover police officers infiltrating criminal gangs, *agents provocateurs*, young female officers acting as 'honey traps', covert listening devices placed in the homes of suspects and staged 'set ups' designed to entrap a suspect are all the makings of a dramatic and enthralling police drama. While some of these practices are a lawful part of investigative policing, case law illustrates that these practices are sometimes used illegally or improperly in order to obtain incriminating evidence against the defendant. This chapter is concerned with the admissibility of evidence which has been obtained either illegally or improperly and we will explore some of the leading cases on entrapment, police trickery and the use of covert listening devices. The admissibility of confession evidence which has been obtained by oppression or as a result of something said or done likely to render the confession unreliable was discussed in Chapter 5 on Confession Evidence. Consequently, this chapter seeks to focus predominantly on other forms of illegally or improperly obtained evidence, although there may be some inevitable overlap with confession evidence.

Generally speaking, all relevant evidence is admissible in criminal proceedings. However, where evidence has been obtained illegally or improperly it might be excluded under a rule of

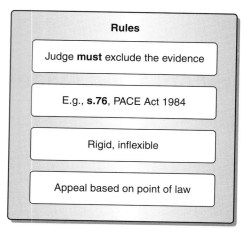
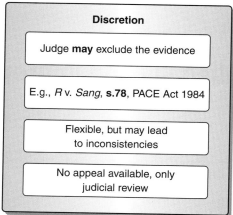

Figure 6.1 Distinguishing rules from discretion

law or through the exercise of judicial discretion.[1] While Chapter 5 concentrated on the exclusionary rule under s. 76, Police and Criminal Evidence Act 1984 (PACE Act 1984), this chapter is more concerned with the exercise of discretion to exclude illegally and improperly obtained evidence under the common law (*R* v. *Sang*[2]) and under statute (s. 78, PACE Act 1984). We will explore the rationale underlying the exercise of such discretion and the extent to which the courts have taken a consistent approach to the exclusion of evidence. The chapter will then consider the types of illegally or improperly obtained evidence that might be excluded by a judge in the exercise of his discretion, including breaches of the PACE Act 1984 and the Codes of Practice, police trickery, agents provocateurs, entrapment and the use of covert listening devices, as well as the human rights implications of such practices. Finally, we will examine the types of situation in which the court might instead take the more severe measure of staying the proceedings as an abuse of process.

6.2 RULES VERSUS DISCRETION

Provided that evidence is deemed to be relevant to the proceedings, it is generally admissible in court. However, where evidence has been obtained illegally or improperly it might be excluded under a rule of law or through the exercise of judicial discretion. Where an exclusionary rule applies, the trial judge *must* exclude the evidence in question, whereas where a discretion is relied upon, the trial judge *may* exclude the evidence but is not obliged to do so (see Figure 6.1). We explored an exclusionary rule under s. 76, PACE Act 1984 which applies specifically to confession evidence in Chapter 5. Section 76 provides that where a confession has been

---

1 For a more detailed consideration of the use of judicial discretion to exclude improperly obtained evidence, see P. Mirfield, *Silence, Confessions and Improperly Obtained Evidence* (Oxford University Press, 1998) and S. Sharpe, *Judicial Discretion and Criminal Investigation* (Sweet & Maxwell, 1998).
2 [1980] AC 402.

obtained by oppression (s. 76(2)(a)) or as a result of something said or done likely to render a confession unreliable (s. 76(2)(b)), the confession must be excluded. The trial judge has no power to override the mandatory rule of law.

Cross-reference

Refer back to Chapter 5 on Confession Evidence for a more detailed look at the applicability of s. 76, PACE Act 1984.

By contrast, there is a discretion to exclude evidence available at common law and also under s. 78 of the Police and Criminal Evidence Act 1984. We will explore the common law discretion to exclude evidence in more detail at paragraph 6.3 below and we will explore s. 78 in more detail at paragraph 6.4 below. However, for now it suffices to state that the case of *R* v. *Sang* provides that the trial judge has a discretion to exclude prosecution evidence if its prejudicial effect outweighs its probative value and s. 78 provides that the discretion exists 'if it appears to the court that, having regard to all the circumstances, including the circumstances in which the evidence was obtained, the admission of the evidence would have such an adverse effect on the fairness of the proceedings that the court ought not to admit it'. Both *R* v. *Sang* and s. 78 provide the trial judge with the power to choose to exclude evidence. Since these are not rules of law, the exclusion of evidence under either *R* v. *Sang* or s. 78 is not mandatory, rather the trial judge may (not must) choose to exclude the evidence. Section 78 applies to all types of prosecution evidence and is not restricted to confession evidence. In deciding whether or not to exercise his discretion under s. 78, the judge will consider the effect that admitting the evidence will have on the fairness of the proceedings.

One significant difference between the application of a rule of law and the exercise of discretion lies in the mechanism of review attaching to each. Where a judge incorrectly applies a rule of law, a defendant may appeal against his conviction on the grounds that the judge erred in law. An appeal court will then determine whether the trial judge was right or wrong in his application of the legal rule. However, the process becomes more difficult where a defendant wishes to challenge the decision of a trial judge during the exercise of his discretion. The only method of challenging a judge's decision under *R* v. *Sang* or s. 78, is through the administrative mechanism of judicial review. A defendant would need to show that the judge's decision was *Wednesbury* unreasonable, i.e. so unreasonable that no reasonable trial judge could come to that decision.[3] The appeal courts are very reluctant to interfere with a trial judge's exercise of his discretion, and it is very difficult to demonstrate that no other reasonable judge would come to the decision that this judge did. It is not enough to show that one judge, or even multiple judges, would have reached a different conclusion. In order for the trial judge's decision to be deemed *Wednesbury* unreasonable, his decision would need to have been an extremely unreasonable one, such that no reasonable judge would come to the same conclusion. This very limited mechanism for review demonstrates the significance of the exercise of judicial discretion and the importance of adopting a

---

3 See *Associated Provincial Picture Houses Ltd* v. *Wednesbury Corp.* [1948] 1 KB 223.

principled approach to the discretionary exclusion of evidence in order to prevent too much inconsistency and unpredictability in its exercise.

Cross-reference

The principles used to justify the exercise of the discretion to exclude evidence under s. 78 of the Police and Criminal Evidence Act 1984 will be explored in paragraph 6.5 below.

The extent to which discretion is an appropriate mechanism for the exclusion of evidence has long been a topic of debate. There are clear advantages to the use of discretion, particularly in terms of the flexibility it offers. However, it has been argued that the use of discretion to solve evidential problems leads to confusion in the law[4] and uncertainty in its exercise,[5] and since there is a lack of control over the judge's decision, his idiosyncrasies and personality may play a significant role.[6]

In the following paragraphs of this chapter we will consider the discretion to exclude at common law and the statutory discretion under s. 78, PACE Act 1984.

6.3   COMMON LAW DISCRETION

The discretion to exclude evidence was initially developed at common law. The next paragraph on the common law discretion covers the position at common law both before the enactment of the Police and Criminal Evidence Act 1984 and after its enactment.

6.3.1   The common law pre-PACE position

The general principle at common law was that evidence would be admissible even where it was obtained as a result of illegal or improper conduct. This principle was encapsulated in the case of *R v. Leatham*,[7] in which Crompton J stated, 'it matters not how you get it; if you steal it even, it would be admissible'. The courts were traditionally not concerned with the provenance of the evidence, but were concerned instead with its probative value. A general discretion to exclude evidence where its prejudicial effect outweighed its probative value was recognised in *R v. Christie*[8] in which the House of Lords stated that a practice had developed in the criminal courts whereby the trial judge indicates to prosecuting counsel that 'in order to ensure a fair trial for the accused, . . . evidence which, although admissible in law, has little value in its direct bearing upon the case, and might indirectly operate seriously to the prejudice of the accused, should not be given against him'.[9]

---

4 See B. Livesey, 'Judicial discretion to exclude prejudicial evidence' [1968] *Cambridge Law Journal* 291 at 302.
5 See C. Williams, 'Judicial discretion in relation to confessions' (1983) 3 *Oxford Journal of Legal Studies* 222 at 235.
6 Ibid.
7 (1861) 8 Cox CC 498.
8 [1914] AC 545 at 564–5.
9 Ibid. at 564.

The principle from *R* v. *Leatham* was cited by Lord Goddard CJ in *Kuruma* v. *R*.[10] This case involved an illegal search of the defendant. In considering the admissibility of evidence discovered as a result of an illegal search, the Privy Council held that the test was relevance; the court was not concerned with how the evidence was obtained. Thus, it must be asked whether the evidence was relevant to a matter in issue. However, the courts recognised a judicial discretion to exclude evidence in the event that admitting the evidence would be unfair to the defendant. Lord Goddard CJ stated: 'No doubt in a criminal case the judge always has a discretion to disallow evidence if the strict rules of admissibility would operate unfairly against an accused'.[11] His Lordship gave the example of evidence obtained through trickery and commented that 'the judge might properly rule it out',[12] although he did not find that the illegal search of the defendant was not sufficient to justify the exercise of the discretion.

Later cases further confirmed the existence of a judicial discretion to exclude evidence where its prejudicial effect outweighed its probative value, and these cases also suggested that the way in which the evidence had been obtained could also be taken into account in the exercise of the discretion. In the case of *Callis* v. *Gunn*,[13] Lord Parker CJ stated that a trial judge might use his discretion to exclude evidence which had been obtained as a result of false representations, threats and bribes. In *R* v. *Payne*,[14] the Court of Appeal held that incriminating evidence that had been obtained through trickery should not have been admitted. In this case, the defendant was arrested on suspicion of driving whilst over the prescribed alcohol limit. He was informed that a medical examination was required to determine if he was suffering from an illness, and on this basis, he consented to the examination. At his trial, the doctor who carried out the medical examination was called to give evidence that the defendant was under the influence of alcohol and therefore unfit to drive. The defendant appealed against his conviction. The Court of Appeal held that the doctor should not have been allowed to give evidence that the defendant was under the influence of alcohol because that evidence had been obtained by tricking the defendant into incriminating himself, and he would not have consented to the examination had he known that the purpose of the examination was to assess his fitness to drive and that the results would be used in evidence against him.

However, commentators note that the discretion was very rarely exercised in practice.[15] For example, in *Jeffrey* v. *Black*,[16] the Divisional Court accepted that 'an irregularity in obtaining evidence does not render the evidence inadmissible'.[17] Thus, the Court held that illegal conduct alone was not sufficient to render evidence inadmissible, but something more was required in order for the trial judge to exercise his discretion to exclude evidence. In this case, the defendant was arrested on suspicion of stealing a sandwich from a pub. After charging the defendant with theft, the police decided to conduct a search of his flat. The search was conducted without the consent of the defendant and was held by the Divisional Court to be an illegal search because it

---

10 [1955] AC 197 at 203.
11 Ibid. at 204.
12 Ibid.
13 [1964] 1 QB 495.
14 [1963] 1 WLR 637.
15 See J. Hunter, 'Judicial discretion: section 78 in practice' [1994] Crim LR 558.
16 [1978] 1 QB 490, DC.
17 Ibid. at 497.

was not related to the alleged theft of the sandwich: 'it is perfectly clear that when they sought to enter his premises, and did enter his premises they were not in the least bit concerned about the sandwich ... I do not accept that the common law has yet developed to the point, ... in which police officers who arrest a suspect for one offence at one point can as a result thereby authorise themselves, ... to go and inspect his house at another place when the contents of his house, ... bear no relation whatever to the offence with which he is charged'.[18] The consequence of the search was that the police found a quantity of cannabis at the defendant's flat. At first instance, the magistrates held that this evidence was inadmissible because it had been obtained illegally. However, the Divisional Court overturned the decision of the magistrates. The Court held that the magistrates (or the trial judge in a Crown Court trial) could only exercise their discretion to exclude the evidence in exceptional cases where there was more than merely illegal conduct. The police must have 'been guilty of trickery or they have misled someone, or they have been oppressive or they have been unfair, or in other respects they have behaved in a manner which is morally reprehensible, then it is open to the justices to apply their discretion and decline to allow the particular evidence to be let in as part of the trial'.[19] The decision in this case demonstrates the low priority that was historically afforded to the citizen's civil rights by the common law.

The common law position is currently reflected in the leading authority of *R* v. *Sang*.[20] In this case, the House of Lords confirmed the existence of a discretion to exclude evidence where its prejudicial effect outweighed its probative value.[21] The defendant in this case was charged with conspiracy to utter (use) forged banknotes and unlawful possession of forged banknotes. He claimed that he had been induced into committing the offence by an *agent provocateur*. He further claimed that he would not have committed the offence but for the inducement. Thus, he argued that he was entrapped into committing the offence. Since previous authorities from the Court of Appeal had already decided that entrapment was no defence in law,[22] counsel for the defendant sought to argue before the trial judge that the judge should exercise his discretion to exclude the evidence of the *agent provocateur*. However, the trial judge ruled that he had no discretion to exclude the prosecution evidence. Consequently, the defendant changed his plea from not guilty to guilty and he appealed to the Court of Appeal on the basis that the trial judge's ruling had been wrong. The Court of Appeal dismissed the appeal, so the defendant appealed to the House of Lords on a point of law of general public importance, namely:

> Does a trial judge have a discretion to refuse to allow evidence – being evidence other than evidence of admission – to be given in any circumstances in which such evidence is relevant and of more than minimal probative value?[23]

---

18 Ibid.
19 Ibid. at 498, per Lord Widgery CJ.
20 Above (n. 2).
21 Ibid. at 437.
22 See *R* v. *McEvilly* (1974) 60 Cr App R 150, *R* v. *Mealey* (1974) 60 Cr App R 59 and *R* v. *Willis* [1976] Crim LR 127.
23 Above (n. 2) at 431.

Lord Diplock gave the leading judgment in the case:

R V. SANG [1980] AC 402
Lord Diplock

[at 435–7]

In no other case . . . has either the Court of Criminal Appeal or the Court of Appeal allowed an appeal upon the ground that either magistrates in summary proceedings or the judge in a trial upon indictment ought to have exercised a discretion to exclude admissible evidence upon the ground that it had been obtained unfairly or by trickery or in some other way that is morally reprehensible; though they cover a wide gamut of apparent improprieties from illegal searches, as in *Kuruma* v. *The Queen* itself and in *Jeffrey* v. *Black* [1978] Q.B. 490 (which must be the high water mark of this kind of illegality) to the clearest cases of evidence obtained by the use of *agents provocateurs* . . .

Nevertheless it has to be recognised that there is an unbroken series of dicta in judgments of appellate courts to the effect that there is a judicial discretion to exclude admissible evidence which has been 'obtained' unfairly or by trickery or oppressively, although except in *Reg.* v. *Payne* [1963] 1 W.L.R. 637, there never has been a case in which those courts have come across conduct so unfair, so tricky or so oppressive as to justify them in holding that the discretion ought to have been exercised in favour of exclusion . . .

. . . the function of the judge at a criminal trial as respects the admission of evidence is to ensure that the accused has a fair trial according to law. It is no part of a judge's function to exercise disciplinary powers over the police or prosecution as respects the way in which evidence to be used at the trial is obtained by them. If it was obtained illegally there will be a remedy in civil law; if it was obtained legally but in breach of the rules of conduct for the police, this is a matter for the appropriate disciplinary authority to deal with. What the judge at the trial is concerned with is not how the evidence sought to be adduced by the prosecution has been obtained, but with how it is used by the prosecution at the trial.

A fair trial according to law involves, in the case of a trial upon indictment, that it should take place before a judge and a jury; that the case against the accused should be proved to the satisfaction of the jury beyond all reasonable doubt upon evidence that is admissible in law; and, as a corollary to this, that there should be excluded from the jury information about the accused which is likely to have an influence on their minds prejudicial to the accused which is out of proportion to the true probative value of admissible evidence conveying that information. If these conditions are fulfilled and the jury receive correct instructions from the judge as to the law applicable to the case, the requirement that the accused should have a fair trial according to law is, in my view, satisfied; for the fairness of a trial according to law is not all one-sided; it requires that those who are undoubtedly guilty should be convicted as well as that those about whose guilt there is any reasonable doubt should be acquitted. However much the judge may dislike the way in which a particular piece of evidence was obtained before proceedings were commenced, if it is admissible evidence probative of the accused's guilt it is no part of his judicial function to exclude it for this reason.

The House of Lords dismissed the defendant's appeal and confirmed that there was no substantive defence of entrapment in English criminal law. The House then turned to the certified question regarding a trial judge's discretion to exclude evidence in a criminal trial. The House held that allowing the trial judge a wide discretion to exclude prosecution evidence which had been obtained by entrapment would be tantamount to permitting the substantive defence of entrapment through the back door. Thus, the House held that there was no general discretion to exclude prosecution evidence merely because it had been obtained improperly or unfairly. The answer given to the certified question was one suggested by Viscount Dilhorne and adopted by four of the five members of the House of Lords in the case. Lord Diplock set out the answer within His Lordship's opinion:

(1) A trial judge in a criminal trial has always a discretion to refuse to admit evidence if in his opinion its prejudicial effect outweighs its probative value.

(2) Save with regard to admissions and confessions and generally with regard to evidence obtained from the accused after commission of the offence, he has no discretion to refuse to admit relevant admissible evidence on the ground that it was obtained by improper or unfair means. The court is not concerned with how it was obtained. It is no ground for the exercise of discretion to exclude that the evidence was obtained as the result of the activities of an *agent provocateur*.[24]

Thus, aside from cases in which it is necessary to protect the privilege against self-incrimination, such as where there is evidence of admissions or evidence obtained from the defendant after the commission of the offence, there is no general judicial discretion to exclude evidence merely on the basis that it has been obtained illegally or improperly. The House of Lords was not concerned with the way in which evidence has been obtained. However, there is a discretion to exclude prosecution evidence if its prejudicial effect outweighs its probative value. As can be seen from the extract from the case above, the House was concerned to ensure that the defendant has a fair trial, so any evidence which might influence the minds of the jurors in a way which is prejudicial to the defendant should be excluded. While the Law Lords were not unanimous on the answer to the certified question, they were unanimous in deciding that the trial judge did not have a discretion to exclude evidence on the grounds that the evidence had been obtained by entrapment. Unfortunately, the opinions of the five Law Lords differed in the scope of the discretion and the decision in *R* v. *Sang* has been criticised by academics because the speeches 'are hard to reconcile'[25] and for being an 'unsatisfactory authority'.[26]

In *The Law of Evidence*, Professor Dennis states as follows:

I. H. DENNIS, *THE LAW OF EVIDENCE*, 5TH EDN (SWEET & MAXWELL, 2013)

[at p. 314]

Sang is an unsatisfactory authority from many points of view. The speeches are inconsistent, they give confusing and unclear guidance on the scope of the fairness discretion at common law, and they misleadingly treat as comparable categories of fairness at trial the separate principles that the accused should not be convicted on prejudicial evidence and the principle that the accused should receive fair treatment in the evidence-gathering process. Most fundamentally of all, *Sang* completely failed to address the changing role and powers of the police in the investigation of offences and the implications this might have for the courts as the guardians of the legitimacy of criminal trials.

---

24 Ibid. at 437.
25 Sharpe, *Judicial Discretion and Criminal Investigation* at p. 50.
26 I. H. Dennis, *The Law of Evidence*, 5th edn (Sweet & Maxwell, 2013) at p. 92.

Despite such criticisms of the case, *R* v. *Sang* is the leading authority on the common law discretion to exclude evidence and it is still applied in cases in which the prejudicial effect of the evidence outweighs its probative value.

6.3.2 The common law post-PACE position

As stated above, there are two sources of the discretion to exclude evidence: (1) at common law, and (2) at statute. The case of *R* v. *Sang* is still the leading authority at common law, but s. 78, PACE Act 1984 also provides for a statutory discretion to exclude prosecution evidence. The statutory discretion under s. 78 will be discussed in detail below. This paragraph is concerned with s. 82(3), PACE Act 1984, which specifically preserves the common law discretion. Thus, the enactment of the Police and Criminal Evidence Act 1984 did not render the common law discretion to exclude evidence redundant and both the common law discretion and statutory discretion co-exist.

S. 82(3), POLICE AND CRIMINAL EVIDENCE ACT 1984

Nothing in this Part of this Act shall prejudice any power of a court to exclude evidence (whether by preventing questions from being put or otherwise) at its discretion.

The preservation of the common law discretion to exclude evidence under s. 82(3), PACE Act 1984 means that the common law discretion under *R* v. *Sang* and the statutory discretion under s. 78 co-exist. This in turn raises the question of the extent to which Parliament intended the common law discretion and statutory discretion to serve the same purpose. The statutory discretion under s. 78 is more commonly used in practice, but the common law discretion under *R* v. *Sang* may be relied on where necessary. One such example is in the event that the trial judge rejects an application to exclude evidence under s. 78, but later changes his mind and wishes to exclude the evidence after it has been heard by the jury. In such cases, it is not open to the judge to exclude the evidence under s. 78, because s. 78 only applies to evidence upon which the prosecution *proposes* to rely; thus, it does not apply to evidence which the jury has already heard. Nevertheless, the trial judge may exclude the evidence using the common law discretion under *R* v. *Sang*, which is not restricted to evidence which has not been adduced before the jury. In *R* v. *Sat-Bhambra*,[27] the Court of Appeal stated, *obiter*, that s. 78 ceases to have effect as soon as the evidence is ruled admissible and is adduced before the jury. At this stage, the trial judge may only use s. 82(3) to rule that the evidence is inadmissible. In practical terms, when evidence has already been ruled admissible and adduced in court, a later ruling that that evidence is inadmissible presents obvious difficulties. The trial judge will then have to decide whether simply to direct the jury to ignore the evidence they heard (something which is quite difficult for any person to do once they have heard it) or to take the more costly decision to discharge the jury. In reaching his decision, the trial judge might be influenced by matters such as the significance of the evidence, the degree of any likely prejudicial effect and the stage at which

---

27 (1988) 99 Cr App R 55, CA.

this occurs in the trial and the length of the trial (it may be easier and less costly to discharge a jury if this occurs at the start of the trial as opposed to towards the end of a lengthy trial).

While it may seem strange that the Police and Criminal Evidence Act 1984 preserved the common law discretion to exclude evidence where its prejudicial effect outweighed its probative value, it is clear that there is at least one significant difference between the common law and statutory forms of the discretion, and that s. 82(3) thus does serve a purpose.

6.4 STATUTORY DISCRETION

The statutory discretion to exclude evidence is found under s. 78 of the Police and Criminal Evidence Act 1984.[28]

S. 78(1), POLICE AND CRIMINAL EVIDENCE ACT 1984

In any proceedings the court may refuse to allow evidence on which the prosecution proposes to rely to be given if it appears to the court that, having regard to all the circumstances, including the circumstances in which the evidence was obtained, the admission of the evidence would have such an adverse effect on the fairness of the proceedings that the court ought not to admit it.

Section 78 is a very significant provision within the Police and Criminal Evidence Act 1984, but it was not contained in the original Police and Criminal Evidence Bill. It was added to the Bill at a late stage in the legislative process. Lord Scarman proposed adding an exclusionary discretion clause to the Bill as it was going through the Committee Stage in the House of Lords and the clause was then revised at the final stages of the legislative process before it became s. 78. Since the Court of Appeal in *R* v. *Fulling*[29] stated that the Police and Criminal Evidence Act 1984 is a codifying Act, a literal approach should be taken in application of s. 78, thus the court should examine the natural meaning of the language in the provision in accordance with the principles set out in *Bank of England* v. *Vagliano Brothers*.[30]

In the case of *R* v. *Mason*,[31] the Court of Appeal considered the scope of s. 78. In this case, the defendant was arrested on suspicion of being involved in an incident of arson after a car was set on fire. The fire had been caused by petrol bombs made with glass bottles containing a flammable liquid. The defendant was questioned by the police with his solicitor present. The police falsely informed the defendant and his solicitor that the defendant's fingerprints had been found on a piece of glass which was allegedly discovered at the crime scene. On the basis of this disclosure, the solicitor advised his client to co-operate with the police interview and

---

28 See A. L.-T. Choo and S. Nash, 'What's the matter with section 78?' [1999] Crim LR 929, M. Gelowitz, 'Section 78 of the Police and Criminal Evidence Act 1984: middle ground or no man's land?' (1990) 106 LQR 327 and K. Grevling, 'Fairness and the exclusion of evidence under section 78(1) of the Police and Criminal Evidence Act 1984' (1997) 113 LQR 667.

29 [1987] QB 426.

30 [1891] AC 107.

31 [1988] 1 WLR 139, CA.

answer all questions. Consequently, the defendant made a full confession to the offence. It later transpired that the police had lied about the piece of glass containing the defendant's fingerprints and no such incriminating evidence linked to the defendant had in fact been found at the scene. At trial, the defence sought to exclude evidence of the confession under either s. 76 or 78 of the Police and Criminal Evidence Act 1984. However, the trial judge ruled that the evidence was admissible because during the police interview the defendant had been aware of his right to remain silent and he had chosen not to. The defendant was convicted and appealed on the grounds that the confession evidence should have been excluded. The Court of Appeal considered the scope of the discretion to exclude under s. 78. Taking first the types of prosecution evidence to which s. 78 applies, while it is true that s. 76, PACE Act 1984 deals specifically with confession evidence, s. 76 provides an exclusionary rule and this does not preclude the exclusionary discretion under s. 78 from also applying to confession evidence. Thus, the Court of Appeal held that s. 78 does apply to confessions as well as to other types of prosecution evidence. In this sense, s. 78 is wider than both the common law discretion under *R* v. *Sang* and the exclusionary rule of law under s. 76, PACE Act 1984. Having determined that s. 78 applies broadly to all types of prosecution evidence, the Court of Appeal also compared the scope of s. 78 with that of the common law and applied a narrow interpretation to s. 78, noting that it 'does no more than to re-state the power which judges had at common law'.[32]

R V. *MASON* [1988] 1 WLR 139, CA
Watkins LJ

[at 143–4]

It is submitted that when a comparison is made between the provisions of those two sections and reference made to *Reg.* v. *Sang* [1980] A.C. 402, it was not the intention of Parliament that section 78 be understood as though the word 'evidence' includes evidence of confessions and admissions. We see no reason whatsoever to put that in our view extremely strained construction upon the plain words used in this section. In our judgment on a proper construction of it the word 'evidence' includes all the evidence which may be introduced by the prosecution into a trial. Thus it is that regardless of whether the admissibility of a confession falls to be considered under section 76(2), a trial judge has a discretion to deal with the admissibility of a confession under section 78 which, in our opinion, does no more than to re-state the power which judges had at common law before the Act of 1984 was passed. That power gave a trial judge a discretion whether solely in the interests of the fairness of a trial he would permit the prosecution to introduce admissible evidence sought to be relied upon, especially that of a confession or an admission. That being so, we now return to the circumstances of the present case.

The Court also strongly disapproved of the deception practised against the solicitor and considered this 'a most reprehensible thing to do', but held that the courtroom was 'not the place to discipline the police'. The Court held that the trial judge had failed to take into account the deception practised against the solicitor when he admitted the confession evidence in court, and that if he had taken this into account, he would have ruled that the confession was inadmissible.

---

32 Ibid. at 144.

Authorities seem to disagree on the scope of the discretion under s. 78 compared to that under *R* v. *Sang*.[33] As noted above, the Court of Appeal in *R* v. *Mason* held that s. 78 merely restates the common law discretion. This view was echoed in *R* v. *Chalkley and Jeffries*[34] where Auld LJ concluded that s. 78 had not enlarged the scope of the discretion under *R* v. *Sang*, and by some academics, such as Carter who commented of s. 78 that '[i]t is hard to detect anything of value that it has added to the common law'.[35] However, some cases have suggested that s. 78 carries wider discretionary powers than *R* v. *Sang*. In *R* v. *Smurthwaite*,[36] Lord Taylor CJ suggested that s. 78 is at least as wide as the common law, this was cited with approval by Lord Nolan in the House of Lords in *R* v. *Khan (Sultan)*,[37] and in *R* v. *Cooke*,[38] Glidewell LJ held that s. 78 is 'substantially wider' than the common law. Thus, the authorities demonstrate some inconsistency in the approach to the interpretation and application of s. 78.

The following paragraph of this chapter considers the traditional principles associated with the application of s. 78 and the extent to which judges apply particular principles in exercising their discretion to exclude evidence under s. 78.

6.5 PRINCIPLES OF EXCLUSION

There is no generally agreed principle governing the exclusion of evidence under s. 78. Judges have been left to interpret both the common law discretion and s. 78 as they see fit, and over the years they have provided different reasons for excluding evidence. Commentators note that this lack of guiding principle has led to inconsistencies in the application of s. 78. Sharpe comments that '[t]he wide and unstructured wording of section 78 of PACE leaves a lacuna in respect of the rationale which is to be employed in the exclusion of illegally or improperly obtained evidence'.[39] Ashworth argues that '[i]t is these inconsistencies which lend urgency to the search for a rationale'.[40] Birch contends that '[t]he more principled the discretion can be said to be, and the more its underlying aims can be articulated, the more consistent will be the decisions made under it'.[41] A clear and principled rationale is necessary in order to ensure a consistent and predictable approach to the application of the discretion under s. 78, but the extent to which the courts currently employ such a principled approach is doubtful.

There are traditionally four principles justifying the exclusion of evidence from a criminal trial. This paragraph explores the principles underlying the exercise of the judicial discretion to exclude evidence under s. 78 of the Police and Criminal Evidence Act 1984. The extent to which judges follow a consistent approach to excluding evidence under s. 78 will be considered. The four principles to be explored are:

---

33 For a detailed discussion on this point, see Dennis, above (n. 26) at pp. 97–103.
34 [1998] QB 848.
35 See P. Carter, 'Evidence obtained by use of a covert listening device' (1997) 113 *Law Quarterly Review* 468.
36 [1994] 4 All ER 426 at 435.
37 [1997] AC 558 at 578.
38 [1995] 1 Cr App R 318 at 328.
39 Above (n. 25) at 157.
40 A. Ashworth, 'Excluding evidence as protecting rights' [1977] Crim LR 723 at 726.
41 D. Birch, 'Excluding evidence from entrapment: what is a fair cop?' [1994] *Current Legal Problems* 73 at 89.

- the reliability principle
- the disciplinary principle
- the protective principle
- the judicial integrity principle.

6.5.1 Reliability principle

The reliability principle is derived from the traditional justification for admitting confession evidence, namely the voluntariness principle. The voluntariness principle provides that only confessions which are voluntarily made should be admissible, and that any confession which has been made involuntarily should be excluded on the basis that it is potentially unreliable. This was expressed in the case of *R* v. *Warickshall*[42] in the following terms: '[a] free and voluntary confession is deserving of the highest credit . . . but a confession forced from the mind . . . comes in so questionable a shape . . . that no credit ought to be given to it; and therefore it is rejected'. The reliability principle is a modern version of the voluntariness principle. The reliability principle is concerned with the way in which the evidence was obtained and the extent to which the reliability of the evidence is affected. Only reliable evidence is admissible; unreliable evidence should be excluded. Ashworth explains that 'determining the truth of the criminal charges is the sole purpose of the criminal trial, and evidence should be admitted or excluded solely on the grounds of reliability'.[43] Thus, unreliable evidence should be excluded in order to remove, so far as possible, the risk of an incorrect verdict. However, adopting the reliability principle allows evidence which has been obtained illegally or improperly to be admissible so long as it is reliable. Thus, the evidence of the possession of a controlled drug which is obtained through an illegal search, as in *Jeffrey* v. *Black*, would be admissible in a trial against the defendant for the possession of that drug, even if the search was entirely unnecessary and irrelevant to the original reason for questioning or arresting the defendant. Thus, the fundamental shortcoming in the reliability principle is that it fails to protect the rights of the defendant.

6.5.2 Disciplinary principle

The disciplinary principle provides that evidence which has been obtained illegally or improperly should be excluded in order to discipline the police and to deter them from future violations of the law or breaches of the Codes of Practice.[44] Ashworth explains that the idea behind this principle was that 'the court should use its position to discourage improper practices in the investigation of crime'.[45] The principle works on the presumption that if the police know that any evidence that they obtain illegally or improperly is going to be excluded, they will be less tempted to resort to such conduct in the future. This principle does not require a causal link between the illegal or improper conduct and the evidence in question; evidence may be excluded under the disciplinary principle even where the violation of the law did not produce

---

42 (1783) 1 Leach CC 263.
43 Above (n. 40) at 723.
44 See Sharpe, above (n. 25) at pp. 29–36 for more detail on the disciplinary principle.
45 Above (n. 40) at 723.

the evidence. For example, in the case of *R* v. *Allen*, the police refused the defendant access to a solicitor. The defendant made a confession, but this was excluded by the trial judge on the basis of the disciplinary principle because 'if the police are allowed to use in court, evidence of suspects whom they hope will incriminate themselves by being denied the advice of a solicitor, they will go on doing so'.[46] However, this case seems to be an anomaly; while the courts strongly disapprove of illegal or improper practices by the police or prosecution, they will not automatically exclude evidence merely in order to discipline the police. Hence, in the same year in *R* v. *Lemsatef*,[47] the Court of Appeal approved the admission of confession evidence, even in cases where the defendant had been denied access to legal advice. In the House of Lords in *R* v. *Sang*, Lord Diplock stated that it was not the role of the courts to discipline the police, rather there is a civil law remedy which should be used where the police break the law and there are disciplinary procedures which may be pursued in cases of improper conduct. Cases post-PACE have further echoed this disapproval of the disciplinary principle as a basis for excluding evidence and have frowned upon the use of the courts as a forum to discipline the police. In *R* v. *Mason*, where the police lied to the defendant's solicitor, the Court of Appeal held that the courts were not the place to discipline the police, and in *R* v. *Delaney*,[48] Lord Lane CJ stated that '[i]t is not part of the duty of the court to rule a statement inadmissible simply in order to punish the police for failure to observe the Code of Practice'.[49]

6.5.3 Protective principle

The protective principle provides that evidence should be excluded where the police have treated the defendant in a way which infringes his fundamental human rights.[50] This principle is advocated by Professor Andrew Ashworth in his article 'Excluding evidence as protecting rights'.[51]

A. ASHWORTH, 'EXCLUDING EVIDENCE AS PROTECTING RIGHTS' [1977] CRIM LR 723

[at 723]

The aim of this article is to argue that neither the reliability principle nor the disciplinary principle is based on sound premises, and to suggest that a third, 'protective' principle provides both a stronger justification for the exclusion of improperly obtained evidence and a plausible explanation of some relevant judicial decisions.

---

46 [1977] Crim LR 163 at 164.
47 [1977] 2 All ER 835.
48 (1989) 88 Cr App R 338, CA.
49 Ibid. at 341. Similarly, in *R* v. *Chalkley and Jeffries* [1998] 2 Cr App R 79, the Court of Appeal stated, *obiter*, that s. 78 should not be used merely to discipline the police. Also see the *Report of the Royal Commission on Criminal Procedure* (Cmnd. 8092, 1981), para. 4.125 and the cases of *R* v. *Keenan* [1990] 2 QB 54, CA and *R* v. *Canale* [1990] 2 All ER 187, CA for further cases expressing similar views.
50 See Sharpe, above (n. 25) at pp. 37–42 and Ashworth, above (n. 40) for more detail on the protective principle.
51 Above (n. 40).

[at 725]

If a legal system declares certain standards for the conduct of criminal investigation – whether they are enshrined in a constitution, detailed in a comprehensive code or scattered in various statutes and judicial precedents – then it can be argued that citizens have corresponding rights to be accorded certain facilities and not to be treated in certain ways. If the legal system is to respect those rights, then it is arguable that a suspect whose rights have been infringed should not thereby be placed at any disadvantage: by 'disadvantage' is meant, here and throughout the article, that evidence obtained by the investigators as a result of the infringement should not be used against the suspect. And the appropriate way of ensuring that the suspect does not suffer this disadvantage is for the court of trial to have the power to exclude evidence by improper methods. The presentation of evidence in court may in this context be viewed as the natural conclusion of a criminal investigation, and it is therefore fitting that the court should protect the defendant from disadvantages resulting from any infringement of his rights during that investigation. The protective principle thus argues that an infringement of an individual's rights (in the broad sense that he is denied something to which he is entitled or subjected to treatment which is improper) supplies a prima facie justification for the exclusion of evidence obtained as a result of that infringement.

Professor Ashworth recognises that a rigid approach whereby any breach of the law automatically leads to the exclusion of evidence assumes that every law protects the liberty of the suspect and that every breach of the law does in fact infringe the liberty of the suspect. Instead, he advocates a qualified protective principle according to which evidence obtained in breach of the law is *liable to* exclusion, unless the court is satisfied that it led to no disadvantage to the defendant. However, a shortcoming of this principle is that it may lead to the exclusion of evidence which is both relevant and reliable, and this may ultimately lead to the acquittal of a guilty defendant. While it was once thought that the enactment of the Human Rights Act 1998 in October 2000 might lead to an increased reliance on the protective principle, commentators have observed that this has not been the case: 'The emphasis on reliability has become more explicit, with the courts declining to accept even blatant breaches of fundamental rights such as Art. 8 rights of respect for privacy as sufficient to render inadmissible the reliable evidence obtained'.[52]

6.5.4 Judicial integrity principle

The judicial integrity principle provides that the courts should not permit the state to rely on evidence which has been obtained as a result of illegal or improper conduct as this would undermine the integrity of the criminal justice system.[53] This principle seeks to protect the integrity of the criminal justice process and the verdict, thereby maintaining public confidence in the criminal legal system. It operates on the basis that the state should set a good example in upholding the law: 'the criminal process is compromised when courts act on

---

52 D. Ormerod and D. Birch, 'The evolution of the discretionary exclusion of evidence' [2004] Crim LR 138 at 153.
53 See A. Zuckerman, 'Illegally-obtained evidence – discretion as a guardian of legitimacy' (1987) *Current Legal Problems* 55.

evidence that has been improperly obtained'.[54] In *The Criminal Process*, Professor Ashworth and Professor Redmayne observe that under this principle, the admission of such evidence undermines the integrity of the court in trying the defendant because the court is simultaneously condoning the illegal or improper behaviour by the police, and condemning the illegal behaviour of the defendant.[55] Professor Dennis advocates a theory of legitimacy within which illegally or improperly obtained evidence should be excluded in order to protect the moral authority of the verdict. He argues that while the other principles discussed above may be factors to be considered in the exercise of the discretion to exclude evidence, the final consideration must be the effect of the illegal or improper conduct on the legitimacy of the verdict.[56]

The integrity principle has been recognised in other jurisdictions, particularly in Canada and Australia. The Canadian Charter of Rights and Freedoms 1982 provides that evidence might be excluded if its admission would tend to 'bring the administration of justice into disrepute'.[57] The Australian courts have applied the integrity principle and have held that evidence should be excluded if its admission would go against the public interest in 'ensuring that the public confidence in the justice system is not undermined by the perception that the courts of law condone or encourage unlawful or improper conduct on the part of those who have the duty to enforce the law'.[58]

On a strict application of the judicial integrity principle, even small or insignificant breaches would lead to the exclusion of evidence. However, this approach would conflict with the reliability principle because it would require the exclusion of any evidence obtained in violation of law or procedure, irrespective of the reliability of that evidence. A preferred approach would be a less strict application of the principle, under which factors such as the severity of the breach, the state of mind of those guilty of the breach, the nature of the offence charged, the reliability of the evidence, and other relevant considerations would be taken into account.

Each of the principles explored below (see Figure 6.2) provides valid arguments for the exclusion of evidence which would have an adverse effect on the fairness of the proceedings, but most of these principles also present shortcomings. It appears that there is no one overarching principle which is relied on consistently by the courts to justify the exclusion of evidence. It may be that judges rely upon a combination of two or more of the principles in the exercise of their discretion under s. 78, but what is evident is that there is no consistency in the approach taken by the courts. In fact, the Court of Appeal has previously stated that '[i]t is undesirable to attempt any general guidance as to the way in which a judge's discretion under section 78 or his inherent powers should be exercised. Circumstances vary infinitely'.[59] In her report on her empirical study at Leeds Crown Court, Mary Hunter observes that the four Crown Court judges

---

54 S. Uglow, 'Covert surveillance and the European Convention on Human Rights' [1999] Crim LR 287 at 289.
55 See A. Ashworth and M. Redmayne, *The Criminal Process*, 4th edn (Oxford University Press, 2010) at p. 346.
56 Above (n. 26) at p. 108.
57 Section 24(2), Charter of Rights and Freedoms 1982.
58 *Ridgeway* v. *R* (1995) 129 ALR 41, per McHugh J at 89. Also see *Bunning* v. *Cross* (1978) 141 CLR 54 and s. 138, Evidence Act 1995.
59 *R* v. *Samuel* [1988] 1 QB 615, per Hodgson J at 630.

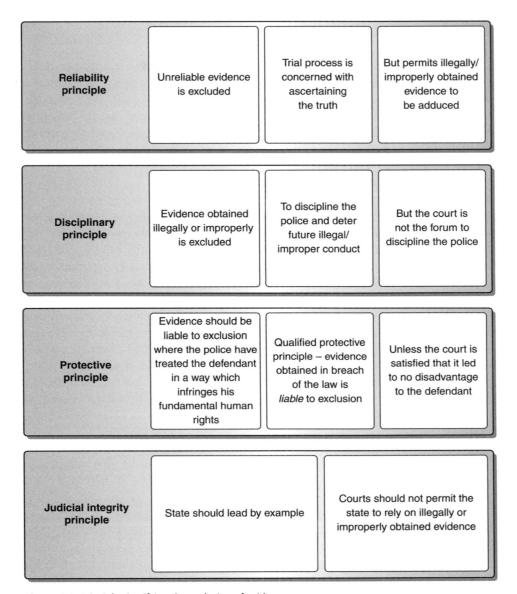

Figure 6.2 Principles justifying the exclusion of evidence

and one High Court judge that she interviewed were either unaware of the principles espoused by academics or aware of them but did not consider them in practice when deciding whether to exclude evidence under s. 78. All of the judges asked agreed that their chief concern in exercising their discretion was the fairness of the proceedings.

The next paragraph of this chapter explores the approaches taken by the courts in respect of different types of illegally or improperly obtained evidence.

6.6   TYPES OF ILLEGALLY OR IMPROPERLY OBTAINED EVIDENCE

The following paragraphs will examine the case law in respect of different types of illegally and improperly obtained evidence. We will begin by looking at examples of breaches of the Police and Criminal Evidence Act 1984 and the Codes of Practice. We will then consider case law relating to the use of police trickery, informants and entrapment and the way in which the courts approach the admissibility of any evidence thereby obtained. Finally, we will explore the admissibility of evidence obtained through the use of covert listening devices.

6.6.1   Breaches of PACE and the Codes of Practice

A breach of the Police and Criminal Evidence Act 1984 constitutes *illegal* conduct while a breach of the accompanying Codes of Practice constitutes *improper* conduct. It is worth noting that sometimes a breach might constitute a breach of both a provision of the PACE Act 1984 and a breach of the Codes of Practice. One such example is the right to access to a solicitor which is provided for by law under s. 58 of the PACE Act 1984 and under para. 6 of Code C. A breach of a provision under the PACE Act 1984 or of a paragraph of its accompanying Codes of Practice will not automatically lead to the exclusion of evidence under s. 78. Case law illustrates that the courts use s. 78 more sparingly, even where there is a clear breach of the Act or a Code of Practice. The Court of Appeal has held that a breach must be regarded as 'significant and substantial' before evidence obtained in consequence of it may be excluded under s. 78.[60] Where the police act with bad faith, this may be sufficient to turn breaches which would not otherwise have been 'significant and substantial' into 'significant and substantial' breaches.[61]

Right to legal advice
The courts regard a suspect's right to legal advice as a fundamental legal right. Consequently, where a suspect is denied access to a solicitor in breach of s. 58 of the PACE Act 1984 and Code C, the breach is likely to be a 'significant and substantial' one and the courts are likely to exclude any evidence which is obtained as a result of that breach. In *R* v. *Samuel*,[62] the defendant was arrested in relation to an armed robbery at a Building Society after he was recognised by a cashier, when he tried to deposit money into his account, as a man who had carried out a robbery about three weeks earlier. The defendant was questioned about the offence and after this interview he requested access to a solicitor. However, his request was refused by a superintendent under s. 58 of the PACE Act 1984 on the grounds that there was a likelihood that other suspects would be inadvertently warned. He was subsequently interviewed on two further occasions without a solicitor present, and he confessed to two burglaries (but not to the armed robbery of the Building Society) in the last of these interviews. He was then charged in relation to the burglaries, and he was again refused access to his solicitor. In a further, final interview,

---

60 See *R* v. *Absolam* (1988) 88 Cr App R 332, CA and *R* v. *Keenan* [1989] 3 WLR 1193, CA.
61 *R* v. *Walsh* (1989) 91 Cr App R 161.
62 Above (n. 59).

the defendant then confessed to the robbery and was charged with this offence. His confession was adduced in evidence at trial and the defendant was convicted. He appealed against his conviction arguing that the trial judge had been wrong to rule that the denial of access to a solicitor was justified and that the trial judge should have excluded the evidence of the confession from the final interview. The Court of Appeal quashed the defendant's conviction and held that the confession ought to have been excluded because its admission would have an adverse effect on the fairness of the proceedings. The court held that the police had wrongly denied the defendant access to his solicitor and also cast doubt on the reason given by the police for refusing such access. The court noted that solicitors are officers of the court and stated that it would only be in rare circumstances that a police officer would refuse access to a solicitor on the basis that there were reasonable grounds for believing that the defendant's solicitor would intentionally interfere with or harm evidence, cause physical injury to other persons, alert other suspects, or hinder the recovery of property.[63] Thus, the refusal of access to a solicitor was unjustified in this case and the defendant 'was denied improperly one of the most important and fundamental rights of a citizen'.[64]

Breaches of Code C

Code C provides the police with guidance on the detention, treatment and questioning of a suspect. Where breaches of Code C are 'significant and substantial' they may lead to the exclusion of evidence obtained in consequence of the breaches, such as in the case of *R* v. *Keenan*.[65] In this case, the Court of Appeal considered the nature of a police interview and held that an informal discussion held with a suspect might constitute an interview and thus be subject to the protections afforded to the questioning of a suspect under Code C. At the trial of the defendant for motoring offences and possession of an offensive weapon, the trial judge admitted evidence of questions put to the defendant and the answers elicited from him at the police station. The defence appealed against the defendant's conviction arguing that this evidence should have been excluded under s. 78 because the police had breached Code C and the admission of the evidence would have an adverse effect on the fairness of the proceedings. The Court referred to three provisions of Code C which are intended to safeguard against 'verballing', the practice by which the police inaccurately record or invent words used by a suspect in an interview. These provisions had been breached in this case:

- a requirement of an accurate and verbatim record of interview made during the course of the interview, unless that is not practicable (Code C, para. 11.3(b)(ii)),
- a requirement that the police record the reason if the interview is not recorded contemporaneously (Code C, para. 11.6),
- a requirement that the suspect is shown the record of interview with a view to signing it or correcting it if he considers it inaccurate (Code C, para. 12.12).

The Court of Appeal held that while 'not every breach or combination of breaches of the Code will justify the exclusion of interview evidence', where there have been 'significant

---

63 Section 58(8), Police and Criminal Evidence Act 1984.
64 Above (n. 59) at 630.
65 [1989] 3 WLR 1193, CA.

and substantial' breaches of the 'verballing' provisions of Code C, this will frequently lead to the exclusion of evidence so obtained under s. 78. In this case, the evidence should have been excluded. The Court also confirmed that it is not the role of the courts to discipline the police, thus the disciplinary principle is not the rationale behind the exclusion of evidence under s. 78.[66]

Similarly, in *R* v. *Absolam*[67] the Court of Appeal held that the evidence of an informal conversation between the defendant and a custody officer should have been excluded. The defendant was arrested for threatening behaviour whilst he was on bail for the possession of cannabis. On his arrival at the police station, the custody officer failed to inform the defendant of his right to legal advice and tried to obtain admissions from the defendant. The custody officer asked the defendant to empty his pockets and the defendant did so. The custody officer asked the defendant 'Is that all?' and the defendant replied 'Yes'. At this stage, the custody officer (knowing that the defendant was on bail for drugs offences) then said to the defendant 'And now put the drugs on the table'. The defendant then produced eight small bags of cannabis resin from inside his trousers. The custody officer said, 'You haven't been selling drugs again, have you?', and the defendant responded 'Yes'. The defendant was then reminded of the caution and asked 'How many of these packets have you sold today?' and the defendant replied 'I do not know'. The custody officer asked 'Were these bags ones that you have left over from selling today?' and the defendant replied 'Yes'. No record was made of the conversation until much later and the record was never shown to the defendant. The defendant denied that the conversation ever took place. The evidence of the conversation was adduced in evidence at trial and the defendant was convicted of possession of cannabis with intent to supply. He appealed against his conviction on the basis that the trial judge should have excluded the evidence of the conversation under s. 78 because its admission would have an adverse effect on the fairness of the proceedings. The Court of Appeal allowed the appeal, substituting the offence of possession of cannabis, and held that there had been serious breaches of the Codes of Practice. Failing to inform the defendant of his right to a solicitor and failing to make a contemporaneous record of the conversation and show it to the defendant were 'significant and substantial' breaches of the Codes of Practice. Consequently, the admissions made by the defendant ought to have been excluded under s. 78 of the PACE Act 1984.

The Court of Appeal has held that the admissions made by the defendant should have been excluded in light of the 'flagrant breaches' of Code C by the police and their 'cynical disregard of the rules'. In *R* v. *Canale*,[68] the defendant was arrested and interviewed at the police station on four separate occasions. The police claimed that he made admissions during the first two interviews, but no contemporaneous record was made of the interviews and the police gave no reason for this (in violation of Code C, paras. 11.3(b)(ii) and 11.6). The defendant made further admissions in the later two interviews and the trial judge permitted all four interviews to be given in evidence. The defendant claimed that he was tricked into making the admissions by promises made by the police and he appealed against his conviction. The Court of Appeal allowed the appeal and emphasised the importance of the protection offered by Code C in terms

---

66 Also see *R* v. *Delaney* (1989) 88 Cr App R 338, CA.
67 (1988) 88 Cr App R 332, CA.
68 (1989) 91 Cr App R 1, CA.

of contemporaneous note-taking. Lord Lane CJ stated that the object of Code C is 'not merely to ensure, so far as possible, that the suspect's remarks are accurately recorded and that he has an opportunity when he goes through the contemporaneous record afterwards of checking each answer and initialling each answer, but likewise it is a protection for the police, to ensure, so far as possible, that it cannot be suggested that they induced the suspect to confess by improper approaches or improper promises'.[69]

A similar level of importance is attached to the requirement that a defendant be cautioned prior to interview. Thus, where the police fail to caution a defendant before asking him questions, the evidence of answers given by the defendant is likely to be excluded at trial. This is essentially what occurred in the case of *R* v. *Nelson*; *R* v. *Rose*.[70] The defendants were two sisters who travelled to the United Kingdom from Jamaica and were found to have cocaine hidden in their luggage. The customs officer who interviewed Nelson had reached the conclusion in his own mind that she was guilty prior to the interview. Nevertheless, he interviewed her without administering the caution first. Consequently, the entire transcript of Nelson's interview should have been excluded under s. 78 because its admission would have an adverse effect on the fairness of the proceedings. The Court of Appeal held that simple questions asked merely to ascertain whether the suitcase belonged to the defendant did not have to be preceded by a caution. The time to caution the defendant arose when the customs officer had a reasonable suspicion that the defendant had committed an offence. Since the customs officer did have reasonable grounds to suspect that Nelson had committed an offence, he should have cautioned her. However, the same could not be said in the case of the other defendant, Rose, who had also been questioned without caution. Evidence of the interview given by Rose was admissible because there had been no such suspicion in respect of Rose until after she had been questioned. Thus, in her case there had been no breach of Code C to warrant the exclusion of the evidence of her interview.

6.6.2 Police trickery, entrapment and *agents provocateurs*

This paragraph deals with cases involving the police using trickery, *agents provocateurs* or other methods of entrapment in order to obtain evidence which incriminates the defendant.[71] These categories do overlap; the cases discussed below have been divided into:

1. cases involving trickery at the police station; and
2. cases involving more elaborate schemes of entrapment and the use of *agents provocateurs*.

Police trickery
Where the police have used trickery in order to obtain evidence of incriminating admissions made by the defendant, the courts will not necessarily exclude that evidence, especially where the evidence is highly reliable. For example, in *R* v. *Bailey and Smith*,[72] the two defendants were

---

69 Ibid. at 1.
70 [1998] 1 Cr App R 399, CA.
71 See Birch, 'Excluding evidence from entrapment: what is a "fair cop"?' (1994) 47 *Current Legal Problems* 73 and G. Robertson, 'Entrapment evidence: manna from heaven, or fruit of the poisoned tree?' [1994] Crim LR 805.
72 (1993) 97 Cr App R 365, CA.

charged with three counts of robbery. They refused to answer questions in police interview, exercising their right to remain silent. The police wanted to obtained more evidence against the defendants, so, having remanded the defendants in custody, the police installed listening devices in a cell and then placed both defendants in the cell together. Unaware that they were being recorded, the defendants made some incriminating admissions about the robberies. The prosecution sought to adduce the recordings in evidence at the defendants' trial, but the defence made an application to exclude the recordings under s. 78 on the grounds that they had been obtained by police trickery, and, therefore, were not made voluntarily. The trial judge ruled that the evidence was admissible and the defendants were convicted. Their appeals against their convictions were dismissed by the Court of Appeal. Simon Brown LJ emphasised the serious nature of the crimes charged, the fact that the recordings were reliable and had not been obtained oppressively and the characteristics of the defendants and held that the trial judge was right to admit the evidence.

R V. *BAILEY AND SMITH* (1993) 97 CR APP R 365, CA
Simon Brown LJ

[at 375]

[W]here, as here, very serious crimes have been committed – and committed by men who have not themselves shrunk from trickery and a good deal worse – and where there has never been the least suggestion that their covertly taped confessions were oppressively obtained or other than wholly reliable, it seems to us hardly surprising that the trial judge exercised his undoubted discretion in the manner he did. If contrary to our view evidence of this sort is generally to be regarded as undesirable and inadmissible, then in our judgment it is for the Codes to be extended accordingly. As the legislation and Codes presently stand, we do not think it unlawful to have obtained, nor unfair to have admitted, these taped conversations.

Whether the courts will exclude evidence obtained as a result of police trickery may depend upon who is deceived by the trick. We have already seen from the case of *R* v. *Mason* that the courts disapproved greatly of the actions of the police in lying to the defendant's solicitor.[73]

R V. *MASON* [1988] 1 WLR 139, CA
Watkins LJ

[at 144]

It is obvious from the undisputed evidence that the police practised a deceit not only upon the appellant, which is bad enough, but also upon the solicitor whose duty it was to advise him. In effect, they hoodwinked both solicitor and client. That was a most reprehensible thing to do. It is not however because we regard as misbehaviour of a serious kind conduct of that nature that we have come to the decision soon to be made plain. This is not the place to discipline the police. That has been made clear

---

73 Above (n. 31).

here on a number of previous occasions. We are concerned with the application of the proper law. The law is, as I have already said, that a trial judge has a discretion to be exercised of course upon right principles to reject admissible evidence in the interests of a defendant having a fair trial. The judge in the present case appreciated that, as the quotation from his ruling shows. So the only question to be answered by this court is whether, having regard to the way the police behaved, the judge exercised that discretion correctly. In our judgment he did not. He omitted a vital factor from his consideration, namely, the deceit practised upon the appellant's solicitor. If he had included that in his consideration of the matter we have not the slightest doubt that he would have been driven to an opposite conclusion, namely, that the confession be ruled out and the jury not permitted therefore to hear of it. If that had been done, an acquittal would have followed for there was no other evidence in the possession of the prosecution.

For those reasons we have no alternative but to quash this conviction.

Before parting with this case, despite what I have said about the role of the court in relation to disciplining the police, we think we ought to say that we hope never again to hear of deceit such as this being practised upon an accused person, and more particularly possibly on a solicitor whose duty it is to advise him unfettered by false information from the police.

Thus, it would appear that intentional deception practised against a solicitor is likely to lead to the exclusion of any evidence obtained in consequence of that deception, while a trick practised against a defendant who has been charged with a serious offence, who has a criminal record or a lifestyle whereby he tricks or deceives others will not automatically lead to the exclusion of incriminating evidence obtained as a result.

Entrapment and agents provocateurs

This paragraph deals with cases of entrapment and the use of *agents provocateurs*. Entrapment involves the police laying a trap for the defendant or an opportunist to fall into. This is a form of police trickery (discussed above), albeit it may result in the police catching the defendant in the act of committing the offence. While entrapment is no substantive defence to an offence in English criminal law,[74] evidence of entrapment may be relevant to the question of the admissibility of evidence obtained as a result of that entrapment.[75] An *agent provocateur* is an undercover police officer or a police informant who incites a defendant to commit a criminal offence which he would not otherwise have committed. The courts distinguish between the use of an undercover police officer who does not incite an offence and an *agent provocateur*, who does. Evidence obtained through the use of an *agent provocateur* may be excluded under s. 78 and a trial judge will have regard to the *Smurthwaite* guidelines in the exercise of his discretion in this regard.

R v. *Christou and Wright*[76] was a case involving entrapment and undercover police officers. The police set up a fake jewellery shop called 'Stardust Jewellers' in Tottenham in north London. The shop was staffed solely by undercover police officers. The aim of the shop was to recover stolen property and to catch those who were handling stolen jewellery. So the police let it be

---

74 *R* v. *Sang* [1980] AC 402.
75 *R* v. *Smurthwaite*; *Gill* [1994] 1 All ER 898, CA.
76 [1992] QB 979, CA.

known that they were willing to buy stolen property and people brought stolen goods into the shop. The shop contained hidden recording equipment and each customer who was trying to sell stolen property was recorded. The defendants in this case each visited the shop on several occasions and they were charged in respect of numerous transactions. The prosecution wished to adduce the recordings in evidence at their trials and this was permitted by the trial judge. The defendants appealed against their convictions arguing that the evidence of the recordings should have been excluded under s. 78 because its admission would have an adverse effect on the fairness of the proceedings. The Court of Appeal dismissed the appeal, holding that the defendants had not been tricked by the police, but they had 'voluntarily applied themselves to the trick'. The Court further stated that the police officers acting as staff in the shop were on 'equal terms' with the customers.

R V. CHRISTOU AND WRIGHT [1992] QB 979
Lord Taylor CJ

[at 986, 988–9]

The police were clearly engaged in a trick or deceit. However, they did not themselves participate in the commission of any offence; nor did they act as 'agents provocateurs' or incite crime. The offences charged had already been committed before the appellants entered the shop and the police, so far from having any dishonest intent, were concerned to return the property to its rightful owners and bring offenders to justice . . . no market was provided which would not have been available elsewhere.

. . .

The judge held that the discretion under section 78 may be wider than the common law discretion identified in *Reg. v. Sang* [1980] A.C. 402, the latter relating solely to evidence obtained from the defendant after the offence is complete, the statutory discretion not being so restricted. However, he held that the criteria of unfairness are the same whether the trial judge is exercising his discretion at common law or under the statute. We agree. What is unfair cannot sensibly be subject to different standards depending on the source of the discretion to exclude it.

In the result the judge concluded that to admit the challenged evidence would not have an adverse effect on the fairness of the trial. He said:

Nobody was forcing the defendants to do what they did. They were not persuaded or encouraged to do what they did. They were doing in that shop exactly what they intended to do and in all probability, what they intended to do from the moment they got up that morning. They were dishonestly disposing of dishonest goods. If the police had never set up the jewellers shop, they would, in my judgment, have been doing the same thing, though of course they would not have been doing it in that shop, at that time. They were not tricked into doing what they would not otherwise have done, they were tricked into doing what they wanted to do in that place and before witnesses and devices who can now speak of what happened. I do not think that is unfair or leads to an unfairness in the trial.

Putting it in different words, the trick was not applied to the appellants; they voluntarily applied themselves to the trick. It is not every trick producing evidence against an accused which results in unfairness. There are, in criminal investigations, a number of situations in which the police adopt ruses or tricks in the public interest to obtain evidence. For example, to trap a blackmailer, the victim may be used as an agent of the police to arrange an appointment and false or marked money may be laid as bait to catch the offender. A trick, certainly; in a sense too, a trick which results in a form of self-incrimination; but not one which could reasonably be thought to involve unfairness. Cases such as *Reg. v. Payne* [1963] 1 W.L.R. 637 and *Reg. v. Mason (Carl)* [1988] 1 W.L.R. 139 are very different from the present case or the blackmail example. In *Reg. v. Mason* as in *Reg. v. Payne* [1963] 1 W.L.R. 637, the defendant was in police custody at a police station. Officers lied to both the defendant and his solicitor. Having no evidence against the defendant, they falsely asserted that his fingerprint had been found in an incriminating place in order to elicit admissions from him. After advice from his solicitor, the defendant made admissions. This court quashed his conviction.

... The judge's exercise of his discretion could only be impugned if it was unreasonable according to *Wednesbury* principles ... In our judgment, not only can the judge's conclusion on this issue not be so stigmatised; we think he was right.

In *Williams and another* v. *DPP*,[77] the police set up a trap in order to catch opportunist thieves. They left a van unattended and unsecured on a busy high street in an area with a high crime rate. The van contained a load of what appeared to be cigarette packets, but they were in fact dummy packets. The police then hid themselves in a nearby location and waited for people to steal the cigarettes. The appellants gave in to temptation and were convicted of interfering with a motor vehicle, or something carried in it, with an intent to commit theft contrary to s. 9(1), Criminal Attempts Act 1981. On appeal by case stated, the Divisional Court considered the extent to which the police had been acting as *agents provocateurs* to the offence. The Court held that the police had done nothing to force, persuade, encourage or coerce the appellants, and they had not participated in, incited, counselled or procured the commission of the offence; thus they had not acted as *agents provocateurs* in this situation. In fact, the appellants had acted voluntarily in the absence of any pressure from the police and with full understanding of their own dishonesty. The Court held that the admission of the evidence of the police would not have any adverse effect on the fairness of the proceedings; consequently, it was rightly admitted by the justices.

The case of *R* v. *Stagg (Colin)*[78] provides an example of the police using a female undercover police officer as a 'honey trap' to snare a defendant who they thought fit the profile of a killer. The defendant in this case was tricked into incriminating himself in the murder of Rachel Nickell on Wimbledon Common. The undercover police officer pretended to be romantically interested in the defendant and they exchanged sexual fantasies. She taped a conversation that she had with the defendant about the Wimbledon Common murder in which she told him that she enjoyed hurting people. Although the defendant went along with the conversation about violent sexual fantasies, he claimed that he did so because he was interested in her romantically, but he denied committing the offence. The officer said to the defendant, 'If only you had done the Wimbledon Common murder, if only you had killed her, it would be all right.' The defendant replied 'I'm terribly sorry, but I haven't'. Despite his denial, the defendant was prosecuted for the

---

77 (1993) 98 Cr App R 209, CA.
78 Unreported, 14 September 1994, Central Criminal Court.

murder. The evidence of the recording was excluded by the trial judge, Ognall J, who threw the case out and directed an acquittal.

The case of *R* v. *Smurthwaite*; *Gill*[79] laid down important guidelines in respect of the evidence obtained through the use of undercover police officers. These are known as the *Smurthwaite* guidelines. The appeal involved two separate cases which were heard together in light of their similar facts. Both defendants were convicted of soliciting to murder: Smurthwaite was convicted of soliciting another person to murder his wife and Gill was convicted of soliciting another person to murder her husband. The defendants were caught when they each unwittingly solicited undercover police officers who were posing as contract killers to carry out the killings. The appeals against conviction centred around the admission of evidence of what was said by the defendants to the undercover police officers which had been recorded on tape. The Court of Appeal held that the trial judges in each case had been right to admit the evidence and it provided guidelines to be considered in relation to evidence which is obtained through the use of *agents provocateurs*.

R V. *SMURTHWAITE*; *GILL* (1994) 98 CR APP R 437
Lord Taylor CJ

[at 440–1]

In our judgment, section 78 has not altered the substantive rule of law that entrapment or the use of an *agent provocateur* does not *per se* afford a defence in law to a criminal charge. A purely evidential provision in a statute, which does not even mention entrapment or *agent provocateur*, cannot, in our view, have altered a substantive rule of law enunciated so recently by the House of Lords. Had Parliament intended to alter the substantive law, it would have done so in clear terms.

However, that is not to say that entrapment, *agent provocateur*, or the use of a trick are irrelevant to the application of section 78. The right approach to the 1984 Act, a codifying Act, is that stated in *Fulling (1987) 85 Cr.App.R. 136, [1987] Q.B. 426*, following the principles laid down in *Bank of England v. Vagliano [1891] A.C. 107, 144*. That is simply to examine the language of the relevant provision in its natural meaning and not to strain for an interpretation which either reasserts or alters the pre-existing law. Viewed in that way, the phrase emphasised by Mr. Worsley clearly permits the Court to have regard to 'the circumstances in which the evidence was obtained' and to exclude it, but only if it 'would have such an adverse effect on the fairness of the proceedings that the Court ought not to admit it.' Thus, the fact that the evidence has been obtained by entrapment, or by *agent provocateur*, or by a trick does not of itself require the judge to exclude it. If, however, he considers that in all the circumstances the obtaining of the evidence in that way would have the adverse effect described in the statute, then he will exclude it . . .

In exercising his discretion whether to admit the evidence of an undercover officer, some, but not an exhaustive list, of the factors that the judge may take into account are as follows: Was the officer acting as an *agent provocateur* in the sense that he was enticing the defendant to commit an offence he would not otherwise have committed? What was the nature of any entrapment? Does the evidence consist of admissions to a completed offence, or does it consist of the actual commission of an offence?

---

79 (1994) 98 Cr App R 437.

How active or passive was the officer's role in obtaining the evidence? Is there an unassailable record of what occurred, or is it strongly corroborated? In *Christou and Wright (1992) 95 Cr.App.R. 264, [1992] 1 Q.B. 979*, this Court held that discussions between suspects and undercover officers, not overtly acting as police officers, were not within the ambit of the Codes under the 1984 Act. However, officers should not use their undercover pose to question suspects so as to circumvent the Code. In *Bryce (1992) 95 Cr.App.R. 320, [1992] 4 All E.R. 567*, the Court held that the undercover officer had done just that. Accordingly, a further consideration for the judge in deciding whether to admit an undercover officer's evidence, is whether he has abused his role to ask questions which ought properly to have been asked as a police officer and in accordance with the Codes.

Beyond mentioning the considerations set out above, it is not possible to give more general guidance as to how a judge should exercise his discretion under section 78 in this field, since each case must be determined on its own facts.

The Court acknowledged the decision of the House of Lords in *R* v. *Sang* which made it clear that there is no substantive defence of entrapment or *agent provocateur* in English criminal law, but it recognised that entrapment, the use of an *agent provocateur* or trickery was not necessarily irrelevant to the application of s. 78. If the admission of evidence would have such an adverse effect on the fairness of the proceedings that the court ought not to admit it, then it would be excluded. The Court held that the phrase 'fairness of the proceedings' under s. 78 referred both to the fairness to the defendant and the fairness to the public. In this sense, the discretion to exclude evidence under s. 78 is wider than that under the common law, which is only concerned with the fairness to the defendant.

The *Smurthwaite* guidelines provide a list of factors which a judge may take into account in deciding whether to exercise his discretion to exclude evidence under s. 78. The list is not exhaustive, so other relevant factors may be taken into account as the judge sees fit:

- **Was the officer acting as an *agent provocateur* in the sense that he was enticing the defendant to commit an offence he would not otherwise have committed?**
  If the officer enticed the defendant to commit an offence which he would not have committed without the presence of the officer, the evidence is more likely to be excluded. However, if the defendant would have committed the offence irrespective of the police officer or if the officer did not entice the defendant to commit the offence, the evidence is more likely to be excluded.
- **What was the nature of any entrapment?**
  There is no real guidance as to the meaning of this factor. The court will consider exactly what the police operation entailed. Where the defendant was 'entrapped', the extent to which he voluntarily committed the offence or was coerced into doing so may be taken into account.
- **Does the evidence consist of admissions to a completed offence, or does it consist of the actual commission of an offence?**
  The nature of the evidence obtained as a result of police operation will also be considered. While the use of undercover operations may be permissible in order to obtain evidence of the commission of an offence, it should not be used as a means to circumvent the Codes of Practice in order to secure admissions from the defendant without safeguards such as a legal adviser for the defendant and a contemporaneous record of interview.

- **How active or passive was the officer's role in obtaining the evidence?**
  If the officer plays an active role in obtaining the evidence, he is more likely to have influenced the commission of the offence and this may be more likely to render the evidence inadmissible under s. 78. However, if the officer took a passive role in obtaining the evidence, this may mean that the evidence is more likely to be admissible.

- **Is there an unassailable record of what occurred, or is it strongly corroborated?**
  Where there is an unassailable record of what occurred or the evidence is strongly corroborated, it is more likely to be more reliable and is therefore more likely to be admissible. However, where there is no record confirming what occurred or there is no corroborating evidence, the evidence is less reliable and may be more likely to be excluded under s. 78.

- **Has the undercover officer abused his role to ask questions which ought properly to have been asked as a police officer and in accordance with the Codes?**
  If the police officer was on equal terms to the defendant (as in *R* v. *Christou and Wright*), then the evidence obtained is less likely to be excluded. However, the position will be different if the police officer has acted as though he were not on equal terms with the defendant and he has abused his role by effectively acting as a police officer. Where the officer has used his position to question the defendant and elicit incriminating evidence from him in a way which ought to have been governed by the Codes of Practice, then the evidence obtained as a result of that questioning is more likely to be excluded under s. 78.

A couple of years after the Court of Appeal decision in *R* v. *Smurthwaite*; *Gill*, the House of Lords confirmed in *R* v. *Latif and Shahzad*[80] that s. 78 of the PACE Act 1984 could be used to exclude evidence obtained by entrapment. While reiterating that entrapment is no defence in English law, the decision ignited the alternative possibility that in entrapment cases the proceedings could be stayed for an abuse of process. The doctrine of abuse of process will be considered in more detail in paragraph 6.7 below when we will revisit this case. For now, it suffices to consider the approach of the House to the issue of excluding evidence obtained as a result of an entrapment under s. 78. The defendants in *R* v. *Latif and Shahzad* were involved in a plan to export 20 kg of heroin from Pakistan to the United Kingdom. Shahzad offered to supply the heroin to a third party, X, and X was to carry the drugs from Pakistan to the United Kingdom. X was in fact an informer employed by the US Drugs Enforcement Administration. The plan was that Shahzad would arrange for the drugs to be distributed in the United Kingdom. X met with Shahzad and the other defendant, Latif, at a hotel in London where they discussed delivery and payment details. The bags supposedly containing the drugs were delivered to Shahzad by a British customs officer who (acting without lawful authority and on the instructions of his superiors) was pretending to be in possession of the drugs on behalf of X. The conversations between the customs officer and the defendants were recorded and adduced in evidence. Both defendants were convicted of being knowingly concerned in the fraudulent evasion of the prohibition on importation of a controlled drug (more commonly referred to as smuggling) contrary to s. 170 of the Customs and Excise Management Act 1979. They appealed against their convictions on three grounds. The first ground related to an application by the defence that the proceedings should be stayed on the ground of abuse of process. The House held that the

---

80 [1996] UKHL 16.

trial judge had been entitled to conclude that the proceedings should not be stayed in this case. This ground will be discussed at paragraph 6.7 below. The second ground of appeal concerned the application of s. 78 of the PACE Act 1984. The defence argued that the evidence of the recordings should have been excluded under s. 78, but while the House confirmed that s. 78 could in principle be used to exclude evidence obtained by entrapment, the trial judge was right not to use it in this case. The House agreed with the trial judge that admitting the evidence of the tape recordings had not prejudiced the defendants, irrespective of the conduct of the informer and customs officer. The incriminating statements had been made in a recording and so were reliable; the defendants were not deprived of any rights. In this case, the defendants were not vulnerable and unwilling and the informer had not invited the defendants to commit the offence, but had merely given them the opportunity to commit the offence. The third ground of appeal should be mentioned for the sake of completeness. This concerned the unlawful actions of the third party, a customs officer, whose voluntary conduct broke the chain of causation. The House of Lords agreed and held that the defendants could not be liable for the full offence and a conviction for an attempt was substituted.

In *Teixeira de Castro* v. *Portugal*,[81] the European Court of Human Rights distinguished between 'cases where the undercover agent's action created a criminal intent that had previously been absent and those in which the offender had already been predisposed to commit the offence'.[82] The Court held that where police officers incite a defendant to supply them with drugs and the defendant would not otherwise have committed the offence, this, and the use of the evidence at the defendant's trial, constitutes a violation of the defendant's right to a fair trial under Article 6 of the European Convention on Human Rights. The defendant in *Nottingham City Council* v. *Amin*[83] relied on this case in his argument that he had been incited by undercover police officers to commit a criminal offence that he would not otherwise have committed. The defendant was a taxi driver who was not licensed to pick up passengers in a certain area. He was flagged down in that area by undercover police officers and subsequently charged with using his vehicle in an area for which he was not licensed. The evidence of the police officers was excluded at trial under s. 78 and the prosecution appealed against this decision by way of case stated. However, Lord Bingham CJ in the Divisional Court distinguished this case from *Teixeira de Castro* v. *Portugal* and held that while the criminal activity in the present case was much more minor, 'the facts … simply cannot lend themselves to the construction that this defendant was in any way prevailed upon or overborne or persuaded or pressured or instigated or incited to commit the offence'.[84] The admission of the evidence in this case would not have had an adverse effect on the fairness of the proceedings and the magistrate ought to have admitted the evidence at trial. In the later House of Lords' decision in *R* v. *Looseley*, Lord Hoffmann sought to clarify Lord Bingham's test in *Nottingham City Council* v. *Amin*:

> Many cases place emphasis upon the question of whether the policeman can be said to have caused the commission of the offence, rather than merely providing an opportunity for the accused to commit it with a policeman rather than in secrecy with someone else. . . .

---

81 (1999) 28 EHRR 101.
82 Ibid. at [32].
83 [2000] 1 WLR 1071.
84 Ibid. at 1080–1.

In referring to whether the defendant would have behaved in the same way if the opportunity had been offered by anyone else, Lord Bingham CJ obviously did not mean only that the defendant would have responded in the same way to someone who was not a policeman. Since the defendant in such cases ex hypothesi does not know that he is dealing with a policeman, such a condition would invariably be satisfied. What he meant was that the policemen behaved like ordinary members of the public in flagging the taxi down. They did not wave £50 notes or pretend to be in distress . . . The test of whether the law enforcement officer behaved like an ordinary member of the public works well . . . [85]

A similar conclusion to that in *Nottingham City Council* v. *Amin* was reached in the case of *R* v. *Shannon*.[86] The defendant in this case was an actor called John Shannon (stage name, John Alford), who was starring in a television drama called 'London's Burning'. He was caught up in a sting by a newspaper when an undercover journalist, posing as an Arab sheikh, supplied drugs to the journalist. The defendant was convicted of supplying a controlled drug to the journalist and he appealed against his conviction. The Court of Appeal dismissed the appeal and held that the defendant had not been incited to commit the offence by the journalist.

The cases above illustrate that evidence obtained through entrapment or the use of an *agent provocateur* may be excluded under s. 78 if its admission would have such an adverse effect on the fairness of the proceedings that the court ought not to admit it. In deciding whether to exercise the discretion to exclude the evidence the judge will take into account the factors listed in the *Smurthwaite* guidelines, such as the degree of involvement by the undercover officer and the extent to which the officer incited the commission of an offence which would not otherwise have been committed. *R* v. *Latif and Shahzad* and some of the other cases discussed above also involved the use of listening devices which recorded the conversations of the defendants. The paragraph below deals with the admissibility of evidence obtained through the use of covert listening devices.

6.6.3 Covert listening devices

Where the police illegally or improperly use a covert listening device to record conversations that the defendant has with another person, the evidence of the recordings is admissible provided that it is relevant.[87] This is subject to the trial judge's discretion to exclude the evidence under s. 78 of the PACE Act 1984 if its admission would have such an adverse effect on the fairness of the proceedings that the court ought not to admit it. The first key case on the use of covert listening devices was *R* v. *Khan (Sultan)*.[88] In this case, the defendant visited the

---

85 [2001] UKHL 53 at [50], [54] and [55].
86 [2001] 1 WLR 51.
87 See P. B. Carter, 'Evidence obtained by use of a covert listening device' (1997) 113 LQR 468, D. Ormerod, 'ECHR and the exclusion of evidence: trial remedies for Article 8 breaches' [2003] Crim LR 61, J. R. Spencer, 'Bugging and burglary by the police' [1997] *Cambridge Law Journal* 6, P. Tain, 'Covert surveillance, *R v Khan* and the European Convention' (1996) 140 *Solicitors Journal* 785 and S. Uglow, 'Covert surveillance and the European Convention on Human Rights' [1999] Crim LR 287.
88 [1997] AC 558, HL.

house of a man whom the police suspected to be involved in the supply of heroin. The police obtained authority to install a covert listening device on the outside of the house and they recorded conversations between the defendant and others during which the defendant made statements incriminating himself in the importation of £100,000-worth of heroin. The prosecution conceded that the police had perpetrated a civil trespass and some small amount of damage by installing the device on the outside of the building, and that the use of the device intruded on the privacy of the occupants of the house. The trial judge admitted the evidence of the recorded conversations at the defendant's trial for being knowingly concerned in the fraudulent evasion of the prohibition of the importation of a Class A drug. Since the trial judge refused to exclude the evidence of the recordings under s. 78, the defendant pleaded guilty and appealed first to the Court of Appeal, and then to the House of Lords. The House dismissed the appeal and emphasised the fact that the test for the admissibility of any evidence at court is relevance, and that relevant evidence is admissible, even if it was illegally obtained. The House acknowledged that the test of relevance is subject to the trial judge's discretion to exclude evidence under the common law or s. 78, but the House upheld the trial judge's decision here since the admission of the evidence did not have such an adverse effect on the fairness of the proceedings that the judge ought to have excluded it under s. 78. It was clear in this case that the evidence was reliable and it was relevant to the guilt of the defendant; consequently, the tape recordings were admissible. The House considered that, strictly speaking, the intrusion on the privacy of the occupants constituted a breach of Article 8 of the European Convention on Human Rights, but that this was outweighed by the public interest in the detection of criminal conduct of great gravity.

The defendant appealed to the European Court of Human Rights, arguing that the illegal use of the covert listening device had violated his right to a private life under Article 8 of the European Convention on Human Rights, and that the admission of this illegally obtained evidence at his trial had violated his right to a fair trial under Article 6.[89] The European Court of Humans Rights ruled that there had in fact been a violation of Article 8 because the use of the listening equipment was illegal, but that this did not automatically mean that there was a violation of Article 6, and there was no such violation in this case. The Court emphasised that its role was not to determine whether particular types of evidence were admissible in principle, or should have been in this specific case, but rather, 'The question which must be answered is whether the proceedings as a whole, including the way in which the evidence was obtained, were fair. This involves an examination of the "unlawfulness" in question and, where violation of another Convention right is concerned, the nature of the violation found.'[90] The Court pointed to s. 78 of the PACE Act 1984 and observed that this provided the domestic courts with an adequate procedure to deal with the admissibility of illegally obtained evidence: 'it is clear that, had the domestic courts been of the view that the admission of the evidence would have given rise to substantive unfairness, they would have had a discretion to exclude it under section 78 of PACE'.[91]

---

89 See *Khan* v. *United Kingdom* (2001) 31 EHRR 45, ECHR.

90 Ibid. at [34]. Note that provided the European Court of Human Rights is satisfied that there is a domestic procedure in place to deal with the admissibility of evidence, it will not interfere in the decision of a domestic court in an individual case: see *Schenk* v. *Switzerland* (1991) 13 EHRR 242, which was similar to the case of *Khan* v. *United Kingdom*.

91 *Khan* v. *United Kingdom* at [39].

The case of *R* v. *Chalkley and Jeffries*[92] raised very similar issues to *R* v. *Khan (Sultan)* and also reached the European Court of Human Rights. The defendants in this case were suspected of being involved in planning serious robberies. In order to gather further evidence to prosecute the defendants, the police arrested one of the defendants and his wife for credit card fraud in order to remove them from their house. The police then unlawfully entered the defendant's house and installed a covert listening device. The defendant was then released and conversations were recorded which incriminated the defendant. The trial judge ruled that the evidence of these tape recordings was admissible at the defendant's trial for conspiracy to commit robbery; consequently, the defendant pleaded guilty and appealed on the basis that the trial judge had been wrong to admit the evidence. The Court of Appeal held that the trial judge had been correct to admit the evidence. The Court applied s. 78 narrowly, holding that 'there is no discretion to exclude evidence unless its quality was or might have been affected by the way in which it was obtained'.[93] In this case, the Court was satisfied that the police conduct did not affect the quality of the evidence of the recordings; thus, the evidence was admissible. However, the Court considered that the trial judge had incorrectly conducted a balancing exercise in doing so, thus confusing the issue of fairness under s. 78 with the test for staying proceedings as an abuse of process. The Court stated that the purpose of the discretion under s. 78 was not for the judge to show his disapproval of the conduct of police officers, but rather it was to consider whether it would be unfair to the *defendants* to admit the evidence in question. Professor Dennis criticises the decision and comments that the Court of Appeal decision was 'unsatisfactory' for several reasons, such as for misstating the test under s. 78 as applying to the *defendants* only rather than more generally to the *proceedings*, which encompasses both the prosecution and the defendant.[94] The defendant appealed to the European Court of Human Rights on the same basis, as did the appellant in *Khan* v. *United Kingdom*. In *Chalkley* v. *United Kingdom*,[95] the government also conceded that the installation of the listening device had been illegal, but the Court held that although there had been a violation of the defendant's right to a private life under Article 8 of the European Convention on Human Rights, there was no violation of the defendant's right to a fair trial under Article 6 since the domestic courts had followed the procedure provided under s. 78.

Khan v. *United Kingdom* was also followed by the European Court of Human Rights in *Allan* v. *United Kingdom*,[96] in which it was held that the police breached Article 8 by planting an informant in the cell in which the defendant was being held and recording the conversations between them in order to obtain incriminating admissions from the defendant. However, the Court held that the use of the recordings in evidence at trial did not violate Article 6. A similar approach was adopted by the European Court of Human Rights in

---

92 Above (n. 34).
93 Ibid. at 875.
94 For further discussion on this, see above (n. 26) at 99–103.
95 (2003) 37 EHRR 30.
96 (2003) 36 EHRR 12.

PG v. *United Kingdom*,[97] in which the Court held that the police violated Article 8 in respect of the use of covert listening devices at the defendant's home and in his cell at the police station, but these violations did not lead to a violation of Article 6 when evidence of the recordings was admitted in evidence. In *R* v. *P*,[98] the House of Lords considered the use of evidence obtained through the interception of telephone communications and held that there was no violation of Article 6 of the European Convention on Human Rights even where the evidence was obtained unlawfully. The House held that the requirement of fairness under Article 6 is comparable to that under s. 78 of the PACE Act 1984. In *R* v. *Mason*,[99] the defendants were convicted of armed robberies after evidence of incriminating conversations recorded in the police cells was admitted in evidence at trial. While the evidence had been obtained in breach of Article 8 of the European Convention on Human Rights, the PACE Act 1984 and the Codes of Practice, the Court of Appeal held that there was no unfairness which warranted the exclusion of the evidence under s. 78. The Court called for some regulation of the use of covert listening devices in police stations.

Previously, the law relating to the use of covert listening devices was confusing and unclear. This led to violations of the law and breaches of Article 8 of the European Convention on Human Rights where covert listening devices were used for the investigation of criminal offences. Since the cases discussed above were decided, Parliament has enacted the Regulation of Investigatory Powers Act 2000 which regulates the powers of the police to intercept communications and use surveillance to gather evidence.

6.7 STAYING PROCEEDINGS AS AN ABUSE OF PROCESS

As we have seen from the discussion of the cases above, a trial judge can stay proceedings as an abuse of process as an alternative to excluding the improperly obtained evidence under s. 78.[100] The next paragraph focuses on the test for the doctrine of abuse of process in this context. In *R* v. *Horseferry Road Magistrates Court, ex parte Bennett*,[101] the House of Lords held that criminal proceedings could be stayed on the grounds that there has been an abuse of process as a result of improper conduct by the police or prosecution. The doctrine of abuse of process was considered in detail by Lord Steyn in *R* v. *Latif and Shahzad*. The House of Lords considered a ground of appeal based upon an argument that the proceedings should have been stayed as an abuse of process since the conduct of the customs officer and the informer had tainted the proceedings to such a degree. However, the House of Lords rejected this argument, holding that it was not an affront to the public conscience to allow the prosecution to proceed.

---

97 (2008) 46 EHRR 51.
98 [2002] 1 AC 14, HL.
99 [2002] Crim LR 841, CA.
100 See A. L.-T. Choo, 'Halting criminal prosecutions: the abuse of process doctrine revisited' [1995] Crim LR 864 and A. Clarke, 'Safety or supervision? The unified ground of appeal and its consequences in the law of abuse of process and exclusion of evidence' [1999] Crim LR 108.
101 [1994] 1 AC 42, HL.

R V. LATIF AND SHAHZAD [1996] 1 WLR 104
Lord Steyn

[at 112–13]

It is now necessary to consider the legal framework in which the issue of abuse of process must be considered. The starting point is that entrapment is not a defence under English law. That is, however, not the end of the matter. Given that Shahzad would probably not have committed the particular offence of which he was convicted, but for the conduct of Honi and customs officers, which included criminal conduct, how should the matter be approached? This poses the perennial dilemma . . . If the court always refuses to stay such proceedings, the perception will be that the court condones criminal conduct and malpractice by law enforcement agencies. That would undermine public confidence in the criminal justice system and bring it into disrepute. On the other hand, if the court were always to stay proceedings in such cases, it would incur the reproach that it is failing to protect the public from serious crime. The weaknesses of both extreme positions leaves only one principled solution. The court has a discretion: it has to perform a balancing exercise. If the court concludes that a fair trial is not possible, it will stay the proceedings. That is not what the present case is concerned with. It is plain that a fair trial was possible and that such a trial took place. In this case the issue is whether, despite the fact that a fair trial was possible, the judge ought to have stayed the criminal proceedings on broader considerations of the integrity of the criminal justice system. The law is settled. Weighing countervailing considerations of policy and justice, it is for the judge in the exercise of his discretion to decide whether there has been an abuse of process, which amounts to an affront to the public conscience and requires the criminal proceedings to be stayed: *Reg. v. Horseferry Road Magistrates' Court, Ex parte Bennett* [1994] 1 A.C. 42. *Ex parte Bennett* was a case where a stay was appropriate because a defendant had been forcibly abducted and brought to this country to face trial in disregard of extradition laws. The speeches in *Ex parte Bennett* conclusively establish that proceedings may be stayed in the exercise of the judge's discretion not only where a fair trial is impossible but also where it would be contrary to the public interest in the integrity of the criminal justice system that a trial should take place. An infinite variety of cases could arise. General guidance as to how the discretion should be exercised in particular circumstances will not be useful. But it is possible to say that in a case such as the present the judge must weigh in the balance the public interest in ensuring that those that are charged with grave crimes should be tried and the competing public interest in not conveying the impression that the court will adopt the approach that the end justifies any means.

In my view the judge took into consideration the relevant considerations placed before him. He performed the balancing exercise. He was entitled to take the view that Shahzad was an organiser in the heroin trade, who took the initiative in proposing the importation. It is true that he did not deal with arguments about the criminal behaviour of the customs officer. That was understandable since that was not argued before him. If such arguments had been put before him, I am satisfied that he would still have come to the same conclusion. And I think he would have been right. The conduct of the customs officer was not so unworthy or shameful that it was an affront to the public conscience to allow the prosecution to proceed. Realistically, any criminal behaviour of the customs officer was venial compared to that of Shahzad.

In these circumstances I would reject the submission that the judge erred in refusing to stay the proceedings.

In determining whether allowing the case to continue would constitute an abuse of process, the courts must ask: would it constitute an affront to the public conscience or be offensive to ordinary notions of fairness? If the answer is yes, the trial judge can stay the entire proceedings. The leading case on staying proceedings as an abuse of process as a result of entrapment is *R* v. *Looseley* which was heard together in the House of Lords with *Attorney General's Reference (No. 3 of 2000)*.[102] In *R* v. *Looseley*, an undercover police officer contacted the defendant and asked if he could get him some heroin. The defendant confirmed that he could and then supplied the police officer with heroin on three separate occasions. The defendant was convicted on charges of supplying a Class A drug. The defence argued that the proceedings should be stayed as an abuse of process, or, alternatively, that the evidence of the police officer should be excluded under s. 78. The trial judge rejected both arguments and the defendant changed his plea to guilty and appealed. The Court of Appeal dismissed the appeal and the defendant appealed to the House of Lords. The House of Lords also upheld the defendant's convictions. The House held that the undercover officer did no more than present himself as an ordinary customer and he did not incite the commission of an offence which the defendant would not otherwise have committed. Consequently, the trial judge had been entitled to refuse to stay the proceedings or to exclude the evidence under s. 78.

In *Attorney General's Reference (No. 3 of 2000)*, two undercover police officers sold contraband cigarettes to the defendant at a cheap price and asked him if he could get them some heroin. At first the defendant said that he could not get heroin at short notice and that he was 'not into heroin', but he eventually agreed to supply them with some as a return favour and he was subsequently charged with supplying a Class A drug. The trial judge in this case stayed the proceedings as an abuse of process on the ground that the police had incited the commission of an offence which the defendant would not otherwise have committed. The Attorney General referred the case to the Court of Appeal, which held that the trial judge had been wrong to stop the trial. A point of law of public importance was then certified and the case reached the House of Lords. The House of Lords held that the trial judge had been entitled to stay the proceedings in this case because the officers did more than merely provide the defendant with an opportunity to commit the offence. In fact, the officers in this case incited the offence by offering the defendant an inducement. The House again confirmed that there is no substantive defence of entrapment in English law, but held that it was open to a trial judge to stay the proceedings as an abuse of process or to exclude evidence obtained as a result of the entrapment under s. 78. The House held that there was a need to balance the need to uphold the rule of law by convicting and punishing those who did commit criminal offences with the need to prevent the police from acting in a manner which constituted an affront to the public conscience or offended ordinary notions of fairness.

---

102 [2001] UKHL 53.

R V. LOOSELEY AND ATTORNEY GENERAL'S REFERENCE (NO. 3 OF 2000) [2001] UKHL 53

Lord Nicholls of Birkenhead

1. My Lords, every court has an inherent power and duty to prevent abuse of its process. This is a fundamental principle of the rule of law. By recourse to this principle courts ensure that executive agents of the state do not misuse the coercive, law enforcement functions of the courts and thereby oppress citizens of the state. Entrapment, with which these two appeals are concerned, is an instance where such misuse may occur. It is simply not acceptable that the state through its agents should lure its citizens into committing acts forbidden by the law and then seek to prosecute them for doing so. That would be entrapment. That would be a misuse of state power, and an abuse of the process of the courts. The unattractive consequences, frightening and sinister in extreme cases, which state conduct of this nature could have are obvious. The role of the courts is to stand between the state and its citizens and make sure this does not happen.

. . .

16. Thus, although entrapment is not a substantive defence, English law has now developed remedies in respect of entrapment: the court may stay the relevant criminal proceedings, and the court may exclude evidence pursuant to section 78. In these respects *R v Sang* [1980] AC 402 has been overtaken. Of these two remedies the grant of a stay, rather than the exclusion of evidence at the trial, should normally be regarded as the appropriate response in a case of entrapment. Exclusion of evidence from the trial will often have the same result in practice as an order staying the proceedings. Without, for instance, the evidence of the undercover police officers the prosecution will often be unable to proceed. But this is not necessarily so. There may be real evidence, or evidence of other witnesses. Exclusion of all the prosecution evidence would, of course, dispose of any anomaly in this regard. But a direction to this effect would really be a stay of the proceedings under another name. Quite apart from these practical considerations, as a matter of principle a stay of the proceedings, or of the relevant charges, is the more appropriate form of remedy. A prosecution founded on entrapment would be an abuse of the court's process. The court will not permit the prosecutorial arm of the state to behave in this way.

17. I should add that when ordering a stay, and refusing to let a prosecution continue, the court is not seeking to exercise disciplinary powers over the police, although staying a prosecution may have this effect. As emphasised earlier, the objection to criminal proceedings founded on entrapment lies much deeper. For the same reason, entrapment is not a matter going only to the blameworthiness or culpability of the defendant and, hence, to sentence as distinct from conviction. Entrapment goes to the propriety of there being a prosecution at all for the relevant offence, having regard to the state's involvement in the circumstance in which it was committed.

. . .

25. Ultimately the overall consideration is always whether the conduct of the police or other law enforcement agency was so seriously improper as to bring the administration of justice into disrepute. Lord Steyn's formulation of a prosecution which would affront the public conscience is substantially to the same effect: see *R v Latif* [1996] 1 WLR 104, 112. So is Lord Bingham of Cornhill CJ's reference to conviction and punishment which would be deeply offensive to ordinary notions of fairness: see *Nottingham City Council v Amin* [2000] 1 WLR 1071, 1076. In applying these formulations the court has regard to all the circumstances of the case.

Lord Nicholls held that the following factors might be taken into account:

- *The nature of the offence.* The use of pro-active techniques is more needed and, hence, more appropriate, in some circumstances than others. The secrecy and difficulty of detection, and the manner in which the particular criminal activity is carried on, are relevant considerations.
- *The reason for the particular police operation.* It goes without saying that the police must act in good faith and not, for example, as part of a malicious vendetta against an individual or group of individuals. Having reasonable grounds for suspicion is one way good faith may be established, but having grounds for suspicion of a particular individual is not always essential. Sometimes suspicion may be centred on a particular place, such as a particular public house. Sometimes random testing may be the only practicable way of policing a particular trading activity.
- *The nature and extent of police participation in the crime.* The greater the inducement held out by the police, and the more forceful or persistent the police overtures, the more readily may a court conclude that the police over-stepped the boundary: their conduct might well have brought about commission of a crime by a person who would normally avoid crime of that kind. In assessing the weight to be attached to the police inducement, regard is to be had to the defendant's circumstances, including his vulnerability. This is not because the standards of acceptable behaviour are variable. Rather, this is a recognition that what may be a significant inducement to one person may not be so to another. For the police to behave as would an ordinary customer of a trade, whether lawful or unlawful, being carried on by the defendant will not normally be regarded as objectionable.
- *The defendant's criminal record.* The defendant's criminal record is unlikely to be relevant unless it can be linked to other factors grounding reasonable suspicion that the defendant is currently engaged in criminal activity.

Lord Nicholls stated that the key consideration for the courts in deciding whether to stay proceedings as an abuse of process is whether the conduct of the police 'was so seriously improper as to bring the administration of justice into disrepute'. His Lordship approved of the tests provided by Lord Steyn ('an affront to the public conscience') and Lord Bingham ('deeply offensive to ordinary notions of fairness') and stated that the court must have regard to the circumstances of the individual case.[103]

---

103 The case of *R* v. *Sutherland and others*, unreported, 29 January 2002, Nottingham Crown Court provides an example of a case in which the trial judge stayed proceedings as an abuse of process. This case involved numerous defendants who were charged with murder. The police acted in bad faith when they recorded legally privileged conversations between the defendants and their solicitors.

6.8 CIVIL PROCEEDINGS

The admissibility of illegally or improperly obtained evidence has been a more contentious issue within the criminal courts. In civil proceedings, the court may control the evidence by giving directions as to the issues on which it requires evidence, the nature of the evidence which it requires, and the way in which the evidence is to be placed before the court.[104] The court may also use its power to exclude evidence which would otherwise be admissible.[105] The admissibility of covertly obtained evidence in civil proceedings was considered in the case of *Jones* v. *University of Warwick*,[106] in which the claimant sued her employer, the defendant, for damages after she suffered an injury to her wrist at work. A hidden camera was used in the claimant's home to record footage of the claimant using her allegedly injured wrist. The district judge excluded the evidence in light of the improper method used to obtain it by illegally gaining entry to the claimant's home. The defendant appealed and the High Court held that the evidence should have been admitted in evidence. The claimant then appealed to the Civil Division of the Court of Appeal. The Court held that the violation of Article 8 of the European Convention on Human Rights was a relevant consideration for the court in deciding whether to exclude the evidence under r. 32.1 of the Civil Procedure Rules 1998. The Court took the view that the illegal conduct was not so outrageous that the defence should be struck out, and furthermore, 'it would be artificial and undesirable for the actual evidence, which is relevant and admissible', not to be placed before the trial judge. Thus, the Court did not consider it right to interfere with the judge's decision not to exclude the evidence. However, the Court expressed its disapproval of the illegal conduct by ordering the defendants to pay the costs of the proceedings required to resolve this issue.

6.9 CONCLUSION

The statutory discretion to exclude evidence under s. 78 would appear to be more commonly relied upon than the common law equivalent under *R* v. *Sang*. However, evidence will not automatically be excluded merely because it has been obtained illegally or improperly. Case law has shown that breaches of the PACE Act 1984 and the Codes of Practice must be 'significant and substantial' if the discretion to exclude is to be exercised. Even where the police have been guilty of trickery or entrapment, this will not necessarily lead to the exclusion of evidence thereby obtained. Only where the police incite or instigate the offence will the discretion be likely to be exercised. While the courts have refused to recognise a substantive defence of entrapment, the possibility of the abuse of process doctrine leading to a stay in proceedings has been increasingly recognised by the courts. However, the test for staying proceedings is much higher than for the exercise of the discretion.

---

104 Rule 32.1(1), Civil Procedure Rules 1998.
105 Rule 32.1(2), Civil Procedure Rules 1998.
106 [2003] 1 WLR 954.

to play in the law on hearsay. Quite the contrary, in recent years there hav landmark decisions which have sought to interpret the statutory provisions and have developed the law further. Most notably, there is a string of cases which status of implied assertions that were previously admissible at common law and statutory framework has overturned the House of Lords' decision in *R* v. *Kearley (No. 1)*.[2] There has also been some extremely significant jurisprudence regarding the extent to which the admissibility of hearsay evidence where the witness is unavailable to give evidence due to fear violates the defendant's right to a fair trial, and, more particularly, his right to examine or have examined witnesses against him under Article 6(3)(d) of the European Convention on Human Rights.[3] These cases have highlighted some of the challenges that still trouble the law on hearsay; and these landmark cases, as well as cases decided since these decisions, will be discussed in this chapter.

Hearsay evidence is best explained by way of an example: where a witness, W, makes a statement to another person, X, about something that W directly perceived, X cannot be called to give evidence in court of the matter perceived by W because it is hearsay evidence. The evidence cannot be received by the court in this manner because X has no personal knowledge of the matter in question, but is relying on what was said to him by W. Hearsay evidence is generally inadmissible because it is inherently unreliable and it is difficult to challenge in court. The law requires that only the best evidence be put before the tribunal of fact, and, thus, W (who is the only person who can give the best evidence here) must be called to give evidence of what he personally perceived. However, sometimes it is not possible to call W to give evidence of the matter: he might have died since the statement was made, or he may have moved away and might now be untraceable. In such circumstances, the trial judge may allow the evidence to be adduced in court by another witness. Before such hearsay evidence is deemed to be admissible in court, the trial judge must consider factors, such as the likely reliability of the evidence and the difficulty that the defence may have in challenging the evidence.

7.2 WHAT IS HEARSAY?

Hearsay is a statement made by a person other than in oral evidence, which is adduced in court in order to prove that the matter stated in the statement was or is true. In *R* v. *Sharp*, Lord Havers adopted the definition of hearsay in *Cross on Evidence*:[4]

> an assertion other than one made by a person while giving oral evidence in the proceedings is inadmissible as *evidence of any fact asserted*.[5]

---

2 [1992] 2 AC 228, HL. For the post-Criminal Justice Act 2003 approach to implied assertions, see *R* v. *Singh* [2006] 1 WLR 1564, *R* v. *MK* [2007] EWCA Crim 3150, *R* v. *Chrysostomou* [2010] EWCA Crim 1403, *R* v. *Elliott* [2010] EWCA Crim 2378 and *R* v. *Twist* [2011] EWCA Crim 1143, discussed at paragraph 7.4.1 below.

3 See the Supreme Court decision in *R* v. *Horncastle* [2010] 2 AC 373, SC and the decision of the European Court of Human Rights in *Al-Khawaja* v. *United Kingdom* (2012) 54 EHRR 23 discussed at paragraph 7.5.1 below.

4 *Cross on Evidence*, 6th edn (Oxford University Press,1985) at p. 38.

5 [1988] 1 WLR 7, HL at 11.

Under the Criminal Justice Act 2003 statutory framework, s. 114(1) now provides that '[i]n criminal proceedings a statement not made in oral evidence in the proceedings is admissible as evidence of any matter stated if . . .'. Thus, according to this section, hearsay is a statement not made in oral evidence which is adduced as evidence of any matter stated. In *R* v. *Twist*, Hughes LJ stated that the words 'admissible as evidence of any matter stated' require us to ask what it is that a party is seeking to prove.[6] Thus, there are two essential aspects to the definition of hearsay:

1. **the place** – the first aspect relates to where the statement was made. The statement must be made out of court (i.e. other than while giving oral evidence in court); and
2. **the purpose** – the second aspect relates to why the party seeking to rely on the statement wishes to adduce it in evidence. If the purpose of adducing the statement is to prove that what was said was true, then it is hearsay. However, if the purpose for adducing the evidence is something other than proving the truth of its contents (for instance, to prove instead that the witness was present by establishing that he or she spoke), then it is not hearsay evidence. Such evidence is instead deemed original evidence and it is admissible. Thus, the statement in question will necessarily contain something descriptive which is capable of being true or false.

The case of *Sparks* v. *R*[7] provides an example of inadmissible hearsay evidence. The defendant was a white man who was charged with indecently assaulting a 3-year-old girl. One of the issues at trial was the race of the alleged attacker because shortly after the attack the girl told her mother that the man who assaulted her 'was a coloured boy'. In light of her age, the girl did not give evidence, but the defendant wanted to adduce evidence of the statement in order to show that he did not assault the girl. While the girl's statement was unambiguous and likely to be reliable, nevertheless the trial judge held that it was hearsay, and thus it was inadmissible at trial. The Privy Council upheld this decision on appeal. The mother was not permitted to give evidence of what her daughter had said to her because the statement went to the issue of the race of the alleged attacker and the purpose of the defendant in adducing the statement was clearly to prove that the statement was true and that he was not the attacker. This case is significant because of the reliability of the statement made by the girl. There was no evidence to suggest that the girl was lying, but since the statement was hearsay, its reliability was overlooked and it was deemed to fall within the rule against hearsay.

The key difference between hearsay evidence and original evidence is the *purpose* for which the party seeks to rely on the statement in court (see Figure 7.1 for the difference between hearsay and original evidence). In *Subramaniam* v. *Public Prosecutor*,[8] Mr L. M. D. De Silva in the Privy Council stated that:

> Evidence of a statement made to a witness by a person who is not himself called as a witness may or may not be hearsay. It is hearsay and inadmissible when the object of the evidence is to establish the truth of what is contained in the statement. It is not hearsay and is admissible when it is proposed to establish by the evidence, not the truth of the statement, but the fact that it was made. The fact that the statement was made, quite apart

---

6 [2011] EWCA Crim 1143 at [6].
7 [1964] AC 964, PC.
8 [1956] 1 WLR 965, PC.

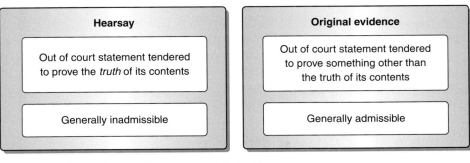

Figure 7.1 Difference between hearsay and original evidence

from its truth, is frequently relevant in considering the mental state and conduct thereafter of the witness or of some other person in whose presence the statement was made.[9]

If the purpose of adducing the evidence is to prove that what was said by the maker of the statement was true, then the statement is hearsay and generally inadmissible, but if there is some other purpose for adducing the evidence, then the statement is original evidence and admissible. By way of an example, imagine that X is a witness to the end of a fight, in which V is seriously injured. After witnessing the attack, X says to Y, 'I saw Fred running away'. If X is unavailable to give evidence in court, the prosecution may wish to call Y to give evidence of what X said to him. However, if the purpose of adducing the evidence of what X said was to prove the truth of its contents, i.e. that Fred was running away, then Y will not be permitted to give that evidence as it will be inadmissible hearsay. However, if, instead, the purpose of adducing the evidence was to prove something other than the truth of its contents, e.g. to prove that X was at the scene or that he spoke, then Y will be able to give evidence of what X said as this will be original evidence.

Broadly speaking, there are three categories of non-hearsay statements:

- statements which are admitted as circumstantial evidence of the state of mind of a person,
- statements which are admitted as circumstantial evidence of a state of affairs, and
- statements which are admitted as circumstantial evidence of the identity of a person or the origin of a person or an object.

Each of these categories will be explored in turn.

7.2.1 Evidence of state of mind

The first category of admissible non-hearsay statements consists of statements which are admitted as circumstantial evidence of the state of mind of the maker of the statement. These might be statements as evidence of the state of mind of a third party or the defendant.

(i) Evidence of the state of mind of a third party
Either the prosecution or the defence might seek to rely on statements made by a third party as evidence of the state of mind of the maker of that statement. Examples of cases in which statements

---

9 Ibid. at 970.

were admitted as evidence of the state of mind of the maker include *Ratten* v. *R*,[10] *R* v. *Gilfoyle*[11] and *R* v. *Blastland*.[12]

Ratten v. *R* is an example of a case in which the prosecution sought to adduce a statement as evidence of the state of mind of the maker. The defendant in this case was charged with the murder of his wife. The prosecution called evidence from an emergency telephone operator who stated that a sobbing female called the emergency services from the deceased's address and said, 'Get me the police, please'. This evidence was held to be admissible and not hearsay because it was not adduced to prove the truth of its contents, but rather to prove the state of mind of the maker (i.e. that the deceased was hysterical and that she asked for the police). From this the jury would be able to infer that the deceased was fearful of an impending attack. This decision was upheld by the Privy Council on appeal. Thus, evidence will not be hearsay and will be admissible if the purpose of adducing the evidence is to prove the state of mind or knowledge of the maker of the statement. *R* v. *Gilfoyle* is an example of a case in which the defendant sought to adduce a statement as evidence of the state of mind of the maker. The defendant in this case was convicted of the murder of his wife who had died in what appeared to be a case of suicide. The defendant wished to adduce suicide notes in the deceased's handwriting in order to prove that his wife had been thinking about committing suicide. The trial judge ruled that the suicide notes were inadmissible hearsay, but the Court of Appeal held that the suicide notes were admissible as circumstantial evidence of the state of mind of the deceased.

We saw previously in Chapter 2 the case of *R* v. *Blastland*. This is another authority for the principle that evidence may be admissible to prove the state of mind of the maker of the statement. The defendant in *R* v. *Blastland* was charged with buggery and murder relating to the death of a 12-year-old boy. The defendant admitted engaging in sexual activity with the boy, but denied killing him. He claimed that after having sex with the boy, he ran away because he had seen another man, Mark, nearby, and worried that Mark had witnessed the sexual activity. The defendant claimed that Mark must have committed the murder and wanted to call evidence that Mark had told witnesses that a boy had been murdered before the body was found. At first instance, the trial held that the evidence was inadmissible. On appeal, the House of Lords held that if the statements of the witnesses were adduced to prove the truth of their contents (i.e. that a boy had been murdered), then the statements would be inadmissible hearsay. However, if the evidence was adduced to prove the state of mind of the maker (i.e. to prove that M knew about the murder before the body was found), then the statements would be admissible as original evidence. However, the House of Lords considered the relevance of the evidence and held that Mark's knowledge was not relevant to the issue of whether the defendant had killed the boy. What was relevant was how Mark had come by his knowledge and he might have come by that knowledge in a number of different ways. Thus, since the jury could not infer the source of that knowledge, they could not infer that Mark was the killer, and the evidence was deemed to be inadmissible on the basis that it

---

10 [1972] AC 378, PC.
11 [1996] 3 All ER 883.
12 [1986] AC 41, HL.

was irrelevant. The House was reluctant to create a new common law exception to the rule against hearsay.

> **Cross-reference**
> Refer back to Chapter 2 for detail on the critique of the case of *R* v. *Blastland* [1986] AC 41, HL.

(ii) Evidence of the state of mind of the defendant

Either the prosecution or the defence might seek to rely on statements which provide evidence of the state of mind of the defendant. Examples of cases in which statements were admitted as evidence of the state of mind of the maker include *Jones* v. *DPP*[13] and *Subramaniam* v. *Public Prosecutor.*

Jones v. *DPP* is a House of Lords authority on similar fact evidence. In this case the defendant was convicted of the murder of a young girl guide. He had a previous conviction for rape of a girl guide in similar circumstances in which he ran a defence of alibi. The defendant also relied on alibi as a defence in relation to the murder charge. However, he initially put forward a false alibi and later relied on a different alibi, claiming that he provided the first false alibi because he had been in trouble with the police before and he had worried that he was unable to account for his whereabouts on the relevant night. The defendant also claimed that when he had returned home on the night of the murder, he had had a conversation with his wife and he provided the details of this conversation as further evidence of his alibi defence. The prosecution claimed that the false alibi and the defendant's account about his conversations with his wife were strikingly similar to the defence which he ran at the trial for rape. The prosecution case was that the evidence of these statements from the defendant was admissible as evidence of the state of mind of the defendant when he was presented with allegations and needed to lie about his whereabouts. The defendant appealed against his conviction for murder. The case reached the House of Lords, which held that the trial judge had been right to permit the prosecution to rely upon the evidence.

In *Subramaniam* v. *Public Prosecutor*, the Privy Council held that evidence of threats made to the defendant were not hearsay where the defendant was relying on the defence of duress as they were not being adduced in order to prove that they were true, i.e. that the threats would be carried out. Rather, they were admissible as original evidence to prove that the threats were made, and therefore, to prove the defendant's state of mind, i.e. that he was acting under the pressure of such threats.

7.2.2 Evidence of state of affairs

The second category of admissible non-hearsay statements consists of statements which are admitted as circumstantial evidence of a state of affairs. An example of such an admissible statement can be seen in the case of *Woodhouse* v. *Hall*.[14] This case involved a prosecution for the management of a brothel contrary to s. 33 of the Sexual Offences Act 1956. The defendant

---

13 [1962] AC 635.
14 (1981) 72 Cr App R 39.

ran a 'massage parlour' which was alleged to be operating as a brothel. Police officers gave evidence of conversations that they had had with women employed at the premises as masseuses. The women were said to have offered the police officers 'hand relief'. The Divisional Court held that a brothel was a place where 'two or more women were offering sexual services'. The police officers were permitted to give evidence as to the offers of sexual services that had been made to them by the women. This was not hearsay evidence because the purpose of adducing the evidence was to prove that the offers were made and thus to prove that the premises was being used as a brothel, not to prove that the offers were true. Thus it was held to be admissible evidence.

However, in the case of *R* v. *Harry*,[15] the Court of Appeal reached a different conclusion. The cases discussed in this paragraph involved the admissibility of implied assertions.[16] An implied assertion is evidence of a statement made and/or conduct by a person from which the existence of a fact can be inferred and the statement was based on a belief in that fact and it is adduced in order to prove the truth of the fact. For example, take a case in which the issue is whether the defendant is a drug dealer or not. Imagine first that X called at the defendant's house and said to a police officer, 'Bertie sells drugs' (Bertie being the nickname of the defendant). This would be an express assertion and the prosecution would seek to adduce the evidence of the statement in order to prove its truth, i.e. that Bertie does indeed sell drugs. If the prosecution wished to call the police officer to give evidence of the statement by X, this would constitute hearsay and would be inadmissible. Imagine now that Y says to a police officer, 'Is Bertie there? I want to buy some drugs'. This would be an implied assertion because it is not Y's intention to assert that Bertie sells drugs, but the statement is based upon Y's belief that Bertie will sell him drugs, and the fact that Bertie sells drugs can be inferred from both Y's conduct in calling and asking for Bertie and from his statement that he wishes to buy drugs. In *R* v. *Harry* the Court of Appeal held that the defendant could not rely on evidence that people had telephoned the defendant's flat, asked for his co-defendant and asked about buying drugs as implied assertions by those who had telephoned the flat that the co-defendant was a drug dealer. These statements were inadmissible hearsay.

This approach to implied assertions was approved by the majority of the House of Lords in the case of *R* v. *Kearley (No. 1)*. In this case, the defendant was charged with possession of a controlled drug with intent to supply, contrary to s. 5(3) of the Misuse of Drugs Act 1971. Only a small quantity of drugs was found at his home. However, while the police were searching the defendant's house, they claimed that there had been eleven telephone calls to the house in which the callers asked for the defendant by his nickname, 'Chippie', and asked for drugs. In addition to this, seven people visited the house asking for the defendant and offering to buy drugs for cash. The prosecution sought to call the police officers to give evidence of the telephone calls and the visits and of the conversations that they had had with the callers and visitors on each occasion. The prosecution wanted to adduce this evidence in order to prove that

15 (1988) 86 Cr App R 105, CA.
16 For further commentary on implied assertions, see T. R. S. Allen, 'Implied assertions as hearsay' (1992) 142 NLJ 1194; A. L.-T. Choo, *Hearsay and Confrontation in Criminal Trials* (Oxford University Press, 1996), ch. 4; M. Hirst, 'Conduct, relevance and the hearsay rule' (1993) 13 *Legal Studies* 54; J. R. Spencer, 'Hearsay, relevance and implied assertions' [1993] CLJ 40; D. Ormerod, 'Reform of implied assertions' (1996) 60 *Journal of Criminal Law* 201; and C. Tapper, 'Hearsay and implied assertions' (1992) 108 LQR 524.

the defendant was in the habit of selling drugs to people, and from this the jury could infer that the defendant had the intention to supply the quantity of drugs which were found in his possession. The trial judge held that the evidence of the conversations from the telephone calls and the visits was admissible and the defendant was convicted. He appealed, but the Court of Appeal upheld the trial judge's decision to admit the evidence. On appeal to the House of Lords, the following question was certified:

> Whether evidence may be adduced at a trial of words spoken (namely a request for drugs to be supplied by the defendant), not spoken in the presence or hearing of the defendant, by a person not called as a witness, for the purpose not of establishing the truth of any fact narrated by the words, but of inviting the jury to draw an inference from the fact that the words were spoken (namely that the defendant was a supplier of drugs).

By a 3:2 majority (Lords Bridge, Ackner and Oliver), the House of Lords overturned the decision of the Court of Appeal and held that the evidence of the conversations between the police and the callers and visitor was inadmissible hearsay because 'evidence of words spoken by a person not called as a witness which are said to assert a relevant fact by necessary implication are inadmissible as hearsay just as evidence of an express statement made by the speaker asserting the same fact would be'.[17] Thus, this case affirmed the inadmissibility of implied assertions despite the fact that the evidence of the implied assertions was likely to be reliable. The decision in this case was criticised by commentators: most notably, in his commentary on *R* v. *Kearley (No. 1)*, Professor Tapper declared that 'the House of Lords has condemned the law to further convolutions of interpretation to determine what implications may be found lurking in statements, both those assertive and non-assertive on their face, and even more problematically in actions'.[18] He further commented that '*Kearley* seems unlikely to be followed, or approved, elsewhere, and may condemn the law of hearsay in England to wallow in a parochial morass of technicality induced by the invitation it extends to the minute dissection and intricate analysis of the corpus of words and acts adduced in evidence'.[19] It would seem that s. 115(3) of the Criminal Justice Act 2003 has overturned the decision in *R* v. *Kearley (No. 1)* because this provision requires that one purpose of the statement is to cause a person to believe the matter, i.e. the statement is meant as an assertion.[20] Thus, implied assertions do not fall within the definition of hearsay under the Criminal Justice Act 2003 and are therefore admissible. This was confirmed by the Court of Appeal in *R* v. *Singh*.[21]

Cross-reference

For more detail on implied assertions and the question of whether s. 115 of the Criminal Justice Act 2003 overturned the position in *R* v. *Kearley (No. 1)*, see paragraph 7.4.1 below.

---

17 *R* v. *Kearley (No. 1)* [1992] 2 AC 228 at 245, per Lord Bridge relying on the support of Lord Ackner and Lord Oliver and the House of Lords decision in *R* v. *Blastland* [1986] AC 41, HL.
18 Tapper, 'Hearsay and implied assertions' (1992) 108 LQR 524 at 527–8.
19 Ibid. at 528.
20 See J. R. Spencer, *Hearsay Evidence in Criminal Proceedings*, 2nd edn (Hart Publishing, 2014) at paras. 3.27–3.28.
21 [2006] 1 WLR 1564.

The House of Lords in *R* v. *Kearley (No. 1)* distinguished the decision in *Woodhouse* v. *Hall* on the basis that the callers in *R* v. *Kearley (No. 1)* were unidentified persons who were merely enquiring about drugs, whereas the women in *Woodhouse* v. *Hall* actually '[offered] herself as a participant in physical acts of indecency for the sexual gratification of men'.[22] While the statements made by the callers in *R* v. *Kearley (No. 1)* were never actually verified by anyone at the premises, i.e. the defendant did not agree to supply drugs to these callers, the women employed in the premises in *Woodhouse* v. *Hall* were in fact offering to participate in sexual conduct. This latter type of statement has been termed 'operative words', i.e. 'words which have a legal effect irrespective of the intention of the person who wrote or spoke them'.[23] Thus, while the statements made by the women in *Woodhouse* v. *Hall* were operative in that they contribute directly to establishing that the premises were being used as a brothel, the same could not be said of the statements in *R* v. *Kearley (No. 1)*, which were never verified nor acted upon by the defendant.

More recently, in the case of *Twist and others*,[24] the Court of Appeal has disapproved of the use of the term 'implied assertion', approving the Law Commission's description of this term as 'a somewhat unfortunate expression'.[25] *R* v. *Twist* involved four cases heard together in the Court of Appeal in which the Court provided guidance on the way in which the hearsay provisions under the Criminal Justice Act 2003 apply to the admissibility of text messages. The principles laid down in this case were intended to be of general application to all forms of communication.[26] Hughes LJ provided guidance on the approach that should be taken to the question of whether the hearsay rules apply. He held that three questions should be asked:

1. What is the relevant fact (matter) which the party seeks to prove?
2. Is there a statement of *that matter* in the communication? If not, no question of hearsay arises (whatever other matters may be contained in the communication).
3. If yes, was one of the purposes (not necessarily the only or dominant purpose) of the maker of the communication that the recipient, or any other person, should believe *that matter* or act upon it as true? If yes, it is hearsay. If no, it is not.[27]

Cross-reference

For more detail on the case of *R* v. *Twist* [2011] EWCA Crim 1143 and the post-CJA 2003 approach to the old cases of 'implied assertions', refer to paragraph 7.4 below.

---

22 See Lord Ackner in *R* v. *Kearley (No. 1)* [1992] 2 AC 228 at 257G.
23 See R. Emson, *Evidence* 5th edn (Palgrave, 2010) at p. 108.
24 [2011] EWCA Crim 1143. For academic commentary on the case, see M. Hirst, 'Hearsay, confessions and mobile telephones' (2011) 75 JCL 482.
25 [2011] EWCA Crim 1143 at [19] and see Law Commission, *Evidence in Criminal Proceedings: Hearsay and Related Topics* (Report No. 245, Cm. 3670, 1997) at para. 7.7.
26 [2011] EWCA Crim 1143 at [1].
27 Ibid. at [17].

7.2.3 Evidence of identity or origin

The third category of admissible non-hearsay statements consists of statements which are admitted as circumstantial evidence of the identity or a person or the origin of an object. One such example is the case of *R* v. *Rice*,[28] in which the prosecution wished to adduce evidence of an airline ticket in the defendant's name in order to prove that the defendant had been on that particular flight. The Court of Appeal held that the ticket was admissible evidence to prove the identity of the person who took the flight. The basis for the decision in *R* v. *Rice* was questioned in *R* v. *Lydon (Sean)*.[29] The Court of Appeal in *R* v. *Lydon (Sean)* referred to a case from the Australian Supreme Court, *R* v. *Romeo*,[30] in which Cox J stated that the airline ticket in *R* v. *Rice* was clearly adduced as proof of the truth of the statement implicit in it, i.e. that someone called Rice was on the flight stated on the ticket.

The defendant in *R* v. *Lydon (Sean)* was convicted of robbery. Somewhere near the location at which the getaway car was found, the police discovered a gun and two pieces of rolled up paper which stated 'Sean rules' and 'Sean rules 85'. The ink used on the paper matched ink found on the barrel of the gun. The trial judge ruled that this evidence was admissible and this ruling was upheld by the Court of Appeal. However, the writings on the pieces of paper were not admitted to prove the truth of their contents, i.e. that Sean ruled, but they were admissible as evidence as to the identity of the person who wrote the statements. Thus, if the jury were satisfied that the gun was linked to the robbery and the pieces of paper were linked to the gun, then the writing on the paper would support the allegation that the defendant was involved in the robbery.

The defendant in *Myers* v. *DPP*[31] was charged with conspiracy to receive stolen cars, and other related offences. The prosecution case alleged that the defendant bought wrecked cars which were identical to cars that had been stolen. The defendant then transferred the registration details of the wrecked cars to the stolen cars and sold the stolen cars. The prosecution called employees of the car manufacturers to prove that the cars were stolen. The employees produced records which had been compiled by workmen when the cars were made. The witnesses had not created the records themselves, but were in charge of keeping the records. The records showed the engine, chassis and cylinder block numbers which were recorded by employees of the car manufacturer as the car was made. The cylinder block number was contained on a secret part of the block and could not be removed. Thus, the cylinder block number on the car and the record were identical, proving that the cars were stolen and passed off as legitimate cars. The defence argued that the evidence of the business records was inadmissible hearsay evidence as it was being adduced by a witness in order to prove the truth of its contents, namely that the men who made the records had entered the numbers that they had seen on the cars at the time of manufacture. As Lord Reid stated:

> The reason why this evidence is maintained to have been inadmissible is that its cogency depends on hearsay. The witness could only say that a record made by someone else showed that, if the record was correctly made, a car had left the works bearing three

---

28 [1963] 1 QB 857.
29 (1987) 85 Cr App R 221.
30 (1982) 30 SASR 243.
31 [1965] AC 1001, HL.

particular numbers. He could not prove that the record was correct or that the numbers which it contained were in fact the numbers on the car when it was made. This is a highly technical point, but the law regarding hearsay evidence is technical, and I would say absurdly technical. So I must consider whether in the existing state of the law that objection to the admissibility of this evidence must prevail.[32]

The reliability of the records could not be tested because the people who created the records were not only not available, but were not even identified to the court. Nevertheless, Lord Morris acknowledged that there was no reason to suppose that the workmen would make false entries and Lord Pearce declared the evidence to be 'fair, clear, reliable and sensible'.[33] However, while there was little danger of the evidence being unreliable or concocted, there was no established exception to the hearsay rule which covered the admissibility of business documents. Thus, by a 3:2 majority (Lords Reid, Morris and Hodson), the House of Lords held that the evidence was wrongly admitted by the Court of Criminal Appeal. Since the rule against hearsay and its exceptions were the result of common law development, it was surprising that the majority in the House of Lords was not prepared to create a new exception to the hearsay rule for business documents and that the House held that the creation of any future exceptions should be left to Parliament.

MYERS V. *DPP* [1965] AC 1001, HL
Lord Reid

[at 1021–2]

I have never taken a narrow view of the functions of this House as an appellate tribunal. The common law must be developed to meet changing economic conditions and habits of thought, and I would not be deterred by expressions of opinion in this House in old cases. But there are limits to what we can or should do. If we are to extend the law it must be by the development and application of fundamental principles. We cannot introduce arbitrary conditions or limitations: that must be left to legislation. And if we do in effect change the law, we ought in my opinion only to do that in cases where our decision will produce some finality or certainty. If we disregard technicalities in this case and seek to apply principle and common sense, there are a number of other parts of the existing law of hearsay susceptible of similar treatment, and we shall probably have a series of appeals in cases where the existing technical limitations produce an unjust result. If we are to give a wide interpretation to our judicial functions questions of policy cannot be wholly excluded, and it seems to me to be against public policy to produce uncertainty. The only satisfactory solution is by legislation following on a wide survey of the whole field, and I think that such a survey is overdue. A policy of make do and mend is no longer adequate. The most powerful argument of those who support the strict doctrine of precedent is that if it is relaxed judges will be tempted to encroach on the proper field of the legislature, and this case to my mind offers a strong temptation to do that which ought to be resisted. I must now explain why I think that to hold this evidence competent would be to change the law.

---

32 Ibid. at 1019F–G.
33 Ibid. at 1034E. It should be noted that Lord Pearce delivered a dissenting opinion in the minority of the House of Lords in *Myers* v. *DPP*.

> It was not disputed before your Lordships that to admit these records is to admit hearsay. They only tend to prove that a particular car bore a particular number when it was assembled if the jury were entitled to infer that the entries were accurate, at least in the main; and the entries on the cards were assertions by the unidentifiable men who made them that they had entered D numbers which they had seen on the cars. Counsel for the respondent were unable to argue that these records fell within any of the established exceptions or to adduce any reported case or any textbook as direct authority for their admission. Only four reasons for their admission were put forward. It was said that evidence of this kind is in practice admitted at least at the Central Criminal Court. Then it was argued that a judge has a discretion to admit such evidence. Then the reasons given in the Court of Criminal Appeal were relied on. And lastly it was said with truth that common sense rebels against the rejection of this evidence.
>
> . . . I ask what the jury would infer from them: obviously that they were probably true records. If they were not capable of supporting an inference that they were probably true records, then I do not see what probative value they could have, and their admission was bound to mislead the jury.

In light of the reluctance of the House of Lords to create a new common law exception to cover business documents, there was an immediate legislative response by Parliament with the enactment of the Criminal Evidence Act 1965 which reversed the decision of the House of Lords in *Myers* v. *DPP*, such that business records were admissible in criminal cases. This position was later governed by the Criminal Justice Act 1988, which created some statutory exceptions that related to documentary evidence. The admissibility of business documents is now covered by s. 117 of the Criminal Justice Act 2003, and such evidence would be admissible today by virtue of s. 114(1)(a) of the Act provided that the requirements under s. 117 are satisfied.

Cross-reference

For more detail on the admissibility of documentary evidence under s. 117 of the Criminal Justice Act 2003, see paragraph 7.5.2 below.

In summary, the purpose of adducing the out-of-court statement is crucial to determining whether the statement is hearsay or not, and thus to determining its admissibility. An out-of-court statement adduced in order to prove the truth of its contents is hearsay evidence which is generally inadmissible. By contrast, an out-of-court statement adduced in order to prove something other than the truth of its contents is original evidence which is generally admissible. The rule against hearsay evidence existed at common law, but the admissibility of hearsay evidence is now governed by the statutory framework found within the Criminal Justice Act 2003. The development of the law is considered in the following paragraph.

7.3 DEVELOPMENT OF THE LAW

At common law, hearsay evidence was generally inadmissible. The rationale for its exclusion was enunciated by Lord Normand in the House of Lords in *Teper* v. *R*:

> The rule against the admission of hearsay evidence is fundamental. It is not the best evidence and it is not delivered on oath. The truthfulness and accuracy of the person

whose words are spoken to by another witness cannot be tested by cross-examination, and the light which his demeanour would throw on his testimony is lost.[34]

Hearsay evidence is not the best evidence because it is not delivered in a courtroom and on oath. It is generally unreliable evidence because the maker of the statement is not present in court and available to be cross-examined in order to check the accuracy of the statement. The tribunal of fact is unable to assess the demeanour of the witness and how their testimony stands up to challenge, and thus, it is difficult for the tribunal to judge the credibility of the maker of the statement.

The common law developed a complicated set of rules to govern the admissibility of hearsay evidence in criminal proceedings. The general rule was that hearsay evidence was deemed to be inadmissible unless one of the exceptions to the rule applied. Most of the exceptions were to be found at common law. However, the common law was unsatisfactory for many reasons: it was complicated, confusing and inflexible as the courts were reluctant to create new exceptions. This inflexibility was most notable in the case of *Myers* v. *DPP*,[35] in which the House of Lords refused to extend the common law exceptions to apply to inherently reliable business documents.

> ### Cross-reference
> For more detail on the case of *Myers* v. *DPP*, see paragraph 7.2.3 above and for more detail on the admissibility of documentary evidence under s. 117 of the Criminal Justice Act 2003, see paragraph 7.5.2 below.

As stated above, the law on hearsay prior to the Criminal Justice Act 2003 was complicated, confusing and often unsatisfactory. A further example of the unsatisfactory nature of the law can be seen in the case of *R* v. *Kearley (No. 1)*.[36] In *R* v. *Kearley (No. 1)*, the House of Lords held that implied assertions were inadmissible despite the fact that the evidence of the implied assertions was likely to be reliable. As we have seen above, the decision in this case was criticised by commentators and it would seem that s. 115(3) of the Criminal Justice Act 2003 has now overturned the decision in *R* v. *Kearley (No. 1)* by ensuring that implied assertions do not fall within the definition of hearsay under the Criminal Justice Act 2003.

> ### Cross-reference
> For more detail on implied assertions and *R* v. *Kearley (No. 1)*, see paragraphs 7.2.2 and 7.4.1.

In 1991, the Royal Commission on Criminal Justice recommended that the law on hearsay be reformed in order to allow the admission of hearsay evidence in court to a greater extent. The rationale for this was to allow the jury to determine the weight to be given to evidence which is relevant, albeit hearsay evidence. The Commission recognised that the law on hearsay evidence in criminal proceedings was 'exceptionally complex and difficult to interpret'[37] and

---

34 [1952] AC 480 at 486.
35 [1965] AC 1001, HL.
36 [1992] 2 AC 228, HL.
37 *Report of the Royal Commission on Criminal Justice* (Cm. 2263, HMSO, 1991), at ch. 8, para. 26.

recommended that the Law Commission should explore the rules of hearsay before reformed. Consequently, the Law Commission published first a Consultation Paper[38] Report[39] which explored the rule against hearsay and made recommendations for reform. The law on hearsay was again considered by Sir Robin Auld in his *Review of the Criminal Courts of England and Wales.*[40] Auld recommended that the law should be reformed to admit of hearsay evidence in criminal proceedings and trust the jury to assess the weight of the evidence. The recommendations of both the Law Commission and Sir Robin Auld ultimately led to the enactment of the reforms in the Criminal Justice Act 2003 which sought to provide more flexibility to the admission of hearsay evidence and place more trust in the tribunal of fact to determine the cogency of such evidence.

7.4 HEARSAY UNDER THE CRIMINAL JUSTICE ACT 2003

As stated above, the Criminal Justice Act 2003 reformed the law on hearsay in criminal proceedings.[41] The Act permits the admission of hearsay evidence in certain specified circumstances. The law on hearsay is now largely covered by the statutory framework under the 2003 Act, although some aspects of the common law have been preserved under s. 118; these will be explored in paragraph 7.6 below. Since the enactment of the Criminal Justice Act 2003, the courts have confirmed that the effect of the Act is that the common law prohibition on the admissibility of hearsay evidence is still the 'default' rule, but that the Act has widened the categories of hearsay evidence which are admissible.[42] The wording of the Criminal Justice Act 2003 takes a positive, inclusionary approach to the admissibility of hearsay evidence as s. 114 (1) provides the circumstances in which hearsay is deemed to be admissible. Thus, hearsay evidence is admissible provided that one of the paragraphs under s. 114(1)(a) to (d) applies.

7.4.1 Definitions

Hearsay is defined by ss. 114 and 115 of the Criminal Justice Act 2003. Section 114(1) provides that 'In criminal proceedings a statement not made in oral evidence in the proceedings is admissible as evidence of any matter stated if . . .'. Thus, hearsay is a statement not made in oral evidence which is adduced as evidence of any matter stated. In *R* v. *Twist*, Hughes LJ stated that it is 'unsurprising' that the words 'admissible as evidence of any matter stated' requires us to ask what it is that a party is seeking to prove. His Lordship noted that most communications will

---

38 Law Commission, *Evidence in Criminal Proceedings and Related Matters* (Consultation Paper No. 138, 1995).
39 Law Commission, *Evidence in Criminal Proceedings: Hearsay and Related Topics* (Report No. 245, Cm. 3670, 1997).
40 Sir Robin Auld, *Review of the Criminal Courts of England and Wales* (2001), available at http://webarchive. nationalarchives.gov.uk/±/http://www.criminal-courts-review.org.uk/ (accessed on 19 July 2014).
41 For commentary on the provisions of the Criminal Justice Act 2003 which relate to hearsay, see Spencer, *Hearsay Evidence in Criminal Proceedings*; D. Birch, 'Hearsay: same old story, same old song?' [2004] Crim LR 556; D. Birch, 'The new law of hearsay: Criminal Justice Act 2003' (2005) 3 *Archbold News* 6–7; and T. Worthern, 'The hearsay provisions of the Criminal Justice Act 2003: so far, not so good?' [2008] Crim LR 431.
42 See *R* v. *Riat* [2013] 1 Cr App R at [3] and *R* v. *Friel (Christopher)* [2012] EWCA Crim 2871 at [18].

contain one or more matters stated, but that this does not necessarily mean that those matters are the matters which the party seeking to adduce the evidence is trying to prove:

> He may sometimes be trying to prove simply that two people were in communication with each other, and not be concerned with the content at all. On other occasions he may be trying to prove the relationship between the parties to the communication but not be in the least concerned with the veracity of the content of it. And there may, of course, be occasions where what he seeks to prove is that a matter stated in the communications is indeed fact. The opening words of section 114 show that it is the last of these situations which engages the rules against hearsay.[43]

The word 'statement' is widely defined under s. 115(2) to include 'any representation of fact or opinion made by a person by whatever means; and it includes a representation made in a sketch, photofit or other pictorial form'. Thus, a hearsay statement covers both representations of fact and opinion made by a person.

S. 115(2), CRIMINAL JUSTICE ACT 2003

A statement is any representation of fact or opinion made by a person by whatever means; and it includes a representation made in a sketch, photofit or other pictorial form.

The hearsay provisions only apply to representations made by a *person*, and do not apply to representations made by a machine, such as CCTV footage. Any such representations are not hearsay statements, and thus are admissible as real evidence.[44] Since the representation can be made by any means, it includes words spoken by a person, a written witness statement by a person, or any other form of written document, such as a police officer's notebook, a medical report, a receipt or a picture or drawing by a person (for instance, a sketch of the suspect). At common law, the hearsay rule also applied to assertions which were made by physical gesture. This is illustrated by the cases of *R* v. *Gibson*[45] and *Chandrasekera* v. *R*.[46] The case of *R* v. *Gibson* involved both a gesture and words spoken simultaneously. The defendant in this case was convicted of unlawfully and maliciously wounding a man with a stone. The victim gave evidence that after he was struck he heard a woman say, 'The person who threw the stone went in there' and that she pointed to the door of the defendant's house. The evidence was adduced in order to prove that the offender had entered the defendant's house, and thus from this it could be inferred that the defendant was the offender. However, the woman had not been identified to the court and therefore her reliability could not be tested. On appeal against conviction, it was held that the evidence of the unidentified woman's statement of identification should have been excluded as inadmissible hearsay. In *Chandrasekera* v. *R*, the defendant was convicted of murder. The victim's throat had been cut, rendering her unable to speak. However, while she was still conscious she made gestures which indicated that the defendant

---

43 [2011] EWCA Crim 1143 at [6].
44 See Spencer, above (n. 20) at para. 3.20.
45 [1887] QBD 537.
46 [1937] AC 220, PC.

had attacked her. When asked directly whether the defendant had caused her injuries, she nodded. The Privy Council held that while the evidence of gestures by the victim was hearsay evidence, it was admissible under an exception to the hearsay rule available under the old common law, namely that it constituted a dying declaration.[47] Thus, the hearsay rule also applied to assertions by physical gesture.

The hearsay provisions also only apply to statements which were made for the purpose of (or if one of the purposes for making the statement was) causing another person to believe the matter or causing another person to act or a machine to operate on the basis that the matter is as stated.

S. 115(3), CRIMINAL JUSTICE ACT 2003

A matter stated is one to which this Chapter applies if (and only if) the purpose, or one of the purposes, of the person making the statement appears to the court to have been –

(a) to cause another person to believe the matter, or
(b) to cause another person to act or a machine to operate on the basis that the matter is as stated.

There has been a string of cases concerning implied assertions and the meaning of a 'matter stated' under s. 115(3) of the Criminal Justice Act 2003. As stated above, this requires us to ask what it is that a party is seeking to prove.[48] Under s. 115(3), hearsay evidence is evidence which is adduced in order to cause another person to believe the matter stated in the statement (i.e. the truth of its contents), or to cause another person to act (or a machine to operate) on the basis of that matter. This means that the hearsay provisions only apply to statements meant as an assertion, and not to implied assertions, thus overturning *R* v. *Kearley (No. 1)*. This was confirmed by the Court of Appeal in *R* v. *Singh*[49] and more recently in *R* v. *Twist*.[50] The defendant in *R* v. *Singh* was charged with conspiracy to kidnap and evidence of calls between the defendant's mobile phones and those of his co-conspirators. In particular, the prosecution adduced evidence of the memories of the mobile phones of the defendant's co-conspirators, which contained the defendant's mobile numbers. The defendant appealed against his conviction on the grounds that the trial judge was wrong to admit the evidence of the memories of the mobile phones because these were implied assertions which are inadmissible, despite the Criminal Justice Act 2003. This argument was rejected by the Court of Appeal, which held that ss. 114 and 118 of the Criminal Justice Act 2003 abolished the old common law rule against hearsay and created a new rule.

---

47 The dying declarations exception to the rule against hearsay was abolished when the hearsay provisions in the Criminal Justice 2003 came into force. However, statements by a deceased would now fall under s. 116(2)(a) of the Criminal Justice Act 2003 as evidence of an unavailable witness due to death, and thus it would be admissible by virtue of s. 114(1)(a) of the Act.

48 Per Hughes LJ in [2011] EWCA Crim 1143 at [6].

49 [2006] EWCA Crim 660.

50 [2011] EWCA Crim 1143. Hughes LJ noted that '[t]he Act does not use the expression "assertion" ... That seems likely to have been because its framers wished to avoid the complex philosophical arguments which beset the common law, as explained in [*Kearley*] ...' at [8].

R V. SINGH [2006] EWCA CRIM 660
Rose LJ

[13] ... Under *Kearley* an unintentional implied assertion was excluded as hearsay. The object of section 115(3) is to draw a line between intentional implied assertions still caught by the hearsay rule and unintentional implied assertions no longer treated as hearsay. Accordingly, only hearsay statements within section 114 are admissible. Section 115(3) means that section 114 does not apply to statements unless the purpose of their maker was to cause belief in the hearer; an unintentional implied assertion remains hearsay, because this is what *Kearley* said, and is now always inadmissible. In the present case, the entries in the telephone memories and on the envelope were unintentional implied assertions outwith section 115(3) and therefore inadmissible.

[14] The interrelationship between sections 114 and 115 is deeply obscure. But, in our judgment, ... the common law rule against the admissibility of hearsay is abolished by the clear express terms to that effect of section 118 ... When sections 114 and 118 are read together they, in our judgment, abolish the common law hearsay rules (save those which are expressly preserved) and create instead a new rule against hearsay which does not extend to implied assertions. What was said by the callers in *Kearley* would now be admissible as direct evidence of the fact that there was a ready market for the supply of drugs from the premises, from which could be inferred an intention by an occupier to supply drugs. The view of the majority in *Kearley*, in relation to hearsay, has been set aside by the Act.

[15] So, in the present case, the telephone entries are not a matter stated within section 115. They are implied assertions which are admissible because they are no longer hearsay. Furthermore they are also admissible under section 118(1)(vii), as statements by an admitted co-conspirator against another party to the enterprise ... A third possible route to admissibility is provided by section 114(2)(d).

The Court held that the new law under the Criminal Justice Act 2003 did not extend to implied assertions, and thus, implied assertions are now no longer hearsay statements and as such are admissible just like any other evidence in the ordinary course of a trial. The appeal was dismissed and the defendant's conviction was upheld.

This was reiterated by the Court of Appeal in *R* v. *Leonard* in which Aikens LJ stated: 'It is clear from section 114(1) and section 118(2) that the common law rules governing the admissibility of hearsay evidence in criminal proceedings are abolished with the exception of the rules preserved by section 118 itself. The common law rules are replaced by the statutory code which governs what is hearsay evidence and when it can be admitted as evidence in criminal proceedings'.[51] The defendant was charged with possession of drugs with intent to supply and two text messages were found on his phone which commented on the quality of the drugs received by the senders of the text messages. One of the text messages read, 'Cheers for yday! Well sound gear:-S! feel well wankered today!' The Court of Appeal held that the messages should not have been admissible because the senders of the messages intended the defendant to believe the matters stated in the messages, namely that the drugs supplied were 'well sound' and that the sender did 'feel well wankered today'. However, the Court of Appeal in *R* v. *Twist*[52] commented that the result would have been different if the prosecution had instead relied upon

---

51 [2009] EWCA Crim 1251 at [30].
52 [2011] EWCA Crim 1143.

the text messages to show that the relationship between the defendant and the sender of the messages was one of drug dealer and customer, rather than to prove the quality of the drugs supplied.[53] The Court in *R* v. *Twist* held that the evidence would have been admissible as an implied assertion if the prosecution had sought to rely on the messages to prove that the defendant was a drug dealer.

In *R* v. *MK*,[54] the Court of Appeal held that evidence of a phone conversation in which the defendant was asked about the availability of drugs and prices was not hearsay because the purpose of the statement was to find out the availability and price of drugs. The evidence did not contain a representation that the defendant was his supplier, but it did constitute an implied assertion of this. It was not the caller's purpose to cause the defendant to believe any representation, nor to act upon its truth. This approach was approved by the Court of Appeal more recently in *R* v. *Twist*.[55] In the case of *R* v. *Chrysostomou*,[56] the Court of Appeal also held that implied assertions are not caught by the hearsay provisions under the Criminal Justice Act 2003. The prosecution sought to adduce text messages which had been found on the defendant's mobile phone as evidence of the defendant's bad character, namely that he was a drug dealer. There were four text messages which read: 'Mate can you get me a henry in for Thursday? I will be in on wed', 'Can I meet you about mid day ish tomorrow for henry? Ta mate and is it still £100?', 'Morning mate, I need 7 g will you do it for 200' and 'If your about sometime today with any stuff on you can you let me know, ta'. The Court of Appeal held that these text messages were admissible as evidence that the defendant was a drug dealer. The Court provided the approach which should be taken to determining the admissibility of a statement which was not given in oral evidence in the proceedings and held that there were three preliminary questions which needed to be asked:

1. Is the evidence relevant?
2. If so, is the evidence a 'statement' within the meaning of s. 115(2) of the Criminal Justice Act 2003?
3. If so, what is the purpose for adducing the statement in evidence?

In this case, it was not disputed that the statements were relevant and the court accepted that the evidence constituted 'statements' under s. 115(2). However, the purpose of the prosecution in adducing the statements was not to prove any matter stated within them, rather the statements were an implied assertion, requiring the jury to infer from the text messages that the defendant was a drug dealer. Since the statements were implied assertions, they were not caught by the hearsay provisions under the Criminal Justice Act 2003 and they were admissible. The Court of Appeal doubted the decision of the House of Lords in *R* v. *Kearley (No. 1)*.

Most recently, in *R* v. *Twist*, the Court of Appeal provided guidance on the way in which the Criminal Justice Act 2003 provisions apply to communications made to, or by, the defendant. The Court preferred that the phrase 'implied assertion' be avoided. The decision of the Court of

---

53 Ibid. at [24].
54 [2007] EWCA Crim 3150.
55 The same approach was followed in *R* v. *Elliott* [2010] EWCA Crim 2378 and this was also approved by the Court of Appeal in *R* v. *Twist*.
56 [2010] EWCA Crim 1403.

Appeal involved four cases which were heard together which all involved text messages sent by mobile telephones, although the Court was keen to state that the principles in the decision apply equally to all forms of communication. The text messages in two of the cases consisted of requests to supply drugs to the sender (where an intention to supply drugs needed to be established for a conviction),[57] and in one case of a request for a gun to be delivered to the sender (in a case of robbery involving a firearm).[58] The fourth case differed in that the text messages relied on were messages sent by the defendant to the complainant. This was a case of rape in which the defendant made admissions which the prosecution sought to rely on to establish that there had been a rape.[59] The Court confirmed again that the Criminal Justice Act 2003 abolished the common law rules of hearsay, except where it was expressly preserved under s. 118. The Court stated that hearsay evidence was generally inadmissible unless it qualified for admission under one of the paragraphs under s. 114(1). It is important to determine two factors:

1. the purpose for which the relevant party seeks to admit the evidence, and
2. the purpose of the maker of the statement.

Where the party sought to prove the truth of a matter stated in the statement and one of the purposes of the maker of the statement was that the recipient or another person should believe the matter stated or act upon it as if it were true, then the evidence would qualify as hearsay and its admissibility would be subject to s. 114(1). Where the evidence is not hearsay, then the usual tests of admissibility must be applied and the evidence must first be deemed to be relevant. The evidence of text messages in this case was not hearsay and was admissible in evidence.

R V. TWIST [2011] EWCA CRIM 1143
Hughes LJ

[8] The Act does not use the expression 'assertion'. Instead it speaks of a 'statement' and the 'matter stated' in it. That seems likely to have been because its framers wished to avoid the complex philosophical arguments which beset the common law, as explained in *DPP v Kearley [1992] 2 AC 228*, as to when an utterance contains an implied assertion. That was a case of telephone calls to the home of the defendant, all seeking the supply of drugs, on which the Crown sought to rely as evidence that he was in the habit of supplying them. The House of Lords held, by a majority, that the calls amounted to 'implied assertions' that the defendant was a drug dealer and that they were for that reason hearsay. It was accepted by counsel in *R v Singh [2006] EWCA Crim 660* ... and held by the court ..., that the evident intention of the Act was to reverse Kearley ... There is no trace of any change of policy in the statute and the policy is unsurprising. The principal underlying reason why hearsay evidence is only admissible in limited circumstances lies in the danger of concoction and the difficulty of testing or contradicting it when the speaker is not in court to be examined upon it ...

---

57 In *R* v. *Twist* and *R* v. *Boothman* [2011] EWCA Crim 1143.
58 In *R* v. *Tomlinson and Kelly* [2011] EWCA Crim 1143.
59 In *R* v. *Lowe* [2011] EWCA Crim 1143.

[9] It is therefore helpful, as it seems to us, that the Act avoids the use of the expression 'assertion' altogether, and with it the difficult concept of the 'implied assertion'. Instead, the Act concentrates the mind on the 'matter stated', which it is sought to prove. This is defined by reference to the purpose of the maker (ie usually the speaker or sender of the communication). The matter stated must be something which the maker intended someone (generally the recipient, since it is to him that the communication is addressed) to believe or to act upon: s 115(3).

. . .

[11] There are therefore two questions which have to be addressed in most cases:

i) what is the matter which it is sought to prove ? (it must of course be a relevant matter), and
ii) did the maker of the communication have the purpose of causing the recipient to believe or to act upon that matter ?

[12] In addressing these questions, and the application of the Act generally, it needs to be remembered that to say that a communication is <u>evidence</u> of a fact (ie tends to prove it) is not the same as saying that that fact is the matter stated in the communication for the purposes of the Act.

. . .

[15] Some communications may contain no statement at all. If, for example, the communication does no more than ask a question, it is difficult to see how it contains any statement. A text message to someone asking 'Will you have any crack tomorrow?' seems to us to contain no statement at all. But even if it be analysed as containing an 'implied assertion' that the recipient is a drug dealer, that fact is still not a 'matter stated' for the purposes of sections 114 and 115(3) because the sender does not have any purpose to cause the recipient to believe that fact or to act upon the basis that it is true. They both know it, and it is the common basis of their communication.

[16] Similarly, it is important when applying the statute to distinguish between:

i) the speaker wishing the hearer to act upon his **message**; and
ii) the speaker wishing the hearer to act upon the basis that a **matter stated in the message is as stated (ie true)**.

Only the second will bring into operation the hearsay rules. If the sender asks whether the recipient will have any crack tomorrow, he does indeed want the recipient to act on his message because he hopes to extract an answer to his question. Even more clearly he does so if he goes one step further and asks for crack to be sold to him tomorrow, because then he hopes to receive a supply. But in neither case does he have the purpose of causing the recipient of his message to believe that the recipient is a drug dealer, or to act on the basis that that is the truth.

[17] Generally, therefore, it is likely to be helpful to approach the question whether the hearsay rules apply in this way:

i) identify what relevant fact (matter) it is sought to prove;
ii) ask whether there is a statement of **that matter** in the communication. If no, then no question of hearsay arises (whatever other matters may be contained in the communication);
iii) if yes, ask whether it was one of the purposes (not necessarily the only or dominant purpose) of the maker of the communication that the recipient, or any other person, should believe **that matter** or act upon it as true ? If yes, it is hearsay. If no, it is not.

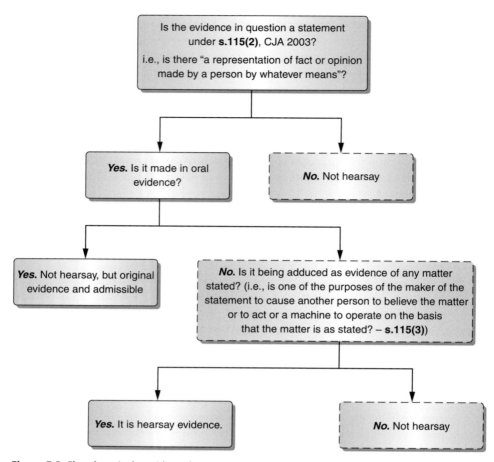

Figure 7.2 Flowchart: is the evidence hearsay?

Thus, in order to determine whether a piece of evidence is hearsay, the relevant fact which the party seeks to prove must first be identified, it must then be asked whether there is a statement of that matter in the communication in question. If so, it must be established whether the evidence is adduced as evidence of any matter stated, i.e. one of the purposes of the maker of the statement is that a person should believe the matter or act upon it (see Figure 7.2 for a flowchart to determine whether evidence is hearsay).

7.4.2 Admissibility

Having determined that a piece of evidence is hearsay, the next question to be determined is whether that hearsay is admissible in court. In *R* v. *Riat (Jaspal)*,[60] the Court of Appeal suggested that there are six successive steps to determining the admissibility of hearsay evidence.

---

60 [2012] EWCA Crim 1509.

R V. RIAT (JASPAL) [2012] EWCA CRIM 1509

[7] The statutory framework provided for hearsay evidence by the CJA 2003 can usefully be considered in these successive steps:

i) Is there a specific statutory justification (or 'gateway') permitting the admission of hearsay evidence (ss.116–118)?
ii) What material is there which can help to test or assess the hearsay (s.124)?
iii) Is there a specific 'interests of justice' test at the admissibility stage?
iv) If there is no other justification or gateway, should the evidence nevertheless be considered for admission on the grounds that admission is, despite the difficulties, in the interests of justice (s.114(1)(d))?
v) Even if prima facie admissible, ought the evidence to be ruled inadmissible (s.78 PACE and/or s.126 CJA)?
vi) If the evidence is admitted, then should the case subsequently be stopped under section 125?

The following paragraphs will consider the gateways of admissibility under s. 114(1) of the Criminal Justice Act 2003. Section 114(1) governs the admissibility of hearsay evidence in criminal proceedings.

S. 114(1), CRIMINAL JUSTICE ACT 2003

In criminal proceedings a statement not made in oral evidence in the proceedings is admissible as evidence of any matter stated if, but only if –

(a) any provision of this Chapter or any other statutory provision makes it admissible,
(b) any rule of law preserved by section 118 makes it admissible,
(c) all parties to the proceedings agree to it being admissible, or
(d) the court is satisfied that it is in the interests of justice for it to be admissible.

As stated above, while the 'default' position under the Criminal Justice Act 2003 is that hearsay evidence is inadmissible, the wording of the Act presents a positive, inclusionary approach to the admission of hearsay evidence. Thus, there are four main circumstances in which hearsay evidence is deemed to be admissible. According to s. 114(1), hearsay evidence is admissible if one of the four paragraphs (a) to (d) is satisfied. These four circumstances of admissibility are presented in Figure 7.3.

In order to determine whether hearsay evidence is admissible under s. 114(1), the flow-chart at Figure 7.4 may be helpful to work through the four paragraphs providing for admissibility. However, it should be noted that the paragraphs are not mutually exclusive; thus, an application to adduce hearsay evidence might be made under more than one paragraph, and a judge might determine that hearsay evidence is admissible under more than one of these paragraphs.

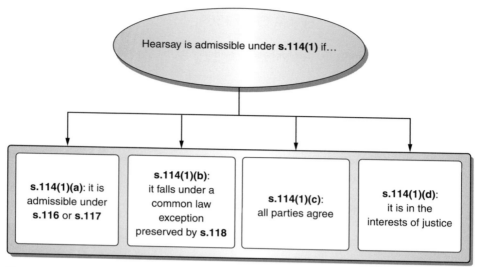

Figure 7.3 Admissibility of hearsay evidence under the Criminal Justice Act 2003

The following text will consider each of the paragraphs of admissibility in turn.

7.5 ADMISSIBILITY UNDER S. 114(1)(A): STATUTORY ADMISSIBILITY

Under s. 114(1)(a) of the Criminal Justice Act 2003, hearsay evidence is admissible if it is admissible by virtue of s. 116 or s. 117 of the Act. Section 116 provides for the admissibility of the evidence of a witness who is unavailable to give evidence. Section 117 provides for the admissibility of a business document. The paragraph below will deal with each of these provisions.

7.5.1 Unavailable witnesses under s. 116

Sometimes a witness to a criminal offence who makes a statement at the time of the incident may not be available to give evidence by the time of the trial, many months later. As the party calling the witness would seek to adduce this evidence in order to prove the truth of what was contained within the statement, the witness statement is hearsay evidence. Where a witness later becomes unavailable, the party seeking to rely on the evidence of the witness might make an application to adduce the witness's written statement in court in place of calling the witness. The witness's written statement, made around the time of the incident, could be read out in court if the trial judge deems it to be admissible. Where the prosecution makes an application to adduce the witness statement of an unavailable witness under s. 114(1), the admissibility of the evidence in the witness statement might be so important to the prosecution case that without it the prosecution case might be much weaker, or even so weak that the case cannot be successfully prosecuted.

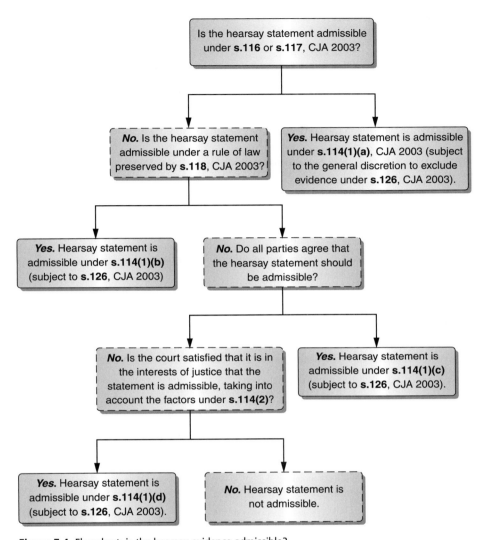

Figure 7.4 Flowchart: is the hearsay evidence admissible?

The defence interest in the statement being deemed inadmissible must also be considered. Where a witness statement is simply read out, the defence will find it very difficult, if not impossible, to challenge matters raised in the statement. The judge must weigh these competing interests and other factors in deciding whether the hearsay evidence is admissible or not.

Section 116(1) provides that hearsay evidence is admissible if three circumstances are satisfied:

- the hearsay evidence must be evidence which would be admissible in oral evidence if the maker of the statement was available (s. 116(1)(a)),
- the maker of the statement is identified to the court's satisfaction (s. 116(1)(b)), and
- the witness is unavailable due to one of the five conditions under s. 116(2) (s. 116(1)(c)).

S. 116, CRIMINAL JUSTICE ACT 2003

(1) In criminal proceedings a statement not made in oral evidence in the proceedings is admissible as evidence of any matter stated if –

    (a) oral evidence given in the proceedings by the person who made the statement would be admissible as evidence of that matter,

    (b) the person who made the statement (the relevant person) is identified to the court's satisfaction, and

    (c) any of the five conditions mentioned in subsection (2) is satisfied.

(2) The conditions are –

    (a) that the relevant person is dead;

    (b) that the relevant person is unfit to be a witness because of his bodily or mental condition;

    (c) that the relevant person is outside the United Kingdom and it is not reasonably practicable to secure his attendance;

    (d) that the relevant person cannot be found although such steps as it is reasonably practicable to take to find him have been taken;

    (e) that through fear the relevant person does not give (or does not continue to give) oral evidence in the proceedings, either at all or in connection with the subject matter of the statement, and the court gives leave for the statement to be given in evidence.

The five conditions of unavailability require that the witness is unavailable because either:

  (i)   the witness has died,

  (ii) the witness is unfit to be a witness due to his bodily or mental condition,

 (iii) the witness is outside the United Kingdom and it is not reasonably practicable to secure his attendance at court,

  (iv) the witness cannot be found despite taking reasonable steps to find him, or

  (v) leave of the court is given due to the witness's fear.

Each of these conditions shall be explored in turn.

(i) Section 116(2)(a): witness has died

This provision echoes the former statutory framework under s. 23 of the Criminal Justice Act 1988.[61] The condition under s. 116(2)(a) of the Criminal Justice Act 2003 does not require much elaboration. Where the maker of the statement is no longer alive, then another person may give evidence of the statement made by the deceased in order to establish that what the deceased said was true. This provision marked an extension of the old common law under which only a witness's 'dying declaration' was admissible as an exception to the rule against hearsay. Dying declarations were a very narrow exception under which the deceased's statement had to relate to the cause of his death and it was only admissible if the prosecution could prove that at the time of making the statement, the deceased had a 'settled, hopeless expectation of impending

---

61 See s. 23(2)(a), Criminal Justice Act 2003 which was repealed on 4 April 2005.

death'.[62] The provision under s. 116(2)(a) is much wider than this, allowing for the admission of a statement made by the deceased about any subject matter and without any requirement of an expectation of death. Provided that oral evidence of the matter would be admissible had the witness been in court and the deceased is identified, then the statement made by the deceased will be admissible under s. 116(1). This provision was applied in the case of *R* v. *Musone*,[63] in which the prosecution sought to adduce evidence of a prisoner's dying declaration ('Musone's just stabbed me') to a fellow prisoner. The evidence was held to be admissible under s. 116(1). A more recent example of the application of s. 116(2)(a) can be found in *R* v. *Friel (Christopher)*.[64] The defendant in this case appealed against his conviction of robbery on the basis that (*inter alia*) the trial judge erred in admitting the hearsay evidence of a witness who had since died. The Court of Appeal held that '[t]here was an obvious gateway for admissibility under section 116(2)(a)'.[65]

Under s. 116(5) a condition under s. 116(2) is to be treated as not satisfied if the condition is attributable to the party seeking to adduce the statement of the witness in evidence or if it is attributable to a person acting on that party's behalf, in order to prevent the witness from giving evidence.

S. 116(5), CRIMINAL JUSTICE ACT 2003

A condition set out in any paragraph of subsection (2) which is in fact satisfied is to be treated as not satisfied if it is shown that the circumstances described in that paragraph are caused –

(a) by the person in support of whose case it is sought to give the statement in evidence, or
(b) by a person acting on his behalf,

in order to prevent the relevant person giving oral evidence in the proceedings (whether at all or in connection with the subject matter of the statement).

Thus, if the party seeking to adduce the statement of the witness in evidence kills the witness or has someone kill the witness on his behalf, the condition under s. 116(2)(a) will not be satisfied and thus the statement of the witness will be inadmissible.

(ii) Section 116(2)(b): witness is unfit by reason of bodily or mental condition

The condition under s. 116(2)(b) requires that the witness is unfit to be a witness due to a bodily or mental condition. A similar provision which allowed for hearsay evidence to be admitted due to the unfitness of the witness also featured in the former legislative framework under s. 23 of the Criminal Justice Act 1988. Section 23(2)(a) stated that 'a statement made by a person in a document shall be admissible in criminal proceedings as evidence of any fact of which direct oral evidence by him would be admissible if . . . the person who made the statement is . . . by

---

62 See *R* v. *Perry* [1909] 2 KB 697. The dying declaration exception was a very narrow exception which did not apply to all statements made on the deathbed: it only applied to statements which related to the cause of the victim's death.
63 [2007] EWCA Crim 1237.
64 [2012] EWCA Crim 2871.
65 Ibid. at [37].

reason of his bodily or mental condition unfit to attend as a witness'. In light of the fact that the unfitness of the witness was also a reason for admitting hearsay evidence under the 1988 Act, it has been suggested that we must presume that the case law relating to s. 23 of the 1988 Act is still relevant.[66] There is one very subtle difference in the wording of these two sections, with the 1988 provision requiring that the witness is unfit to *attend* as a witness while the 2003 Act requires that the witness is unfit to *be* a witness. It is submitted that this difference is of no significance. In *R* v. *Setz-Dempsey*; *R* v. *Richardson*,[67] Beldam LJ commented that the words in s. 23(2)(a) 'are not intended merely to apply to the physical act of getting to court but to the capacity of the witness when there to give evidence'.[68] The 2003 Act clearly covers witnesses who are able to attend court, but by reason of their bodily or mental condition are unfit to give evidence. However, it would be very surprising if the 2003 Act was not also applied to witnesses who are unable to attend court by reason of their bodily or mental condition. It is suggested that the courts will treat s. 116(2)(b) in the same way as its predecessor, and this approach is borne out more recently in the Divisional Court's reference to the provisions being 'in identical terms'[69] and in the Divisional Court's use of the word 'attend' when discussing the section: 'This provision is of course an important one and it is necessary that statements of witnesses who are indeed unfit to attend trial because of their bodily or mental condition should be able to be given, otherwise crimes may well not be brought home'.[70]

The burden of proving that the witness is unfit to give evidence is on the party seeking to adduce the hearsay evidence and the standard of proof is the criminal standard, beyond reasonable doubt.[71] It is for the judge to decide whether a witness is unfit to attend as a witness. The judge is the expert on whether a person is capable of giving evidence, and while a doctor's advice may assist the judge in reaching his decision, it is not conclusive of the matter, even where it is the only or main evidence on the matter.[72]

Some of the pre-2003 cases may assist us in determining the types of condition which might render a witness unavailable under s. 116(2)(b). In *R* v. *Millett*,[73] the Court of Appeal agreed with the trial judge's assessment that a witness was 'unfit to come to court and give evidence because it creates a risk of a permanent and very serious and potentially catastrophic adverse effect on her health and in my judgment that is what this section, Section 23 of the Criminal Justice Act, 1988 was intended to prevent occurring'[74] and held that 'as a matter of law, a witness who runs a modest risk of potentially serious, permanent consequences may properly be found to be unfit to attend as a witness within the meaning of the statute'.[75] In *R* v. *Setz-Dempsey*; *R* v. *Richardson*,[76] a witness, who suffered from a mental disorder, was unable to remember the relevant events after he had been sworn in to give evidence and despite attempting to refresh his

---

66 Spencer above (n. 20) at para. 6.14.
67 (1994) 98 Cr App R 23.
68 Ibid. at 27.
69 See *R (on the application of Meredith)* v. *Harwich Justices* [2006] EWHC 3336 (Admin) at [7].
70 Ibid. at [8].
71 Per Henry LJ in *R* v. *Millett*, unreported, 21 July 2000, CA (Crim Div), Transcript no. 99/07705/W2 at [8].
72 See *R* v. *Lang* [2004] EWCA Crim 1701 at [6] and [9].
73 Above (n. 71).
74 Ibid. at [12].
75 Ibid. at [13].
76 (1994) 98 Cr App R 23.

memory from his witness statement. There was medical evidence that the mental disorder of the witness meant that under stress the witness became very anxious and unable to provide a coherent account and to recall matters. The Court of Appeal held that s. 23(2)(a) of the Criminal Justice Act 1988 was not to be so narrowly construed as to only apply to witnesses who were unable to physically attend court, but it applied equally to witnesses who, having attended court (and indeed, having started to give evidence), did not have the capacity to give evidence.

Section 116(5) applies to all of the conditions under s. 116(2). Thus, the condition under s. 116(2)(b) will not be satisfied if the fact that the witness is unfit is attributable to the party seeking to adduce the statement of the witness in evidence or if it is attributable to a person acting on that party's behalf, in order to prevent the witness from giving evidence. If the condition is attributed to the party, the statement of the witness will be inadmissible.

(iii) Section 116(2)(c): witness is outside the United Kingdom

The condition under s. 116(2)(c) requires that the witness is outside the United Kingdom and it is not reasonably practicable to secure his attendance. This condition was also a feature of the legislative framework under s. 23(2)(b) of the Criminal Justice Act 1988 and the previous case law relating to this condition also still applies. The courts have considered the meaning of the phrase 'reasonably practicable' and what steps the party seeking to rely on the evidence of the witness would need to take to prove to the court that it is not 'reasonably practicable' to secure the attendance of the witness. In *R* v. *C and K*,[77] a key prosecution witness, who was in South Africa, told a police officer that he had changed his mind about coming to the United Kingdom to give evidence at trial. The trial judge ruled that the prosecution could not reasonably secure the witness's attendance and that his witness statement was admissible as his evidence. However, the Court of Appeal held that this expression 'reasonably practicable' had to be judged on the basis of the steps taken, or not taken, by the prosecution. The prosecution in this case had not taken sufficient steps to ascertain the witness's reasons for changing his mind: 'We . . . see force in the contention . . . that further enquiries as to why the witness has changed his mind, and has refused to give evidence via video-link are reasonably required. The police officer who had spoken to the witness on a number of occasions, and met him in South Africa, was "very surprised" by "his sudden change of heart". Further enquiries were, in our view, appropriate.'[78] The Court of Appeal held that a judge deciding on the admissibility of hearsay evidence under s. 116(2)(c) should also consider whether to exclude the evidence using its general discretion to exclude evidence under s. 126 of the Criminal Justice Act 2003 or s. 78 of the Police and Criminal Evidence Act 1984 and stated that '[w]hether it is fair to admit the statement or statements depends, in part, on what efforts should reasonably be made to secure the attendance of the witness or, at least, to arrange a procedure whereby the contents of the statements can be clarified and challenged'.[79] The Court also considered the pre-2003 authority of *R* v. *Radak*, in which a witness who was living in the United States refused to come to court in the United Kingdom to give evidence. The Court of Appeal held in that case that a witness giving evidence through a live television link under s. 32 of the Criminal Justice Act 1988 would also

---

77 [2006] EWCA Crim 197.
78 Ibid. at [25].
79 Ibid. at [24].

constitute attendance for the purposes of s. 23(2)(b) of that Act. Thus, 'attendance' for the purposes of s. 116(2)(c) of the Criminal Justice Act 2003 also covers both physical presence in the courtroom and giving evidence via a live television link.[80]

As stated above, s. 116(5) applies to all of the conditions under s. 116(2). Thus, the condition under s. 116(2)(c) will not be satisfied if the fact that the witness is outside the United Kingdom and it is not reasonably practicable to secure his attendance is attributable to the party seeking to adduce the statement of the witness in evidence or if it is attributable to a person acting on that party's behalf, in order to prevent the witness from giving evidence. Thus, the statement of the witness will be inadmissible.

(iv) Section 116(2)(d): witness cannot be found

The condition under s. 116(2)(d) requires that the witness cannot be found although such steps as it is reasonably practicable to take to find him have been taken. A similar provision was also found in the old law, under s. 23(2)(c) of the Criminal Justice Act 1988. The courts have considered the meaning of the expression 'such steps as it is reasonably practicable to take' in determining the applicability of s. 116(2)(d). In CT v. R,[81] where no request was made to the witness to attend the trial until after the trial had started, the prosecution attempts to secure the attendance of the witness fell well below what was considered reasonable. In R v. Adams,[82] a witness who was required to give evidence at a trial on a Monday was phoned on the Friday before and a message was left for him. He had been notified about the trial date approximately 3 or 4 months before the start of the trial and had indicated then that he would attend, but no further contact had been made with the witness until the last working day before the start of the trial. When the witness did not attend court on the Monday another call was made to him but he did not answer his phone. The trial judge concluded that the witness could not be found and that such steps as were reasonably practicable had been taken to find him, and ruled that his witness statement could be admitted under s. 116(2)(d). The defendant appealed against his conviction and the Court of Appeal held that while the trial judge had been correct to rule that the witness could not be found, the efforts made to notify the witness about the trial did not constitute taking reasonably practicable steps. The Court of Appeal considered the phone call to the witness on the last working day before the trial a 'wholly inadequate approach of those whose duty it was to keep in touch with the witness' and criticised the steps taken to contact the witness:

> the need to keep in touch, to be alive to the witness's needs and commitments is not less now than it ever was; if anything it is rather greater now than it used to be. Leaving contact with a witness such as this until the last working day before the trial is not good enough and it certainly is not such steps as it is reasonably practicable to take to find him. In addition to that, once the message was not known to have been received on the Friday and there was doubt about it, ... reasonably practicable steps which ought to have been taken included a visit to his address and/or to his place of work or agency, or at least contact with those places, perhaps by telephone.[83]

---

80 See R v. E [2010] EWCA Crim 3302 and R v. Cheema [2010] EWCA Crim 1352.
81 [2011] EWCA Crim 2341.
82 [2008] 1 Cr App R 35, CA.
83 Ibid. per Hughes LJ at [13].

In *R* v. *T(D)*,[84] the Court of Appeal was very critical of the informal manner in which the trial judge had dealt with the issue of the witness's absence. The Court of Appeal held that the evidence of a witness had been wrongly admitted where no attempt had been made to explore the steps taken by the police to maintain contact with the witness and find out where she had gone or what information the witness's mother or social security had regarding the witness's whereabouts. There had been no evidence of any attempt to trace the location of the witness's mobile phone activity through cell site analysis, and although submissions were made to the Court of Appeal that this is an expensive technique to be used in such cases, the Court of Appeal was quite critical that there had also been no evidence as to the cost of such analysis either.

R V. *T(D)* [2009] EWCA CRIM 1213
Thomas LJ

The approach to s. 116(2)(d)

25. In the recent decision of this court in *Horncastle* [2009] EWCA Crim 964 the court dealt with the position of witnesses who were in fear. At paragraph 87 the court said:

> It is, however, important that all possible efforts are made to get the witness to court. As is clear, the right to confrontation is a longstanding requirement of the common law and recognised in Article 6(3)(d). It is only to be departed from in the limited circumstances and under the conditions set out in the CJA 2003. The witness must be given all possible support, but also made to understand the importance of the citizen's duty . . .

26. Although the court was in that instance dealing with witnesses who were kept from court through fear, the principle applicable is the same in the case of a witness who is reluctant to come to court and absents himself. It is important that all efforts are made to get the witness to court; this must start with the witness being given all possible support and made to understand the importance of the citizen's duty to give evidence.

27. The right to confrontation is a long-standing right of the common law and is reflected in the European Convention at Article 6(3)(d). The right to confrontation is not to be lightly departed from. The provisions of the Criminal Justice Act 2003, described in *Horncastle* as a carefully crafted code, need to be observed carefully.

28. It seems to us that in a case of this kind, unless there is a written agreed statement of facts, it is simply not possible to proceed to consider an application without evidence as to the steps taken to find the witness.

29. Our conclusion

30. If an agreed statement of facts had been produced in this case, it would have exposed the error in the approach of the learned judge, which was to look at the matter, as if this witness was reluctant from the time when the police started to make enquiries after the PCMH in the month before the trial. It is apparent from the witness's own statement that she was reluctant from the day she made the

---

84 [2009] EWCA Crim 1213.

statement. She said she would not come and therefore was at risk of breaking contact so she could not be found.

31. There was, because matters proceeded so informally before the judge, no attempt to try and explore what steps the police had taken through the well-known programme established for Witness Care to keep contact with her, to explain to her her duty, to try and find where she had gone in the months before the PCMH. No doubt the constabulary at Portsmouth have a Witness Care Unit, but there was no evidence before the judge as to what steps it had taken. Nor was there any evidence when enquiries came to be made in the early part of 2008 and in the month or two before the trial as to what information the witness's mother had about her location, no evidence as to what enquiries had been made of social security (as one assumes that the witness concerned was on social security). She had been on the telephone. There was no evidence as to whether any attempt had been made to trace her through cell site analysis. It is said that all of this might be expensive. It may be. We do not know, however, because there was no evidence about that either.

32. It seems to us, and in particular from the judge's remarks, that there must be a suspicion that this kind of application is being dealt with far too informally. Given the importance of the right to confrontation under our law, it is quite impermissible to proceed with an application of this kind informally.

33. It is to be hoped in applications of this kind that the facts can be agreed, but, if not, evidence must be called and the judge must make findings of fact. With respect to the judge in this case, he did not make any findings. He merely expressed a summary of what he was told. It follows, therefore, first that there was no evidence properly before the judge on which he could have made any findings at all. Secondly, even if the limited matters that had been relied on by the Crown had been facts upon which they had established by evidence, it would have been hopeless to expect a judge to say that such steps as were reasonably practicable had been taken. If there was a problem with the cost of caring for a reluctant witness and finding her, then that needed to be dealt with by evidence. There was no such evidence.

34. In the result, therefore, we are of the clear view that this evidence was wrongly admitted as there was no evidence to establish that such steps as were reasonably practicable to find SD had been taken. It is accepted that if the evidence was wrongly admitted, the conviction cannot be considered safe. In the circumstances, therefore, we have no alternative but to quash this conviction.

The Court of Appeal highlighted the right to confrontation under Article 6(3)(d) of the European Convention on Human Rights and emphasised the importance of a more formal approach to applications under s. 116(2)(d). The Court recommended that a written agreed statement of facts as to the steps taken to find the witness should be produced before such an application is considered.

As with the other provisions above, s. 116(5) provides that where the fact that the witness cannot be found is attributable to the party seeking to adduce the statement of the witness in evidence or if it is attributable to a person acting on that party's behalf, in order to prevent the witness from giving evidence, the condition under s. 116(2)(d) will not be satisfied and the statement of the witness will be inadmissible. The Court of Appeal explained the principle underlying s. 116(5) in *R* v. *Rowley*, stating that a person who deliberately brought about the absence of the witness should not be permitted to benefit from the witness's absence.[85] The Court further held that the conduct of the person seeking to adduce the evidence of the witness 'should have been an effective cause, albeit not the only cause, of the witness's absence'.[86] Thus, where for instance a key prosecution witness cannot be found, partly because he simply does not want to come to court to testify and partly because he has gone into hiding after a threat made by the defendant or his associates acting on his behalf, the conduct of the defendant and his associates would need to be 'an effective cause' of the witness's absence if s. 116(2) is to apply. The rationale for this principle was expressed by the Court of Appeal in *R* v. *Rowley*: 'to hold otherwise would significantly undermine the policy of the legislation'.[87]

(v) Section 116(2)(e): fear of the witness

The condition under s. 116(2)(e) requires that the witness does not give evidence through fear and the court gives leave for the statement to be read in evidence. This provision is intended to prevent the fear of a witness from affecting the admissibility of their evidence. Thus, where a witness is afraid, the court can permit their witness statement to be read in lieu of them attending court to give evidence.[88] This provision was also represented under the former statutory framework in s. 23(3) of the Criminal Justice Act 1988. Section 116(2)(e) requires that 'through fear the relevant person does not give (or does not continue to give) oral evidence in the proceedings, either at all or in connection with the subject matter of the statement, and the court gives leave for the statement to be given in evidence'. This provision applies both to witnesses who are intimidated before they even enter the witness box, as well as those who become intimidated part of the way through giving evidence, i.e. those who do start to give evidence, but then do not 'continue to give' evidence due to fear.[89] The provision also applies to witnesses who do not give evidence 'either at all or in connection with the subject matter of the statement'. This means that it applies to a witness who never steps foot in the witness box, as well as a witness who gives some evidence, but does not give evidence on the subject matter of his witness statement. However, it will not apply to a witness who is willing to testify, but who will not tell the whole truth out of fear;[90] in such a case, the statement of the witness could be admitted instead under s. 114(1)(d) in the interests of justice, or the statement could be admitted under s. 119 of the Criminal Justice Act 2003 as a previous inconsistent statement.

Section 116(3) provides some guidance on the interpretation to be given to the meaning of 'fear', stating that 'fear' is to be widely construed.

---

85 [2013] 1 WLR 895, CA at 901.

86 Ibid. at 902.

87 Ibid.

88 It has been held that the hearsay provisions will not apply to anonymous hearsay evidence (thus, a witness whose anonymity has been preserved due to their fear). Where witness anonymity has been granted, the witness's statement is not to be admitted under s. 114(1) of the Criminal Justice Act 2003 and so cannot be read. In *R* v. *Mayers* [2008] EWCA Crim 2989, the Court of Appeal held that to admit anonymous hearsay evidence would be to rewrite the law and stated that any steps to extend the law to cover anonymous witnesses would have to be taken by Parliament.

89 See *R* v. *Adeojo (Sodiq)* [2013] EWCA Crim 41.

90 *R* v. *Saunders (James Joe)* [2012] EWCA Crim 1185 at [34].

S. 116(3), CRIMINAL JUSTICE ACT 2003

For the purposes of subsection (2)(e) 'fear' is to be widely construed and (for example) includes fear of the death or injury of another person or of financial loss.

Section 116(3) specifies that fear includes fear of the death or injury of a person or fear of financial loss, but the use of the word 'includes' shows that this list is not exhaustive. According to this partial definition, 's.116(3) covers situations where the witness is in fear as a result of threats of death or of injury to himself or another person, or as a result of threats which would result in financial loss, such as threats of damage to property. It has been suggested that "fear" under s.116(3) is so broad that it could even extend to "the consequences of committing perjury"';[91] the suggestion being that a witness who has already lied in their witness statement might rely on their fear that they could be prosecuted for perjury and could lose their job as a result would fall within the section. The Law Commission stated that it would be wrong for a witness who is merely afraid of being prosecuted from benefitting from s.116(2)(e), but the Commission felt it unnecessary to include specific provision to exclude this since no court would think it in the 'interests of justice' that the witness's statement be admitted in such circumstances.[92] Thus, the safeguard within s. 116(4) would enable the judge to refuse to grant leave in these circumstances, preventing the admission of the evidence.

In order to rely on s. 116(2)(e) as a basis for the admissibility of hearsay evidence under s. 114(1)(a), the party seeking to rely on the evidence must apply for leave of the court. This is the only provision for which leave must be formally granted before the evidence can be adduced in court.[93] In deciding whether or not to grant leave, s. 116(4) provides that the court may only grant leave if it considers that the statement ought to be admitted in the interests of justice, having regard to a number of factors in s. 116(4)(a) to (d), namely,

(a) to the statement's contents,
(b) to any risk that its admission or exclusion will result in unfairness to any party to the proceedings (and in particular to how difficult it will be to challenge the statement if the relevant person does not give oral evidence),
(c) in appropriate cases, to the fact that a special measures direction could be made in relation to the relevant person, and
(d) to any other relevant circumstances.

---

91 See A. Heaton-Armstrong, D. Wolchover and A. Maxwell-Scott, 'Obtaining, recording and admissibility of out-of-court witness statements' in A. Heaton-Armstrong, E. Shepherd, G. Gudjonsson and D. Wolchover, *Witness Testimony* (Oxford University Press, 2006) at p. 176.
92 Law Commission, *Evidence in Criminal Proceedings: Hearsay and Related Topics* (Report No. 245, Cm. 3670, 1997) at para. 8.66.
93 Where one of the other conditions under s. 116(2) applies, the evidence of the witness is automatically admissible and the party seeking to adduce the evidence need not apply for the leave of the judge.

S. 116(4), CRIMINAL JUSTICE ACT 2003

Leave may be given under subsection (2)(e) only if the court considers that the statement ought to be admitted in the interests of justice, having regard –

(a) to the statement's contents,

(b) to any risk that its admission or exclusion will result in unfairness to any party to the proceedings (and in particular to how difficult it will be to challenge the statement if the relevant person does not give oral evidence),

(c) in appropriate cases, to the fact that a direction under section 19 of the Youth Justice and Criminal Evidence Act 1999 (c. 23) (special measures for the giving of evidence by fearful witnesses etc) could be made in relation to the relevant person, and

(d) to any other relevant circumstances.

These factors listed under s. 116(4) need only be considered if the application to adduce the hearsay evidence is based upon the fear of an unavailable witness under s. 116(2)(e).[94]

Fear is to be subjectively assessed, so the crucial question is whether the witness himself was in fear, not whether his fear was reasonable.[95] In deciding whether a hearsay statement is admissible under s. 116(2)(e) by virtue of the fact that he will not give oral evidence through fear, there have been a number of recent decisions in the Supreme Court and Court of Appeal which suggest that a strict approach should be taken.[96] Both *R* v. *Riat (Jaspal)*[97] and *R* v. *Shabir (Mohammed Haness)*[98] are authorities for the principle that where an application is made to adduce the evidence of a witness's statement on the basis that the witness does not wish to give evidence due to fear, the evidence of fear itself should be rigorously tested. In *R* v. *Riat (Jaspal)*, the Court held that the manner in which the evidence of fear is tested will depend upon the circumstances of the case and that it is critical that every effort is made to get the witness to testify in court. This means that the court should consider the possibility of using special measures to enable the witness to testify, as stated in s. 116(4)(c). In *R* v. *Shabir (Mohammed Haness)*, the Court of Appeal set out the approach that should be taken in cases in which a witness is in fear, as follows:

R V. *SHABIR (MOHAMMED HANESS)* [2012] EWCA CRIM 2564

(1) The 'default' position is that hearsay evidence is not admissible.

(2) It is a pre-condition to the admission of a hearsay statement that the witness concerned is identified: s.116(1)(b).

---

94 Although, for a suggestion that s. 116(4) applies more generally, see *R (on the application of the CPS)* v. *Uxbridge Magistrates* [2007] EWHC 205 (Admin).

95 *R* v. *Doherty* [2006] EWCA Crim 2716.

96 For example, see *R* v. *Horncastle* [2010] 2 AC 373, *R* v. *Riat* [2013] 1 Cr App R 2 and *R* v. *Shabir (Mohammed Haness)* [2012] EWCA Crim 2564.

97 [2013] 1 Cr App R 2 at [54](ii).

98 [2012] EWCA Crim 2564 at [69].

(3) The necessity to resort to second-hand evidence must be clearly demonstrated. The more central the evidence that is sought to be admitted as hearsay evidence is to the case, the greater the scrutiny that has to be undertaken to see whether or not it should be admitted as hearsay.

(4) Although 'fear' is to be widely construed in accordance with s.116(3) and, specifically, the fear of a witness does not have to be attributed to the defendant, a court has to be satisfied, to the criminal standard, that the proposed witness will not give evidence (either at all or in connection with the subject matter of the relevant statement) 'through fear'. Thus a causative link between the fear and the failure or refusal to give evidence must be proved.

(5) How it is proved that a witness will not give evidence 'through fear' depends upon the background together with the history and circumstances of the particular case. Every effort must be made to get the witness to court to test the issue of his 'fear'. The witness alleging 'fear' may be cross-examined by the defence (if needs be in a voir dire), if necessary using 'special measures' to assist the witness. That procedure may be possible but, in certain cases, may not be appropriate.

(6) If testing by the defence is properly refused (after consideration) then 'it is incumbent on the judge to take responsibility rigorously to test the evidence of fear and to investigate all the possibilities of the witness giving oral evidence in the proceedings'. The manner in which that should be done will depend on the circumstances of the case and upon the witness and will necessarily involve discussions with counsel as to approach and questions to be asked. For example, if a court cannot hear from a witness a tape recording or video of an interview on the question of his 'fear' should, if possible, be made available. The critical thing is that 'every effort is made to get the witness to court'.

(7) In relation to the 'gateway' of s.116(2)(e), leave to admit the statement will only be given if the conditions for passing through a specific 'secondary gateway' are satisfied. They are set out in s.116(4). Overall a court will only admit a statement under s.116(2)(e) if it considers that it is 'in the interests of justice' to do so. In that respect, the court has to have specific regard to the matters set out in s.116(4)(a) to (c).

(8) When a court considers s.116(4)(c), the court should take all possible steps to enable a fearful witness to give evidence notwithstanding his apprehension. 'A degree of (properly supported) fortitude can legitimately be expected in the fight against crime'. A court must therefore have regard to whether (in an appropriate case), a witness would give evidence if a direction for 'special measures' were to be made under s.19 YJCEA 1999.

(9) In this regard it is particularly important that, before the court has ruled on the application to admit under s.116(2)(e), no indication, let alone assurance, is given to a potential witness that his evidence will or may be read if he says he is afraid, because that can only give rise to an expectation that this will, indeed, happen. If it does then the statement will have been admitted on an improper basis; the impact of the evidence will be diminished and that may have further consequences, e.g. An application to the judge under s.125 at the end of the prosecution case to stop the case.

(10) When a judge considers the 'interests of justice' under s.116(4), although he is not obliged to consider all the factors set out in s.114(2)(a) to (i) of the CJA, those factors may be a convenient checklist for him to consider.

(11) Once the judge has concluded that the specific gateways in s.116(4) have been satisfied, the court must consider the vital linked questions of (a) the apparent reliability of the evidence sought to be adduced as hearsay and (b) the practicality of the jury testing and assessing its reliability. In this

regard s.124 (which permits a wide range of material going to credibility of the witness to be adduced as evidence) is vital.

(12) In many cases a judge will not be able to make a decision as to whether to admit an item of hearsay evidence unless he has considered not only the importance of that evidence and its apparent strengths and weaknesses, but also what material is available to help test and assess it, in particular what evidence could be admitted as to the credibility of the witness and the hearsay evidence under s.124. The judge is entitled to expect that 'very full' enquiries as to witness credibility will have been made if it is the prosecution that wishes to put in the hearsay evidence and if it is the defence, they too must undertake proper checks.

The Court of Appeal applied *R* v. *Riat (Jaspal)* and *R* v. *Shabir (Mohammed Haness)* in *R* v. *Harvey (Shelton)*.[99] The Court of Appeal commented that the evidence of fear in this case was of 'significant strength', that the police had made every reasonable effort to get the witnesses to court and that the witnesses were unequivocal in their refusal to attend court and that special measures directions would not have alleviated their concerns.[100] While in recent years the courts appear to have adopted a strict approach to the admissibility of witness statements under s. 116(2)(e), in the earlier decision of *R* v. *Davies*, the Court of Appeal held that the courts may consider a witness statement or the evidence of a police officer who has spoken to the witness as evidence of the witness's fear.[101] The Court of Appeal in *R* v. *Davies* also specifically stated that the trial judge should not test the basis of the witness's fear by calling the witness to give evidence 'since that may undermine the very thing that section 116 was designed to avoid'.[102] However, the approach of the courts in more recent years would appear to suggest that a mere statement of fear contained in a witness statement is unlikely to be sufficient today, and that there must be a more rigorous test of the evidence through the oral testimony of a witness as to their fear, most likely with the use of the special measures provisions contained within the Youth Justice and Criminal Evidence Act 1999.

Cross-reference

Where a witness is afraid to give evidence, an application for a Special Measures Direction might initially be made to encourage the witness to give evidence by providing comfortable conditions for that evidence to be given, and to ultimately try to improve the quality of the witness's evidence. Thus, the hearsay provision under s. 116(2)(e) of the Criminal Justice Act 2003 should be considered alongside the special measures directions under the Youth Justice and Criminal Justice Act 1999. Refer to Chapter 9 on Witnesses for special measures directions.

99 [2014] EWCA Crim 54.
100 Ibid. at [53]–[55].
101 This would be admissible as evidence of the witness's state of mind by virtue of s. 118(1) under rule 4(c) (see paragraph 7.6.3 of this chapter) or if the police officer has made notes on the witness's fear, his could potentially be admissible by virtue of s. 117(4) as a document created for pending criminal proceedings (see paragraph 7.5.2 of this chapter). Circumstantial evidence relating to the state of mind of the witness would also be admissible as non-hearsay evidence (see paragraph 7.2.1 of this chapter).
102 *R* v. *Davies* [2007] 2 All ER 1070 at [14].

Finally, where the witness's fear is attributable to the party seeking to adduce the statement of the witness in evidence or if it is attributable to a person acting on that party's behalf, in order to prevent the witness from giving evidence the condition under s. 116(2)(e) will not be satisfied and the statement of the witness will be inadmissible. This was emphasised by the Court of Appeal in the case of *R* v. *Horncastle*.[103]

R V. *HORNCASTLE* [2009] EWCA CRIM 964
Court of Appeal

83. A witness who is in fear may be as effectively unavailable as a witness who is dead, ill, or overseas. In some cases, the fear will have been induced by or on behalf of the accused. Nor is it always the case that fear induced by or on behalf of the accused is limited to one of overt traceable threats. Sometimes the reputation of the accused and his associates is enough: this is one way in which gangs can maintain their hold on an area. The finding that the fear is induced by or on behalf of the accused may be an inevitable one if the inquiry be made: cui bono? Where the fear is attributable to the accused or his associates, it is an additional factor supporting the admissibility of the evidence, since otherwise a premium is put by the criminal justice system on the intimidation of witnesses.

. . .

86. In our view, the terms of section 116, like the jurisprudence of the ECtHR, do not impose the requirement that the fear must be attributable to the defendant. It is sufficient that the witness is in fear. No doubt Parliament took into account the well known difficulties of ascertaining the source of a witness's fear. Nor does article 6 of the Convention require this. As we have set out, it is our view that in determining whether the requirements of article 6(3)(d) have been met, two of the essential questions are whether there is a justifiable reason for the absence of the witness supported by evidence (see the fifth and sixth propositions that we consider can be derived from the case law of the ECtHR) and whether the evidence is demonstrably reliable or its reliability can properly be tested and assessed. On this analysis, if the witness can give evidence which should be heard by the court in the interests of justice, but is clearly too frightened to come, then it matters not whether that fear was brought about by or on behalf of the defendant – there is a justifiable reason for the absence. The task of the court is to be sure that there are sufficient counterbalancing measures in place (including measures that permit a proper assessment of the reliability of that evidence fairly to take place) and to permit a conviction to be based on it only if it is sufficiently reliable given its importance in the case. The provisions of the CJA 2003 require all this to be done.

As we have seen above, where a witness is unavailable to give oral evidence of a matter, their written witness statement may be admissible as evidence of that matter, provided that the conditions under s. 116(1) are satisfied. Evidence falling within s. 116 is admissible by virtue of s. 114(1)(a) of the Criminal Justice Act 2003. Hearsay evidence may alternatively be admissible under s. 114(1)(a) by virtue of it being a business document under s. 117.

---

103 [2009] EWCA Crim 964.

Cross-reference

For a discussion on the hearsay provisions, Article 6(3)(d) of the European Convention on Human Rights and the European jurisprudence, see paragraph 7.9 below.

7.5.2 Business documents under s. 117

Under s. 114(1)(a) of the Criminal Justice Act 2003, hearsay evidence may be admissible under either s. 116 (unavailable witnesses) or under s. 117 of the Act. Section 117(1) of the Act provides for the admissibility of business documents or other documents. This provision echoes the old provision under s. 24 of the Criminal Justice Act 1988 and was originally prompted by the decision of the House of Lords in *Myers* v. *DPP*.[104] Section 117(1) of the 2003 Act provides that hearsay evidence is admissible if three circumstances are satisfied:

- the hearsay evidence must be evidence which would be admissible in oral evidence as evidence of that matter (s. 117(1)(a)),
- the requirements under s. 117(2) are satisfied (s. 117(1)(b)), and
- the requirements under s. 117(5) are satisfied in a case involving a document prepared for pending or contemplated criminal proceedings (s. 117(1)(c)).

The requirements under s. 117(2) state that the document must have been created or received by a person in the course of a trade, business, profession or other occupation, or as the holder of a paid or unpaid office, and that the person who supplied the information in the statement had or may reasonably be supposed to have had personal knowledge of the matters dealt with.[105]

S. 117, CRIMINAL JUSTICE ACT 2003

(1) In criminal proceedings a statement contained in a document is admissible as evidence of any matter stated if –
  (a) oral evidence given in the proceedings would be admissible as evidence of that matter,
  (b) the requirements of subsection (2) are satisfied, and
  (c) the requirements of subsection (5) are satisfied, in a case where subsection (4) requires them to be.
(2) The requirements of this subsection are satisfied if –
  (a) the document or the part containing the statement was created or received by a person in the course of a trade, business, profession or other occupation, or as the holder of a paid or unpaid office,

---

104 [1965] AC 1001, HL and see paragraph 7.2.3 (above).
105 See *R* v. *Humphris* [2005] EWCA Crim 2030, in which the details of the defendant's previous convictions which had been obtained from a Police National Computer printout were not admissible because the police officers who had entered the information on the computer had no personal knowledge of the matters in question as required by s. 117(2)(b). By contrast, in *Grazette* v. *DPP* [2012] EWHC 3863 (Admin) where details of the 'street name' of a defendant were entered on a police criminal intelligence system, this evidence was admissible under s. 117 because the person who entered the information on the system had or may reasonably be supposed to have had personal knowledge of the matter as required by s. 117(2)(b).

(b) the person who supplied the information contained in the statement (the relevant person) had or may reasonably be supposed to have had personal knowledge of the matters dealt with, and

(c) each person (if any) through whom the information was supplied from the relevant person to the person mentioned in paragraph (a) received the information in the course of a trade, business, profession or other occupation, or as the holder of a paid or unpaid office.

(3) The persons mentioned in paragraphs (a) and (b) of subsection (2) may be the same person.

Section 117(3) states that the person who created or received the document in s. 117(2)(a) and the person who supplied the information contained in the statement in s. 117(2)(b) may be the same person. Where the information in the statement has passed through more than one person, then s. 117(2)(c) requires that each person received the information in the course of a trade, business, profession or other occupation, or as the holder of a paid or unpaid office. Thus, s. 117 allows for the admissibility of multiple hearsay evidence, i.e. hearsay evidence that has passed through a number of people.[106]

Under s. 117(4), there is a further requirement where the document was prepared for the purposes of pending or contemplated criminal proceedings or for a criminal investigation. In these circumstances, the requirements in s. 117(5) must also be satisfied. These are that the witness is unavailable due to any of the conditions in s. 116(2)(a) to (e), or the witness cannot reasonably be expected to have any recollection of the matters dealt with in the statement having regard to the length of time since he supplied the information and other circumstances.

S. 117, CRIMINAL JUSTICE ACT 2003

(4) The additional requirements of subsection (5) must be satisfied if the statement –

(a) was prepared for the purposes of pending or contemplated criminal proceedings, or for a criminal investigation, but

(b) was not obtained pursuant to a request under section 7 of the Crime (International Co-operation) Act 2003 (c. 32) or an order under paragraph 6 of Schedule 13 to the Criminal Justice Act 1988 (c. 33) (which relate to overseas evidence).

(5) The requirements of this subsection are satisfied if –

(a) any of the five conditions mentioned in section 116(2) is satisfied (absence of relevant person etc), or

(b) the relevant person cannot reasonably be expected to have any recollection of the matters dealt with in the statement (having regard to the length of time since he supplied the information and all other circumstances).

---

106 See *Maher* v. *DPP* [2006] EWHC 1271 (Admin) in which it was held that evidence of a registration number of a car which had allegedly caused damage to another car and which had been recorded in the Police Incident Log was not admissible under s. 117. While the document was created by a police clerk in the course of their occupation (s. 117(2)(a)) and the information was supplied by a person with personal knowledge of the matters dealt with (s. 117(2)(b)), it had passed through a further party, namely the girlfriend of the man whose car had been damaged and she did not receive the information in the course of a trade, business, etc. under s. 117(2)(c).

This provision has been held to apply to an entry on a Police National Computer printout.[107] It might also apply, for instance, to notes made in a police officer's notebook, where that officer cannot reasonably be expected to remember the incident at a trial which takes place many years later, or if he becomes unavailable to attend court in the ensuing period, perhaps due to death or unfitness to give evidence.

However, where the court has concerns about the reliability of the statement, due to its contents, the source of the information contained in it, or the way in which or the circumstances in which the information was supplied or received, or the way in which or the circumstances in which the document concerned was created or received, it may make a direction under s. 117(7) that the statement is unreliable. In such circumstances, the statement would not be admissible by virtue of s. 117(6).

S. 117, CRIMINAL JUSTICE ACT 2003

(6) A statement is not admissible under this section if the court makes a direction to that effect under subsection (7).

(7) The court may make a direction under this subsection if satisfied that the statement's reliability as evidence for the purpose for which it is tendered is doubtful in view of –

(a) its contents,

(b) the source of the information contained in it,

(c) the way in which or the circumstances in which the information was supplied or received, or

(d) the way in which or the circumstances in which the document concerned was created or received.

7.6 ADMISSIBILITY UNDER S. 114(1)(B): THE COMMON LAW

Under s. 114(1)(b) of the Criminal Justice Act 2003, hearsay evidence is admissible if it is admissible under one of the common law rules preserved by s. 118 of the Act. Section 118(2) abolishes the common law rules on the admissibility of hearsay evidence, except for those rules preserved by s. 118(1). Section 118(1) preserves a specific list of eight common law rules governing the admissibility of hearsay evidence in criminal proceedings.

S. 118, CRIMINAL JUSTICE ACT 2003

(1) The following rules of law are preserved.

...

(2) With the exception of the rules preserved by this section, the common law rules governing the admissibility of hearsay evidence in criminal proceedings are abolished.

---

107 *R (on the application of Wellington)* v. *DPP* [2007] EWHC 1061 (Admin).

The eight common law rules preserved by s. 118(1) are as follows:

1. Public information
2. Reputation as to character
3. Reputation or family tradition
4. *Res gestae*
5. Confessions
6. Admissions by agents
7. Common enterprise
8. Expert evidence.

Since s. 118(1) merely preserves the common law (as opposed to placing the rules onto a statutory footing), it is necessary to refer to the common law for each rule in determining its applicability. Each of the rules will be considered briefly in turn below.

7.6.1 Public information

The first common law rule preserved by s. 118(1) relates to public information. This rule specifies certain categories of public documents which are admissible hearsay evidence. In particular, published works which deal with matters of a public nature (e.g. histories, scientific works, dictionaries and maps) are admissible as evidence of those public facts stated in them; public documents and record, such as public registers (i.e. the register of births, deaths and marriages or the land register), court records, treaties and pardons, are admissible as evidence of facts stated in them;[108] and evidence of a person's age, date of birth or place of birth is admissible without the person presenting the information having personal knowledge of the matter in question.

S. 118(1), CRIMINAL JUSTICE ACT 2003

1   *Public information etc*

Any rule of law under which in criminal proceedings –

(a) published works dealing with matters of a public nature (such as histories, scientific works, dictionaries and maps) are admissible as evidence of facts of a public nature stated in them,
(b) public documents (such as public registers, and returns made under public authority with respect to matters of public interest) are admissible as evidence of facts stated in them,
(c) records (such as the records of certain courts, treaties, Crown grants, pardons and commissions) are admissible as evidence of facts stated in them, or
(d) evidence relating to a person's age or date or place of birth may be given by a person without personal knowledge of the matter.

---

108 The first three types of public document or information are also preserved in civil proceedings by virtue of s. 7(2)(a)–(c) of the Civil Evidence Act 1995.

This is a narrow rule of admissibility as it only applies to documents or information which are of a public nature.

7.6.2 Reputation

The next two common law rules preserved by s. 118(1) relate to reputation: one rule relates to reputation as to character, and the other to reputation or family tradition.

S. 118(1), CRIMINAL JUSTICE ACT 2003

2   *Reputation as to character*

Any rule of law under which in criminal proceedings evidence of a person's reputation is admissible for the purpose of proving his good or bad character.

3   *Reputation or family tradition*

Any rule of law under which in criminal proceedings evidence of reputation or family tradition is admissible for the purpose of proving or disproving –

(a) pedigree or the existence of a marriage,
(b) the existence of any public or general right, or
(c) the identity of any person or thing.

The first of these rules provides that evidence of a person's reputation is admissible hearsay evidence in criminal proceedings for the purpose of proving his good or bad character.[109] This rule originates from the case of *R* v. *Rowton*.[110] So, a witness may be called to give evidence of the general reputation of the defendant in the community in order to prove that the defendant is of either good or bad character.

The second rule provides that evidence of reputation or family tradition is admissible in order to prove or disprove one of three matters, namely,

- pedigree[111] or existence of a marriage,[112]
- the existence of a public or general right, or
- the identity of a person or thing.[113]

7.6.3 *Res gestae*

The fourth common law rule preserved by s. 118(1) relates to *res gestae*. *Res gestae* statements are statements which are made so closely connected with a particular event that the possibility

---

109 This rule is also preserved in civil proceedings by virtue of s. 7(3)(a) of the Civil Evidence Act 1995.
110 (1865) LE & Ca 520.
111 'Pedigree' here refers to blood relationships.
112 This rule also applies in respect of proving or disproving the existence of a civil partnership: see s. 84(5) of the Civil Partnership Act 2004.
113 This rule is also preserved in civil proceedings by virtue of s. 7(3)(b) of the Civil Evidence Act 1995.

of the statement being a lie or a mistaken statement are minimal. *Res gestae* statements are admissible hearsay evidence because they are more likely to be reliable than other hearsay statements.

S. 118(1), CRIMINAL JUSTICE ACT 2003

4   *Res gestae*

Any rule of law under which in criminal proceedings a statement is admissible as evidence of any matter stated if –

(a) the statement was made by a person so emotionally overpowered by an event that the possibility of concoction or distortion can be disregarded,
(b) the statement accompanied an act which can be properly evaluated as evidence only if considered in conjunction with the statement, or
(c) the statement relates to a physical sensation or a mental state (such as intention or emotion).

There are three types of *res gestae* statement. These are:

- spontaneous statements ('excited utterances')
- statements accompanying an act
- statements relating to a physical sensation or a mental state.

(i) Spontaneous statements

Spontaneous statements are statements which are made by a person who was so emotionally overpowered by an event that the possibility of concoction or distortion can be disregarded.[114] Such statements are often referred to as 'excited utterances'. The leading case on spontaneous *res gestae* statements is the House of Lords' authority of *R* v. *Andrews*.[115] The victim was attacked after someone knocked on the door to his flat and he answered it. Having been wounded, he went to the flat below for help. When the police arrived, the victim informed the officers that one of his attackers was called 'Donald' (this was the first name of the defendant). As the victim died from his wounds, the police officers were called to give evidence of this statement. The trial judge, Court of Appeal and House of Lords held that while this evidence was hearsay, it was admissible as a *res gestae* statement. Lord Ackner delivered the leading opinion in the House of Lords. His Lordship stated that a trial judge faced with an application to admit evidence under the doctrine of *res gestae* must first ask himself whether the possibility of concoction or distortion can be disregarded. In order to answer this question, the judge must consider the circumstances in which the statement was made in order to determine whether the event was sufficiently spontaneous. This will require the judge to question whether the event was still operating at the time of the statement and whether it dominated the thoughts of the

---

114 Section 118(1), rule 4(a).
115 [1987] AC 281, HL.

victim, such that his statement was an instinctive reaction and there was no real opportunity for reasoned reflection.[116]

The case of *Ratten* v. *R* was considered earlier in relation to implied assertions.[117] This was a case involving the question of the admissibility of the deceased's emotional state and statement to an emergency services operator which was held to be admissible in the trial against the defendant for murder as it was adduced to prove the state of mind of the maker, rather than the truth of its contents. In the Privy Council, Lord Wilberforce also held that the statement would be admissible as *res gestae* because the statement was so closely connected in time and place to the event and the emotion in the woman's voice demonstrated that the event was operating on her mind at the time.

Another example of *res gestae* is the case of *R* v. *Turnbull*.[118] The defendant was charged with murder after an argument in a pub car park led to the death of a man. Immediately after he had been stabbed, the victim entered the pub and said that 'Tommo' (the defendant's nickname) had stabbed him. He later died. The statement of the deceased was admissible at trial as *res gestae* because it was so closely connected in time and place to the event that the possibility for concoction or distortion was negligible. Similarly, in *R* v. *Lawson*,[119] the defendant was heard arguing with his wife. She was later found to be badly burned and in a confused state and was heard to utter the words 'you have really got me now'. After she died the defendant was convicted of manslaughter. The trial judge ruled that the statement was admissible both as a dying declaration and as part of the *res gestae*. The Court of Appeal upheld this decision and held that the evidence would be part of the *res gestae* if the judge was satisfied that it was made at a time when the deceased was so emotionally overpowered by an event that the possibility of concoction or distortion could be ruled out. This paragraph was recently applied in the case of *R* v. *Saunders (James Joe)*[120] in which the Court of Appeal held that the trial judge had been right to admit evidence of the victim's statement to his wife that he had just been stabbed by the defendant.

(ii) Statements accompanying an act

Another type of *res gestae* is a statement that accompanies an act which can only properly be evaluated as evidence if considered in conjunction with the statement.[121] Thus, this applies to statements which explain a relevant act. An example is the case of *R* v. *Edwards*,[122] in which the defendant was charged with the murder of his wife. A week before the murder, the deceased had visited a neighbour in order to ask the neighbour to look after a carving knife and an axe, telling the neighbour that her husband threatened her with these and she felt safer with them out of the way. This statement was held to be admissible as an explanation for the act of handing the knife and axe to the neighbour.

---

116 Ibid. per Lord Ackner at 300–1.
117 See paragraph 7.2.1 above.
118 (1984) 80 Cr App R 104.
119 [1998] Crim LR 883.
120 [2012] EWCA Crim 1185.
121 Section 118(1), rule 4(b).
122 (1872) 12 Cox CC 230.

(iii) Statements relating to a physical sensation or mental state

This type of *res gestae* is a statement which relates to a physical sensation or a mental state (such as intention or emotion).[123] The statement must be closely connected to a physical sensation or mental state. The case of *R* v. *Edwards* (mentioned above) could also fall under this category of *res gestae* as the statement made to the neighbour was a statement which related to the state of mind of the wife, demonstrating that she felt threatened by her husband and that she was worried that her life was at risk. Another example is the case of *R* v. *Gilfoyle* (mentioned above), in which the defendant sought to adduce suicide notes written by his wife as evidence of her suicidal state of mind. The deceased had also informed her friends that her husband had asked her to write suicide notes. The Court of Appeal held that these statements to the deceased's friends were admissible as evidence of the state of mind of the deceased, to show that she was not suicidal.

7.6.4 Confessions

The next two common law rules preserved by s. 118(1) relate to confessions and admissions. Rule 5 provides that the common law relating to confessions applies and rule 6 provides that the common law relating to admissions made by agents of the defendant applies.

S. 118(1), CRIMINAL JUSTICE ACT 2003

5   Confessions etc

Any rule of law relating to the admissibility of confessions or mixed statements in criminal proceedings.

6   Admissions by agents etc

Any rule of law under which in criminal proceedings –

(a) an admission made by an agent of a defendant is admissible against the defendant as evidence of any matter stated, or

(b) a statement made by a person to whom a defendant refers a person for information is admissible against the defendant as evidence of any matter stated.

The law relating to the admissibility of confession evidence is governed by both statute and common law. Sections 76, 76A and 77 of the Police and Criminal Evidence Act 1984 provide rules of law relating to admissibility and s. 78, PACE Act 1984 provides a judicial discretion to exclude such evidence.

Cross-reference

Refer to Chapter 5 on Confession evidence for a more detailed exploration of the admissibility of confession evidence.

---

123   Section 118(1), rule 4(c).

Confessions made by agents of the defendant refers to confessions made on the defendant's behalf by his agent, such as confessions made by the defendant's solicitor or barrister.

7.6.5 Common enterprise

The seventh common law rule preserved by s. 118(1) relates to common enterprise (namely, conspiracy and joint enterprise). This rule provides that where one party to a common enterprise makes a statement, the common law relating to that statement applies.

S. 118(1), CRIMINAL JUSTICE ACT 2003

7 *Common enterprise*

Any rule of law under which in criminal proceedings a statement made by a party to a common enterprise is admissible against another party to the enterprise as evidence of any matter stated.

The statement is admissible against another party to that enterprise as evidence of any matter stated therein. The statement must have been made in furtherance of the common enterprise and in the course of the enterprise.[124] However, the statement may not be used as evidence of another party's participation in the common enterprise without independent evidence of that fact.[125]

7.6.6 Expert evidence

The final common law rule preserved by s. 118(1) relates to expert evidence. This rule provides that where evidence is given by an expert witness, the common law rules relating to expert evidence apply.

S. 118(1), CRIMINAL JUSTICE ACT 2003

8 *Expert evidence*

Any rule of law under which in criminal proceedings an expert witness may draw on the body of expertise relevant to his field.

The expert may draw upon the body of expertise relevant to his field; thus, he may rely on works of authority which are regarded under the common law as admissible hearsay evidence.[126]

These common law rules are preserved by s. 118(1) of the Criminal Justice Act 2003 and are admissible hearsay statements by virtue of s. 114(1)(b) of the Act.

---

124 *R* v. *Devonport and Pirano* [1996] 1 Cr App R 221 and *R* v. *Jones* [1997] 2 Cr App R 119, CA.
125 *R* v. *Smart and Beard* [2002] EWCA Crim 772 and *Donat* (1986) 82 Cr App R 173 at 179.
126 See *R* v. *Abadom* (1983) 76 Cr App R 48.

> **Cross-reference**
> Refer to Chapter 12 on Opinion and expert evidence for a discussion of the evidence given by expert witnesses in criminal proceedings.

7.7 ADMISSIBILITY UNDER S. 114(1)(C): ALL PARTIES AGREE

The third way in which a hearsay statement may be admissible is by virtue of s. 114(1)(c) of the Criminal Justice Act 2003. This provision is self-explanatory. Where all the parties to the proceedings agree that the hearsay evidence should be admissible, then it may be admitted under s. 114(1)(c) of the Criminal Justice Act 2003.

7.8 ADMISSIBILITY UNDER S. 114(1)(D): INTERESTS OF JUSTICE

The final way in which a hearsay statement may be admitted in court is under s. 114(1)(d) of the Criminal Justice Act 2003, which provides for the admissibility of a hearsay statement where it would be in the interests of justice that the statement be admitted. This section provides the judge with a discretion to include hearsay evidence where it is not caught by one of the other paragraphs under s. 114(1). As such, it is often referred to as the 'safety valve' provision.

Sections 114(1)(a) to (d) are alternatives, so a party may seek to make an application to adduce hearsay evidence under more than one of the paragraphs under s. 114(1). As such, he may decide to make a second, alternative application under s. 114(1)(d) in addition to an application under one of the other paragraphs.[127] Section 114(1)(d) is available in law for all types of hearsay (including confession evidence), and any party to criminal proceedings may rely on this inclusionary discretion in an application to the court.[128] In deciding whether to admit hearsay evidence under s. 114(1)(d), the court must have regard to the factors set out in s. 114(2). These include:

- the probative value of the statement (assuming it to be true) in relation to a matter in issue in the proceedings, or how valuable it is for the understanding of other evidence in the case;
- what other evidence has been, or can be, given on the matter or evidence;
- how important the matter or evidence is in the context of the case as a whole;
- the circumstances in which the statement was made;
- how reliable the maker of the statement appears to be;
- how reliable the evidence of the making of the statement appears to be;
- whether oral evidence of the matter stated can be given and, if not, why it cannot;
- the amount of difficulty involved in challenging the statement;
- the extent to which that difficulty would be likely to prejudice the party facing it.

---

127 *R* v. *Y* [2008] 1 WLR 1683.
128 Ibid. Also see n. 88 above in relation to anonymous hearsay evidence which is not admissible under s. 114(1) of the Criminal Justice Act 2003: *R* v. *Mayers* [2008] EWCA Crim 2989.

This list is not exhaustive, so any other factors that the court considers to be relevant can also be taken into account.

S. 114(2), CRIMINAL JUSTICE ACT 2003

In deciding whether a statement not made in oral evidence should be admitted under subsection (1)(d), the court must have regard to the following factors (and to any others it considers relevant) –

(a) how much probative value the statement has (assuming it to be true) in relation to a matter in issue in the proceedings, or how valuable it is for the understanding of other evidence in the case;
(b) what other evidence has been, or can be, given on the matter or evidence mentioned in paragraph (a);
(c) how important the matter or evidence mentioned in paragraph (a) is in the context of the case as a whole;
(d) the circumstances in which the statement was made;
(e) how reliable the maker of the statement appears to be;
(f) how reliable the evidence of the making of the statement appears to be;
(g) whether oral evidence of the matter stated can be given and, if not, why it cannot;
(h) the amount of difficulty involved in challenging the statement;
(i) the extent to which that difficulty would be likely to prejudice the party facing it.

While, in practice, counsel may make an application to adduce hearsay on more than one ground, the Court of Appeal has been keen to warn judges to be careful in the application of the inclusionary discretion under s. 114(1)(d) of the Criminal Justice Act 2003. In *R* v. *Saunders (James Joe)*, the Court of Appeal noted that s. 114(1)(d) 'is drafted in vague terms and is an unruly horse'.[129] The Court stated that there 'is considerable authority to the effect that this paragraph must be cautiously and narrowly construed and applied' and cited *R* v. *Z*,[130] in which the Court of Appeal warned that s. 114(1)(d) 'is to be cautiously applied, since otherwise the conditions laid down by Parliament in s.116 would be circumvented'.[131] The Court went on to state that while the Court of Appeal would not readily interfere with the trial judge's exercise of the inclusionary discretion under s. 114(1)(d), where the judge's decision is 'marred by legal error' or where he had failed to take into account relevant matters under s. 114(2), or where he has reached a conclusion that no sensible tribunal could have reached, the Court will interfere with his decision.[132]

In *M* v. *R*,[133] the Court held that the conditions laid down in s. 116 in respect of unavailable witnesses were indeed circumvented because had reasonable steps been taken to locate the complainant witness, she would probably have been located and could have been called to give live evidence at trial. There was no evidence at hand to suggest that she would not have complied with a witness summons. Consequently, the Court of Appeal held that in considering

---

129 [2012] EWCA Crim 1185 at [34].
130 [2009] EWCA Crim 20.
131 Ibid. at [20].
132 This approach accords with the grounds of judicial review generally found in public law.
133 [2011] EWCA Crim 2341.

an application under s. 114(1)(d), the trial judge should have paid particular attention to s. 114(2)(c) and (g): 'the important factor set out in section 114(2)(g) should have led to the response that the oral evidence of the complainant could have been given, and if it was unavailable that was through the failure of the prosecution to take reasonable steps to secure the attendance of the complainant'.[134] The Court concluded in this case that the trial judge had failed to place proper weight on s. 114(2)(c) and that his consideration of s. 114(2)(g) was flawed.

Where a witness has been given notice about the court date and warned to attend court, but nevertheless fails to attend court to give evidence for personal reasons which are not sufficient to engage the gateways under s. 116, the question of whether his statement should be admitted in the interests of justice under s. 114(1)(d) was considered in *EED* v. *R*.[135] The Court of Appeal reminded itself that the defendant is entitled to examine witnesses against him and held that the circumstances in which the evidence of an available but reluctant witness may be admitted in the interests of justice are limited.[136]

7.9 HEARSAY AND ARTICLE 6(3)(D)

The admissibility of hearsay evidence raises a further issue of the defendant's right to confrontation.[137] Article 6(3)(d) of the European Convention on Human Rights provides that everyone charged with a criminal offence has the minimum right 'to examine or have examined witnesses against him and to obtain the attendance and examination of witnesses on his behalf under the same conditions as witnesses against him'. This means that every defendant has the right to cross-examine prosecution witnesses. The extent to which the hearsay provisions under the Criminal Justice Act 2003 operate to violate the defendant's right to examine witnesses under Article 6(3)(d) has been the subject of both domestic and European jurisprudence.[138] In *Al-Khawaja and Tahery* v. *United Kingdom*,[139] the European Court of Human Rights held that there was a violation of Article 6(1) read in conjunction with Article 6(3)(d) where the conviction was based solely or to a decisive degree on the evidence of a witness whom the defendant did not have the opportunity to cross-examine: 'the Court doubts whether any counterbalancing factors would be sufficient to justify the introduction in evidence of an untested statement which was the sole or decisive basis for the conviction of an applicant'. However, the Court held that in exceptional cases where the witness was kept from giving evidence due to fear which was induced by the defendant, then admitting the witness statement of the witness might be justified. In *R* v. *Horncastle*,[140] the Supreme Court considered the effect of the jurisprudence of

---

134 Ibid. at [13].
135 [2010] EWCA Crim 1213.
136 Ibid. at [21].
137 For a theoretical discussion on the right to confrontation, see M. Redmayne, 'Confronting confrontation' in P. Robert and J. Hunter, *Criminal Evidence and Human Rights* (Hart Publishing, 2012) at pp. 283–307.
138 For further discussion on the dialogue between the Supreme Court and the European Court of Human Rights, see I. H. Dennis, 'Case comment: *Al-Khawaja and Tahery v United Kingdom*' [2012] Crim LR 375; I. H. Dennis, 'Case comment: *R v Riat*' [2013] Crim LR 60; M. Redmayne, 'Hearsay and human rights: *Al-Khawaja* in the Grand Chamber' [2012] 75(5) MLR 865.
139 (2009) 49 EHRR 1.
140 [2010] 2 AC 373, SC.

the European Court of Human Rights and decided not to follow the approach adopted by the European Court of Human Rights. In reaching this decision, the Supreme Court drew a distinction between the inquisitorial system on the continent and the English adversarial system. Lord Phillips pointed out that on the continent the evidence of witnesses was often used without the defendant having the chance to cross-examine the witness, whereas the English adversarial system is entirely different in that the admission of a witness statement and the inability of the defence to cross-examine falls under the exception rather than the rule.[141] Lord Phillips drew on the fact that the European jurisprudence acknowledged that Article 6(3)(d) was not absolute, but emphasised that the European jurisprudence lacks clarity on the application of the exceptions to Article 6(3)(d). His Lordship further stated that, '[t]he sole or decisive rule has been introduced into the Strasbourg jurisprudence without discussion of the principle underlying it or full consideration of whether there was justification for imposing the rule as an overriding principle applicable equally to the continental and common law jurisdictions'.[142] Thus, Lord Phillips held that the exceptions to the hearsay rule enacted by Parliament in the Criminal Justice Act 2003 are not subject to the 'sole and decisive rule'.[143] Both the Court of Appeal and the Supreme Court[144] in *R* v. *Horncastle* were confident that the safeguards written into the Criminal Justice Act 2003 by Parliament protected against any violation of Article 6(3)(d) and therefore that the 'sole and decisive rule' was unnecessary in England.[145] The Supreme Court held that the Criminal Justice Act 2003 already strikes the right balance of protecting the defendant's right to a fair trial and protecting the interests of the victim and society.[146]

In December 2011, the case of *Al-Khawaja and Tahery* v. *United Kingdom* was again heard before the European Court of Human Rights' Grand Chamber.[147] In this decision, the Grand Chamber revisited its position in relation to the Criminal Justice Act 2003 and concluded that the 'sole and decisive rule' should not be so rigidly applied, such that where a hearsay statement is the sole or decisive evidence against a defendant, its admission will not automatically lead to a breach of Article 6(1) of the European Convention on Human Rights. However, in such circumstances the proceedings must be subject to 'the most searching scrutiny'.[148] The Grand Chamber held that the fact that a conviction is based solely or to a decisive extent on the statement of an absent witness constitutes a very important factor to balance in the scales and one which would require sufficient counterbalancing factors.[149] The Court then examined the procedural safeguards within the Criminal Justice Act 2003 and under s. 78 of the Police and Criminal Evidence Act 1984 and the common law, and concluded that the safeguards 'are, in principle, strong safeguards designed to ensure fairness'.[150]

---

141 Ibid. at [59] to [62].
142 Ibid. at [14].
143 Ibid.
144 It is worth noting that the Court of Appeal in *R* v. *Horncastle* sat as an enlarged bench of five Law Lords and the Supreme Court sat as an enlarged bench of nine Supreme Court Justices.
145 [2010] 2 AC 373 at [92].
146 Ibid. at [108].
147 (2012) 54 EHRR 23.
148 Ibid. at [147].
149 Ibid.
150 Ibid. at [151].

The Court of Appeal has since considered the dialogue between the Supreme Court in *R* v. *Horncastle* and the European Court of Human Rights in *Al-Khawaja and Tahery* v. *United Kingdom*. In *R* v. *Ibrahim*,[151] the Court of Appeal considered the differences between the approaches of the UK Supreme Court and the European Court of Human Rights. The Court of Appeal concluded that while the Supreme Court declined to apply the 'sole and decisive' test, the Grand Chamber held that this test remained part of the European jurisprudence. The Court of Appeal held that to the extent that there are differences in the approaches of the courts, the Court of Appeal was bound by the decision of the Supreme Court.[152] Thus, the courts in the United Kingdom will follow the decision of the Supreme Court in *R* v. *Horncastle* and will weigh the defendant's right to a fair trial and inherent right to confrontation against the safeguards written into the Criminal Justice Act 2003. As a recent example, in *R* v. *Adeojo (Sodiq)*, the Court of Appeal held that 'in the absence of an opportunity for the defence to cross-examine the decisive witness against the [defendant] the admission of the evidence was not to be permitted unless the jury could safely conclude that it was reliable'.[153] The reliability of the evidence could be assessed by reference to the safeguards and counterbalancing measures present and the Court of Appeal identified the safeguards and counterbalancing measures in this case in reaching its conclusion that the trial judge had rightly admitted the evidence.

7.10   OTHER PROVISIONS

There are a few other provisions relating to hearsay evidence which require a brief mention.

7.10.1 Multiple hearsay

Section 121 of the Criminal Justice Act 2003 provides an additional requirement for the admissibility of multiple hearsay. Multiple hearsay is a hearsay statement that has passed through a number of people, such that the maker of the original statement and the person wishing to give evidence of that statement are quite removed. For obvious reasons, such evidence is more unreliable than first-hand hearsay, and, as such, the Criminal Justice Act 2003 imposes an additional requirement before it is admissible in court. Multiple hearsay is excluded under s. 121(1) unless one of three exceptions in s. 121(1)(a) to (c) applies:

(a) either of the statements is admissible under section 117, 119 or 120,
(b) all parties to the proceedings so agree, or
(c) the court is satisfied that the value of the evidence in question, taking into account how reliable the statements appear to be, is so high that the interests of justice require the latter statement to be admissible for that purpose.

---

151 [2012] EWCA Crim 837.
152 This approach was also followed in *R* v. *Riat (Jaspal)* [2013] 1 Cr App R 2.
153 [2013] EWCA Crim 41 at [80], following *R* v. *Riat (Jaspal)* [2013] 1 Cr App R 2 at [32].

7.10.2 Capability to make a statement

Under s. 123 of the Criminal Justice Act 2003, where a statement is made by a person who did not have the required capability to make a statement at the time it was made, the statement is not admissible. The capability of the witness is assessed under s. 123(3), and a person has the required capability if he is capable of understanding questions put to him about the matters stated, and giving answer to such questions which can be understood.

7.10.3 Previous statements

Cross-reference
Sections 119 and 120 of the Criminal Justice Act 2003 deal with inconsistent statements by witnesses and other previous statements of witnesses respectively. These are covered in Chapter 10 (Trial procedure and witness testimony).

7.10.4 Section 9 statements

Since witness statements are hearsay statements, it is necessary to briefly mention the alternative procedure for reading a witness statement of a witness who is not required to come to court to give evidence by any of the parties to the criminal proceedings. Where the parties agree that the witness need not come to court (usually because their evidence is not contentious and needs no challenge), the statement can be read under s. 9 of the Criminal Justice Act 1967. This is known as a 'section 9' statement.

Cross-reference
Refer to Chapter 10 on Witness testimony for more information about section 9 statements.

7.11 SAFEGUARDS

In addition to those set out above,[154] there are three further safeguards which are set out in separate provisions; these are designed to ensure, as far as it is possible to do so, that the hearsay evidence which is admitted under s. 114(1) is reliable. Under s. 124 of the Criminal Justice Act 2003, evidence may be adduced to challenge the credibility of the maker of a statement who does not appear as a live witness in court. Under s. 125 of the Criminal Justice Act 2003, the trial judge has the power to stop a case and order an acquittal or a retrial where, after the close of the

---

154 Section 117(6) and (7) provide safeguards in respect of hearsay evidence admitted under s. 117, s. 116(4) provides safeguards in respect of hearsay evidence admitted under s. 116(2)(e) and s. 114(2) adds a further level of factors to be considered where a judge exercises his discretion to admit hearsay evidence under s. 114(1)(d).

prosecution case, the case is based wholly or partly on a hearsay statement and the evidence is important in the case and is so unconvincing that a conviction would be unsafe.

Finally, under s. 126(1) of the Criminal Justice Act 2003, the trial judge has a discretion to exclude hearsay evidence if the court is satisfied that the case for excluding the statement, taking account of the danger that to admit it would result in undue waste of time, substantially outweighs the case for admitting it, taking account of the value of the evidence. Despite its heading, 'court's general discretion to exclude evidence', the discretion to exclude under s. 126(1) is relatively narrow in scope since it applies where the value of the evidence is substantially outweighed by the undue waste of time that its admission would cause.[155] This is further supported by s. 126(2) which expressly preserves the discretion to exclude evidence under s. 78 of the Police and Criminal Evidence Act 1984 and at common law.

7.12 CIVIL HEARSAY

In civil proceedings, hearsay evidence is generally admissible. Section 1 of the Civil Evidence Act 1995 provides that evidence shall not be excluded in civil proceedings on the ground that it is hearsay. However, the Act does lay down a number of conditions to be followed. Under s. 2(1) of the Act, a party proposing to adduce hearsay evidence must give such notice to the other parties in the proceedings as is reasonable and practicable in the circumstances for the purpose of enabling him or them to deal with any matters arising from its being hearsay, unless this requirement is waived under s. 2(3). The procedure for giving such notice is provided by rules 33.2 and 33.3 of the Civil Procedure Rules. Under s. 3 of the Civil Evidence Act 1995, where a party adduces hearsay evidence and does not call the person who made the statement to give evidence, then any other party to the proceedings may call that witness to cross-examine him on his statement, provided that the court has given leave for that party to do so. Section 4(1) provides that in assessing the weight to be attached to the hearsay evidence, 'the court shall have regard to any circumstances from which any inference can reasonably be drawn as to the reliability or otherwise of the evidence'. Section 4(2) states that the court may have regard to the following factors:

- whether it would have been reasonable and practicable for the party by whom the evidence was adduced to have produced the maker of the original statement as a witness;
- whether the original statement was made contemporaneously with the occurrence or existence of the matters stated;
- whether the evidence involves multiple hearsay;
- whether any person involved had any motive to conceal or misrepresent matters;
- whether the original statement was an edited account, or was made in collaboration with another or for a particular purpose;
- whether the circumstances in which the evidence is adduced as hearsay are such as to suggest an attempt to prevent proper evaluation of its weight.

---

155 Although in *R* v. *Atkinson (Darren Courtney)* [2011] EWCA Crim 1746, the Court of Appeal held that the trial judge was right to have excluded hearsay evidence under s. 126 after balancing the interests of both the defendant and his co-defendant and concluding that the interest of the co-defendant in excluding the evidence far outweighed the defendant's interest in having the evidence admitted.

Section 5(1) of the Civil Evidence Act 1995 provides that hearsay evidence will not be admissible if at the time of making the statement the witness was not competent as a witness. This means that he was 'suffering from such mental or physical infirmity, or lack of understanding, as would render a person incompetent as a witness in civil proceedings'.

Finally, section 5(2) provides that evidence attacking or supporting the credibility of the witness is admissible, as is evidence of previous inconsistent statements, provided that such evidence would have been admissible had the witness been called to give evidence.

7.13   CONCLUSION

The statutory framework under the Criminal Justice Act 2003 sought to increase the admissibility of hearsay evidence and to simplify the old common law, which was confusing and complicated. It is clear that while the Criminal Justice Act 2003 has made some attempts to simplify the law (for example, by eradicating the doctrine of implied assertions), the law is by no means now clear and simple. The appeal courts have resisted challenges to the statutory position regarding implied assertions and the appeal courts and the Grand Chamber of the European Court of Human Rights have recently been embroiled in a complicated and protracted consideration of the potential violation of the right to a fair trial under Article 6(1) through the denial of the right of confrontation protected by Article 6(3)(d) where a witness is unavailable to give evidence due to fear. The admissibility of hearsay evidence has always been a contentious and complicated area of law, and it appears that it will remain so as the law continues to develop.

Summary

- Hearsay is a statement made by a person other than in oral evidence, which is adduced in court in order to prove that the matter stated in the statement was or is true. Under the Criminal Justice Act 2003 statutory framework, s. 114(1) provides that: in criminal proceedings a statement not made in oral evidence in the proceedings is admissible as evidence of any matter stated if:
  - it is admissible under s. 116 or s. 117 (s. 114(1)(a))
  - it is admissible under a common law rule preserved by s. 118 (s. 114(1)(b))
  - all of the parties agree to it being admissible (s. 114(1)(c))
  - it is in the interests of justice to admit the evidence (s. 114(d)).
- If there is some other purpose for adducing the evidence, then the statement is original evidence and admissible. A statement is admissible as a non-hearsay statement if it is admitted as circumstantial evidence of the state of mind of a person, or of a state of affairs, or of the identity of a person or the origin of a person or an object.
- Under s. 115(2), 'statement' is widely defined and includes 'any representation of fact or opinion made by a person by whatever means; and it includes a representation made in a sketch, photofit or other pictorial form'.

- Under s. 115(3), the hearsay provisions only apply to statements which were made for the purpose of (or if one of the purposes for making the statement was) causing another person to believe the matter or causing another person to act or a machine to operate on the basis that the matter is as stated. This means that the hearsay provisions only apply to statements meant as an assertion, and not to implied assertions, thus overturning *R* v. *Kearley (No. 1)* [1992] 2 AC 228, HL, *R* v. *Singh* [2006] 1 WLR 1564 and *R* v. *Twist* [2011] EWCA Crim 1143.
- Under s. 116 evidence of a witness who is unavailable to give evidence is admissible if:
  - the evidence would be admissible in oral evidence if the maker of the statement was available (s. 116(1)(a)),
  - the maker of the statement is identified (s. 116(1)(b)), and
  - the witness is unavailable due to his death, he is unfit to be a witness due to his bodily or mental condition, he is outside the United Kingdom and it is not reasonably practicable to secure his attendance at court, he cannot be found despite taking reasonable steps to find him, or due to the witness's fear (s. 116(1)(c)).
- Under s. 116(5) the conditions under s. 116(2) are not to be treated as satisfied if the condition is attributable to the party seeking to adduce the statement of the witness in evidence or if it is attributable to a person acting on that party's behalf, in order to prevent the witness from giving evidence.
- Under s. 117 a document is admissible if it was created or received by a person in the course of a trade, business, profession or other occupation, or as the holder of a paid or unpaid office, and the person who supplied the information had or may reasonably be supposed to have had personal knowledge of the matters dealt with.
- Under s. 114(1)(b) of the Criminal Justice Act 2003, hearsay evidence is admissible if it is admissible under one of the common law rules preserved by s. 118 of the Act.
- *Res gestae* statements are statements which are made so closely connected with a particular event that the possibility of the statement being a lie or a mistaken statement are minimal. *Res gestae* statements are admissible hearsay evidence because they are more likely to be reliable than other hearsay statements.
- Under s. 114(1)(d), a hearsay statement is admissible if it is in the interests of justice to admit it. The court must have regard to the factors listed under s. 114(2), such as the probative value of the statement, the other evidence available, the importance of the matter, the circumstances in which the statement was made, the reliability of the maker of the statement and the evidence of the making of the statement, whether oral evidence can be given on the matter, the difficulty in challenging the statement, and the extent to which it would be likely to prejudice the other party.

For discussion . . .

1. With reference to case law, explain the difference between an inadmissible hearsay statement and an admissible non-hearsay statement.
2. To what extent have Parliament and the Court of Appeal done away with the doctrine of implied assertions?

3. How far did the Criminal Justice Act 2003 go in preserving the common law exceptions to the rule against hearsay?

4. To what extent are the cases of *R* v. *Horncastle* [2010] 2 AC 373 and *Al-Khawaja* v. *United Kingdom* (2012) 54 EHRR 23 satisfactory and consistent?

5. Critically evaluate the safeguards contained within the Criminal Justice Act 2003 with respect to the law on hearsay.

Further reading

D. Birch, 'Criminal Justice Act 2003: (4) hearsay – same old story, same old song?' [2004] Crim LR 556.
In this article, written shortly after the Criminal Justice Act 2003 received Royal Assent, the author explores the implications of the statutory framework with respect to hearsay evidence and is critical of the reforms.

A. L.-T. Choo, *Hearsay and Confrontation in Criminal Trials* (Oxford University Press, 1996).
This is a leading monograph on hearsay evidence. While it was written before the Criminal Justice Act 2003, it provides a valuable evaluation of the rationale for the rule against hearsay, the operation of the hearsay rule and the statutory and common law exceptions to the rule as they stood in 1996.

M. Hirst, 'Hearsay, confessions and mobile telephones' (2011) 75(6) *Journal of Criminal Law* 482–502.
This article considers the implications of the case of *R* v. *Twist* [2011] EWCA Crim 1143 and highlights some of the problems surrounding the admissibility of message and call logs found on mobile phones. The author points to some mistakes made by the Court of Appeal and argues that only the Supreme Court now has the power to remove the problem case of *R* v. *Kearley* [1992] AC 228, HL.

P. Mirfield, 'A final farewell to Kearley' (2012) 128 *Law Quarterly Review* 331–7.
This is a case commentary on the Court of Appeal decisions in *R* v. *Leonard* [2009] EWCA Crim 1251 and *R* v. *Twist* [2011] EWCA Crim 1143. The piece revisits the case of *R* v. *Kearley* [1992] AC 228, HL and comments on the likely demise of the doctrine of implied assertions post-*Twist*.

J. R. Spencer, *Hearsay Evidence in Criminal Proceedings*, 2nd edn (Hart Publishing, 2014).
This is the leading text on hearsay evidence. The book provides a comprehensive and up-to-date critical evaluation of the statutory framework on hearsay evidence and the case law since the enactment of the Criminal Justice Act 2003.

M. Stockdale and J. Clough, 'Confessions and the Criminal Justice Act 2003' (2013) 77(3) *Journal of Criminal Law* 231–54.
This article considers the Law Commission's intentions regarding the admissibility of confession evidence under the Criminal Justice Act 2003. It argues that the Law Commission's Report left several issues relating to the admissibility of confessions unclear. The article explores the jurisprudence since the hearsay provisions of the Criminal Justice Act 2003 have come into force and considers the scope and effect of s. 128(2) of the Act.

8 Character evidence

8.1 INTRODUCTION

'Character evidence' is evidence that relates to a person's disposition to act in a particular way. This might include evidence of the tendency of a defendant to commit certain types of offence (bad character) or evidence of no previous convictions (good character), or evidence of the tendency of a witness to tell lies (bad character) or to undertake charity work (good character). This chapter explores the admissibility of character evidence in criminal and civil proceedings. This chapter is chiefly concerned with the admissibility of evidence of bad character relating to a defendant or a witness in criminal proceedings. It will also explore the admissibility of evidence of the defendant's good character in criminal proceedings, and, to a lesser extent, the admissibility of character evidence in civil evidence. Evidence of bad character is widely construed and might be shown by evidence of previous convictions, evidence of the commission of a criminal offence which did not result in prosecution, evidence of an acquittal or evidence of reprehensible behaviour. Evidence of good character might typically include evidence that the defendant or witness has no previous convictions or evidence of charitable behaviour. The law relating to the admissibility of character evidence is governed by both statute and case law. In particular, the Criminal Justice Act 2003 provides a statutory framework which governs the admissibility of evidence of bad character of a defendant and of a non-defendant in criminal proceedings,[1] while the admissibility of evidence of good character and the directions that a trial judge should give a jury on evidence of good character is governed by case law.

8.2 CONSIDERATIONS IN DETERMINING ADMISSIBILITY

The admissibility of evidence of bad character is a matter that must be determined by the trial judge. It has always been a controversial issue for the courts and is dominated by two competing interests: (1) the propensity and/or credibility of the witness, and (2) the prejudicial effect of the admission of such evidence.

8.2.1 Propensity and credibility

Before the admissibility of any evidence falls to be determined by the trial judge, the judge must be satisfied that the evidence is relevant to a matter in issue in the proceedings.

> **Cross-reference**
> Refer back to Chapter 2 for a more detailed discussion on the meaning of relevance.

On the one hand, it might be argued in favour of the admissibility of character evidence that the evidence of a defendant's previous convictions or misconduct is relevant to propensity or his credibility. Evidence of propensity is evidence of previous behaviour which goes towards proving that a person has a tendency to act in a particular way, and is most likely to be adduced in relation to a defendant (the likelihood that the defendant is guilty of the offence charged). Where there is evidence that the defendant has behaved in a particular way in the past which is similar to the later behaviour from which the alleged offence emanates, evidence of this past misconduct may be relevant to the likelihood that the defendant has committed the offence charged. Similarly, it can be argued that evidence of a defendant's good character (i.e. evidence that the defendant has no previous convictions) is relevant to the likelihood that the defendant did not commit the offence charged. Evidence of credibility is evidence which goes towards

---

1 For commentary on the provisions of the Criminal Justice Act 2003 which relate to evidence of bad character, see G. Durston, 'Bad character evidence and non-party witnesses under the Criminal Justice Act 2003' [2004] 8(4) E & P 233–9, G. Durston, 'The impact of the Criminal Justice Act 2003 on similar fact evidence' [2004] 68(4) JCL 307–13, R. Munday, 'What constitutes "other reprehensible behaviour" under the bad character provisions of the Criminal Justice Act 2003' [2005] Crim LR 24–43, R. Munday, 'Bad character rules and riddles: "explanatory notes" and true meanings of s. 103(1) of the Criminal Justice Act 2003' [2005] Crim LR 337–54, R. Munday, 'Cut-throat defences and the "propensity to be untruthful" under s. 104 of the Criminal Justice Act 2003' [2005] Crim LR 624–37, R. Munday, 'Round up the usual suspects! Or what we have to fear from Part II of the Criminal Justice Act 2003' (2005) 169 JPN 328, P. Plowden, 'Making sense of character evidence' (2005) 155 NLJ 47, J. R. Spencer, 'Bad character gateways' (2005) 155 NLJ 650, P. Tain, 'Bad character' (2004) 148(48) SJ 1449, C. Tapper, 'The Criminal Justice Act 2003: Part 3: Evidence of bad character' [2004] Crim LR 533–55, R. Taylor, M. Wasik and R. Leng, *Blackstone's Guide to the Criminal Justice Act 2003* (Oxford University Press, 2004), ch. 8.

proving that a person is less worthy of belief. Credibility is a matter which may be relevant to a defendant or a non-defendant witness. Where there is evidence that a witness has lied in the past, especially where those lies were the subject of a conviction for perjury, evidence of these previous lies may be relevant to the likelihood that the witness is telling the truth. If the evidence of bad character is relevant to the propensity or credibility of the witness (or both), the evidence should be put before the jury in order that the jury is fully informed. It is then for the jury to place weight upon that evidence at its discretion (within the guidance given by the judge on the law).

8.2.2 Prejudicial effect of admission

However, there is a competing argument against the admission of evidence of a defendant's bad character: that is that the evidence of previous convictions or other bad character might have a prejudicial effect on the jury (or other tribunal of fact), who might convict on the basis of previous convictions, rather than the evidence relating to the offence charged. It is important to safeguard the defendant's right to a fair trial in order to protect the integrity of the criminal justice system, but this is not to say that evidence of bad character should always be excluded.

Research into the effect of the admission of evidence of a defendant's bad character on the tribunal of fact has been carried out in studies involving mock jurors and mock magistrates. In 1995, the Home Office commissioned an experimental study at the University of Oxford at the request of the Law Commission.[2] In this study, it was shown that jurors were more likely to convict a defendant of an offence if evidence of previous convictions for similar offences was adduced than if no previous convictions were adduced or previous convictions for offences which were dissimilar were adduced. In an article published in the *Criminal Law Review* in 2000, Professor Sally Lloyd-Bostock reported on the 1995 study.[3] She concluded that the study showed that there was evidence that the admission of the defendant's previous convictions in a jury trial can have a prejudicial effect on the trial and increases the chances of conviction.

S. LLOYD-BOSTOCK, 'THE EFFECTS ON JURIES OF HEARING ABOUT THE DEFENDANT'S PREVIOUS CRIMINAL RECORD: A SIMULATION STUDY' [2000] CRIM LR 734

[at 753]

The results clearly confirm that evidence of previous convictions can have a prejudicial effect, especially where there is a recent previous conviction for a similar offence. Significant effects were found even though no information about the previous conviction other than the offence was provided, and where there was only one previous conviction. It may well be that greater effects would be found for a longer

---

2 See a summary of the study carried out at the University of Oxford in 1995 at appendix D of the Law Commission's Consultation Paper, *Evidence in Criminal Proceedings: Previous Misconduct of a Defendant* (No. 141) at para. D63. This study is not to be confused with the Jury Project at the University of Oxford Penal Research Unit in the 1970s, which was also funded by the Home Office.

3 S. Lloyd-Bostock, 'The effects on juries of hearing about the defendant's previous criminal record: a simulation study' [2000] Crim LR 734.

criminal record, especially one including several similar previous convictions. The findings concerning the effects of a previous conviction for indecent assault on a child in particular show the potential for such convictions to be highly prejudicial. It appears that, in addition to any effect of similarity to the current charge, the nature of the offence produces a more general negative evaluation, including a perceived propensity to commit a range of other offences.

... Participants appear to be drawing on beliefs about typical offenders and patterns of offending which include not only beliefs about the likelihood that offenders will commit similar offences in future, but also beliefs that offenders who commit certain types of crime typically *do not* commit certain others.

[After acknowledging the limitations of the mock study, Professor Lloyd-Bostock stated at 754–5:]

Nonetheless, the central findings of this and already existing research are consistent and make theoretical sense. Very thin information about a previous conviction (the name of the offence) is evidently sufficient to evoke a quite rich stereotype, so that a similar recent conviction (especially for sexual abuse of a child) is potentially damaging for no reason that the law permits. The Law Commission quote Sir Rupert Cross's response to criticism that the CLRC did not refer to empirical evidence as follows:

> But would the CLRC have been any wiser with regard to the crucial question whether disclosure of the record increases the risk of the conviction of an innocent man?

If we assume that, amongst defendants with similar previous convictions, some are innocent of the current offence, we have good grounds to infer that routinely revealing previous convictions would indeed increase the risk of convicting an innocent man.

As juries only act as the tribunal of fact in a very small percentage of criminal trials,[4] it is also important to investigate the effect of the admission of such evidence on the decisions of lay magistrates who hear the majority of criminal trials.[5] In 2006, Professor Lloyd-Bostock published an article on the results of a further study that she carried out into the effect on lay magistrates of the admission of previous convictions and evidence that the defendant is of good character in summary trials.[6] Interestingly, Professor Lloyd-Bostock also examined the question of speculation and the effect on lay magistrates of no evidence being adduced as to the character of the defendant. This study was carried out after the reforms to the law on bad character brought in by the Criminal Justice Act 2003. She concludes that the admission of previous convictions before the lay magistrates is compelling and that providing very limited information about the nature of a previous conviction was potentially damaging, whereas the provision of no information or evidence of the good character of the defendant did not have as much of an impact as is often expected.

---

4 It has been noted that jury trials represent only a very small percentage of criminal cases. Some estimates put this figure at less than 1% of criminal cases, while others state that it is somewhere between 1% and 2% of cases. See A. Sanders, R. Young and M. Burton, *Criminal Justice*, 4th edn (Oxford University Press, 2010) at p. 554 and S. Lloyd-Bostock and C. Thomas, 'The continuing decline of the English jury' in N. Vidmar (ed.), *World Jury Systems* (Oxford University Press, 2000) at p. 61.

5 The vast majority of criminal cases (over 95%) are dealt with in the magistrates' courts. See A. Ashworth and M. Redmayne, *The Criminal Process*, 4th edn (Oxford University Press, 2010) at p. 323 and Sanders, Young and Burton, *Criminal Justice* at p. 554.

6 S. Lloyd-Bostock, 'The effects on lay magistrates of hearing that the defendant is of "good character", being left to speculate, or hearing that he has a previous conviction' [2006] Crim LR 189.

S. LLOYD-BOSTOCK, 'THE EFFECTS ON LAY MAGISTRATES OF HEARING THAT THE DEFENDANT IS OF "GOOD CHARACTER", BEING LEFT TO SPECULATE, OR HEARING THAT HE HAS A PREVIOUS CONVICTION' [2006] CRIM LR 189

[at 210–12]

As with the simulated jurors, it seems that very sparse information is sufficient to evoke a quite rich and potentially damaging stereotype. Significant effects were found even though only minimal information about the previous offence was provided (namely the offence charged), and there was only one conviction. The probative value of such information, without any details of the earlier offence and its circumstances, is arguably very limited. As in the Jury Study, the effects shown are not large, but they are significant and follow a consistent pattern. The results with bench verdicts indicate that they may make the difference between a guilty and a not-guilty verdict . . . For the magistrates, hearing about an old conviction could be as powerful as hearing about a recent one. Any previous conviction, recent or old, affected magistrates' assessments of the defendant's likely guilt and verdicts unfavourably, unless it was both recent and dissimilar to the current charge.

On the other hand, absence of information, or information that the defendant is of good character, had a weaker impact than is sometimes assumed. It seems that it is specific, concrete information that does the damage . . . Good character . . . did produce significantly more favourable ratings of the defendant's tendency to commit the kind of crime he was on trial for and his desert of punishment. However, . . . did not benefit the defendant when it came to assessments of his guilt . . .

. . . the potentially prejudicial nature of information specifying a similar or particularly serious previous offence is clear, and is apparent in the responses of magistrates who are presumably alert to the importance of not allowing it to prejudice them. The speed of the magistrates' deliberations confirmed that they are using well-developed decision categories rather than more elaborate and conscious 'from scratch' reasoning. On the other hand, the study did not confirm that 'guessed at' previous convictions have an important prejudicial effect, nor that evidence of 'good character' is in itself very influential when it comes to decisions on guilt.

As Professor Lloyd-Bostock states, further research into the effects of adducing evidence of bad character and evidence of good character is needed in order to determine more precisely the extent to which such evidence has a prejudicial effect on the verdict delivered by a lay tribunal of fact. However, there are limitations to the research that can be carried out since the jury members do not give reasons for their decision in reaching a verdict and the secrecy rule prevents any investigation into their deliberations.[7]

---

7 The common law rule prohibiting any investigation into the deliberations of the jury has been traced back to the eighteenth-century case of *Vaise* v. *Delaval* (1785) 1 Durn & E 11. The secrecy rule was also affirmed in *Ellis* v. *Deheer* [1922] 2 KB 113 and the European Court of Human Rights held that it was 'a crucial and legitimate feature of English trial law' in *Gregory* v. *United Kingdom* (1997) 25 EHRR 577. More recently, the House of Lords held that the secrecy rule was an absolute rule in *R* v. *Mirza*; *R* v. *Connor and Rollock* [2004] 1 AC 1118. However, an interesting dissenting opinion was provided by Lord Steyn who took the view that the Court of Appeal should be allowed to investigate into jury deliberations in 'exceptional circumstances'.

8.3 DEVELOPMENT OF THE LAW

Prior to the enactment of the Criminal Justice Act 2003, the law relating to the admissibility of evidence of bad character had developed through statute and case law. The law recognised the need to balance the competing interests of admitting probative evidence of bad character and ensuring that the defendant receives a fair trial. Prior to the Criminal Evidence Act 1898, the defendant's rights during his own trial were limited. The defendant was not competent to give evidence in his own defence, but, nevertheless, evidence of the defendant's bad character was admissible in certain circumstances. The Criminal Evidence Act 1898 was a significant piece of legislation in that it allowed the defendant to give evidence at his own trial. This development also brought with it the inevitable question of how a defendant witness should be treated during the process of giving evidence. Thus, this same Act also governed the law on the cross-examination of the defendant about his bad character.

The Criminal Evidence Act 1898 provided for a general rule that excluded evidence of a defendant's bad character, thus the prosecution were not permitted to cross-examine the defendant or any other defence witness with a view to adducing evidence of the defendant's bad character.[8] It was often said that the defendant was protected from such cross-examination by a 'shield'. However, there were a number of exceptions to this general rule both under statute and at common law. Under s. 1(3), Criminal Evidence Act 1898, a judge could give leave for a defendant to be cross-examined about his bad character if:

- the cross-examination was relevant to guilt,[9]
- the defendant attempted to establish his good character,[10]
- the defendant cast imputations on the character of a prosecution witness,[11] or
- the defendant gave evidence against a co-defendant.[12]

At common law, evidence of a defendant's propensity to act in a particular way ('similar fact evidence') was admissible in exceptional circumstances, namely where there was a 'strong degree of probative force'. In the case of *DPP* v. *Boardman*,[13] the House of Lords held that there must be a 'striking similarity' between the evidence of previous criminal behaviour and the facts of the offence currently alleged. Lord Salmon stated that '[t]he similarity would have to be so unique or striking that common sense makes it inexplicable on the basis of coincidence'.[14] However, this phrase, 'striking similarity', was disapproved in the House of Lords' later decision of *DPP* v. *P*[15] in which the House held that similar fact evidence was admissible if its probative value outweighs its prejudicial effect.

---

8 Section 1(3), Criminal Evidence Act 1898 (as amended).
9 Section 1(3)(i). See also *R* v. *Chitson* [1909] 2 KB 945, CA and *Jones* v. *DPP* [1962] AC 635, HL.
10 Section 1(3)(i).
11 Section 1(3)(ii). See also *Selvey* v. *DPP* [1970] AC 304, HL and *R* v. *Britzman and Hall* [1983] 1 WLR 350, CA.
12 Section 1(3)(iii). See also *R* v. *Murdoch and Taylor* [1965] AC 574, HL, *R* v. *Davis* [1975] 1 WLR 345, CA, *R* v. *Varley* [1982] 2 All ER 519, CA and *R* v. *Randall* [2004] 1 WLR 56, HL.
13 [1975] AC 421, HL.
14 Ibid. at 462.
15 [1991] 2 AC 447, HL.

In an article in 2004, Professor Tapper highlighted the need for reform of the law relating to evidence of bad character. He examined the problems with the law under the Criminal Evidence Act 1898 and described the former legal framework as one 'of incoherence, complexity and uncertainty'.

C. TAPPER, 'CRIMINAL JUSTICE ACT 2003: PART 3: EVIDENCE OF BAD CHARACTER' [2004] CRIM LR 533

[at 535–6]

[The law] undoubtedly suffered from a dearth of conceptual underpinning . . . The situation was seen as one of incoherence, complexity and uncertainty . . .

There was, in particular, no coherence between the rules relating to the admissibility of evidence of the bad character of the accused when adduced in chief with that of the permitted use of evidence of his bad character in cross-examination. So too, there was little effective protection of the character of witnesses other than the accused under the rigour of cross-examination, while the accused was accorded protection as a witness . . .

The complexity of the law was inherent in its very structure. Thus in the case of the use of evidence of the bad character of the accused in chief to show his guilt of the offence with which he were currently charged, a distinction had first to be made between evidence of bad character which flowed directly from the facts of the offence with which he were charged, and his bad character as otherwise manifest. This could involve difficult tasks of delineation of what did and did not flow directly from the facts of the offence, for example, abuse and minor assaults before a homicidal attack, or assaults on others at around the same time. Then assuming such a distinction could be made, a determination of whether the other matters did show the bad character of the accused, and if they did, whether they were sufficiently relevant to proof of the offence charged. All of this had to be established before the exclusionary rule for evidence of the accused's bad character so adduced were brought into play at all. It was only then that the court could address its mind to the question of whether an exception to the general exclusionary rule, such as that for evidence of 'similar facts' applied. Nor was this the end of the matter for even though that exception came to be denominated in terms of the balance of probative value and prejudicial effect so resulting, many thought a further stage to arise in which the court should consider whether a discretion cast in identical terms to exclude the evidence ought to be applied.

The provisions of the Criminal Justice Act 2003 reflected the proposals set out in the Government White Paper *Justice for All* which was published in 2002[16] and the White Paper followed the Law Commission Report, *Evidence of Bad Character in Criminal Proceedings* and the *Review of the Criminal Courts of England and Wales* carried out by Auld LJ, both published in 2001. Both Auld LJ and the Law Commission criticised the law on bad character as set out under the Criminal Evidence Act 1898. The White Paper suggested reforming the law to allow evidence of bad character relating to both defendants and witnesses to be adduced if relevant. According to the White Paper, a defendant would often be inhibited from adducing bad

---

16 Government White Paper, *Justice for All* (Cm. 5563, 2002).

by the defendant was a reprisal attack for this previous gun attack. Stanley Burnton LJ held that:

> the evidence of the three incidents was evidence that was alleged to do with the evidence of the murder in question. The words of the statute are straightforward, and clearly apply to evidence of incidents alleged to have created the motive for the index offence. Indeed, where the evidence is reasonably relied upon for motive, it would be irrational to introduce a temporal requirement. Take these examples. A man is wounded in a shooting. He is hospitalised for 6 months. On discharge, he is alleged to have shot the man who is alleged to have been his attacker. In another case, the reprisal is the day after the first attack. In the second case, the evidence of the first attack is not bad character for the purposes of section 98, in the first it is.[29]

Thus the Court held that s. 98 'includes no express or obviously implicit temporal qualification'[30] and thus there need not be a nexus in time between the alleged offence and the misconduct in question. The Court of Appeal did not follow the cases of *R* v. *Tirnaveanu*[31] and *R* v. *McNeill (Tracy)*[32] in which the Court of Appeal had held that the words 'to do with' in s. 98(a) required that there be some nexus in time between the offence and the evidence of misconduct. In *R* v. *Sule (Sahid)*, the Court of Appeal distinguished *R* v. *Tirnaveanu* and *R* v. *McNeill (Tracy)* on the basis that in neither of the latter two cases 'was the bad character evidence relied upon as showing a motive for the index offence, and what was said by the Court in its judgments has no application to such a case, which was not before the Court'.[33] The Court also commented *obiter* that even if s. 98(a) did contain a temporal requirement, it would have been satisfied since the three gun attacks and the alleged murder all took place within a period of three months.

As stated above, there are earlier authorities which set out a temporal requirement between the alleged offence and the misconduct. Although these cases were not followed in the more recent case of *R* v. *Sule (Sahid)*, they were not overruled. There is a distinguishing feature between these cases: *R* v. *Sule (Sahid)* involved the admissibility of evidence of incidents which occurred prior to the offence with which the defendant was charged and the Court of Appeal seemed to distinguish the former cases on the basis that they did not involve demonstrating motive for the offence charged. However, in both *R* v. *Tirnaveanu* and *R* v. *McNeill (Tracy)*, the evidence in question related to incidents which occurred post-offence. In *R* v. *Tirnaveanu*, the Court of Appeal held that there was not a sufficient nexus between the offence charged and the evidence that the prosecution sought to adduce. The charges related to the illegal entry of Romanian immigrants into the United Kingdom. The defendant was alleged to have posed as a solicitor and assisted immigrants to enter the United Kingdom illegally through the use of forged documentation. The prosecution had wanted to adduce evidence that the defendant had

29 Ibid. at [12].
30 Ibid. at [11].
31 [2007] EWCA Crim 1239.
32 [2007] EWCA Crim 2927.
33 Above (n. 28) at [11]. (Also see the extract from *R* v. *Sule (Sahid)* below.)

had previous dealings with immigrants and they relied on s. 98(a); however, the Court held that there was not enough of a temporal nexus for the evidence to fall within s. 98(a).[34]

R V. *TIRNAVEANU* [2007] EWCA CRIM 1239
Thomas LJ

[at [23]–[24]]

The basis on which it was contended before us by the prosecution that the evidence which they sought to adduce was 'to do' with the facts of the alleged offence was that it was evidence which was central to the case in that it related to proving that the appellant was the person who had committed the offences charged in the various counts. We do not accede to that submission. As counsel for the prosecution accepted, if his submission was right, then in any case, where the identity of the defendant was in issue (including, by way of example, cases of sexual misconduct), the prosecution would be able to rely on this exclusion to adduce evidence of misconduct on other occasions which helped to prove identity. It seems to us that the exclusion must be related to evidence where there is some nexus in time between the offence with which the defendant is charged and the evidence of misconduct which the prosecution seek to adduce. In the commentary in the Criminal Law Review to *R v T* [2007] Crim LR 165, it was argued that the court in *Machado* and *McIntosh* had taken too narrow a view of s.98 thereby permitting prejudicial evidence to be admitted on the threshold test of relevance alone with no gateway having to be satisfied. We do not agree – the application of s.98 is a fact specific exercise involving the interpretation of ordinary words.

We respectfully agree with Professor J R Spencer, QC *Evidence of Bad Character* at paragraph 2.23 where he suggests that there is a potential overlap between evidence that has to do with the alleged facts of the offence and evidence that might be admitted through one of the gateways in section 101(1). As he observes in relation to the example he took of prior misconduct being the reason for the commission of the offence, such evidence could be admitted either as 'to do' with the offence or as important explanatory evidence under s.101(1)(c):

In practice nothing of any legal significance depends on which of these two routes it is by which the evidence comes in.

In *R* v. *McNeill (Tracy)*, the defendant's behaviour after the alleged offence was held on appeal not to fall within s. 98(a). The defendant was convicted of making threats to kill towards her neighbour. The prosecution had sought to adduce evidence that, two days later, the defendant had made a threat to burn down her block of flats and those living in them to a housing officer. The Court of Appeal held that this evidence did fall within s. 98(a) and that s. 98 was to be broadly construed. Of course, both of these cases above must now be read in light of the Court of Appeal decision in *R* v. *Sule (Sahid)*, discussed above.

---

34 Since the evidence did not fall within the exclusion under s. 98(a), it did fall within the definition of 'bad character' under s. 98 generally. However, the Court held that the evidence was admissible under s. 101(1)(d) as 'it was relevant to an important matter in issue between the defendant and the prosecution – whether it was the appellant who had committed the offences and not some other person' ([2007] EWCA Crim 1239, per Thomas LJ at [26]).

R V. *SULE (SAHID)* [2012] EWCA CRIM 1130
Stanley Burnton LJ

[at [9]–[11]]

The judge carefully considered the admission of the evidence of the three earlier submissions and handed down a detailed written ruling. He held that the evidence of the 3 incidents was highly relevant and had to do with the alleged facts of the offence with which the defendants were charged within the meaning of section 98 of the 2003 Act. Mr Price seeks to challenge this decision, on the basis that such facts must have a nexus in time with the alleged offence, and the incidents in question had no such nexus. For the proposition that there must be such a nexus he relies principally on the judgment of this Court in *McNeill* [2007] EWCA Crim 2927 and *Tirnaveanu* [sic] [2007] EWCA Crim 1239, [2007] 2 Cr App R 23.

We are clear that the Applicant's reliance on these authorities is misplaced. In *McNeill*, the evidence was of a threat made by the defendant subsequent to the alleged offence. It was held that because of the proximity of time between the offence and the threat, the evidence of the threat was 'to do with' the evidence of the alleged earlier offence. It is understandable that chronological proximity may be required in such a case, where otherwise the evidence of bad character is little more than evidence of propensity. In *Tirnaveanu* [sic] similarly, the evidence of bad character was in essence evidence of further similar offending, by the defendant, and again some chronological proximity may be required if the provisions of section 103 are not to be circumvented.

In neither of those cases was the bad character evidence relied upon as showing a motive for the index offence, and what was said by the Court in its judgments has no application to such a case, which was not before the Court. Section 98 includes no express or obviously implicit temporal qualification.

In *R* v. *Abaphai and others*,[35] the Court of Appeal considered the scope of s. 98(b) and held that it was of wide application. Thus, not only did it encompass conduct by prosecuting authorities, but it also covered the situation where a co-defendant blackmailed the defendant in connection with the offence with which they were jointly charged. Therefore, evidence that a co-defendant has intimidated or blackmailed the defendant in connection with the case or its investigation or prosecution would be admissible, just as it would have been before the Criminal Justice Act 2003. This paragraph might therefore apply to situations where a co-defendant blackmails a defendant in order to influence them to take sole responsibility for the offence for which they are jointly charged, or to conceal or dispose of evidence related to the offence, or to hide the co-defendant's participation in the offence from the investigating officers. Such evidence would be admissible since it falls within s. 98(b) and it would not be subject to the application of the gateway under s. 101(1).

8.4.1 Reputation

Evidence of reputation is also excluded from the reach of the gateways under the Criminal Justice Act 2003 by s. 118(1), which preserves the common law rule under which a person's

---

35 [2011] EWCA Crim 917.

reputation is admissible for the purposes of proving his bad character[36] in criminal proceedings.

8.4.2 Misconduct

The term 'misconduct' under s. 98 is defined within the Act, although the definition of this word appears in the interpretation section to Chapter 1 of Part 11 of the Act, s. 112, rather than within a subsection of s. 98 itself. Thus, under s. 112 'misconduct' is defined as 'the commission of an offence or other reprehensible behaviour'.

S. 112, CRIMINAL JUSTICE ACT 2003

'misconduct' means the commission of an offence or other reprehensible behaviour

---

In order to appreciate the full meaning of 'bad character' it is necessary to read these two sections together. Thus, by amalgamating these definitions evidence of bad character becomes 'evidence of, or a disposition towards, the commission of an offence or other reprehensible behaviour'.

Thus, this provision expands the definition of 'bad character' under s. 98 to cover 'reprehensible behaviour' (see Figure 8.2). The Explanatory Notes to the Criminal Justice Act 2003 state that '[t]his is intended to be a broad definition and to cover evidence that shows that a person has committed an offence, or has acted in a reprehensible way (or is disposed to do so) as well as evidence from which this might be inferred'.[37] Evidence of the commission of an offence obviously includes evidence of a previous conviction, so previous convictions are clearly evidence of bad character under the Criminal Justice Act 2003.[38] 'Evidence of the commission of an offence' under s. 98 has also been held to cover offences committed after the alleged offence with which the court is concerned,[39] cautions,[40] an absolute discharge after a finding by a jury that the defendant was unfit to plead,[41] allegations which were stayed as an abuse of process,[42] a decision by the CPS not to prosecute the accused,[43] as well as evidence of prior 'risky driving' which had never resulted in a charge, let alone in a prosecution.[44] Before the enactment of the Criminal Justice Act 2003, the House of Lords held in *R* v. *Z*,[45] that evidence of a previous acquittal could be adduced as

---

36 Or his good character.
37 Home Office, Explanatory Notes to the Criminal Justice Act 2003, para. 353.
38 This has been held to include convictions from a court in a different jurisdiction: see *R* v. *Kordasinski* [2007] 1 Cr App R 17. See J. R. Spencer, 'Are foreign convictions admissible as evidence of bad character?' (2007) 2 *Archbold News* 6–9.
39 *R* v. *Adenusi* (2007) 171 JP 169.
40 *R* v. *Weir* [2006] 1 WLR 1885.
41 *R* v. *Renda and others* [2006] 1 WLR 2948.
42 *R* v. *Smith and others* [2006] 2 Cr App R 4.
43 *R* v. *Ngyeun* [2008] EWCA Crim 585.
44 *R* v. *McKenzie* [2008] RTR 22.
45 [2000] 3 WLR 117, HL.

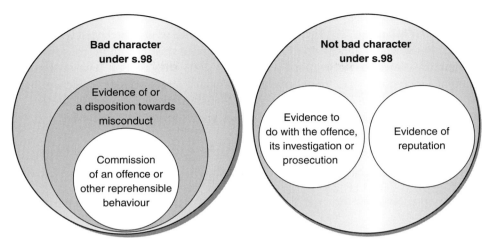

Figure 8.2 Meaning of bad character under s. 98

similar fact evidence; although in *R* v. *O'Dowd*,[46] the defendant maintained his innocence in relation to rape allegations for which he had been acquitted and the Court of Appeal held that the evidence of these acquittals should not have been adduced since it had resulted in the trial of collateral issues and significantly lengthened the proceedings at hand. However, the wide definitions provided by ss. 98 and 112 clearly demonstrate that the definition of bad character is not restricted to just previous convictions. Bad character under the Act also includes evidence that the defendant has committed a criminal offence, irrespective of whether he has actually been convicted of it in a court of law, as well as evidence of a disposition towards committing criminal offences.

8.4.3 Reprehensible behaviour

The definition of bad character further encompasses evidence of 'reprehensible behaviour' by the defendant, as well as evidence of the defendant's disposition towards reprehensible behaviour. In *R* v. *Weir and others*,[47] Kennedy LJ stated that, '[t]he definition of "misconduct" in section 112(1) is very wide. It makes it clear that behaviour may be reprehensible, and therefore misconduct, though not amounting to the commission of an offence'.[48] In *R* v. *Renda and others*,[49] Sir Igor Judge stated that, 'as a matter of ordinary language, the word "reprehensible" carries with it some element of culpability or blameworthiness'.[50]

Munday criticises the definitions under ss. 98 and 112, commenting: 'The meaning of "the commission of an offence" is tolerably clear. But what, one might ask, ought a court to treat

---

46 [2009] 2 Cr App R 16.
47 Above (n. 40).
48 Ibid. at 1911.
49 Above (n. 41).
50 Ibid. at 2953.

under the conflated tag, "evidence of, or of a disposition towards, the commission of *other reprehensible behaviour*"?'[51] There is no definition of this term 'reprehensible behaviour' within the Act, but it would appear that Parliament intended this term to be construed widely. The Explanatory Notes to the Criminal Justice Act 2003 suggest that 'evidence not related to criminal proceedings' (i.e. 'reprehensible behaviour') might include 'evidence that a person has a sexual interest in children or is racist'.[52] Shortly after the Criminal Justice Act 2003 came into force, Munday considered the scope of this phrase in the article below.

R. MUNDAY, 'WHAT CONSTITUTES "OTHER REPREHENSIBLE BEHAVIOUR" UNDER THE BAD CHARACTER PROVISIONS OF THE CRIMINAL JUSTICE ACT 2003' [2005] CRIM LR 24

[at 25]

It comes as something of a surprise to encounter the very expression, 'reprehensible behaviour', in what purports to be a modernising statute. Doubtless, it took a deft wordsmith to come up with this colourful expression. Regrettably, in a criminal context, the word 'reprehensible' is strongly redolent of another age: it is more evocative of Victorian social moralising than representative of the more neutral traits of a statute designed to set the creaking rules of criminal evidence on a modern footing.

. . .

[at 26]

Taking as their point of departure the Wittgenstinian slogan, 'the meaning is the context', lawyers might initially assume that the contexts in which the expression 'bad character' is to be found would indicate with some precision what the legislature intended ['reprehensible behaviour'] to mean. Regrettably, they would be disappointed. 'Bad character' is used in so many different situations in the 2003 Act that it is suggested that no single, coherent contextual pattern can be discerned.

. . .

[at 31–2]

However matters may have looked to those who slipped in the word, 'reprehensible' is not a term to which one can assign a particularly distinct meaning. In basic terms, at times the word denotes serious misdoings, but it can equally signify minor detours from perceived paths of righteousness. As when weighing substances lighter than air, specialist equipment may be called for to assess the term's meaning with any confidence . . . Evidently, the word is somewhat slippery.

. . .

[at 43]

To the extent that a direction is called for, explaining the use to which unfavourable information about an accused may be put, it might be thought appropriate that this protection be afforded to defendants in all cases where the risk is run that the jury might make more of such evidence than is justified. In short,

---

51 See Munday, above (n. 24) at 25.

52 Explanatory Notes to the Criminal Justice Act 2003, para. 355. Although see *R* v. *Weir* above (n. 40) in which it was held that a sexual relationship between an adult man and a girl who was 16 years old at the time that the relationship started would not amount to reprehensible behaviour without any evidence that he had groomed her, or that her parents had expressed any disapproval, or of her immaturity.

since the word 'reprehensible' covers misdoings of widely varying magnitude, courts can give effect to this simply by adhering to more general underlying notions of criminal justice – a notion of fair trial where, despite the more heavy-handed approach of the new legislation, the relevance of evidence remains a strict requirement and, dare one say, where one of the law's prime concerns remains the avoidance of miscarriages of justice.

Thus, Munday suggests that the phrase is difficult to define and he would appear to take the view that the courts should adopt a sensible approach to the admissibility of evidence of bad character rather than strain to find an all-encompassing definition for the term 'reprehensible'. The term 'reprehensible behaviour' has been widely construed by the courts to include: writing rap lyrics planning a violent attack and an interest in images of violent attacks,[53] a husband forging a report from a private eye alleging that his wife was having an adulterous relationship,[54] and the behaviour of the defendant which led to a harassment warning (namely a complaint from a woman that the defendant had gone round to her home twice in relation to a dispute with her ex-partner and while he was not threatening or violent, he 'was intimidating at times in his demeanour'; he also took her car keys and telephone number and returned on the second occasion with two other men).[55]

However, the courts have maintained limits on the term, ensuring that it is not all-encompassing. It has been held that the following did not amount to reprehensible behaviour: shouting at a partner about the care of a young child where the shouting is aggressive but there is no violence,[56] taking an overdose of drugs,[57] the exaggeration by a school pupil to other pupils of an allegation that a teacher had hit her,[58] a sexual relationship between a 34-year-old man and a 16-year-old girl without any evidence of grooming or the disapproval of her parents or of her immaturity,[59] and being arrested and released without charge.[60]

It should be noted that any evidence which does not fall within the definition of bad character under the 2003 Act is admissible, provided that it is relevant and it is not excluded by any other provision such as s. 78, Police and Criminal Evidence Act 1984 or under the common law discretion[61] to exclude prosecution evidence.[62]

Once it has been established that evidence falls under the definition of 'bad character' within s. 98 and s. 112 of the Criminal Justice Act 2003, the question as to its admissibility under one of the available 'gateways' falls to be considered. Different sections of the Criminal Justice Act 2003 govern the admissibility of evidence of bad character of the defendant and of the non-defendant. Section 100(1) provides for the admissibility of bad character evidence of a

---

53 *R* v. *Saleem* [2007] EWCA Crim 1923.
54 *R* v. *Malone* [2006] EWCA Crim 1860.
55 *R* v. *Dalby (Lewis)* [2012] EWCA Crim 701.
56 *R* v. *Osbourne* [2007] EWCA Crim 481. It should be noted that the court stated (at [34]) that while such behaviour did not amount to 'reprehensible behaviour' for the purposes of the Criminal Justice Act 2003, it was 'not . . . to be commended'.
57 *R* v. *Hall-Chung* (2007) 151 SJLB 1020.
58 *R* v. *V* [2006] EWCA Crim 1901.
59 *R* v. *Weir* [2006] 1 WLR 1885.
60 See *R* v. *Hong and another*, reported with *R* v. *Weir*.
61 *R* v. *Sang* [1980] AC 402, HL.
62 See *R* v. *Manister*, which was heard in the Court of Appeal together with *R* v. *Weir*.

non-defendant, while s. 101(1) provides for the admissibility of evidence of the defendant's bad character. Each of these sections will be considered in turn over the next part of this chapter, beginning with the admissibility of evidence of the defendant's bad character under s. 101(1), Criminal Justice Act 2003.

8.5 BAD CHARACTER EVIDENCE OF THE DEFENDANT

The admissibility of evidence of bad character of the defendant is governed by s. 101(1), Criminal Justice Act 2003. This section provides seven instances in which evidence of a defendant's bad character may be admissible. These are known as 'gateways'.

S. 101(1), CRIMINAL JUSTICE ACT 2003

In criminal proceedings evidence of the defendant's bad character is admissible if, but only if –

(a) all parties to the proceedings agree to the evidence being admissible,

(b) the evidence is adduced by the defendant himself or is given in answer to a question asked by him in cross-examination and intended to elicit it,

(c) it is important explanatory evidence,

(d) it is relevant to an important matter in issue between the defendant and the prosecution,

(e) it has substantial probative value in relation to an important matter in issue between the defendant and a co-defendant,

(f) it is evidence to correct a false impression given by the defendant, or

(g) the defendant has made an attack on another person's character.

These gateways provide for the method by which evidence of the defendant's bad character is to become admissible at trial. In R v. *Highton and others*,[63] the Court of Appeal drew a distinction between the gateways which provide for the *admissibility* of such evidence and the separate question of the *use* to which such evidence can be put once admitted: s. 101(1) itself 'states that it is dealing with the question of admissibility and makes no reference to the effect that admissible evidence as to bad character is to have'.[64] In this case, this meant that where evidence was admitted under s. 101(1)(g) (which covers situations where the defendant has made an attack on another person's character), it may be used as evidence of the defendant's propensity to commit offences as well as to the defendant's credibility, despite the fact that s. 101(1)(d) specifically refers to the propensity of the defendant. Thus, the gateways act only as a mechanism by which evidence of the defendant's bad character can be adduced in court, and the question of what the jury or magistrates may use this evidence for is a distinct question which will depend upon 'the matters to which it is relevant rather than upon the gateway through which it was admitted'.[65]

63 [2005] 1 WLR 3472.
64 Ibid., per Lord Woolf CJ at 3477.
65 Ibid.

8.5.1 Discretion to exclude

Before exploring each of the gateways under s. 101(1), it is prudent to mention the judicial discretion to exclude unfair evidence. Under s. 78(1), Police and Criminal Evidence Act 1984, the trial judge may exclude prosecution evidence 'if it appears to the court that, having regard to all the circumstances, including the circumstances in which the evidence was obtained, the admission of the evidence would have such an adverse effect on the fairness of the proceedings that the court ought not to admit it.' This provision applies to any prosecution evidence, thus it should be available in relation to any of the gateways under which the prosecution is seeking to adduce evidence of the defendant's bad character. Similarly, the common law discretion to exclude evidence which is prejudicial to the defendant, in *R* v. *Sang*, should also be available.

> **Cross-reference**
> Refer to Chapter 5 on 'Confession evidence' and Chapter 6 on 'Improperly obtained evidence' for a more detailed discussion on the application of the general discretion to exclude evidence under s. 78(1), Police and Criminal Evidence Act 1984.

However, the Criminal Justice Act 2003 also contains its own statutory discretion to exclude evidence of bad character where its admission would have such an adverse effect on the fairness of the proceedings that the court ought not to admit it. This can be found under s. 101(3), Criminal Justice Act 2003, but it only applies to two of the seven gateways, namely gateway (d) and gateway (g). Where either of these gateways is relied upon, the evidence of the defendant's bad character will be admissible subject to the discretion to exclude evidence under s. 101(3).

S. 101, CRIMINAL JUSTICE ACT 2003

(3) The court must not admit evidence under subsection (1)(d) or (g) if, on an application by the defendant to exclude it, it appears to the court that the admission of the evidence would have such an adverse effect on the fairness of the proceedings that the court ought not to admit it.

(4) On an application to exclude evidence under subsection (3) the court must have regard, in particular, to the length of time between the matters to which that evidence relates and the matters which form the subject of the offence charged.

The wording of this subsection is almost identical to the wording of the general discretion to exclude evidence under s. 78(1), Police and Criminal Evidence Act 1984; however, there is one significant difference. Once the trial judge has determined that the admission of the evidence would have an adverse effect on the fairness of the proceedings, the two provisions differ in terms of the degree of discretion afforded to the trial judge. While s. 78(1) provides that the trial judge '*may* refuse to allow' unfair evidence to be admissible, s. 101(3) provides less discretion in that it states that the judge '*must* not admit' such evidence.[66]

---

66 Author's emphasis.

Where the defence makes an application to exclude evidence of bad character under s. 101(3), Criminal Justice Act 2003, s. 104(4) of the Act provides that the court must also take into account the length of time between the matters relating to the evidence of bad character and the offence charged.

8.5.2 The 'gateways'

There are seven gateways which provide for the admissibility of evidence of the bad character of the defendant under s. 101(1), Criminal Justice Act 2003 (see Figure 8.3). Provided that one of these gateways applies, the evidence of bad character is admissible under s. 101(1). Under s. 101(1), such evidence is admissible where:

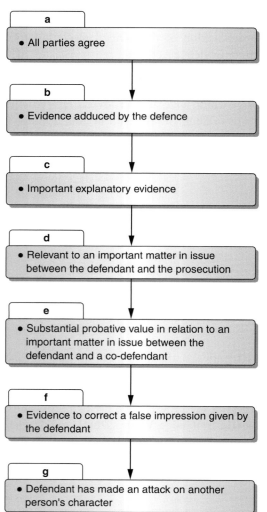

Figure 8.3 The gateways of admissibility under s. 101(1)

a
- All parties agree

b
- Evidence adduced by the defence

c
- Important explanatory evidence

d
- Relevant to an important matter in issue between the defendant and the prosecution

e
- Substantial probative value in relation to an important matter in issue between the defendant and a co-defendant

f
- Evidence to correct a false impression given by the defendant

g
- Defendant has made an attack on another person's character

(a) all parties agree to the evidence being admissible;
(b) the evidence is adduced by the defendant;
(c) it is important explanatory evidence;
(d) it is relevant to an important matter in issue between the defendant and the prosecution;
(e) it has substantial probative value in relation to an important matter in issue between the defendant and a co-defendant;
(f) it is evidence to correct a false impression given by the defendant; or
(g) the defendant has made an attack on another person's character.

Gateway (a): all parties agree

Under s. 101(1)(a), where all the parties in the proceedings agree to the admissibility of the evidence, then it will be admissible. This gateway is relatively straightforward; if the defendant does not object to evidence of his own bad character being adduced, then it will be admissible provided that the prosecution and any co-defendants also agree to the evidence being admissible. The leave of the court is not required to adduce the evidence under s. 101(1)(a). In *R* v. *Hussain*,[67] the two co-defendants were running 'cut-throat' defences. They both had previous convictions for offences of dishonesty and they wished to adduce the bad character of each other. Since counsel for each of the defendants realistically expected that the defendants' convictions would be admissible under another gateway (and the prosecutor was also in agreement), they agreed to admit the previous convictions of each defendant under s. 101(1)(a). Leave of the trial judge was not required. Where evidence of the defendant's bad character is adduced under s. 101(1)(a), it is good practice for the evidence to be presented to the jury in the form of a written formal admission under s. 10, Criminal Justice Act 1967.

Gateway (b): adduced by the defendant

Under s. 101(1)(b), evidence of the bad character of the defendant is either 'adduced by the defendant himself or is given in answer to a question asked by him in cross-examination and intended to elicit it'. Gateway (b) applies where counsel for the defendant asks a prosecution witness about the defendant's bad character in cross-examination, or where the defendant gives evidence at his own trial and adduces his own bad character during examination-in-chief by his own counsel.[68] Once the requirements of s. 101(1)(b) have been satisfied, the court has no discretion to refuse to allow the evidence of the defendant's bad character to be adduced.[69] There may be good reason for the defendant to be upfront about any previous convictions that he has. As Murphy and Glover state:

> There is sometimes a valid reason for the accused to put his bad character before the jury. Where his previous convictions are relatively minor, or are for offences quite different in nature from the offence with which he is now charged, it may do no harm, and may even

---

67 [2008] EWCA Crim 1117.
68 For example, see *R* v. *Tollady (Kim)* [2010] EWCA Crim 2614, *R* v. *Gruber* [2010] EWCA Crim 1821, *R* v. *Lodge (Moya)* [2009] EWCA Crim 2651 and *R* v. *Lafayette (Anthony Lascelles)* [2008] EWCA Crim 3238.
69 *R* v. *Edwards* [2005] EWCA Crim 3244 at [1].

be advantageous to show the jury that the accused has no history of character related to the kind of offence charged. If the accused remains silent about his character, there is always the risk that the jury may speculate about it, and by bringing the subject up, the accused may even gain some credit for frankness.[70]

Gateway (c): important explanatory evidence

Under gateway (c), evidence of a defendant's bad character is admissible if 'it is important explanatory evidence'. Under the old common law, background evidence which provided evidence of the history of the case was admissible if without that evidence the case before the jury would be difficult to understand.[71] Under the Criminal Justice Act 2003, gateway (c) applies to background evidence which is needed by the jury to understand the facts of the case. 'Important explanatory evidence' is defined under s. 102 as evidence without which the jury would find it 'impossible or difficult properly to understand other evidence in the case', and that the evidence has 'substantial' value for understanding the case as a whole.

S. 102, CRIMINAL JUSTICE ACT 2003

... evidence is important explanatory evidence if –

(a) without it, the court or jury would find it impossible or difficult properly to understand other evidence in the case, and

(b) its value for understanding the case as a whole is substantial.

The Explanatory Notes to the Act describe 'explanatory evidence' as something which, 'whilst not going to the question of whether the defendant is guilty, is necessary for the jury to have a proper understanding of other evidence being given in the case by putting it in its proper context'.[72] If the case is generally understandable without the additional evidence of bad character, then the evidence should not be admitted.[73] The Explanatory Notes then provide an example of 'a case involving the abuse by one person of another over a long period of time. For the jury to understand properly the victim's account of the offending and why they did not seek help from, for example, a parent or other guardian, it might be necessary for evidence to be given of a wider pattern of abuse involving that other person.'[74] Section 102(b) of the Criminal Justice Act 2003 also provides a further requirement that the evidence has 'substantial' probative value for understanding the case as a whole. This latter requirement is known as an 'enhanced relevance' test and it places a necessary restriction on the evidence which may be admitted under this gateway, thus evidence which is not really

---

70 P. Murphy and R. Glover, *Murphy on Evidence*, 13th edn (Oxford University Press, 2013) at pp. 168–9.
71 See *R* v. *Pettman* (unreported), 5 May 1985, CA.
72 Explanatory Notes to the Criminal Justice Act 2003, para. 360. This description is actually used in relation to the similar provision for the admissibility of evidence of a non-defendant's bad character under s. 100(1)(a), but is also helpful in relation to s. 101(1)(c).
73 Ibid. at para. 361.
74 Ibid. at para. 360.

relevant to a matter in issue or evidence which only goes to a trivial issue in the case would not be admissible under gateway (c).

The following two cases serve as examples of cases in which evidence was rightly admitted under s. 101(1)(c). In *R* v. *Chohan*,[75] the prosecution witness as to identity in a robbery case was permitted to give evidence as to the reasons for her recognition of the defendant. She described that she met the defendant during heroin dealings. This evidence was admissible under s. 101(1)(c) as important explanatory evidence in the sense that it explained the basis of her identification of the defendant. In *R* v. *Suleman (Omar Mohammed)*,[76] the defendant was charged with various counts of arson and public nuisance. The Court of Appeal dismissed an appeal against the decision of the trial judge to admit evidence of previous fires which occurred a year or two before those which formed the offences with which the defendant was charged, but for which the defendant was never indicted. The prosecution case was that one person was responsible for all of the fires. The trial judge admitted evidence of the fires as important explanatory evidence under s. 101(1)(c) since it would have been misleading for the jury to hear about only some of the fires (evidence of the previous fires was also admissible under s. 101(1)(d)).

In *R* v. *Davis*,[77] the Court of Appeal held that the trial judge was wrong to have admitted the evidence as 'important explanatory evidence' under s. 101(1)(c). The Court considered the application of gateway (c) in a case involving an allegation that the defendant had killed his girlfriend after she told him that she was having an affair. The trial judge admitted the evidence of the defendant's ex-girlfriend of 20 years previously to the effect that the defendant had been jealous and violent during their relationship and that it would be difficult for the jury properly to understand the evidence of the defendant's conduct towards his girlfriend without this evidence and that the value of the evidence for understanding the case as a whole was substantial. Thus, the Court of Appeal held that the trial judge should not have admitted the evidence as 'important explanatory evidence' under s. 101(1)(c).

R V. *DAVIS* [2008] EWCA CRIM 1156
Rix LJ

33. Gateway (c), important explanatory evidence, no doubt reflects the common law rule which permitted background or explanatory material where the account otherwise to be placed before the court would be incomplete and incomprehensible . . . the gateway is now governed by the new statutory language and has to be seen in its overall setting.

34. That setting permits evidence of propensity under gateway (d) where it is 'relevant to an important matter in issue', but subject to the additional safeguards of s. 101(3) and (4) and (where appropriate) s. 103(3). That would suggest that evidence of propensity should not readily slide in under the guise of important background evidence, and that evidence which is admitted under gateway (c) should not readily be used, once admitted, for a purpose, such as propensity, for which additional safeguards or different tests have first to be met. Similarly, evidence may be admitted under gateway (f)

---

75 Reported with *R* v. *Edwards*, above (n. 69).
76 [2012] EWCA Crim 1569.
77 [2008] EWCA Crim 1156.

'to correct a false impression given by the defendant' subject to the requirements of s. 105, and it would seem odd if such evidence should be admitted under gateway (c) qua background, where its real importance was to correct a false impression, without meeting the requirements of s. 105. A similar point could be made in relation to gateway (g), which requires an attack on another person's character, where the additional safeguards of s. 101(3) and (4) again apply. However, evidence can of course be admitted via more than one gateway, and evidence admitted under the more stringent conditions of gateway (d) as 'relevant to an important matter in issue' might well thereafter be available for more general purposes.

. . .

36. . . . there must be a danger in admitting such evidence merely as 'explanatory', however important, if the use to which it is really intended to put it is as evidence of propensity, where the statutory tests and safeguards are different. We consider that such considerations require that the statutory test for gateway (c) should be applied cautiously where it is argued to overlap with a submitted case of propensity . . .

41. In our judgment, we think that the judge, highly experienced as he is, nevertheless in our case erred . . . The evidence of the wife's killing and the issue of provocation were in our judgment entirely comprehensible to the jury without their knowing of Rosie Thorne . . . certainly nothing that happened between him and Rosie Thorne some 20 years earlier could throw any light on it, let alone amount to important explanatory evidence, whose value for understanding the case as a whole was substantial, without which the jury would find it impossible or difficult properly to understand other evidence in the case . . .

42. . . . the judge quite properly had difficulties with a submission that he should admit the evidence under gateway (d). And yet, the real purpose of its admission under gateway (c), it seems to us, was to inform the jury that the appellant had a propensity for violence and aggression, including at least the threats of death, even in the absence of provocation . . . That is not important explanatory evidence, it is evidence of a propensity, or evidence to meet the appellant's case of provocation by seeking to show that he could kill (even though he never before had) without provocation. It seems to us that however hard one presses the word 'properly' in the statutory test of 'impossible or difficult properly to understand' it is illegitimate to press it as far as admitting the evidence of Rosie Thorne simply on the ground that it might possibly go a certain distance to meet the appellant's case at trial. The evidence of Rosie Thorne was not intended to *explain* or help the jury to *understand* the other evidence in the case, but to *contradict* the appellant's case, from a distance of some twenty years, as to the dynamics of his relationship with his wife and the circumstances leading up to her death. A fortiori it is difficult to see that Rosie Thorne's evidence had a 'substantial' value for understanding the case as a whole.

The courts have been keen to maintain a limit on the evidence which falls under the category of 'important explanatory evidence'. As such, there have been several decisions in which the Court of Appeal has upheld trial judges' decisions not to admit the evidence under s. 101(1)(c). Two examples are *R* v. *Smith*[78] and *R* v. *Beverley (Elijah)*.[79] In *R* v. *Smith*, the defendant had been charged with sexual offences against children. The trial judge refused to admit evidence of previous sexual acts with children under gateway (c) (although he did rule

---

78 Reported with *R* v. *Edwards*, above (n. 69).
79 [2006] EWCA Crim 1287.

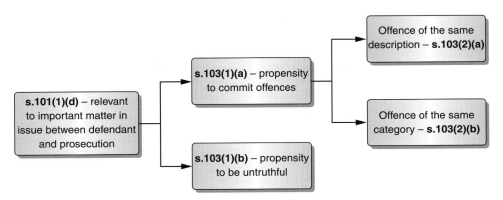

Figure 8.4 Gateway (d): relevant to an important matter in issue between the defendant and prosecution

that it was admissible under gateway (d)). The Court of Appeal upheld the trial judge's decision not to admit the evidence under s. 101(1)(c) and provided a 'word of caution for the future about the general undesirability of the jury being required to explore satellite issues one stage removed from the charges they are trying unless this is really necessary'.[80] In *R* v. *Beverley (Elijah)*, the Court of Appeal held that the two paragraphs under s. 102 ((a) and (b)) were cumulative. In this case, evidence of the defendant's previous convictions for possession of cannabis and possession of cannabis with intent to supply was adduced under s. 101(1)(c) at the defendant's trial for conspiracy to import cocaine. The Court of Appeal held that evidence of these previous convictions should not have been admitted by the trial judge under s. 101(1)(c) because these previous convictions were not important explanatory evidence under s. 102 of the Criminal Justice Act 2003. The Court stated that the jury were not disabled or disadvantaged in understanding any of the evidence against the defendant without having the evidence of these two previous convictions and that there never should have been an application under gateway (c).

It would seem that s. 78, Police and Criminal Evidence Act 1984 can apply in relation to s. 101(1)(c), thus the court may exercise its discretion to exclude the evidence of the defendant's bad character where its admission would have an adverse effect on the fairness of the proceedings.[81]

Gateway (d): relevant to an important matter between prosecution and defendant
Under s. 101(1)(d), evidence of a defendant's bad character is admissible if it is 'relevant to an important matter in issue between the defendant and the prosecution'[82] (see Figure 8.4). According to Rose LJ in *R* v. *Hanson*, s. 101(1)(d) is likely to be one of the gateways most commonly relied on in bad character applications.[83] Section 101(1)(d) provides that only

---

80 Above (n. 69), per Scott Baker LJ at [86].
81 See *R* v. *Highton*, above (n. 63).
82 According to s. 109(1), Criminal Justice Act 2003, in assessing the relevance of evidence, the court should assume that the evidence is true, unless it appears to the court on material before it that no court or jury could reasonably find it to be true (s. 109(2)).
83 [2005] EWCA Crim 824 at [5].

prosecution evidence is admissible under gateway (d).[84] Section 103(1) provides a definition of 'matters in issue between the defendant and the prosecution' as including evidence of the defendant's propensity to commit offences of the kind with which he is charged and evidence of the defendant's propensity to be untruthful, i.e. his credibility.

S. 103(1), CRIMINAL JUSTICE ACT 2003

For the purposes of section 101(1)(d) the matters in issue between the defendant and the prosecution include –

(a) the question whether the defendant has a propensity to commit offences of the kind with which he is charged, except where his having such a propensity makes it no more likely that he is guilty of the offence;

(b) the question whether the defendant has a propensity to be untruthful, except where it is not suggested that the defendant's case is untruthful in any respect.

Thus, this gateway allows for the admission of evidence that is relevant to:

1. the propensity of the defendant to commit a particular type of offence, and
2. the defendant's credibility.

It should be noted that in *R* v. *Highton*, Lord Woolf CJ pointed out that s. 103(1) is not exhaustive: 'section 103(1) prefaces section 103(1)(a) and (b) with the word "include". This indicates that the matters in issue may extend beyond the two areas mentioned in this subsection'.[85] Thus, it would appear that while gateway (d) allows for the admission of evidence relevant to the defendant's propensity to commit certain offences and his propensity to be untruthful, it may also be relevant to other matters in issue between the defendant and the prosecution. Whether the courts will choose to interpret this provision broadly or not remains to be seen.

In any event, s. 103(2) elaborates on the types of previous convictions that fall under limb s. 103(1)(a), relating to the propensity of the defendant to commit offences of the type with which he is charged. This section provides that any evidence that the defendant has committed an offence of the 'same description' as the one with which he is charged, or an offence of the 'same category' as the one with which he is charged would be admissible as evidence of his propensity to commit offences of the kind with which he is charged. This will be considered in more detail below.

It would also appear that unlike s. 101(1)(c) and (e), s. 101(1)(d) contains no 'enhanced relevance' test. Thus, the matters in issue between the defendant and the prosecution need not have substantial probative value.

PROPENSITY TO COMMIT OFFENCES   Section 103(1)(a) defines a matter in issue between the prosecution and the defence as 'the question whether the defendant has a propensity to commit offences of the kind with which he is charged, except where his having such a

---

84 See s. 103(6), Criminal Justice Act 2003.
85 Above (n. 63) at 3477.

propensity makes it no more likely that he is guilty of the offence'. It should be noted from the outset that under s. 103(1)(a), such evidence will not be admissible where the defendant's propensity to commit offences of the kind with which he is charged makes it no more likely that the defendant is guilty of the offence in question. The kind of offences that may be admitted as evidence of the defendant's propensity are set out in s. 103(2) and they cover offences of the 'same description' or of the 'same category' as the one with which the defendant is charged.

S. 103(2), CRIMINAL JUSTICE ACT 2003

Where subsection (1)(a) applies, a defendant's propensity to commit offences of the kind with which he is charged may (without prejudice to any other way of doing so) be established by evidence that he has been convicted of –

(a) an offence of the same description as the one with which he is charged, or

(b) an offence of the same category as the one with which he is charged.

Offences of the 'same description' and offences of the 'same category' are further defined under s. 103(4).[86]

S. 103, CRIMINAL JUSTICE ACT 2003

(4) For the purposes of subsection (2) –
  (a) two offences are of the same description as each other if the statement of the offence in a written charge or indictment would, in each case, be in the same terms;
  (b) two offences are of the same category as each other if they belong to the same category of offences prescribed for the purposes of this section by an order made by the Secretary of State.
(5) A category prescribed by an order under subsection (4)(b) must consist of offences of the same type.

Section 103(4)(a) provides that two offences are of the 'same description' where the statement of offence on an indictment would be the same. This is a very narrow category, requiring the previous conviction to be essentially the same offence as the offence charged, albeit there is some leeway in that the offence charged may be prosecuted on a different basis from the offence for which the defendant has previously been convicted. Thus, where a defendant has previously been convicted of an offence of fraud by false representation, this offence would be of the 'same description' as an offence of fraud by abuse of position since both are charged contrary to s. 1 of the Fraud Act 2006 and the statement of offence on the

---

86 Sections 103(7)–(11), Criminal Justice Act 2003 were inserted into the 2003 Act by the Coroners and Justice Act 2009 on 15 August 2010. These provisions deal with how the court should determine whether foreign convictions are of the same description or category as the offence charged.

indictment would simply read 'Fraud, contrary to s. 1 of the Fraud Act 2006'.[87] Section 103(4)(b) provides that two offences are of the 'same category' where they belong to the same category of offences as prescribed by the Secretary of State. There are currently two prescribed categories of offences which can be found in the Schedule annexed to the Criminal Justice Act 2003 (Categories of Offences) Order 2004. The two prescribed categories are: the Theft Category under Part 1 and the Sexual Offences (Persons under the age of 16) Category under Part 2. The offences listed as falling under the Theft category are: theft, robbery, burglary (if there was an intention to steal under s. 9(1)(a), Theft Act 1968 or a theft or attempted theft under s. 9(1)(b), Theft Act 1968), aggravated burglary (if there was a burglary as described previously), taking a motor vehicle or other conveyance without authority, aggravated vehicle-taking, handling stolen goods, going equipped, making off without payment, acting as a secondary party to one of the listed offences, or attempting to commit an offence so specified. The offences listed as falling under the sexual offences category apply only to offences against a person under the age of 16. They are too numerous to list, but they include: rape of a person under the age of 16, assault by penetration of a person under the age of 16, sexual assault of a person under the age of 16, causing a person under the age of 16 to engage in sexual activity without consent, intercourse with a girl under 16 and intercourse with a girl under 13.

Section 103(2) is subject to a discretionary provision under s. 103(3) to exclude the evidence of a previous conviction of the same description or same category, if it would be unjust to admit it by reason of the time that has passed since the conviction, or for any other reason.

S. 103(3), CRIMINAL JUSTICE ACT 2003

Subsection (2) does not apply in the case of a particular defendant if the court is satisfied, by reason of the length of time since the conviction or for any other reason that it would be unjust for it to apply in his case.

The Court of Appeal considered the application of s. 101(1)(d) in the case of *R* v. *Hanson*. It is clear from s. 103(2) itself and from the Court of Appeal decision, that propensity may be established under gateway (d) even where the defendant has not been convicted of an offence of the same description or category as the offence with which he is charged. Section 103(2) provides that evidence of the defendant's propensity 'may (without prejudice to any other way of doing so) be established by ...'. In *R* v. *Hanson*, Rose LJ stated that, '[i]n referring to offences of the same description or category, section 103(2) is not exhaustive of the types of conviction which might be relied upon to show evidence of propensity to commit offences of the kind charged'.[88] This was confirmed by the Court of Appeal in *R* v. *Johnson*,[89] in which it was held that previous conviction for burglary and attempted theft should have been admissible as evidence of the defendant's propensity to commit the offence he was being tried for, namely conspiracy to burgle. The Court of Appeal held that

---

87 See *Archbold 2013* (Sweet & Maxwell) at para. 21–364.
88 Above (n. 83) at [8].
89 [2009] EWCA Crim 649.

the trial judge had been wrong to refuse to admit the evidence of the previous convictions because they did not fall under the same description or category as conspiracy to burgle. The Court confirmed that the words of s. 103(2) allow for a wide approach to be taken, such that propensity may be established by evidence of the commission of offences of the same description or category, or by other means.

R V. JOHNSON [2009] EWCA CRIM 649
Maurice Kay LJ

20. The error of the judge was to consider that the prosecution could not establish propensity because conspiracy to burgle is not an 'offence of the same description' or an 'offence of the same category' as burglary or another substantive offence of dishonesty. The true position is that the relevant propensity 'may (without prejudice to any other way of doing so)' be established by an offence of the same description within the meaning of s. 103(2)(a) or an offence of the same category within the meaning of s. 103(2)(b). However, as the words we have emphasised make clear, other ways of establishing propensity are not excluded. What s. 103(2) does is to provide permissive and simple ways of establishing propensity. Where they do not apply, propensity may still be established by other means. So if two men have individual records for relevant offences of burglary, there is no obvious reason why those records should not be used to establish a relevant propensity if they are later charged together with an offence of conspiracy to burgle. It would be absurd if their previous individual records could be used to establish propensity if they were later charged with a joint offence of burglary (as the appellants concede that they could) but they could not be used to establish propensity if the later charge were one of conspiracy to burgle.

Thus, it is clear that the defendant's propensity may also be proved through the admission of a previous conviction for an offence of a different description or category. Rose LJ continues in *R* v. *Hanson*, '[n]or, however, is it necessarily sufficient, in order to show such propensity, that a conviction should be of the same description or category as that charged'.[90] Thus, just because a defendant has a previous conviction for the same offence, it does not mean that that conviction is automatically admissible to show the defendant's propensity to prove the offence charged. The Court held that there are three questions to be considered where propensity to commit the kind of offence with which he is charged is relied upon. These are:

1. Does the history of conviction(s) establish a propensity to commit offences of the kind charged?
2. Does that propensity make it more likely that the defendant committed the offence charged?
3. Is it unjust to rely on the conviction(s) of the same description or category; and, in any event, will the proceedings be unfair if they are admitted?[91]

---

90 Above (n. 83) at [8].
91 Ibid.

R V. HANSON [2005] EWCA CRIM 824
Rose LJ

9. There is no minimum number of events necessary to demonstrate such a propensity. The fewer the number of convictions the weaker is likely to be the evidence of propensity. A single previous conviction for an offence of the same description or category will often not show propensity. But it may do so where, for example, it shows a tendency to unusual behaviour or where its circumstances demonstrate probative force in relation to the offence charged: compare *Director of Public Prosecutions v P* [1991] 2 AC 447, 460–461. Child sexual abuse or fire setting are comparatively clear examples of such unusual behaviour but we attempt no exhaustive list. Circumstances demonstrating probative force are not confined to those sharing striking similarity. So, a single conviction for shoplifting, will not, without more, be admissible to show propensity to steal. But if the modus operandi has significant features shared by the offence charged it may show propensity.

Propensity may be established by evidence of a number of convictions for the same offence, or it might be established by evidence of just one previous conviction for the same offence along with evidence of a similar method of commission or evidence of other previous misconduct with particular similar facts which make it more likely that the defendant is guilty of the offence charged. Prior to the Criminal Justice Act 2003, this latter type of evidence was known as similar fact evidence and its admissibility was governed by common law. In *DPP* v. *Boardman*, the House of Lords held that similar fact evidence would only be admissible if it was 'strikingly similar' to the offence alleged to have been committed. However, the 'striking similarity' requirement was a strict test which meant that it was difficult to adduce similar fact evidence at trial. This narrow approach was mitigated by the House of Lords' later authority of *DPP* v. *P*, in which the House held that similar fact evidence is admissible if its probative force outweighs its prejudicial effect.

The admissibility of similar fact evidence is now covered by s. 101(1)(d) of the Criminal Justice Act 2003. An example of a post-Criminal Justice Act 2003 case with similar facts is *R* v. *Chopra*.[92] In this case, the Court of Appeal held that in order for evidence of previous offending to be admissible under s. 101(1)(d) to establish propensity, '[t]here will have to be sufficient similarity to make it more likely that each allegation is true. The likelihood or unlikelihood of innocent coincidence will, we are sure, continue to be a relevant and sometimes critical test'.[93] The defendant was a dentist who was charged with indecently assaulting three of his female teenage patients in similar ways on three different occasions. The issue on appeal was whether the trial judge was right to direct the jury that the evidence of one complainant was admissible in support of the evidence of another provided that there was no possibility that the complainants had colluded or contaminated the evidence of each other. The Court of Appeal held that there was 'sufficient connection and similarity between the allegations which were made to make them cross-admissible under the ... Act'[94] and that the proceedings would not be unfair if

---

92 [2006] EWCA Crim 2133.
93 Ibid. at [24].
94 Ibid. at [22].

the previous conduct was admitted in evidence. It is for the jury to consider whether 'each similar complaint makes each other similar complaint the more likely'.[95] A similar case is that of *R* v. *Somanathan*,[96] in which the defendant was a Hindu priest who was accused of raping a woman who attended his temple. The complainant was vulnerable at the time of the alleged attack, her marriage having recently broken down. The defendant visited her at her flat, which is where the alleged rape took place. Two other women had also given previous accounts of the way in which the defendant had sexually harassed them. These two women had also been vulnerable and the defendant had sought to visit each of their homes, but had cancelled the visits after finding out that he would not be alone with the women. The account that the women gave of the sexual approaches made to them bore a resemblance to the account given by the complainant of similar conduct by the defendant. Thus, the Court of Appeal held that the evidence of these two women was admissible under s. 101(1)(d) as evidence of the defendant's propensity to act in such a way.

In *R* v. *Brima*,[97] the Court of Appeal held that in deciding on the admissibility of evidence under s. 101(1)(d), the trial judge's task is to consider whether the evidence of bad character is capable of establishing the defendant's propensity to commit offences and it is for the jury to decide whether the evidence of bad character actually does establish propensity. In this case, the appellant was charged with murder and it was the prosecution case that he had stabbed the victim with a knife. The appellant had two previous convictions: one for assault occasioning actual bodily harm in which the defendant had stabbed the victim in the leg with a knife, and the other for robbery in which the defendant held a knife to the victim's throat while demanding the victim's trainers and top. The prosecution argued that these convictions demonstrated that the appellant had a propensity to commit offences of violence with knives. However, it was argued on behalf of the appellant that the previous convictions do not establish propensity because severe force was used in the murder but was not used in the previous convictions. The Court of Appeal held that the trial judge had been right to admit evidence of these previous convictions and that the role of the trial judge is not to determine whether the previous convictions actually do establish propensity (this is a question of fact for the jury), but it is the judge's role only to determine whether the previous convictions had the *capacity* to establish propensity.

PROPENSITY TO BE UNTRUTHFUL   Section 103(1)(b) of the Criminal Justice Act 2003 defines a matter in issue between the prosecution and the defence as 'the question whether the defendant has a propensity to be untruthful, except where it is not suggested that the defendant's case is untruthful in any respect'. Where the prosecution does not allege that the defendant is lying in his defence, then it may not use evidence of the defendant's bad character to demonstrate a propensity to be untruthful.[98] Thus, where the defendant has

---

95 Ibid. at [30].
96 Reported with *R* v. *Weir*, above (n. 40).
97 [2006] EWCA Crim 408.
98 In *R* v. *Campbell* [2007] EWCA Crim 1472 at [29], Lord Phillips CJ comments that such cases will be 'comparatively rare'.

previous convictions for dishonesty offences or perjury, these may only be adduced to demonstrate a propensity to be untruthful where it is the prosecution's case that the defendant is lying.[99]

R V. HANSON [2005] EWCA CRIM 824
Rose LJ

13. As to propensity to untruthfulness, this, as it seems to us, is not the same as propensity to dishonesty. It is to be assumed, bearing in mind the frequency with which the words honest and dishonest appear in the criminal law, that Parliament deliberately chose the word 'untruthful' to convey a different meaning, reflecting a defendant's account of his behaviour, or lies told when committing an offence. Previous convictions, whether for offences of dishonesty or otherwise, are therefore only likely to be capable of showing a propensity to be untruthful where, in the present case, truthfulness is an issue and, in the earlier case, either there was a plea of not guilty and the defendant gave an account, on arrest, in interview, or in evidence, which the jury must have disbelieved, or the way in which the offence was committed shows a propensity for untruthfulness, for example, by the making of false representations.

In *R* v. *Campbell*,[100] the Court of Appeal reiterated the point made in *R* v. *Highton*, that there is a distinction between determining the admissibility of evidence under one of the s. 101 gateways and the use to which that evidence may be put.[101] The Court rejected a submission by the appellant that the jury are restricted in the use to which they can put evidence once it has been admitted through a particular gateway under s. 101(1). Once the judge has determined whether the evidence is admissible under a gateway as a matter of law, the jury are to be given the freedom to apply their common sense to the matter and to use that evidence in any respect in which it is relevant. The Court took the view that to distinguish between propensity to commit offences and credibility is 'unrealistic'. Lord Phillips CJ stated that: 'To direct them only to have regard to it for some purposes and to disregard its relevance in other respects would be to revert to the unsatisfactory practices that prevailed under the old law'. His Lordship continued: '[i]f the jury learn that a defendant has shown a propensity to commit criminal acts they may well at one and the same time conclude that it is more likely that he is guilty and that he is less likely to be telling the truth when he says that he is not'.[102]

---

99 Lord Phillips CJ also makes the point that it does not follow that evidence as to the defendant's propensity to be untruthful will always be relevant where there is an issue as to the credibility of the defendant since the defendant's propensity to be untruthful will 'not normally be capable of being described as an *important matter* in issue between the defendant and the prosecution' (see *R* v. *Campbell* at [30]).

100 Above (n. 98).

101 See Lord Woolf CJ in *R* v. *Highton and others* above (n. 63) at 3477.

102 Above (n. 98) at [28].

R V. CAMPBELL [2007] EWCA CRIM 1472
Lord Phillips CJ

27 What should a jury's common sense tell them about the relevance of the fact that a defendant has, or does not have, previous convictions? It may tell them that it is more likely that he committed the offence with which he is charged if he has already demonstrated that he is prepared to break the law, the more so if he has demonstrated a propensity for committing offences of the same nature as that with which he is charged. The extent of the significance to be attached to previous convictions is likely to depend upon a number of variables, including their number, their similarity to the offence charged and how recently they were incurred and the nature of his defence.

28 In considering the inference to be drawn from bad character the courts have in the past drawn a distinction between propensity to offend and credibility. This distinction is usually unrealistic. If the jury learn that a defendant has shown a propensity to commit criminal acts they may well at one and the same time conclude that it is more likely that he is guilty and that he is less likely to be telling the truth when he says that he is not.

29 Section 101(1)(d) of the 2003 Act renders admissible bad character evidence where it is 'relevant to an important matter in issue between the defendant and the prosecution'. Section 103(1)(b) provides that matters in issue between the prosecution and defence include 'the question whether the defendant has a propensity to be untruthful, except where it is not suggested that the defendant's case is untruthful in any respect'. It will be comparatively rare for the case of a defendant who has pleaded not guilty not to involve some element that the prosecution suggest is untruthful. It does not, however follow, that, whenever there is an issue as to whether the defendant's case is truthful, evidence can be admitted to show that he has a propensity to be untruthful.

30 The question of whether a defendant has a propensity for being untruthful will not normally be capable of being described as an important matter in issue between the defendant and the prosecution. A propensity for untruthfulness will not, of itself, go very far to establishing the commission of a criminal offence. To suggest that a propensity for untruthfulness makes it more likely that a defendant has lied to the jury is not likely to help them. If they apply common sense they will conclude that a defendant who has committed a criminal offence may well be prepared to lie about it, even if he has not shown a propensity for lying whereas a defendant who has not committed the offence charged will be likely to tell the truth, even if he has shown a propensity for telling lies. In short, whether or not a defendant is telling the truth to the jury is likely to depend simply on whether or not he committed the offence charged. The jury should focus on the latter question rather than on whether or not he has a propensity for telling lies.

31 For these reasons, the only circumstance in which there is likely to be an important issue as to whether a defendant has a propensity to tell lies is where telling lies is an element of the offence charged. Even then, the propensity to tell lies is only likely to be significant if the lying is in the context of committing criminal offences, in which case the evidence is likely to be admissible under section 103(1)(a).

DISCRETION TO EXCLUDE   Under s. 101(3), where evidence of the defendant's bad character is held to be admissible under s. 101(1)(d), the trial judge has the discretion to exclude the evidence. The discretion is only triggered in the event that the evidence is admissible under either gateway (d) or (g) and if the defendant has made an application to exclude the evidence.[103] If the trial judge takes the view that 'the admission of the evidence would have such an adverse effect on the fairness of the proceedings that the court ought not to admit it', then he *must* exclude the evidence.[104] In exercising this discretion to exclude the evidence, s. 101(4) states that the judge must also have regard to 'the length of time between the matters to which that evidence relates and the matters which form the subject of the offence charged'. Thus, the older the conviction, the more likely the judge will be to exclude it under s. 101(3), although this is certainly not a factor which will automatically render an old or a 'spent' conviction inadmissible. The judge will need to consider the age of the conviction in addition to other factors which weigh upon whether its admission would have an adverse effect on the fairness of the proceedings.

J. R. SPENCER, *EVIDENCE OF BAD CHARACTER*, 2ND EDN (HART PUBLISHING, 2009)

[at paras. 4.79–4.80]
[Professor Spencer predicts that:]

... the basis of the argument will often be that admitting the evidence would result in 'moral prejudice' – in other words, it would inflame the jury against the defendant and predispose them to convict him in order to punish him for what he did before, even though they are not convinced that he is guilty of the offence of which he is currently accused.

In my view, this is not a sensible basis on which the courts should exclude 'bad character' evidence which is adduced to show propensity. It should do so, in my view, where the evidence consists of incidents which are trivial. It should be prepared to do so if the evidence is plain and stale ... But if evidence is relevant, in that it would make a tribunal of reasonable people more inclined to convict, it should in principle be admitted. As suggested earlier ..., the real dangers with bad character evidence are its use to bolster up a weak case in which there is little or no other evidence, and the risk that it will divert the attention of the court into time-wasting 'satellite issues'. If this is so, the discretion to exclude should be exercised with an eye to these matters, rather than to the allegedly inflammatory nature of the evidence it is sought to exclude. In principle, it cannot be right to exclude evidence that is clearly relevant for fear that it might make the fact-finders shocked or angry with the accused. Were this so, it would make it impossible for the criminal justice system to deal with the most serious cases or offenders.

In *R* v. *Hanson*, the Court of Appeal held that a number of factors may be taken into account by the judge when considering the fairness of the proceedings under s. 101(3). The Court stated that the following matters should be taken into account: the degree of similarity between the previous conviction and the offence charged, the gravity of the past and present offences, the

---

103 Professor Spencer comments that such applications are likely to be common (see J. R. Spencer, *Evidence of Bad Character*, 2nd edn (Hart Publishing, 2009), at para. 4.79).
104 The Court of Appeal in *R* v. *Hanson* above (n. 83) at [10] noted that the words 'must not admit' in s. 101(3) make this stronger than s. 78(1) of the Police and Criminal Evidence Act 1984 which states that the judge 'may refuse to allow' the evidence to be admitted.

strength of the prosecution case (the less evidence there is against the defendant, the less likely it will be just to admit his previous convictions) and the date of the commission of the offence (where there is a significant gap between the date of commission and the date of conviction). Where the conviction is particularly old and it shares no special feature with the offence charged, the age of the conviction should be considered as its admission is more likely to have an adverse effect on the fairness of the proceedings, unless it shows a continuing propensity. Finally, the Court considered it necessary to examine each previous conviction individually, rather than look at the offences as a whole.

Gateway (e): substantial probative value regarding an important matter between defendant and co-defendant

Under s. 101(1)(e), evidence of a defendant's bad character is admissible if it 'has substantial probative value in relation to an important matter in issue between the defendant and a co-defendant'.[105] Prior to the Criminal Justice Act 2003, evidence of the defendant's bad character was admissible if the defendant gave evidence against a co-defendant.[106] Gateway (e) under s. 101(1) of the Criminal Justice Act 2003 applies to evidence which is adduced by the co-defendant or which is given by a witness in cross-examination by the co-defendant, so this gateway is not available to the prosecution.[107] Where co-defendants are running cut-throat defences, this gateway might be used by a co-defendant to adduce evidence of the defendant's bad character. Under s. 101(1)(e), the evidence must have 'substantial probative value'; this means that the evidence will not be admissible if it is only of marginal or trivial value. Similarly, the evidence must relate to an 'important matter' between the defendant and co-defendant, thus any evidence which relates only to a marginal or trivial matter will be inadmissible.[108] Unlike gateways (d) and (g), there is no discretion to exclude any evidence which meets the threshold in gateway (e). Thus, once the trial judge has decided that the evidence is of substantial probative value in relation to an important matter between the defendant and a co-defendant, the trial judge may not exclude it by using s. 101(3), Criminal Justice Act 2003, nor by relying on s. 78, Police and Criminal Evidence Act 1984, nor by invoking the defendant's right to a fair trial under Article 6 of the European Convention on Human Rights.[109]

Evidence of bad character which is admissible under s. 101(1)(e) may go to any matter to which the jury considers it relevant. Thus, it may be relied upon as evidence of the defendant's propensity to commit offences or it may be relied upon as evidence of the defendant's credibility. Where the evidence goes to the defendant's credibility, s. 104(1) provides that it only applies to the extent that the defendant has undermined the defence of the co-defendant.

---

105 According to s. 109(1), Criminal Justice Act 2003, in assessing the probative value of evidence, the court should assume that the evidence is true, unless it appears to the court on material before it that no court or jury could reasonably find it to be true (s. 109(2)).
106 See s. 1(3)(iii), Criminal Evidence Act 1898.
107 Section 104(2), Criminal Justice Act 2003.
108 See the Explanatory Notes to the Criminal Justice Act 2003 at para. 375.
109 See *R* v. *Musone (Ibrahim)* [2007] 1 WLR 2467.

S. 104, CRIMINAL JUSTICE ACT 2003

(1) Evidence which is relevant to the question whether the defendant has a propensity to be untruthful is admissible on that basis under section 101(1)(e) only if the nature or conduct of his defence is such as to undermine the co-defendant's defence.

In *R* v. *Edwards and Rowlands*,[110] the defendants were convicted of conspiracy to supply a Class A drug. They ran cut-throat defences and Edwards obtained leave from the trial judge to adduce evidence of Rowlands' previous convictions under s. 101(1)(e). The Court of Appeal held that the question of whether the evidence had substantial probative value was 'ultimately a question for the judge on his "feel" of the case' and that '[o]nce admitted ... what weight the jury was to attach to the evidence was an entirely different matter'.[111]

Examples of cases in which evidence was successfully admitted under s. 101(1)(e) include *R* v. *Najib*[112] and *R* v. *Mitchell (Michael)*.[113] In *R* v. *Najib*, the defendant, N, and a co-defendant were jointly charged with murder and arson with intent to endanger life in respect of an arson attack at the victim's house. The two defendants blamed each other for the attack and N's co-defendant sought to rely upon evidence that N had set fire to the victim's brother's car a year previously. This evidence was held to be admissible under s. 101(1)(e) as evidence of substantial probative value relating to an important matter in issue between the defendant and the co-defendant. In *R* v. *Mitchell (Michael)*, the defendant was charged with attempted murder and possession of a firearm with intent to endanger life. The prosecution case was that the defendant shot at a police officer who was chasing him. The defendant claimed that the gun belonged to his younger cousin and co-defendant, and that he had taken the gun from his co-defendant in order to protect him. The defendant claimed that the gun had accidentally discharged as he jumped down from a wall. The co-defendant denied that the gun belonged to him and relied upon s. 101 (1)(e) to adduce evidence that the defendant had used a similar story after he had been found in possession of a knife by a prison officer on a previous occasion.

Gateway (f): correct a false impression given by the defendant

Under s. 101(1)(f), evidence of a defendant's bad character is admissible if it is 'evidence to correct a false impression given by the defendant'. Prior to the Criminal Justice Act 2003, evidence of the defendant's bad character was admissible where the defendant asserted that he was of good character.[114] Gateway (f) must be read together with s. 105(1) which states that the defendant gives a false impression if he makes an express or implied assertion which gives the jury a false or misleading impression of the defendant.[115] An example of an express assertion

---

110 Above (n. 69).
111 Ibid., per Scott Baker LJ at [27].
112 [2013] EWCA Crim 86.
113 [2010] EWCA Crim 783.
114 The defendant could be cross-examined as to his bad character where he attempted to establish his good character under s. 1(3)(ii), Criminal Evidence Act 1898.
115 Section 105(1)(a), Criminal Justice Act 2003.

would be where the defendant states that he is of good character when in fact he is not, while an implied assertion would include giving evidence of good behaviour which implies that the defendant is of good character when he is not. A simple assertion by the defendant that he is not guilty of the offence charged is not sufficient to be treated as a false impression.[116] This gateway also includes making an assertion by conduct,[117] and the Explanatory Notes to the Criminal Justice Act 2003 give the example of a defendant giving a false impression through his appearance or dress: 'if a defendant were to give a false impression by suggesting he were a priest, he could not escape this provision simply by not making such an assertion verbally but choosing to wear a clerical collar'.[118]

S. 105, CRIMINAL JUSTICE ACT 2003

(1) For the purposes of section 101(1)(f) –
   (a) the defendant gives a false impression if he is responsible for the making of an express or implied assertion which is apt to give the court or jury a false or misleading impression about the defendant;
   (b) evidence to correct such an impression is evidence which has probative value in correcting it.
   . . .
(4) Where it appears to the court that a defendant, by means of his conduct (other than the giving of evidence) in the proceedings, is seeking to give the court or jury an impression about himself that is false or misleading, the court may if it appears just to do so treat the defendant as being responsible for the making of an assertion which is apt to give that impression.
(5) In subsection (4) 'conduct' includes appearance or dress.

This gateway applies where the defendant is responsible for making the assertion. This does not mean that the assertion has to be made by the defendant specifically during the trial, but the provision is much wider and under s. 105(2) it is said to also encompass assertions made by the defendant in police interview, upon being charged, as well as assertions made by another defence witness, or made by a witness in cross-examination by the defence where the question intended to elicit the assertion or was likely to do so, or assertions made by any person out of court which the defendant adduces during proceedings. Under s. 105(3), a defendant is not to be treated as being responsible for the assertion if he disassociates himself from it or withdraws it.

S. 105, CRIMINAL JUSTICE ACT 2003

(2) A defendant is treated as being responsible for the making of an assertion if –
   (a) the assertion is made by the defendant in the proceedings (whether or not in evidence given by him),
   (b) the assertion was made by the defendant –

---

116 See *R* v. *Somanathan*, reported in *R* v. *Weir* above (n. 40) at 1901.
117 See s. 105(4) and (5).
118 See para. 376.

(i) on being questioned under caution, before charge, about the offence with which he is charged, or

(ii) on being charged with the offence or officially informed that he might be prosecuted for it, and evidence of the assertion is given in the proceedings,

(c) the assertion is made by a witness called by the defendant,

(d) the assertion is made by any witness in cross-examination in response to a question asked by the defendant that is intended to elicit it, or is likely to do so, or

(e) the assertion was made by any person out of court, and the defendant adduces evidence of it in the proceedings.

(3) A defendant who would otherwise be treated as responsible for the making of an assertion shall not be so treated if, or to the extent that, he withdraws it or disassociates himself from it.

According to s. 105(7), only prosecution evidence is admissible under s. 101(1)(f). The prosecution may adduce evidence to correct the false impression created by the defendant. Section 105(6) provides that the evidence is admissible under s. 101(1)(f) only to the extent that it corrects the false impression given by the defendant. Evidence admitted under this gateway may not be excluded under s. 101(3).

The following cases are examples of situations in which evidence of the defendant's bad character was admissible to correct a false impression given by the defendant. In *R* v. *Gillespie (Peter Hugh)*,[119] it was held that the defendant's previous fraudulent conduct was admissible under s. 101(1)(f) to correct the impression that the defendant had given the jury that he was of good character and that 'his bankruptcy had been a "sad and unfortunate" incident' when in fact it was the result of the defendant's fraudulent conduct.[120] In *R* v. *Wylie (Peter Ernest)*,[121] it was held that the defendant's previous conviction for an offence under the Insolvency Act 1986 could be adduced to correct the false impression given by the defendant when he claimed that he had never been in trouble before. In *R* v. *Amponsah*,[122] the defendant was charged in relation to smuggling drugs into the United Kingdom. Evidence was adduced to the effect that the defendant was a 'hard-working woman of good character' and in cross-examination she gave evidence that she did not tell lies. The court was satisfied that the defendant had created a false impression of herself and thus evidence of her previous conviction for theft was admissible under s. 101(1)(f). In *R* v. *Kiernan*,[123] the defendant gave evidence that he had a previous conviction, that he had 'learned his lesson' by serving his prison sentence for that offence. Thus, he gave the false impression that he was a reformed character, but in fact the defendant had absconded years ago after a previous conviction and was 'on the run' at the time of his arrest. The Court of Appeal held that the trial judge had been right to allow the defendant to be cross-examined on his absconding. Finally, in

---

119 [2011] EWCA Crim 3152.

120 The evidence of bad character in this case was also admitted under s. 101(1)(c) and (d), Criminal Justice Act 2003.

121 [2010] EWCA Crim 3110.

122 [2005] EWCA Crim 2993.

123 [2008] EWCA Crim 972.

R v. *Somanathan*,[124] the defendant put himself forward as a man of good character with no previous convictions and as a priest who had a good reputation at his Hindu temple, and who had never behaved inappropriately towards women who attended his temple. Evidence of two women who claimed to have been sexually harassed by the defendant was admissible to correct this false impression that he had given of himself.

Gateway (g): attack on another person's character

Under s. 101(1)(g), evidence of a defendant's bad character is admissible if 'the defendant has made an attack on another person's character'. Prior to the Criminal Justice Act 2003, the prosecution was permitted to adduce evidence of the defendant's bad character where the defendant cast imputations against prosecution witnesses.[125] The provision under s. 101(1)(g) is much wider in that it applies to any other person, and not just witnesses.[126] Only prosecution evidence is admissible under s. 101(1)(g).[127] Section 101(1)(g) is further explained within s. 106(1), and it includes three scenarios, namely:

1. The defendant adduces evidence attacking the other person's character.[128] This applies to an attack on any other person and is, therefore, wider than the previous position under the Criminal Evidence Act 1898 which was restricted to situations where the defendant attacked the character of a prosecution witness.

2. The defendant or his legal representative[129] asks questions in cross-examination which are intended or likely to elicit the evidence.[130] This might apply where the defence cross-examines another witness about that witness's previous convictions or other evidence of bad character, or where the defence cross-examines a witness as to another person's character with a view to adducing evidence of bad character. Under this provision, the evidence must be adduced intentionally or by questions which were likely to elicit the answers they did. Thus, where the witness volunteers the information in the absence of such questions, gateway (g) will not apply.

3. Evidence is given of an imputation made by the defendant under caution or upon charge about the other person.[131] This might apply where a police officer gives evidence as to the defendant's response upon arrest or on charge, or where such an attack was made by the defendant during the police interview which is then adduced in court.

---

124 Reported in *R* v. *Weir*, above (n. 40).
125 The defendant could be cross-examined as to his bad character where he cast imputations on the character of prosecution witnesses under s. 1(3)(ii), Criminal Evidence Act 1898.
126 See *R* v. *Nelson* [2006] EWCA Crim 3412 at [14] to [15]. Although the Court of Appeal stated (at [16]) that 'it would be unusual for evidence of a defendant's bad character to be admitted when the only basis for doing so was an attack on the character of a non-witness who is also a non-victim. The fairness of the proceedings would normally be materially damaged by doing so'.
127 Section 106(3), Criminal Justice Act 2003.
128 Section 106(1)(a), Criminal Justice Act 2003.
129 Appointed to conduct a cross-examination on his behalf under s. 38(4), Youth Justice and Criminal Evidence Act 1999.
130 Section 106(1)(b), Criminal Justice Act 2003.
131 Section 106(1)(c), Criminal Justice Act 2003.

S. 106, CRIMINAL JUSTICE ACT 2003

(1) For the purposes of section 101(1)(g) a defendant makes an attack on another person's character if –

(a) he adduces evidence attacking the other person's character,

(b) he (or any legal representative appointed under section 38(4) of the Youth Justice and Criminal Evidence Act 1999 (c. 23) to cross-examine a witness in his interests) asks questions in cross-examination that are intended to elicit such evidence, or are likely to do so, or

(c) evidence is given of an imputation about the other person made by the defendant –

(i) on being questioned under caution, before charge, about the offence with which he is charged, or

(ii) on being charged with the offence or officially informed that he might be prosecuted for it.

Section 106(2) deals with the meaning of 'evidence attacking the other person's character' within s. 101(1)(g). This section uses similar terminology to that found under ss. 98 and 112, Criminal Justice Act 2003, so this gateway applies to evidence that the other person has committed an offence, or that he has behaved, or is disposed to behave, in a reprehensible way.

S. 106, CRIMINAL JUSTICE ACT 2003

(2) In subsection (1) 'evidence attacking the other person's character' means evidence to the effect that the other person –

(a) has committed an offence (whether a different offence from the one with which the defendant is charged or the same one), or

(b) has behaved, or is disposed to behave, in a reprehensible way; and 'imputation about the other person' means an assertion to that effect.

The following cases provide examples of cases in which evidence of the defendant's bad character has been held to be admissible under s. 101(1)(g). In *R* v. *Ball*,[132] the defendant, who was convicted of rape, made disparaging comments to the police about the complainant, stating that she was sexually promiscuous. The trial judge admitted his previous convictions on the basis that these comments constituted an attack on her character and had triggered gateway (g). In *R* v. *Benabbou (Fouad)*,[133] the Court of Appeal held that the trial judge had been right to admit evidence of the defendant's previous conviction for robbery because the defendant had accused the victim of making up a false allegation to hide their own wrongdoing. In *R* v. *Chrysostomou*,[134] the trial judge admitted evidence of the defendant's bad character under s. 101(1)(g) after he attacked the victim by alleging that she took cocaine and that she owed him money. In

---

132 Reported with *R* v. *Renda*, above (n. 41).
133 [2012] EWCA Crim 1256.
134 [2010] EWCA Crim 1403.

R v. *Dowds*,[135] the defendant was charged with burglary. Evidence of his previous convictions for burglary were admissible under s. 101(1)(g) because the defendant had, in answer to questions in cross-examination, given evidence that his co-defendant had committed a burglary the day before the burglary with which they were charged. In *R* v. *Hearne*,[136] the defendant was convicted of burglary after he broke into an aviary. He claimed that he had done so in order to free wild birds that the owner was keeping illegally. This was deemed to be an attack on the owner's character, and, thus, the defendant's previous convictions were admissible under s. 101(1)(g). Finally, evidence of the defendant's previous convictions in *R* v. *Highton*[137] were admissible after the defendant stated at trial that the complainants had lied to the police, and in *R* v. *Carp*,[138] the defendant's previous convictions were admissible after he cross-examined the complainant about her violent background. The Court of Appeal stated in these latter two cases that where evidence is admissible under s. 101(1)(g), it may be used to establish the defendant's propensity to commit offences as well as his credibility.

DISCRETION TO EXCLUDE   As stated above in respect of gateway (d), where evidence of the defendant's bad character is held to be admissible under s. 101(1)(g), the defendant may make an application to the trial judge to exclude the evidence under s. 101(3). Under s. 101(3), the judge must exclude the evidence where it appears to the court that its admission would have an adverse effect on the fairness of the proceedings. It is up to the trial judge how he exercises his discretion to exclude the evidence under s. 101(3).[139]

8.5.3 Offences committed by the defendant when a child

Section 108(2), Criminal Justice Act 2003 provides that where the defendant is aged 21 or over, evidence of a previous conviction for an offence that he committed when under the age of 14 is generally not admissible, even once the threshold for one of the gateways under s. 101(1) has been satisfied. However, this is subject to two exceptions: (1) where both offences are indictable only, and (2) where the court is satisfied that it is in the interests of justice that the evidence be admitted.

8.5.4 Other provisions governing defendant's bad character

Section 27(3), Theft Act 1968 applies where the defendant is charged with handling stolen goods and guilty knowledge is in issue and provides for the admissibility of certain evidence to prove that the defendant knew or believed the goods to be stolen. In particular, evidence that the defendant handled stolen goods not more than twelve months earlier and evidence that the defendant had been convicted of theft or of handling stolen goods within the past five years is admissible as evidence of guilty knowledge in respect of the current charge.

---

135 Reported with *R* v. *Bovell* [2005] EWCA Crim 1091.
136 [2009] EWCA Crim 103.
137 Above (n. 63).
138 Which was reported with *R* v. *Highton*, above (n. 63).
139 See *R* v. *Nelson* [2006] EWCA Crim 3412.

8.6 BAD CHARACTER EVIDENCE OF A NON-DEFENDANT

The admissibility of evidence of bad character of a non-defendant is governed by s. 100(1), Criminal Justice Act 2003. This section provides three instances in which evidence of a non-defendant's bad character may be admissible, namely where it is important explanatory evidence, it has substantial probative value in relation to a matter of issue in the proceedings and is of substantial importance in the case, or where all parties agree.

S. 100(1), CRIMINAL JUSTICE ACT 2003

In criminal proceedings evidence of the bad character of a person other than the defendant is admissible if and only if –

(a) it is important explanatory evidence,
(b) it has substantial probative value in relation to a matter which –
    (i) is a matter in issue in the proceedings, and
    (ii) is of substantial importance in the context of the case as a whole, or
(c) all parties to the proceedings agree to the evidence being admissible.

The definition of bad character under s. 98, Criminal Justice Act 2003 also applies to the admissibility of a non-defendant's bad character under s. 100. Section 100 can be invoked by any of the parties in the case, thus the prosecution, the defendant or a co-defendant might seek to rely on s. 100 in order to adduce evidence of the bad character of a non-defendant. Under s. 100(4), Criminal Justice Act 2003, where a party wishes to adduce evidence of the bad character of a non-defendant under either s. 100(1)(a) or s. 100(1)(b), he must first apply to the court for leave to do so.

S. 100(4), CRIMINAL JUSTICE ACT 2003

Except where subsection (1)(c) applies, evidence of the bad character of a person other than the defendant must not be given without leave of the court.

It should be noted that once the conditions under s. 100(1) are met, then the trial judge has no discretion to exclude the evidence under the Criminal Justice Act 2003.[140] Section 100(1) is different from s. 101(1) in this respect since s. 101(3) provides a discretion to exclude such evidence, but this does not apply to s. 100(1).

The Court of Appeal has confirmed that s. 100(1) applies to evidence of either a non-defendant's propensity to commit offences or to his credibility (or, indeed, to both). Moses LJ stated that s. 100(1) 'is not limited in such a way as to exclude evidence either of the propensity of a non defendant or his credibility. Both may have substantial probative value in relation to a matter which is in issue in the proceedings'.[141]

---

140 *R* v. *Braithwaite* [2010] 2 Cr App R 18.
141 See *R* v. *H* [2009] EWCA Crim 2899 at [15].

8.6.1 Important explanatory evidence

Under s. 100(1)(a), evidence of the bad character of a non-defendant is admissible if it is 'important explanatory evidence'. This is similar to s. 101(1)(c) in respect of evidence of the bad character of a defendant. Section 100(2) further defines 'important explanatory evidence' as evidence without which the jury would 'find it impossible or difficult properly to understand other evidence in the case'. It must also be evidence that provides substantial value for understanding the case as a whole.

S. 100(2), CRIMINAL JUSTICE ACT 2003

For the purposes of subsection (1)(a) evidence is important explanatory evidence if –

(a) without it, the court or jury would find it impossible or difficult properly to understand other evidence in the case, and

(b) its value for understanding the case as a whole is substantial.

8.6.2 Substantial probative value regarding matter in issue of substantial importance

Under s. 100(1)(b), evidence of the bad character of a non-defendant is admissible if 'it has substantial probative value' in relation to 'a matter in issue in the proceedings' and is of 'substantial importance in the context of the case as a whole'. Section 100(3) provides a number of factors which the court must have regard to in assessing the probative value of the evidence, including the nature and number of the events,[142] when those events occurred,[143] the nature and extent of any similarities between the instances of misconduct,[144] and the extent to which the evidence shows that the same person was responsible for the misconduct each time.[145] This list is non-exhaustive, so the court may also take into account any other factors that it considers relevant.

S. 100(3), CRIMINAL JUSTICE ACT 2003

In assessing the probative value of evidence for the purposes of subsection (1)(b) the court must have regard to the following factors (and to any others it considers relevant) –

(a) the nature and number of the events, or other things, to which the evidence relates;

(b) when those events or things are alleged to have happened or existed;

---

142 Section 100(3)(a), Criminal Justice Act 2003.
143 Section 100(3)(b), Criminal Justice Act 2003.
144 Section 100(3)(c), Criminal Justice Act 2003.
145 Section 100(3)(d), Criminal Justice Act 2003.

(c) where –
   (i) the evidence is evidence of a person's misconduct, and
   (ii) it is suggested that the evidence has probative value by reason of similarity between that misconduct and other alleged misconduct, the nature and extent of the similarities and the dissimilarities between each of the alleged instances of misconduct;
(d) where –
   (i) the evidence is evidence of a person's misconduct,
   (ii) it is suggested that that person is also responsible for the misconduct charged, and
   (iii) the identity of the person responsible for the misconduct charged is disputed, the extent to which the evidence shows or tends to show that the same person was responsible each time.

In *R* v. *Brewster and another*,[146] two co-defendants sought leave to cross-examine the complainant on her previous convictions on the basis that the facts of the convictions had substantial probative value in relation to her creditworthiness. The Court of Appeal gave some guidance as to how a trial judge should approach s. 100(1)(b). Pitchford LJ stated that 'the trial judge's task will be to evaluate the evidence of bad character which it is proposed to admit for the purpose of deciding whether it is reasonably capable of assisting a fair-minded jury to reach a view whether the witness's evidence is, or is not, worthy of belief. Only then can it properly be said that the evidence is of substantial probative value on the issue of creditworthiness'. The Court held that it is not necessary for the party seeking to rely on s. 100(1)(b) to establish that the bad character demonstrates a tendency towards untruthfulness. This is a question for the jury to determine. The Court stated that the judge should consider the following questions:

1. whether creditworthiness is a matter in issue which is of substantial importance in the context of the case as a whole;
2. if so, whether the bad character relied upon is of substantial probative value in relation to that issue.

8.6.3 All parties agree

Under s. 100(1)(c), evidence of the bad character of a non-defendant is admissible if all parties agree to its admissibility. This is similar to s. 101(1)(a) in respect of evidence of a defendant's bad character.

8.7 GOOD CHARACTER EVIDENCE OF THE DEFENDANT

Evidence of the defendant's good character is admissible and may go towards establishing that the defendant is credible or that the defendant is less likely to have committed the offence charged, or both.[147] Evidence of good character might be evidence that the defendant has no previous

---

146 [2011] 1 WLR 601.
147 See R. Munday, 'What constitutes a good character?' [1997] Crim LR 247.

convictions, evidence of a good reputation[148] in the community or amongst friends, or evidence of admirable or praiseworthy conduct. In *R* v. *Rowton*,[149] it was held that the defendant (who was a schoolmaster charged with indecently assaulting a schoolboy) could not adduce evidence of specific examples of previous good conduct. The defendant had wanted to adduce evidence from character witnesses to the effect that the defendant was of good character and evidence that he had a history of admirable conduct. It was held that a character witness could only give evidence as to his knowledge of the general good reputation of the defendant in a general sense. The witness was not permitted to give evidence as to particular instances of good conduct by the defendant. This case has been subject to much criticism, and while it has never officially been overruled, it is generally ignored by the courts. Nevertheless, the approach in *R* v. *Rowton* was applied in *R* v. *Redgrave*.[150] The defendant in this case had been arrested after he allegedly made sexual approaches to two male plain-clothed police officers in a public lavatory. The defendant sought to adduce evidence of specific details of his heterosexual relationships with girlfriends, but the court held that this was inadmissible. These two cases are unlikely to be applied today, and the courts do permit evidence of specific instances of previous conduct to be adduced on behalf of the defendant to demonstrate a lack of propensity and the credibility of the defendant.

In the House of Lords' decision in *R* v. *Aziz*,[151] Lord Steyn considered the rationale for the requirement that a trial judge should direct the jury as to a defendant's good character:

R V. *AZIZ* [1996] AC 41, HL
Lord Steyn

[at 50–1]

... in recent years there has been a veritable sea-change in judicial thinking in regard to the proper way in which a judge should direct a jury on the good character of a defendant. It has long been recognised that the good character of a defendant is logically relevant to his credibility and to the likelihood that he would commit the offence in question. That seems obvious. The question might nevertheless be posed: why should a judge be obliged to give directions on good character? The answer is that in modern practice a judge almost invariably reminds the jury of the principal points of the prosecution case. At the same time he must put the defence case before the jury in a fair and balanced way. Fairness requires that the judge should direct the jury about good character because it is evidence of probative significance. Leaving it entirely to the discretion of trial judges to decide whether to give directions on good character led to inconsistency and to repeated appeals. Hence there has been a shift from discretion to rules of practice and *Vye* was the culmination of this development.

The leading case on evidence of good character is the case of *R* v. *Vye*,[152] in which the Court of Appeal laid down directions to be given to a jury in relation to the good character. Prior to *R* v. *Vye*,

---

148 Note that according to s. 99(2) of the Criminal Justice Act 2003, s. 118 of the Act preserves the admissibility of a person's reputation for the purposes of proving his good character.
149 (1865) Le & Ca 520, CCR.
150 (1982) 74 Cr App R 10, CA.
151 [1996] AC 41, HL.
152 [1993] 1 WLR 471, CA.

there was no clear guidance for the courts in directing juries on the use of evidence of good character. For instance, in *R* v. *Berrada*,[153] the trial judge failed to direct the jury properly because he made no mention of the fact that the defendant was of good character. The Court of Appeal held that the trial judge should have directed the jury that the defendant's good character was relevant to his credibility. This type of direction as to credibility is now the first limb of the *Vye* direction. The defendant in *R* v. *Vye* was a 50-year-old man who had no previous convictions. On appeal against his conviction in this case, he argued that the trial judge had failed to properly direct the jury on the defendant's good character. The Court of Appeal held that there are two directions which a judge might give on the good character of the defendant: the first provides that the defendant's good character is relevant to his credibility, and the second provides that the defendant's good character is relevant to his guilt or innocence (i.e. his propensity), because it makes him less likely to have committed the offence charged. The Court held that:

1. A direction as to the relevance of evidence of the defendant's good character to his *credibility* is to be given where the defendant testified or made pre-trial answers or statements. This is known as limb 1. A direction based on this limb can only be given (and must be given) where the defendant has either given evidence at trial or has made admissions or 'mixed' statements pre-trial, such as by answering questions in police interview. Where the defendant makes wholly exculpatory statements, a limb 1 direction is not required.[154]
2. A direction as to the relevance of evidence of the defendant's good character to the likelihood of his having committed the offence charged (i.e. to his *propensity*) is to be given, whether or not he has testified, or made pre-trial answers or statements. This is known as limb 2. A direction based on this limb should be given by the trial judge in all cases, irrespective of whether the defendant has testified or made pre-trial statements.
3. Where there are two defendants, jointly charged, and one defendant (D1) is of good character but the other defendant (D2) is of bad character, the same rules above apply because D1's right to a good character direction outweighs the risk of prejudice to D2.

R V. *VYE* [1993] 1 WLR 471
Lord Taylor CJ

[at 474]

These three appeals are all based upon criticisms of the judges' directions in regard to good character. At one time, these issues would not have been regarded even as arguable in this court. The trial judge was understood to have a broad discretion to comment on the defendant's good character or not as he thought fit. The principle applied by this court was that the judge had no obligation to give directions on good character or even to remind the jury of it: Rex v. Aberg [1948] 2 K.B. 173; Reg. v. Smith [1971] Crim.L.R. 531.

---

153 (1989) 91 Cr App R 131, CA.
154 See *R* v. *Aziz* above (n. 151) in which Lord Steyn stated (at 51) that 'It is clear beyond any doubt that *Vye* is only concerned with mixed statements. And the position remains that a wholly exculpatory statement is not evidence of any fact asserted.'

Since about 1989 however, there has been a dramatic change. This court has been inundated with appeals based upon the judge's alleged misdirection or failure to give any direction to the jury about good character. Save in one respect, clear principles have not emerged and Mr. Martin Wilson on behalf of the Crown in these appeals described the present situation as 'something of a lottery.' After drawing our attention to all the relevant authorities reported and unreported since 1989, Mr. Wilson submitted that this court should now give clear guidance as to the relevant principles.

[at 479]

... in our judgment the following principles are to be applied. (1) A direction as to the relevance of his good character to a defendant's credibility is to be given where he has testified or made pre-trial answers or statements. (2) A direction as to the relevance of his good character to the likelihood of his having committed the offence charged is to be given, whether or not he has testified, or made pre-trial answers or statements. (3) Where defendant A of good character is jointly tried with defendant B of bad character, (1) and (2) still apply.

Where a trial judge fails to follow *Vye* and does not give appropriate directions as to the defendant's good character, the defendant has a good ground of appeal and is likely to succeed in overturning his conviction.

In *R* v. *Aziz* the House of Lords considered the question of whether two defendants, who had been charged with fraud offences against the Inland Revenue, could be treated as of good character (and thus whether they were entitled to a *Vye* direction) after admitting that they had lied on mortgage application forms. Both defendants had no previous convictions. The House of Lords held that the defendants could be treated as of good character. The House held, *obiter*, that a trial judge has the discretion not to give a good character direction if it would be an 'insult to common sense' to do so.

R V. *AZIZ* [1996] AC 41, HL
Lord Steyn

[at 53]

A good starting point is that a judge should never be compelled to give meaningless or absurd directions. And cases occur from time to time where a defendant, who has no previous convictions, is shown beyond doubt to have been guilty of serious criminal behaviour similar to the offence charged in the indictment. A sensible criminal justice system should not compel a judge to go through the charade of giving directions in accordance with *Vye* in a case where the defendant's claim to good character is spurious. I would therefore hold that a trial judge has a residual discretion to decline to give any character directions in the case of a defendant without previous convictions if the judge considers it an insult to common sense to give directions in accordance with *Vye*.

A defendant still has the right to a *Vye* direction where he admits to the police that he has lied previously (as in *R* v. *Aziz*) and where he admits that he has committed other offences in the past or admits to other, previous reprehensible behaviour. The court is likely to disregard any previous convictions which are trivial, obviously unrelated to the offence charged,[155] or spent (i.e. they were committed a long time ago).[156] Equally, just because a person has previous convictions does not mean that they cannot be treated as of good character – the trial judge also retains a discretion to refuse to give a *Vye* direction where it would be an 'insult to common sense'.[157]

8.8   CIVIL PROCEEDINGS

In civil proceedings, the key test for the admissibility of character evidence is relevance; character evidence is admissible if it is relevant to a fact in issue or if it is itself in issue[158] in the case. If the character evidence is probative of a fact in issue, it will then be for the judge in the case to determine whether to admit the evidence, having regard to the overriding objective under rule 1.2 of the Civil Procedure Rules 1998 and dealing with the case justly.[159]

Section 4(1) of the Rehabilitation of Offenders Act 1974 provides that evidence of a party's previous conviction will not be admissible in civil proceedings if the conviction is 'spent', unless justice cannot be done without its admission under s. 7(3) of the 1974 Act.

8.9   CONCLUSION

Evidence relating to a witness's character is relevant to proceedings for two potential reasons. It may go towards the credibility of a witness or, where that witness is a defendant in the proceedings, it may go towards establishing his propensity to behave in a particular way. The law allows for evidence of both bad character and good character to be adduced in certain circumstances in order to prove or disprove matters relating to credibility or propensity. Evidence of the good character of the defendant is admissible at common law, and in relevant cases the trial judge is required to direct the jury as to the relevance of the evidence of good character in relation to the credibility of the defendant or his propensity to behave in a particular way (*Vye* direction). The Criminal Justice Act 2003 provides a comprehensive statutory framework governing the admissibility of evidence of a witness's bad character and seeks to ensure a balance between promoting a liberal approach to allowing relevant evidence to be adduced and safeguarding against the prejudicial effect of the admissibility of bad character evidence on a defendant. As such, the Act contains discretionary provision to allow for the exclusion of bad character evidence where it appears to the court that its admission would have an adverse effect on the fairness of the proceedings.

---

155 See *R* v. *Gray* [2004] EWCR Crim 1074.
156 See *R* v. *Durbin* [1995] 2 Cr App R 84.
157 See *R* v. *Doncaster* (2008) JP 202.
158 For example, in cases of defamation the character of the claimant is in issue.
159 *O'Brien* v. *Chief Constable of South Wales Police* [2005] 2 AC 534.

Summary

- Character evidence may be relevant to propensity or credibility. Evidence of propensity is evidence of previous behaviour which goes towards proving that a person has a tendency to act in a particular way. Evidence of credibility is evidence which goes towards proving that a person is less worthy of belief.
- Consideration must be given to the prejudicial effect of the admission of character evidence.
- 'Bad character' is defined under the Criminal Justice Act 2003 as evidence of or a disposition towards misconduct. 'Misconduct' is defined under s. 112 as the commission of an offence or other reprehensible behaviour.
- Evidence of a defendant's bad character is admissible if it falls under one of the seven gateways under s. 101(1), Criminal Justice Act 2003, namely that: all parties agree, it is adduced by the defendant or elicited from a prosecution witness in cross-examination, it is important explanatory evidence, it is relevant to an important matter in issue between the defendant and the prosecution, it has substantial probative value in relation to an important matter in issue between the defendant and a co-defendant, it is evidence to correct a false impression given by the defendant, or the defendant has made an attack on another person's character.
- Where evidence of the defendant's bad character is admissible under gateway (d) or (g), the judge must exclude it under s. 101(3) if its admission would have an adverse effect on the fairness of the proceedings, taking into account the age of the convictions (s. 101(4)).
- Evidence of a non-defendant's bad character is admissible if it falls under one of the three paragraphs under s. 100(1), Criminal Justice Act 2003, namely that: it is important explanatory evidence, it has substantial probative value in relation to a matter in issue and is of substantial importance in the context of the case as a whole, or all parties agree.
- Where the defendant is of good character, the judge must direct the jury in accordance with *R* v. *Vye*. If the defendant testified or made pre-trial admissions, the judge should direct the jury that the defendant's good character is relevant to his credibility (limb 1). In all cases, the judge should direct the jury that the defendant's good character is relevant to his propensity (limb 2).

For discussion . . .

1. Critically evaluate the meaning of 'bad character' under the Criminal Justice Act 2003.
2. To what extent is the discretion to exclude evidence under s. 101(3), Criminal Justice Act 2003 merely a reproduction of s. 78, Police and Criminal Evidence Act 1984?
3. In what ways can the prosecution establish the propensity of the defendant to commit offences under s. 101(1)(d)?
4. Compare and contrast the gateways that provide for the admissibility of the bad character of the defendant with those provisions applicable to a non-defendant.
5. Explain when a defendant is entitled to a good character direction and the nature of the direction that the trial judge will give.

Further reading

S. Brown and B. Steventon, 'The admissibility of bad character evidence' [2008] *Coventry Law Journal* 1.
This article explores the statutory regime relating to evidence of bad character under the Criminal Justice Act 2003 and the criminological research carried out into the effect of adducing bad character evidence at trial. The authors examine each of the gateways under s. 101(1) and discuss the key decisions of the Court of Appeal in the cases of *R* v. *Hanson* and *R* v. *Highton*.

S. Lloyd-Bostock, 'The effects on lay magistrates of hearing that the defendant is of "good character", being left to speculate, or hearing that he has a previous conviction' [2006] Crim LR 189.
This article provides a report on a study carried out into the effect that the admission of evidence of the defendant's bad character has on a lay bench of magistrates.

R. Munday, 'What constitutes a good character?' [1997] Crim LR 247.
This article considers the development of the common law relating to the admission of evidence of good character in criminal proceedings. The author argues that the law is too rigid, and calls for reform.

R. Munday, 'What constitutes "other reprehensible behaviour" under the bad character provisions of the Criminal Justice Act 2003?' [2005] Crim LR 24.
This article explores the meaning of 'bad character' under the Criminal Justice Act 2003. The article focuses particularly on the meaning of 'reprehensible behaviour' and the interpretation that might be given to this term by the courts.

J. R. Spencer, *Evidence of Bad Character*, 2nd edn (Hart Publishing, 2009).
This is the leading text on evidence of bad character. The book provides a critical evaluation of the statutory framework on bad character evidence.

C. Tapper, 'Criminal Justice Act 2003: Part 3: Evidence of bad character' [2004] Crim LR 533.
This article was published shortly after the Criminal Justice Act 2003 was enacted. The article compares the position under the old law with the framework under the Criminal Justice Act 2003. It summarises the reasons for the reforms and considers the principles behind the reforms. The author argues that the reforms have failed to achieve simplicity and that they represent a missed opportunity, making further reform necessary.

9 Witnesses

9.1 INTRODUCTION

This chapter and the next chapter will concentrate on witnesses and the testimony given by witnesses in court respectively. In particular, this chapter will focus on three considerations which arise prior to a witness stepping into the witness box. The first of these is whether the witness is indeed competent to give evidence and whether they may be compelled to do so if they refuse. (See Figure 9.1.) The rules relating to the competence and compellability of witnesses to give evidence for the prosecution or for the defence will be examined. The second issue arising in this chapter relates to the giving of evidence sworn or unsworn. Most witnesses who give evidence will do so after being sworn (i.e. after either taking the oath or affirming in the witness box), but some witnesses (particularly child witnesses) will give evidence unsworn; the rules relating to sworn and unsworn evidence will be considered. Finally, we will explore the

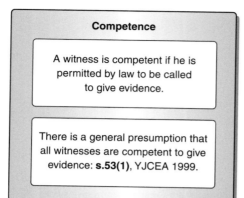

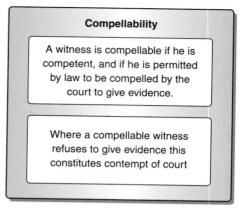

Figure 9.1 Terminology

problem of witness intimidation and calling vulnerable witnesses to give evidence. Where important prosecution witnesses are vulnerable or intimidated, their protection becomes crucial to the continuation of the case. We will consider the special measures which might be adopted in order to enhance the quality of the evidence of a vulnerable or intimidated witness and to provide protection whilst giving evidence. The statutory framework governing special measures directions has in recent years been supported by further statutory provisions which permit judges to grant witness anonymity orders in certain circumstances to further protect the identity of vulnerable or intimidated witnesses.

9.2 COMPETENCE AND COMPELLABILITY

9.2.1 General presumption of competence and compellability

There is a general statutory presumption that all witnesses are competent to give evidence in criminal proceedings irrespective of their age.[1]

S. 53(1), YOUTH JUSTICE AND CRIMINAL EVIDENCE ACT 1999

At every stage in criminal proceedings all persons are (whatever their age) competent to give evidence.

The presumption in favour of the competence of a witness is subject to an exception under s. 53(3), Youth Justice and Criminal Evidence Act 1999 in respect of a witness who is unable to understand questions put to him and to give answers which can be understood. This provision replaced the test of 'intelligible testimony' found under s. 33A(2A), Criminal Justice Act 1988 (repealed by the Youth Justice and Criminal Evidence Act 1999) and at common law.[2]

---

1 Section 53(1), Youth Justice and Criminal Evidence Act 1999.
2 See the case of *DPP* v. *M* [1998] QB 913 in which the Divisional Court held that the trial court should not refuse to allow a child to give evidence by virtue of her age alone (in this case the complainant was just 4 years old at the time

S. 53(3), YOUTH JUSTICE AND CRIMINAL EVIDENCE ACT 1999

A person is not competent to give evidence in criminal proceedings if it appears to the court that he is not a person who is able to –

(a) understand questions put to him as a witness, and
(b) give answers to them which can be understood.

Where the competence of a witness (whether a child or an adult) is disputed by the court or a party to proceedings, the court will determine the issue of the competence of the witness to give evidence.[3] The burden of proving that the witness is competent is on the party calling the witness, and the court must be satisfied of the competence of the witness to the lower, civil standard of proof (i.e. on a balance of probabilities).[4]

Cross-reference
The procedure for determining the competence of a witness will be considered in more detail in the context of the competence of child witnesses in paragraph 9.3 below.

There is a further general presumption that all competent witnesses are compellable to give evidence,[5] although this is subject to some exceptions detailed below. Where a witness is both competent to give evidence and compellable but refuses to do so, he is in contempt of court.

9.2.2 Competence and compellability of the defendant

For the prosecution
Although there is a general presumption in favour of the competence of a witness, there are specific rules which relate to the competence of the defendant to give evidence for the prosecution (see Table 9.1 for a summary of the rules). Section 53(4) provides a further exception to the general presumption according to which a defendant is not a competent witness to give evidence for the prosecution.

S. 53(4), YOUTH JUSTICE AND CRIMINAL EVIDENCE ACT 1999

A person charged in criminal proceedings is not competent to give evidence in the proceedings for the prosecution . . .

---

of trial), but the court should assess the child witness's competence by questioning the child or watching a video of the child and considering whether the child is able to understand questions and to answer them in a manner which is coherent and comprehensible, and thus whether he is capable of giving intelligible testimony in accordance with s. 33A(2A), Criminal Justice Act 1988 (repealed by the Youth Justice and Criminal Evidence Act 1999).

3 Section 54(1), Youth Justice and Criminal Evidence Act 1999.
4 Section 54(2), Youth Justice and Criminal Evidence Act 1999.
5 Per Lord Wilberforce in *Hoskyn* v. *Metropolitan Police Commissioner* [1979] AC 474.

Thus, while a defendant is competent under the general presumption to give evidence as part of the defence case, he may not appear as a witness on behalf of the prosecution.[6] This also means that where a defendant is jointly tried with a co-defendant, the co-defendant may not give evidence for the prosecution, but may only give evidence in his own defence.

In his own defence

In accordance with the general presumption under s. 53(1), Youth Justice and Criminal Evidence Act 1999, the defendant is today a competent witness to give evidence in his own defence, but this has not always been the case. Historically, defendants were not permitted to speak even in their own defence and it was not until the enactment of the Criminal Evidence Act 1898 that defendants were finally deemed to be competent witnesses for the first time. However, even though a defendant is now competent to give evidence in his own defence, he may not be compelled to do so. This is in line with the privilege against self-incrimination which provides that a defendant should not be forced to answer questions which might tend to incriminate him.

Although the defendant is not competent to give evidence for the prosecution, where the defendant is jointly tried with a co-defendant, he may give evidence in his own defence against that co-defendant. The defendant might wish to give evidence in his own defence against a co-defendant where they are running incompatible defences, such as a 'cut-throat' defence – a defence by which both defendants blame each other.

The defendant is a competent witness to give evidence in support of his own defence, but in accordance with s. 1(1), Criminal Evidence Act 1898, he may not be compelled to give evidence (he has the right to remain silent), but may do so only upon his own application. Where the defendant does decide to testify, he is treated like any other witness: he must testify from the witness box or other place from which the other witnesses give their evidence, unless otherwise ordered by the court,[7] and he may be subject to a criminal charge of perjury if he should lie on oath. Only in exceptional circumstances will a defendant be excused from giving evidence from the witness box, such as through infirmity. In *R* v. *Symonds*,[8] the defendant had given evidence and been cross-examined from the dock rather than from the witness box. Swift J stated that:

> This was an unusual course for the trial to take and an improper one . . . an accused person shall have an opportunity of giving evidence on his own behalf in the same way and from the same place as the witnesses for the prosecution. It is not right to deprive him of the benefit . . . There may be cases in which a prisoner is so infirm that he cannot walk from the dock to the witness box without inconvenience or pain. There may be cases where the prisoner exhibits violence which may be more easily quelled in the dock than in the witness box. But apart from cases of such a nature the right of the prisoner to give his evidence from the witness box should not be interfered with . . .[9]

---

6 This rule originates from the common law; see the case of *R* v. *Rhodes* [1899] 1 QB 77 in which Lord Russell of Killowen CJ stated (at 80): 'It is clear that the limitation of the right of a person charged with an offence to give evidence is that he may be called for the defence, and for the defence alone.'

7 Section 1(4), Criminal Evidence Act 1898 (as amended by the Youth Justice and Criminal Evidence Act 1999).

8 (1925) 18 Cr App R 100.

9 Ibid. at 101.

Similarly, in *R* v. *Farnham Justices*,[10] the defendant applied for judicial review of the court's policy requiring defendants to give evidence from the dock rather than from the witness box. The defendant argued that he had been unfairly prejudiced by being prevented from giving evidence from the witness box like other witnesses had, and that justice was not seen to be done. The Divisional Court allowed the application and quashed the defendant's conviction for driving offences. The Court held that only in exceptional circumstances could the justices refuse to allow the defendant the right to testify from the witness box, and only where there was some misconduct or other such consideration justifying the denial of this right. Watkins LJ stated that '[j]ustices must not give defendants what may seem to some the perplexing choice as to where they give evidence. Their place is in the witness box and nowhere else unless, as I have said, there is some striking, particular, unusual reason for preventing a defendant going from the dock to the witness box.'[11]

By giving evidence in his own defence, the defendant opens himself up to cross-examination by the prosecution and by counsel for any co-defendants in the case, as well as to examination-in-chief by his own counsel. The defendant can be asked questions in cross-examination that go to the matters in issue in the case even though the questions might tend to incriminate the defendant.

The effect of silence at trial

The 'right to silence' or the defendant's right not to testify in his own defence at trial is enshrined in s. 35(4), Criminal Justice and Public Order Act 1994, which states that:

This section does not render the accused compellable to give evidence on his own behalf, and he shall accordingly not be guilty of contempt of court by reason of a failure to do so.

Where the defendant exercises his right to silence and decides not to testify,[12] or where the defendant does decide to testify, but once in the witness box he refuses to answer questions put to him,[13] he opens himself up to adverse inferences being drawn against him for his silence.

S. 35, CRIMINAL JUSTICE AND PUBLIC ORDER ACT 1994

(2) Where this subsection applies, the court shall, at the conclusion of the evidence for the prosecution, satisfy itself (in the case of proceedings on indictment [with a jury], in the presence of the jury) that the accused is aware that the stage has been reached at which evidence can be given for the defence and that he can, if he wishes, give evidence and that, if he chooses not to give evidence, or having been sworn, without good cause refuses to answer any question, it will be permissible for the court or jury to draw such inferences as appear proper from his failure to give evidence or his refusal, without good cause, to answer any question.

(3) Where this subsection applies, the court or jury, in determining whether the accused is guilty of the offence charged, may draw such inferences as appear proper from the failure of the accused to give evidence or his refusal, without good cause, to answer any question.

---

10 [1991] RTR 309.
11 Ibid. at 313.
12 Section 35(2), Criminal Justice and Public Order Act 1994.
13 Section 35(3), ibid.

The leading case on the operation of s. 35, Criminal Justice and Public Order Act 1994 is *R* v. *Cowan*.[14] In this case the Court of Appeal set out the directions that a trial judge should give in cases where the defendant does not testify.

- the judge must direct the jury that the burden of proof remains on the prosecution and that the prosecution must prove the case beyond reasonable doubt;
- the judge must make it clear that the defendant is entitled to remain silent – that is his right and his choice;
- silence on its own is not enough to establish the guilt of the defendant;[15]
- the jury must be satisfied that the prosecution has a prima facie case – only then may it draw any inferences from the defendant's failure to give evidence; and
- despite evidence relied on to explain his silence, if the defendant's silence can only be attributed to the defendant having no explanation, or none that would stand up to cross-examination, the jury may draw adverse inferences.

Cross-reference

Refer to Chapter 4 on Silence for discussion about ss. 34–37, Criminal Justice and Public Order Act 1994, which detail the other circumstances in which adverse inferences may be drawn against the defendant for his silence.

By choosing not to testify,[16] the defendant is not guilty of contempt of court and s. 35, Criminal Justice and Public Order Act 1994 does not render the defendant compellable to give evidence.[17] At the close of the prosecution case, the court must be satisfied that the defendant is aware that the stage in the trial has been reached where the defendant may give evidence if he so wishes, and that 'if he chooses not to give evidence, or having been sworn, without good cause refuses to answer any question, it will be permissible for the court or jury to draw such inferences as appear proper from his failure to give evidence or his refusal, without good cause, to answer any question'.[18] The judge must ask counsel for the defendant (in the presence of the jury):

> Have you advised your client that the stage has now been reached at which he may give evidence and, if he chooses not to do so or, having been sworn, without good cause refuses to answer any question, the jury may draw such inferences as appear proper from his failure to do so?[19]

---

14 [1996] QB 373, CA.

15 In accordance with s. 38(3), Criminal Justice and Public Order Act 1994.

16 See *R* v. *Cox* [2013] EWCA Crim 1025 in which the defendant's application for leave to appeal against his conviction was dismissed on the basis that he had not shown that he was unfit to make a decision as to whether to give evidence or not. The Court of Appeal relied upon the fact that those representing the defendant had carefully advised the applicant and recorded the advice given and the applicant's decision in accordance with the procedure in *R* v. *Bevan* (1994) 98 Cr App R 354.

17 Section 35(4), Criminal Justice and Public Order Act 1994.

18 Section 35(2), ibid.

19 *The Consolidated Criminal Practice Direction*, IV.44.3 (available at www.justice.gov.uk/guidance/courts-and-tribunals/courts/procedure-rules/criminal/pd_consolidated.htm).

Where counsel indicates that he has advised his client accordingly, then the case will continue; where counsel has not advised his client, the judge will briefly adjourn the case in order that counsel might do so. Where the defendant is representing himself, the judge will address the defendant in the presence of the jury in the following terms:

> You have heard the evidence against you. Now is the time for you to make your defence. You may give evidence on oath, and be cross-examined like any other witness. If you do not give evidence or, having been sworn, without good cause refuse to answer any question the jury may draw such inferences as appear proper. That means they may hold it against you. You may also call any witness or witnesses whom you have arranged to attend court. Afterwards you may also, if you wish, address the jury by arguing your case from the dock. But you cannot at that stage give evidence. Do you now intend to give evidence?[20]

Under s. 35(1), Criminal Justice and Public Order Act 1994, no adverse inferences may be drawn against the defendant for his failure to testify or answer questions in the witness box if either the defendant's guilt is not in issue,[21] or 'it appears to the court that the physical or mental condition of the accused makes it undesirable for him to give evidence'.[22] In an article on the approach of the courts to s. 35(1)(b), Owusu-Bempah states that s.35(1)(b) 'has the potential to act as a safeguard for vulnerable defendants against an indiscriminate application of adverse inferences which can be drawn under s.35, notwithstanding the possibility of a legitimate explanation for silence'.[23] But Owusu-Bempah argues that the provision 'has been applied too restrictively and is therefore failing to fulfil its potential' and concludes that 'a clearer and less restrictive interpretation of s. 35(1)(b) might be necessary to satisfy the interests of justice'.[24]

The meaning of s. 35(1)(b) was considered by the Court of Appeal in the case of *R* v. *Friend*.[25] The case involved a 14-year-old defendant who was convicted of murder. The court heard evidence that the defendant had an IQ of 63 and a mental age of 9 years old, but that he was less suggestible than the average person. The defendant failed to give evidence at trial and argued on appeal against his conviction that the judge should not have directed the jury that adverse inferences could be drawn against him for his failure to testify, in accordance with s. 35(1)(b), Criminal Justice and Public Order Act 1994. The Court of Appeal dismissed the appeal and held that the clear purpose of s. 35(1)(b) is 'to mitigate any injustice to a person who is physically or mentally handicapped' and the language of the section gives the trial judge a wide discretion.[26] The Court refused to accept that the defendant's low mental age meant that he should have had immunity from adverse inferences being drawn, particularly in light of the fact that defence counsel had not raised the issue of whether the defendant was fit to plead at trial. The Court of Appeal held that the trial judge could not be said to have applied the wrong test because there was 'no right test' for the exercise of judicial discretion in relation to s. 35(1)(b), and that it was

---

20 Ibid. at IV.44.5.
21 Section 35(1)(a), Criminal Justice and Public Order Act 1994.
22 Section 35(1)(b), ibid.
23 A. Owusu-Bempah, 'Judging the desirability of a defendant's evidence: an unfortunate approach to s. 35(1)(b) of the Criminal Justice and Public Order Act 1994' [2011] Crim LR 690 at 691.
24 Ibid. See also the extract from this article below.
25 [1997] 1 WLR 1433, CA.
26 Ibid. at 1441.

not necessary to supplement the Act with a test because the wording of the section was clear. The trial judge had considered all relevant factors, including the expert evidence as to the psychiatric assessment of the defendant. Otton LJ suggested that: 'A physical condition might include a risk of an epileptic attack; a mental condition, latent schizophrenia where the experience of giving evidence might trigger a florid state.'[27] This case reached the Court of Appeal in a second appeal in 2004,[28] and on this occasion the defendant's conviction was quashed on the basis of new expert evidence which suggested that the defendant suffered from Attention Deficit Hyperactivity Disorder and that 'he did not have the cognitive or psychological function or capacity to participate effectively in the trial as a result of, firstly, his level of mental impairment; secondly, inattentiveness and lack of ability to concentrate; and thirdly, his emotional state; and that it was thus undesirable for him to give evidence'.[29] The Court of Appeal stated that in light of the new evidence, '[i]t is clear that the judge would not have ruled in favour of drawing any adverse inference, certainly in respect of the failure to give evidence, and ... probably also in respect of the interview or silence at the first interview' and that even if there had been some direction, 'the judge would still have had to direct the jury with reference to the new evidence and ... he would in the light of the new evidence certainly have directed the jury in quite different terms as regards any inference from silence'.[30]

ABENAA OWUSU-BEMPAH, 'JUDGING THE DESIRABILITY OF A DEFENDANT'S EVIDENCE: AN UNFORTUNATE APPROACH TO S. 35(1)(B) OF THE CRIMINAL JUSTICE AND PUBLIC ORDER ACT 1994' [2011] CRIM LR 690

[at 703–4]

... s. 35(1)(b) does little to advance the rationale behind the CJPOA. Despite assertions that adverse inferences from silence are merely an application of common sense, the failure of a vulnerable defendant to testify on the grounds of an existing physical or mental condition can hardly be considered a reliable indication of guilt. Neither does a defendant's non-participation at the trial stage have any likely impact on the efficient investigation of crime or the prevention of ambush defences, key concerns for those advocating reform prior to the CJPOA. Added to the unfortunately restrictive approach of the courts is the lack of consistency within the case law, making it difficult for a defendant to determine whether testifying will be in his best interest.

The courts are under no obligation to interpret s. 35(1)(b) so narrowly. In other words, they need to adopt a clearer and less restrictive interpretation. In order to achieve this, judges should be required to:

1) consider specifically the impact which a defendant's condition will have on the quality of his evidence as well as the risks to his health;

---

27 Ibid. at 1442. In *R* v. *Kavanagh* [2005] EWHC 820 (Admin) it was held that merely suffering from a mental condition, such as depression, was not sufficient on its own, it also had to be proved that this condition made the defendant giving evidence 'undesirable'.
28 *R* v. *Friend (No. 2)* [2004] EWCA Crim 2661.
29 Ibid. at [20].
30 Ibid. at [30] and [31] respectively.

2) where the case concerns a young defendant, consider age as an important factor in making a decision on the applicability of s. 35(1)(b); the availability of special measures should not influence this decision;

3) consider the issue of s. 35(1)(b) even in the absence of supportive evidence from the defence; and

4) where the jury are invited to draw adverse inferences, direct them that silence is not necessarily an indicator of guilt, that there are possible innocent explanations for silence, and remind them of any submission the defence has made in this regard.

Such measures would increase protection against the risks of injustice and wrongful conviction to many more defendants. They would also show a greater appreciation and acknowledgment for the fact that silence does not necessarily imply guilt, and would express a greater concern for fairness in the trials of young and vulnerable defendants.

9.2.3 Competence and compellability of a co-defendant

Where the defendant is jointly tried with a co-defendant, the defendant is competent to give evidence on behalf of a co-defendant (for instance, a co-defendant might wish to call the defendant if they are running compatible defences), but he is not compellable (because of his privilege against self-incrimination). (See Table 9.1 for a summary of the rules.) A co-defendant is also not competent to give evidence against the defendant for the prosecution (because no defendant charged in the proceedings may give evidence for the prosecution).[31] However, where the defendant ceases to be a co-defendant, he will become both competent and compellable for either the prosecution or the defendant.[32] A co-defendant ceases to be a co-defendant in the following situations:

- upon acquittal (e.g. after a successful submission of no case to answer),
- where *nolle prosequi* is entered on direction of the Attorney-General (this is a formal discontinuance of proceedings, where the defendant is deemed to have been acquitted),
- on a guilty plea, or
- by making a successful application for a separate trial.

Where a former co-defendant gives evidence against the defendant for the prosecution, this is known as 'turning Queen's evidence'. In *R* v. *McEwan*,[33] the defendant had originally been jointly charged with a co-defendant, but the co-defendant pleaded guilty to the offence. The Court of Appeal confirmed that under s. 35(5), Youth Justice and Criminal Evidence Act 1999, '. . . if a person pleads guilty to the indictment, he is no longer incompetent to give evidence for the prosecution against others charged on that indictment' and 'that is sufficient to render him a person no longer charged, until he applies to set aside that plea'.[34]

---

31 Section 53(4), Youth Justice and Criminal Evidence Act 1999.
32 Section 53(5), ibid.
33 [2011] EWCA Crim 1026.
34 Ibid. at [13] and [15] respectively.

9.2.4 Competence and compellability of a spouse or civil partner

The rules governing the competence and compellability of the spouse or civil partner of the accused fall under s. 53(1), Youth Justice and Criminal Evidence Act 1999 and s. 80, Police and Criminal Evidence Act 1984 (PACE Act 1984) (see Table 9.1 for a summary of the rules).[35] The basic principle of competence provides that the spouse or civil partner of the defendant is competent to give evidence in criminal proceedings under the general presumption of competence contained within s. 53(1), Youth Justice and Criminal Evidence Act 1999. These rules relate only to a current spouse or civil partner of the defendant, and do not apply in respect of a person with whom the defendant is cohabiting in a long-term relationship. In *R* v. *Pearce*, it was held that 'the words [of s. 80, PACE Act 1984] are clear and are not capable of being expanded so as to embrace a relationship to which they plainly do not apply'.[36] The Court of Appeal refused to extend the applicability of s. 80, PACE Act 1984 to an unmarried partner of the defendant with whom he is cohabiting since 'if the concession were to be widened it is not easy to see where logically the widening should end'.[37]

Section 80A, PACE Act 1984 provides that where a spouse or civil partner does not give evidence in the proceedings, the prosecution shall not make any comment about this to the jury in his closing speech. However, this prohibition does not apply to the trial judge, who may make reference to the failure of the spouse or civil partner to give evidence. In *R* v. *Davey*,[38] prosecuting counsel commented on the fact that the defendant had not called his wife to give evidence. While the Court of Appeal considered this to be 'wrong' and 'plainly a material irregularity' and commented that the judge might well have intervened,[39] the Court was satisfied that the summing up of the trial judge properly addressed the comment by directing the jury not to speculate on the reason for the wife not giving evidence:

R V. DAVEY [2006] EWCA CRIM 565
Mr Justice Aikens

[21] If there had been no comment at all from the judge in his summing-up, then we might have been concerned that this conviction was unsafe and it might have had to have been quashed. But the fact is that the judge did address prosecuting counsel's comment that Mrs Davey had not given evidence. He properly directed the jury that it must not speculate on why the appellant's wife was not called and that it must not speculate on what her evidence might have been. The judge's direction is emphatic and clear in its terms. This court must work upon the assumption that a jury will follow a direction that a judge gives in his summing-up. In our view this direction clearly and emphatically directed the jury to put out of its mind any speculation as to why the appellant's wife was not called and what she might have said. That specific comment reinforced the judge's general comment which he had already made in his summing-up . . . that the jury must try the case on the evidence and must not speculate on what other evidence there might have been.

35 Section 80, Police and Criminal Evidence Act 1984 was amended by the Civil Partnership Act 2004 (Sch. 27, para. 97(4)) to apply equally to civil partners.
36 [2002] 1 WLR 1553 at [12], per Kennedy LJ.
37 Ibid.
38 [2006] EWCA Crim 565.
39 *R* v. *Whitton* [1998] Crim LR 492.

[22] We cannot accept Mr Sweeney's submission that the direction of the judge was too anodyne and should have been given in stronger terms. We have concluded that the firm directions of the judge were quite sufficient to correct and dissipate any prejudice that might have been caused to the appellant by the impermissible comment from the Crown. Accordingly we have concluded that the conviction was safe and that this appeal must be dismissed.

For the prosecution

Historically, the spouse of a defendant was neither competent, nor compellable as a witness for the prosecution. However, today the spouse or civil partner of the defendant is competent to give evidence against the defendant; in this respect the spouse or civil partner is treated as any ordinary witness. Thus, a spouse or civil partner of the defendant is a competent witness against the defendant in accordance with the general presumption of competence under s. 53(1), Youth Justice and Criminal Evidence Act 1999.[40] However, the spouse or civil partner of the defendant generally cannot be compelled to give evidence for the prosecution (and against the defendant). The rationale for this rule is found in the sanctity of marriage and the historical notion that husband and wife are one unit, as well as in the interests of the State in preventing the breakdown of marriages. Accordingly, the spouse or civil partner of a defendant should not be forced to play a part in the prosecution case against the defendant by testifying for the prosecution. It was recognised that there was an increased risk that the witness would perjure himself or herself in protecting the defendant.

J. BRABYN, 'A CRIMINAL DEFENDANT'S SPOUSE AS A PROSECUTION WITNESS' [2011] CRIM LR 613

[at 614]

The original general incompetence of a defendant's spouse for the prosecution owed much to the 'doctrine of unity' of husband and wife, also the perceived danger of promoting perjury, a belief in public repugnance at the sight of one spouse testifying against another and the undesirability of the resulting implacable discord and disharmony between the spouses. A blunt rule also had the practical merits of simplicity, predictability and minimising risks of unfair inferences from refusal to testify.

By the latter half of the 20th century, the 'doctrine of unity' had little credence. In its absence, in a society of increased gender equality and committed individualism, nothing could justify denying a willing spouse the choice of testifying and the trial court access to a willing spouse's evidence, hence general competence.

. . .

General compellability was another matter. There was no strong lobby demanding that change . . . The fact a spouse had testified against the defendant was thought highly likely to cause serious and prolonged, often terminal marital conflict, even where internal violence and abuse did not indicate the marriage already had failed or was likely to fail . . . Furthermore, unwilling spouses should not generally

---

40 Recently affirmed by the Court of Appeal in *R* v. *L* [2008] EWCA Crim 973 at [27], per Lord Phillips CJ.

be exposed to a clash of duties to both prosecution and the defendant, forced to contribute to causing the serious economic and social consequences that followed prosecution of the defendant, nor driven to commit perjury or contempt to protect the defendant.

However, an opposing view was put forward by Wigmore who argued that a spouse should be compelled to give evidence in the interests of the pursuit of truth in a criminal trial:

> In an age which has so far rationalized, depolarized, and dechivalrized the marital relation and the spirit of femininity as to be willing to enact complete legal and political equality and independence of man and woman, this marital privilege is the merest anachronism, in legal theory, and an indefensible obstruction to truth, in practice.[41]

There are exceptions to the rule that the spouse or civil partner of a defendant cannot be compelled to give evidence on behalf of the prosecution. The spouse or civil partner of the defendant may be compelled to give evidence for the prosecution where the defendant has been charged with one of the specified offences under s. 80(3), PACE Act 1984. These specified offences relate to an assault or sexual offence allegedly committed against a person under the age of 16, or an assault against the spouse or civil partner, or any inchoate or accessorial form of liability in respect of such offences.

S. 80(3), POLICE AND CRIMINAL EVIDENCE ACT 1984

In relation to the spouse or civil partner of a person charged in any proceedings, an offence is a specified offence for the purposes of subsection (2A) above if –

(a) it involves an assault on, or injury or threat of injury to, the spouse or civil partner or a person who was at the material time under the age of 16;
(b) it is a sexual offence alleged to have been committed in respect of a person who was at the material time under that age; or
(c) it consists of attempting or conspiring to commit, or of aiding, abetting, counselling, procuring or inciting the commission of, an offence falling within paragraph (a) or (b) above.

J. BRABYN, 'A CRIMINAL DEFENDANT'S SPOUSE AS A PROSECUTION WITNESS' [2011] CRIM LR 613

[at 614]

In 1972 the Criminal Law Revision Committee recommended ... the compellability of the defendant's spouse with respect to offences against that spouse, citing the public interest in the prosecution of serious domestic violence, protection against familial pressure not to testify and

---

41 *Wigmore on Evidence*, 3rd edn (1940), vol. VIII, p. 232 (cited in *Hoskyn* v. *Metropolitan Police Commissioner* [1979] AC 474 at 483). See also R. Munday, 'Sham marriages and spousal compellability' (2001) 65 JCL 336.

the absence of proven problems with compellability to date. The Committee also favoured compellability with respect to violent and sexual offences against children of the defendant's household under sixteen, again citing the seriousness of some offences and protection against familial intimidation but also the exceptional difficulty in proving many such cases in the absence of spousal testimony, especially where the child could not testify, and the relatively frequent complicity of the spouses. The Committee rejected extension of this protection to children generally as over inclusive but the extension was made by the EW legislature twelve years later, apparently in response to some 'high profile cases of child sex abuse'.

R V. L [2008] EWCA CRIM 973
Lord Phillips of Worth Matravers CJ

Policy

27. . . . it is helpful to consider the policy behind the current restrictions on the compellability of a wife to give evidence against her husband. The rule against compelling a wife to give evidence against her husband has its origin in the common law. It used to be the case that, subject to limited exceptions, a wife not merely was not compellable, but was not competent, to give evidence against her husband in a criminal trial. In *Hoskyn* v *Metropolitan Police Commissioner* [1979] AC 474 Lord Wilberforce at p. 488 said that this was because of

> the identity of interest between husband and wife and because to allow her to give evidence
> would give rise to discord and to perjury and would be, to ordinary people, repugnant.

28. It was, however, not obvious that it was repugnant to permit, or even require, a wife to give evidence against her husband in all circumstances. In some circumstances at least it might be said to be repugnant that, through absence of a wife's evidence, a husband might fail to be convicted of serious criminality. Thus Wigmore on Evidence, 3rd ed. (1940), p. 232, described the rule that precluded a wife from giving evidence against her husband as:

> the merest anachronism, in legal theory, and an indefensible obstruction to truth, in practice.

29. In the interests of the due conviction of the guilty, Parliament has severely curtailed the restriction upon a wife giving evidence against her husband. A wife is now a competent witness against her husband in all circumstances – see section 53 of the Youth Justice and Criminal Evidence Act 1999. A wife is compellable where her evidence is in respect of offences of violence towards herself or violence or sexual offences against children under sixteen years of age. Compellability in the latter instance reflects, *inter alia*, the desirability of convicting fathers who have committed violent or sexual offences against their children; offences in relation to which a wife may well be both a cogent and a reluctant witness.

Despite the exceptions to the general rule found under s. 80(3), PACE Act 1984, a spouse or civil partner who is also a co-defendant in the proceedings is not compellable to give evidence for the prosecution. This is stated in s. 80(4), PACE Act 1984 and exists in order to protect his or her privilege against self-incrimination.

S. 80(4), POLICE AND CRIMINAL EVIDENCE ACT 1984

No person who is charged in any proceedings shall be compellable by virtue of subsection (2) or (2A) above to give evidence in the proceedings.

The case of *R* v. *L*[42] raised some interesting questions regarding the evidence of the spouse of the appellant. In this case, the appellant had been charged with various sexual offences including rape, sexual activity with a family member and indecent assault against his daughter; many of the counts charged were specimen counts. Five of the specimen counts of indecent assault related to offences allegedly committed against the complainant while she was aged under 16; the remaining charges related to offences allegedly occurring when the complainant was aged 16 or over. Under s. 80, PACE Act 1984, the appellant's wife would only have been a compellable witness in respect of the allegations occurring when the complainant was aged under 16. The wife had given the police a statement which related to the charges on the indictment that allegedly took place when the complainant was aged 19; thus, the trial judge ruled that the wife was not a compellable witness for the prosecution. The prosecution subsequently sought to admit the wife's witness statement under s. 114(1), Criminal Justice Act 2003. The defendant appealed on the basis that the trial judge had been wrong to refer to parts of the statement after ruling that he had the power to admit the statement in the interests of justice under s. 114(1)(d). The Court of Appeal held that there was no obligation on the police to warn the wife that she was not compellable for the prosecution before taking a statement from her, especially since this might have inhibited the investigation.[43] The Court held that s. 80, PACE Act 1984 does not bar the admission of such a witness statement in evidence where the wife has voluntarily made the statement, and 'the risk of marital discord will not be in play if that statement is subsequently placed in evidence to the same extent as if the wife is asked to give oral evidence to the jury that implicates her husband'.[44] The Court did acknowledge the 'obvious paradox in excusing the wife from giving evidence, but then placing before the jury in the form of a hearsay statement the very evidence that she does not wish to give'[45] and held that whether it would be just to admit the witness statement would depend upon the facts of the individual case. In this particular case, the Court was satisfied that there was 'no injustice in admitting the statement' because '[t]he law has made it clear that the interests of convicting a husband of child abuse take precedence over the demands of marital duty and harmony that would otherwise protect the wife from being compelled to give evidence'.[46]

For the accused

The spouse or civil partner of the defendant is a competent witness to give evidence on behalf of the defendant in accordance with the general presumption of competence under s. 53(1), Youth Justice and Criminal Evidence Act 1999. The spouse or civil partner is generally compellable by the defendant under s. 80(2), PACE Act 1984.

---

42 [2008] EWCA Crim 973.
43 Ibid. at [31].
44 Ibid. at [35].
45 Ibid.
46 Ibid. at [36].

> ## S. 80(2), POLICE AND CRIMINAL EVIDENCE ACT 1984
>
> In any proceedings the spouse or civil partner of a person charged in the proceedings shall, subject to subsection (4) below, be compellable to give evidence on behalf of that person.

The one exception to this rule applies where the spouse or civil partner of the defendant is also a co-defendant; in these circumstances, s. 80(4), PACE Act 1984 provides that the spouse or civil partner is not compellable, in accordance with the privilege against self-incrimination.

For a co-defendant
The spouse or civil partner of the defendant is also competent to give evidence on behalf of any co-defendant under the general presumption of competence (s. 53(1), Youth Justice and Criminal Evidence Act 1999). However, the spouse or civil partner is only compellable to give evidence for a co-defendant where the defendant is charged with a specified offence under s. 80(3), PACE Act 1984. The spouse or civil partner will not be compellable if they are also charged in the proceedings as a co-defendant (s. 80(4), PACE Act 1984).

Former spouse or former civil partner
Where the witness was formerly a spouse or civil partner of the defendant but they have now divorced or the civil partnership is dissolved, the former spouse or civil partner is treated as any ordinary witness as if they have never been married or in a civil partnership. Thus, a former spouse or former civil partner is competent and compellable as a witness. This is provided in statute under s. 80(5) and (5A), PACE Act 1984.

9.2.5 Competence and compellability of other witnesses

In light of the general presumption of competence under s. 53(1), Youth Justice and Criminal Evidence Act 1999, all witnesses who do not fall within s. 53(3) and (4) are competent to give evidence. In light of the general presumption that all competent witnesses are compellable, there will only be a few circumstances (as shown above) in which witnesses are not compellable. Below are some further examples:

The Sovereign
The Sovereign is a competent witness, but is not compellable to give evidence.

Judges
Judges are competent witnesses. Judges should only be called to give evidence as a last resort; and judges are not compellable to give evidence on matters related to and resulting from the exercise of their judicial function.[47]

---

47 *Warren* v. *Warren* [1997] QB 488.

Table 9.1 Summary of the rules relating to the competence and compellability of various key witnesses

Party	Competent?	Compellable?
Accused for prosecution	No, under s. 53(4), YJCEA 1999	No, because not competent
Accused for defence	Yes, under the general presumption of competence: s. 53(1), YJCEA 1999	No, due to the privilege against self-incrimination
Co-defendant for prosecution	No, unless he ceases to be a co-defendant: s. 53(4)–(5), YJCEA 1999	No, because not competent
Co-defendant for defence	Yes, under the general presumption of competence: s. 53(1), YJCEA 1999	No, due to the privilege against self-incrimination
Spouse or civil partner for prosecution	Yes, under the general presumption of competence: s. 53(1), YJCEA 1999	No, unless specified offence under s. 80(3), PACE: (i) assault on spouse or civil partner or person under 16; (ii) sexual offence on person under 16; (iii) inchoate or accessorial liability relating to (i) or (ii). But not compellable if spouse is also a co-defendant: s. 80(4), PACE.
Spouse or civil partner for defence	Yes, under the general presumption of competence: s. 53(1), YJCEA 1999	Yes: s. 80(2), PACE. Unless spouse is also a co-defendant: s. 80(4), PACE.
Spouse or civil partner for co-defendant	Yes, under the general presumption of competence: s. 53(1), YJCEA 1999	No, unless specified offence under s. 80(3), PACE. But not compellable if spouse or civil partner is also a co-defendant: s. 80(4), PACE.
Former spouse or former civil partner	Yes, under the general presumption of competence: s. 53(1), YJCEA 1999	Yes, under s. 80(5) and (5A), PACE

Jurors

Jurors may not be questioned about the details of the deliberations of the jury after the verdict has been given. Disclosing (and indeed soliciting) details of jury deliberations constitutes contempt of court under s. 8(1), Contempt of Court Act 1981.[48] However, jurors are competent and compellable to give evidence of any impropriety or misconduct which occurs prior to the verdict being delivered or outside the jury room.[49]

---

48 See also the case of *R* v. *Mirza*; *R* v. *Connor and Rollock* [2004] 1 AC 1118 in which the House of Lords affirmed this principle, thus preserving the secrecy rule relating to jury deliberations. For further discussion of this case see N. Monaghan, 'Protecting the secret deliberations of the jury in the interests of efficiency – has the law "lost its moral underpinning"? Lord Steyn's dissent in *R v Mirza*; *R v Connor and Rollock*' in *Dissenting Judgments in the Law* (Wildy, Simmonds & Hill, 2012).

49 See *R* v. *Young* [1995] QB 324, a case in which the jurors consulted a Ouija board in a hotel in which they had been sequestered for the night.

9.3 SPECIAL CASES OF COMPETENCE

9.3.1 Competence of a child witness in criminal proceedings

Unreliability: the historical perspective

Historically, there was considerable reticence about the admissibility and reliability of the evidence of child witnesses. In *R* v. *Wallwork*, Lord Goddard CJ commented about the evidence of a 5-year-old girl who was called as a witness, '[t]he court deprecates the calling of a child of this age as a witness . . . it seems to us to be unfortunate that she was called and, with all respect to the learned judge, I am surprised that he allowed her to be called. The jury could not attach any value to the evidence of a child of five; it is ridiculous to suppose that they could . . . There must be corroborative evidence if a child of tender years and too young to understand the nature of an oath is called, but in any circumstances to call a little child of the age of five seems to us to be most undesirable, and I hope it will not occur again.'[50] Similarly, in *R* v. *Wright and Ormerod* (another case involving the competence of a 5-year-old child as a witness), Ognall J referred to *R* v. *Wallwork* with approval, stating that 'the validity of, and good sense behind, that proposition has remained untrammelled in the practice of the criminal courts'.[51] However, in recent years there has been a growing acceptability of the evidence of even very young child witnesses. In the case of *R* v. *Barker*,[52] the complainant was just 3 years old and she was called as a witness as the complainant in a sexual abuse case. In this case, Lord Judge CJ commented on the evidence of young child witnesses, stating that allowance must be made for child witnesses in the trial process, that there should be no stigma of unreliability attached to the evidence of a child witness, and that provided the statutory criteria for competence are satisfied, then it is for the jury to determine the credibility of the child witness.

R V. *BARKER* [2010] EWCA CRIM 2
Lord Judge CJ

[40] We emphasise that in our collective experience the age of a witness is not determinative on his or her ability to give truthful and accurate evidence. Like adults some children will provide truthful and accurate testimony, and some will not. However children are not miniature adults, but children, and to be treated and judged for what they are, not what they will, in years ahead, grow to be. Therefore, although due allowance must be made in the trial process for the fact that they are children with, for example, a shorter attention span than most adults, none of the characteristics of childhood, and none of the special measures which apply to the evidence of children carry with them the implicit stigma that children should be deemed in advance to be somehow less reliable than adults. The purpose of the trial process is to identify the evidence which is reliable and that which is not, whether it comes from an adult or a child. If competent, as defined by the statutory criteria, in the context of credibility in the forensic process, the child witness starts off on the basis of equality with every other witness. In trial by jury, his or

---

50 (1958) 42 Cr App R 153 at 160–1.
51 (1990) 90 Cr App R 91 at 94.
52 [2010] EWCA Crim 2.

her credibility is to be assessed by the jury, taking into account every specific personal characteristic which may bear on the issue of credibility, along with the rest of the available evidence.

[41] The judge determines the competency question, by distinguishing carefully between the issues of competence and credibility. At the stage when the competency question is determined the judge is not deciding whether a witness is or will be telling the truth and giving accurate evidence. Provided the witness is competent, the weight to be attached to the evidence is for the jury.

Competence: the statutory criteria

Today, children are competent witnesses. As stated at paragraph 9.2 above, there is a general presumption under s. 53(1), Youth Justice and Criminal Evidence Act 1999 that all witnesses are competent to give evidence, no matter what their age. However, this general presumption is subject to an exception in respect of a witness who is unable to understand questions put to him and to give answers which can be understood under s. 53(3), Youth Justice and Criminal Evidence Act 1999.

S. 53(3), YOUTH JUSTICE AND CRIMINAL EVIDENCE ACT 1999

A person is not competent to give evidence in criminal proceedings if it appears to the court that he is not a person who is able to –

(a) understand questions put to him as a witness, and
(b) give answers to them which can be understood.

Where the issue arises as to the competence of a young child to give evidence in criminal proceedings, the court will determine the issue of competence. Either the court itself or a party to proceedings may dispute the competence of a witness.[53] Under s. 54(2), Youth Justice and Criminal Evidence Act 1999, the party calling the witness bears the burden of proving, on a balance of probabilities, that the witness is competent. The hearing as to the competence of a witness will take place in the absence of the jury, in a *voir dire*,[54] and expert evidence may be called on the matter of competence.[55] If the court considers it necessary, the court may question the witness in the presence of the parties.[56] In reaching its conclusion as to the competence of the witness, the court must treat the witness as having the benefit of any special measures directions which the court has given, or proposes to give that witness.[57]

Section 53 largely reflects the test regarding child witnesses which existed at common law. In *R v. D (Criminal Evidence: Child Witness)*,[58] the Court of Appeal provided guidance on the competence of a child witness to give evidence which was based upon: whether the child

---

53 Section 54(1), Youth Justice and Criminal Evidence Act 1999.
54 Section 54(4), Youth Justice and Criminal Evidence Act 1999.
55 Section 54(5), ibid.
56 Section 54(6), ibid.
57 Section 54(3), ibid.
58 (1995) *The Times*, 15 November.

understands questions put to him, his ability to communicate, his ability to give a coherent and comprehensive account of his evidence, and his maturity to distinguish between fact and fantasy. Thus the test for competency of child witnesses was whether they could understand questions and give a coherent and intelligible account of their evidence. A significant factor was their ability to differentiate between truth and fiction. If a child was able to so differentiate, then they could give evidence and it was for the jury to decide whether the child was telling the truth.

9.3.2 Competence of a child witness in civil proceedings

The position with regard to child witnesses in civil proceedings is a little different.[59] While the criminal courts have tended to permit the evidence of young child witnesses, the civil courts have operated on a presumption against the competence and compellability of such young witnesses. However, the Supreme Court has now ruled that it should not be only in exceptional cases that a child witness is called to give oral evidence in family proceedings; thus, the presumption against children giving oral evidence has been removed.[60] Instead, the Supreme Court has held that it should be for individual family courts to determine on a case-by-case basis when a child witness should give evidence and whether any steps can be taken to improve the quality of the child's evidence and minimise the risk of harm to the child.[61]

9.3.3 Competence of a mentally ill witness

As with child witnesses, a mentally ill witness is generally competent to give evidence under the general presumption of competence within s. 53(1), Youth Justice and Criminal Evidence Act 1999. However, where the witness is unable to understand questions put to him and to give answers which can be understood, he will not be competent to give evidence.[62] In the case of *R* v. *Sed*,[63] the Court of Appeal approved the distinction that the trial judge drew between the competence of the complainant and her reliability, the former being a question of law for the judge to determine, and the latter a question of fact for the jury. This case involved a complainant who suffered from Alzheimer's disease. After watching a video interview with the witness, the trial judge ruled that the witness was competent to give evidence despite the fact that she did not understand all the questions put to her or that all her answers were understandable. The trial judge was, nevertheless, satisfied that she understood and was understood

---

59 See A. Brammer and P. Cooper, 'Still waiting for a meeting of minds: child witnesses in the criminal and family justice systems' [2011] Crim LR 925 for a comparison of the approach taken to the evidence of child witnesses in criminal and family proceedings and the effect of the recent Supreme Court decision in *Re W (Children) (Family Proceedings: Evidence)* [2010] UKSC 12.

60 *Re W (Children) (Family Proceedings: Evidence)* [2010] UKSC 12.

61 Brammer and Cooper point out in the article at n. 59 above that since there is no statutory framework in civil proceedings which is equivalent to the special measures provided for under the Youth Justice and Criminal Evidence Act 1999, the civil justice system is not set up for the use of special measures, and thus, the system may have to 'borrow' a criminal court with the appropriate technical video and live link equipment in order to give effect to some special measures.

62 Section 53(3), Youth Justice and Criminal Evidence Act 1999.

63 [2004] 1 WLR 3218.

sufficiently for a jury to evaluate her evidence. In the case of *DPP* v. *R*,[64] the High Court drew a distinction between a witness who is unable to understand questions and give intelligible answers, and a witness who suffers a loss of memory: '[r]ecollection is quite different from competence'.[65] A witness who merely suffers the latter is not an incompetent witness. The Court held that although the evidence of the witness in this case may have needed treating with some care as a result of the fact that the witness had learning difficulties, the problem at trial was not her competence, but it was her loss of memory.

While the issue of the competence of the witness is a question of law for the judge to decide, the question of the credibility of that evidence is a question of fact for the jury to determine (in a case involving a jury). Thus, where a witness suffers from a mental illness and is deemed to be competent to give evidence, then it is left to the jury to determine the weight that should be attached to that evidence. Members of the jury are free to disregard any evidence that they consider lacks credibility as a result of the mental illness.[66]

9.3.4 Reviewing competence at trial

In *DPP* v. *R*,[67] the High Court held that the competence of the witness should be assessed both at the time when consideration is given to the admission of a video recorded interview and throughout the trial (particularly when the time comes for cross-examination of the witness). Thus, where the witness has given examination-in-chief via a video interview, which the prosecution has already adduced prior to the issue of the competence of the witness arising, the video will not become retrospectively 'inadmissible'. However, if the witness is deemed to be incompetent and thus is not cross-examined, 'the court may well place little or no weight on the video recorded interview, precisely because it cannot be tested in cross-examination'.[68] Similarly, in *R* v. *Powell*,[69] the child witness was merely 3 years old. She was deemed to be competent at the time that the video interview was recorded, but it became clear in cross-examination that she did not understand the questions asked, she was not able to give answers that could be understood, and she did not comprehend the importance of telling the truth. The Court of Appeal held that her competence to give evidence should have been reviewed at this stage and the case should have been withdrawn from the jury since no reasonable jury properly directed could convict on the basis of the evidence adduced.

9.4 SWORN AND UNSWORN EVIDENCE

Where the court decides that the witness is competent to give evidence, consideration must also be given to whether the witness may give sworn evidence or whether his evidence must be heard unsworn.

---

64 [2007] EWHC 1842 (Admin).
65 Ibid. at [21].
66 *R* v. *Hill* (1851) 2 Denison 254; 169 ER 495.
67 [2007] EWHC 1842 (Admin).
68 Ibid. at [16].
69 [2006] EWCA Crim 3.

9.4.1 Competence to give sworn evidence

Under s. 55(2), Youth Justice and Criminal Evidence Act 1999, a witness may only give sworn evidence if he is aged 14 years or older and he has a sufficient appreciation of the solemnity of the occasion and of the particular responsibility to tell the truth which is involved in taking an oath. The court has no discretion to allow a child under the age of 14 to give sworn evidence.

S. 55(2), YOUTH JUSTICE AND CRIMINAL EVIDENCE ACT 1999

The witness may not be sworn for that purpose (i.e. giving evidence on oath) unless –

(a) he has attained the age of 14, and
(b) he has a sufficient appreciation of the solemnity of the occasion and of the particular responsibility to tell the truth which is involved in taking an oath.

There is a general presumption in favour of the witness giving sworn evidence if he is able to give intelligible testimony.[70] If a witness is able to give intelligible testimony, he is presumed to have a sufficient appreciation of the matters mentioned in s. 55(2)(b) unless any evidence is adduced to the contrary. A witness is deemed to be able to give 'intelligible testimony' if he is able to understand questions put to him as a witness and give answers to them which can be understood.[71] Where evidence is adduced to the contrary, then it is for the party seeking to have the witness sworn to prove, on a balance of probabilities, that the witness has attained the necessary age and has sufficient appreciation of the matters mentioned.[72] Any hearing as to the competence of the witness to give sworn evidence is conducted in the absence of the jury,[73] but in the presence of the parties,[74] and expert evidence may be called on the matter.[75]

The test of 'intelligible testimony' under s. 55(8) largely reflects the common law test prior to the enactment of the 1999 Act, under which a child aged 14 or above was generally presumed to be competent to give sworn evidence, but where such a child's competence was questioned, the test laid down in *R* v. *Hayes* questioned 'whether the child has sufficient appreciation of the solemnity of the occasion and the added responsibility to tell the truth, which is involved in taking an oath over and above the duty to tell the truth which is an ordinary duty of normal social conduct'.[76] The child witness would be asked whether he understands the nature of the oath, the importance of telling the truth and whether he has sufficient understanding of the solemnity of the occasion in giving sworn evidence.

---

70 Section 55(3), Youth Justice and Criminal Evidence Act 1999.
71 Section 55(8), ibid.
72 Section 55(4), ibid.
73 Section 55(5), ibid.
74 Section 55(7), ibid.
75 Section 55(6), ibid.
76 [1977] 1 WLR 238.

9.4.2 Competence to give unsworn evidence

Where a person (of any age) is competent to give evidence, but is not competent to give sworn evidence under s. 55(2), he must give his evidence unsworn.[77] Thus, a child under the age of 14 will give his evidence unsworn, as will a person aged 14 or over who does not have a sufficient appreciation of the solemnity of the occasion and of the particular responsibility to tell the truth which is involved in taking an oath. Where s. 56(1) applies (the witness is under 14 or does not have a sufficient appreciation of the solemnity of the occasion and of the particular responsibility to tell the truth), a deposition of unsworn evidence may be taken for the purposes of criminal proceedings as if that evidence had been given on oath.[78] Where a witness has given unsworn evidence but it later appears to the Court of Appeal that the witness should have given sworn evidence, this alone will not provide sufficient grounds to quash a conviction.[79]

Under s. 96, Children Act 1989, where a child who is called as a witness does not, in the opinion of the court, understand the nature of an oath, the child's evidence may be heard unsworn if the court is satisfied that the child understands that it is his duty to speak the truth, and has sufficient understanding to justify his evidence being heard.[80]

9.5 OATHS AND AFFIRMATIONS

Oral evidence must be given under oath (subject to the rules on unsworn evidence above). Where a witness is called to give oral evidence in proceedings, he must first take the oath or affirm. This is done immediately upon the witness stepping into the witness box and prior to the witness beginning his evidence. The witness may choose either to take the oath or to affirm. Both oaths and affirmations are binding on the witness and if the witness is later found to have lied under oath (or having affirmed), he may be prosecuted for perjury.

9.5.1 The oath

Section 1(1), Oaths Act 1978 prescribes that the person taking the oath shall hold the Bible in his uplifted hand and shall repeat the words of the oath. The words of the oath in its Christian form are:

> *I swear by Almighty God that the evidence which I shall give shall be the truth, the whole truth, and nothing but the truth.*

A different form of words is provided for other faiths and the witness is asked what oath they would like to take prior to swearing. A failure to comply with the precise form of words or with the requirement that the Bible be taken in a raised hand does not automatically invalidate the oath; rather the oath is valid if it is taken in a way binding and intended to be binding upon the

---

77 Section 56(1) and (2), Youth Justice and Criminal Evidence Act 1999.
78 Section 56(3), ibid.
79 Section 56(5), ibid.
80 Section 96(2), Children Act 1989.

conscience of the witness.[81] In the case of *R* v. *Kemble*,[82] the witness, who was Muslim, took the oath while holding the New Testament. The defendant appealed against his conviction on the ground that the oath had been administered incorrectly. However, the Court of Appeal dismissed the appeal and held that whether the administration of an oath was lawful depended on two things: (1) whether the oath appeared to the court to be binding on the conscience of the witness, and (2) if so, whether the witness himself considered the oath to be binding on his conscience. In this particular case, the witness gave evidence to the Court of Appeal that irrespective of the religious book he held, he considered his oath to be binding upon his conscience.[83]

9.5.2 The affirmation

Where a person called to give evidence objects to being sworn, he may instead give his evidence after making a solemn affirmation.[84] The affirmation may also be taken by 'a person to whom it is not reasonably practicable without inconvenience or delay to administer an oath in the manner appropriate to his religious belief as it applies in relation to a person objecting to be sworn'.[85] An affirmation is of the same force and effect as the oath,[86] and thus it is just as binding as an oath and can similarly lead to a prosecution for perjury where a witness lies in evidence after taking the solemn affirmation. Section 6(1), Oaths Act 1978 provides the wording of the affirmation as follows:

> *I, do solemnly, sincerely and truly declare and affirm that the evidence which I shall give shall be the truth, the whole truth, and nothing but the truth.*

In the case of *R* v. *Bellamy*,[87] the Court of Appeal held that, although the trial judge was right to investigate the competence of the mentally ill witness, after ruling that she was competent to give evidence, the judge was wrong to then question her on her theological beliefs and understanding and rule that she should affirm rather than take the oath.

9.6 VULNERABLE AND INTIMIDATED WITNESSES

This section of the text explores the ways in which the courts can assist vulnerable and intimidated witnesses in giving evidence through the use of special measures in order to improve the quality of their evidence. Some of the measures introduced under the Youth Justice and Criminal Evidence Act 1999 include the giving of evidence behind a screen which

---

81 See *R* v. *Chapman* [1980] Crim LR in which the defendant did not take the Bible in his raised hand as specified in the Oaths Act 1978.
82 [1990] 1 WLR 1111.
83 See J. Cooper QC, 'Oaths and affirmations' (2012) 176 JPN 114 for an argument that the oath is no guarantee of the truth and see G. Lindhorst, 'To swear or not to swear?' (2012) 176 JPN 178 for a response and different perspective, namely that taking the oath or affirming 'is meant to impress upon the witness the importance of the act of giving evidence and of seeking to tell the truth to the best of one's ability'.
84 Section 5(1), Oaths Act 1978.
85 Section 5(2), ibid.
86 Section 5(4), ibid.
87 (1986) 82 Cr App R 222 at 225.

shields the witness so that they cannot see the defendant, the use of a live link to enable the witness to give evidence from another room, the use of video recorded evidence, excluding the defendant's family or friends from the courtroom, and, for young children, the removal of wigs and gowns by the judge and counsel in court. The special measures provisions have been described by Professor Jenny McEwan as, 'the government's response to the problems which face vulnerable witnesses in the intimidating courtrooms. [The Youth Justice and Criminal Evidence Act 1999] recognises that the stress, and in some cases, humiliation involved in giving evidence may cause potential witnesses to refuse to participate. Meanwhile, fears are growing that criminal defendants and their supporters are increasingly ready to use fear to deter witnesses from testifying against them.'[88]

9.6.1 The rationale for the special measures directions

Since ss. 16 to 33, Youth Justice and Criminal Evidence Act 1999 came into force on 24 July 2002 (with the exception of s. 28 which at the time of writing is still not fully in force), the courts have had the power to order a special measures direction for certain eligible witnesses. These provisions govern the special measures directions available and the rules relating to the eligibility of witnesses for special measures.

The special measures were introduced in order to protect witnesses who are vulnerable or intimidated and improve the quality of the testimony they give: '. . . the Act addresses various problems relating to vulnerable witnesses, not simply for the purpose of protecting and supporting such persons but also in the interests of maximising the evidence available in criminal courts and improving its quality'.[89] By protecting vulnerable and intimidated witnesses, the use of special measures is intended to encourage witnesses to give evidence against a defendant despite their fears, and to assist witnesses to give the 'best evidence' that they can (improving the quality[90] of their evidence by relieving the stress of giving evidence and by improving the recall and communication of the witness).[91] Thus, the rationale behind the special measures provisions is threefold:

- to protect vulnerable and intimidated witnesses,
- to maximise the evidence available in court, and
- to improve the quality of the witness testimony.

The special measures also serve to ensure that the witness is available to be challenged by the defence, allowing the defence the opportunity to cross-examine the witness and to fully test the

---

88 J. McEwan, 'In defence of vulnerable witnesses: the Youth Justice and Criminal Evidence Act 1999' (2000) 4 E&P 1 at 1.
89 D. Birch and R. Leng, *Blackstone's Guide to the Youth Justice and Criminal Evidence Act 1999* (Blackstone Press Ltd, 2000) at p. 1.
90 'Quality' is defined in s. 16(5) of the Act 'in terms of completeness, coherence and accuracy', and 'coherence' refers to 'a witness's ability in giving evidence to give answers which address the questions put to the witness and can be understood both individually and collectively'. For more information, see paragraph 9.6.3 below on the statutory framework.
91 For a detailed discussion of the 'best evidence' principle, see Birch and Leng, *Blackstone's Guide to the Youth Justice and Criminal Evidence Act 1999* at pp. 26–9.

prosecution case. In the absence of special measures directions, where a key prosecution witness refuses to give evidence due to fear, the prosecution may have little choice but to make an application that the witness's statement be read out in court. The rules governing the admissibility of hearsay statements given by unavailable witnesses are found in ss. 114(1)(a) and 116, Criminal Justice Act 2003.

Cross-reference

Refer to Chapter 7 for more detail on the hearsay provisions and the circumstances in which a witness statement (which is, of course, a hearsay statement) may be read in evidence due to the unavailability of the witness.

However, the reading of a key witness's statement in evidence without having that witness available to be cross-examined would inevitably be highly objectionable to the defence. Where an application by the prosecution to read out such a statement is refused, then unless the prosecution feels that it has enough evidence to prosecute without that witness's evidence, it will offer no evidence and the judge will direct an acquittal. Thus, one aim of the provisions governing special measures directions was to avoid unjustified acquittals, either through prosecutions being dropped due to the fear of a key witness by encouraging witnesses to give evidence, or through the evidence given by a vulnerable or intimidated witness being of poor quality.

Although largely welcome, the special measures provisions have not entirely escaped controversy. Professor Diane Birch and Roger Leng acknowledge that 'fears have been expressed that new means for receiving evidence may undermine the oral and adversarial traditions of the criminal trial or work unfairness for defendants'.[92] In an adversarial trial, value is attached to evidence given orally in court. When a witness gives live evidence from the witness box the tribunal of fact is able to assess the credibility of the witness, not just by listening to the content of the testimony, but also by examining the witness's appearance and demeanour while giving evidence. However, such an assessment of the witness is somewhat limited by the use of some special measures, such as where evidence is given by the witness in another room via a live link or where the evidence was pre-recorded.

J. MCEWAN, 'SPECIAL MEASURES FOR WITNESSES AND VICTIMS' IN M. MCCONVILLE AND G. WILSON, *THE HANDBOOK OF THE CRIMINAL JUSTICE PROCESS* (OXFORD UNIVERSITY PRESS, 2002), PP. 237–51

[at p. 237]

In the adversarial trial, evidence is adduced by one of the parties and is challenged by the other. In practical terms using oral evidence best achieves this. Hence trials tend to be oral, and to depend heavily on witness testimony. The finder of fact, when choosing between disputed versions of events, is therefore forced to decide which of the various witnesses called is not telling the truth. To this end, magistrates and juries tend to examine not only the content of oral testimony, but also the appearance

---

92 Ibid. See also D. Birch, 'A better deal for vulnerable witnesses?' [2000] Crim LR 223 for further critique of the provisions.

and demeanour of witnesses. It may be relevant that a witness is tall or heavily built. The demeanour of the witness whilst actually giving evidence is also thought to be significant. The more confidently the witness performs, the more likely he or she is to be believed. Hence a witness who struggles to comprehend the questions asked, or whose powers of self-expression are very weak, either as a permanent matter or temporarily in the context of the courtroom, is at considerable disadvantage. Where this witness is the victim of a crime, there is a danger that the criminal will be acquitted and go unpunished only because fluent, convincing oral evidence is not forthcoming at the trial.

... The object [of the Youth Justice and Criminal Evidence Act 1999] has been to retain the orality of proceedings so far as is possible. At the same time, the Act recognizes that for some witnesses oral communication is particularly difficult, and the courtroom a particularly difficult place in which to communicate.

9.6.2 What are the special measures directions?

The special measures which may be used in respect of an eligible vulnerable or intimidated witness are found under ss. 23 to 33, Youth Justice and Criminal Evidence Act 1999. They are:

- screening the witness from the accused (s. 23),
- giving evidence via live link (s. 24),
- giving evidence in private (s. 25),
- removal of wigs and gowns (s. 26),
- video-recorded evidence-in-chief (s. 27),
- video-recorded cross-examination or re-examination (s. 28),
- examination of witness through an intermediary (s. 29), and
- provision of an aid to communication (s. 30).

Screens
A screen is probably one of the simplest special measures used. Where this special measure is employed, a screen is used to shield the witness from the defendant in order that the witness cannot see the defendant while giving evidence. Under s. 23(1), a screen may be used to prevent the witness from seeing the defendant while giving testimony or being sworn in court. Section 23(2) requires that the screen must not prevent the witness from being able to see, and to be seen by the judge and jury (if there is one), the legal representatives acting in the proceedings, and any interpreter or other person appointed to assist the witness.

The use of screens actually pre-dates the Youth Justice and Criminal Evidence Act 1999, being used previously mainly in respect of child witnesses. In *R* v. *DJX*,[93] a case involving allegations of sexual abuse against a number of child complainants, the trial judge was informed through Social Services that the child complainants might be reluctant or unwilling to give evidence. The judge considered the fact that cases sometimes collapsed for this very reason and decided to use a screen to prevent the child witnesses from seeing the dock. The

---

93 (1990) 91 Cr App R 36.

defendants appealed against their convictions on the grounds that the use of the screens had been prejudicial to the defendants. However, the Court of Appeal held that the trial judge's decision was 'a perfectly proper, and indeed a laudable attempt to see that this was a fair trial: fair to all, the defendants, the Crown and indeed the witnesses'.[94] There is also some authority pre-dating the Youth Justice and Criminal Evidence Act 1999 which supports the use of screens in respect of adult witnesses. In *R* v. *Cooper and Schaub*[95] the Court of Appeal held that although the use of screens was generally confined to child witnesses and was prejudicial to the defendant, they could be used in respect of an adult witness in the most exceptional cases. Now, under the Youth Justice and Criminal Evidence Act 1999, a screen can be used in respect of both child witnesses, and vulnerable or intimidated adult witnesses. The only limitation applied is that witnesses must be 'eligible' under either s. 16 or s. 17, Youth Justice and Criminal Evidence Act 1999.

> **Cross-reference**
>
> The eligibility rules under ss. 16 and 17, Youth Justice and Criminal Evidence Act 1999 are discussed below.

Section 23(1), Youth Justice and Criminal Evidence Act 1999 provides for a special measures direction that allows for the witness 'to be prevented by means of a screen *or other arrangement* from seeing the accused' (author's emphasis). This means that the direction under s. 23 might actually provide for an alternative arrangement to a screen by which the witness is prevented from seeing the accused. There is an example of such an arrangement in the early authority of *R* v. *Smellie*,[96] in which the defendant was ordered to sit on the stairs leading out of the dock so that he was out of sight of the complainant, but could still hear her, when she was giving evidence. Lord Coleridge J held that '[i]f the judge considers that the presence of the prisoner will intimidate a witness there is nothing to prevent him from securing the ends of justice by removing the former from the presence of the latter'.[97] However, Birch and Leng argue that:

> . . . it is clearly potentially a more prejudicial course of action than the erection of a screen. Not only does it focus the attention of the jury on the accused as the likely source of the witness's discomfiture, it also prevents them from assessing his reaction to the evidence the witness gives and (potentially at least) makes it harder for the accused to have proper contact with those responsible for representing him without drawing attention to himself in a way which appears to run counter to the notion of hiding him in the first place.[98]

The latter requirement that the defendant is able to communicate with his legal representatives and participate in the trial is one which has been held to be important in ensuring that the defendant receives a fair trial under Article 6, European Convention on Human Rights, which guarantees the right of the defendant to participate effectively in his trial.[99] Thus, it is highly

---

94 Ibid., per Lane LCJ at 41.
95 [1994] Crim LR 531.
96 (1920) 14 Cr App R 128.
97 Ibid. at 130.
98 Birch and Leng, *Blackstone's Guide to the Youth Justice and Criminal Evidence Act 1999* at p. 57.
99 See *T* v. *UK and V* v. *UK* [2000] Crim LR 187.

unlikely that an arrangement such as that which occurred in *R* v. *Smellie* would be acceptable today. Nevertheless, the 1999 Act does permit some arrangement other than the use of a screen in preventing the witness from seeing the accused. Where there is some reason preventing the use of a screen, moving the defendant to another part of the courtroom, such that he is still clearly able to communicate with his lawyers, might be acceptable under s. 23(1) and under Article 6. However, such a situation is unlikely to arise and should be rarely employed; where the use of a screen is possible, this method of preventing the witness from seeing the defendant while giving evidence should be preferred.

Live links

An alternative special measure to a screen is the use of a live television link. Under s. 24(1), Youth Justice and Criminal Evidence Act 1999 a special measures direction may be given to provide for the witness to give evidence via a live link. Using this special measure, the witness is not sat in the courtroom but may be sat in another room within the court building, and a television link is used so that everyone in the courtroom (including the defendant and the jury) can see the witness. The witness will only be able to see one person (the person speaking) at a time, either the judge or counsel who is conducting the examination-in-chief or cross-examination. A witness who is eligible under either s. 16 or s. 17 may use a live link for their testimony.

The use of live links in cases involving child witnesses also pre-dates the Youth Justice and Criminal Evidence Act 1999. Under s. 32, Criminal Justice Act 1988 a child witness in a case involving sexual or violent offences could be cross-examined via a live television link. This provision was repealed by the Youth Justice and Criminal Evidence Act 1999 insofar as it related to child witnesses. Section 32, Criminal Justice Act 1988 still exists in an amended form and provides for a witness's evidence (other than the defendant) to be given via a live television link in cases where the witness is outside the United Kingdom.[100]

Evidence in private

Under s. 25(1), Youth Justice and Criminal Evidence Act 1999, the judge may direct that specified persons are excluded from the court during the giving of the witness's evidence. However, the direction may not be used to exclude the defendant, his legal representatives or a person appointed to assist the defendant, such as an interpreter.[101] This measure may be used to exclude from court persons such as members of the defendant's family, his friends or associates, and even members of the press. McEwan comments that 'The press was hostile to the introduction of the power, under s. 25, to exclude them from the trial, although the government has stressed that it is not to be undertaken lightly. After discussion with members of the press, an amendment was added to permit one media representative to remain if the court is cleared.'[102] In addition to the requirement that the witness fall under the eligibility provisions under ss. 16 and 17, this special measures direction is subject to a further restriction. A direction to exclude

---

100 See paragraph 9.7 on live television links below.
101 Section 25(2), Youth Justice and Criminal Evidence Act 1999.
102 McEwan, 'In defence of vulnerable witnesses: the Youth Justice and Criminal Evidence Act 1999' (2000) 4 E&P 1 at 12.

specified persons from court only applies where the proceedings relate to sexual offences, or if it appears to the court that there are reasonable grounds for believing that any person other than the accused has sought, or will seek, to intimidate the witness in connection with testifying in the proceedings.[103] Thus, this provision is justified on the basis that it provides only a very narrow exception to the principle of open justice.[104]

Removal of wigs and gowns

Section 26, Youth Justice and Criminal Evidence Act 1999 provides for the removal of wigs and gowns during the giving of a witness's evidence. The removal of wigs and gowns during a child witness's testimony also pre-dates the Youth Justice and Criminal Evidence Act 1999, but this provision provides that such a measure might also be used in respect of vulnerable adult witnesses. The wishes of the witness will be considered by the court in accordance with s. 19(3)(a), Youth Justice and Criminal Evidence Act 1999.

Video-recorded evidence

Section 27(1), Youth Justice and Criminal Evidence Act 1999 provides for the examination-in-chief of a witness to be pre-recorded and the video of this played in court. This provision is currently in force and applies to any eligible witness whether they are eligible under s. 16 or s. 17, Youth Justice and Criminal Evidence Act 1999. Under s. 27(2), the whole recording or part of the recording may be excluded from evidence if the court considers that it is not in the interests of justice to admit it. In considering the admissibility of the video-recording or part of it, the court must consider whether any prejudice to the defendant in admitting the evidence is outweighed by the desirability of showing the full interview.[105] Where the witness will not be available to be cross-examined and the parties have not agreed that there is no need for the witness to be available,[106] then the video-recording of the examination-in-chief of the witness will not be admissible.[107] Neither will the video-recording be admissible where insufficient information has been disclosed about the circumstances in which the recording was made.[108] The court may give leave for a witness who has given evidence-in-chief via a video-recording to give further evidence-in-chief, for instance via a live link.[109]

Under s. 28(1), Youth Justice and Criminal Evidence Act 1999, the cross-examination or re-examination of a witness may also be pre-recorded and the video of this played in court. This provision applies where the examination-in-chief of a witness has been recorded in accordance with s. 27. The recording must be made in the presence of such persons as the rules of court or the direction may provide and in the absence of the defendant. Both the judge and the legal representatives must be able to see and hear the examination of the witness and to communicate with the persons in whose presence the recording is being made, and the defendant must be able to see and hear any such examination and to communicate with any legal representative acting

---

103 Section 25(4), Youth Justice and Criminal Evidence Act 1999.
104 Home Office Report, *Speaking Up for Justice* (June 1998).
105 Section 27(3), Youth Justice and Criminal Evidence Act 1999.
106 See s. 27(4)(a)(ii), ibid.
107 Section 27(4)(a), ibid.
108 Section 27(4)(b), ibid.
109 Section 27(5)(b)(ii) and (9), ibid.

for him.[110] At the time of writing, s. 28 is only partially in force; in fact, it is the only special measure not to be fully enacted. The Ministry of Justice is carrying out a pilot of s. 28 in the Crown Court at Kingston-Upon-Thames, Leeds and Liverpool in cases in which there may be a delay in holding the trial or which lend themselves to pre-trial cross-examination of a vulnerable witness by the nature of the case.

In the following passage, McEwan considers the rationale for the use of video-recorded evidence, as well as the advantages and disadvantages of receiving evidence in this way in a criminal trial:

J. MCEWAN, 'IN DEFENCE OF VULNERABLE WITNESSES: THE YOUTH JUSTICE AND CRIMINAL EVIDENCE ACT 1999' (2000) 4 E&P 1

[at 7–10]

In the Pigot Report the arguments in favour of the videotaped interview for potential child witnesses were rehearsed. One of the main points in its favour was the advantage attached to obtaining evidence as soon as possible after the event. This is particularly true in relation to young children, whose memories may fade more quickly than those of adults. Children are, unlike adults, the responsibility of social services who, typically, become aware of problems within the family before the police. Cases are referred early on to the Joint Child Protection team who conduct the interview. Although a contemporaneous account may be preferable in the case of other categories of vulnerable witness, it must be asked how this would in practice be achieved. Even in the case of an adult within the care of the social services or the National Health Service, it is unlikely that cases would be referred early to investigating teams trained to interview in this way. The likelihood of a reasonably contemporaneous account being committed to videotape is therefore remote. Further, if the ground for using a videotaped interview for an adult witness is fear (see below) the probability is that the recording will be made very shortly before trial, after securing permission from a judge at a plea and directions hearing. The justification of increased accuracy through contemporaneity would not apply. The rationale for this special measure, it seems, lies entirely in the reduction of stress – which may, in the view of some critics, merely make it easier for the witness to lie. A logical problem arises from making a measure of this kind available to some witnesses. Apparently in their case, the measure is justified if the quality of their evidence would be enhanced, as long as the defence is not unduly handicapped by the procedure. But if the defence are not generally unfairly disadvantaged by use of a measure, why should it not be available to all witnesses whose evidence would be enhanced, not merely to those who fit the description of eligible witnesses?

. . .

The use of videorecorded interviews at trial presents a variety of awkward legal points. For some purposes, a videotape is a memory-refreshing document. In addition, the video may amount to a previous consistent or inconsistent statement. Should a tape exist but not be presented in lieu of evidence in chief at the trial, the witness may undergo cross-examination on any discrepancies between what is said at trial and what was said in the interview.

. . .

Assuming that most videotaped cross-examinations would feature a prosecution witness, a real concern is that the defence could be severely prejudiced by having to cross-examine in advance of the

110 Section 28(2), ibid.

trial, before they have heard other prosecution witnesses give evidence. Rightly or wrongly, defence advocates may feel disadvantaged by the absence of the jury. They will have to conduct cross-examinations without any indication of jury reaction. Meanwhile, the disadvantage for a prosecution witness for whom the measure is employed is that a last-minute change of plea to guilty does not spare them the ordeal of cross-examination. The effectiveness of the provision will depend largely on the ability of prosecutors to provide full disclosure in good time. Baroness Mallalieu's experience of disclosure by social services of records relating to children in care made her sceptical that the documents would be available in time, raising the spectre of the child having to be cross-examined twice.

Intermediaries

Section 29(1), Youth Justice and Criminal Evidence Act 1999 came into force on 23 February 2004 and it provides for any examination of the witness to be conducted through an interpreter or other person approved by the court as an intermediary. Only witnesses who are eligible under s. 16 (i.e. witnesses under the age of 18, or the quality of whose evidence is likely to be diminished by a mental or physical disorder) may apply for a special measure under s. 29.[111] Under s. 29(2), the function of an intermediary is to communicate, to the witness, questions put to that witness, and to then communicate the witness's answers to counsel, and to explain such questions or answers so far as necessary to enable them to be understood by the witness or counsel. Under s. 29(5), an intermediary must make a declaration that he will faithfully perform his function as intermediary. The examination of the witness through an intermediary must be made in the presence of such persons as the rules of court or the direction may provide. Both the judge and the legal representatives must be able to see and hear the examination of the witness and to communicate with the intermediary, and the jury must be able to see and hear the examination.[112]

The Court of Appeal considered the use of special measures directions in respect of witnesses with severe communication difficulties in *R* v. *Watts*.[113] This case involved allegations of sexual assault by a care worker against four women suffering from mental disorders. All of the women suffered difficulty in communicating; one of the complainants could only communicate by the movement of her eyes, and the service manager of the care home, who knew her well, acted as an interpreter when she gave evidence. An intermediary was also present during the interview.

---

111 The courts also have a common law power to order the use of an intermediary for defendants who require assistance with communicating: see *R (on the application of C)* v. *Sevenoaks Youth Court* [2010] 1 All ER 735 and *R (on the application of AS)* v. *Great Yarmouth Youth Court* [2011] EWHC 2059 (Admin). Section 33BA of the Youth Justice and Criminal Evidence Act 1999 (introduced by the Coroners and Justice Act 2009) will provide the court with the power to direct that the defendant be permitted to give evidence through an intermediary, but at the time of writing this provision is not yet in force.

112 Section 29(3), Youth Justice and Criminal Evidence Act 1999.

113 [2010] EWCA Crim 1824.

R V. WATTS [2010] EWCA CRIM 1824
Mr Justice Mackay

[17] Less than half a generation ago the criminal courts would not have contemplated attempting to receive evidence from persons in the position of these complainants. The Youth Justice and Criminal Evidence Act 1999 ('the 1999 Act') introduced a radical new regime by which special measures were made available to enable vulnerable witnesses (including witnesses with major communication difficulties) to give evidence, or to improve the quality of the evidence. This is the first occasion on which the evidence of complainants suffering from such profound levels of disability has been brought to the court's attention . . .

[18] The parliamentary intention which emerges from the 1999 Act is that those who are competent to give evidence should be assisted to do so. It is well understood that competence is not the same as reliability (see *MacPherson* [2006] 1 Cr App R 30); *Barker* [2010] EWCA Crim 4). Provided the court is satisfied that the witness is able to understand the question put to him (or her) and give answers to them which can be understood, the competency test is satisfied. The Act further contemplates the reception of evidence in circumstances where a witness who satisfies the statutory test as to competence, may nevertheless lack sufficient communication skills to give evidence without the use of an intermediary. The use of intermediaries forms an integral part of the structure of the special measures regime. In the present case, . . . two of the complainants gave evidence with the assistance of an intermediary (one of whom was not registered) by means of a process which was seen by the jury. Although arrangements were for a registered intermediary to be available to assist at trial, if required, Miss Munro decided that she should not cross-examine the complainants. The judge described that decision as understandable, but the opportunity for cross-examination (with all the attendant difficulties) was available, at least in relation to JR and JB. Instead of formal cross-examination of the witnesses, Miss Munro focused her attention, and that of the jury, on the areas of evidence which advanced the defendant's case that the allegations against him were false.

[19] Further, although section 27(4) contemplates an inability to cross-examine as a reason for refusing to admit evidence in chief obtained by special measures, the Act leaves that decision to the discretion or judgment of the court. It therefore countenances the possibility that such evidence can be admitted even where no direct cross-examination is possible.

Aid to communication

Finally, under s. 30, Youth Justice and Criminal Evidence Act 1999, while giving evidence the witness may be provided with such device as the court considers appropriate with a view to enabling questions or answers to be communicated to or by the witness despite any disability or disorder or other impairment which the witness has or suffers from. This special measure only applies to witnesses who are eligible under s. 16 of the 1999 Act. For example, in the case of *R* v. *Watts* (above), one of the complainants suffered from profound cerebral palsy and other similar disabilities. She gave evidence using an electronic communicator device to respond to questions. The device was in the form of a tablet computer mounted on her wheelchair. The tablet computer gave the witness access to a number of electronic grids containing drawings, pictures or symbols and a square for Yes or No. The witness activated a switch when a cursor reached the picture or symbol that she desired and then an electronic 'voice' would vocalise the image.

9.6.3 The statutory framework

Having explored all of the special measures available, it is necessary to consider the statutory framework governing the eligibility of these special measures. The framework has been criticised for being 'of such complexity that the potential for courts to make errors is greatly increased'.[114] The structure of the provisions within the Youth Justice and Criminal Evidence Act 1999 is relatively complicated, and the special rules that apply to child witnesses and complainants in sexual cases make the framework even more confusing. Professor Diane Birch comments that '[t]he new statutory framework is not, sadly, a model of simplicity'.[115]

Section 19, Youth Justice and Criminal Evidence Act 1999 is the starting point for considering whether a special measures direction may be granted (see Figure 9.2). Under s. 19(1), any party may make an application for a special measures direction or the court may raise the issue. The court must first determine whether the witness is eligible to receive a special measures direction under either s. 16 (vulnerable witnesses) or s. 17 (intimidated witnesses) of the 1999 Act. Where the witness is deemed to be eligible under either of these sections, the court must then determine whether any of the special measures would *improve the quality of the evidence*, and give a direction providing for the appropriate measure to apply.

The rules relating to eligibility for special measures are found under ss. 16 and 17, Youth Justice and Criminal Evidence Act 1999. Section 16 covers the eligibility of vulnerable witnesses, while s. 17 deals with the eligibility of intimidated witnesses.

J. MCEWAN, 'IN DEFENCE OF VULNERABLE WITNESSES: THE YOUTH JUSTICE AND CRIMINAL EVIDENCE ACT 1999' (2000) 4 E&P 1

[at 4]

The concept of vulnerability is extended by the Act beyond the traditional categories of witnesses: generally, children, those with a learning disability and complainants in sexual cases. Also included are intimidated witnesses, and witnesses who suffer fear or distress in relation to giving evidence at a criminal trial. They are now included in the statutory categories of 'eligible' witness ... If a witness is 'eligible', and the court takes the view that, without a special measure to assist, the quality of the witness's evidence is likely to be diminished, it may make a special measures direction. This might be in response to an application by a party, or the issue may be raised by the court of its own motion.

Vulnerable witnesses: eligibility under s. 16
Section 16 provides that a witness may be eligible to receive a special measure on grounds of age or incapacity. A witness is eligible under s. 16(1) if the witness is:

---

114 McEwan, 'In defence of vulnerable witnesses: the Youth Justice and Criminal Evidence Act 1999' (2000) 4 E&P 1 at 13.
115 Birch, 'A better deal for vulnerable witnesses?' [2000] Crim LR 223 at 240. See also L. Hoyano, 'Variations on a theme by Pigot: special measures directions for child witnesses' [2000] Crim LR 250 for further acknowledgement of the complexity of the statutory framework.

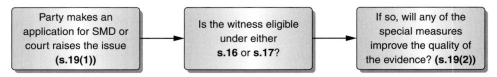

Figure 9.2 Process for applying for a special measures direction

- under the age of 18[116] at time of hearing; or
- the quality of the evidence is likely to be diminished by reason of mental disorder or because the witness has a 'significant impairment of intelligence and social functioning'; or
- the quality of the evidence is likely to be diminished because the witness has a physical disability or is suffering from a physical disorder.

Thus, this section applies to witnesses who may be vulnerable due to their age or either a physical or mental disability. Under s. 16(1)(a), a witness is eligible for any of the special measures under ss. 23 to 30 if he is under 18 years of age. Where an application is made for a special measure on the grounds that the witness suffers from a physical or mental disorder or a 'significant impairment of intelligence and social functioning' under s. 16(1)(b), then in order to direct that a special measure be used, the court must take the view that the quality of the evidence is likely to be diminished by reason of that disorder. The term 'quality' is defined in s. 16(5), which states that:

S.16(5), YOUTH JUSTICE AND CRIMINAL EVIDENCE ACT 1999

references to the quality of a witness's evidence are to its quality in terms of completeness, coherence and accuracy; and for this purpose 'coherence' refers to a witness's ability in giving evidence to give answers which address the questions put to the witness and can be understood both individually and collectively.

In considering eligibility under s. 16(1)(b), the court must also consider any views expressed by the witness.[117] Where a witness is eligible for a special measure under s. 16, he is eligible for any of the measures within ss. 23 to 30.[118] (See Figure 9.3.)

Intimidated witnesses: eligibility under s. 17

Section 17 provides that a witness may be eligible to receive a special measure on grounds of fear or distress about testifying. A witness is eligible under s. 17(1) if the court is satisfied that the quality of the witness's evidence is likely to be diminished by reason of fear or distress in

---

116 This provision was amended by s. 98, Coroners and Justice Act 2009, which increased the age to 18. This amendment came into force in June 2011.
117 Section 16(4), Youth Justice and Criminal Evidence Act 1999.
118 Section 18(1)(a), Youth Justice and Criminal Evidence Act 1999 (although it is worth noting again that s. 28 is not yet in force).

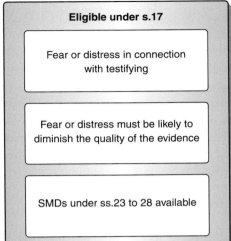

Figure 9.3 The eligibility rules for special measures

connection with testifying. In determining the eligibility of the witness under s. 17(1), the court is to take into account the factors listed in s. 17(2), namely:

- the nature and alleged circumstances of the offence to which the proceedings relate;
- the age of the witness;
- the social and cultural background and ethnic origins of the witness (if the court considers it relevant);
- the domestic and employment circumstances of the witness (if the court considers it relevant);
- any religious beliefs or political opinions of the witness (if the court considers it relevant);
- any behaviour towards the witness on the part of the defendant, members of the family or associates of the defendant, or any other person who is likely to be an accused or a witness in the proceedings.

In considering eligibility under s. 17(1), the court must also consider any views expressed by the witness.[119]

Under s. 17(4), a complainant in respect of a sexual offence who is a witness in the proceedings relating to that offence is eligible for a special measures direction under s. 17, unless the witness has informed the court of his wish not to be so eligible.

> **Cross-reference**
> Refer to Chapter 10 on the special rules relating to the cross-examination of sexual complainants.

---

119 Section 17(3), Youth Justice and Criminal Evidence Act 1999.

Under s. 17(5), a witness in proceedings relating to a 'relevant offence'[120] is eligible for a special measures direction under s. 17, unless the witness has informed the court of the witness's wish not to be so eligible.

Where a witness is eligible for a special measure under s. 17, he is eligible for any of the measures within ss. 23 to 28.[121] (See Figure 9.3.)

Improving the quality of the evidence

As stated above, a witness who is deemed to be eligible for a special measures direction under s. 16 or s. 17 of the 1999 Act will not automatically be granted a direction. Section 19(2) provides that where the witness is deemed to be eligible under s. 16 or s. 17, the court must then determine whether any of the special measures would *improve the quality of the evidence*. The court should then select any appropriate special measure or a combination of appropriate special measures. The measure selected (or any combination of measures selected) should in the opinion of the court be likely to maximise so far as practicable the quality of such evidence.[122] Section 19(3) provides that in deciding whether a special measure would be likely to improve or maximise the quality of the witness's evidence, the court must consider all the circumstances of the case, including any views expressed by the witness; and whether the special measure might inhibit another party to proceedings from effectively testing the evidence.

9.6.4 Special provisions for child witnesses

Further special provisions under the Youth Justice and Criminal Evidence Act 1999 apply in the case of any child witness who is under the age of 18 (and therefore eligible under s. 16(1)(a)). In the case of such witnesses, the court must also have regard to s. 21 before considering whether a special measure would improve the quality of the evidence of the witness under s. 19(2). In particular, the court must have regard to s. 21(3) to (7) before considering the test under s. 19(2).[123]

The primary rule and its limitations

According to s. 21(3), the primary rule in the case of children under the age of 18 is that the examination-in-chief of such a witness should be undertaken via video-recording (in accordance with s. 27), and that any evidence which is not given by video-recording (such as where there is no pre-recording of the examination-in-chief) should be via a live television link (in

---

120 A 'relevant offence' is an offence listed in Schedule 1A to the 1999 Act and includes murder and manslaughter, where a firearm or knife was used or carried; an offence under s. 18, s. 20, s. 47 or s. 38, Offences Against the Person Act 1861, where a firearm or knife was used to cause the injuries or, in the case of s. 38, to carry out the assault, or where the knife or firearm was carried; having an offensive weapon, or an article with a blade or point, in a public place; and offences under the Firearms Act 1968.
121 Section 18(1)(b), Youth Justice and Criminal Evidence Act 1999 (although it is worth noting again that s. 28 is not yet in force).
122 Section 19(2), Youth Justice and Criminal Evidence Act 1999.
123 Section 21(2), Youth Justice and Criminal Evidence Act 1999.

accordance with s. 24). Under s. 21(3), the cross-examination and re-examination of the child witness should also be undertaken via a live link. This primary rule is subject to the limitations set down in s. 21(4):

- the first limitation relates to the availability of the special measure in question;
- the second limitation is the discretion to exclude any video-recording (or part of it) if the court is of the opinion, having regard to all the circumstances of the case, that it should be excluded in the interests of justice;[124]
- the third limitation is that if the witness informs the court of the witness's wish that the rule should not apply, then it will not apply to the extent that the court is satisfied that this would not diminish the quality of the witness's evidence;[125] and
- the fourth limitation is that the evidence will not be given by video-recording if the court is satisfied that it would not be likely to maximise the quality of the witness's evidence so far as practicable.

Where a witness's testimony falls to be received live in court, then the court must direct that a screen be used in accordance with s. 23, unless the witness informs the court that he does not want the use of a screen and the court is satisfied that this would not diminish the quality of the witness's evidence, or where the court considers that a screen would not be likely to maximise the quality of the witness's evidence.[126] Under s. 21(4C), the court must take into account: the age and maturity of the witness; his ability to understand the consequences of giving live evidence in court or with the use of a screen; the relationship between the witness and the defendant; the witness's social and cultural background and ethnic origins; and the nature and alleged circumstances of the offence.

9.7 LIVE TELEVISION LINKS

In certain circumstances, live television links may be used to receive any witness's evidence. Section 51, Criminal Justice Act 2003 governs the use of live links in criminal proceedings and applies to witnesses who are not necessarily vulnerable or intimidated. Under s. 51, a witness (other than the defendant) may give evidence via a live link if the court is satisfied that it is in the interests of the efficient or effective administration of justice and suitable facilities for receiving evidence through a live link are available.[127] In deciding whether to allow the witness's evidence to be given via a live link, the court must consider all the circumstances of the case, including:

- the availability of the witness;
- the need for the witness to attend in person;
- the importance of the witness's evidence to the proceedings;

---

124 As per s. 27(2), Youth Justice and Criminal Evidence Act 1999.
125 See s. 21(4)(ba), Youth Justice and Criminal Evidence Act 1999.
126 See s. 21(4A) and (4B), Youth Justice and Criminal Evidence Act 1999.
127 Section 51(4), Criminal Justice Act 2003.

- the views of the witness;
- the suitability of the facilities; and
- whether a direction might tend to inhibit any party to the proceedings from effectively testing the witness's evidence.[128]

In a Crown Court trial, the judge may direct the jury, if he thinks it necessary, that the evidence given through a live link must be given the same weight as if the witness had been in court.[129]

Where a witness is outside the United Kingdom, evidence may be given via a live link under s. 32, Criminal Justice Act 1988. A recent example of a slightly more unusual case is that of *R* v. *Holli Reed*,[130] in which the important evidence of a defence witness as to fact was a soldier serving in the British Army who was stationed in Cyprus at the time of the trial. Counsel for the defence, Stephen Akinsanya, applied to the trial judge to use a Skype application on his iPad2 to link to the witness's computer in Cyprus. The trial judge allowed the iPad2 to be set up in front of the jury and the witness's evidence to be received in this way.[131]

In civil proceedings, rule 32.3 of the Civil Procedure Rules states that the court may allow a witness to give evidence through a video link or by other means.

9.8   VIDEO-RECORDED EVIDENCE

Section 137(1), Criminal Justice Act 2003 is not yet in force, but when it is brought into force, it will provide for a video recording of a witness's evidence (other than the defendant), to be admitted as evidence-in-chief, provided that:

- the person claims to be an eyewitness to the offence;
- the video recording of the statement was taken at a time when events were fresh in the witness's memory;
- the offence is indictable;
- the witness's recollection of events is likely to be significantly better at the time he gave the recorded account than by the time of the trial; and
- it is in the interests of justice to admit the recording, having regard to whether the recording is an early and reliable account from the witness, the quality is adequate, and any views which the witness may have about using the recording for this purpose.

This provision will not be limited to vulnerable or intimidated witnesses as the provisions under the Youth Justice and Criminal Evidence Act 1999 are, but it will apply to any witness who fulfils the criteria within s. 137 (listed above).

---

128 Section 51(6) and (7), Criminal Justice Act 2003.
129 Section 54(2), Criminal Justice Act 2003.
130 Unreported, 22 August 2011, Luton Crown Court.
131 For further detail on this case, refer to S. Akinsanya, 'New technology saves the day' (2012) *Counsel Magazine*, February issue, at 19.

9.9 WITNESS ANONYMITY ORDERS

In January 2010, a new statutory framework was brought into force to permit witnesses to give evidence anonymously. The provisions are found in ss. 86 to 90, Coroners and Justice Act 2009. These provisions replace the short-lived Criminal Evidence (Witness Anonymity) Act 2008 which was enacted as a temporary emergency measure following the House of Lords' decision in *R* v. *Davis*,[132] a case which restricted the courts' ability to permit witnesses to give evidence anonymously at trial. In this case, Lord Bingham stated that '[i]t is a long-established principle of the English common law that, subject to certain exceptions and statutory qualifications, the defendant in a criminal trial should be confronted by his accusers in order that he may cross-examine them and challenge their evidence'.[133] His Lordship took the view that the anonymity granted to the witnesses by the trial judge in this case 'hampered the conduct of the defence in a manner and to an extent which was unlawful and rendered the trial unfair'.[134]

In an article in the Criminal Law Review, Ormerod, Choo and Easter consider the rationale behind the anonymity provisions as well as the disadvantages that these present to a defendant in a criminal trial:

D. ORMEROD, A. CHOO AND R. EASTER, 'CORONERS AND JUSTICE ACT 2009: THE "WITNESS ANONYMITY" AND "INVESTIGATION ANONYMITY" PROVISIONS' [2010] CRIM LR 368

[at 368–9]

The debate about the circumstances in which it may be permissible for the Crown to secure a conviction based on the evidence of an anonymous witness engages issues which are numerous, complex and controversial. These include: the need to secure evidence in serious cases in which increasingly commonly witnesses are unwilling to provide evidence for fear of reprisals; the need to protect witnesses and their rights to security and privacy; the disadvantages faced by the defendant and whether these render the process so unfair as to deny the accused a fair trial; the extent to which defendants can claim a right to 'confront' their accuser and whether this is infringed; whether a process can be designed to ensure sufficient safeguards for the rights of the defendant and the witness.

The potential disadvantages to the defendant are significant and substantial: it is impossible to investigate fully the credibility of the anonymous witness; the defendant is worse off than if hearsay is adduced against him or her; the defendant has no opportunity to assess the demeanour of the witness; the defendant's cross-examination is less likely to be effective; the defendant's ability to examine witnesses is unequal to the Crown's; there is a potential conflict with art. 6(3)(d) . . .; there is no opportunity to confront the witnesses; the defendant is more reliant than normal on the disclosure process; the defendant's relationship with his or her counsel may be put under strain where counsel

---

132 [2008] UKHL 36. See also I. Dennis, 'The right to confront witnesses: meanings, myths and human rights' [2010] Crim LR 255 for a theoretical approach to the right to confrontation.

133 [2008] UKHL 36 at [5].

134 Ibid. at [35].

alone sees the witness; the jury may be likely to treat the use of anonymous witness evidence as implicit evidence that the accused is violent and/or responsible for intimidation. The witness denied anonymity faces at worst a risk to life, at minimum a loss of respect for privacy. The issue is not, of course, one of 'balancing' the respective rights; it is a question of when the defendant's right to a fair trial ought to be qualified to protect witnesses' rights . . .

The statutory framework

Section 86(1), Coroners and Justice Act 2009 defines a 'witness anonymity order' as a court order 'that requires such specified measures to be taken in relation to a witness in criminal proceedings as the court considers appropriate to ensure that the identity of the witness is not disclosed in or in connection with the proceedings'. The kinds of measures that may be required to be taken are set out in s. 86(2) and include measures ensuring that:

- the witness's name and other identifying details are withheld or removed from materials in the proceedings;
- the witness may use a pseudonym;
- the witness is not asked questions that might lead to the identification of the witness;
- the witness is screened;[135]
- the witness's voice is subjected to modulation.[136]

Applying for a witness anonymity order

An application for a witness anonymity order may be made by either the prosecution or the defence.[137] Where an application is made by the prosecution, then under s. 87(2) the prosecutor must disclose the identity of the witness to the court (unless the court instructs otherwise), but the prosecution need not disclose the witness's identity or any information that might enable the witness to be identified to the defence or any other party. Where an application is made by the defence, then under s. 87(3), the defence must disclose the identity of the witness to the court and to the prosecution, but the defence need not disclose the witness's identity or any information that might enable the witness to be identified to any co-defendant, or his legal representatives, or any other party. Section 87(6) provides that the court must give every party to the proceedings the opportunity to be heard where an application for a witness anonymity order is made, although the court may hear one or more parties in the absence of a defendant and his or her legal representatives, if it appears to the court to be appropriate to do so in the circumstances.[138]

---

135 Although the witness may not be screened to such an extent that the witness cannot be seen by the judge or other members of the court, or the jury (s. 86(4)(a), Coroners and Justice Act 2009).
136 Although the witness's voice should not be modulated to such an extent that the witness's natural voice cannot be heard (s. 86(4)(b), Coroners and Justice Act 2009).
137 Section 87(1), Coroners and Justice Act 2009.
138 Ibid.

The conditions

A witness anonymity order may be made by the court where three conditions (A, B and C) in s. 88, Coroners and Justice Act 2009 are met.[139]

- Condition A is set out in s. 88(3) of the Act and provides that the witness anonymity order must be necessary in order to protect the safety of the witness or another person or to prevent any serious damage to property, or to prevent real harm to the public interest.
- Condition B is that, having regard to all the circumstances, the effect of the proposed order would be consistent with the defendant receiving a fair trial: s. 88(4).
- Condition C is that the importance of the witness's testimony is such that in the interests of justice the witness ought to testify, and the witness would not testify if the proposed order were not made, or there would be real harm to the public interest if the witness were to testify without the proposed order being made: s. 88(5).

In considering whether the witness anonymity order is necessary in order to protect the safety of the witness or another person or to prevent any serious damage to property, the court must have particular regard to any reasonable fear on the part of the witness that they or another person would suffer death or injury, or that there would be serious damage to property, if the witness were to be identified.[140]

Other considerations

The court must also have regard to the considerations in s. 89(2), Coroners and Justice Act 2009, namely:

- the general right of a defendant in criminal proceedings to know the identity of a witness;
- the extent to which the credibility of the witness would be a relevant factor;
- whether evidence given by the witness might be the sole or decisive evidence implicating the defendant;
- whether the witness's evidence could be properly tested without his or her identity being disclosed;
- whether there is any reason to believe that the witness has a tendency or any motive to be dishonest, having regard to any previous convictions and to any relationship between the witness and the defendant or any associates of the defendant;
- whether it would be reasonably practicable to protect the witness by any other means.

Under s. 90(2), Coroners and Justice Act 2009, the judge must give the jury such warning as the judge considers appropriate to ensure that the witness anonymity order does not prejudice the defendant.

---

139 Section 88(2), Coroners and Justice Act 2009.
140 Section 88(6), ibid.

9.10   CONCLUSION

The principle of orality in adversarial proceedings demands that evidence is received in court via the oral testimony of witnesses. Thus, the approach taken by the law is one that promotes the reception of all relevant oral witness testimony. It is only in rare circumstances that a witness will be deemed incompetent to give evidence in criminal proceedings or that a witness will not be compellable; most witnesses are both competent to give evidence in criminal proceedings and they may be compelled to do so by law. However, the law recognises that there are some sensitive situations in which witnesses may not wish to give evidence through fear of the repercussions, or, although they have no objection to doing so, the witness may be particularly vulnerable due to their age or their status as the complainant in a case involving an allegation of sexual abuse. As such, the law has developed a statutory framework to provide some protective measures to vulnerable and intimidated witnesses in order that the quality of their evidence is maximised. As we have seen, the interest at the heart of these measures is the improvement of the quality of the oral testimony received by the tribunal of fact.

Summary

- There is a general presumption under s. 53(1), Youth Justice and Criminal Evidence Act 1999 that all witnesses are competent to give evidence, irrespective of age. A witness will not be competent to give evidence if they are unable to understand and answer questions (s. 53(3)) or if they are charged in the proceedings (s. 53(4)).
- The defendant is not competent to give evidence for the prosecution (s. 53(4), Youth Justice and Criminal Evidence Act 1999). Although he is competent to give evidence in his own defence, he is not compellable (s. 1(1), Criminal Evidence Act 1898). However, adverse inferences may be drawn against a defendant who fails to testify (s. 35, Criminal Justice and Public Order Act 1994).
- The rules governing the compellability of a spouse or civil partner are found within s. 80, Police and Criminal Evidence Act 1984. A spouse or civil partner is not compellable to give evidence for the prosecution or a co-defendant unless s. 80(3) applies, but is compellable to give evidence for the defence. A spouse or civil partner will not be compellable if also charged in proceedings.
- Only a witness who is aged 14 or over and has a sufficient appreciation of the solemnity of the occasion and of the particular responsibility to tell the truth may give sworn evidence (s. 55(2), Youth Justice and Criminal Evidence Act 1999). Otherwise, a witness will give evidence unsworn (s. 56(1)).
- Where a witness is eligible under s. 16, Youth Justice and Criminal Evidence Act 1999 (vulnerable witness), by age or a mental or physical disorder which is likely to diminish the quality of the evidence given, a special measures direction under ss. 23 to 30 may be used to improve the quality of the evidence.

- Where a witness is eligible under s. 17, Youth Justice and Criminal Evidence Act 1999 (intimidated witness), by reason of fear or distress in connection with testifying, a special measures direction under ss. 23 to 28 may be used to improve the quality of the evidence.
- Where a witness is aged under 18, the court must consider the primary rule under s. 21(3), Youth Justice and Criminal Evidence Act 1999 which provides for the special measures direction under s. 27 (video-recorded examination-in-chief), and for evidence not given by video-recording to be given in accordance with s. 24 (live link).
- Under s. 51, Criminal Justice Act 2003, a witness (other than the defendant) may give evidence via a live link if the court is satisfied that it is in the interests of the efficient or effective administration of justice and suitable facilities for receiving evidence through a live link are available. Under s. 32, Criminal Justice Act 1988, a witness who is outside the United Kingdom may give evidence via a live link.
- A witness may give evidence anonymously under s. 86, Coroners and Justice Act 2009 if Conditions A to C, contained within s. 88, are satisfied: A – it is necessary in order to protect safety or prevent serious damage to property, or real harm to the public interest; B – the order is consistent with the defendant receiving a fair trial; and C – the importance of the witness's testimony is such that in the interests of justice the witness ought to testify.

For discussion . . .

1. What is the justification for the principle that a spouse or civil partner is not compellable to give evidence for the prosecution against the defendant? To what extent is this valid in modern society?
2. Should very young children be deemed incompetent to give evidence in criminal proceedings? If not, in what circumstances should the courts hear such evidence, and how should this evidence be assessed?
3. How is competence to give sworn evidence determined? Should unsworn evidence be treated differently to evidence which has been given under oath or after affirming?
4. Explain the rationale for the introduction of special measures directions under the Youth Justice and Criminal Evidence Act 1999. What are the criticisms that may be levelled at the use of such measures?
5. What are the arguments for and against the use of witness anonymity orders in a criminal trial?

Further reading

D. Birch, 'A better deal for vulnerable witnesses?' [2000] Crim LR 223.
This article critically evaluates the reforms under the Youth Justice and Criminal Evidence Act 1999, with particular focus on competence and special measures. The paper praises the reforms for acknowledging that adult witnesses may also be vulnerable witnesses, but criticises the Act for being rushed through Parliament without a sufficient consultation process.

J. Brabyn, 'A criminal defendant's spouse as a prosecution witness' [2011] Crim LR 613.
This paper considers the law relating to the competence of the defendant's spouse as a witness for the prosecution. The author offers an analysis of the rationale for the legal position and discusses the recent

Court of Appeal decision in the case of *R* v. *L* [2008] EWCA Crim 973. Finally, the author offers an alternative approach based upon Australian law.

A. Brammer and P. Cooper, 'Still waiting for a meeting of minds: child witnesses in the criminal and family justice systems' [2011] Crim LR 925.
This article compares the approaches taken in the criminal and the family justice systems to the evidence of child witnesses and considers the effect of the recent Supreme Court decision in the case of *Re W (Children) (Family Proceedings: Evidence)* [2010] UKSC 12. The paper criticises the fact that the civil system is not set up for the use of special measures and there is no statutory framework comparable to the Youth Justice and Criminal Evidence Act 1999.

I. Dennis, 'The right to confront witnesses: meanings, myths and human rights' [2010] Crim LR 255.
This article provides a theoretical analysis of the principle that a defendant in criminal proceedings has a right to be confronted by his accusers. It argues that the right to confrontation is not a single right, but instead a bundle of rights which, although closely linked, are also distinguishable. These are: the right to public trial, the right to face-to-face confrontation, the right to cross-examination, and the right to know the identity of the accuser.

L. Ellison, *The Adversarial Process and the Vulnerable Witness* (Oxford University Press, 2002).
This monograph critically evaluates the special measures directions under the Youth Justice and Criminal Evidence Act 1999. The book acknowledges the attempt made by the reforms to improve the treatment of vulnerable and intimidated witnesses while maintaining adversarial principles, such as that of orality. The book criticises the approach taken and highlights its limitations. A comparative analysis of the law in the Netherlands is also provided.

J. McEwan, 'Special measures for witnesses and victims' in M. McConville and G. Wilson (eds.), *The Handbook of the Criminal Justice Process* (Oxford University Press, 2002), pp. 237–51.
This chapter analyses the provisions relating to vulnerable and intimidated witnesses under the Youth Justice and Criminal Evidence Act 1999 and explores the special measures directions in some detail.

J. Spencer and M. Lamb, *Children and Cross-Examination: Time to Change the Rules?* (Hart Publishing, 2003).
This book explores the use of the evidence of child witnesses in trials and argues that further reforms in the United Kigdom are needed. Various contributors consider comparative positions in countries such as Australia, New Zealand, Austria and Norway. Professor Spencer offers a concluding chapter in which he questions whether video-recorded cross-examination under s. 28, Youth Justice and Criminal Evidence Act 1999 is workable and whether it solves the problems arising from the cross-examination of children. He argues that adversarial cross-examination could be 'tamed' in respect of child witnesses and that cross-examination could even be dispensed with as a result of the hearsay provisions of the Criminal Justice Act 2003.

10 Trial procedure and witness testimony

10.1 INTRODUCTION

While the previous chapter focused on issues arising prior to a witness giving testimony, such as the types of witnesses that may be called or compelled to give evidence at trial and any special measures that might be employed to improve the quality of the evidence given by vulnerable or intimidated witnesses, this chapter is concerned with trial procedure and the process by which the court receives the testimony of witnesses. The chapter begins by exploring the role of the advocate at trial and the purpose of advocacy, as well as the order of proceedings in both criminal and civil trials. A significant focus of this chapter is the examination of witnesses on oath: consideration will be given to the purpose of examination-in-chief, cross-examination and re-examination of witnesses and the types of questions (leading or non-leading questions) which may be asked of witnesses at each of these stages. The procedure for dealing with the use of a document to refresh a witness's memory will be explained, such as where a witness refreshes his memory from his witness statement before going into court, or a police officer refreshes his memory from his incident notebook during his testimony. The exceptions to the rule that prior consistent statements are not admissible as evidence of consistency will be explored. The chapter will look at the way in which unfavourable and hostile witnesses who give evidence may be treated, and finally, the special rules relating to the cross-examination of complainants in sexual offence cases will be examined.

10.2   THE ROLE OF THE ADVOCATE

Before exploring the procedure at trial and the testimony of witnesses, it is worth consider-ing the role of the advocate at trial.[1] The English legal system is an adversarial one and the trial process is based upon the adversarial model which 'is characterised by two opposing parties gathering, selecting and presenting evidence for trial' and as being concerned with 'proof' rather than with 'truth', a consideration which dominates the inquisitorial model.[2] Oral advocacy consequently has an important function in the adversarial model of the trial, presenting and testing the evidence before the tribunal of fact. In most cases an advocate will represent the defendant 'to represent the language and legal points that arise from that complexity of thoughts and words. The advocate then becomes the personifica-tion of the client in the courtroom'.[3] Professional duties are imposed upon the advocate. An advocate's primary obligation is to the court: both barristers and solicitors have a duty not to deceive or knowingly or recklessly mislead the court.[4] A barrister has a duty to 'promote and protect fearlessly and by all proper and lawful means the lay client's best interests';[5] thus counsel in a civil case and defence counsel in a criminal case must fight vehemently in the interests of his client. In a criminal case in the Crown Court, counsel will often adopt emotive language in seeking to persuade the jury to acquit the defendant. However, in a criminal case, the prosecutor is a 'minister of justice' who must 'be seen to be detached and calm'[6] and whose job is to provide, dispassionately, the factual basis upon which the prosecution case against the defendant is brought: '. . . counsel for the prosecution . . . are to regard themselves as ministers of justice, and not to struggle for a conviction'.[7] Since the prosecutor is not fighting for a conviction, he should not use highly emotive language in his closing speech, in order that the jury are able to give their verdict in accordance with the evidence, rather than 'under the influence of feelings excited by the speeches on one side or the other'.[8]

10.3   TRIAL PROCEDURE

This paragraph seeks to provide some context for what follows in this chapter by setting out broadly the order of proceedings in both criminal and civil trials.

---

1 For further discussion see S. Solley QC, 'The role of the advocate' in M. McConville and G. Wilson (eds.), *The Handbook of the Criminal Justice Process* (Oxford University Press, 2002), pp. 311–22.
2 See J. Hodgson, 'Conceptions of the trial in inquisitorial and adversarial procedure' in A. Duff et al. (eds.), *The Trial on Trial* (Hart Publishing, 2006), vol. II, pp. 223–42 at 224.
3 Above (n. 1) at p. 313.
4 See Part III, para. 302, Code of Conduct of the Bar of England and Wales, 8th edn and Chapter 5, O(5.1), Solicitors Regulation Authority Code of Conduct 2011.
5 Part III, para. 303(a), Code of Conduct of the Bar of England and Wales, 8th edn.
6 Above (n. 1) at p. 317.
7 See Crompton J in *R* v. *Puddick* (1865) 4 F & F 497 at 499.
8 Ibid.

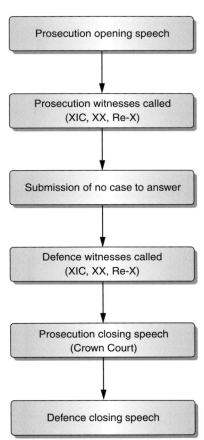

Figure 10.1 Procedure in a criminal trial

10.3.1 Criminal trial

Criminal trials may take place either in a magistrates' court or in a Crown Court. (See Figure 10.1.) Summary trials take place in a magistrates' court before a district judge or bench of lay magistrates. Trials on indictment take place in the Crown Court before a jury. Immediately before a trial begins in the Crown Court, a jury of twelve lay members of the public chosen at random will be empanelled and sworn in as jurors in the case. The clerk of the court will then read out the charge against the defendant and put him in the jury's charge with the words 'It is your charge, having heard the evidence, to say whether he be guilty or not'. Prosecution counsel will then open the Crown's case. In a magistrates' court, there is no jury to be empanelled, but the clerk of the court will put the information (the equivalent to the indictment in the Crown Court) to the defendant and the defendant will enter his plea. Where the defendant pleads not guilty, the trial will then begin with the prosecution opening the Crown's case.

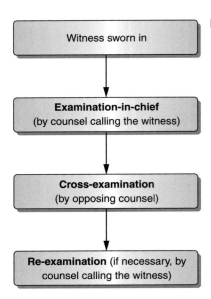

Figure 10.2 Examination of witnesses

The Crown's case begins with an opening speech by prosecution counsel.[9] Where the case is tried in the magistrates' court, the opening speech is usually brief since the magistrates hearing the case are experienced fact-finders and the case may very well be simpler than a case tried on indictment. In the Crown Court, prosecuting counsel's opening speech will be delivered to a lay bench of jurors who may well have never stepped foot inside a courtroom before, therefore, counsel may spend some time explaining the charge to the jury and setting out the witnesses he intends to call and summarising the evidence that they will give. After the opening speech, prosecution counsel will call the Crown's first witness. The first witness to give evidence is usually the complainant (if there is one), and the witness will be sworn before being examined-in-chief by prosecuting counsel. After the examination-in-chief, the witness will then be open to cross-examination by the defence.[10] The prosecution may then (if necessary) ask questions in re-examination, before the witness is released. (See Figure 10.2.) The prosecution will call each of its witnesses, who will be examined-in-chief, cross-examined, and possibly re-examined, in this way until every prosecution witness has been called. Some witnesses will not be called to give live evidence in court, but their witness statement may be read out in court if agreed by the defence; this is known as a s. 9 statement[11] and is dealt with in paragraph 10.4 below. At the end of the prosecution case, the trial has reached its 'half time' point and it is then open to the

---

9 This is not obligatory and in the magistrates' court, counsel may choose not to make an opening speech where the case is relatively straightforward.
10 See paragraph 10.5.3 below for a detailed discussion of the provisions of the Youth Justice and Criminal Evidence Act 1999 which place limitations on the defendant personally conducting the cross-examination of certain protected witnesses and on the types of questions that may be asked in cross-examination of a complainant in a sexual offence case.
11 Section 9, Criminal Justice Act 1967.

defence to make a submission of no case to answer, should the defence wish to do so.[12] If the submission is accepted, an acquittal will be directed and the jury will be discharged; but if the submission is rejected, the trial will continue with the defence case.

In a summary trial, the defence has a right to make either an opening speech or a closing speech. It is usual practice for defence counsel to forgo an opening speech in favour of making a closing speech. In a Crown Court the defence has a limited right to make an opening speech (in addition to his closing speech), but this is only exercisable where the defence is calling evidence as to the facts other than the evidence of the defendant. The defence will then call its evidence, starting with the defendant (if he chooses to give evidence) unless the court directs otherwise.[13]

Cross-reference

Refer back to Chapter 9 for a discussion of the right to silence and the effect of the defendant's silence at trial under s. 35, Criminal Justice and Public Order Act 1994.

Where the defendant does choose to give evidence at trial, he will be sworn in before being examined-in-chief by defence counsel. After the examination-in-chief, the defendant will be tendered to the prosecution for cross-examination. He may then be re-examined by defence counsel. The same process will be followed until all defence witnesses have been called; this marks the close of the defence case.

In a summary trial, at the close of the defence case the defence has the right to make either an opening speech or a closing speech and will usually opt for the latter. The prosecution does not have the right to make a closing speech.[14] In a Crown Court trial, the prosecution will deliver a closing speech before the defence does the same. The defence closing speech is made after the prosecution closing speech, so that the defence has the last word. In the closing speech, counsel will summarise his case and draw on the evidence which supports his theory of the case. Counsel may comment on the evidence during speeches only and may not do so during the testimony of the witnesses. After the closing speeches, the magistrates in a summary trial will then retire to consider their verdict. In a Crown Court trial, the final stage of the trial before the jury retires to consider its verdict is the judge's summing up. In his summing up, the judge will summarise the evidence given by each of the witnesses, he will direct the jury on the law, including the burden and standard of proof, the charges faced by the defendant and the elements of the offence that need to be proved by the prosecution, as well as any other evidential issues which arise in the course of the trial and which may need to be explained to the jury. After summing up, the judge will send the jury out to consider its verdict. Initially, the judge will direct the jury to reach a unanimous decision upon which all twelve of them are agreed. If they are unable to do so and a

---

12 In determining whether there is a case to answer or not the judge (in a Crown Court trial) should apply the test in *R* v. *Galbraith* [1981] 1 WLR 1039. The judge should stop the case where there is no evidence that the crime has been committed by the defendant, or where there is some evidence but it is of a tenuous character. The equivalent test is set out for summary trials under rule 37.3(c) of the Criminal Procedure Rules.

13 Section 79, Police and Criminal Evidence Act 1984.

14 In a summary trial, either the prosecution or the defence can make an application to deliver a second speech. If one party is permitted to do so, then the other party must also be given the opportunity to make a second speech.

minimum of two hours and ten minutes have passed,[15] the judge may accept a majority verdict upon which at least ten jurors are agreed.

10.3.2 Civil trial

A civil trial may take place in the county court or the high court. In a civil case, the trial will begin with a short opening statement by counsel for the claimant. The trial judge may then invite counsel for the other party to make an opening statement. The claimant's case is presented first: the witnesses whose statements have been served by the claimant will be called to give evidence. Each witness will be examined-in-chief by counsel for the claimant, before then being cross-examined by counsel for the defence and possibly re-examined by counsel for the claimant. This process will be followed in respect of every witness called by the claimant until the close of the claimant's case. The defence case will follow with the defence calling its witnesses. Each defence witness will be examined-in-chief by counsel for the defence, before then being cross-examined by counsel for the claimant, and possibly re-examined by counsel for the defence. At the conclusion of all of the evidence, closing submissions will be made by counsel for the claimant, then by counsel for the defence. Finally, a reply will be made on behalf of the claimant. The trial judge will then consider his decision.

10.4 EXAMINATION-IN-CHIEF

Where a witness is called to give evidence and takes the oath or affirms, the first stage of the witness's testimony will be given in examination-in-chief. The witness will be examined-in-chief by counsel calling the witness: so a prosecution witness will be examined-in-chief by prosecuting counsel, and the defendant or any other defence witnesses will be examined-in-chief by defence counsel. The purpose of examination-in-chief is to draw out the witness's account of events (i.e. to get the witness to be the narrator of his own story) and to elicit any facts which strengthen the case of the side calling the witness. The role of counsel in conducting an examination-in-chief of a witness is to get the witness to give a structured and chronological account of what he witnessed; counsel must not give the account or put words into the witness's mouth. As such, there is a restriction on the types of questions that might be asked by counsel in examination-in-chief; counsel may only ask non-leading questions and is prohibited from asking leading questions.[16]

10.4.1 Non-leading questions

Non-leading questions are open-ended questions which do not suggest an answer to the witness, but instead allow the witness to tell their story in their own words. As a general rule, it has been stated that non-leading questions will begin with the words: who, what, when,

---

15 Section 17, Juries Act 1974 provides for a two-hour minimum, but an extra ten minutes was added to this by the *Practice Direction (Crime: Majority Verdict)* [1970] 1 WLR 916 in order to allow the jury time to move between the courtroom and the deliberation room, to settle down and to elect a foreman.

16 The rationale and scope of the rule against asking leading questions in examination-in-chief is explored by Adrian Keane and Rudi Fortson in 'Leading questions – a critical analysis' [2011] Crim LR 280.

where, how, why.[17] For example, 'where were you on 25 March?', 'who were you with?', 'what was he wearing?' By contrast, leading questions are questions which suggest the answer that is sought. Questions which assume the existence of certain facts which have yet to be adduced orally in court are leading questions. For example, 'did he have blood on his shirt?', 'was he a metre away from you?', 'was she wearing a blue dress?' Leading questions are not permitted in examination-in-chief because the evidence must come from the witness in the witness box, rather than from that witness's advocate. As Iain Morley QC points out in *The Devil's Advocate*, 'If you lead, the tribunal knows you have suggested the answer, and so the value of the evidence is diminished'.[18] However, although leading questions are not generally permitted in examination-in-chief, they may be put to a witness in certain circumstances, such as at the start of a witness's evidence in relation to introductory and non-contentious matters. For instance, where there is no dispute as to the witness's presence in a particular place at a particular time, the question 'were you in your office on 25 March?' Leading questions may also be asked in examination-in-chief of a witness whom the judge has ruled to be a hostile witness.

Cross-reference

The testimony of hostile witnesses is dealt with below at paragraph 10.4.4.

10.4.2 Refreshing memory

Out of court

Where a witness is called to give evidence in court they are often asked to recall details about events which occurred at an earlier date, sometimes many months or years ago. Prosecution witnesses will usually give a witness statement to the police contemporaneously to the incident outlining their account. The defendant (and any defence witnesses) as to fact will also give the defence solicitor a written account of the incident; the defendant's account is known as the defendant's 'proof of evidence'. A witness who is called to give evidence at court will give evidence in examination-in-chief from memory, without his witness statement, which is most likely to have been made at some date several months earlier, closer to the events which the witness is being called to testify about. In order to avoid the process of giving evidence becoming merely a memory test,[19] the witness is permitted to use his witness statement (or proof of evidence in the case of the defendant) to refresh his memory of events before giving evidence, but this must take place outside the courtroom.[20] He may not use his witness

---

17 For example, see R. McPeake (ed.), *Advocacy*, 15th edn (Oxford University Press, 2010), at pp. 145–6. Although it has been noted that this technique will not necessarily prevent leading. See Adrian Keane and Rudi Fortson, 'Leading questions – a critical analysis' [2011] Crim LR 280 at 287 where the following example is given: 'Thus, if the assault has yet to be established, it is implicitly leading ... to ask "When did D hit you?"'

18 Morley QC, *The Devil's Advocate*, 2nd edn (Sweet & Maxwell, 2009) at p. 138.

19 In *R* v. *Richardson* [1971] 2 QB 484 at 489, Sachs LJ cited with approval the Supreme Court of Hong Kong in *Lau Pak Ngam* v. *The Queen* [1966] Crim LR 443, 'Testimony in the witness-box becomes more a test of memory than of truthfulness if witnesses are deprived of the opportunity of checking their recollection beforehand by reference to statements or notes made at a time closer to the events in question.'

20 *R* v. *Richardson* [1971] 2 QB 484.

statement to refresh his memory during the course of giving evidence and this applies even where the court adjourns during the witness's testimony.

Lord Justice Sachs explained the practice of the courts regarding the use of memory refreshing documents in the case of *R* v. *Richardson*:[21]

R V. *RICHARDSON* [1971] 2 QB 484, CA
Sachs LJ

[at 489–90]

... it is the practice of the courts not to allow a witness to refresh his memory in the witness-box by reference to written statements unless made contemporaneously ... witnesses for the prosecution in criminal cases are normally (though not in all circumstances) entitled, if they so request, to copies of any statements taken from them by police officers ... witnesses for the defence are normally, as is known to be the practice, allowed to have copies of their statements and to refresh their memories from them at any time up to the moment when they go into the witness-box ... no one has ever suggested that in civil proceedings witnesses may not see their statements up to the time when they go into the witness-box. One has only to think for a moment of witnesses going into the box to deal with accidents which took place five or six years previously to conclude that it would be highly unreasonable if they were not allowed to see them.

It is true that by the practice of the courts of this country a line is drawn at the moment when a witness enters the witness-box ...

The courts, however, must take care not to deprive themselves by new, artificial rules of practice of the best chances of learning the truth. The courts are under no compulsion unnecessarily to follow on a matter of practice the lure of the rules of logic in order to produce unreasonable results which would hinder the course of justice. Obviously it would be wrong if several witnesses were handed statements in circumstances which enabled one to compare with another what each had said. But there can be no general rule (which, incidentally, would be unenforceable, unlike the rule as to what can be done in the witness-box) that witnesses may not before trial see the statements which they made at some period reasonably close to the time of the event which is the subject of the trial. Indeed, one can imagine many cases, particularly those of a complex nature, where such a rule would militate very greatly against the interests of justice.

It used to be the case that a distinction was drawn between contemporaneous and non-contemporaneous documents. While a witness was permitted to refresh his memory in the witness box from a document which had been made contemporaneously to the incident, documents which were not made contemporaneously to the incident could only be read before the witness was called into the witness box. However, this distinction between contemporaneous and non-contemporaneous documents has now been abandoned. In *R* v. *Da Silva*,[22] the Court of Appeal held that the trial judge had discretion in the interests of justice to allow a witness to refresh his memory from a non-contemporaneous statement where:

- the witness indicates that he cannot now recall the details of events because of the lapse of time since they took place;

---

21 Ibid.
22 [1990] 1 All ER 29.

- the witness made a statement much nearer the time of the events and that the contents of the statement represented his recollection at the time he made it;
- the witness had not read the statement before coming into the witness box; and
- the witness wished to have an opportunity to read the statement before he continued to give evidence.

It does not matter whether the witness leaves the witness box in order to read the witness statement, but it must be taken away from him when he re-enters the witness box to continue giving evidence and he cannot refer to it again when giving evidence.

In court

Under s. 139, Criminal Justice Act 2003, a witness who is giving evidence in the witness box may refresh his memory from a document that the witness made or verified. This section applies most frequently to a police officer who wishes to use his notebook to refresh his memory of the incident. Section 139 provides that a witness may refresh his memory at any stage from a document made or verified by him at an earlier time providing that he:

- states in oral evidence that the document records his recollection of the matter at that earlier time; and
- his recollection of the matter is likely to have been significantly better at that time than it is at the time of his oral evidence.

The party calling the witness will usually make the application to use a document to refresh the witness's memory and this will usually take place during the examination-in-chief of the witness. Such an application can be made irrespective of whether the witness refreshed his memory from the document out of court prior to beginning his or her evidence. However, since the statutory provision clearly states that the witness may refresh his memory from the document 'at any stage', then such an application is not restricted to examination-in-chief and might potentially instead be made in re-examination. Where the document is used to refresh the witness's memory in examination-in-chief, then the witness can also be cross-examined upon the document. The jury may also be allowed to see the document if it would assist them in assessing the credibility of the witness.[23]

The document which has been used to refresh the witness's memory is not automatically admitted into evidence and will not necessarily become an exhibit even if the witness is cross-examined on the document, as long as the cross-examination goes no further than the parts used for refreshing memory. However, where counsel asks questions which go beyond the parts of the document which were used to refresh the witness's memory, then the document may become an exhibit.

10.4.3 Previous consistent statements

There is a general rule (known as the rule against narrative) that a witness's out of court statement which is consistent with the current testimony of the witness is not admissible as

---

23 *R* v. *Bass* [1953] 1 QB 680, CA.

evidence of consistency.[24] Thus, a witness may not be asked in examination-in-chief whether he has made a previous statement which is consistent with his testimony. In the recent case of *R* v. *Chinn*, Aikens LJ stated that:

> Broadly speaking, the common law position was that previous consistent out of court statements by witnesses were inadmissible as evidence of the facts stated in them. They were hearsay evidence and they did no more than confirm what the witness said in oral evidence in court. The prohibition on adducing such evidence was known variously as 'the rule against self-corroboration' or 'the rule against narrative'.[25]

The reason for this rule against adducing previous consistent statements is to prevent the deliberate concoction of evidence by a witness who might repeat a statement to various people before the trial and then seek to rely on the statements made to those people as previous consistent statements. An example of the inadmissibility of a previous consistent statement is to be found in the case of *R* v. *Roberts*[26] in which the defendant had been charged with the murder of a girl. At his trial the defendant gave evidence that he had shot her after his gun went off accidentally. He had made a previous consistent statement to his father days after the shooting, that his defence would be one of accident. The trial judge ruled that this previous statement made to his father was inadmissible and this ruling was upheld by the Court of Appeal on two grounds:

1. it was inadmissible hearsay if it was tendered to prove the truth of its contents, and
2. it was inadmissible as a previous consistent statement if it was tendered to support the credibility of the defendant by showing that his story was consistent.

R V. *ROBERTS* [1942] 1 ALL ER 187, CA
Humphreys J

[at 191]

The rule relating to this is sometimes put in this way, that a party is not permitted to make evidence for himself. That law applies to civil cases as well as to criminal cases. For instance, if A and B enter into an oral contract, and some time afterwards there is a difference of opinion as to what were the actual terms agreed upon and there is litigation about it, one of those persons would not be permitted to call his partner to say: 'My partner a day or two after told me what his view of the contract was and that he had agreed to do' so and so. So, in a criminal case, an accused person is not permitted to call evidence to show that, after he was charged with a criminal offence, he told a number of persons what his defence was going to be, and the reason for the rule appears to us to be that such testimony has no evidential value. It is because it does not assist in the elucidation of the matters in dispute that the evidence is said to be inadmissible on the ground that it is irrelevant. It would not help the jury in this case in the least to be told that the appellant said to a number of persons, whom he saw while he was waiting his trial, or on bail if he was on bail: that his defence was this, that or the other.

---

24 *R* v. *Roberts* [1942] 1 All ER 187.
25 [2012] EWCA Crim 501 at [41].
26 [1942] 1 All ER 187.

However, there are a number of exceptions to the rule against previous consistent statements and these will be considered below.[27]

Statements rebutting allegations of fabrication

The first common law exception to the rule against narrative arises where it is suggested to a witness in cross-examination that he has recently fabricated his evidence. In such a situation, a previous consistent statement is admissible to rebut that allegation and show that the witness made a statement at some earlier time which is consistent with the current testimony of the witness. This would usually be dealt with in re-examination by the party calling the witness. An example of the operation of this common law exception can be seen in the case of *R* v. *Oyesiku*.[28] The defendant in this case was charged with assaulting a police officer in the execution of his duty and he was remanded in custody. The defendant's wife had witnessed the incident and she immediately (before visiting her husband in custody) went to her husband's solicitors and made a written statement about the incident she had witnessed, stating that the police officer had been the aggressive party in the incident. At the defendant's trial, his wife was called as a witness for the defence and she was cross-examined by the prosecution who alleged that she had fabricated her evidence in collaboration with her husband. The trial judge ruled that evidence of a previous consistent statement was admissible in re-examination of the wife to rebut the allegation of fabrication. The solicitor could also be called as a witness to prove that the wife had given a statement of her account of the incident at the solicitor's office immediately after the incident and before she had visited her husband in custody, thus showing that there was no opportunity for the wife to concoct her story with her husband.

At common law in criminal proceedings, the statement adduced to rebut the allegation of fabrication was evidence going towards credibility, thus it could only be used to prove that the witness was not lying and not as evidence of the truth of the statement. However, this has been extended by s. 120(2), Criminal Justice Act 2003, which states that '[i]f a previous statement by the witness is admitted as evidence to rebut a suggestion that his oral evidence has been fabricated, the statement is admissible as evidence of any matter stated of which oral evidence by the witness would be admissible'. Thus, a previous consistent statement adduced to rebut an allegation of fabrication provides evidence of the credibility of the witness as well as evidence of the truth of the statement. Such a statement is also admissible as evidence of the witness's credibility and the truth of the statement in civil proceedings under s. 6(2) and (5), Civil Evidence Act 1995.

Memory refreshing documents

The use of a document to refresh the memory of a witness in court has been explored above.[29] As stated above, where a document is used to refresh the witness's memory in the witness box and the cross-examination of the witness goes beyond the parts of the

---

27 See M. O'Floinn and D. Ormerod, 'Social networking material as criminal evidence' [2012] Crim LR 486 at 494 for consideration of the admissibility of previous consistent statements on social networking websites under s. 120, Criminal Justice Act 2003.

28 (1971) 56 Cr App R 240, CA.

29 Refer to paragraph 10.4.2 above.

document which were used for refreshing the witness's memory, the document may be exhibited. Under the common law, any statements in the document which are admissible would only be evidence of the consistency of the witness and would not be evidence of the truth of contents of the statements.[30] However, s. 120(3), Criminal Justice Act 2003 extends the scope of the common law. It provides that where a document, containing a statement made by the witness, is used to refresh the witness's memory during examination-in-chief, and the witness is cross-examined upon that document, and the document is adduced in evidence, then the statement used by the witness to refresh his memory is admissible as evidence of any matter stated.[31] Thus, the statement is evidence of the truth of its contents and also goes to the consistency of the witness. In *R* v. *Chinn*, the Court of Appeal has held that s. 120(3) only applies where the witness successfully refreshes his memory from a document while giving evidence:

> ... section 120(3) contemplates that the witness *does* refresh his memory by examining the relevant statement in the out of court document. The effect of that is that his *oral* evidence about the facts of which he has refreshed his memory are admissible oral evidence in the normal way. The novelty in section 120(3) is that those statements in the document used to refresh the witness's evidence also become admissible evidence of the matters stated therein.[32]

However, the Court held that where the witness fails to refresh his memory from the document, s. 120(3) does not apply.

Evidence of previous identification
Where a witness makes an out-of-court statement identifying the defendant, either the witness identifying the defendant or any other person present who witnessed the identification can give evidence of the identification. At a formal identification carried out at the police station a police officer will be present and will be able to give evidence of the identification (although the admissibility of identification evidence is subject to the judicial discretion to exclude evidence under s. 78, Police and Criminal Evidence Act 1984 where that evidence has been obtained as a result of 'significant and substantial' breaches of the guidance on identification procedures set out in Code D). It is important to allow evidence of a previous identification to be adduced in court in order to avoid the practice of identifying the defendant in the dock. Dock identifications are frowned upon because of the obvious and inherent risk that such an identification would be prejudicial to a defendant.

Cross-reference
Refer to Chapter 11 for a detailed examination of identification procedures under Code D.

Under s. 120(4) and (5), where a witness gives evidence identifying the defendant as the offender, any previous statement made by the witness which identifies or describes a person,

---

30 See *R* v. *Virgo* (1978) 67 Cr App R 323 and *R* v. *Chinn* [2012] EWCA Crim 501.
31 See *R* v. *Chinn* [2012] EWCA Crim 501 at [44].
32 Ibid. at [47].

object or place is also admissible as evidence of the truth of the witness's evidence, provided that the witness indicates that to the best of his belief he made the statement and that it states the truth. The evidence of the previous statement also goes to the consistency of the witness. In *R* v. *Chinn*, the Court of Appeal considered the application of s. 120(5):

> The previous statement of a witness will have identified or described a person, object or place that is connected with an alleged offence or other relevant event. A description of a person, object or place that is made in a vacuum is of no use in criminal proceedings. The description or identification has to be put in the relevant context because the person, or object or place is being described or identified for a particular purpose in the criminal proceedings. Thus the witness may say in the statement that it was Mr X who was at the ABC Bar on a certain day at a certain time. That statement identifies Mr X in this way because it is that identification at that place and time that is relevant; probably to an alleged offence at the ABC Bar at a particular time. The same must be true of an object and a place.[33]

The Court held that s. 120(5) does not apply solely to statements which only identify a person, object or place and no more, but it applies to statements that identify a person, object or place in the course of a more general narrative. Section 120(5) would not, however, apply to any parts of the witness's statement that go beyond identifying or describing the defendant, an object or a place; these parts would remain inadmissible hearsay.

No recollection of events
Under s. 120(4) and (6), Criminal Justice Act 2003, where a witness no longer remembers a matter and cannot reasonably be expected to remember the matter[34] but he made a statement when the matters were fresh in his memory, that previous statement is admissible as evidence of any matter stated, provided that the witness indicates in evidence that to the best of his belief he made the statement, and that to the best of his belief it states the truth.

Complaint by complainant
Under the common law, there is an exception to the rule against narrative which applies to complainants in sexual cases. Where the complainant made a complaint of a sexual offence to another person voluntarily shortly after the offence took place, the person to whom the complaint was made could give evidence of the fact that the complainant had made a complaint and of the details of the complaint. Such evidence is admissible to demonstrate the consistency of the complainant's evidence, and, where consent is in issue, to demonstrate that the complainant's conduct was inconsistent with consent.[35] This has now been extended by s.120(4)

---

33 Ibid. at [57].
34 It is for the judge to determine whether the witness no longer remembers and could reasonably be expected to remember the matter. This is an objective assessment, although the judge will take into account factors such as the characteristics of the particular witness, the nature of the particular incident, the circumstances in which it occurred and other factors such as what has happened to the witness between the time of the incident and the trial: *R* v. *Chinn* [2012] EWCA Crim 501 at [62]–[63].
35 *R* v. *Osborne* [1905] 1 KB 551, CCR.

and (7), Criminal Justice Act 2003 beyond the scope of sexual cases to any offence. Further, while the common law rule only applied to complaints made at the first opportunity, s. 120(7) no longer contains such a requirement. When s. 120(7), Criminal Justice Act 2003 was first enacted there was a requirement under s. 120(7)(d) that the complaint be made as soon as could reasonably be expected after the alleged conduct, but this has since been repealed by s. 112, Coroners and Justice Act 2009.

Section 120(7) provides that the evidence of a previous complaint witness is admissible as evidence of any matter stated, provided that the witness gives evidence that to the best of his belief he made the statement and that to the best of his belief it states the truth. It also provides evidence of the consistency of the witness. However, the exception under s. 120(7) only applies where:

- the witness claims to be a person against whom an offence has been committed,[36]
- the offence is one to which the proceedings relate,[37]
- the statement consists of a complaint made by the witness (whether to a person in authority or not) about conduct which would, if proved, constitute the offence or part of the offence,[38]
- the complaint was not made as a result of a threat or a promise,[39] and
- before the statement is adduced the witness gives oral evidence in connection with its subject matter.[40]

Res gestae *statements*

Res gestae statements are admissible as an exception to the rule against narrative. A *res gestae* statement is a statement which was made contemporaneously with the relevant incident.[41] Such a statement is evidence of the consistency of the witness and is also evidence of the truth of the statement since it is also an exception to the rule against hearsay (this has been dealt with in Chapter 7 on Hearsay).

Statements made on accusation

Where the defendant is confronted with an accusation or incriminating facts, any statement that he makes on accusation is admissible evidence of the reaction of the defendant to show the consistency of the witness. So, if on an earlier occasion, the witness denies the commission of an offence on accusation, the exculpatory statement of denial is admissible as evidence of consistency to show the attitude of the defendant,[42] but it is not evidence of the truth of the denial. Where the statement made on accusation is inculpatory or a 'mixed' statement (partly inculpatory and partly exculpatory), then the previous statement will be

---

36 Section 120(7)(a).
37 Section 120(7)(b).
38 Section 120(7)(c).
39 Section 120(7)(e).
40 Section 120(7)(f).
41 *R* v. *Fowkes*, The Times, 8 March 1856.
42 See *R* v. *Tooke* (1990) 90 Cr App R 417, CA in which it was held that the statement must be relevant and spontaneous and that the trial judge has discretion whether to admit the evidence or not.

admissible under s. 76(1), PACE Act 1984 as confession evidence to prove the truth of the statement.

> **Cross-reference**
>
> Refer to Chapter 5 on Confession evidence for a more detailed discussion of mixed statements and the admissibility of confession evidence and the rules of exclusion under s. 76(2), PACE Act 1984.

10.4.4 Unfavourable and hostile witnesses

This paragraph deals with problematic witnesses and explores the distinction between witnesses who are merely unfavourable to the case of the party calling them, and witnesses who are deemed hostile by the judge.

Unfavourable witnesses

An unfavourable witness is one who fails to 'come up to proof'. This means that the witness does not say in testimony what he was expected to say in examination-in-chief, i.e. what was in his witness statement or proof of evidence, or he may even go so far as to give evidence of the opposite of that which he was called to give. An unfavourable witness may be an honest witness who has simply forgotten the details of the matter about which he is asked, or he may be an honest but mistaken witness. We have already learnt that counsel may not generally lead a witness in examination-in-chief or cross-examine the witness on any previous inconsistent statements or his bad character. Similarly, counsel may not cast imputations on the credibility of his own witness because he adduces the evidence of that witness in order to prove that the witness is truthful and credible. On that basis, counsel may not, having called the witness, subsequently argue that the witness is not credible. Where it transpires that a witness is an unfavourable witness, counsel can do little other than hope that the testimony of any other witnesses that he calls (if indeed there are any), or other evidence in the case, prove the matters which the unfavourable witness fails to testify favourably upon. If it does, counsel will invite the jury to prefer the evidence of those witnesses that contradict the unfavourable witness.

Hostile witnesses

By contrast, a hostile witness is one who, in the opinion of the judge, demonstrates a hostile mind[43] in examination-in-chief, who clearly intends not to tell the truth to the court. A witness may only be deemed to be a hostile witness with the leave of the judge. A hostile witness does not come up to proof but he is not merely a mistaken or forgetful witness. Rather, a hostile witness is one who deliberately chooses to give evidence which contradicts his original witness statement or proof of evidence whether due to fear, hostility or an unwillingness to be involved in the proceedings.

---

43 *Greenough* v. *Eccles* (1859) 5 CBNS 786 at 794.

R. MUNDAY, 'HOSTILE WITNESSES AND THE ADMISSION OF WITNESS STATEMENTS UNDER SECTION 23 OF THE CRIMINAL JUSTICE ACT 1988' [1991] CRIM LR 349

Hostile witnesses

In order to be declared hostile, a witness must have convinced the court by his answers to questions and/or demeanour in the courtroom that he simply will not tell the truth. Merely failing to come up to proof will not suffice; *animus* must be evident, whether it emerges in examination-in-chief or in cross-examination. At common law it is virtually certain that, once pronounced hostile, it is permissible to put leading questions to one's own witness. But not until the advent of section 3 of the Criminal Procedure Act 1865 was it clearly made possible to cross-examine hostile witnesses on their previous inconsistent statements. The 1865 Act, which will apply in all cases where the hostile witness has actually testified, provides:

> A Party producing a Witness ... may, in case the Witness shall, in the Opinion of the Judge, prove adverse, ... by Leave of the Judge, prove that he has made at other Times a Statement inconsistent with his present Testimony; but before such last-mentioned Proof can be given the Circumstances of the supposed Statement, sufficient to designate the particular Occasion, must be mentioned to the Witness, and he must be asked whether or not he has made such Statement.

Where a witness fails to come up to proof, counsel should not immediately make an application to treat the witness as a hostile witness (unless there is such a degree of hostility that this really is the only possible course of action). Instead, counsel should usually first ask the witness to refresh his memory.[44] As stated above, in order to be entitled to treat a witness as a hostile witness, counsel must apply to the judge for leave to do so. The application is made before the judge in the absence of the jury and decides whether the witness is hostile or whether he is merely an unfavourable witness. The judge takes into account the demeanour of the witness and any previous inconsistent statements made by the witness. The witness should only be questioned in the absence of the jury in exceptional circumstances.[45]

A witness who has been declared a hostile witness by the trial judge is treated differently to an unfavourable witness since imputations may indeed be cast on the credibility of a hostile witness. Section 3, Criminal Procedure Act 1865 deals with the extent to which a witness may be discredited by the party calling the witness. Where the judge rules that the witness is hostile, and gives leave, counsel may ask leading questions in examination-in-chief (thus the witness is effectively cross-examined) on a previous statement that is inconsistent with his current testimony, such as by asking the witness whether he made the previous statement and about the circumstances of that statement.[46] However, counsel is not permitted to impeach the

---

44 *R* v. *Maw* [1994] Crim LR 841.
45 *R* v. *Darby* [1989] Crim LR 817.
46 In *R* v. *Fraser* (1956) 40 Cr App R 160, CCA it was held that if the Crown is in possession of a previous inconsistent statement which directly contradicts a prosecution witness's testimony, counsel for the prosecution has a duty to apply to the judge for leave to cross-examine the witness as hostile.

credit of the witness by general evidence of bad character. Upon cross-examination on a previous inconsistent statement, if the witness accepts the truth of his previous inconsistent statement, then that statement will stand as his evidence on the facts. If the witness does not accept the truth of his previous inconsistent statement, the statement will go to the credibility of the witness. The jury will be directed by the judge about the dangers of relying on the evidence of a witness who has contradicted himself, and that they should decide whether the witness was credible at all before considering what part of his evidence they could accept.[47] Under s. 119(1), Criminal Justice Act 2003, where a witness in criminal proceedings admits making a previous inconsistent statement, or such a statement is proved under s. 3, Criminal Procedure Act 1865, the jury will also be directed that the previous inconsistent statement is admissible as evidence of any matter stated of which oral evidence by him would be admissible. However, it is implicit in s. 119 that a previous inconsistent statement will not become part of the witness's evidence where the witness is not declared a hostile witness under s. 3, Criminal Procedure Act 1865 and does not admit making a previous inconsistent statement.[48] In civil proceedings, a previous inconsistent statement is admissible as the truth of its contents.[49]

10.4.5 Agreed statements

An agreed statement is also known as a 's. 9 statement'. Where a statement is 'agreed' under s. 9, Criminal Justice Act 1967, the statement of the witness may be read in court and that statement will stand as the evidence of that witness. As such, the witness will not be called to give oral evidence, and thus will not be cross-examined. All parties to the proceedings must agree to the witness statement being read as a s. 9 statement. If one party to the proceedings does not agree to the witness statement being read out in court, then the witness must be called to give oral evidence and will be open to cross-examination on the evidence given, or the evidence of the witness may not be relied upon by the party relying on the evidence of the witness. Under s. 9, Criminal Justice Act 1967, a written statement made by a witness is admissible as the oral evidence of that witness if:

- the statement is signed by the witness;
- the statement contains a declaration by the witness;[50]
- before the hearing at which the statement is tendered in evidence, a copy of the witness statement is served by the party proposing to tender it, on each of the other parties to the proceedings; and
- none of the other parties objects to the statement being tendered in evidence under this section (notice of any objections must be served within seven days from the service of the copy of the statement).

---

47 *R* v. *Maw*, above (n. 44).
48 See *R* v. *Maw*, ibid. and *R* v. *Golder* [1960] 1 WLR 1169 for the common law position.
49 Section 1, Civil Evidence Act 1995.
50 The declaration is to be to the effect that it is true to the best of his knowledge and belief and that he made the statement knowing that, if it were tendered in evidence, he would be liable to prosecution if he wilfully stated in it anything which he knew to be false or did not believe to be true.

The purpose of s. 9, Criminal Justice Act 1967 is to promote efficiency in both cost and time; reading agreed statements avoids witnesses being called where their evidence is not in dispute. Agreed statements are usually statements which are non-contentious, such as the medical evidence of a doctor in a case involving an offence against the person if the injuries are not in dispute, or the evidence of a forensic scientist if the defendant does not dispute that evidence.

10.5 CROSS-EXAMINATION

When a witness is called to give evidence-in-chief and takes the oath or affirms, he opens himself up to cross-examination by the other side. The cross-examination of a witness takes place after that witness has given evidence-in-chief. In cross-examination, counsel is permitted to (and should) ask leading questions.[51]

> **Cross-reference**
> Refer back to paragraph 10.4.1 above for the distinction between leading and non-leading questions.

Cross-examination has two main purposes:

- the first is to undermine the evidence of the witness, with the ultimate objective of weakening the case for the opposition; and
- the second purpose is for counsel to establish his own case.

In establishing his own case, the cross-examining party must put each part of his case upon which the witness can give evidence to the witness. If part of the case is not put to the witness in cross-examination, counsel will be deemed to have accepted the witness's account on that point and will not be permitted to put forward any different account or explanation of this in his closing speech. However, where the omission is accidental, the trial judge has discretion to recall the witness so that counsel's client's case may be put to the witness.[52] Although cross-examination requires counsel to ask questions designed to undermine the evidence of the witness, counsel must not ask questions in order to insult or vilify the witness. This is reflected in the Bar's Code of Conduct, according to which counsel 'must not make statements or ask questions which are merely scandalous or intended or calculated only to vilify, insult or annoy either a witness or some other person'.[53] However, despite the recent rise in solicitor

---

51 See Iain Morley QC, *The Devil's Advocate*, ch. 8 for an excellent explanation of the techniques that should be employed during cross-examination.

52 See *R* v. *John Seigley* (1911) 6 Cr App R 106 and *R* v. *Wilson* [1977] Crim LR 553. This latter case involved a lengthy and complicated trial during which defence counsel attacked the credibility of a prosecution witness. Prosecuting counsel obtained leave to cross-examine the defendant as to his previous convictions, but forgot to pursue this line of questioning during the cross-examination. The trial judge permitted the defendant to be recalled so that questions about his previous convictions could be put to him. The Court of Appeal held that there was no material irregularity here.

53 Part VII, para. 708(g), Code of Conduct of the Bar of England and Wales, 8th edn.

advocates, there does not seem to be equivalent guidance from the Solicitors Regulation Authority.[54]

In cross-examining a witness, counsel's question may go beyond the scope of the issues covered during examination-in-chief. However, there are some limitations on what may be asked in cross-examination.

10.5.1 No cross-examination on inadmissible evidence

First and foremost, counsel may not cross-examine a witness on evidence that has been ruled inadmissible. The same rules relating to the admissibility of evidence in examination-in-chief also apply to cross-examination. Thus, counsel may not adduce inadmissible evidence in cross-examination. One way to circumvent this rule can be found where the evidence is inadmissible hearsay contained in a document. Where counsel hands the document to the witness during cross-examination and the witness gives evidence that the contents of the document are true then the contents of the document become the testimony of the witness and may be adduced in court.

10.5.2 Rule of finality on collateral issues

It is clear that a witness may be cross-examined on matters which are relevant to an issue in the case. However, counsel may also cross-examine a witness on collateral issues, such as asking questions about the credibility of the witness. Thus, a witness may be asked about the reliability of their memory, or about their reasons for remembering a particular fact, or about the opportunity they had to make a particular observation or gain particular knowledge. A witness may be cross-examined to show that their evidence is inconsistent, improbable or wrong, or to highlight any omissions in their evidence to demonstrate that their evidence is unreliable and not credible. Finally, where the credibility of a witness is challenged, counsel may wish to cross-examine the witness about their bad character, including any previous convictions that they may have or any reprehensible behaviour that they have demonstrated in the past, such as evidence of racial prejudice, violent behaviour, or, perhaps, drug abuse. Any cross-examination on the bad character of a witness may only take place with the leave of the trial judge and is subject to the rules relating to the admissibility of a witness's bad character under ss. 100 (bad character of a non-defendant witness) and 101 (bad character of a defendant witness), Criminal Justice Act 2003. However, there is some control over the questions that may be put to the witness. There is a general rule that any answer which is given by the witness in cross-examination on a collateral issue is final, so counsel may not call evidence in rebuttal of the answer given by the witness (this is known as the rule of finality on collateral issues).

---

54 Although there appears to be nothing within the Solicitors Regulation Authority, Code of Conduct 2011 that deals specifically with this point, the SRA has published a 'Statement of standards for solicitor higher court advocates' which provides some guidance regarding appropriate techniques when questioning vulnerable witnesses (at www.sra.org.uk/solicitors/accreditation/higher-rights/competence-standards.page (accessed on 19 July 2014).

There are a number of exceptions to the general rule of finality on collateral issues where evidence may be adduced in order to rebut the answer given by the witness regarding his own credibility. For instance, if a witness refutes that he is not a credible witness but denies that he has previous convictions or that he is biased, evidence may be called in rebuttal of that denial to undermine the credibility of the witness.

Previous inconsistent statements

Where, in cross-examination, a witness admits that he made a previous inconsistent statement no further evidence of that previous inconsistent statement may be adduced in accordance with the finality rule. However, where a witness denies that he has made a previous inconsistent statement and the statement is relevant to a fact in issue, evidence may be adduced in rebuttal of the denial in order to prove that the previous inconsistent statement was indeed made. Evidence of the previous statement may only be used to discredit the witness and is not evidence of the truth of the previous inconsistent statement. Sections 4 and 5 of the Criminal Procedure Act 1865 provide for the procedure to be followed in such a situation. Under s. 4, another witness may be called to prove that an earlier statement was made. Section 4 applies to both oral and written statements made by the witness, but before another witness can be called to prove the previous inconsistent statement, the circumstances of the statement must be mentioned to the witness, and the witness must be asked whether he or she made the statement. Under s. 5, a written statement may be produced and put to the witness; thus, section 5 only applies to written previous inconsistent statements. Under this section, the written statement need not be shown to the witness, but counsel must have the written statement in his possession and must draw the witness's attention to the statement before adducing evidence of the inconsistency.

Previous convictions

Where a witness is cross-examined about his bad character and admits that he has previous convictions but claims that he is innocent of the crime he was convicted of, then no evidence may be adduced to rebut his claims. However, where the witness denies having any previous convictions, counsel cross-examining the witness may prove the convictions under s. 6, Criminal Procedure Act 1865 in order to undermine the credibility of the witness. However, spent convictions may not be adduced in either civil proceedings[55] or in criminal proceedings if it can reasonably be avoided.[56] Further, in criminal proceedings, no one is permitted to refer in open court to a spent conviction without the authority of the judge, which may only be given in the interests of justice.[57]

Evidence of a general reputation for lying

Evidence may be adduced to prove that a witness (X) has a general reputation for telling lies. Another witness (Y) may be called to give evidence that he knows that X has such a general reputation and that he would not believe X himself. The party calling Y may not adduce

55 See s. 4(1), Rehabilitation of Offenders Act 1984.
56 See the *Consolidated Criminal Practice Direction*, Part I at I.6.4.
57 Ibid. at I.6.6.

evidence of the details of incidents where X has been untruthful, but Y may be cross-examined by X's counsel on specific incidents.

Bias

Evidence may be called to rebut a witness's denial of bias in relation to the case generally (such as through being bribed to give particular evidence), or in relation to specific parties in the case (such as having a grudge against a party or having an affair with a party in the case).

Evidence of medical condition affecting reliability

The final exception to the rule of finality on collateral issues relates to witnesses who suffer from a medical condition which might affect their reliability. In such cases, medical evidence may be adduced to prove that the witness suffers from some physical condition or abnormality of mental functioning which might affect his reliability.[58]

10.5.3 Cross-examination of witnesses by defendant

Sometimes in criminal proceedings, a defendant might decide not to be represented by a solicitor or barrister, but instead might choose to conduct his defence himself. In such situations, the defendant will deliver his own opening and closing speeches to the magistrates or jury, and will conduct his own examination-in-chief and cross-examination of witnesses. While it is perfectly permissible for a defendant to conduct his own defence, this becomes controversial where the complainant or other prosecution witnesses are either children or vulnerable or intimidated witnesses. The following paragraph explores the situations in which a defendant is prevented from personally conducting the cross-examination of a witness in criminal proceedings. Sections 34 to 36 of the Youth Justice and Criminal Evidence Act 1999 provide for a prohibition on the defendant conducting a cross-examination personally where the prosecution is for a sexual offence and the complainant in the case is to be cross-examined (s. 34) or the prosecution witness is a child (s. 35).

SS. 34–35, YOUTH JUSTICE AND CRIMINAL EVIDENCE ACT 1999

34 Complainants in proceedings for sexual offences

No person charged with a sexual offence may in any criminal proceedings cross-examine in person a witness who is the complainant, either –

(a) in connection with that offence, or

(b) in connection with any other offence (of whatever nature) with which that person is charged in the proceedings.

---

58 See *Toohey* v. *Metropolitan Police Commissioner* [1965] AC 595 at 608 where Lord Pearce gave two examples: (1) of an eyewitness suffering from a cataract at the time of the incident who, according to medical evidence, could not possibly have seen the incident from the distance claimed, and (2) of a witness suffering from a mental illness whereby he experiences delusions and, according to medical evidence, this makes him incapable of giving reliable evidence.

35 Child complainants and other child witnesses

(1) No person charged with an offence to which this section applies may in any criminal proceedings cross-examine in person a protected witness, either –

(a) in connection with that offence, or

(b) in connection with any other offence (of whatever nature) with which that person is charged in the proceedings.

(2) For the purposes of subsection (1) a 'protected witness' is a witness who –

(a) either is the complainant or is alleged to have been a witness to the commission of the offence to which this section applies, and

(b) either is a child or falls to be cross-examined after giving evidence in chief (whether wholly or in part) –

(i) by means of a video recording made (for the purposes of section 27) at a time when the witness was a child, or

(ii) in any other way at any such time.

(3) The offences to which this section applies are –

(a) any offence under –

[(iva) any of sections 33 to 36 of the Sexual Offences Act 1956]

(v) the Protection of Children Act 1978[, or]

[(vi) Part 1 of the Sexual Offences Act 2003[or any relevant superseded enactment];]

(b) kidnapping, false imprisonment or an offence under section 1 or 2 of the Child Abduction Act 1984;

(c) any offence under section 1 of the Children and Young Persons Act 1933;

(d) any offence (not within any of the preceding paragraphs) which involves an assault on, or injury or a threat of injury to, any person.

[(3A) In subsection (3)(a)(vi) 'relevant superseded enactment' means –

(a) any of sections 1 to 32 of the Sexual Offences Act 1956;

(b) the Indecency with Children Act 1960;

(c) the Sexual Offences Act 1967;

(d) section 54 of the Criminal Law Act 1977.]

(4) In this section 'child' means –

(a) where the offence falls within subsection (3)(a), a person under the age of [18]; or

(b) where the offence falls within subsection (3)(b), (c) or (d), a person under the age of 14.

(5) For the purposes of this section 'witness' includes a witness who is charged with an offence in the proceedings.

Under s. 34, Youth Justice and Criminal Evidence Act 1999, a person who has been charged with a sexual offence is prohibited from cross-examining in person the complainant, either in connection with that offence or in connection with any other offence that the defendant is charged with. A 'sexual offence' is defined under s. 62 to include any offence under Part 1 of the Sexual Offences Act 2003[59] or any offence that has been superseded by these legislative provisions.[60]

59 This includes the main sexual offences under the 2003 Act, such as rape, assault by penetration, sexual assault and causing a person to engage in sexual activity without consent, as well as such offences as they relate to children.
60 This includes offences such as burglary with intent to rape, unlawful intercourse, indecent assault and other offences listed in s. 62(1A), Youth Justice and Criminal Evidence Act 1999.

Under s. 35(1), Youth Justice and Criminal Evidence Act 1999, a person who has been charged with a specified offence is prohibited from cross-examining in person a 'protected witness', either in connection with that offence or in connection with any other offence that the defendant is charged with. Under s. 35(2), a 'protected witness' is either a complainant or a witness to the commission of the offence who is also either a child or a witness who is the subject of a special measures direction under s. 27 (gave evidence-in-chief via a video-recording) at the time when the witness was a child.

> **Cross-reference**
>
> Refer back to Chapter 9 for a detailed discussion on special measures directions for vulnerable and intimidated witnesses.

Section 35(1) applies only to specified sexual offences listed under s. 35(3)(a)[61] and s. 35(3A),[62] kidnapping, false imprisonment, cruelty to persons under 16, and any offence involving an assault on, or injury or a threat of injury to, any person. For the purposes of these provisions, a child is a person under the age of 18 where the offence is one under s. 35(3)(a), or under the age of 14 where the offence is one under s. 35(3)(b) or (c).

There is a further provision under s. 36, Youth Justice and Criminal Evidence Act 1999 which prohibits the defendant from personally conducting the cross-examination of other witnesses which do not fall within ss. 34 and 35 of the Act. Although the application of this section is wider in scope in that it can apply in respect of any witness, the court may only make such a prohibitive direction if it would improve the quality of the evidence given by the witness and it would not be contrary to the interests of justice to make the direction.

S. 36, YOUTH JUSTICE AND CRIMINAL EVIDENCE ACT 1999
36 Direction prohibiting accused from cross-examining particular witness

(1) This section applies where, in a case where neither of sections 34 and 35 operates to prevent an accused in any criminal proceedings from cross-examining a witness in person –
   (a) the prosecutor makes an application for the court to give a direction under this section in relation to the witness, or
   (b) the court of its own motion raises the issue whether such a direction should be given.
(2) If it appears to the court –
   (a) that the quality of evidence given by the witness on cross-examination –
      (i) is likely to be diminished if the cross-examination (or further cross-examination) is conducted by the accused in person, and
      (ii) would be likely to be improved if a direction were given under this section, and

---

61 The offences listed are any offences under ss. 33 to 36, Sexual Offences Act 1956 (these relate to keeping a brothel, letting premises or permitting premises to be used as a brothel), the protection of Children Act 1978 (this relates to offences involving indecent photographs of children) and Part 1 of the Sexual Offences Act 2003 (including offences such as rape, assault by penetration, sexual assault and causing a person to engage in sexual activity without consent, as well as such offences as they relate to children).

62 This section includes relevant offences that have been superseded by the Sexual Offences Act 2003.

(b) that it would not be contrary to the interests of justice to give such a direction,

the court may give a direction prohibiting the accused from cross-examining (or further cross-examining) the witness in person.

(3) In determining whether subsection (2)(a) applies in the case of a witness the court must have regard, in particular, to –

(a) any views expressed by the witness as to whether or not the witness is content to be cross-examined by the accused in person;

(b) the nature of the questions likely to be asked, having regard to the issues in the proceedings and the defence case advanced so far (if any);

(c) any behaviour on the part of the accused at any stage of the proceedings, both generally and in relation to the witness;

(d) any relationship (of whatever nature) between the witness and the accused;

(e) whether any person (other than the accused) is or has at any time been charged in the proceedings with a sexual offence or an offence to which section 35 applies, and (if so) whether section 34 or 35 operates or would have operated to prevent that person from cross-examining the witness in person;

(f) any direction under section 19 which the court has given, or proposes to give, in relation to the witness.

(4) For the purposes of this section –

(a) 'witness', in relation to an accused, does not include any other person who is charged with an offence in the proceedings; and

(b) any reference to the quality of a witness's evidence shall be construed in accordance with section 16(5).

Under s. 36, Youth Justice and Criminal Evidence Act 1999, the defendant may be prohibited from cross-examining in person a witness where the witness is neither a complainant in a sexual offence (under s. 34) or a protected witness (for the purposes of s. 35) or a co-defendant in the proceedings.[63] A direction may be given by the court either after an application by the prosecution or by the court of its own motion if it appears to the court that the quality[64] of the evidence given by the witness on cross-examination is likely to be diminished if the cross-examination is conducted by the defendant in person and would be likely to be improved if a direction were given under s. 36, and it would not be contrary to the interests of justice to give such a direction.[65] Under s. 36(3), the court must have regard to:

- any views expressed by the witness;
- the nature of the questions likely to be asked;
- any behaviour on the part of the accused generally and in relation to the witness;
- any relationship between the witness and the accused;

---

63 Section 36(4)(a), Youth Justice and Criminal Evidence Act 1999.

64 According to s. 36(4)(b), Youth Justice and Criminal Evidence Act 1999, 'quality' is assessed under s. 16(5) in terms of 'completeness, coherence and accuracy'; and 'coherence' refers to 'a witness's ability in giving evidence to give answers which address the questions put to the witness and can be understood both individually and collectively'.

65 Section 36(2), Youth Justice and Criminal Evidence Act 1999.

- whether any person (other than the accused) is or has at any time been charged in the proceedings with a sexual offence or an offence to which s. 35 applies, and (if so) whether s. 34 or s. 35 prevents that person from cross-examining the witness in person;
- any special measures direction which the court has given, or proposes to give, in relation to the witness.

Where a defendant is prohibited from conducting a cross-examination in person under either s. 34, s. 35 or s. 36 and the court decides that it is necessary in the interests of justice for the witness to be cross-examined, the court must appoint a qualified legal representative to cross-examine the witness in the interests of the defendant.[66] In cases where the defendant has been prevented from conducting a cross-examination in person under s. 34, s. 35 or s. 36, the judge must give the jury a warning (if the judge considers it necessary to do so) to ensure that the defendant is not prejudiced.

10.5.4 Cross-examination as to sexual history of a complainant

There are significant limitations to the questions that may be asked by the defence when cross-examining a complainant in a sexual case.[67] Section 41 of the Youth Justice and Criminal Evidence Act 1999 prohibits counsel from asking questions or adducing evidence about the sexual history or behaviour of the complainant; however, s. 41 also provides for exceptions to this rule where the trial grants leave.[68]

S. 41, YOUTH JUSTICE AND CRIMINAL EVIDENCE ACT 1999
41 Restriction on evidence or questions about complainant's sexual history

(1) If at a trial a person is charged with a sexual offence, then, except with the leave of the court –
  (a) no evidence may be adduced, and
  (b) no question may be asked in cross-examination, by or on behalf of any accused at the trial, about any sexual behaviour of the complainant.
(2) The court may give leave in relation to any evidence or question only on an application made by or on behalf of an accused, and may not give such leave unless it is satisfied –
  (a) that subsection (3) or (5) applies, and
  (b) that a refusal of leave might have the result of rendering unsafe a conclusion of the jury or (as the case may be) the court on any relevant issue in the case.
  . . .
(6) For the purposes of subsections (3) and (5) the evidence or question must relate to a specific instance (or specific instances) of alleged sexual behaviour on the part of the complainant (and accordingly nothing in those subsections is capable of applying in relation to the evidence or question to the extent that it does not so relate).

---

66 See s. 38(1) and (4), Youth Justice and Criminal Evidence Act 1999.
67 The sexual offences that this provision applies to are set out in s. 62, Youth Justice and Criminal Evidence Act 1999.
68 See O'Floinn and Ormerod, above (n. 27) at 501–4 for consideration of the admissibility of evidence of sexual history found on social networking websites.

(7) Where this section applies in relation to a trial by virtue of the fact that one or more of a number of persons charged in the proceedings is or are charged with a sexual offence –

(a) it shall cease to apply in relation to the trial if the prosecutor decides not to proceed with the case against that person or those persons in respect of that charge; but

(b) it shall not cease to do so in the event of that person or those persons pleading guilty to, or being convicted of, that charge.

Leave may be granted by the judge in the circumstances under either s. 41(3) or s. 41(5) and if a refusal to grant leave might render a conviction unsafe.[69] For leave to be granted under s. 41, the questions asked by counsel must also relate to a specific instance of alleged sexual behaviour by the complainant.[70] If leave is granted under s. 41 in a trial in which the defendant who is charged with a sexual offence is jointly tried with a co-defendant, s. 41 will still apply in the event of the defendant pleading guilty or being convicted of the sexual offence.[71] However, where the prosecutor decides to discontinue the case involving the sexual offence against the defendant, s. 41 will cease to apply to the trial.[72]

Granting leave under s. 41(3)

S. 41, YOUTH JUSTICE AND CRIMINAL EVIDENCE ACT 1999

(3) This subsection applies if the evidence or question relates to a relevant issue in the case and either –

(a) that issue is not an issue of consent; or

(b) it is an issue of consent and the sexual behaviour of the complainant to which the evidence or question relates is alleged to have taken place at or about the same time as the event which is the subject matter of the charge against the accused; or

(c) it is an issue of consent and the sexual behaviour of the complainant to which the evidence or question relates is alleged to have been, in any respect, so similar –

(i) to any sexual behaviour of the complainant which (according to evidence adduced or to be adduced by or on behalf of the accused) took place as part of the event which is the subject matter of the charge against the accused, or

(ii) to any other sexual behaviour of the complainant which (according to such evidence) took place at or about the same time as that event,

that the similarity cannot reasonably be explained as a coincidence.

(4) For the purposes of subsection (3) no evidence or question shall be regarded as relating to a relevant issue in the case if it appears to the court to be reasonable to assume that the purpose (or main purpose) for which it would be adduced or asked is to establish or elicit material for impugning the credibility of the complainant as a witness.

---

69 See s. 41(2), Youth Justice and Criminal Evidence Act 1999.
70 Section 41(6).
71 Section 41(7)(b).
72 Section 41(7)(a).

Leave may be granted to cross-examine the complainant on his or her sexual behaviour where the questions counsel wishes to ask relate to something other than consent[73] (leave is not required where the questions relate to the defendant's belief in consent).[74] Where the questions counsel wishes to ask do relate to consent, leave may be granted if the questions relate to sexual behaviour of the complainant which is alleged to have taken place at or about the same time as the offence.[75] This has been interpreted narrowly by the House of Lords:

> I was initially tempted to think that the words 'at or about the same time as the event' could be given a wide meaning certainly a few hours perhaps a few days when a couple were continuously together. But that meaning could not reasonably be extended to cover a few weeks which are relied on in the present case and I consider in the event that even if read with Article 6 they must be given a narrow meaning which would not allow the evidence or cross examination in the present case or in other than cases where the acts relied on were really contemporaneous.[76]

Finally, leave may be granted if the questions relate to any sexual behaviour of the complainant which is so similar to the circumstances of the alleged offence and the similarity cannot be reasonably explained as coincidence,[77] or to any other sexual behaviour of the complainant that took place at the same time as the alleged offence and the similarity cannot be reasonably explained as coincidence.[78] However, the trial judge will not grant leave under s. 41(3) where it appears to the court to be reasonable to assume that the purpose (or main purpose) for which the evidence would be adduced is to impugn the credibility of the complainant as a witness.[79]

Granting leave under s. 41(5)

S. 41, YOUTH JUSTICE AND CRIMINAL EVIDENCE ACT 1999

(5) This subsection applies if the evidence or question –
   (a) relates to any evidence adduced by the prosecution about any sexual behaviour of the complainant; and
   (b) in the opinion of the court, would go no further than is necessary to enable the evidence adduced by the prosecution to be rebutted or explained by or on behalf of the accused.

Under s. 41(5), leave may be granted to cross-examine the complainant on his or her sexual behaviour where the questions counsel wishes to ask relate to evidence adduced by the prosecution in examination-in-chief about the complainant's sexual behaviour, and the

73 Section 41(3)(a).
74 Section 42(1)(b).
75 Section 41(3)(b).
76 Per Lord Slynn in *R* v. *A (Complainant's Sexual History)* [2002] 1 AC 45, HL at 55–6.
77 Section 41(3)(c)(i).
78 Section 41(3)(c)(ii).
79 Section 41(4).

cross-examination will go no further than is necessary to rebut or explain the evidence adduced by the prosecution.

The leading authority on s. 41 is the House of Lords' decision in *R* v. *A (Complainant's Sexual History)*,[80] in which the House of Lords considered a question certified by the Court of Appeal, namely whether the exclusion of the sexual history between the defendant and complainant under s. 41, Youth Justice and Criminal Evidence 1999 violated the defendant's right to a fair trial under Article 6 of the European Convention on Human Rights.

R V. A (COMPLAINANT'S SEXUAL HISTORY) [2001] UKHL 25
Lord Slynn

1. My Lords, in recent years it has become plain that women who allege that they have been raped should not in court be harassed unfairly by questions about their previous sex experiences. To allow such harassment is very unjust to the woman; it is also bad for society in that women will be afraid to complain and as a result men who ought to be prosecuted will escape.

2. That such questioning about sex with another or other men than the accused should be disallowed without the leave of the court is well established. It was recognised in section 2 of the Sexual Offences (Amendment) Act 1976 which provided that without the leave of the judge there should be no evidence or cross-examination by or on behalf of the defendant of a complainant's sexual experience with a person other than the accused. Leave was only to be given by the judge 'if and only if he is satisfied that it would be unfair to that defendant to refuse to allow the evidence to be adduced or the question to be asked'.

3. Such a course was necessary in order to avoid the assumption too often made in the past that a woman who has had sex with one man is more likely to consent to sex with other men and that the evidence of a promiscuous woman is less credible.

4. Evidence of previous sex with the accused also has its dangers. It may lead the jury to accept that consensual sex once means that any future sex was with the woman's consent. That is far from being necessarily true and the question must always be whether there was consent to sex with this accused on this occasion and in these circumstances.

5. But the accused is entitled to a fair trial and there is an obvious conflict between the interests of protecting the woman and of ensuring such fair trial. Such conflict is more acute since the Human Rights Act 1998 came into force. The question is whether one of these interests should prevail or whether there must be a balance so that fairness to each must be accommodated and if so whether it has been achieved in current legislation. That is essentially the question which arises in this case. I gratefully adopt the statement of the facts and the relevant statutory provisions set out in the text of the speech prepared by my noble and learned friend Lord Steyn.

6. The question certified by the Court of Appeal which gave leave to appeal to your Lordships' House is 'May a sexual relationship between a defendant and complainant be relevant to the issue of consent so as to render its exclusion under section 41 of the Youth Justice and Criminal Evidence Act 1999 a contravention of the defendant's right to a fair trial?'

...

---

80 [2001] UKHL 25. Applied in *R* v. *S* [2010] EWCA Crim 1579, *R* v. *Miah (Zunur)* [2006] EWCA Crim 1168 and *R* v. *X* [2005] EWCA Crim 2995.

9. It is apparent that prima facie the restriction placed on the court's power to give leave seriously limits the opportunities for cross-examination or the adducing of evidence on behalf of the accused . . .

10. The need to protect women from harassment in the witness box is fundamental. It must not be lost sight of but I suspect that the man or woman in the street would find it strange that evidence that two young people who had lived together or regularly as part of a happy relationship had had sexual acts together, must be wholly excluded on the issue of consent unless it is immediately contemporaneous. The question whether such evidence should be believed and whether it is sufficient to establish consent or even belief in consent are different matters. The man and woman in the street might also find it strange that evidence may be given and cross-examination allowed as to belief in consent but not to consent itself when the same evidence was being relied on. That distinction has been recognised in the cases but without in any way resiling from a strong insistence on the need to protect women from humiliating cross-examination and prejudicial but valueless evidence, it seems to me clear that these restrictions in section 41 prima facie are capable of preventing an accused person from putting forward relevant evidence which may be evidence critical to his defence, whether it is as to consent or to belief that the woman consented. If thus construed section 41 does prevent the accused from having a fair trial then it must be declared to be incompatible with the Convention.

. . .

Lord Steyn

46. It is of supreme importance that the effect of the speeches today should be clear to trial judges who have to deal with problems of the admissibility of questioning and evidence on alleged prior sexual experience between an accused and a complainant. The effect of the decision today is that under section 41(3)(c) of the 1999 Act, construed where necessary by applying the interpretative obligation under section 3 of the Human Rights Act 1998, and due regard always being paid to the importance of seeking to protect the complainant from indignity and from humiliating questions, the test of admissibility is whether the evidence (and questioning in relation to it) is nevertheless so relevant to the issue of consent that to exclude it would endanger the fairness of the trial under article 6 of the convention. If this test is satisfied the evidence should not be excluded.

The House of Lords held that it was a matter for the trial judge to determine whether evidence of a previous consensual sexual relationship was relevant in any given case. The House acknowledged that in some cases evidence of a previous consensual sexual relationship might be relevant to the issue of consent and (in order to ensure that s. 41 of the Youth Justice and Criminal Evidence Act 1999 is compliant with Article 6 of the European Convention on Human Rights) leave might be given, in certain circumstances, for the cross-examination of a complainant as to a previous consensual sexual relationship. Section 41 should be construed by having regard to the interpretative obligation under s. 3 of the Human Rights Act 1998 to read and give effect to domestic legislation, so far as it is possible to do so, in a way which is compatible with the Convention rights. Consideration ought also to be given to the need to seek to protect a complainant from indignity and humiliating questions.

In his article in the *Criminal Law Review* published shortly after the enactment of the Youth Justice and Criminal Evidence Act 1999, Neil Kibble provides a critique of the provisions relating to evidence of the sexual history of a complainant.

N. KIBBLE, 'THE SEXUAL HISTORY PROVISIONS: CHARTING A COURSE BETWEEN INFLEXIBLE LEGISLATIVE RULES AND WHOLLY UNTRAMMELLED JUDICIAL DISCRETION?' [2000] CRIM LR 274

(at 276–7)

The scope of the new legislation is, ... wider than that of the Sexual Offences (Amendment) Act 1976 in three significant respects. First, the new legislation is not restricted to rape offences. Second, section 41 does not restrict itself to evidence or questions concerning the sexual experience of the complainant 'with a person other than the defendant'. Sexual behaviour with the defendant also falls within the scope of the legislation. The legislation therefore ends the automatic presumption that the prior sexual behaviour of the complainant with the accused is relevant to consent. Third, the reference in section 41 to 'sexual behaviour' is arguably wider than the 'sexual experience' of the earlier Act.

One issue that may give rise to difficulty is whether evidence that the complainant made previous false complaints constitutes evidence of sexual behaviour. The government was emphatic that it does not: 'it is about untruthful conduct on prior occasions. There is a very clear difference.' But the difference is clear only in respect of those cases in which the complainant has *admitted* the falsity of the complaint. In such cases, no reference to evidence of sexual behaviour is required, nor is sexual behaviour even implied. However, there may be cases in which the defendant seeks to introduce evidence of prior false complaint where the complainant *denies* the falsity of the complaint. In these cases, evidence of sexual behaviour may well be required to show that the complaint was false. It could be argued that in such cases the evidence should be regarded as evidence of sexual behaviour, therefore falling within the scope of the provisions. This would raise the problem that such evidence would appear to be excluded by section 41(4), which provides that no evidence shall be regarded as relevant to an issue in the trial if its purpose is to impugn the credibility of the complainant. Given section 41(4), it is likely that the courts will determine that evidence of false complaint (whether admitted or otherwise) does not constitute evidence of sexual behaviour. Experience in other jurisdictions certainly suggests that courts will find a way to admit evidence of false complaints, even where the legislation would appear to require its exclusion. A greater danger lies in the admission of evidence of false complaint where falsity is denied. The possibility of distraction and of prejudicial impact must raise doubts as to the admissibility of such evidence. At the very least, ... nothing less than a strong factual foundation for concluding that the prior complaint was false should be sufficient to support a decision to admit the evidence.

...

(at 284–6)

Relevance, probative value and prejudicial impact

..., the reference in section 41(3) of the YJCEA to a relevant issue in the case 'that is not an issue of consent' shows the clear legislative intention to exclude evidence or questions concerning sexual behaviour where the grounds for its relevance are that the sexual behaviour makes it more likely that the woman consented on this occasion. However, . . . the YJCEA, . . . provides for two specific exceptions, contained in section 41(3)(b) and (c).

The exception in section 41(3)(b), allowing evidence or questioning where it relates to behaviour alleged to have taken place 'at or about the same time' as the alleged offence, was the product of a Lords amendment. The original Bill specified that the sexual behaviour should have taken place within 24 hours of the event, but it was accepted during the Lords debates that this restriction was somewhat arbitrary and the provision was amended accordingly. Lord Bingham C.J., among others, argued that the provision was flawed because it did not give a judge any discretion to admit evidence that fell outside the time frame (unless the issue was belief in consent). One of the grounds of his objection was that evidence that a complainant has had sexual intercourse with four different men on the four nights prior to the alleged offence was relevant to consent and should be admitted. This would appear to be a version of the propensity argument and is not, it is submitted, a persuasive objection. However, there is a more significant problem with the exception contained in section 41(3)(b). As Lord Bingham noted, the recognition of the 24-hour window (even in amended form) calls into question the Government's view on the relevance of prior sexual history to consent. Why does otherwise irrelevant evidence suddenly become relevant merely because it occurs within the 24-hour period?

The second exception recognised within the YJCEA provisions raises a similar problem. Section 41(3)(c) recognises the relevance of sexual behaviour to consent where it is so similar that it cannot reasonably be explained as a coincidence. Not in the original Bill, the provision was introduced in response to the 'Romeo and Juliet' scenario recounted by Baroness Mallalieu.[81] Notwithstanding the Government's insistence that the exception should be construed narrowly, the recognition of the exception calls into question once again the coherence of the Government's position on the relevance of evidence of sexual behaviour. The 'similar fact' exception to the non-admissibility of character evidence regarding the accused is not based on the premise that it is only at this point that the evidence becomes relevant. Rather, the exception rests on the premise that only at this point does the probative value of the evidence outweigh its prejudicial effect. This argument *acknowledges* the relevance of the evidence outside of the exception, but recognises that other factors require its exclusion. A similar argument could have been made with regard to prior sexual history on the issue of consent: its tenuous relevance, especially given the absence of a complaint on the previous occasions; its prejudicial effect, and its tendency to distract the jury from the real issues in the trial require its exclusion, save in the two enumerated exceptions. This would be a coherent position to take . . . The Government's position is neither persuasive nor coherent, and this must make the provisions more vulnerable to challenge in the courts.

10.6 RE-EXAMINATION

Counsel may conduct a re-examination of his own witness if he wishes to, but there are some limitations on the questions that may be asked. Counsel is not permitted to raise new issues in

---

81 Kibble explains this example in these terms at footnote 38: 'Baroness Mallalieu advanced a scenario in which a complainant was alleging that she had been raped by a man who had climbed up onto her balcony into her bedroom, and in which she had on several occasions both prior to and since the alleged rape (outside the restriction "at or about the same time as the event") invited men to re-enact the *Romeo and Juliet* balcony scene prior to having sexual intercourse with them.'

re-examination, thus it cannot be used to ask questions that counsel may have neglected to ask in examination-in-chief. Instead, re-examination is used to clarify any ambiguities in the witness's testimony that may have arisen during cross-examination in order to repair any damage done to the witness's credibility in cross-examination. Re-examination is treated like examination-in-chief in the sense that only non-leading questions may be asked.

10.7 CONCLUSION

While the principle of orality in adversarial proceedings demands that live oral evidence is received from a witness, the rules of procedure govern the manner in which testimony is elicited from a witness. The party calling the witness may ask the witness questions with a view to getting the witness to tell their story in their own words; thus, the types of questions which may be asked of a witness in examination-in-chief are necessarily limited to non-leading questions which do not put words into a witness's mouth. In order to test the reliability of a witness's testimony and to put the opposing case, the opposing party is also permitted to ask questions of the witness in cross-examination. In contrast to the type of questions asked in examination-in-chief, the questions asked in cross-examination are deliberately leading in order that the answers given by the witness are restricted as far as possible. Special procedural rules are also adopted where a witness wishes to use a document to refresh his memory, where a witness proves to be hostile and where a complainant in sexual offence is cross-examined. These rules are designed to manage the manner in which the testimony is elicited in order to ensure that the evidence put before the tribunal of fact is relevant and reliable.

Summary

- The purpose of examination-in-chief is to get the witness to give a structured and chronological account of what he witnessed. Counsel may only ask non-leading questions in examination-in-chief and is prohibited from asking leading questions.
- When a witness is called to give evidence-in-chief and takes the oath or affirms, he opens himself up to cross-examination. In cross-examination, counsel should ask leading questions. Cross-examination has two main purposes: (1) to undermine the evidence of the witness, with the ultimate objective of weakening the case for the opposition; and (2) to establish your case.
- Re-examination is used to clarify any ambiguities in the witness's testimony that may have arisen during cross-examination. Counsel is not permitted to raise new issues in re-examination. Only non-leading questions may be asked in re-examination.
- Non-leading questions are open-ended questions which do not suggest an answer to the witness, but instead allow the witness to tell their story in their own words. Leading questions are questions which suggest the answer that is sought.
- Outside the courtroom, a witness is permitted to use his witness statement to refresh his memory of events before giving evidence. He may not use his witness statement to refresh his memory during the course of giving evidence.

- Under s. 139, CJA 2003, a witness who is giving evidence in the witness box may refresh his memory from a document that he made or verified at an earlier time providing that he states in oral evidence that the document records his recollection of the matter at that earlier time and his recollection of the matter is likely to have been significantly better at that time than it is at the time of his oral evidence.
- The rule against narrative provides that a witness may not be asked in examination-in-chief whether he has made a previous statement which is consistent with his testimony. The exceptions to this rule apply to statements rebutting allegations of fabrication, memory refreshing documents, evidence of previous identification, witnesses with no recollection of events, complaints by complainants, *res gestae* statements and statements made on accusation.
- An unfavourable witness is one who fails to 'come up to proof', i.e. he does not say what he was expected to say in examination-in-chief. A hostile witness is one who, in the opinion of the judge, demonstrates a hostile mind in examination-in-chief, who clearly intends not to tell the truth to the court.
- The rule of finality on collateral issues provides that any answer which is given by a witness in cross-examination on a collateral issue is final. The exceptions to this rule apply to previous inconsistent statements, previous convictions and bias that the witness denies, evidence of a general reputation for lying and evidence of a medical condition affecting reliability.
- A defendant in a sexual case is prohibited from cross-examining in person the complainant (s. 34, YJCEA 1999). A defendant who has been charged with a specified offence is prohibited from cross-examining in person a 'protected witness' (s. 35(1), YJCEA 1999). A defendant is prohibited from personally cross-examining a witness if it would improve the quality of the evidence given by the witness and it would not be contrary to the interests of justice (s. 36, YJCEA 1999).
- A complainant in a sexual case may not be cross-examined on his or her sexual history without the leave of the judge, which may be granted in the circumstances under either s. 41(3) or s. 41(5), YJCEA 1999 and if a refusal to grant leave might render a conviction unsafe.

For discussion . . .

1. Before beginning his testimony, a witness is allowed to refresh his memory from his witness statement, but once he has begun his testimony he can no longer do so. Consider the justification for this distinction.
2. What is the rationale for the rule against narrative? What is the rationale behind each of the exceptions to this rule?
3. Explain the difference between a hostile witness and an unfavourable witness.
4. What is the rationale for the rule of finality on collateral issues? What is the rationale behind each of the exceptions to this rule?
5. Consider the extent to which s. 41, YJCEA 1999 is consistent with the defendant's right to a fair trial.

Further reading

D. Birch, 'Rethinking sexual history evidence: proposals for fairer trials' [2002] Crim LR 531.
Professor Birch considers in this article whether the limitations placed on the admissibility of sexual history evidence by s. 41, Youth Justice and Criminal Evidence Act 1999 and the House of Lords' decision in *R* v. *A (Complainant's Sexual History)* [2002] 1 AC 45. Professor Birch provides a persuasive argument that the law is theoretically flawed and inconsistent with good evidence doctrine. She argues that a better solution is to rethink the legislation. This article should be read in conjunction with Professor Temkin's response in the 2003 *Criminal Law Review.*

D. Birch, 'Untangling sexual history evidence: a rejoinder to Professor Temkin' [2003] Crim LR 370.
In this article Professor Birch writes a response to Professor Temkin's article in the 2003 *Criminal Law Review* (below) defending her article in the 2002 *Criminal Law Review* (above). While acknowledging that rape myths pose a threat to fair trials, Professor Birch suggests the creation of a Working Group to look for new ways to dispel rape myths and argues that s. 41 is not the appropriate manner of doing so. Instead, she supports the approach that places trust in juries to assess the evidence.

I. Morley, *Devil's Advocate* (Sweet & Maxwell, 1993).
An excellent book on the dos and don'ts of advocacy. It is a book highly praised by practitioners and provides a practical approach to performing well in court.

R. Pattenden, 'The hostile witness' (1992) 56 *Journal of Criminal Law* 414.
This article explores the problems that have arisen in connection with treating a witness as a hostile witness. Professor Pattenden argues that the discretion to allow counsel to treat a witness as hostile is important for the aim of discovering the truth and she warns against the narrow interpretation of s. 3, Criminal Procedure Act 1865.

M. Stone, 'Essential tactics of criminal evidence' (2011) 175 JPN 107, 121, 137.
This is an article in three parts in which Stone sets out essential tactics for presenting or challenging disputed eyewitness testimony in criminal trials.

J. Temkin, 'Sexual history evidence – beware the backlash' [2003] Crim LR 217.
In this article, Professor Temkin writes a response to Professor Birch's article from the 2002 *Criminal Law Review* (above). Professor Temkin argues in defence of the provisions under s. 41, Youth Justice and Criminal Evidence Act 1999 and considers whether s. 41 provides greater protection to defendants.

11 Corroboration and identification evidence

11.1 INTRODUCTION

This chapter is concerned with the way in which unreliable evidence is handled by the court at trial. Evidence might be unreliable in a variety of situations and for a variety of reasons. For example, where a witness receives an inducement or payment in respect of giving evidence, where a co-defendant runs a 'cut-throat' defence, or where a defendant tells lies about the offence, their testimony might be unreliable. Quite controversially, in relatively recent times the evidence of children and complainants of sexual offences was deemed to be inherently unreliable and it required a mandatory corroboration warning by the judge. Evidence of visual identification is notoriously unreliable. We have all suffered that embarrassing moment where you think you've just spotted someone you know and you wave at them only to realise that you've made a mistake and you have no idea who the person you've just waved at is. With this in mind, it is relatively easy to see how evidence of identification can be extremely unreliable, even where a witness honestly believes that they are right. The challenge faced by the courts in each of these circumstances is to ensure that evidence which is adduced before the jury is reliable or that there are sufficient safeguards in place to ensure that the jury members do not place undue weight on unreliable evidence in reaching their verdict. The most common way for the courts to deal with unreliable evidence is by giving the jury a care warning in which they are warned about the potential unreliability of the evidence and that they should be careful about the weight that they attach to it. This chapter explores the circumstances in which care or cautionary warnings must or may be given by a trial judge and the nature of those warnings.

11.2   CORROBORATION

Evidence is more reliable if it is supported by other evidence. The law used to require that unreliable evidence was supported by other independent evidence (known as 'corroborating evidence'). Historically, certain forms of evidence (such as evidence given by children, the evidence of an accomplice or evidence by a complainant of a sexual offence) were thought to be so inherently unreliable that juries were warned about the danger of convicting the defendant on the basis of such evidence if it was not accompanied by independent corroborating evidence. While these forms of evidence are no longer subject to such presumptions, occasionally the evidence of a witness might be considered unreliable and a trial judge might need to give the jury a care warning, known as a '*Makanjuola* warning'.[1]

> **Cross-reference**
>
> A *Makanjuola* care warning is derived from the case of *R* v. *Makanjuola*. This case is now the leading authority on corroboration and it will be discussed at paragraph 11.2.5 below.

11.2.1 Meaning of corroboration

Today there is no general rule in England and Wales that the evidence of a witness must be corroborated. This means that witness testimony is generally admissible in court irrespective of whether or not there is independent evidence which supports the evidence of the witness, and a conviction can be based upon the uncorroborated evidence of a witness. Similarly, there is no general rule that uncorroborated evidence must also be subject to a care warning. Thus, there is no need for the trial judge to warn the jury about the dangers of convicting the defendant on uncorroborated evidence. Until recently, in Scotland, there has been a legal requirement of corroboration; so, for instance, where a defendant confessed to an offence but there was no independent evidence supporting the confession, the defendant could not be convicted. However, on the basis of recommendations made in the Carloway Report,[2] the Scottish

---

1 *R* v. *Makanjuola* [1995] 1 WLR 1348, CA.
2 *The Carloway Review: Report and Recommendations* (17 November 2011) available at www.scotland.gov.uk/About/Review/CarlowayReview/Contents (accessed on 19 July 2014).

government has recently proposed the abolition of the requirement of corroboration and this is likely to become law very soon.[3]

There are two definitions of 'corroboration'. The technical definition given by Lord Reading CJ in *R* v. *Baskerville*,[4] is that corroboration is 'independent testimony' which supports a particular piece of evidence. The non-technical definition of corroboration does not require that the evidence is independent, and thus it is merely 'supporting evidence'.

R V. *BASKERVILLE* [1916] 2 KB 658
Lord Reading CJ

[at 667]

We hold that evidence in corroboration must be independent testimony which affects the accused by connecting or tending to connect him with the crime. In other words, it must be evidence which implicates him, that is, which confirms in some material particular not only the evidence that the crime has been committed, but also that the prisoner committed it ... corroborative evidence is evidence which shows or tends to show that the story of the accomplice that the accused committed the crime is true, not merely that the crime has been committed, but that it was committed by the accused.

Although there is no general rule requiring corroboration as a matter of law, there are a few statutory offences which require corroboration before a defendant may be convicted of the offence. These offences are perjury, speeding and an attempt to commit offences with a statutory legal requirement of corroboration, and these are discussed below.

11.2.2 Legal requirement of corroboration

Some statutory offences carry a legal requirement of independent corroborating evidence. These include, namely, perjury, speeding and an attempt to commit offences with a statutory legal requirement of corroboration.[5]

Perjury

Perjury is the offence of wilfully making a statement under oath 'which he knows to be false or does not believe to be true'.[6] Thus, a witness who gives evidence at trial under oath will commit perjury if he either tells a lie or makes a statement that he does not believe to be true. Under s. 13, Perjury Act 1911, a person cannot be convicted of perjury 'solely upon the evidence of one witness as to the falsity of any statement alleged to be false'. This means that s. 13 is only

---

3 See s. 57 of the Criminal Justice (Scotland) Bill, introduced on 20 June 2013, available at www.scottish. parliament.uk/parliamentarybusiness/Bills/65155.aspx (accessed on 19 July 2014). (Bills of the Scottish Parliament refer to 'sections', rather than 'clauses' as per UK Bills.)
4 [1916] 2 KB 658.
5 The special verdict of not guilty by reason of insanity under s. 2, Trial of Lunatics Act 1883 cannot be returned by a jury unless two or more registered medical practitioners have given written or oral evidence (see s. 1, Criminal Procedure (Insanity and Unfitness to Plead) Act 1991).
6 Section 1, Perjury Act 1911.

relevant where the defendant is alleged to have committed perjury by making a false statement (as opposed to by making a statement which he did not believe to be true).[7] In such cases, corroborating evidence is required as to the 'falsity of the statement' in order to convict a person of perjury, thus, a defendant cannot be convicted of this form of perjury on the basis of the evidence of one witness alone: 'there can be no conviction on the evidence of one witness alone; there must be one witness and something else in addition'.[8] This does not necessarily mean that there must be evidence from two witnesses; it is sufficient if the corroboration comes from one witness and a confession.[9] In *R* v. *Peach*,[10] the Court of Appeal also held that it was sufficient if the evidence came from two witnesses who each heard a confession by the defendant on the same occasion.

R V. *PEACH* [1990] 1 WLR 976
Lord Lane CJ

[at 979–80]

There seem to this court to be two separate problems to be solved in these circumstances. First of all, is there evidence of falsity, that is to say, falsity of the evidence sworn on oath? Secondly, if so, is the further requirement of section 13 satisfied?

Despite the arguments of counsel, we have no hesitation in saying that evidence to the effect that the defendant has confessed that his sworn statement was false, is evidence of the statement's falsity. Apart from any other reason, if that were not so, then in the majority of cases, that is to say, cases where the only person who knows that the sworn statement was untrue is the defendant himself, he will never be convicted, however often he asserted the untruthfulness of the statement which he has made on oath.

That leaves the second question, namely, is section 13 satisfied if two witnesses testify to having heard the defendant admit the falsity on the same occasion? One reads the section and asks whether in those circumstances the jury is being asked to convict of perjury solely upon the evidence of one witness as to the falsity of the statement alleged to be false. The answer on any view seems to us to be certainly not. The evidence is evidence of the falsity and there are two witnesses testifying to it. That interpretation does no violence to the reasons given by Byles J. in *Reg. v. Hook*, Dears. & B. 606, 616, to which reference has just been made, and is giving the words of the Act of 1911, so it seems to us, the only meaning which, in the view of this court, they can be said to bear. The plain words of the Act also have the advantage of resolving the not inconsiderable conflict between the various pre-1911 decisions to which reference has been made.

The application of s. 13 was recently explored by the Court of Appeal in *R* v. *Cooper (John).*[11]

---

7 Corroboration is not necessary where the prosecution alleges that the defendant made a statement which he did not believe to be true.
8 Per Lord Reading CJ in *R* v. *Threlfall* (1914) 10 Cr App R 112 at 117.
9 Per Avory J, ibid. at 114.
10 [1990] 1 WLR 976.
11 [2010] EWCA Crim 979.

R V. COOPER (JOHN) [2010] EWCA CRIM 979
Lord Judge CJ

11. In unequivocal terms therefore, the evidence of one witness as to the falsity of the statement given in evidence is not enough to found a conviction. For this purpose there must be at least two pieces of evidence, at least one of which must be independent of the witness called to establish the falsity of the statement. There must be some evidence 'in addition' to that witness. This may be provided by two or more witnesses, it may be provided by one witness and a document, for example, a confession by the defendant, or an incriminating letter written by him. But the necessary further evidence must be independent of the witness whose evidence requires corroboration, coming from a source independent of him. Material which is not independent of the testimony to be corroborated is not capable of amounting to corroboration.

12. The prohibition is absolute: unlike many of the common law corroboration requirements, it is not open to the jury to convict if, having given due regard to the warning against returning a conviction in the absence of corroboration, it is, notwithstanding the absence of corroboration, convinced of the truthfulness of the witness.

In this case, the Lord Chief Justice quashed the defendant's conviction for perjury because there was no corroborating evidence as to the falsity of the defendant's statement. The only evidence relied upon by the prosecution in this case was the evidence of a witness, and the Court of Appeal held that business documents prepared by that witness which, taken on their own did not establish the falsity, could not constitute corroborating evidence. The Court held that 'the two areas of evidence [were] not independent of each other'.[12]

Speeding
Under s. 89(2), Road Traffic Regulation Act 1984, a person cannot be convicted of speeding under s. 89(1) solely on the opinion evidence of one witness to the effect that the vehicle was travelling in excess of the speed limit. Thus, independent corroborating evidence as to speed is required in order to convict a defendant of speeding under s. 89(1). It is not enough that one witness gives evidence of his opinion as to the defendant's guilt. However, where a police officer gives the only evidence as to the speed of the vehicle, and his testimony is based on 'objectively determined phenomena', such as skid marks, damage to the vehicle, there is no violation of s. 89(2).[13]

Attempts
Under s. 2(2)(g), Criminal Attempts Act 1981, where a statutory offence contains a requirement of corroboration before the defendant can be convicted in respect of the full offence, then any attempt to commit that offence also carries the requirement of corroboration. Thus, if a defendant were charged with attempting to commit perjury by making a false statement, he could not be convicted solely on the basis of the evidence of one witness.

---

12 Ibid. at [17].
13 *Crossland* v. *DPP* [1988] 3 All ER 712.

11.2.3 Unreliable witnesses

Historically, certain special categories of witness were deemed to be so inherently unreliable that their testimony warranted mandatory corroboration warnings. Where the prosecution case was based upon the evidence of a child, evidence of the defendant's accomplice or evidence from the complainant of a sexual offence, the trial judge would warn the jury of the danger of convicting the defendant on such evidence without independent corroborating evidence.

Special categories of witness

Children, complainants of sexual offences and accomplices fell into special categories of prosecution witness who were deemed to be inherently unreliable on the basis of social prejudices which existed at the time. The testimony of children was considered to be of particular concern because children were thought to be fanciful and prone to make-belief. Similarly, complainants of sexual offences, who were statistically more often women, were deemed to be unreliable witnesses because they were likely to lie or give evidence of fantasy, rather than the truth.

Finally, very little trust was placed in the testimony of an accomplice. An accomplice might give evidence against a defendant in one of two ways. He might agree to give evidence against the defendant as a prosecution witness, possibly in exchange for the prosecution dropping a more serious charge or all charges, or simply after a guilty plea (this is known as 'turning Queen's evidence'), or he might give evidence against the defendant while himself a co-defendant (this is known as running a 'cut-throat' defence). Where an accomplice gave evidence against a defendant as a prosecution witness, he was deemed to be unreliable because he was likely to have his own purpose to serve in giving evidence for the prosecution against the defendant.[14] Consequently, corroboration was a legal requirement in such situations. However, where an accomplice did not give evidence for the prosecution but nonetheless made accusations against the defendant, there was no legal requirement for a full corroboration warning, but it was at the discretion of the trial judge to decide whether a warning should be given to the jury and the form that such a warning should take.[15] More recently, in *R* v. *Jones; Jenkins*,[16] the Court of Appeal held that the trial judge had erred in failing to warn the jury to treat an accomplice's evidence with caution. The Court held that it would be useful for the trial judge to consider four points to put to the jury in such cases:

1. the jury should consider the case for and against each defendant separately;
2. the jury should decide the case on the basis of all of the evidence, including the evidence of each defendant's co-defendant;
3. the jury should bear in mind that co-defendants may have an interest to serve or an axe to grind; and
4. the jury should assess the evidence of co-defendants in the same way as that of the evidence of any other witness in the case.

---

14 *R* v. *Prater* [1960] 2 QB 464.
15 See *R* v. *Knowlden* (1981) 77 Cr App R 94, CA and *R* v. *Cheema* [1994] 1 WLR 147, CA.
16 [2004] 1 Cr App R 5, CA.

R v. *Jones*; *Jenkins* was followed by the Court of Appeal in *R* v. *Petkar and Farquhar*,[17] in which the Court of Appeal expressed some concerns about the points outlined by Auld LJ in *R* v. *Jones*; *Jenkins*:

R V. PETKAR AND FARQUHAR [2003] EWCA CRIM 2668
Rix LJ

74. . . . First, we would regard the danger of a warning regarding the evidence of cut-throat co-defendants not so much that which was canvassed and dismissed in Jones and Jenkins, namely that it may indicate to the jury that the *judge* had formed an adverse view as to their defences, but rather that it serves to devalue the evidence of both co-defendants in the eyes of the *jury*. It might be said that if the jury should regard the evidence of each defendant with a somewhat jaundiced eye on his 'interest to serve' or his grinding axe, that goes far, in a real cut-throat defence, to undermine the defence of each.

75. Secondly, we wonder whether Auld LJ's third constituent to his direction (the warning) lies easily with his fourth constituent: and thus whether the distinction which a warning to be wary of a co-defendant's evidence is really designed to elucidate is that between evidence in a co-defendant's own defence (which has to be treated like that of any other witness) and evidence which incriminates the co-defendant.

Despite the potential for unreliability where accomplices run cut-throat defences, the failure to give the jury a warning to treat the evidence with caution will not automatically render a conviction unsafe.[18]

Improper motive
Putting aside these specific categories of witness, witnesses may prove to be unreliable for a range of reasons. It was held in *R* v. *Beck*[19] that where there was evidence that the testimony of a witness might be tainted by an improper motive, the trial judge was obliged to give the jury a warning to proceed with caution. In the *Criminal Law Review*, Professor Diane Birch considers the warning derived from the case of *R* v. *Beck*.

D. J. BIRCH, 'CORROBORATION: GOODBYE TO ALL THAT?' [1995] CRIM LR 524

[at 528–30]

. . . the Criminal Bar Association questioned whether abolishing the corroboration rules without replacement left the accused with sufficient safeguard against conviction on the evidence of witnesses of dubious veracity. The Law Commission retorted that adequate protection was to be found in the judge's existing obligation to direct the jury on the evidence. This consists (a) of a general duty to put the defence case fairly to the jury and, in doing so, to draw attention to items of the prosecution case which are actually or potentially unreliable or open to criticism; and more crucially (b) in specific cases, to give a

---

17 [2003] EWCA Crim 2668 at [74], CA.
18 *R* v. *Okuwa* [2010] EWCA Crim 832.
19 [1982] 1 WLR 461.

warning about certain witnesses who may have an interest of their own to serve in giving evidence. This type of warning, attributed to *Beck*, is, although mandatory, free of the criticism that has beset the corroboration rules, and therefore the Law Commission was content that some cases formerly dealt with as corroboration cases should, if the witness has an axe to grind, be brought within the *Beck* warning instead. The superiority of *Beck* derives first from the fact that the obligation it creates is witness-specific, arising only where there is material to suggest that a particular witness's evidence may be tainted by an improper motive; secondly from its flexibility (the terms of the warning are that the jury is advised to proceed with caution in approaching the evidence of the witness in question, but the strength of the advice varies according to the facts of the case), and thirdly from its avoidance of complexity: there is no magic formula to be followed as to the way in which other evidence may be resorted to to support the witness's testimony.

...

What *Beck* did, ... was to limit the cases in which a full warning was required ... The ... likely possibility, is that *Beck* applies in all cases where, ... there is 'material to suggest that a witness's evidence may be tainted by an improper motive'. It is not necessary, nor is it possible, to be specific about the form an improper motive may take, for common sense suggests that it may take any number of forms: spite, ill will, the levelling of old scores and financial gain are but a few examples ...

Cross-reference

Witnesses may give false or misleading evidence because they have their own particular purpose to serve or another motive for lying. You should refer to the case of *R* v. *Lucas* at paragraph 11.6 below for the direction that the trial judge will give a jury in the event of a defendant admitting that he has told lies on a previous occasion.

The overriding rule

Aside from the special categories of witness identified above who warranted a full corroboration warning by law, a trial judge also had a more general duty to warn the jury about convicting the defendant on the basis of the uncorroborated evidence of any witness whose testimony is potentially unreliable. Mirfield outlines the general duty of the judge in an article written prior to the leading authority of:

> ... the trial judge is under a general duty, in every case, to ensure that the accused's defence is put fairly and adequately to the jury. This rule, described in *Spencer* as the 'overriding rule', will come into play whenever the circumstances suggest a doubt about the truthfulness of a witness who testifies against the accused.[20]

In the case of *R* v. *Spencer*,[21] the House of Lords held that while the categories of witness requiring a full warning were closed, the trial judge had a general duty to warn the jury of the danger of convicting the defendant on the evidence of other suspect witnesses without corroboration. The facts of this particular case involved witnesses who were patients at a secure

---

20 P. Mirfield, '"Corroboration" after the 1994 Act' [1995] Crim LR 448 at 449.
21 [1987] AC 128, HL.

hospital, had criminal records and suffered from mental disorders. In such a case, the House of Lords held that the trial judge should (as he did in this case) direct the jury to approach the evidence of the patients 'with great caution' because of their mental condition and criminal background. The House emphasised the overriding rule that the trial judge 'must put the defence fairly and adequately'.[22]

Cross-reference

Where a person who falls within the definition of a 'mentally handicapped' person within s. 77, Police and Criminal Evidence Act 1984 confesses to a criminal offence in the absence of an independent person, and the prosecution of that person depends wholly or substantially on the evidence of that confession, the trial judge shall warn the jury of the special need for caution before convicting that person on the basis of the confession. Section 77, Police and Criminal Evidence Act 1984 is discussed at paragraph 11.2.6 below, and in more detail in Chapter 5 on Confession evidence.

11.2.4 Corroboration no longer legally required

The corroboration requirements in respect of children, complainants in sexual offences and accomplices no longer exist. The abolition of the legal requirement of corroboration was justified on the basis that the full corroboration warning was very technical and complicated, it was not clear that the warning was effective, and it was difficult to justify in respect of these specific categories of witness. According to John Hartshorne, '[t]he motivation for abolishing the corroboration warning was the appreciation that it had become cumbersome and difficult to follow by juries, and that the warning was in many cases misleading if not insulting'.[23] The authors of *Blackstone's Guide to the Criminal Justice and Public Order Act 1994* provide further explanation of the rationale for the reforms:

M. WASIK AND R. TAYLOR, *BLACKSTONE'S GUIDE TO THE CRIMINAL JUSTICE AND PUBLIC ORDER ACT 1994* (BLACKSTONE PRESS, 1995)

[at p. 47]

Whether all this complexity in any way furthered its intended purpose of protecting the accused from evidence likely to be unreliable or fabricated is open to doubt and there was a school of thought that the warning could actually operate to the detriment rather than to the benefit of the accused . . .

Quite apart from the issues of complexity, effectiveness and the impact on cases involving children, there was also the issue of whether it was appropriate to treat members of a class of witnesses differently on that account rather than emphasising the issue of the credibility and reliability of the individual witness. Branding all members of a class as being prone to give unreliable or false testimony was a type of discrimination which sat increasingly uneasily with contemporary notions of equal

---

22 Per Lord Ackner, ibid. at 142.
23 J. Hartshorne, 'Corroboration and care warnings after *Makanjuola*' (1998) 2(1) E&P 1.

treatment and respect for the individual, particularly in respect of sexual complainants who tend more frequently to be women rather than men. Although the rule applies equally to male as well as female complainants, it was perceived in some quarters as an insult to women and as an unholy relic of the bygone days when it could be intellectually respectable to argue that women were less objective, accurate or honest witnesses than men.

The mandatory warning in respect of the evidence of children was abolished in 1988, and in 1991 the Law Commission recommended that the mandatory warning in respect of the evidence of accomplices and complainants of sexual offences should also be abolished.[24] The mandatory warnings for these specific categories of witness have since been abolished by statute. Section 34(2), Criminal Justice Act 1988 abolished the mandatory warning in respect of the uncorroborated evidence of a child and s. 32(1), Criminal Justice and Public Order Act 1994 abolished the mandatory warning in respect of the uncorroborated evidence of an accomplice or a complainant of a sexual offence.

S. 34(2), CRIMINAL JUSTICE ACT 1988

Any requirement whereby at a trial on indictment it is obligatory for the court to give the jury a warning about convicting the accused on the uncorroborated evidence of a child is abrogated . . .

S. 32(1), CRIMINAL JUSTICE AND PUBLIC ORDER ACT 1994

(1) Any requirement whereby at a trial on indictment it is obligatory for the court to give the jury a warning about convicting the accused on the uncorroborated evidence of a person merely because that person is –
(a) an alleged accomplice of the accused, or
(b) where the offence charged is a sexual offence, the person in respect of whom it is alleged to have been committed,
is hereby abrogated.

P. MIRFIELD, '"CORROBORATION" AFTER THE 1994 ACT' [1995] CRIM LR 448

[at 460]

Suspect witnesses will not go away just because the corroboration warning rules have gone, nor does the Law Commission suggest that they will. It would be possible simply to close the book on the categories of case with which those rules dealt and the categories which developed by analogy from them. Probably, the book *is* now closed as regards children and complainants in sexual cases, so that all

---

24 Law Commission Report, *Corroboration of Evidence in Criminal Trials* (Law Com. No. 202, Cm. 1620, 1991).

> that remains is the judge's general duty to put the defence case fairly and adequately to the jury. The Commission argues that *Beck* and *Spencer* will continue to have force in future. It has been argued here that their survival is less clearly established than the Commission suggests, and that these chapters too may have had their day.
>
> If, as seems more likely, the courts do regard the cautionary direction cases as surviving the Act, there is obvious merit in the Commission's argument, by reverse analogy, that they should be extended to cover accomplice cases. However, the authorities support the application of *Beck* to all improper motive cases – though not to any witness 'with a purpose of his own to serve', given the restricted, technical meaning in law of that term – and there is thus no reason for courts to feel constrained to use cautionary directions only where the witness is an accomplice or at risk of conviction in connection with the matters at issue in the case. Indeed, if the well-known statement in *Beck* about the obligation of trial judges in improper motive cases is correct, those directions *must* be given. Finally, there is neither authority nor good sense in the Commission's proposal that the judge should not give a direction where confident of the sincerity of the particular witness. It may be supposed that there will be plenty of meat here for the courts to get their teeth into.

As a result of these statutory reforms, where children, complainants of sexual offences or accomplices give evidence at trial, the judge is no longer obliged to warn the jury about the dangers of convicting upon their uncorroborated evidence. However, there may be occasions where the credibility or reliability of a witness is of a tenuous nature, such that a warning would be desirable. Shortly after the abolition of the legal requirements of corroboration for certain categories of witness, the Court of Appeal ruled that in cases where there is evidence that a witness is unreliable, it is open to the trial judge to give the jury a discretionary care warning, known as a '*Makanjuola* warning'.

11.2.5 Discretionary care warning

Makanjuola *warning*
In *R* v. *Makanjuola*,[25] the Court of Appeal acknowledged that the original justification for the old mandatory corroboration warnings was still current, namely that some witnesses may lie for their own purposes or for other reasons, or even for no reason at all. Consequently, the Court held that a trial judge should have the discretion to give the jury a warning about convicting the defendant on the basis of the uncorroborated evidence of any witness who may be unreliable.

R V. MAKANJUOLA [1995] 1 WLR 1348
Lord Taylor CJ

[at 1350–2]

The underlying rationale of the corroboration rules . . . was that accomplices may well have purposes of their own to serve and complainants about sexual offences may lie or fantasise for unascertainable reasons or no reason at all. That rationale, it is argued, cannot evaporate overnight. So the traditional

---

25 [1995] 1 WLR 1348.

warnings to juries should continue. The statute removes the requirement to give them but the judge is still free to do so and he should . . .

Whether, as a matter of discretion, a judge should give any warning and if so its strength and terms must depend upon the content and manner of the witness's evidence, the circumstances of the case and the issues raised. The judge will often consider that no special warning is required at all. Where, however the witness has been shown to be unreliable, he or she may consider it necessary to urge caution. In a more extreme case, if the witness is shown to have lied, to have made previous false complaints, or to bear the defendant some grudge, a stronger warning may be thought appropriate and the judge may suggest it would be wise to look for some supporting material before acting on the impugned witness's evidence. We stress that these observations are merely illustrative of some, not all, of the factors which judges may take into account in measuring where a witness stands in the scale of reliability and what response they should make at that level in their directions to the jury. We also stress that judges are not required to conform to any formula and this court would be slow to interfere with the exercise of discretion by a trial judge who has the advantage of assessing the manner of a witness's evidence as well as its content.

To summarise.

(1) Section 32(1) abrogated the requirement to give a corroboration direction in respect of an alleged accomplice or a complainant of a sexual offence, simply because a witness falls into one of those categories.

(2) It is a matter for the judge's discretion what, if any warning, he considers appropriate in respect of such a witness as indeed in respect of any other witness in whatever type of case. Whether he chooses to give a warning and in what terms will depend on the circumstances of the case, the issues raised and the content and quality of the witness's evidence.

(3) In some cases, it may be appropriate for the judge to warn the jury to exercise caution before acting upon the unsupported evidence of a witness. This will not be so simply because the witness is a complainant of a sexual offence nor will it necessarily be so because a witness is alleged to be an accomplice. There will need to be an evidential basis for suggesting that the evidence of the witness may be unreliable. An evidential basis does not include mere suggestion by cross-examining counsel.

(4) If any question arises as to whether the judge should give a special warning in respect of a witness, it is desirable that the question be resolved by discussion with counsel in the absence of the jury before final speeches.

(5) Where the judge does decide to give some warning in respect of a witness, it will be appropriate to do so as part of the judge's review of the evidence and his comments as to how the jury should evaluate it rather than as a set-piece legal direction.

(6) Where some warning is required, it will be for the judge to decide the strength and terms of the warning. It does not have to be invested with the whole florid regime of the old corroboration rules.

(7) It follows that we emphatically disagree with the tentative submission made by the editors of *Archbold, Criminal Pleading, Evidence & Practice*, vol. 1 in the passage at paragraph 16.36 quoted above. Attempts to re-impose the straitjacket of the old corroboration rules are strongly to be deprecated.

(8) Finally, this court will be disinclined to interfere with a trial judge's exercise of his discretion save in a case where that exercise is unreasonable in the *Wednesbury* sense . . .

It is entirely for the judge to decide upon whether such a warning should be given to the jury, and, if it is to be given, the precise terms of the warning. These matters will depend upon the circumstances of the case before the judge and the degree to which the witness in question has been shown to be unreliable. Since the decision whether or not to give a warning under *Makanjuola* and the terms of such a warning are discretionary, it is very difficult to challenge a trial judge's decisions on the matter. The Court of Appeal was keen to highlight its disinclination to interfere with a trial judge's exercise of his discretion in this regard, and thus, the only possible challenge would be to judicially review the trial judge's decision on the basis that it was '*Wednesbury* unreasonable'.[26] This is a very high bar to reach since it involves showing that the decision of the trial judge was so unreasonable that no other reasonable tribunal would have ever reached that decision, and in subsequent authorities the Court of Appeal has refused to interfere with the exercise of trial judges' discretion for this very reason.[27] In light of this, it is of the utmost importance that counsel should ensure he has made his representations on the matter to the trial judge in the absence of the jury and before closing speeches and the judge's summing up as per point (4) in the extract from *R* v. *Makanjuola* above. In *R* v. *Walker*,[28] the Court of Appeal allowed an appeal on the basis that the trial judge did not give a *Makanjuola* warning in a rape case in which the complainant had retracted the allegation in a letter to the defendant. The Court was critical of the failure of counsel and the judge to consider the issue of such a warning together before closing speeches.

The Court of Appeal in *R* v. *Makanjuola* held that there must be some evidential basis upon which it is suggested that the witness is unreliable, and this cannot be based solely upon the fact that the witness is an accomplice or complainant of a sexual offence. While the categories of witnesses requiring a full corroboration warning by law have now been abrogated by statute, there are still some types of witness who are more likely to give unreliable testimony and in respect of whom a *Makanjuola* warning is likely to be required. The Court gave examples of witnesses who have lied or made previous false allegations, or where the witness is shown to hold a grudge against the defendant. In *R* v. *Muncaster*,[29] the Court of Appeal has subsequently held that the decision in *R* v. *Makanjuola* was not confined to the old categories of witnesses whose evidence required corroboration, but that the guidance provided by the Court was of general application. Where the trial judge does exercise his discretion to give a corroboration warning in accordance with *R* v. *Makanjuola*, the judge should identify any independent supporting evidence for the jury, and if there is no such evidence, then he should direct the jury that there is no independent supporting evidence.[30]

---

26 See *Associated Provincial Picture Houses Ltd* v. *Wednesbury Corporation* [1947] 2 All ER 680, HL.

27 See *R* v. *R* [1996] Crim LR 815, *R* v. *LJL* [1999] Crim LR 489 and *R* v. *Gregory* (2000) unreported, 28 February 2000, case no. 9904313 Y3, in which the Court of Appeal refused to interfere with the trial judges' exercise of discretion in each case on the basis that it had not been *Wednesbury* unreasonable.

28 [1996] Crim LR 742.

29 [1999] Crim LR 409.

30 In *R* v. *MB (Appeal Against Conviction)* [2000] Crim LR 181, the Court of Appeal held that the judge's failure to direct the jury that there was no independent supporting evidence could have resulted in the jury treating evidence improperly as corroborating evidence.

Cell confessions

Caution must usually be exercised where the prosecution case relies wholly or substantially on the evidence of an unrecorded confession by the defendant which is made to another prisoner while in a prison cell. Reliance on such a cell confession will usually warrant a *Makanjuola* warning. In *Benedetto* v. *R*,[31] the Privy Council recognised the potential for unreliability raised by reliance on a cell confession made to a prisoner who is awaiting trial and equated evidence of a cell confession to evidence of identification by an eyewitness, the unreliability of which has long been acknowledged:[32]

> evidence of the kind on which the Crown relies in this case, where an untried prisoner claims that a fellow untried prisoner confessed to him that he was guilty of the crime for which he was then being held in custody, raises an acute problem which will always call for special attention in view of the danger that it may lead to a miscarriage of justice.[33]

The Privy Council also drew attention to the significant distinction between evidence of cell confessions and eyewitness identification evidence and provided guidance to a trial judge on how to direct the jury in respect of such evidence.

BENEDETTO V. *R* [2003] UKPC 27
Lord Hope

32. The problem which is presented by cell confessions is, of course, different. In the case of identification evidence it is that a wholly honest and convincing witness who has sincerely convinced himself and whose sincerity carries conviction is not infrequently mistaken, and that the value of such evidence is notoriously difficult to assess . . . In the case of a cell confession it is that the evidence of a prison informer is inherently unreliable, in view of the personal advantage which such witnesses think they may obtain by providing information to the authorities. Witnesses who fall into this category tend to have no interest whatsoever in the proper course of justice. They are men who, as Simon Brown LJ put in *R v Bailey* [1993] 3 All ER 513, 523j, tend not to have shrunk from trickery and a good deal worse. And they will almost always have strong reasons of self-interest for seeking to ingratiate themselves with those who may be in a position to reward them for volunteering confession evidence. The prisoner against whom that evidence is given is always at a disadvantage. He is afforded none of the usual protections against the inaccurate recording or invention of words used by him when interviewed by the police. And it may be difficult for him to obtain all the information that is needed to expose fully the informer's bad character.

. . .

34. In *Pringle's case* [2003] UKPC 9 at [30] the Board recognised that it was not possible to lay down any fixed rules about the directions which the judge should give to a jury about the evidence which one prisoner gives against another prisoner about things done or said while they are both together in custody. But . . . a judge must always be alert to the possibility that the evidence by one prisoner against another is tainted by an improper motive, and the possibility that this may be so has to be regarded with

---

31 [2003] UKPC 27.
32 See Lord Bingham in *R* v. *Forbes* [2001] 1 AC 473 at 478–9, para. 6.
33 Per Lord Hope, [2003] UKPC 27 at [31].

particular care where a prisoner who has yet to face trial gives evidence that the other prisoner has confessed to the very crime for which he is being held in custody. The following guidance was then given:

> The indications that the evidence may be tainted by an improper motive must be found in the evidence. But this is not an exacting test, and the surrounding circumstances may provide all that is needed to justify the inference that he may have been serving his own interest in giving that evidence. Where such indications are present, the judge should draw the jury's attention to these indications and their possible significance. He should then advise them to be cautious before accepting the prisoner's evidence.

> 35. ... there are two steps which the judge must follow when undertaking this exercise ... The first is to draw the jury's attention to the indications that may justify the inference that the prisoner's evidence is tainted. The second is to advise the jury to be cautious before accepting his evidence ... it is the responsibility of the judge to examine the evidence for himself so that he can instruct the jury fully as to where these indications are to be found and as to their significance ... it is the responsibility of the judge to [explain] to the jury that they must be cautious before accepting and acting upon that evidence.

Not every case involving a cell confession will necessarily require a warning by the trial judge. From *Benedetto* v. *R* and *R* v. *Pringle*[34] it seems that a cell confession made to a prisoner with a criminal record or a motive to lie may warrant a warning, but there may be no need for a warning in a case which does not bear those characteristics. In *R* v. *Stone*,[35] the Court of Appeal stated that 'a summing-up should be tailored by the judge to the circumstances of the particular case', such that:

> If an alleged confession, for whatever reason, would not have been easy to invent, it would be absurd to require the judge to tell the jury that confessions are often easy to concoct. Similarly, ... in a case where the defence has deliberately not cross-examined the informant as to motive of hope of advantage, the law does not require the judge to tell the jury that, merely because the informant was a prisoner, there may have been such a motive.[36]

By the same token, where a prisoner who gives evidence of a cell confession is so discredited in cross-examination that the prosecution itself renounces the evidence, no special warning will be necessary. The case of *R* v. *Causley*[37] involved such evidence of cell confessions allegedly made to three convicts who were discredited in cross-examination. The trial judge's warning to the jury that they should be cautious in relying upon the evidence of these alleged confessions was held to be adequate, the Court of Appeal rejecting an appeal on the grounds that the direction did not warn of the dangers of convicting on the evidence of a convict in sufficiently strong terms. In a commentary on this case, Professor Birch notes that '[t]he present case provides a good example of a situation where a judicial warning of the need for caution was

---

34 [2003] UKPC 9.
35 [2005] EWCA Crim 105.
36 Ibid. at [84].
37 [1999] Crim LR 572.

rightly given even where any juror with half a brain could see that the witnesses were, individually and collectively, a most unreliable bunch'.[38] The decision was based upon the individual circumstances of the case and this was a case in which it would have been obvious to the jury that the evidence was unreliable because of the fact that it was so discredited in cross-examination to be renounced by the party relying on it. While cell confessions are potentially unreliable, there is no rule requiring a fixed care warning merely because a case involves such a confession. Whether a warning is appropriate or not is for the trial judge to determine and will depend upon the individual facts of the case. The 'need for great caution' when dealing with cell confessions and the need 'to direct the jury in clear terms to exercise caution when considering an alleged cell confession' was also recently acknowledged in the case of *R* v. *Nudds*.[39]

11.2.6 Mandatory care warning

Confessions by 'mentally handicapped' people

Under s. 77(1), Police and Criminal Evidence Act 1984, where the prosecution case depends wholly or substantially on the confession of a person who is mentally handicapped, and the confession was not made in the presence of an independent person,[40] the trial judge must warn the jury of the special need for caution before convicting the defendant on the basis of the confession. Section 77(2) applies to cases tried summarily and provides that where such a warning would be given under s. 77(1), the magistrates must treat the case as one in which there is a special need for caution before convicting the defendant on the basis of the confession.

S. 77, POLICE AND CRIMINAL EVIDENCE ACT 1984

(1) Without prejudice to the general duty of the court at a trial on indictment [with a jury] to direct the jury on any matter on which it appears to the court appropriate to do so, where at such a trial –

    (a) the case against the accused depends wholly or substantially on a confession by him; and

    (b) the court is satisfied –

        (i) that he is mentally handicapped; and

        (ii) that the confession was not made in the presence of an independent person,

the court shall warn the jury that there is special need for caution before convicting the accused in reliance on the confession, and shall explain that the need arises because of the circumstances mentioned in paragraphs (a) and (b) above.

(2) In any case where at the summary trial of a person for an offence it appears to the court that a warning under subsection (1) above would be required if the trial were on indictment [with a jury], the court shall treat the case as one in which there is a special need for caution before convicting the accused on his confession.

---

38 Ibid. at 573.
39 [2008] EWCA Crim 148 at [45], CA.
40 According to s. 77(3), PACE Act 1984, an '"independent person" does not include a police officer or a person employed for, or engaged on, police purposes'.

Cross-reference

Refer back to Chapter 5 on Confession evidence for a more detailed consideration of s. 77, PACE Act 1984 and for the meaning of 'mentally handicapped' under the Act.

11.3 VISUAL IDENTIFICATION EVIDENCE

Evidence of identification is notoriously unreliable. There have been numerous miscarriages of justice which have been caused by reliance on the evidence of an eyewitness or eyewitnesses who have mistakenly (albeit honestly) identified the defendant as the offender. These cases illustrate the problematic nature of identification evidence and provide some explanation for the special treatment afforded to identification evidence today, particularly where the case against the defendant is based wholly or substantially upon the accuracy of the identification evidence of an eyewitness whom the defendant alleges to be mistaken. Furthermore (and somewhat disconcertingly), the reliability of eyewitness identification evidence is not necessarily increased by multiple similar eyewitness accounts; some of the most notorious miscarriages of justice caused by unreliable eyewitness identification evidence have involved the testimony of numerous eyewitnesses. One notable example is the case of Adolf Beck who was mistakenly convicted twice of offences which he did not commit on the basis of eyewitness evidence.[41] In 1895, Beck was convicted of defrauding a woman of her jewellery after he was identified by eleven women as the man who had stolen their jewellery in a similar way. These women gave evidence at Beck's trial and he was convicted and sentenced to imprisonment. In 1904, after he had been released, Beck was again arrested on a similar charge. This time, he was identified by four women who claimed that Beck had defrauded them and he was again convicted on the basis of this identification evidence. However, shortly after Beck's conviction, the frauds started again and the real perpetrator, a man called John Smith, was apprehended. It later transpired that John Smith was responsible for the crimes for which Adolf Beck had been convicted both in 1895 and 1904 and that all fifteen witnesses as to identification in those previous trials had been mistaken. The case of Adolf Beck clearly illustrates the inherent unreliability of identification evidence, even by multiple eyewitnesses. This miscarriage of justice caused public outrage and an inquiry into the case was set up in 1904.[42] The case was also significant in that it led to the creation of the Court of Criminal Appeal in 1907.

The case of Adolf Beck was not an anomaly. After Beck's case, there were further miscarriages of justice which were also caused by reliance on the evidence of mistaken witnesses as to identification. In Scotland in 1909, Oscar Slater was wrongly convicted of murder on the basis of the evidence of mistaken identification of two witnesses who said they saw him leaving the scene of the murder, and twelve other witnesses placed him at the scene.[43] Slater served nearly twenty years in prison for a murder he did not commit before his conviction was quashed. In 1972,

---

41 E. R. Watson (ed.), *The Trial of Adolf Beck: Notable British Trials* (W. Hodge, 1924).

42 *Report of Committee of Inquiry into Case of Adolf Beck* (Cd. 2315, 1904), Parliamentary Papers, 1905, vol. LXII.

43 See A. C. Doyle, *The Case of Oscar Slater* (New York, 1912) and W. Roughead, *Trial of Oscar Slater* (W. Hodge, 1910).

Luke Dougherty was wrongly convicted of shoplifting on the mistaken identification evidence of two witnesses. It later transpired that Dougherty could not have committed the offence since he had an alibi which was corroborated by fifty other people. As police officers are professionally trained to have better skills of observation, they should, in theory at least, make more reliable eyewitnesses.[44] However, one infamous miscarriage of justice was caused by the mistaken identification evidence of police officer witnesses as well as civilian witnesses. In 1969, Lazlo Virag was convicted of stealing money from parking meters and using a firearm to resist arrest. Virag was wrongly identified by eight witnesses, five of whom were police officers. Virag was sent to prison and served five years before it was discovered that he was not the perpetrator.

11.3.1 Mistaken identification

In 1972, the Criminal Law Revision Committee acknowledged '[w]e regard mistaken identification as by far the greatest cause of actual or possible wrong convictions'.[45] The latter cases of Luke Dougherty and Lazlo Virag led to a Departmental Committee being set up to review the law on identification evidence. The Committee was chaired by Lord Devlin and it published a Report in 1976.[46] The problem with identification evidence was clearly explained in the Devlin Report.

THE DEVLIN REPORT (1976)

4.11 The strength of evidence of visual identification depends upon the power of recognition, that is, of observation and memory combined. It is obvious that the power of recognition will be greater if the witness is already familiar with the person he sees. Familiarity does not, however, do away with the problem entirely. It may mean that the witness's power to memorise a face can hardly be challenged, but his power of observation may be. A man is unlikely to be mistaken about a very familiar face at which he has had a good look, but he might be mistaken about it on a fleeting glimpse . . .

4.25 Our own view is that identification ought to be specially regarded by the law simply because it is evidence of a special character in that its reliability is exceptionally difficult to assess. It is impervious to the usual tests. The two ways of testing a witness are by the nature of his story – is it probable and coherent? – and by his demeanour – does he appear to be honest and reliable? . . . But in identification evidence there is no story; the issue rests upon a single piece of observation . . . If a man thinks he is a good memoriser and in fact is not, that fact will not show itself in his demeanour . . .

. . .

8.1 We are satisfied that in cases which depend wholly or mainly on eyewitness evidence of identification there is a special risk of wrong conviction. It arises because the value of such evidence is exceptionally difficult to assess; the witness who has sincerely convinced himself and whose sincerity carries conviction is not infrequently mistaken.

---

44 In *R* v. *Reid* [1990] 1 AC 363, it was acknowledged that the identification evidence of police officers can be just as unreliable as that of civilians.

45 Criminal Law Revision Committee on Evidence, 11th Report (1972) at para. 196.

46 Lord Devlin, *Report to the Secretary of State for the Home Department of the Departmental Committee on Evidence of Identification in Criminal Cases* (Cmnd. 338, HMSO, 1976) (the Devlin Report). Chapters 2 and 3 of the Report explore the cases of Luke Dougherty and Lazlo Virag respectively.

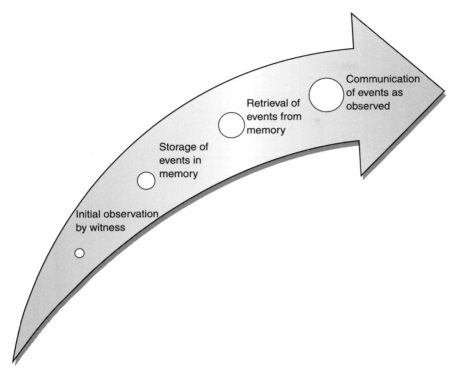

Figure 11.1 Factors affecting accuracy of identification evidence

A significant problem with eyewitness identification evidence lies in the difficulty in challenging the evidence in cross-examination. This is particularly true in the case of an honest but mistaken witness, and even more so in the case of such a witness who is confident in his or her evidence. The miscarriages of justice discussed above illustrate the consequences of reliance on mistaken identification evidence. Much psychological research has been carried out into the reasons why eyewitness identification evidence is so inherently unreliable.[47] There are several factors which could potentially affect the accuracy of identification evidence, and these include factors which relate to observation, memory and retrieval, and finally, communication (see Figure 11.1).

1. Observation – reliable identification evidence first requires that the witness's initial observation of the perpetrator is accurate.
2. Memory and retrieval – once the observation has taken place, the accuracy of the evidence will depend upon the witness's ability to remember what he has seen. This includes the ability to

---

47 For example, see B. L. Cutler and S. D. Penrod, *Mistaken Identification: The Eyewitness, Psychology, and the Law* (Cambridge University Press, 1995), D. B. Fishmann and E. F. Loftus, 'Expert psychological testimony on eyewitness identification' (1978) 4 *Law & Psychology Review* 87, E. F. Loftus, 'Unconscious transference in eyewitness identification' (1976) 2 *Law & Psychology Review* 93, E. F. Loftus, D. Wolchover and D. Page, 'General review of the psychology of witness testimony' in A. Heaton-Armstrong, E. Shepherd, G. Gudjonsson and D. Wolchover (eds.), *Witness Testimony Psychological, Investigative and Evidential Perspectives* (Oxford University Press, 2006).

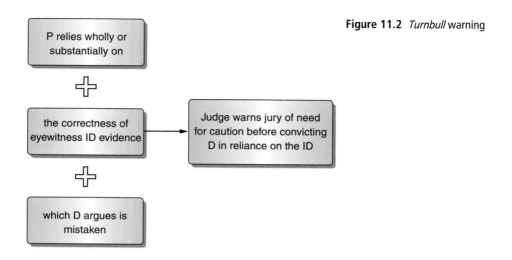

Figure 11.2 *Turnbull* warning

store the memory and its details, as well as the ability to retrieve that memory when required, and often some time after the initial observation has taken place.

3. Communication – finally, accurate and reliable identification evidence also requires that the witness is able to communicate the events in such a way that they accurately reflect the initial observation.

In light of the inherent unreliability of eyewitness identification evidence, it is necessary to ensure that there are sufficient safeguards in place to protect against the risk of miscarriages of justice. To this end, the common law has developed a special warning which is given in cases in which the prosecution case is wholly or substantially dependent upon identification evidence which the defendant argues is mistaken. This is known as a '*Turnbull* warning' and will be discussed below.

11.3.2 *Turnbull* guidelines

The leading authority on dealing with cases involving eyewitness identification evidence is *R* v. *Turnbull*.[48] The case of *Turnbull* provides the trial judge with guidelines on how to deal with identification cases and on the warning that the judge should give the jury in such cases (see Figure 11.2). A *Turnbull* warning is not given in every case involving an identification of the defendant by an eyewitness. *Turnbull* warnings are reserved for cases in which the prosecution relies either wholly or substantially upon the correctness of identification evidence of one or more eyewitnesses whom the defendant argues is or are mistaken. In such cases, the trial judge should warn the jury of the special need for caution before convicting the defendant in reliance on the correctness of the identification. In *R* v. *Turnbull*, Lord Widgery CJ stated that the risk of miscarriages of justice can be reduced if trial judges were to sum up to juries as follows:

---

48 [1977] QB 224.

R V. TURNBULL [1977] QB 224
Lord Widgery CJ

[at 228]

First, whenever the case against an accused depends wholly or substantially on the correctness of one or more identifications of the accused which the defence alleges to be mistaken, the judge should warn the jury of the special need for caution before convicting the accused in reliance on the correctness of the identification or identifications. In addition he should instruct them as to the reason for the need for such a warning and should make some reference to the possibility that a mistaken witness can be a convincing one and that a number of such witnesses can all be mistaken. Provided this is done in clear terms the judge need not use any particular form of words.

Secondly, the judge should direct the jury to examine closely the circumstances in which the identification by each witness came to be made. How long did the witness have the accused under observation? At what distance? In what light? Was the observation impeded in any way, as for example by passing traffic or a press of people? Had the witness ever seen the accused before? How often? If only occasionally, had he any special reason for remembering the accused? How long elapsed between the original observation and the subsequent identification to the police? Was there any material discrepancy between the description of the accused given to the police by the witness when first seen by them and his actual appearance? If in any case, whether it is being dealt with summarily or on indictment, the prosecution have reason to believe that there is such a material discrepancy they should supply the accused or his legal advisers with particulars of the description the police were first given. In all cases if the accused asks to be given particulars of such descriptions, the prosecution should supply them. Finally, he should remind the jury of any specific weaknesses which had appeared in the identification evidence.

As can be seen from the extract above, Lord Widgery CJ also stated that the judge should direct the jury that a mistaken witness can be a convincing one. The jury should be reminded that a witness as to identification can be honest, convinced as to what they have seen, as well as convincing in the evidence that they give, but yet mistaken.[49] The cases of Adolf Beck, Oscar Slater, Luke Dougherty, Lazlo Virag, and many others, all illustrate that multiple witnesses can all be mistaken and the trial should remind the jury of this fact. After this, Lord Widgery CJ states that the trial judge should then examine the circumstances of the identification (see below).

Cases of recognition
It might be thought that where an eyewitness identifies a person whom he knows well, possibly even a relative, such recognition is more reliable. While this may be true, Lord Widgery CJ also pointed out that it is important to warn jurors that while cases of recognition may be more reliable than cases in which the witness has identified a stranger, nevertheless this should not be taken to mean that cases of recognition need no warning. People do make mistakes in cases of recognition, and even when recognising close relatives and friends; thus, such cases also fall within the scope of a *Turnbull* warning.

---

49 This was reiterated in the Privy Council by Lord Griffiths in *Scott* v. *R* [1989] AC 1242.

R V. *TURNBULL* [1977] QB 224
Lord Widgery CJ

[at 228]

Recognition may be more reliable than identification of a stranger; but even when the witness is purporting to recognise someone whom he knows, the jury should be reminded that mistakes in recognition of close relatives and friends are sometimes made.

In *R* v. *Ley*,[50] Scott Baker LJ pointed out that there are varying degrees of recognition and that '[t]he degree of familiarity of the witness with the person he or she is identifying is very relevant just as are the circumstances of the identification itself'.[51]

Quality of the evidence
Whether or not the evidence of identification will be left for the jury to consider depends primarily upon the quality of the evidence. This is a matter for the trial judge to determine. Lord Widgery CJ gave guidance on the approach to be taken by the trial judge.

R V. *TURNBULL* [1977] QB 224
Lord Widgery CJ

[at 228–30]

If the quality is good and remains good at the close of the accused's case, the danger of a mistaken identification is lessened; but the poorer the quality, the greater the danger.

In our judgment when the quality is good, as for example when the identification is made after a long period of observation, or in satisfactory conditions by a relative, a neighbour, a close friend, a workmate and the like, the jury can safely be left to assess the value of the identifying evidence even though there is no other evidence to support it: provided always, however, that an adequate warning has been given about the special need for caution. Were the courts to adjudge otherwise, affronts to justice would frequently occur.

. . .

When, in the judgment of the trial judge, the quality of the identifying evidence is poor, as for example when it depends solely on a fleeting glance or on a longer observation made in difficult conditions, the situation is very different. The judge should then withdraw the case from the jury and direct an acquittal unless there is other evidence which goes to support the correctness of the identification.

Thus, the first task of the trial judge is to make an assessment of the quality of the evidence based upon factors such as whether the evidence depends solely on a fleeting glance,[52] and the

---

50   [2007] 1 Cr App R 25.
51   Ibid. at para. 19.
52   The guidelines laid down in *R* v. *Turnbull* were designed to deal precisely with cases in which the identification was made on the basis of a fleeting glance: per Lord Widgery CJ in *R* v. *Oakwell* [1978] 1 WLR 32.

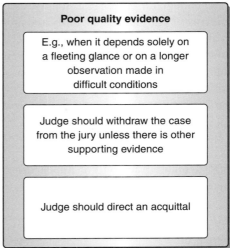

Figure 11.3 *Turnbull* warning: assessing the quality of the identification evidence

circumstances of the observation by the witness (see Figure 11.3). Factors affecting the circumstances of the observation were mentioned in an earlier extract and include:

- the length of time that the accused was in the witness's view,
- the distance between the accused and the witness,
- the light at the time,
- whether or not the observation was impeded by anything,
- whether or not the witness had seen the accused before,
- the lapse of time between the original observation and the identification,
- the discrepancy between the first description of the accused given to police by the witness and the actual appearance of the accused.

Where the trial judge takes the view that the quality of the identification evidence is good, then he may safely leave the jury to assess the value of the evidence, even if there is no independent supporting evidence. He should also be sure to warn the jury about the special need for caution in convicting the defendant on the basis of such evidence. However, if the trial judge determines that the quality of the identifying evidence is poor, then the judge should withdraw the case from the jury and direct an acquittal, unless there is other corroborating evidence which supports the correctness of the identification. Where the quality of the identification evidence is poor but there is other supporting evidence, then the trial judge can leave the case to be determined by the jury and there is no general duty on the judge to direct the jury not to convict the defendant solely on the basis of the identification evidence.[53]

The trial judge also has a duty to remind the jury of any specific weaknesses in the identification evidence, and a failure to do so may lead to the conviction being quashed.[54] It

53 *R* v. *Ley* [2007] 1 Cr App R 25 at para. 31.
54 *R* v. *Irvin* [2007] EWCA Crim 2701.

is not enough for the judge to simply refer to counsel's submissions about the weaknesses in the evidence.[55] The judge 'must fairly and properly summarise for the jury such specific weaknesses as arguably are exposed by the evidence'.[56] Finally, according to *R* v. *Turnbull*, the trial judge should point out to the jury any evidence which is capable of supporting the evidence of identification. He should also inform the jury if there is any evidence which the jury might think was supporting evidence but which in fact is not. Where a trial judge significantly fails to follow the *Turnbull* guidelines, any conviction will be quashed on appeal.[57]

11.3.3 Description evidence

In *R* v. *Gayle*,[58] the Court of Appeal drew a distinction between evidence of identification and mere evidence of description.

> ### *R* V. *GAYLE* [1999] 2 CR APP R 130
> **Henry LJ**
>
> [at 135]
>
> [There is a] qualitative difference between identification evidence and what the judge called 'evidence of description'. The special need for caution before conviction on identification evidence is because, as experience has often shown, it is possible for an honest witness to make a mistaken identification. But the danger of an honest witness being mistaken as to distinctive clothing, or the general description of the person he saw (short or tall, black or white etc., or the direction in which he was going) are minimal. So the jury can concentrate on the honesty of the witness, in the ordinary way.

Since the risk of a miscarriage of justice is lower with evidence of description, there is no need in such cases for the trial judge to follow *R* v. *Turnbull* and warn the jury of the special need for caution before convicting the defendant on the basis of that evidence.

11.4 IDENTIFICATION PROCEDURES

There are specific identification procedures which must be followed by the police in cases in which the identity of the perpetrator is disputed. Code D[59] of Codes of Practice which are issued under s. 66 of the Police and Criminal Evidence Act 1984 provides guidance to the police on identification procedures. Paragraph 1.1 states that Code D 'concerns the principal methods used by police to identify people in connection with the investigation of offences and the keeping of accurate and reliable criminal records'. Paragraph 1.2 provides that 'identification

---

55 *R* v. *Fergus* (1994) 98 Cr App R 313.
56 Ibid. at 321.
57 *R* v. *Reid* [1990] 1 AC 363.
58 [1999] 2 Cr App R 130.
59 The latest version of Code D came into effect on 7 March 2011 and can be found at www.gov.uk/government/publications/pace-code-d-2011 (accessed on 19 July 2014).

by an eyewitness arises when a witness who has seen the offender committing the crime and is given an opportunity to identify a person suspected of involvement in the offence in a video identification, identification parade or similar procedure' and sets out the purpose of the identification procedures, which are:

- to test the witness's ability to identify the suspect as the person they saw on a previous occasion, and
- to provide safeguards against mistaken identification.

In cases in which an eyewitness witnesses the offender committing the offence or sees them shortly thereafter or close to the scene of the crime, the first description given by the eyewitness must be recorded.[60] Code D is divided into three alternative scenarios, dealing with (1) suspects who are not known, (2) suspects who are known and available, and (3) suspects who are known but not available.

11.4.1 Identity of the suspect not known

Where the identity of the suspect is not known, the police may take the witness to a particular place in the local area to see if they are able to identify the suspect.[61] The police must take care not to draw the witness's attention to any particular individual. If the identity of the suspect is not known to the police, the witness may be shown photographs, computerised images or artist's sketches.[62]

11.4.2 Suspect known and available

In cases in which the suspect is known to the police and available for an identification procedure to be carried out, then one of three procedures will take place, namely a video identification, an identification parade or a group identification.[63] An identification procedure must be held whenever there is an eyewitness who has identified or purported to identify a suspect before an identification procedure has been held, or there is a witness who has not yet had an opportunity to identify the suspect and the suspect disputes the eyewitness evidence, unless holding an identification procedure would not be practicable or would serve no useful purpose.[64] This mandatory obligation on the police to hold an identification procedure where the eyewitness evidence is disputed was introduced into Code D after the House of Lords' decision in *R* v. *Forbes*.[65] An identification officer is responsible for arranging and conducting the identification procedure. An identification officer is an officer who is not below the rank of inspector and who is not involved in the investigation.[66] In choosing which procedure to use, it is important to note that these procedures form a hierarchy; so, the procedure which should be

---

60 Code D, para. 3.1.
61 Code D, para. 3.2.
62 Code D, para. 3.3.
63 Code D, para. 3.4.
64 Code D, para. 3.12.
65 [2001] 1 AC 473, HL.
66 Code D, para. 3.11.

considered first is a video identification. A video identification should be used unless it is not practicable, or an identification parade is both practicable and more suitable,[67] or if a group identification is more suitable than either a video identification or an identification parade and practicable to arrange.[68]

Video identification

A video identification is where the police show the witness moving images of the defendant along with moving images of at least eight other people resembling the defendant so far as possible in age, general appearance and position in life.[69] Any unusual features of the suspect, such as a visible scar, may be either hidden on the defendant and in the same place on each of the other people or replicated on the other people.[70] The moving images should show the people and suspect performing the same sequence of movements or in the same positions and under identical conditions.[71] The suspect's solicitor must have a reasonable opportunity to see the images before they are shown to the witness and any objections should, if practicable, be acted upon. If it is not practicable to so do, this should be recorded.[72] All aspects of the video identification should be documented. In recent years, video identifications have become more commonplace than identification parades (which used to be the preferred method of identification). This is largely due to the relative ease of putting together a group of video clips of people with a similar appearance to the suspect from a bank of videos, compared to the difficulty of finding participants for an identification parade who bear enough of a similarity to the suspect.

Identification parade

An identification parade is where the police present to the witness a parade of at least eight people in addition to the suspect, who resemble the suspect in age, height, general appearance and position in life.[73] Any unusual features of the suspect, such as a visible scar, may be either hidden on the defendant and in the same place on each of the other people or replicated on the other people. Where the feature may not be replicated on the other people, then the feature should be hidden on all participants in the parade, for instance by using a plaster or a hat.[74] The suspect must be shown the participants in the parade before the witness see the line-up and the suspect may make objections to any person or anything else in the parade. Any reasonable objections should be acted upon, unless it is not practicable to so do, in which case this should be recorded.[75] The suspect may select his own position in the line-up.[76] The identification parade should usually be videoed.[77]

---

67 Code D, para. 3.14.
68 Code D, para. 3.16.
69 Code D, Annex A, para. 2.
70 Code D, Annex A, para. 2A. Where features of the people in the moving images need to be concealed or added to, the images should be altered electronically.
71 Code D, Annex A, para. 3.
72 Code D, Annex A, para. 7.
73 Code D, Annex B, para. 9.
74 Code D, Annex B, para. 10.
75 Code D, Annex B, para. 12.
76 Code D, Annex B, para. 13.
77 Code D, Annex B, para. 23.

Group identification

A group identification is where the police place the suspect in a group of people who are passing by or waiting around informally in a specific location, such as a shopping centre or at a railway station.[78] The witness is taken to the location and is asked if they can see the suspect. Group identifications can take place either with the suspect's consent or covertly without their consent.[79] In selecting a location, consideration must be given to the general appearance of people present and the likely numbers of people present.[80] After the group identification has taken place, a photograph or video should be taken of the scene of the group identification.[81] Where the suspect does consent to the group identification, the suspect shall have a reasonable opportunity to have a solicitor present.[82]

11.4.3 Suspect known but not available

Where the identity of the suspect is known to the police but the suspect is not available, the identification officer may hold a video identification, using either moving or still images. The images or video footage may be obtained covertly if necessary.[83] If neither a video identification, identification procedure nor group identification are practicable, the identification officer may arrange a confrontation.[84] A confrontation is only used as a last resort. This is where the suspect is directly confronted by the witness. The consent of the suspect is not required. Any confrontation must take place in the presence of the suspect's solicitor unless this would cause reasonable delay.[85] The confrontation will take place in the police station[86] and the witness must be told in advance that the person they saw may or may not be the person they are to confront.[87]

11.4.4 Breaches of Code D

Where the police fail to follow the identification procedures set out in Code D, this may lead to the exclusion of identification evidence at trial under s. 78, PACE Act 1984. Evidence will only be excluded if its admission would have such an adverse effect on the fairness of the proceedings that it ought not to be admitted. Whether or not evidence will be excluded will depend upon the circumstances of each individual case.[88] A breach of Code D will not automatically lead to the exclusion of evidence, and the Court of Appeal is generally reluctant to interfere with the exercise of a trial judge's discretion unless it is *Wednesbury* unreasonable. In *R* v. *Quinn*,[89] the

---

78 Code D, Annex C, para. 4.
79 Code D, Annex C, para. 2.
80 Code D, Annex C, para. 6.
81 Code D, Annex C, para. 8.
82 Code D, Annex C, para. 13.
83 Code D, para. 3.21.
84 Code D, para. 3.23.
85 Code D, Annex D, para. 4.
86 Code D, Annex D, para. 6.
87 Code D, Annex D, para. 1.
88 See *R* v. *Forbes* [2001] 1 AC 473 at 487 and *R* v. *Popat (No. 2)* [2000] 1 Cr App R 387.
89 [1995] 1 Cr App R 480.

Court of Appeal was not prepared to rule that the trial judge's decision not to exclude the evidence under s. 78 was *Wednesbury* unreasonable, despite the fact that there were several breaches of Code D. The Court held that in directing the jury, the trial judge should have specifically referred to the breaches and then left it to the jury to decide how they would approach these. This was approved by the House of Lords in *R* v. *Forbes*[90] in which Lord Bingham stated:

> In any case where a breach of Code D has been established but the trial judge has rejected an application to exclude evidence to which the defence objected because of that breach, the trial judge should in the course of summing up to the jury (a) explain that there has been a breach of the Code and how it has arisen, and (b) invite the jury to consider the possible effect of that breach.[91]

Cross-reference

Refer to Chapter 6 on improperly obtained evidence for a more detailed discussion on the application of s. 78, PACE Act 1984 and the types of illegality or impropriety which is required in order for a judge to exercise his discretion to exclude evidence under s. 78.

A more drastic alternative to excluding the evidence under s. 78 is to halt the trial. This occurred in *R* v. *Finley*,[92] in which numerous cumulative and seemingly deliberate breaches of Code D led the Court of Appeal to rule that the trial judge should not have left the case to the jury since it was inherently weak. The Court quashed the defendant's conviction because justice was not seen to have been done and the case ought to have been stopped at the close of the prosecution's case.

11.5   OTHER FORMS OF IDENTIFICATION EVIDENCE

While much of this chapter has focused on visual identification evidence and accompanying the identification procedures under Code D, there are other forms of identification evidence which may also raise issues regarding reliability. Suspects may instead be identified by their voice, through photographs or CCTV evidence, via their fingerprints, palm prints or even ear prints, or via a DNA comparison. These forms of identification evidence are discussed briefly below.

11.5.1 Voice identification

Evidence of the identification of a suspect by his voice[93] carries a significant risk of miscarriage of justice and is more difficult than visual identification.[94] The risk of misidentification is higher

---

90 [2001] 1 AC 473.
91 Ibid. at 488, para. 27.
92 [1993] Crim LR 50.
93 See D. Ormerod, 'Sounds familiar? Voice identification evidence' [2001] Crim LR 595 and D. Ormerod, 'Sounding out expert voice identification' [2002] Crim LR 771.
94 *R* v. *R (David Anthony)* [2000] Crim LR 183.

when the listener is a lay listener (as opposed to an expert in voice recognition) and where the quality of the recording is poor. In England and Wales, voice recognition evidence by an expert is generally admissible in court and the evidence of a lay listener would only be admissible as factual evidence, and not as evidence of opinion.[95] In *R* v. *O'Doherty*[96] (an appeal from Northern Ireland), the Court of Appeal distinguished between forms of voice analysis. The Court held that expert evidence would only generally be admissible if it were supported by acoustic analysis and that no prosecution should be brought in Northern Ireland if it is based only on auditory analysis evidence which is in itself inadmissible. In the more recent case of *R* v. *Flynn*,[97] the Court of Appeal held that the key to determining whether evidence of voice identification evidence should be admissible or not is the degree of familiarity of the witness with the suspect's voice.[98] Thus, where a lay listener is more familiar with the voice of the suspect, the evidence of voice recognition is more likely to be admissible. In order to safeguard against miscarriages of justice, the Court also held that where the prosecution seek to rely on evidence of voice recognition it is desirable that an expert should be instructed to provide an opinion on the identification. Finally, the Court held that the jury must be carefully directed so as to warn them of the dangers of misidentification. In *R* v. *Hersey*,[99] the Court of Appeal held that the jury should be directed along the lines of the *Turnbull* direction given in visual identification cases: the trial judge should warn the jury about the risks of misidentification, should point out to the jury the fact that an honest witness might be mistaken, and the reasons why they might be mistaken, as well as the strengths and weaknesses in the evidence.[100]

11.5.2 Photographs and video evidence

In some cases, the prosecution might seek to adduce photographic or video evidence of the offence or offender, such as from security cameras or CCTV cameras.[101] Such evidence is admissible in evidence because it is relevant to whether the offence was committed, and the identity of the offender.[102] The prosecution might show the jury the photographs or footage and invite them to conclude that the person in the photographs or footage is the defendant. In such cases, the jury members are not acting as experts, but they 'are called upon to do no more than the average person in domestic, social and other situations does from time to time, namely to say whether he is sure that a person shown in a photograph is the person he is then at'.[103] While a full *Turnbull* direction is not necessary, the jury should be warned about the risk of mistaken identification[104] and should be told to consider whether the appearance of the defendant has

---

95 *R* v. *Robb* (1991) 93 Cr App R 161.
96 [2003] 1 Cr App R 5.
97 [2008] 2 Cr App R 20.
98 Also see *R* v. *R (David Anthony)* [2000] Crim LR 183.
99 [1998] Crim LR 281.
100 See also *R* v. *Chenia* [2002] EWCA Crim 2345.
101 R. Costigan, 'Identification from CCTV: the risk of injustice' [2007] Crim LR 591.
102 *R* v. *Dodson and Williams* [1984] 1 WLR 971.
103 Ibid. at 979.
104 *R* v. *Blenkinsop* [1995] 1 Cr App R 7.

changed or not since the photograph was taken or the footage recorded.[105] According to Watkins LJ:

> ... the quality of the photographs, the extent of the exposure of the facial features of the person photographed, evidence, or the absence of it, of a change in a defendant's appearance and the opportunity a jury has to look at a defendant in the dock and over what period of time are factors, among other matters of relevance in this context in a particular case, which the jury must receive guidance upon from the judge when he directs them as to how they should approach the task of resolving this crucial issue.[106]

In *Attorney General's Reference (No. 2 of 2002)*,[107] the Court of Appeal summarised the law on the circumstances in which photographic evidence is admissible from which the jury could be invited to conclude that the defendant is the person in the photograph.

ATTORNEY GENERAL'S REFERENCE (NO. 2 OF 2002) [2002] EWCA CRIM 2373
Rose LJ

[at [19]]

In our judgment, on the authorities, there are, as it seems to us, at least four circumstances in which, subject to the judicial discretion to exclude, evidence is admissible to show and, subject to appropriate directions in the summing-up, a jury can be invited to conclude that the defendant committed the offence on the basis of a photographic image from the scene of the crime:

(i)   where the photographic image is sufficiently clear, the jury can compare it with the defendant sitting in the dock (*Dodson and Williams*);

(ii)   where a witness knows the defendant sufficiently well to recognise him as the offender depicted in the photographic image, he can give evidence of this (*Fowden and White, Kajala v Noble, Grimer, Caldwell and Dixon and Blenkinsop*); and this may be so even if the photographic image is no longer available for the jury (*Taylor v Chief Constable of Chester*);

(iii) where a witness who does not know the defendant spends substantial time viewing and analysing photographic images from the scene, thereby acquiring special knowledge which the jury does not have, he can give evidence of identification based on a comparison between those images and a reasonably contemporary photograph of the defendant, provided that the images and the photograph are available to the jury (*Clare and Peach*);

(iv)   a suitably qualified expert with facial mapping skills can give opinion evidence of identification based on a comparison between images from the scene (whether expertly enhanced or not) and a reasonably contemporary photograph of the defendant, provided the images and the photograph are available for the jury (*R. v Stockwell (1993) 97 Cr App R 260, R. v Clarke [1995] 2 Cr App R 425 and R. v Hookway [1999] Crim LR 750*).

---

105 Above (n. 102).
106 Ibid. at 979.
107 [2002] EWCA Crim 2373.

These days, personal information about people is more readily available in the public domain through social media websites, such as Facebook, Twitter and YouTube. People post both photographs and video footage of themselves online and these may be viewed by the broader public. In the case of *R* v. *Alexander*,[108] the identification of the defendant had taken place informally through Facebook when two prosecution witnesses in the case went through Facebook to look for the profiles of the offenders. The Court of Appeal held that evidence of the identification through Facebook was not necessarily invalid, but the fact that this informal identification procedure was not properly documented was a clear disadvantage to the defendants. The evidence was admissible and it was for the jury to decide upon its reliability after proper directions from the trial judge. The Court acknowledged that there is likely to be an increase in this type of identification via social networking websites and that the police should ensure that they obtain as much detail as possible about the identification, including the available images that were examined and a statement as to what occurred.

11.5.3 Facial mapping evidence

Where photographic evidence or video footage is adduced at court and identification is in issue, a facial mapping expert may be called to give expert evidence to assist the jury.[109] Evidence of facial mapping may be relied upon in support of other evidence or it might be the sole evidence in the case.[110] An expert in facial mapping may give opinion evidence of his comparison of the images and a photograph of the accused, but it must be made clear to the jury that this is the subjective opinion of the expert.[111] As facial mapping is a relatively new technique of identification, the trial judge should ensure that he warns the jury that caution should be exercised when evaluating the expert's evidence.[112]

11.5.4 Lip reading evidence

Where there is video evidence from which a lip reading expert is able to deduce what is being said by the people in the video, that evidence is admissible in court. However, the trial judge must warn the jury as to its limitations and the inherent risks of error.[113]

11.5.5 Identification by fingerprints, palm prints, shoe prints, ear prints, etc.

Fingerprints and palm prints have long been used as a form of identification. Each person has a unique fingerprint, which remains the same throughout their life. In light of this, the courts have accepted evidence of identification by fingerprints as the sole evidence to prove the identity of the suspect.[114] Evidence of identification by fingerprints must be given by an expert witness

---

108 [2013] 1 Cr App R 26.
109 See *R* v. *Stockwell* (1993) 97 Cr App R 260 and *R* v. *Clarke* [1995] 2 Cr App R 425.
110 See *R* v. *H (Stephen James) (A juvenile)* [1999] Crim LR 750 and *R* v. *Mitchell* [2005] EWCA Crim 731.
111 *R* v. *Atkins* [2010] 1 Cr App R 8.
112 *R* v. *Gardner* [2004] EWCA Crim 1639.
113 *R* v. *Luttrell* [2004] 2 Cr App R 31.
114 *R* v. *Castleton* (1910) 3 Cr App R 74.

and the jury must be warned that the evidence does not conclusively prove that the defendant is guilty of the offence.[115] As with any expert evidence, the jury is free to accept or reject the evidence of an expert as they see fit. A fingerprint comparison is conducted by looking for similarities in the ridge characteristics between two fingerprints. The admissibility of fingerprint evidence will depend upon the degree of similarity between the fingerprints of the defendant and the fingerprints found at the scene of the crime.[116] Other factors which might affect the admissibility of the fingerprint evidence are the size of the fingerprint from the scene of the crime and the quality and clarity of the fingerprint.[117] In *R* v. *Smith*,[118] the Court of Appeal observed that a precondition to being on the Home Office register of fingerprint experts was that the expert must have undertaken a training course run by the police. The Court held that the court, not the police, is the arbiter of who is a competent fingerprint expert. A defendant should have access to independent fingerprint experts who have not been trained by the police.

Other prints from which a defendant might be identified are the impressions made by the shoes of the offender. While an expert in footwear impressions could give evidence of his opinion as to the similarity of such impressions based upon his experience, the Court of Appeal has disapproved of the use of mathematical formulae to reach likelihood ratios on the basis that this method was unreliable. The Court considered that there were too many variables and uncertainties in such a calculation.[119]

Even ear prints left at the scene of a crime have been used as a method of identification. In *R* v. *Kempster (No. 2)*,[120] the Court of Appeal held that the evidence of an expert in ear prints comparison is admissible at court. However, the evidence of an identification by ear print evidence would only be probative of identification where the minutiae of the ear print ('the small anatomical features such as notches, nodules or creases in the ear structure') can be identified and matched or where the gross features ('the main cartilaginous folds') of the ear print provide a precise match.

11.5.6 Dock identifications

In television dramas involving a court scene, there is often a dramatic moment when the witness giving evidence is asked 'do you see the attacker in this room today?' and the witness replies, 'yes, it was him' while pointing to the defendant in the dock. This is known as a dock identification and this procedure is not generally permitted to take place as a first identification.

---

115 *R* v. *Buckley* (1999) 163 JP 561.

116 Until relatively recently, sixteen matching points of ridge characteristics were usually required to prove with certainty that a fingerprint from the scene matched the defendant's fingerprint. In *R* v. *Buckley* (1999) 163 JP 561, it was stated that at least eight matching points were usually required before a judge would exercise his discretion to admit the fingerprint evidence. However, by 2001 a non-numerical approach to fingerprint comparison was adopted by the Association of Chief Police Officers whereby a fingerprint officer would carry out the identification and this would then be checked by two others who are fingerprint experts: see *R* v. *Smith* [2011] 2 Cr App R 16.

117 Above (n. 114).

118 [2011] 2 Cr App R 16.

119 *R* v. *T* [2011] 1 Cr App R 9.

120 [2008] 2 Cr App R 19.

The reason for this is because dock identifications are very prejudicial to the defendant. In *R* v. *Johnson*,[121] Lord Woolf CJ explained this further:

> ... if someone is seen in the dock of a court and is identified, or if the person is identified on an identification parade, it is very easy subsequently not to be identifying the person originally observed at the scene of the crime, but the person seen in the circumstances just described. For that reason the practice of identification at court is now frowned upon. Dock identifications are not normally to be permitted in the course of proceedings.[122]

11.6 LIES AND THE *LUCAS* DIRECTION

Where a defendant tells lies about matters relating to the offence charged (e.g. where he provides a false alibi), the prosecution might seek to rely on the fact that he has lied to support the case that the defendant is guilty of the offence, or the jury might seek to infer that the defendant is guilty from the lies. However, just because a defendant has told lies about the offence does not automatically mean that he is guilty. The courts have acknowledged that there are a variety of reasons why a defendant might tell lies:

> Defendants in criminal cases may have lied for many reasons, for example to bolster a true defence. They may feel that they are wrongly implicated and although innocent that nobody will believe them and so they lie just to conceal matters which look bad but which in truth are not bad. They may lie to protect someone else. They may lie because they are embarrassed or ashamed about other conduct of theirs which is not the offence charged. They may lie out of panic or confusion. All sorts of reasons.[123]

Consequently, careful directions must be given to the jury about how they should approach lies told by the defendant and when such lies may be used to corroborate evidence of guilt. The leading authority on this is the case of *R* v. *Lucas*[124] and the direction given to the jury is known as a '*Lucas* direction'. In *R* v. *Goodway*, the Court of Appeal held that *Lucas* was of general application in any case in which lies told by the defendant are or may be used as evidence to support the defendant's guilt.[125] Thus, where the prosecution relies on lies told by the defendant, or where such lies might be used by the jury to support the prosecution case that the defendant is guilty (as opposed to being mere evidence as to the credibility of the defendant),[126] a *Lucas* direction should be given.[127]

---

121 [2001] 1 Cr App R 26.
122 Ibid. at para. 17.
123 Per Auld J in *R* v. *Burge and Pegg* (1993) at Winchester Crown Court, reported in [1996] 1 Cr App R 163.
124 [1981] QB 720.
125 *R* v. *Goodway* (1994) 98 Cr App R 11 at 17.
126 Where the defendant's lies go only to the credibility of the defendant, a *Lucas* direction is not needed: see *R* v. *Smith* [1995] Crim LR 305.
127 *R* v. *Burge and Pegg* [1996] 1 Cr App R 163, followed in *R* v. *Williams* [2012] EWCA Crim 2516.

> ### R V. LUCAS [1981] QB 720
> ### Lord Lane CJ
>
> [at 724]
>
> To be capable of amounting to corroboration the lie told out of court must first of all be deliberate. Secondly it must relate to a material issue. Thirdly the motive for the lie must be a realisation of guilt and a fear of the truth. The jury should in appropriate cases be reminded that people sometimes lie, for example, in an attempt to bolster up a just cause, or out of shame or out of a wish to conceal disgraceful behaviour from their family. Fourthly the statement must be clearly shown to be a lie by evidence other than that of the accomplice who is to be corroborated, that is to say by admission or by evidence from an independent witness.
>
> As a matter of good sense it is difficult to see why, subject to the same safeguards, lies proved to have been told in court by a defendant should not equally be capable of providing corroboration. In other common law jurisdictions they are so treated . . .

In *R* v. *Goodway*,[128] the Court also stated that:

> The jury must be satisfied that there is no innocent motive for the lie and should be reminded that people sometimes lie, for example, in an attempt to bolster a just cause, or out of shame, or out of a wish to conceal disgraceful behaviour.

Thus, a trial judge must direct the jury that if they wish to rely on lies told by the defendant to support evidence of the defendant's guilt, they must be satisfied that:

- the lie is deliberate,
- it relates to a material issue,
- there is no innocent motive for the lie – the motive for the lie must be a realisation of guilt (the jury should be reminded that people sometimes lie for a number of reasons, such as, in an attempt to bolster a just cause, or out of shame, or out of a wish to conceal disgraceful behaviour, or out of a desire to protect another person), and
- the statement must be clearly shown to be a lie by other evidence (e.g. by an admission or by the evidence of an independent witness).

A *Lucas* direction should not be given in every case in which the defendant gives evidence, even if the jury considers that the defendant has lied about one or more matters. In *R* v. *Burge and Pegg*,[129] the Court of Appeal held that a *Lucas* direction should not be given in a 'normal case where there is a straight conflict of evidence' and that if a *Lucas* direction was given in such a case, it would 'add complexity and do more harm than good'.[130] A *Lucas* direction should only be given in cases in which there is a danger that the jury may use the evidence of lies as evidence which is probative of guilt (rather than credibility). The Court identified four circumstances in which a *Lucas* direction is usually required. These are:

---

128 Above (n. 125) at 15.
129 [1996] 1 Cr App R 163.
130 Ibid. at 173.

    (i) Where the defence relies on an alibi.

   (ii) Where the judge considers it desirable or necessary to suggest that the jury should look for support or corroboration of one piece of evidence from other evidence in the case, and amongst that other evidence draws attention to lies told, or allegedly told, by the defendant.

  (iii) Where the prosecution seek to show that something said, either in or out of the court, in relation to a separate and distinct issue was a lie, and to rely on that lie as evidence of guilt in relation to the charge which is sought to be proved.

  (iv) Where although the prosecution have not adopted the approach to which we have just referred, the judge reasonably envisages that there is a real danger that the jury may do so.[131]

In *R* v. *Middleton*,[132] the Court of Appeal sought to summarise the authorities on the issue of lies told by a defendant.[133]

R V. *MIDDLETON* [2001] CRIM LR 251
Judge LJ

18. ... People do not always tell the truth. Laudable as it may be to do so, whatever the circumstances, they do not, or cannot, always bring themselves to face up to reality. Innocent people sometimes tell lies even when by doing so they create or reinforce the suspicion of guilt. In short, therefore, while lying is often resorted to by the guilty to hide and conceal the truth, the innocent can sometimes misguidedly react to a problem, or postpone facing up to it or attempt to deflect ill-founded suspicion, or fortify their defence by telling lies. For example, a married man who has had consensual sexual intercourse with a woman and is then faced with an allegation of raping her will sometimes untruthfully deny the act of sexual intercourse at all, in order selfishly to avoid embarrassment to him of his wife's discovery of his infidelity or, less selfishly perhaps, the consequent anguish that the knowledge may cause to her and to their children.

19. The purpose of giving the *Lucas* direction, as with many others intended to assist a jury with its proper approach to issues of evidence, is to avoid the risk that they may adopt what in different contexts Professor Sir John Smith described in his commentary on *R v Smith* [1995] Crim.L.R. 940, as 'forbidden reasoning' ...

20. In the present context this, in short, is to assume that lying demonstrates, and is consistent only with, a desire to conceal guilt, or, putting it another way, to jump from the conclusion that the defendant has lied to the further conclusion that he must therefore be guilty. That is an understandable inference a jury may sometimes draw from evidence about lies told by a defendant. However, as we know, on their own lies do not prove guilt, and they may sometimes be told by defendants who are indeed innocent.

---

131 Ibid.

132 23 March 2000, Court of Appeal, Criminal Division (Case No. 9904593 W3), [2001] Crim LR 251.

133 The Court took great care to emphasise that it was 'not ... intending to suggest a reformulation of principle or undermining the existing authorities' (at [23]).

21. Assuming that a lie, or lies, have been told, the ultimate question for the jury is, why did this defendant tell this lie, or these lies, in this particular case? Just as the jury should be warned, for example, not to misuse use [sic] their knowledge of a defendant's previous convictions, so when the defendant has lied, in order to avoid the prohibited reasoning, the jury will often need to be warned – perhaps more accurately, reminded – of the reality, namely that an innocent defendant may sometimes lie and that the inference of guilt does not automatically follow.

22. Where, however, there is no risk that the jury may follow the prohibited line of reasoning, then a *Lucas* direction is unnecessary. On the whole, approaching the matter generally, it is inherently unlikely that such a direction will be appropriate in relation to lies which the jury conclude that the defendant must have told them in his evidence. In this situation, the consequence of the jury rejecting the defendant's evidence is usually covered by the general directions of law on the burden and standard of proof, and if a *Lucas* direction about lies told by the defendant in his evidence to the jury is given, it will often be circular and therefore confusing in its effect.

Judge LJ was careful to point out that the Court of Appeal did not seek to reformulate the law or undermine any existing cases on the matter, but the judgment was intended to set out the principles derived from those cases. His Lordship commented that the large number of reported decisions from the Court of Appeal on this matter had 'tended to obscure the essential simplicity of the principle' and that the issue of whether or not a *Lucas* direction should be given should be analysed in the context of each individual case.[134]

11.7   CONCLUSION

The law necessarily seeks to safeguard against the admissibility of evidence which is likely to be or which is at risk of being unreliable. Where potentially unreliable evidence is adduced in court, the trial judge will be particularly concerned to ensure that the jury does not place undue weight on the evidence in reaching its verdict. This is usually achieved through the use of a care warning in which the trial judge will warn the jury about the potential unreliability of the evidence and about the need for caution in convicting the defendant on the basis of that evidence alone. Care warnings are used in certain circumstances, such as where doubt is cast upon the reliability of a witness's evidence because perhaps the witness has been offered an inducement to give evidence, in which case the trial judge has the discretion to give the jury a *Makanjuola* warning against convicting the defendant on the basis of unreliable, uncorroborated evidence. Similarly, where the prosecution case is based wholly or substantially upon identification evidence which the defendant claims is mistaken, the trial judge will assess the quality of the identification evidence and may decide to withdraw the case from the jury entirely, or to leave the evidence for the jury to assess along with a warning about the dangers of convicting on the basis of the accuracy of the identification evidence.

---

134 Ibid. at [18] and [23].

Summary

- There are two definitions of 'corroboration'. The technical *Baskerville* definition is that corroboration is 'independent testimony' which supports a particular piece of evidence. The non-technical definition of corroboration does not require that the evidence is independent, and thus it is merely 'supporting evidence'.
- There is no general rule in England and Wales that the evidence of a witness must be corroborated. However, some statutory offences require corroboration before a defendant may be convicted of the offence, namely perjury, speeding and an attempt to commit offences with a statutory legal requirement of corroboration.
- The mandatory warning in respect of the evidence of children was abolished by s. 34(2), Criminal Justice Act 1988. The mandatory warning in respect of the uncorroborated evidence of an accomplice or a complainant of a sexual offence was abolished by s. 32(1), Criminal Justice and Public Order Act 1994.
- A trial judge has the discretion to give the jury a warning about convicting the defendant on the basis of the uncorroborated evidence of a witness who may be unreliable. This is known as a *Makanjuola* warning and it is a matter for the judge's discretion what, if any warning, he considers appropriate. There will need to be an evidential basis for suggesting that the evidence of the witness may be unreliable.
- Identification evidence by an eyewitness is notoriously unreliable and has been responsible for many notorious miscarriages of justice.
- Where the prosecution relies either wholly or substantially upon the correctness of identification evidence of an eyewitness which the defendant argues is mistaken, a *Turnbull* warning should be given.
- The trial judge should warn the jury of the special need for caution before convicting the defendant in reliance on the correctness of the identification. The trial judge should also direct the jury that a mistaken witness can be a convincing one and that a number of witnesses can all be mistaken, and should then examine the circumstances of the identification.
- Code D provides guidance to the police on the use of identification procedures. The Code provides a hierarchy of procedures to be used in cases in which the suspect is known and available. The preferred procedure is a video identification. If this cannot be held, the police should hold an identification parade, and, if this cannot be held, the police should hold a group identification. A confrontation is a last resort and should only be held where the identity of the suspect is known but he is not available.
- Where identification evidence is obtained in breach of Code D, it will not automatically be excluded at trial under s. 78, PACE Act 1984. Whether or not the trial judge will exercise his discretion under s. 78 to exclude such evidence will depend upon the circumstances of the individual case.
- Where the prosecution relies on lies told by the defendant, or where such lies might be used by the jury to support the prosecution case that the defendant is guilty, a *Lucas* direction should be given. The jury members should be told that they can only rely on the lie as evidence of guilt if they are satisfied that the lie was deliberate, it relates to a material issue, there was no innocent motive for the lie, and the lie was admitted or proved by other evidence.

For discussion . . .

1. What was the rationale for the abolition of the legal requirement of corroboration in cases involving sexual complainants and children? To what extent does *R* v. *Makanjuola* offer adequate protection against convictions on the evidence of unreliable witnesses?
2. Critically evaluate the law relating to the admissibility of cell confessions.
3. Consider why evidence of visual identification is so unreliable. What steps does the legal system take to safeguard against miscarriages of justice?
4. To what extent are the courts willing to admit other forms of evidence of identification? Are the legal procedures used in gathering such evidence satisfactory?
5. What is a *Lucas* direction and what is the rationale for giving such a direction?

Further reading

P. Bogan QC and A. Roberts, *Identification: Investigation, Trial and Scientific Evidence* (Jordan Publishing, 2011).

This book provides a comprehensive analysis of all aspects of identification evidence, including the powers and duties of the police on the collection of identification evidence and the conduct of identification procedures, the admissibility of identification evidence at court and the scientific aspects of DNA profiling, fingerprint and skin impression evidence, handwriting comparisons, voice identification and evidence obtained through dog tracking.

R. Costigan, 'Identification from CCTV: the risk of injustice' [2007] Crim LR 591.

In this article, the author explores the law relating to identification via CCTV evidence and argues that psychological research into identification from CCTV footage must inform decisions on the admissibility of such evidence and the warnings that should be given to the jury in order to prevent miscarriages of justice.

J. Hartshorne, 'Corroboration and care warnings after *Makanjuola*' (1998) 2(1) E&P 1.

Published a few years after the decision in *R* v. *Makanjuola*, this article explores the scope of the *Makanjuola* guidelines and offers an insight into the way in which the guidelines operate in practice. The author argues that the guidelines do not offer a balance between protecting the defendant and the needs of justice, and suggests that a better course of action would have been to have adopted a suggestion of the Law Commission.

P. Mirfield, '"Corroboration" after the 1994 Act' [1995] Crim LR 448.

This article considers the effect of the abolition of the mandatory corroboration requirements in respect of accomplices and complainants in sexual cases and whether a cautionary direction might survive the Criminal Justice and Public Order Act 1994. It should be noted that this article was written before the leading authority of *R* v. *Makanjuola*.

D. Ormerod, 'Sounds familiar? Voice identification evidence' [2001] Crim LR 595.

In this article, the author considers the dangers of using voice identification and voice recognition evidence and suggests safeguards to be invoked in order to prevent miscarriages of justice where voice identification evidence is relied upon.

A. Roberts, 'The problem of mistaken identification: some observations on process' (2004) 8 E&P 100. This is a leading article on mistaken identification in which the author explores the dangers inherent in eyewitness identification evidence and the importance of safeguarding against misidentification and consequent miscarriages of justice. He argues that any departure from pre-trial procedures should be taken seriously by the courts and warns that the risk of miscarriages of justice remains if such breaches are not guarded against.

12 Opinion and expert evidence

12.1 INTRODUCTION

A witness is called to give evidence at trial about matters which they have personally perceived. A witness is generally not permitted to give evidence about their opinion since the opinion of a non-expert witness is not relevant. However, the opinion of expert witnesses is relevant and admissible. Doctors, forensic scientists, psychologists and forensic accountants are all examples of the types of expert who may be called to give evidence in the criminal and civil courts. Many experts will have studied and practised in their chosen field for years, while others may have no qualifications at all. Since expert witnesses are called to give evidence about matters on which they are deemed to have specialist knowledge (above and beyond that of the average juror or other fact-finder), it is perhaps unsurprising that the evidence of expert witnesses is often held in very high regard by fact-finders. However, there have been several significant, and some very high profile, cases in which doubt has been cast upon the accuracy and reliability of the evidence of expert witnesses.[1] This raises questions about who is deemed to be an expert and how this is decided, as well as questions about the extent to which jurors are deferential to expert opinion evidence. The weight of the evidence of an expert witness is a matter for the jury and jurors are told to treat the evidence of expert witnesses in the same way as any other evidence in the case; thus, jurors are free to accept or disregard the evidence as they see fit.

---

1 Cases include *R* v. *Dallagher* [2002] EWCA Crim 1903, *R* v. *Clark (Sally)* [2003] EWCA Crim 1020, *R* v. *Cannings (Angela)* [2004] EWCA Crim 1 and *R* v. *Harris and others* [2005] EWCA Crim 1980.

However, where an issue in a case falls beyond the scope of the knowledge and education of the jury, there is clearly a real danger that jurors may treat an expert witness differently to other witnesses in the case, placing significant weight on the evidence of the expert. Where the evidence of the expert is unreliable or inaccurate, the potential for a miscarriage of justice to occur is very high and the consequences are potentially very damaging to the criminal justice system as a whole.

This chapter considers the rules relating to the admissibility of opinion evidence, both in relation to non-expert witnesses and experts. The first part of this chapter distinguishes between evidence of fact and opinion evidence and focuses on the evidence given by non-expert witnesses. The general rule against opinion evidence is explained and rationalised. In the second part of this chapter, we will consider the types of matters upon which expert opinion evidence is deemed to be necessary and admissible and who may be regarded as an expert witness. Finally, we will explore the Law Commission's proposals for reform in relation to expert evidence received in criminal proceedings.

12.2   OPINION EVIDENCE

This paragraph introduces evidence of opinion and deals with the distinction between evidence of fact and opinion evidence. The general rule at common law is that evidence of fact is admissible at trial (subject to the usual exceptions explored through this textbook), while evidence of the opinion of a non-expert witness is generally inadmissible at trial. This paragraph explores the general rule in more detail and considers the rationale for the exclusion of opinion evidence.

12.2.1 Distinguishing fact and opinion

The first important issue to consider is the distinction between evidence of fact and evidence of opinion. The law seeks to draw a distinction between facts which are perceived by a witness and the inferences (or opinions) which are drawn from the perception of those facts. A witness's function in a trial is to state facts: he or she will give evidence about matters that he or she has personally perceived. For example, an eyewitness to a robbery will likely give evidence about the physical appearance of the robbers, what they were wearing, what they were carrying, what they did, who they spoke to, etc. Similarly, an eyewitness to a road accident might give evidence as to the position of any cars or pedestrians prior to the accident, which vehicles or people moved, how they moved and in which order they moved. These are all matters of fact, and provided that these were all matters which were indeed personally perceived by the witness, then he or she may give evidence about them. By contrast, an opinion is a matter which is inferred from an accumulation of facts or from a sequential series of facts. A person who provides their opinion on a matter draws inferences from those perceived facts. The drawing of inferences is not usually a function of a witness, but it is a function of the tribunal of fact. Thus, a non-expert witness cannot usually give evidence of the inferences which they drew from the facts that they perceived (i.e. as to their opinion). Thus, the opinions that an eyewitness to a road accident might draw from the facts that he or she perceived could be that the car was speeding and that the driver was drunk. These opinions might be inferred from facts such as: the car was going faster than other cars in the vicinity, the brakes screeched before the car came to a halt, he noticed tyre marks on the road after the event, the driver's breath smelt of alcohol, he was unsteady on his feet, his eyes were bloodshot and his speech was slurred. It is important to be able to distinguish between matters of fact and matters of opinion as the law is generally concerned to exclude evidence of opinion. However, we will see below that there are a number of exceptions to this general rule which apply to expert witnesses and even to non-expert witnesses in cases where the fact and opinion are difficult to separate.

12.2.2 General rule at common law

The general rule at common law is that evidence of the opinion of a non-expert witness is inadmissible. As Bingham LJ stated in *R* v. *Robb*, 'The cardinal rule in English legal proceedings, whether criminal or civil, is that witnesses may only give oral evidence of what they personally heard, saw, did or witnessed. They may not, in general, express opinions as to what happened or may have happened.'[2] Thus, non-expert witnesses can only give evidence about matters that they have personally perceived, i.e. they can give evidence as to the details of what they saw or heard or said (this is known as 'perception evidence'). A non-expert witness generally may not give evidence of their opinions. The rationale for the exclusion of non-expert opinion evidence is that such evidence is irrelevant to the trial process:

> It frequently happens that a bystander has a complete and full view of an accident. It is beyond question that, while he may inform the court of everything that he saw, he may not express any opinion on whether either or both of the parties were negligent. The reason commonly assigned is that this is the precise question the court has to decide, but, in truth, it is because his opinion is not relevant. Any fact that he can prove is relevant, but his opinion is not. The well-recognised exception in the case of scientific or expert witnesses depends on considerations which, for present purposes, are immaterial. So, on the trial of the issue in the civil court, the opinion of the criminal court is equally irrelevant.[3]

It is the role of the tribunal of fact to draw inferences from the facts presented in evidence by witnesses and to reach opinions as to what happened. A witness who provides his opinion on the facts would therefore be usurping the role of the tribunal of fact and there is a risk that the jury might be influenced by the inferences drawn by the witness.

There are two exceptions to the general rule that opinion evidence is inadmissible; the most obvious exception being opinion evidence given by an expert witness. Expert witnesses may give evidence as to their opinion on a particular matter because of their special knowledge and skill in that matter. This and the other exceptions to the general rule will be discussed below.

---

2 (1991) 93 Cr App R 161 at 164.
3 Per Lord Goddard CJ in *Hollington* v. *Hewthorn & Co.* Ltd [1943] KB 587 at 595.

12.2.3 Exceptions to the general rule

As stated above, there are two exceptions to the general prohibition on the admissibility of opinion evidence at trial. These are: (1) where a non-expert witness gives evidence of their opinion that is based on facts which they have personally perceived; and (2) where an expert witness gives evidence on a matter requiring specialised knowledge or skill.

The first exception applies in respect of non-expert witnesses: a non-expert may provide his opinions on facts that he has personally perceived where it is virtually impossible or very difficult to separate the facts from the opinion (and provided that the matter in question does not require special knowledge or expertise). A non-expert can give evidence about matters including the speed that a car he observed was travelling at, or that the defendant was the person that he saw committing the crime, or about the identity of an object, or of the age or emotional state of another person. For example, a non-expert witness who gives evidence of facts which he personally perceived about the defendant, such as that the defendant's breath smelt of alcohol, his eyes were bloodshot, his speech was slurred and he was unsteady on his feet, may give evidence of his opinion inferred from those facts that the defendant was drunk.[4] The second exception applies to matters which are beyond the knowledge or skill of ordinary jurors and judges, i.e. matters which require specialised knowledge or skill. Expert witnesses are permitted to draw inferences from facts because of their specialised knowledge or skill, thus the opinion evidence of an expert witness is admissible at trial. The question of when expert evidence is required and who may give opinion evidence as an expert will be considered in paragraph 12.3 below.

12.3 WHEN IS EXPERT EVIDENCE REQUIRED?

The opinion evidence of an expert is admissible at trial where the court is concerned with a matter or matters which fall outside the scope of the knowledge and skill of the jury or the judge. The question of whether an expert witness is required to give evidence is a matter of law for the trial judge to determine. The judge will consider whether the matter in issue in the case requires specialised knowledge or skill which falls beyond the knowledge and skill of the jury or the judge. If it does, an expert may be called to give evidence of his opinion; but if it does not, no expert will be required. Examples of when expert evidence is required are provided in paragraph 12.3.1 below.

12.3.1 Matters requiring expert knowledge

As stated above, an expert witness can be called to give evidence about any matter which is deemed to fall outside the knowledge of the tribunal of fact. There are countless matters upon

---

4 See *R* v. *Davies* [1962] 1 WLR 1111, in which a non-expert witness was permitted to give evidence that in his opinion the defendant was drunk, provided that he stated the facts upon which he based that inference. However, the witness was not permitted to give evidence as to the ultimate issue in the case, namely whether the defendant was unfit to drive through drink or drugs.

which experts have been called to give their opinion at court; and, as science and technology continue to develop, further matters may require expert opinion. It is not prudent to attempt to list all matters requiring expertise, but the following cases provide some common examples of matters which require special expert knowledge:

- mental disorders suffered by the defendant or a witness
- scientific evidence
- other cases.

(i) Mental disorder

Expert evidence is required in cases where the defendant's defence is based upon his suffering from a mental disorder or where a witness is said to be incapable of giving credible evidence by the fact of his suffering from a mental disorder. Precedent shows that expert evidence is required in cases where the defendant pleads the defences of insanity (where expert evidence is required as to the question of whether the defendant was suffering from a disease of the mind for the purposes of the *M'Naghten Rules*)[5] or diminished responsibility (where expert evidence is required as to the question of whether the defendant was suffering from an abnormality of mental functioning at the time of the killing).[6] In *Toohey* v. *MPC*,[7] the House of Lords held that where a witness is suffering from a mental disorder, expert evidence is required as to the question of whether that disorder renders the witness incapable of giving reliable evidence. Although, no expert evidence is required as to the question of whether a witness who is not suffering from a mental disorder is telling the truth.[8]

(ii) Scientific evidence

The jury may require assistance with scientific evidence and some forms of identification evidence, such as the assessment of facial mapping evidence, handwriting comparisons, ear prints, lip reading and DNA evidence.

Facial mapping evidence may be called where the identification of the defendant is in issue and an expert is required to give evidence in relation to a comparison between an image of the defendant and the defendant himself. For example, in *R* v. *Stockwell*[9] a facial mapping expert was permitted to give his opinion as to whether a face in photographic stills taken from security cameras was the defendant. However, as with all expert evidence, the jury were to be directed that they were not bound by the evidence of the expert. In *R* v. *Atkins*,[10] the Court of Appeal held that the fact that facial mapping was not based upon a statistical database was not a reason for excluding this type of evidence. An expert in facial mapping is permitted to give evidence of his assessment as to whether the defendant could be identified in photographic images, and, in doing so, he could use terms which expressed a degree of probability of the images being the

---

5 See the case of *R* v. *Holmes* [1953] 1 WLR 686 which deals with this point and the *M'Naghten Rules* (1843) 10 Cl & F 200 on insanity.
6 See *R* v. *Bailey* (1977) 66 Cr App R 31.
7 [1965] AC 595, HL.
8 See *R* v. *Pinfold and MacKenney* [2003] EWCA Crim 3643 (discussed below).
9 (1993) 97 Cr App R 260.
10 [2010] 1 Cr App R 8.

same. The expert's assessment was based upon his experience, rather than upon a statistical database, but the jury was nevertheless entitled to be informed of the expert's assessment. However, the Court reiterated that it should be made clear to the jury that the expert's evidence is subjective opinion.

An expert in comparing handwriting may be called to give his opinion as to whether a sample of handwriting was written by a particular person or not.[11] An expert may give opinion evidence as to the identification of the defendant by an ear print.[12] Lip reading evidence where an expert lip reads from a video was also potentially admissible.[13]

Expert evidence which compares DNA profiles obtained from the scene of the crime with DNA profiles obtained from the defendant is admissible. In *R v. Doheny and Adams*,[14] the Court of Appeal provided guidance on the procedure which should be adopted in cases involving DNA evidence.

R V. DOHENY AND ADAMS [1997] 1 CR APP R 369
Phillips LJ

[at 374–5]

1. The scientist should adduce the evidence of the DNA comparisons together with his calculations of the random occurrence ratio.
2. Whenever such evidence is to be adduced, the Crown should serve upon the Defence details as to how the calculations have been carried out which are sufficient for the defence to scrutinise the basis of the calculations.
3. The Forensic Science Service ('FSS') should make available to a defence expert, if requested, the databases upon which the calculations have been based.

It seems to us that these suggestions are sound, and we would endorse them. We would add that it is important that any issue of expert evidence should be identified and, if possible, resolved before trial and this area should be explored by the Court in the pre-trial review.

When the scientist gives evidence it is important that he should not overstep the line which separates his province from that of the Jury.

He will properly explain to the Jury the nature of the match ('the matching DNA characteristics') between the DNA in the crime stain and the DNA in the blood sample taken from the Defendant. He will properly, on the basis of empirical statistical data, give the Jury the random occurrence ratio – the frequency with which the matching DNA characteristics are likely to be found in the population at large. Provided that he has the necessary data, and the statistical expertise, it may be appropriate for him then to say how many people with the matching characteristics are likely to be found in the United Kingdom – or perhaps in a more limited relevant sub group, such as, for instance, the Caucasian sexually active males in the Manchester area.

---

11 See *R v. Silverlock* [1894] 2 QB 766, in which a solicitor was called as an expert witness to give evidence on a comparison of handwriting.
12 See *R v. Dallagher* [2002] EWCA Crim 1903 and *R v. Gilfoyle (No. 2)* [2001] 2 Cr App R 57.
13 See *R v. Luttrell* [2004] 2 Cr App R 31.
14 [1997] 1 Cr App R 369.

This will often be the limit of the evidence which he can properly and usefully give. It will then be for the Jury to decide, having regard to all the relevant evidence, whether they are sure that it was the Defendant who left the crime stain, or whether it is possible that it was left by someone else with the same matching DNA characteristics.

The scientist should not be asked his opinion on the likelihood that it was the Defendant who left the crime stain, nor when giving evidence should he use terminology which may lead the Jury to believe that he is expressing such an opinion.

It has been suggested that it may be appropriate for the statistician to expound to the Jury a statistical approach to evaluating the likelihood that the Defendant left the crime stain, using a formula which gives a numerical probability weighting to other pieces of evidence which bear on that question. This approach uses what is known as the Bayes Theorem. In the case of *Dennis John Adams* (Transcript 26th April 1996) this Court deprecated this exercise in these terms at p.30:

> To introduce Bayes Theorem, or any similar method, into a criminal trial plunges the Jury into inappropriate and unnecessary realms of theory and complexity deflecting them from their proper task.

> We would strongly endorse that comment.

The summing up

When the Judge comes to sum up the Jury are likely to need careful directions in respect of any issues of expert evidence and guidance to dispel any obfuscation that may have been engendered in relation to areas of expert evidence where no real issue exists. The Judge should explain to the Jury the relevance of the random occurrence ratio in arriving at their verdict and draw attention to the extraneous evidence which provides the context which gives that ratio its significance, and that which conflicts with the conclusion that the Defendant was responsible for the crime stain. Insofar as the random occurrence ratio is concerned, a direction along these lines may be appropriate, although any direction must always be tailored to the facts of the particular case:

> Members of the Jury, if you accept the scientific evidence called by the Crown, this indicates that there are probably only four or five white males in the United Kingdom from whom that semen stain could have come. The Defendant is one of them. If that is the position, the decision you have to reach, on all the evidence, is whether you are sure that it was the Defendant who left that stain or whether it is possible that it was one of that other small group of men who share the same DNA characteristics.

This decision was revisited more recently in *R* v. *Bates*,[15] in which the Court of Appeal was asked to consider the admissibility of partial profile DNA evidence. The Court held that there was nothing in *R* v. *Doheny and Adams* to suggest that evidence based on partial profiles must be ruled inadmissible in every case. Moore-Bick LJ stated that:

> We can see no reason why partial profile DNA evidence should not be admissible provided that the jury are made aware of its inherent limitations and are given a sufficient

---

15 [2006] EWCA Crim 1395.

explanation to enable them to evaluate it. There may be cases where the match probability in relation to all the samples tested is so great that the judge would consider its probative value to be minimal and decide to exclude the evidence in the exercise of his discretion, but this gives rise to no new question of principle and can be left for decision on a case by case basis.[16]

Thus, the jury must be carefully directed in relation to expert evidence concerning DNA, especially where the case involved partial profile DNA evidence. The Court of Appeal has held that it is important to distinguish between the issues of admissibility and weight of DNA evidence:[17] the question of admissibility of expert evidence relating to DNA is one of law for the judge to determine, while the question of assessment of that evidence is one for the jury. It has been held that 'expert evidence of a scientific nature is not admissible where the scientific basis on which it is advanced is insufficiently reliable for it to be put before the jury'.[18] However, a suitably experienced forensic science expert may give his evaluative opinion evidence about DNA evidence even where the expert was not able to give a random match probability, provided that the limited basis of the evaluation was made clear to the jury.[19]

Finally, expert evidence may be called in relation to a comparison between broken glass found on the defendant's shoes and broken glass found at the scene of the crime. In *R* v. *Abadom*,[20] a scientist was called to give evidence as to the refractive index of the glass. In this case, it was also held that in giving his expert opinion, a scientist may consult and use statistical data compiled by others.[21]

(iii) Other cases requiring expert evidence

Expert evidence may be called as to the physical and mental effect of cocaine on users of the drug and the different methods of taking cocaine.[22]

12.3.2 Matters not requiring expert knowledge

The following cases provide examples of matters which do not require special expert knowledge and can be assessed by a jury. The cases generally show that no expert evidence is required to draw conclusions about:

- the state of mind or reactions of a witness,
- his capacity to understand an issue, where that witness does not suffer from a mental illness,
- the meaning of ordinary words used in Acts of Parliament, or
- age or identity.

---

16 Ibid. at [30].
17 *R* v. *Reed, Reed and Garmson* [2010] 1 Cr App R 23.
18 Ibid. at [111].
19 *R* v. *Dlugosz*; *R* v. *Pickering*; *R* v. *MDS* [2013] 1 Cr App R 32, CA and see Andrew Roberts [2013] Crim LR 684.
20 [1983] 1 WLR 126.
21 Also applied in *R* v. *Jackson* [1996] 2 Cr App R 420.
22 *R* v. *Skirving* [1985] QB 819.

(i) State of mind or reactions

The jury does not need the help of an expert to decide what the intentions of the defendant were where the defendant has no psychiatric problems. Thus, in *R* v. *Chard*,[23] where the defendant was charged with murder, the trial judge was right to exclude psychiatric evidence as to the defendant's intentions at the time of the killing because the defendant had no abnormality of mind and was not raising the defence of diminished responsibility or insanity at trial. The Court of Appeal held that the jury does not need the assistance of an expert witness to determine what the intentions of a man with a normal mind were.

R V. *CHARD* (1972) 56 CR APP R 268
Roskill LJ

[at 270–1]

. . . one purpose of jury trials is to bring into the jury box a body of men and women who are able to judge ordinary day-to-day questions by their own standards, that is, the standards in the eyes of the law of theoretically ordinary reasonable men and women. That is something which they are well able by their ordinary experience to judge for themselves. Where the matters in issue go outside that experience and they are invited to deal with someone supposedly abnormal, for example, supposedly suffering from insanity or diminished responsibility, then plainly in such a case they are entitled to the benefit of expert evidence. But where, as in the present case, they are dealing with someone who by concession was on the medical evidence entirely normal, it seems to this Court abundantly plain, on first principles of the admissibility of expert evidence, that it is not permissible to call a witness, whatever his personal experience, merely to tell the jury how he thinks an accused man's mind – assumedly a normal mind – operated at the time of the alleged crime with reference to the crucial question of what that man's intention was. As I have already said, this applicant was by concession normal in the eyes of the law.

Similarly, in *R* v. *Wood*,[24] where the defendant who was charged with murder raised the partial defence of suicide pact under s. 4 of the Homicide Act 1957, the Court of Appeal held that expert psychiatric evidence as to the likelihood of there being a suicide pact was rightly excluded by the trial judge. The defence of suicide pact does not involve any medical tests, but instead requires the jury to consider factual questions of whether the defendant was acting in pursuance of a suicide pact and whether he had a settled intention of dying in pursuance of that pact. These were questions which were within the knowledge and experience of the jury. Even if the defendant suffered from an abnormal personality (falling short of a mental disorder) which rendered him susceptible to excessive behaviour under stressful conditions, the case raised no issues which fell outside the knowledge and experience of the jury.

---

23 (1972) 56 Cr App R 268.
24 [1990] Crim LR 264.

> **Cross-reference**
>
> Compare this decision to the decision in *R* v. *Bailey* (1977) 66 Cr App R 31 (above), in which it was held that expert evidence as to the mental condition of the defendant is admissible in cases in which the defendant raises the defence of diminished responsibility under s. 2 of the Homicide Act 1957. The differences between the defences of suicide pact and diminished responsibility are significant: the latter requires proof of an abnormality of mental functioning, something which clearly falls outside of the expertise of the jury, while the former merely requires consideration of factual matters within the jury's expertise.

In the leading case of *R* v. *Turner*,[25] the Court of Appeal held that the jury did not need the help of an expert psychiatrist in order to determine the reactions of a person who is not suffering from any mental disorder. The defendant in this case was charged with the murder of his girlfriend. The prosecution case was that he killed her by hitting her with a hammer. He pleaded the partial defence of provocation, claiming that he suffered a loss of control when she told him that she had had affairs with other men and that she was pregnant by another man. The defence wanted to adduce opinion evidence from a psychiatrist to the effect that, while the defendant was not suffering from a mental illness, his personality was such that he was likely to be telling the truth. The trial judge ruled that the evidence was inadmissible and the defendant appealed against his conviction for murder. The Court of Appeal held that the trial judge had rightly excluded the evidence since there was no question of the defendant suffering a mental illness. The Court also held that psychiatric evidence is not admissible to prove that the defendant is likely to be telling the truth; this is a matter for the jury to determine.

R V. TURNER [1975] 1 QB 834
Lawton LJ

[at 841–3]

The first question ... is whether the psychiatrist's opinion was relevant. A man's personality and mental make-up do have a bearing upon his conduct. A quick-tempered man will react more aggressively to an unpleasing situation than a placid one. Anyone having a florid imagination or a tendency to exaggerate is less likely to be a reliable witness than one who is precise and careful. These are matters of ordinary human experience. Opinions from knowledgeable persons about a man's personality and mental make-up play a part in many human judgments. In our judgment the psychiatrist's opinion was relevant. Relevance, however, does not result in evidence being admissible: it is a condition precedent to admissibility. Our law excludes evidence of many matters which in life outside the courts sensible people take into consideration when making decisions. Two broad heads of exclusion are hearsay and opinion ... the psychiatrist's report contained a lot of hearsay which was inadmissible. A ruling on this ground, however, would merely have trimmed the psychiatrist's evidence: it would not have excluded it altogether. Was it inadmissible because of the rules relating to opinion evidence?

---

25 [1975] 1 QB 834.

The foundation of these rules was laid by Lord Mansfield in *Folkes* v. *Chadd* (1782) 3 Doug. K.B. 157 and was well laid: the opinion of scientific men upon proven facts may be given by men of science within their own science. An expert's opinion is admissible to furnish the court with scientific information which is likely to be outside the experience and knowledge of a judge or jury. If on the proven facts a judge or jury can form their own conclusions without help, then the opinion of an expert is unnecessary. In such a case if it is given dressed up in scientific jargon it may make judgment more difficult. The fact that an expert witness has impressive scientific qualifications does not by that fact alone make his opinion on matters of human nature and behaviour within the limits of normality any more helpful than that of the jurors themselves; but there is a danger that they may think it does.

What, in plain English, was the psychiatrist in this case intending to say? First, that the defendant was not showing and never had shown any evidence of mental illness, as defined by the Mental Health Act 1959, and did not require any psychiatric treatment; secondly, that he had had a deep emotional relationship with the girl which was likely to have caused an explosive release of blind rage when she confessed her wantonness to him; thirdly, that after he had killed her he behaved like someone suffering from profound grief. The first part of his opinion was within his expert province and outside the experience of the jury but was of no relevance in the circumstances of this case. The second and third points dealt with matters which are well within ordinary human experience. We all know that both men and women who are deeply in love can, and sometimes do, have outbursts of blind rage when discovering unexpected wantonness on the part of their loved ones; the wife taken in adultery is the classical example of the application of the defence of 'provocation'; and when death or serious injury results, profound grief usually follows. Jurors do not need psychiatrists to tell them how ordinary folk who are not suffering from any mental illness are likely to react to the stresses and strains of life. It follows that the proposed evidence was not admissible to establish that the defendant was likely to have been provoked. The same reasoning applies to its suggested admissibility on the issue of credibility. The jury had to decide what reliance they could put upon the defendant's evidence. He had to be judged as someone who was not mentally disordered. This is what juries are empanelled to do. The law assumes they can perform their duties properly. The jury in this case did not need, and should not have been offered, the evidence of a psychiatrist to help them decide whether the defendant's evidence was truthful.

... we are firmly of the opinion that psychiatry has not yet become a satisfactory substitute for the common sense of juries or magistrates on matters within their experience of life.

In *R* v. *Turner*, the Court of Appeal considered the foundation of the rule that opinion evidence is inadmissible and the rationale for the rule. Where the matter in issue in the case falls within the knowledge of the jury or within what can be described as normal human nature and behaviour, the evidence of an expert with 'impressive scientific qualifications' will not be more helpful than the jurors' own knowledge, but the Court considered that there was a 'danger' that the jury might place undue weight on the evidence of such an expert simply because of the expert's qualifications. This case provided a relatively restrictive approach to the admissibility of expert evidence and laid the foundations for a series of later cases in which the courts refused to admit the evidence of an expert to speak as to the reliability of a witness where there was no evidence that the witness was suffering from a mental illness.

Following *R* v. *Turner*, the courts took a restrictive approach to the admissibility of expert evidence where a witness was not said to suffer from a mental illness; namely that no expert evidence was generally needed as to the reliability of the witness. Thus, the courts held that while there are mental conditions other than mental illness which may require expert evidence, there is no need to call a psychiatrist to give his expert opinion on how a person who does not suffer from mental illness might react to the stresses and strains of life.[26] In *R* v. *Weightman*,[27] the defendant was charged with the murder of her child. She made a number of admissions to the killing and the prosecution adduced these in evidence at her trial. However, the defendant suffered from a histrionic personality which meant that she was theatrical, emotional in her expression and often said things in order to attract attention. Nevertheless, since the defendant did not suffer from a recognised mental illness, the trial judge refused to allow expert evidence from a psychiatrist to be given. The Court of Appeal dismissed the appeal and ruled that the trial judge had been right to exclude this expert evidence. McCowan LJ held that the defendant's personality was 'not something which is beyond the experience of normal non-medical people ... The jurors ... would know that there are people like that ... In our judgment they would not have been helped by having a psychiatrist talking about 'emotional superficiality' and 'impaired capacity to develop and sustain deep or enduring relationships'.[28] His Lordship then quoted Lawton LJ's judgment in *R* v. *Turner*, that 'dressed up in scientific jargon it may make judgment more difficult'.[29]

Similarly, where the issue in a murder trial is whether the deceased may have committed suicide, psychological evidence as to the state of mind of the deceased which does not show mental illness is not generally admissible at the defendant's trial for murder. In *R* v. *Gilfoyle*,[30] the defendant was charged with the murder of his pregnant wife. He was convicted at his trial after defence counsel called no evidence in his defence. However, on appeal, the defence sought to adduce fresh evidence as to the state of mind of the deceased in order to show that she had committed suicide. The defence sought to call a psychologist expert witness to give evidence about his 'psychological autopsy' on the deceased based upon his assessment of her medical records which disclosed that she suffered from depression and mood swings. The expert had also studied the deceased's diary entries and questioned her family and friends, and his opinion was that these all supported the defence case that the deceased committed suicide. However, the Court of Appeal rejected this argument and held that the evidence tendered from the psychologist was not expert evidence of a kind which should properly be placed before a jury. The Court questioned the validity of the evidence and held that the conclusions drawn were unstructured and speculative and 'not the stuff of which admissible expert evidence is made'.[31] The Court also commented that 'we very much doubt whether assessing levels of happiness or unhappiness is a task for an expert rather than jurors and none of the points which he makes about the "suicide" notes is outwith the experience of a jury'.[32] Thus, the Court took the view that drawing inferences about the happiness of the deceased is a matter within the jury's remit.

---

26 See *R* v. *Strudwick* (1994) 99 Cr App R 326, citing *R* v. *Weightman* (1991) 92 Cr App R 291.
27 (1991) 92 Cr App R 291.
28 Ibid. at 297.
29 Ibid.
30 [2001] 2 Cr App R 5.
31 Ibid. at [25] per Rose LJ.
32 Ibid.

Where the witness suffers from no mental illness and is capable of giving reliable evidence, no expert evidence is required to assist the jury in determining whether the witness is in fact telling the truth; this is a matter of fact upon which the jury members are able to decide. In *R* v. *MacKenney and Pinfold*,[33] the defendants were convicted of four counts of murder and one count of murder respectively. At trial, the defence had sought to adduce expert evidence from a psychologist (who had no medical qualifications), who would give evidence of his conclusions drawn from observing a prosecution witness (a third co-defendant who had pleaded guilty to six murders and who then gave evidence for the prosecution), that while the witness was capable of giving reliable evidence, he had a psychopathic personality which meant that he might choose not to do so. The trial judge ruled that this evidence was inadmissible and the defendants appealed. The Court of Appeal dismissed the appeal and confirmed that the question of the credibility of a witness is a matter for the jury and that they did not need the help of an expert witness in reaching their conclusions. The Court went on to state that the expert evidence of a psychiatrist (not a psychologist) would be admissible in relation to the credibility of a witness only where the capacity of that witness to give truthful evidence was a fact in issue. However, this case was referred back to the Court of Appeal for a second time twenty years later by the Criminal Cases Review Commission on the grounds that new evidence that the prosecution witness had retracted his statements incriminating the defendants rendered their convictions unsafe.[34] The Court of Appeal recognised that 'the approach of this court has over the years developed and is now more generous towards the admission of expert evidence than was once the case'.[35] The Court considered the admissibility of expert evidence as to the credibility of the witness and held that the evidence was admissible irrespective of the absence of an examination of the witness by the expert, provided that the evidence disclosed that the witness suffered a medical abnormality. Thus, the absence of any physical examination was not a decisive factor in determining the admissibility of the evidence, although it was a matter for the jury to take into account when considering the weight of the expert evidence. The Court quashed the defendants' convictions on the basis that the prosecution witness's evidence was so uncreditworthy as to be 'worthless'. The Court held that some limits to the types of expert evidence which is admissible were necessary and approved the judgment of Roch LJ in *R* v. *O'Brien*:

> First the abnormal disorder must not only be of the type which might render a confession or evidence unreliable, there must also be a very significant deviation from the norm shown ... Second, there should be a history pre-dating the making of the admissions or the giving of evidence which is not based solely on a history given by the subject, which points to or explains the abnormality or abnormalities.
>
> If such evidence is admitted, the jury must be directed that they are not obliged to accept such evidence. They should consider it if they think it right to do so, as throwing light on the personality of the defendant and bringing to their attention aspects of that personality of which they might otherwise have been unaware.[36]

---

33 (1983) 76 Cr App R 271.
34 *R* v. *Pinfold and MacKenney* [2003] EWCA Crim 3643.
35 See [2003] EWCA Crim 3643 at [14].
36 Unreported, 25th January 2000, Court of Appeal (Criminal Division); [2000] Crim LR 676.

Thus, there must be some type of abnormality which renders the evidence given by the witness unreliable, and there must be some previous independent evidence as to the abnormality. Once the evidence has been admitted, the jury should be directed that they are free to accept or reject the evidence of the expert as they see fit.

(ii) Defendant's capacity to understand an issue

Where the defendant has an IQ of 69 or less, expert evidence may be adduced in relation to the defendant's capacity to understand an issue. In *R v. Masih*,[37] the defendant and his co-defendants were charged with rape. The defendant had an IQ of 72, so he was on the borderline of sub-normal intelligence. The defence wished to adduce expert evidence as to the defendant's level of intelligence, his immaturity and his limited ability to understand people. There was evidence to suggest that the defendant may have been persuaded to have sexual intercourse with the complainant by a co-defendant in order to prevent the defendant from giving evidence against the co-defendant. The trial judge held that the expert evidence was inadmissible, and the defence appealed against conviction. The Court of Appeal held that the evidence was rightly held to be inadmissible, and that generally speaking expert evidence is not admissible as to the defendant's IQ, unless the IQ was lower (69 or less).

(iii) Ordinary words

Expert evidence is not permitted as to the meaning of words used in legislation which were in ordinary use in the English language. However, in *DPP v. A & BC Chewing Gum*,[38] it was held that expert evidence as to whether cards found in packets of bubble gum were likely to deprave and corrupt children was admissible.

(iv) Age and identity

A non-expert may give his opinion as to the age of a person.[39] Expert evidence is not required where the age of an unknown person depicted in a photograph is in issue; assessing the age of the person is a matter within the remit of the jury.[40] Similarly, where a witness gives evidence identifying that something or someone is what he saw on a previous occasion, he is providing his opinion as to the accuracy of that identification. Such evidence is admissible from a non-expert witness.[41]

Having considered when expert evidence can be given on a matter, the next question to determine is, who constitutes an expert? This will be considered in paragraph 12.3.3 below.

12.3.3 Who is an expert?

The question of whether a witness is competent to give evidence as an expert witness is a matter of law for the judge to decide. It is clear from the case law on the competence of expert witnesses

---

37 [1986] Crim LR 395.
38 [1968] 1 QB 159.
39 *R v. Cox* [1898] 1 QB 179.
40 *R v. Land* [1998] 1 Cr App R 301.
41 *Fryer v. Gathercole* (1849) 154 ER 1209.

that there is no requirement that an expert possesses formal qualifications in the area on which he is to give evidence, or that his skill or experience in the area arises due to his business or profession; it is sufficient that the witness has skill or knowledge in the area. Thus, in *R* v. *Silverlock*,[42] a solicitor was called as an expert witness to give evidence on a comparison of handwriting. The solicitor had been studying handwriting for years before the trial as a hobby, and he was deemed to be an expert on the comparison of handwriting. Lord Russell stated that an expert witness must be '*peritus*', meaning that the witness must be skilled and have adequate knowledge in the particular area. Similarly, in *R* v. *Clare & Peach*,[43] a police officer who had 'closely and analytically' watched the video film of a violent disturbance at a football match was deemed to be an expert on the video. The Court of Appeal was satisfied that the police officer had 'special knowledge' of the video, as he had watched the film about forty times and had examined it in slow motion, one frame at a time, with the facility to rewind and play the video as many times as he needed.

In *R* v. *Robb*,[44] Bingham LJ considered how the courts might identify a field as one which requires expertise, as well as what qualifies a witness to give evidence of his opinion as an expert. His Lordship began by looking at '[t]he old-established, academically-based sciences such as medicine, geology or metallurgy, and the established professions such as architecture, quantity surveying or engineering' and he stated that these 'present no problem. The field will be regarded as one in which expertise may exist and any properly qualified member will be accepted without question as an expert'.[45] However, Bingham LJ acknowledged that there are many other areas which may also require expert evidence, and on which expert evidence is habitually given in court, such as expert evidence relating to fingerprints,[46] handwriting and accident reconstruction, opinions as to the 'market value of land, ships, pictures or rights', and as to 'the quality of commodities, or on the literary, artistic, scientific or other merit of works alleged to be obscene'. His Lordship stated that while the courts would accept these types of evidence, they 'would not accept the evidence of an astrologer, a soothsayer, a witch-doctor or an amateur psychologist'. Bingham LJ summarised the approach that the courts should have to the question of whether a person is an expert:

> the essential questions are whether study and experience will give a witness's opinion an authority which the opinion of one not so qualified will lack, and (if so) whether the witness in question is *peritus* in Lord Russell's sense.[47]

As we have seen above, in *R* v. *Silverlock* Lord Russell stated that an expert witness must be '*peritus*', meaning that the witness must be skilled and have adequate knowledge in the area on which he is to give evidence.

---

42 [1894] 2 QB 766.
43 [1995] 2 Cr App R 333.
44 (1991) 93 Cr App R 161.
45 Ibid. at 164.
46 See S. Cole and A. Roberts, 'Certainty, individualization and the subjective nature of expert fingerprint evidence' [2012] Crim LR 824.
47 (1991) 93 Cr App R 161 at 164.

12.3.4 Reliability of expert witnesses

As a result of several appeals over the past twelve years, the reliability of the evidence of expert witnesses has been subject to closer scrutiny by academics and the courts. The Law Commission published a Consultation Paper on the reliability of expert evidence in 2009[48] and this was followed by a Law Commission Report, in 2011.[49] In the Consultation Paper, the Law Commission raised concerns about the reliability of expert evidence and the 'pressing danger' of wrongful convictions[50] and recognised that '[e]xpert evidence is sometimes admitted too readily'.[51] The danger inherent in admitting unreliable expert evidence is that the jury will be too quick to defer to the expert on the basis of his expertise. One of the key cases cited by the Law Commission was *R* v. *Dallagher*[52] in which the defendant was convicted of murder on the basis of an ear print identification of the defendant. Two expert witnesses conducted an ear print comparison on ear prints found on a window which the murderer used to enter the victim's home and identified the defendant as the offender. This evidence was held to be admissible at trial and the defence appealed against the conviction on the ground that the evidence should have been excluded. The defence relied upon the evidence of three expert witnesses who doubted the reliability of the evidence given by the prosecution experts. The Court of Appeal quashed the conviction because the fresh defence evidence might reasonably have affected the jury's verdict had it been given at trial.

The paragraphs below consider some high-profile cases involving unreliable expert opinion evidence. The first selection of cases highlighted deal with mothers who were accused of the murder of their own babies after expert evidence was put before the jury as to the probability of their babies dying from Sudden Infant Death Syndrome. The second category of cases considered focuses on the use of expert evidence as to the childhood memories of an adult complainant in historic sexual abuse cases.

Sudden Infant Death Syndrome cases

In 2003, the Court of Appeal held that Sally Clark's convictions for the murder of her two baby sons were unsafe because the expert evidence relied upon at trial was flawed.[53] The defendant's two sons died aged 8 weeks and 11 weeks respectively. A post mortem concluded that the first baby had died as a result of Sudden Infant Death Syndrome (SIDS), but the post mortem for the second baby concluded that the baby died from being shaken. This conclusion led the pathologist to revisit the first post mortem and he then revised his conclusions and stated that the first baby had been smothered to death. The prosecution called expert evidence at trial to the effect that the chances of two babies in one family dying

---

48 Law Commission,*The Admissibility of Expert Evidence in Criminal Proceedings in England and Wales: A New Approach to the Determination of Evidentiary Reliability* (Consultation Paper No. 190, April 2009).
49 Law Commission Report, *Expert Evidence in Criminal Proceedings in England and Wales* (Law Com No. 325, March 2011).
50 Such as in the cases of *R* v. *Dallagher* [2002] EWCA Crim 1903, *R* v. *Clark (Sally) (No. 2)* [2003] EWCA Crim 1020 and *R* v. *Cannings* [2004] EWCA Crim 1.
51 Above (n. 48) at para. 2.12.
52 [2002] EWCA Crim 1903.
53 *R* v. *Clark (Sally) (No. 2)* [2003] EWCA Crim 1020.

from SIDS was one in 73 million, and the defendant was convicted. On a second appeal to the Court of Appeal, the defence called new evidence of previously undisclosed microbiological reports relating to one of the children. These reports revealed that it was possible to conclude that the child had died from natural causes. The Court of Appeal held that this was crucial evidence and that the failure to disclose these reports before trial rendered the convictions unsafe. The Court was also highly critical of the statistical evidence of the one in 73 million chance of both babies dying from SIDS, stating that it 'was tantamount to saying that without consideration of the rest of the evidence one could be just about sure that this was a case of murder'.[54] Sally Clark's appeal was a high-profile case and the success of the defence and Court of Appeal's criticisms of the expert evidence led to another high-profile appeal in *R* v. *Cannings*.[55] Angela Cannings was convicted of the murder of two of her three children who all died in infancy. The prosecution based its case on the unlikely chance of three such deaths occurring in one family. On appeal, the defence adduced fresh medical evidence to the effect that the deaths were due to SIDS. The Court of Appeal quashed her convictions and held that there was substantial medical opinion which suggested that three sudden, unexplained infant deaths could occur naturally in one family, and that the multiple deaths did not necessarily lead to the conclusion that they must have resulted from the deliberate infliction of harm. Since death by natural causes could not be excluded as a reasonable possibility, the convictions should be quashed. This case was followed a year later by *R* v. *Kai-Whitewind*[56] in which the defendant appealed against her conviction for the murder of her 3-month-old baby. The conviction was based upon the conflicting evidence of expert witnesses, but the Court of Appeal distinguished this case from *R* v. *Cannings* because in *R* v. *Kai-Whitewind* there was other evidence which supported the conviction.[57] Further appeals against convictions based upon shaken baby syndrome followed. In *R* v. *Holdsworth*,[58] the Court of Appeal quashed the conviction of a woman convicted of murdering her 2-year-old son. The Court cautioned against the reliance on scientific knowledge in cases where there was no other evidence to support the expert opinion. Where the expert opinion is fundamental to the prosecution case, special caution was required. In *R* v. *Henderson and others*,[59] three appeals involving shaken baby syndrome were heard together. The Court of Appeal provided guidance on managing expert evidence and directing the jury so as to ensure that they reach a verdict which can be justified on a logical basis.[60]

---

54 Ibid. at [175].
55 [2004] 1 WLR 2607.
56 [2005] 2 Cr App R 31.
57 See also *R* v. *Harris and others* [2005] EWCA Crim 1980, which involved four separate appeals against convictions for murder, manslaughter and inflicting grievous bodily harm. The cases were all shaken baby syndrome cases. The appeals were based upon fresh medical research which threw doubt on the safety of the convictions. The Court of Appeal considered each case in turn and held that such cases should be dealt with on a case-by-case basis.
58 [2008] EWCA Crim 971.
59 [2010] EWCA Crim 1269.
60 Ibid. at [202].

R V. HENDERSON AND OTHERS [2010] EWCA CRIM 1269
Moses LJ

[217] There are two features of the content of a summing-up in cases such as these which, we suggest, are important. First, a realistic possibility of an unknown cause must not be overlooked. In cases where that possibility is realistic, the jury should be reminded of that possibility. They should be instructed that unless the evidence leads them to exclude any realistic possibility of an unknown cause they cannot convict. In cases where it is relevant to do so, they should be reminded that medical science develops and that which was previously thought unknown may subsequently be recognised and acknowledged. As it was put by Toulson L.J., 'today's orthodoxy may become tomorrow's outdated learning' (*R v Holdsworth [2008] EWCA Crim 971* at [57]). In cases where developing medical science is relevant, the jury should be reminded that special caution is needed where expert opinion evidence is fundamental to the prosecution [57].

[218] Second, the jury need directions as to how they should approach conflicting expert evidence. *Kai-Whitewind* teaches that the mere fact that expert differs from expert is no ground for withdrawing the case from the jury. But how is the jury to approach such a conflict? To suggest, in cases where the expert evidence is fundamental to the case, that the jury should approach that expert opinion in the same way as they do in every other criminal case, is inadequate. It is difficult enough for Family Division judges to express their reasons for accepting or rejecting conflicting expert evidence, despite their experience. Juries, we suggest, should not be left in cases requiring a higher standard of proof to flounder in the formation of a general impression. A conclusion cannot be left merely to impression. In the appeal of Henderson, Dr Leestma gave, if we may say so, a most beguiling impression, courteous and understated as it was. But there were, as we have concluded, sound reasons relating to his experience in comparison with Dr Al-Sarraj for rejecting what he told us. Lacking the experience of Family Division judges, a jury needs to be directed as to the pointers to reliable evidence and the basis for distinguishing that which may be relied upon and that which should be rejected.

[219] In *Harris* the court pointed out the assistance given by Cresswell J. [271]. That guidance is of assistance not only to judges, practitioners and experts themselves, but also to a jury. If the issue arises, a jury should be asked to judge whether the expert has, in the course of his evidence, assumed the role of an advocate, influenced by the side whose cause he seeks to advance. If it arises, the jury should be asked to judge whether the witness has gone outside his area of expertise. The jury should examine the basis of the opinion. Can the witness point to a recognised, peer-reviewed, source for the opinion? Is the clinical experience of the witness up-to-date and equal to the experience of others whose evidence he seeks to contradict?

[220] Of course, none of these features will determine the case. Not all of these features are even relevant in every case. But we seek to emphasise the importance of guiding the jury as to the proper approach to conflicting opinions. An overall impression can never be the substitute for a rational process of analysis. The jury are not required to produce reasons for their conclusion. Nevertheless, the judge should guide them by identifying those reasons which would justify either accepting or rejecting any conflicting expert opinion on which either side relies.

[221] We acknowledge the danger of being over-prescriptive in relation to directions to the jury. But judges, we suggest, need to remember that their directions are part of the means by which they ensure that a case which depends on expert evidence proceeds to its conclusion on a logically justifiable basis.

Finally, in *R* v. *Arshad*,[61] the Court of Appeal dismissed an appeal against conviction for murder on the basis that the judge's summing-up had been fair. The judge was not required to expressly state to the jury that there was a special need for caution, as long as that was the effect of the summing-up.

This long string of appeals based upon cases involving expert evidence on shaken baby syndrome demonstrates the difficulties facing the courts when the jury hears complicated medical evidence from experts whose opinions often conflict, such as ensuring that conflicting evidence is presented to the jury clearly such that the jury is aware of all of the possible causes of death and assisting the jury to evaluate the expert evidence through the judge's summing-up.

CHILDHOOD MEMORIES[62]   In *R* v. *Anderson*,[63] the Court of Appeal cast doubt over the reliability of expert evidence of an adult's childhood memories. The Court branded the reports provided by the expert in this case 'controversial' and held that '[i]t is also highly unlikely, given the state of medical opinion that this court will receive the evidence of the kind put forward by Professor Conway in the near future'.[64] The Court referred to the earlier decision of *R* v. *JH and R* v. *TG*,[65] in which such evidence from the same expert was accepted by the Court of Appeal. However, the Court commented that it was 'unaware at that time of significant criticisms of Professor Conway's methodology which have led to the court's declining to receive his evidence'[66] and in light of this the Court expressed its doubts about whether *R* v. *JH and R* v. *TG* would be decided in the same way today.

12.3.5 Procedural matters

Section 127 of the Criminal Justice Act 2003 provides that an expert witness may base his opinion on a statement which has been prepared by another person for the purposes of criminal proceedings, provided that that person had or may reasonably have been supposed to have personal knowledge of the matters stated in the statement.[67]

Where one party seeks to rely on the evidence of an expert witness, that party must give notice to the other side. Thus, rule 33.4 of the Criminal Procedure Rules requires the party seeking to rely on expert evidence to serve it on the court and the other party in the case as soon as is practicable.

Where an expert gives evidence at trial, the jury must be directed carefully by the judge so as to ensure that they treat that evidence like the evidence of any other witness given in the trial. Thus, the jury must not be directed that they must accept the evidence of the expert,[68] but, while

---

61 [2012] EWCA Crim 18.

62 See S. Ring, 'Due process and the admission of expert evidence in recovered memory in historic child sexual abuse cases: lessons from America' (2012) 16(1) E&P 66.

63 [2012] EWCA Crim 1785.

64 Ibid. at [18].

65 Also reported as *R* v. *X (Childhood Amnesia)* [2006] 1 Cr App R 10.

66 Above (n. 63) at [9] and see *R* v. *S* [2006] EWCA Crim 1404, *R* v. *E* [2009] EWCA Crim 1370 and *R* v. *H* [2011] EWCA Crim 2344 referred to by the Court of Appeal.

67 Thus, s. 127 of the Criminal Justice Act 2003 allows for the admissibility of the hearsay evidence of other identified persons who have prepared statements for the purposes of criminal proceedings.

68 *R* v. *Lanfear* [1968] 2 QB 77.

it is important for the jury to know that they are not bound by expert evidence, there is no requirement that the jury be directed using specific wording.[69]

12.4 THE ULTIMATE ISSUE RULE

The 'ultimate issue rule' provides that a witness is not permitted to give evidence of his opinion on the ultimate issue. The rationale for this rule is that the determination of the ultimate issue in the case is one for the tribunal of fact, and allowing a witness to express an opinion on this issue could usurp the functions of the tribunal of fact. Traditionally, the rule was applied to both expert witnesses and non-expert witnesses. In *DPP v. A & BC Chewing Gum*,[70] an expert witness was not permitted to give evidence as to whether the images on collectible cards found in packets of bubble gum tended to corrupt and deprave children because this was the ultimate issue to be determined by the justices as the tribunal of fact. However, the rule was abolished by s. 3, Civil Evidence Act 1972 for the purposes of expert witnesses giving evidence in civil proceedings. In criminal proceedings, the rule appears to be disregarded in relation to expert witnesses, who frequently provide their opinion on the ultimate issue in a case. In *R v. Stockwell*,[71] Taylor LCJ held that:

> Whether an expert can give his opinion on what has been called the ultimate issue, has long been a vexed question . . . if there is such a prohibition, it has long been more honoured in the breach than the observance . . . The rationale behind the supposed prohibition is that the expert should not usurp the functions of the jury. But since counsel can bring the witness so close to opining on the ultimate issue that the inference as to his view is obvious, the rule can only be, as the authors of the last work referred to say, a matter of form rather than substance. In our view an expert is called to give his opinion and he should be allowed to do so. It is, however, important that the judge should make clear to the jury that they are not bound by the expert's opinion, and that the issue is for them to decide.[72]

Thus, in respect of expert witnesses the ultimate issue rule no longer applies.

12.5 REFORM

In light of several high-profile miscarriages of justice involving unreliable expert evidence, the Law Commission reviewed the law on the admissibility of expert evidence[73] and published its

---

69 *R v. Fitzpatrick* [1999] Crim LR 832.
70 [1968] 1 QB 159.
71 (1993) 97 Cr App R 260.
72 Ibid. at 265–6.
73 See L. Heffernan and M. Coen, 'The reliability of expert evidence: reflections on the Law Commission's proposals for reform' (2009) 73 JCL 488, G. Edmond and A. Roberts, 'The Law Commission's Report on Expert Evidence in Criminal Proceedings' [2011] Crim LR 844, K. Shaw, 'Expert evidence reliability; time to grasp

Consultation Paper, *The Admissibility of Expert Evidence in Criminal Proceedings in England and Wales: A New Approach to the Determination of Evidentiary Reliability* in 2009.[74] In the Consultation Paper, the Law Commission proposed that there should be a new reliability test to determine the admissibility of expert evidence. The Law Commission explored the approach of the courts in the United States and based its proposed test on the leading American case of *Daubert*.[75] In 2011, the Law Commission published its final report on the admissibility of expert evidence, *Expert Evidence in Criminal Proceedings in England and Wales*.[76] This Report was accompanied by a Draft Criminal Evidence (Experts) Bill in which the Commission recommended a new statutory reliability-based admissibility test.[77] The Commission also recommended that trial judges be provided with a list of statutory factors to help them apply the reliability test.[78] According to the Draft Bill, expert opinion evidence would not be admissible, unless it is adjudged to be sufficiently reliable to go before a jury.[79] Expert opinion evidence would be sufficiently reliable to be admitted if the opinion is soundly based and the strength of the opinion is warranted having regard to the grounds on which it is based.[80] Opinions based upon a hypothesis which has not been sufficiently scrutinised, which is based upon an unjustifiable assumption or flawed data, which relies on a method which was not properly carried out or not appropriate, or where the opinion relies on an inference which was not properly reached, would not be sufficiently reliable.[81]

12.6 CONCLUSION

Opinion evidence is generally inadmissible at trial because the drawing of inferences from given facts is a function of the tribunal of fact. However, the two main exceptions to this rule are: (1) opinion evidence given by a non-expert based upon facts personally perceived, and (2) opinion evidence given by an expert on a matter requiring special skill or knowledge which goes beyond the knowledge of the tribunal of fact. While an expert witness may give his opinion as to the ultimate issue in a case, a non-expert witness may not. The question of who may give expert evidence on any given matter is a legal one for the judge to determine.

---

the nettle' (2011) 75 JCL 368, G. Edmond, 'Is reliability sufficient? The Law Commission and expert evidence in international and interdisciplinary perspective: part 1' (2012) 16(1) E&P 30 and T. Ward, 'Expert evidence and the Law Commission: implementation without legislation?' [2013] Crim LR 561 on the Law Commission recommendations.

74 Law Commission, *The Admissibility of Expert Evidence in Criminal Proceedings in England and Wales: A New Approach to the Determination of Evidentiary Reliability* (Consultation Paper No. 190, April 2009).

75 *Daubert* v. *Merrell Dow Pharmaceuticals Inc.* 509 US 579 (1993). See also S. Cole and A. Roberts, 'Certainty, individualization and the subjective nature of expert fingerprint evidence' [2012] Crim LR 824.

76 Law Commission Report, *Expert Evidence in Criminal Proceedings in England and Wales* (Law Com No. 325, March 2011).

77 Ibid. at para. 3.36.

78 Ibid. at para. 3.62.

79 Clause 1(2), Draft Criminal Evidence (Experts) Bill.

80 Clause 4(1), Draft Criminal Evidence (Experts) Bill.

81 Clause 4(2), Draft Criminal Evidence (Experts) Bill.

An expert must have sufficient skill or knowledge in the area concerned, but need not possess formal qualifications. In recent years, the reliability of some types of expert evidence has been subject to scrutiny as a result of several high-profile miscarriages of justice. As a result, the Law Commission has reported on the reliability and admissibility of such evidence in criminal proceedings, and has proposed a new test of admissibility based upon the American approach. At the time of writing, Parliament has yet to respond to the Law Commission's recommendations with legislation and we wait to see if the Commission's draft Bill will be adopted.

Summary

- The law distinguishes between facts, which are perceived by a witness, and inferences (or opinions), which are drawn from the perception of those facts. The drawing of inferences is a function of the tribunal of fact.
- The general rule at common law is that evidence of the opinion of a non-expert witness is inadmissible. There are two exceptions to this general rule, namely (1) where a non-expert witness gives opinion evidence that is based on facts which they have personally perceived, and (2) where an expert witness gives evidence on a matter requiring specialised knowledge or skill.
- An expert witness can be called to give evidence about any matter which is deemed to fall outside the knowledge of the tribunal of fact.
- Expert evidence is required in cases where the defendant's defence is based upon his suffering from a mental disorder, such as where the defendant pleads the defences of insanity (see *R* v. *Holmes* [1953] 1 WLR 686) and diminished responsibility (see *R* v. *Bailey* (1977) 66 Cr App R 31).
- The jury does not need the help of an expert to decide what the intentions of the defendant were where the defendant has no psychiatric problems (see *R* v. *Chard* (1972) 56 Cr App R 268).
- The jury may require assistance with scientific evidence and some forms of identification evidence.
- The jury did not need the help of an expert psychiatrist in order to determine the reactions of a person who is not suffering from any mental disorder (*R* v. *Turner* [1975] 1 QB 834).
- The question of whether a witness is competent to give evidence as an expert is a matter of law for the judge to decide. The expert need not possess formal qualifications; it is sufficient that the witness has skill or knowledge in the area (see *R* v. *Silverlock* [1894] 2 QB 766).
- In recent years, the reliability of expert evidence has been subject to scrutiny, particularly in the field of shaken baby syndrome (see *R* v. *Clark (Sally) (No. 2)* [2003] EWCA Crim 1020 and *R* v. *Cannings* [2004] 1 WLR 2607).
- The 'ultimate issue rule' provides that a non-expert witness is not permitted to give evidence of his opinion on the ultimate issue. However, expert witnesses in criminal and civil proceedings may give opinion evidence about the ultimate issue.

For discussion . . .

1. Identify the principles derived from the cases of *Toohey* v. *MPC* [1965] AC 595 and *R* v. *Pinfold and MacKenney* [2003] EWCA Crim 3643 and explain how the cases are reconcilable.
2. Critically evaluate the decision of the Court of Appeal in *R* v. *Turner* [1975] 1 QB 834.
3. Explain how the courts determine the competence of an expert witness.
4. How does the law safeguard against wrongful conviction in cases involving expert evidence? Do you think the safeguards are sufficient?
5. Explain the effect of the ultimate issue rule. To what extent does the rule have any significance in respect of expert evidence today?

Further reading

L. Heffernan and M. Coen, 'The reliability of expert evidence: reflections on the Law Commission's proposals for reform' (2009) 73 JCL 488.
This article explores the law governing the reliability of expert evidence and analyses the recommendation made by the Law Commission in its Consultation Paper for a new statutory rule requiring the trial judge to assess the reliability of expert evidence as a matter of admissibility. The article considers the American approach upon which the proposed test was based, and the authors consider the challenges that such a test would present.

J. Jackson, 'The ultimate issue rule: one rule too many?' [1984] Crim LR 75.
This article considers the ultimate issue rule. The author provides a robust criticism of the rule and calls for its abolition.

Law Commission, *The Admissibility of Expert Evidence in Criminal Proceedings in England and Wales: A New Approach to the Determination of Evidentiary Reliability* (Consultation Paper No. 190, April 2009).
In this Consultation Paper, the Law Commission proposed that the admissibility of expert evidence should be subject to a reliability test. The proposal was based upon the US test from *Daubert* v. *Merrell Dow Pharmaceuticals Inc.* 509 US 579 (1993). The Consultation Paper was followed by the Law Commission's Report in 2011.

Law Commission Report, *Expert Evidence in Criminal Proceedings in England and Wales* (Law Com No. 325, March 2011).
The publication of this Report followed the Consultation by the Law Commission. In the Report, the Law Commission formally recommended a new reliability-based admissibility test for expert evidence in criminal proceedings. The Law Commission proposes that the test should be applied in appropriate cases, rather than routinely. The test provides that expert opinion evidence would only be admitted if it is adjudged to be sufficiently reliable to go before a jury. The Report was accompanied by a draft Criminal Evidence (Experts) Bill.

P. Roberts, 'Towards the principled reception of expert evidence of witness credibility in criminal trials' (2004) 8 E&P 215.
This paper provides a case commentary on the decision in *R* v. *Pinfold and MacKenney* [2003] EWCA Crim 3643.

T. Ward, 'Expert evidence and the Law Commission: implementation without legislation?' [2013] Crim LR 561.

This article considers the recommendations made by the Law Commission in its Report on expert evidence and the current common law on admissibility. The author argues that the exclusionary discretion could and should be used to exclude any prosecution evidence which is not soundly based or which is expressed in unduly strong terms. The author argues that the current common law combined with the exclusionary discretion are sound, albeit inadequately applied in some cases.

13 Disclosure

13.1 INTRODUCTION

This chapter explores the provisions that govern the process of pre-trial disclosure. The law on disclosure has been the subject of extensive discussion amongst academics and practitioners.[1] This is a controversial area, and the arguments balancing the interests of all the parties in a case are well rehearsed. The concept of pre-trial prosecution disclosure supports the defendant's right to a fair trial or fair hearing under Article 6 of the European Convention on Human Rights by ensuring that the defendant is aware of the evidence against him before trial. The rules on disclosure also assist in the administration of justice by ensuring that the issues that will arise at trial are identified at an early stage; this reduces the length of court hearings and ensures that the justice system is more cost efficient. Brief consideration will be given to the civil disclosure process before a more detailed examination of disclosure in the criminal justice system. The

---

1 See M. Redmayne, 'Criminal Justice Act 2003 (1) disclosure and its discontents' [2004] Crim LR 441; R. Leng, 'Defence strategies for information deficit: negotiating the CPIA' (1997) 1 E&P 215; J. Sprack, 'The Criminal Procedure and Investigations Act 1996: (1) the duty of disclosure' [1997] Crim LR 308; S. Sharpe, 'Article 6 and the disclosure of evidence in criminal trials' [1999] Crim LR 273; and M. Redmayne, 'Process gains and process values: the Criminal Procedure and Investigations Act 1996' (1997) 60 MLR 79.

chapter will provide an overview of the disclosure process in criminal proceedings before looking at the two different types of disclosure: disclosure of 'used' material, where the prosecution discloses to the defence any material on which it intends to rely, and disclosure of 'unused' material, which is governed by the Criminal Procedure and Investigations Act 1996. The Criminal Procedure and Investigations Act 1996 (as amended by the Criminal Justice Act 2003) lays down a framework for the disclosure of unused material. The 1996 Act also first introduced the concept of defence disclosure into the criminal justice system, requiring that the defence disclose its case in advance of trial through the service of a defence statement. Finally, the chapter will consider the non-disclosure of material which is subject to public interest immunity (PII), the secretive manner in which some PII applications are made and the effect of this on the defendant's right to a fair trial under Article 6.

13.2   RATIONALE

The rules on disclosure are of fundamental importance in the context of both civil and criminal litigation and deserve consideration within the study of the law of evidence because the principle of disclosure is synonymous with an open and transparent justice system. Where the rules of disclosure are not followed, there may be serious and permanent consequences in trial proceedings. As Lord Bingham stated, '. . . the lack of an obligation on the prosecution to disclose material in their possession has led to notorious miscarriages of justice'.[2] In the case of *R* v. *Keane*,[3] Lord Taylor CJ stated that where the material in the possession of the prosecution 'may prove the accused's innocence or avoid a miscarriage of justice, then the balance comes down resoundingly in favour of disclosing it'. The rules of disclosure in both civil and criminal proceedings seek to balance competing interests. Prosecution material should be disclosed to the defence in the interest of ensuring that the defendant has a fair trial, and this is important due to the imbalance in the resources of the prosecution compared to those of the defence; the disclosure rules seek to go some way towards achieving 'equality of arms'. However, this must be balanced against non-disclosure by the prosecution of certain material in order to protect the public interest. Lord Bingham observed that, '[t]he difficulty is obvious: the defendant's right to a fair trial may be compromised if the material is not disclosed to him, the public interest jeopardized if it is'.[4] The fundamental principle of disclosure is linked generally to the defendant's right to a fair trial or fair hearing under Article 6 of the European Convention on Human Rights. The European Court of Human Rights has stated that:

> The Court considers that it is a requirement of fairness under art 6(1), indeed one which is recognised under English law, that the prosecution authorities disclose to the defence all material evidence for or against the accused and that the failure to do so in the present case gave rise to a defect in the trial proceedings.[5]

---

2 T. Bingham, *The Rule of Law* (Penguin, 2011) at p. 91.
3 [1994] 1 WLR 746.
4 Above (n. 2) at p. 98.
5 See *Edwards* v. *United Kingdom* (1992) 15 EHRR 417 at para. 36.

More specifically in criminal proceedings, disclosure is linked to the minimum right under Article 6.3(a) which states that the defendant has a right 'to be informed promptly, in a language which he understands and in detail, of the nature and cause of the accusation against him'. Thus, the defendant has the right to know the nature of the case against him. Further, the principle of disclosure requires that the defence have access to material which enables them to conduct an effective cross-examination of prosecution witnesses or call witnesses which may support the case for the defence; thus this is linked to the minimum right under Article 6.3(d) which provides that the defendant has a right 'to examine or have examined witnesses against him and to obtain the attendance and examination of witnesses on his behalf under the same conditions as witnesses against him'.[6] The defence is also subject to rules of disclosure and the underlying rationale for the requirement that the defence disclose his defence prior to trial is to prevent the ambush of the prosecution by the defence.[7]

13.3 DISCLOSURE IN CIVIL PROCEEDINGS

In civil proceedings, all parties to proceedings are subject to obligations of pre-trial disclosure. The rationale underlying the rules on disclosure is consistent with the notion that parties should have access to all evidence or information that is relevant to the proceedings and to the issues in the case. Thus, the disclosure process carries tones of the inquisitorial approach by advocating access to relevant information. This also eliminates the element of surprise and the possibility that one party might lose his or her case as a result of being ambushed by the defence or by the testimony of an unexpected witness. Consequently, this approach is focused on the objective of truth finding.

Part 31 of the Civil Procedure Rules 1998 governs the process of pre-trial disclosure in civil proceedings. In civil proceedings, parties will initially exchange statements of case, which set out the basis of the claim being brought or the defence being run by the relevant party. Parties will also then be obliged to make disclosure of a list of documents that they have in their possession and which they rely on in support of their case or which adversely affect their case or another party's case or support another party's case.[8] The party providing the list must also then make these documents available for inspection by other parties in the case.[9] However, any documents which are subject to privilege or public interest immunity will not need to be subject to inspection, nor any where it would be disproportionate to the issues in the case to permit inspection of the document.[10]

---

6 This argument was accepted by the European Court of Human Rights in *Edwards* v. *United Kingdom* (1992) 15 EHRR 417 at para. 32.

7 In *R* v. *Penner* [2010] EWCA Crim 1155, the Court of Appeal recently confirmed that the Criminal Procedure Rules have abolished 'trial by ambush' and stated that trial by ambush is no longer permissible.

8 Rule 31.6, Civil Procedure Rules 1998.

9 Rule 31.3, ibid.

10 Rule 31.3(2), ibid.

> **Cross-reference**
>
> The issue of public interest immunity will be considered at paragraph 13.8 of this chapter. Privilege and public interest immunity will both be considered in Chapter 14.

The parties in proceedings must also serve on other parties any witness statements that they intend to rely on at trial.[11] In civil proceedings, the witness statements served will stand as the evidence-in-chief of the witness who gives evidence.[12] If a witness is not called to give evidence, the witness statement may be adduced as hearsay evidence.[13]

13.4 OVERVIEW OF DISCLOSURE IN CRIMINAL PROCEEDINGS

The disclosure process begins at an early stage in proceedings with the disclosure of used material. In summary cases, the prosecution will make disclosure of the initial details of the prosecution case, known as 'advance information' (or AI) to the defence. In cases tried on indictment, the prosecution will serve on the defence a bundle of witness statements upon which they intend to rely. The next stage of the disclosure process involves initial prosecution disclosure of unused material. The prosecution will serve unused material under s. 3, Criminal Procedure and Investigations Act 1996. The defence must (or 'may' if the case is tried summarily) then serve a defence statement. The prosecution will continue to review the material that they have in their possession and will serve any further unused material under their continuing duty of disclosure. Finally, the defence may serve an updated defence statement, if appropriate. (See Figure 13.1.)

13.5 DISCLOSURE OF USED MATERIAL

The prosecution disclosure of used material is separate to the obligations under the Criminal Procedure and Investigations Act 1996. According to the *Attorney General's Guidelines on Disclosure*,[14] prosecutors should consider the potential need to disclose material at an early stage in proceedings in the interests of justice and fairness in a case. The prosecution is also under a continuing duty from the arrest of a defendant to committal proceedings to decide whether disclosure is necessary in the interests of justice.[15] One example given in the Guidelines is in cases where the material disclosed might significantly affect a bail decision or that might enable the defence to contest the committal proceedings.[16] In addition to this, there are formal requirements of disclosure of advance information in relation to matters dealt with summarily.

---

11 Rule 32.4, ibid.
12 Rule 32.5(2), ibid.
13 Rule 32.5(1), ibid.
14 *Attorney General's Guidelines on Disclosure*, available at www.gov.uk/government/publications/attorney-generals-guidelines-on-disclosure-2013 (accessed on 19 July 2014).
15 *R* v. *DPP, ex parte Lee* [1999] 1 WLR 1950.
16 Above (n. 14) at para. 55.

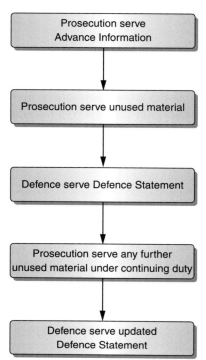

Figure 13.1 Overview of disclosure process

13.5.1 Advance information

The first disclosure made to the defence is advance information (or AI) and this applies only in summary only and either way matters. This information is designed to provide the defence with any used material which supports the allegation against the defendant. The Advance Information Rules are contained in Part 10 of the Criminal Procedure Rules 2013[17] and the Attorney General's Guidelines on Disclosure.[18] They require the prosecution to disclose initial details of the prosecution in any case that can be tried summarily. The relevant material must be disclosed at or before the start of the day of the first hearing at the magistrates' court.[19] Advance information must include:

- a summary of the evidence on which the case will be based, or
- witness statements or documents setting out the facts on which the case will be based, or
- a combination of both a summary and such witness statements and documents, and
- the defendant's previous convictions.[20]

---

17 Available at www.legislation.gov.uk/uksi/2013/1554/part/10/made (accessed on 19 July 2014).
18 Above (n. 14).
19 Part 21.2, Criminal Procedure Rules 2011. Part 21 of the Criminal Procedure Rules 2011 does not apply to indictable only offences which are committed to the Crown Court under s. 51, Crime and Disorder Act 1998.
20 Part 21.3, Criminal Procedure Rules 2011.

13.5.2 Trial on indictment

Where the defendant is sent to the Crown Court for trial under s. 51, Crime and Disorder Act 1998, the prosecution will serve both used material, including details of the charges against the defendant, the witness statements of witnesses the prosecution intends to rely on, and a schedule of unused material, alongside the material which should be disclosed as part of initial prosecution disclosure under s. 3, Criminal Procedure and Investigations Act 1996.

13.6 DISCLOSURE UNDER THE CRIMINAL PROCEDURE AND INVESTIGATIONS ACT 1996

The Criminal Justice Act 2003 made substantial amendments to the disclosure rules under the Criminal Procedure and Investigations Act 1996. The amendments under the Criminal Justice Act 2003 largely reflected the government's White Paper, *Justice for All*,[21] which was in itself the government's response to Auld LJ's *Review of the Criminal Courts of England and Wales*.[22] The Criminal Justice Act 2003 reformed the law significantly in relation to both the initial duty of prosecution disclosure and the obligations of disclosure on the defence. In the extract from *R v. H & C*[23] below, Lord Bingham justifies the reforms to the rules of disclosure and the obligation on the prosecution.

R V. H & C [2004] UKHL 3
Lord Bingham

14 Fairness ordinarily requires that any material held by the prosecution which weakens its case or strengthens that of the defendant, if not relied on as part of its formal case against the defendant, should be disclosed to the defence. Bitter experience has shown that miscarriages of justice may occur where such material is withheld from disclosure. The golden rule is that full disclosure of such material should be made.

15 This is a field in which domestic practice has developed markedly, although not always consistently, over the last 20 years. Until December 1981, the prosecution duty was to make available, to the defence, witnesses whom the prosecution did not intend to call, and earlier inconsistent statements of witnesses whom the prosecution were to call: see *Archbold, Pleading, Evidence and Practice in Criminal Cases*, 41st ed (1982), paras 4–178–4–179. Guidelines issued by the Attorney General in December 1981 (*Practice Note (Criminal Evidence: Unused Material)* [1982] 1 All ER 734) extended the prosecution's duty of disclosure somewhat, but laid down no test other than one of relevance ('has some bearing on the offence(s) charged and the surrounding circumstances of the case') and left the decision on disclosure to the judgment of the prosecution and prosecuting counsel.

---

21 *Justice for All* Cm. 5563, TSO, 2002.
22 Auld LJ, *Review of the Criminal Courts of England and Wales* (TSO, 2001). Archived at www.criminal-courts-review.org.uk.
23 [2004] UKHL 1.

16 In *R v Ward (Judith)* [1993] 1 WLR 619, 674 this limited approach to disclosure was held to be inadequate:

> An incident of a defendant's right to a fair trial is a right to timely disclosure by the prosecution of all material matters which affect the scientific case relied on by the prosecution, that is, whether such matters strengthen or weaken the prosecution case or assist the defence case. This duty exists whether or not a specific request for disclosure of details of scientific evidence is made by the defence. Moreover, this duty is continuous: it applies not only in the pre-trial period but also throughout the trial.

The rule was stated with reference to scientific evidence, because that is what the case concerned, but the authority was understood to be laying down a general test based on relevance: see *R v Keane* [1994] 1 WLR 746, 752.

17 The Criminal Procedure and Investigations Act 1996 gave statutory force to the prosecution duty of disclosure, but changed the test. Primary disclosure must be made under section 3(1)(a) of any prosecution material which has not previously been disclosed to the accused and which in the prosecutor's opinion might undermine the case for the prosecution against the accused. Secondary disclosure under section 7(2)(a) is to be made, following delivery of a defence statement, of previously undisclosed material which might be reasonably expected to assist the accused's defence. Section 32 of the Criminal Justice Act 2003 ... has amended section 3(1)(a) of the 1996 Act so as to require primary disclosure of any previously undisclosed material 'which might reasonably be considered capable of undermining the case for the prosecution against the accused or of assisting the case for the accused'. Whether in its amended or unamended form, section 3 does not require disclosure of material which is either neutral in its effect or which is adverse to the defendant, whether because it strengthens the prosecution or weakens the defence. This rule was not criticised by the appellants' counsel, unsurprisingly since a defendant cannot complain that the defence (and the judge and jury) are not alerted to the existence of material which, if revealed, would lessen his chance of acquittal. The information which came to light in the course of the European Court proceedings in *Edwards and Lewis* 22 July 2003 (that Edwards had been involved in the supply of heroin before the start of the undercover operation: judgment, para 16) would not have been disclosable under the present rule, since that information could only have thrown doubt on his contention that he thought he was dealing with jewellery and on any contention that he had been induced to commit the offence of which he was convicted.

13.6.1 Initial duty of disclosure by prosecution

After service of advance information, the prosecution must disclose to the defence any unused material which 'might reasonably be considered capable of undermining the case for the prosecution against the accused or of assisting the case for the accused'. This initial duty of prosecution disclosure is contained within s. 3, Criminal Procedure and Investigations Act 1996.

S. 3(1), CRIMINAL PROCEDURE AND INVESTIGATIONS ACT 1996 (AS AMENDED BY S. 32, CRIMINAL JUSTICE ACT 2003)

The prosecutor must –

(a) disclose to the accused any prosecution material which has not previously been disclosed to the accused and which might reasonably be considered capable of undermining the case for the prosecution against the accused or of assisting the case for the accused, or
(b) give to the accused a written statement that there is no material of a description mentioned in paragraph (a).

The Criminal Justice Act 2003 made some important changes to the original provisions of the Criminal Procedure and Investigations Act 1996 on disclosure. Section 32 amended s. 3, Criminal Procedure and Investigations Act 1996, abolishing the previous two-stage prosecution disclosure process (of primary prosecution disclosure and secondary prosecution disclosure), under which defence disclosure was linked to the defendant's right to full prosecution disclosure, and replacing it with one single stage of prosecution disclosure. The previous process involved a subjectively applied test of primary prosecution disclosure whereby the prosecution had to disclose material which 'in the prosecutor's opinion might undermine the case for the prosecution against the accused', but this controversial test was criticised for placing too much discretion in the hands of the individual prosecutor.[24] The current test is an objective one, such that the prosecution must disclose material which 'might reasonably be considered capable of' either undermining the prosecution case or assisting the defence case. In the case of *R* v. *Vasiliou*[25] it was held that the previous convictions of prosecution witnesses was material which might undermine the prosecution case, so any previous convictions of witnesses that the prosecution proposes to call must be disclosed under s. 3. Under s. 7A, Criminal Procedure and Investigations Act 1996, the prosecution is also under a continuing duty to review any decisions on disclosure.

13.6.2 Defence disclosure

The concept of defence disclosure was introduced by the Criminal Procedure and Investigations Act 1996, but it has also been subject to very significant changes by the amendments in the Criminal Justice Act 2003. We will explore the background to the introduction of defence disclosure as this is important in understanding the arguments in favour of having defence obligations of disclosure as well as the arguments against such an onus.

Background
Prior to the Criminal Procedure and Investigations Act 1996, the law relating to disclosure was governed by common law, under which the defence was not obliged to disclose its case before

---

24 For example, see Sharpe, 'Article 6 and the disclosure of evidence in criminal trials' [1999] Crim LR 273.
25 [2000] Crim LR 845.

trial. In 1981, the Phillips Royal Commission rejected any suggestion that the defence should formally be obliged to disclose its case. However, the Phillips Commission did recommend that the defence should give advance notice of specific defences, such as those dependent on scientific or medical evidence.[26] In 1993, the Runciman Royal Commission[27] 'felt that the courts had swung the pendulum too far in favour of the defence'.[28] It was suggested, for the first time, that the defence should be subject to a duty to disclose its case prior to trial. The primary justifications put forward for such a duty were: the need to reduce surprise at trial, to protect the prosecution from 'ambush' defences, and to assist the prosecution in its preparation of its case. The Runciman Royal Commission also argued that there were efficiency considerations to be made by imposing a duty of disclosure on the defence: it was suggested that defence disclosure might lead to the prosecution dropping the case, or to an early guilty plea, or to fixing an earlier trial date, and permit more accurate estimates of the length of the trial.

A notable result of the 1993 Report was the powerful dissent by Michael Zander QC.[29] Zander's dissenting arguments were (and still are) extremely convincing. Zander took the view that it was 'contrary to principle' to make a defendant respond to the prosecution case until it had been presented at trial:[30] a defendant should be fully entitled to put the prosecution to proof and run no defence. He argued that it was not the job of a defendant to be helpful to the prosecution or the system – his only task is to defend himself.[31] This is inherent in the fundamental principle that the burden of proof rests on the prosecution – the case is brought against the defendant by the state. He also argued that 'ambush' defences were rare and not a problem within the criminal justice system as the defence was usually identifiable from a defendant's interview, if not, from the facts and prosecution witness statements.[32] As far as considerations of efficiency were concerned, Zander stated that these arguments were 'unconvincing';[33] in fact, efficiency was far from the major consideration from the defendant's point of view. He questioned why a defendant should be forced to assist the prosecution and system with efficiency (either cost or time efficiency), when it is the prosecution and system making allegations against the defendant. While a defendant does not need to be malicious, he should not be forced to assist in the prosecution against himself. In fact, Zander suggested that defence disclosure may cause more delays as the prosecution asks for further particulars, and will result in more cost, as conferences will be required prior to drafting a defence statement, counsel's advice may be sought and the solicitor or counsel will spend time drafting the defence statement.[34]

Despite these persuasive criticisms of the 1993 Report, the government followed the Report's recommendations and s. 5 of the Criminal Procedure and Investigations Act 1996 provided that

---

26 Royal Commission on Criminal Procedure, *Report* (Cm. 8092, HMSO, 1981) paras. 8.20–8.22.
27 Royal Commission on Criminal Justice, *Report* (Cm. 2263, HMSO, 1993), pp. 91–100.
28 Ibid. at ch. 6, para. 49.
29 Royal Commission on Criminal Justice, *Note of Dissent by Professor Michael Zander* (Cm. 2263, HMSO, 1993), pp. 221–3.
30 Ibid. at para. 1.
31 Ibid. at para. 2.
32 Ibid. at para. 3.
33 Ibid. at para. 7.
34 Ibid. at para. 9.

a defendant who is to be tried on indictment must disclose a defence case statement. Under this original legislation, a defence case statement had to set out, in general terms, the nature of the defence; matters on which the defendant took issue with the prosecution and reasons; if the defendant was to rely on an alibi, then the particulars of that alibi (name and address of alibi witness, or, if these were not known, any information which might be of material assistance in finding the witness). Prior to the Criminal Justice Act 2003, the requirements of defence disclosure used to be less detailed than prosecution disclosure and there was a tactical decision to be made by defence lawyers as to how much detail to include in the defence statement (it was important to include enough information to trigger secondary prosecution disclosure[35] and avoid the defence sanctions for non-disclosure, but not too much to give away too many details of the defence case). In his *Review of the Criminal Courts of England and Wales*, Auld LJ concluded that the CPIA 1996 'has not worked well'.[36] Despite acknowledging that 'the 1996 Act was logical in principle',[37] his Lordship stated that it was 'unworkable', that there was a poor practice of disclosure, a lack of trust between parties and that lengthy trials had not fallen as intended. Auld LJ also concluded that the scheme was costly to the Crown Prosecution Service and the police.[38] In proposing a number of changes to the law on disclosure, Auld LJ further stated that there was a need for service of a defence statement 'as an aid to early identification of the issues, and in consequence, an efficient process and one that is fair both to the defence and to the prosecution as the representative of the public interest'.[39] However, the requirements of defence disclosure under the Criminal Procedure and Investigations Act 1996 were changed by virtue of the amendments made by the 2003 Act which have placed a further, more detailed onus of disclosure on the defence (the details of these will be discussed later).

Defence case statement

As we know, the Criminal Procedure and Investigations Act 1996 also places duties of disclosure on the defence. In a summary case, s. 6 of the Act applies which provides that the defence *may* serve a defence statement on the prosecution. (See Figure 13.2.) By contrast, in a case which is to be tried on indictment, s. 5 of the 1996 Act applies which provides that the defence *must* serve a defence statement on the prosecution. (See Figure 13.3.) Thus, service of a defence statement is voluntary for matters tried summarily, but obligatory for more serious matters tried on indictment. Service of the defence statement must take place within 14 days of prosecution disclosure where the defence statement is voluntarily disclosed under s. 6, or within 21 days of prosecution disclosure where the defence statement is disclosed under s. 5

---

35 The concept of secondary prosecution disclosure is now obsolete as a result of the amendments by the Criminal Justice Act 2003, which amalgamated the previous two-stage prosecution disclosure into a one-stage process.

36 Above (n. 22), ch. 10 at para. 121.

37 Ibid., para. 153.

38 It is worth noting that this had indeed been predicted by Michael Zander QC in his dissent to the proposals for the Criminal Procedure and Investigations Act 1996 made by the Runciman Commission in 1993 (see Royal Commission on Criminal Justice, *Note of Dissent by Professor Michael Zander*, pp. 221–3).

39 Above (n. 22), ch. 10 at para. 156. See Redmayne, 'Criminal Justice Act 2003 (1): disclosure and discontents' [2004] Crim LR 441 for an analysis of the principle of defence disclosure.

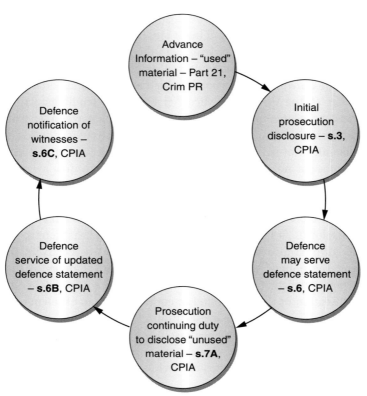

Figure 13.2 Disclosure process for summary trial

(compulsory disclosure).[40] There are also sanctions for faults in defence disclosure, including for non-disclosure, service out of time and providing inconsistent defences in the defence statement. The sanctions involve the drawing of adverse inferences against the defence and are contained under s. 11, Criminal Procedure and Investigations Act 1996.

Cross-reference

The sanctions for non-disclosure by the defence under s. 11, Criminal Procedure and Investigations Act 1996 will be considered in more detail at paragraph 13.6.7 below.

Contents of a defence statement

Section 6A of the Criminal Procedure and Investigations Act 1996 (which was inserted into the Criminal Procedure and Investigations Act 1996 by s. 33(2) of the Criminal Justice Act 2003) sets out the required contents of a defence statement.

---

40 Criminal Procedure and Investigations Act 1996 (Defence Disclosure Time Limits) Regulations 1997, regs. 2 and 3.

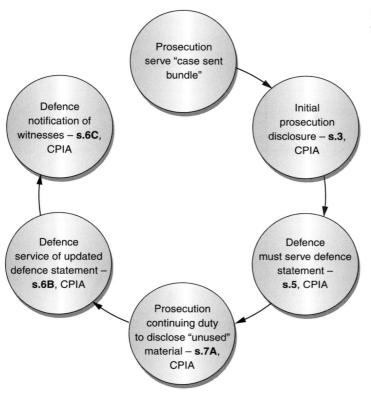

Figure 13.3 Disclosure process for trial on indictment

S. 6A, CRIMINAL PROCEDURE AND INVESTIGATIONS ACT 1996 (AS INSERTED BY S. 33(2), CRIMINAL JUSTICE ACT 2003)

(1) For the purposes of this Part a defence statement is a written statement –
   (a) setting out the nature of the accused's defence, including any particular defences on which he intends to rely,
   (b) indicating the matters of fact on which he takes issue with the prosecution,
   (c) setting out, in the case of each such matter, why he takes issue with the prosecution, and
   (d) indicating any point of law (including any point as to the admissibility of evidence or an abuse of process) which he wishes to take, and any authority on which he intends to rely for that purpose.
(2) A defence statement that discloses an alibi must give particulars of it, including –
   (a) the name, address and date of birth of any witness the accused believes is able to give evidence in support of the alibi, or as many of those details as are known to the accused when the statement is given;
   (b) any information in the accused's possession which might be of material assistance in identifying or finding any such witness in whose case any of the details mentioned in paragraph (a) are not known to the accused when the statement is given.

(3) For the purposes of this section evidence in support of an alibi is evidence tending to show that by reason of the presence of the accused at a particular place or in a particular area at a particular time he was not, or was unlikely to have been, at the place where the offence is alleged to have been committed at the time of its alleged commission.

Under s. 6A(1), Criminal Procedure and Investigations Act 1996, the defence statement requires the defence to:

- set out the nature of the accused's defence, including any particular defences on which he intends to rely;
- indicate the matters of fact on which the accused takes issue with the prosecution;
- set out why the accused takes issue with each matter; and
- indicate any point of law which the accused wishes to take and any authorities he intends to rely upon.

Further, where the defence is alibi, the accused must provide particulars of any alibi witnesses, including the name, address and date of birth of the witness, or, if those details are not known, then any information that the defendant has about the witness which might be of material assistance in finding the witness.[41]

Amendments to the Criminal Procedure and Investigations Act 1996 by s. 34 of the Criminal Justice Act 2003 now require the defence to notify the prosecution of any witnesses the defence intends to call. This provision inserted s. 6C into the 1996 Act which stipulates that if witnesses are to be called on behalf of the defendant, the defence must also now provide the details of those witnesses, including their name, address and dates of birth, or if those details are not known, then any information that the defendant has about the witness which might be of material assistance in finding the witness.[42]

S. 6C, CRIMINAL PROCEDURE AND INVESTIGATIONS ACT 1996 (AS INSERTED BY S. 34, CRIMINAL JUSTICE ACT 2003)

(1) The accused must give to the court and the prosecutor a notice indicating whether he intends to call any persons (other than himself) as witnesses at his trial and, if so –
   (a) giving the name, address and date of birth of each such proposed witness, or as many of those details as are known to the accused when the notice is given;
   (b) providing any information in the accused's possession which might be of material assistance in identifying or finding any such proposed witness in whose case any of the details mentioned in paragraph (a) are not known to the accused when the notice is given.

Proposed amendments to the Criminal Procedure and Investigations Act 1996 by s. 33 of the Criminal Justice Act 2003 will require the defence to serve an updated defence statement closer

---

41 Section 6A(2), Criminal Procedure and Investigations Act 1996.
42 Section 6C(1), Criminal Procedure and Investigations Act 1996.

to the start of the trial, but this amendment has not yet been brought into force.[43] There is also a further proposed amendment inserting s. 6D into the 1996 Act which will require that the defence notifies the prosecution of any expert witnesses the defence intends to call. However, this amendment has not yet been brought into force.

S. 6D, CRIMINAL PROCEDURE AND INVESTIGATIONS ACT 1996 (AS INSERTED BY S. 35, CRIMINAL JUSTICE ACT 2003 BUT NOT YET IN FORCE)

(1) If the accused instructs a person with a view to his providing any expert opinion for possible use as evidence at the trial of the accused, he must give to the court and the prosecutor a notice specifying the person's name and address.
(2) A notice does not have to be given under this section specifying the name and address of a person whose name and address have already been given under section 6C.
(3) A notice under this section must be given during the period which, by virtue of section 12, is the relevant period for this section.

13.6.3 Duty of continuing review

The prosecution has a continuing duty of disclosure of unused material under s. 7A, CPIA 1996. This means that the prosecution must review the material in its possession to ensure that all unused material which 'might reasonably be considered capable of undermining the prosecution case or assisting the case for the defence' is disclosed to the defence. If there is no such further evidence to disclose, the prosecution should communicate this to the defence.

13.6.4 Section 8 applications

Where the defence believes that the prosecution has further material in its possession which should have been disclosed to the defence under the 1996 Act and it has failed to do so, the defence may make an application to the court for an order that the prosecution should comply with the disclosure under s. 8, Criminal Procedure and Investigations Act 1996 (this is known as a s. 8 application). A s. 8 application may only be made provided that the defence has served a defence statement on the prosecution and, in order to be successful in the application for disclosure, the defendant must show that he has reasonable cause to believe that the prosecution material requested might reasonably be expected to assist his defence. The burden of proof is on the defence to show that he reasonably believes that there is prosecution material that may assist his defence. However, s. 8 applications may not be used as a 'fishing expedition' and the provision prevents speculative applications for disclosure of prosecution material by requiring the defence to specify in the application the material which it wants the prosecution to disclose and explain why it is thought that the prosecutor has that material. The defence will also need to justify why that material should be disclosed to the defence (i.e. why it might undermine the case for the prosecution or assist the

---

43 Section 6B, Criminal Procedure and Investigations Act 1996.

defence case). It is of course open to the prosecution to make representations to the court to the effect that material should not be disclosed on the grounds that it is not in the public interest for it to be disclosed (public interest immunity applications are dealt with below at paragraph 13.8).

13.6.5 Consequences of non-disclosure

The 1996 Act provides for consequences for both the prosecution and the defence if they fail to follow the disclosure rules. The sanctions for faults with defence disclosure cover a wider range of disclosure faults and are arguably more onerous than the consequences for prosecution failure to observe disclosure time limits.

13.6.6 Prosecution failure to observe time limits

Section 10 of the Criminal Procedure and Investigations Act 1996 applies where the prosecution fails to comply with initial prosecution disclosure or with the continuing duty of disclosure within the specified time limits. According to s. 10(2), non-disclosure by the prosecution is not in itself grounds for staying the proceedings as an abuse of process. However, where the non-disclosure also involves such a delay in proceedings to the extent that the defendant is denied the right to a fair trial, this may constitute grounds for staying the proceedings for abuse of process.[44]

S.10, CRIMINAL PROCEDURE AND INVESTIGATIONS ACT 1996

(1) This section applies if the prosecutor –
  (a) purports to act under section 3 after the end of the period which, by virtue of section 12, is the relevant period for section 3, or
  (b) purports to act under section 7A(5) after the end of the period which, by virtue of section 12, is the relevant period for section 7A.
(2) Subject to subsection (3), the failure to act during the period concerned does not on its own constitute grounds for staying the proceedings for abuse of process.
(3) Subsection (2) does not prevent the failure constituting such grounds if it involves such delay by the prosecutor that the accused is denied a fair trial.

Although the consequences for the prosecution for failing to observe the disclosure time limits may be very grave in the event that proceedings are stayed, this section does not grant an automatic sanction for non-disclosure. Instead s. 10(3) provides that the failure combined with a delay violating the defendant's right to a fair trial may be enough to support an argument of abuse of process and result in a stay of proceedings. There is no sanction on the prosecution comparable to that on the defence whereby it might be open to the tribunal of fact to hold faults in disclosure against the prosecution. Thus, even where the defence has had to force the hand of the prosecution by making a successful application for disclosure under s. 8, there are no sanctions on the prosecution for the non-disclosure.

---

44 Section 10(3), Criminal Procedure and Investigations Act 1996.

13.6.7 Sanctions for defence non-disclosure

Under s. 11 of the CPIA 1996, a defendant may be subject to sanctions for failing to comply with the provisions relating to defence disclosure. Faults that may fall under s. 11 and thus warrant sanction include failure to serve a defence statement, serving it out of time, setting out inconsistent defences in the defence case statement, running a different defence at trial from that in the defence case statement, or calling alibi evidence without having complied with s. 5(7). Each of these faults will have repercussions for the defendant as s. 11(5) permits the court or jury to draw 'such inferences as appear proper in deciding whether the accused is guilty' from such lack of compliance.[45] Further, any other party may, with leave of the court, 'make such comment as appears proper'.[46] However, s. 11(10) makes it clear that the court or jury may not convict the defendant of an offence solely on the basis of inferences drawn under s. 11(5). This must be communicated to the jury in any case where the judge directs them that they may draw inferences from his disclosure failure.

S. 11, CRIMINAL PROCEDURE AND INVESTIGATIONS ACT 1996

(5) Where this section applies –
  (a) the court or any other party may make such comment as appears appropriate;
  (b) the court or jury may draw such inferences as appear proper in deciding whether the accused is guilty of the offence concerned.

. . .

(10) A person shall not be convicted of an offence solely on an inference drawn under subsection (5).

These defence sanctions are controversial, particularly when one considers, first, that there are no equivalent sanctions for prosecution non-disclosure, and, secondly, that it is prosecution non-disclosure which has been responsible for many notorious miscarriages of justice in recent years. In the recent case of *R* v. *Rochford*[47] the Court of Appeal held that the court did not have the power to make an order that the defendant comply with the disclosure rules under s. 6A and then punish the defendant for contempt of court upon non-compliance. The Court of Appeal held that the sanctions to be imposed upon a defendant for failing to comply with the disclosure rules were set out under s. 11(5) and that:

> Any order such as a judge might make would be no more than an emphatic articulation of the statutory obligation created by section 5(5) and 6A. The sanction for non-compliance is explicit in the statute in section 11. It is not open to the court to add an additional extra-statutory sanction of punishment for contempt of court.[48]

Subsections (2), (3) and (4) set out the circumstances in which the defence sanctions may apply.

---

45 Section 11(5)(b), Criminal Procedure and Investigations Act 1996.
46 Section 11(5)(a), Criminal Procedure and Investigations Act 1996.
47 [2011] 1 WLR 534.
48 Ibid. at para. 18.

S. 11, CRIMINAL PROCEDURE AND INVESTIGATIONS ACT 1996

(1) This section applies in the three cases set out in subsections (2), (3) and (4).

(2) The first case is where section 5 applies and the accused –

    (a) fails to give an initial defence statement,

    (b) gives an initial defence statement but does so after the end of the period which, by virtue of section 12, is the relevant period for section 5,

    (c) is required by section 6B to give either an updated defence statement or a statement of the kind mentioned in subsection (4) of that section but fails to do so,

    (d) gives an updated defence statement or a statement of the kind mentioned in section 6B(4) but does so after the end of the period which, by virtue of section 12, is the relevant period for section 6B,

    (e) sets out inconsistent defences in his defence statement, or

    (f) at his trial –

        (i) puts forward a defence which was not mentioned in his defence statement or is different from any defence set out in that statement,

        (ii) relies on a matter which, in breach of the requirements imposed by or under section 6A, was not mentioned in his defence statement,

        (iii) adduces evidence in support of an alibi without having given particulars of the alibi in his defence statement, or

        (iv) calls a witness to give evidence in support of an alibi without having complied with section 6A(2)(a) or (b) as regards the witness in his defence statement.

(3) The second case is where section 6 applies, the accused gives an initial defence statement, and the accused –

    (a) gives the initial defence statement after the end of the period which, by virtue of section 12, is the relevant period for section 6, or

    (b) does any of the things mentioned in paragraphs (c) to (f) of subsection (2).

(4) The third case is where the accused–

    (a) gives a witness notice but does so after the end of the period which, by virtue of section 12, is the relevant period for section 6C, or

    (b) at his trial calls a witness (other than himself) not included, or not adequately identified, in a witness notice.

In summary, the court or jury may be able to draw adverse inferences against the defendant where the defendant:

- fails to serve a defence statement that he is required to serve under s. 5 or does so out of time,
- serves a defence statement under s. 6 out of time,
- fails to serve an updated defence statement as required by s. 6B or does so out of time,[49]
- serves a defence statement setting out inconsistent defences,
- puts forward a defence at trial that was not mentioned in the defence statement or is different from that in his defence statement,

---

49 Although, note that s. 6B is not yet in force.

- relies on a matter which was not mentioned in his defence statement (in breach of s. 6A),
- adduces evidence of an alibi or calls an alibi witness without having provided the particulars of the alibi or alibi witness in his defence statement,
- serves a witness notice under s. 6C but does so out of time,[50] or
- calls a witness who was not identified in a witness notice under s. 6C.[51]

The leave of the court is required in some circumstances before prosecuting counsel or counsel for a co-defence may comment to the jury about the defence fault in disclosure. These circumstances are set out in subsections (6) and (7):

S. 11, CRIMINAL PROCEDURE AND INVESTIGATIONS ACT 1996

(6) Where –
    (a) this section applies by virtue of subsection (2)(f)(ii) (including that provision as it applies by virtue of subsection (3)(b)), and
    (b) the matter which was not mentioned is a point of law (including any point as to the admissibility of evidence or an abuse of process) or an authority, comment by another party under subsection (5)(a) may be made only with the leave of the court.
(7) Where this section applies by virtue of subsection (4), comment by another party under subsection (5)(a) may be made only with the leave of the court.

The leave of the court must be obtained where the defendant has failed to mention a point of law or authority in his defence statement which he relies on in court or (when s. 6C comes into force) where he serves a witness notice under s. 6C out of time or calls a witness who was not identified in a witness notice.

Where the defence fault is that the defendant relies on a different defence in court to that set out in his defence statement, the court must have regard to the considerations under s. 11(8) which take into account the extent of the differences in the defences and whether there is any justification for it before deciding whether the sanctions under s. 11(5) are to apply.

S. 11, CRIMINAL PROCEDURE AND INVESTIGATIONS ACT 1996

(8) Where the accused puts forward a defence which is different from any defence set out in his defence statement, in doing anything under subsection (5) or in deciding whether to do anything under it the court shall have regard –
    (a) to the extent of the differences in the defences, and
    (b) to whether there is any justification for it.

Further, when the provisions under s. 6B come into force in relation to witness notices, where the defendant does serve a witness notice and fails to include or adequately identify a witness in

---

50 Although, note that s. 6C is not yet in force.
51 Ibid.

the notice, the court must have regard to whether there is any justification for the failure before deciding whether the sanctions under s. 11(5) apply.

S. 11, CRIMINAL PROCEDURE AND INVESTIGATIONS ACT 1996

(9) Where the accused calls a witness whom he has failed to include, or to identify adequately, in a witness notice, in doing anything under subsection (5) or in deciding whether to do anything under it the court shall have regard to whether there is any justification for the failure.

As the detail required in a defence case statement has increased with the amendments brought in by the Criminal Justice Act 2003 (and as they continue to do so with the amendments coming into force incrementally), so too do the number of sanctions for non-compliance by the defence. The absence of corresponding sanctions for prosecution non-disclosure is disproportionate to the detailed provisions relating to defence sanctions.

13.7   UNUSED MATERIAL

There is a Code of Practice which supplements the Criminal Procedure and Investigations Act 1996 and imposes duties upon the investigating police officers to record and retain information and material gathered or generated during investigation.[52] Where there is doubt as to whether proceedings will be instituted against the defendant, the material should be retained until the decision has been made.[53] Material should be kept until the conclusion of the proceedings,[54] and, where the defendant is convicted, material should be kept until the release of the defendant or for six months from the date of conviction.[55] Where there is an appeal against conviction in progress or the Criminal Cases Review Commission is considering an application in respect of the case, then the investigator should also keep the material.[56]

Where the investigator (or disclosure officer) believes that the defendant will plead not guilty at a summary trial, or that the offence will be tried in the Crown Court, the disclosure officer must prepare a schedule of unused material (i.e. a schedule which lists material that has been retained and that does not form part of the case against the defendant).[57] The disclosure officer will compile a list of non-sensitive material (a schedule of non-sensitive material) as well as a schedule of sensitive material (i.e. material that it is not in the public interest to disclose).[58]

---

52 Part II, Criminal Procedure and Investigations Act 1996 (s. 23(1)).
53 Criminal Procedure and Investigations Act 1996 Code of Practice at para. 5.7.
54 Ibid. at para. 5.8.
55 Ibid. at para. 5.9.
56 Ibid. at para. 5.10.
57 Ibid. at para. 6.2.
58 Ibid. at paras. 6.3 and 6.4.

13.8 PUBLIC INTEREST IMMUNITY

While the prosecution is subject to initial duties of disclosure, non-disclosure may be justified on grounds of public interest immunity (or PII) where, for instance, the material is of a sensitive nature. As stated above, the prosecution must compile a sensitive schedule of material which may be covered by public interest immunity. If the prosecution wishes to apply for immunity from having to disclose certain material or information, it must make a public interest immunity application to the court. Evidence which may be covered by public interest immunity includes:

- documents relating to national security,
- confidential information,
- the identity of police informants or undercover officers,
- details of premises used for police surveillance,
- details of other crime detection methods, or
- information relating to the welfare of children.

Section 21(2) of the Criminal Procedure and Investigations Act 1996 expressly preserved the common law position on public interest immunity in criminal proceedings. Thus, it is necessary to consider the case law on public interest immunity. In the case of *R* v. *Ward*[59] it was held that it is for the court, not for the prosecution, to make the final decision as to whether immunity from disclosure should be granted. Further guidance on public interest immunity was set out by the Court of Appeal in the case of *R* v. *Davis*.[60] The Court held that the prosecution has a general duty to make voluntary disclosure of material (today this is in accordance with its obligations under the Criminal Procedure and Investigations Act 1996). Where the prosecution claims that it should not be required to disclose material on ground of public interest immunity there are three forms in which the application might be made.[61] The nature of the application made in any given case will depend on the material that the prosecution seeks to protect.

13.8.1 *Inter partes* application

Under the first type of public interest immunity application, the prosecution must notify the defence that it is applying to the court in respect of non-disclosure and must inform the defence of the category of the material in question. The defence may then make representations in court opposing the application. This is known as an *inter partes* application since both parties are in court during the application.

13.8.2 *Ex parte* application with notice

However, the court recognised that, in some situations, revealing the category of material to the defence would also reveal the information that the prosecution is trying to protect (i.e. that it is not in the public interest to reveal). In such situations, the prosecution should notify the defence

---

59 [1993] 1 WLR 619.
60 [1993] 1 WLR 613.
61 The procedure for applications for public interest immunity is now contained within Part 22 of the Criminal Procedure Rules 2013.

that the application is going to be made to the court, but not of the category of material that it concerns. The application is then made *ex parte* with notice (i.e. only the prosecution is permitted to attend the public interest immunity application at court to make representations – the defence may not attend, but is aware that the application is taking place). If the court considers that the application should have been made *inter partes*, then it will so order.

13.8.3 *Ex parte* without notice

Finally, where even notifying the defence that a public interest immunity application is going to be made will in itself reveal the very material that the prosecution is seeking to protect, the prosecution will make an *ex parte* application without notice (i.e. only the prosecution is permitted to attend the court hearing to make representations, and the defence is not notified that the hearing is taking place). If the court thinks that notice should be given to the defence or that the application should have been made *inter partes*, it will so order. This type of application is rarely used and highly controversial.

Throughout this chapter, the protection of the defendant's right to a fair trial under Article 6 of the European Convention on Human Rights has been a recurring interest. In assessing whether the defendant had a fair trial, the court looks at the overall fairness of the proceedings. The Criminal Procedure and Investigations Act 1996 is generally compatible with the defendant's right to a fair trial under Article 6. Where the police or the prosecution fail to collate and retain 'unused' evidence in breach of their duties under the Criminal Procedure and Investigations Act 1996, there may be a breach of the defendant's fair trial under Article 6. However, Article 6 does not require that the defence should have unlimited access to prosecution material.

In *Rowe and Davis* v.*UK*,[62] the European Court of Human Rights held that there had been a violation of the defendant's right to a fair trial under Article 6 of the European Convention on Human Rights where the prosecution withheld evidence from the defence on grounds of public interest immunity without consulting the judge. As stated above, in the earlier case of *R* v. *Ward*,[63] the Court of Appeal held that it was for the judge and not the prosecution to make decisions on the disclosure of material which it may be in the public interest to withhold.

R V.*WARD* [1993] 1 WLR 619
Glidewell, Nolan and Steyn LJJ

[at 681]

... when the prosecution acted as judge in their own cause on the issue of public interest immunity in this case they committed a significant number of errors which affected the fairness of the proceedings. Policy considerations therefore powerfully reinforce the view that it would be wrong to allow the prosecution to withhold material documents without giving any notice of that fact to the defence. If, in a wholly exceptional case, the prosecution are not prepared to have the issue of public interest immunity determined by a court, the result must inevitably be that the prosecution will have to be abandoned.

---

62 (2000) 30 EHRR 1.
63 [1993] 1 WLR 619.

In *R* v. *Governor of Brixton Prison, ex parte Osman*[64] Mann LJ said of the balancing exercise in respect of decisions on public interest immunity: '... a judge is balancing on the one hand the desirability of preserving the public interest in the absence of disclosure against, on the other hand, the interests of justice'.[65] Section 15 of the Criminal Procedure and Investigations Act 1996 provides that the court has a duty to continually monitor its decisions on public interest immunity. If the court orders non-disclosure of material before the trial begins, that decision is not necessarily final. The court may change its mind and order disclosure at a later stage, at which point it is up to the prosecution whether they make disclosure of the material in question or offer no further evidence in the case.

In the case of *Edwards and Lewis* v. *UK*,[66] important evidence was withheld from the defence on grounds of public interest immunity. The European Court of Human Rights held that there had been a violation of Article 6.1 and stated that the procedure followed to determine public interest immunity issues conflicted with the requirements of adversarial proceedings and equality of arms and failed to sufficiently safeguard the interests of the defendants. The Court held that:

> It is in any event a fundamental aspect of the right to a fair trial that criminal proceedings, including the elements of such proceedings which relate to procedure, should be adversarial and that there should be equality of arms between the prosecution and defence. The right to an adversarial trial means, in a criminal case, that both prosecution and defence must be given the opportunity to have knowledge of and comment on the observations filed and the evidence adduced by the other party.[67]

The Court acknowledged that there is sometimes a need to withhold information from the defendant on grounds of public interest immunity. However, the Court was concerned that in such cases where the defendant is to be deprived of material in his defence, the procedures adopted must safeguard the rights of the defendant:

> ... In some cases it may be necessary to withhold certain evidence from the defence so as to preserve the fundamental rights of another individual or to safeguard an important public interest. Nonetheless, only such measures restricting the rights of the defence which are strictly necessary are permissible under Article 6(1). Furthermore, in order to ensure that the accused receives a fair trial, any difficulties caused to the defence by a limitation on its rights must be sufficiently counterbalanced by the procedures followed by the judicial authorities ...[68]

The case of *Edwards and Lewis* v. *UK* called into question the use of *ex parte* applications without notice. This procedure has long proved controversial and the use of special independent counsel has been suggested as a way of getting round the problem of an unrepresented defendant. Special independent counsel have been used in some proceedings involving issues

---

64 [1991] 1 WLR 281, DC.
65 Ibid. at 288.
66 (2004) 40 EHRR 593.
67 Ibid. at [52].
68 Ibid. at [53].

of national security in immigration appeals, but independent counsel are not yet common place in standard criminal proceedings and the procedure of employing independent counsel is not without problems itself. In the recent leading House of Lords' decision on public interest immunity applications in criminal proceedings, Lord Bingham provided guidance on the procedure to be followed by judges hearing such applications and considered the potential use of special independent counsel.

R V. H & C [2004] UKHL 3
Lord Bingham

18 Circumstances may arise in which material held by the prosecution and tending to undermine the prosecution or assist the defence cannot be disclosed to the defence, fully or even at all, without the risk of serious prejudice to an important public interest ... some derogation from the golden rule of full disclosure may be justified but such derogation must always be the minimum derogation necessary to protect the public interest in question and must never imperil the overall fairness of the trial.

...

21 The years since the decision in *R v Davis* [1993] 1 WLR 613 and enactment of the Criminal Proceedings and Investigations Act 1996 have witnessed the introduction in some areas of the law of a novel procedure designed to protect the interests of a party against whom an adverse order may be made and who cannot (either personally or through his legal representative), for security reasons, be fully informed of all the material relied on against him. The procedure is to appoint a person, usually called a 'special advocate', who may not disclose to the subject of the proceedings the secret material disclosed to him, and is not in the ordinary sense professionally responsible to that party, but who, subject to those constraints, is charged to represent that party's interests ... The courts have recognised the potential value of a special advocate even in situations for which no statutory provision is made. Thus the Court of Appeal invited the appointment of a special advocate when hearing an appeal against a decision of the Special Immigration Appeals Commission in *Secretary of State for the Home Department v Rehman* [2003] 1 AC 153, paras 31–32, and in *R v Shayler* [2003] 1 AC 247, para 34, the House recognised that this procedure might be appropriate if it were necessary to examine very sensitive material on an application for judicial review by a member or former member of a security service.

22 There is as yet little express sanction in domestic legislation or domestic legal authority for the appointment of a special advocate or special counsel to represent, as an advocate in PII matters, a defendant in an ordinary criminal trial, as distinct from proceedings of the kind just considered. But novelty is not of itself an objection, and cases will arise in which the appointment of an approved advocate as special counsel is necessary, in the interests of justice, to secure protection of a criminal defendant's right to a fair trial. Such an appointment does however raise ethical problems, since a lawyer who cannot take full instructions from his client, nor report to his client, who is not responsible to his client and whose relationship with the client lacks the quality of confidence inherent in any ordinary lawyer-client relationship, is acting in a way hitherto unknown to the legal profession. While not insuperable, these problems should not be ignored, since neither the defendant nor the public will be fully aware of what is being done. The appointment is also likely to cause practical problems: of delay, while the special counsel familiarises himself with the detail of what is likely to be a complex case; of expense, since the introduction of an additional, high-quality

advocate must add significantly to the cost of the case; and of continuing review, since it will not be easy for a special counsel to assist the court in its continuing duty to review disclosure, unless the special counsel is present throughout or is instructed from time to time when need arises. Defendants facing serious charges frequently have little inclination to co-operate in a process likely to culminate in their conviction, and any new procedure can offer opportunities capable of exploitation to obstruct and delay. None of these problems should deter the court from appointing special counsel where the interests of justice are shown to require it. But the need must be shown. Such an appointment will always be exceptional, never automatic; a course of last and never first resort. It should not be ordered unless and until the trial judge is satisfied that no other course will adequately meet the overriding requirement of fairness to the defendant. In the Republic of Ireland, whose legal system is, in many respects, not unlike that of England and Wales, a principled but pragmatic approach has been adopted to questions of disclosure and it does not appear that provision has been made for the appointment of special counsel . . .

Lord Bingham emphasised that the public interest immunity regime was compatible with the Convention rights and the jurisprudence of the European Court of Human Rights: 'there is no dissonance between the principles of domestic law and those recognised in the Convention jurisprudence'.[69] Lord Bingham provided guidance on the considerations required in criminal cases involving public interest immunity applications.

R V. H & C [2004] UKHL 3
Lord Bingham

36 When any issue of derogation from the golden rule of full disclosure comes before it, the court must address a series of questions.

(1) What is the material which the prosecution seek to withhold? This must be considered by the court in detail.

(2) Is the material such as may weaken the prosecution case or strengthen that of the defence? If No, disclosure should not be ordered. If Yes, full disclosure should (subject to (3), (4) and (5) below) be ordered.

(3) Is there a real risk of serious prejudice to an important public interest (and, if so, what) if full disclosure of the material is ordered? If No, full disclosure should be ordered.

(4) If the answer to (2) and (3) is Yes, can the defendant's interest be protected without disclosure or disclosure be ordered to an extent or in a way which will give adequate protection to the public interest in question and also afford adequate protection to the interests of the defence?

This question requires the court to consider, with specific reference to the material which the prosecution seek to withhold and the facts of the case and the defence as disclosed, whether the prosecution should formally admit what the defence seek to establish or whether disclosure short of full disclosure may be ordered. This may be done in appropriate cases by the preparation of summaries or extracts of evidence, or the provision of documents in an edited or anonymised form, provided the documents supplied are in each instance approved by the judge. In appropriate cases

---

69 *R* v. *H & C* [2004] UKHL 3 at [33].

the appointment of special counsel may be a necessary step to ensure that the contentions of the prosecution are tested and the interests of the defendant protected (see para 22 above). In cases of exceptional difficulty the court may require the appointment of special counsel to ensure a correct answer to questions (2) and (3) as well as (4).

(5) Do the measures proposed in answer to (4) represent the minimum derogation necessary to protect the public interest in question? If No, the court should order such greater disclosure as will represent the minimum derogation from the golden rule of full disclosure.

(6) If limited disclosure is ordered pursuant to (4) or (5), may the effect be to render the trial process, viewed as a whole, unfair to the defendant? If Yes, then fuller disclosure should be ordered even if this leads or may lead the prosecution to discontinue the proceedings so as to avoid having to make disclosure.

(7) If the answer to (6) when first given is No, does that remain the correct answer as the trial unfolds, evidence is adduced and the defence advanced?

   It is important that the answer to (6) should not be treated as a final, once-and-for-all, answer but as a provisional answer which the court must keep under review.

Despite approving of the public interest immunity procedure adopted by the courts, Lord Bingham in the House of Lords reiterated that the use of *ex parte* applications without notice would be extremely rare and even questions whether such cases should proceed at all if the material being withheld from the defence would be 'of significant help to the defendant'. In such cases, Lord Bingham states that 'there must be a very serious question whether the prosecution should proceed, since special counsel, even if appointed, cannot then receive any instructions from the defence at all'.[70]

Today, the procedure for making a public interest immunity application is found under rule 22.3 of the Criminal Procedure Rules. Rule 22.3(2)(b) provides that an application to withhold material on grounds of public interest immunity should be made initially in writing to the court, any other person who the prosecutor thinks would be directly affected by disclosure of the material, and the defendant, but only to the extent that serving it on the defendant would not disclose what the prosecutor thinks ought not to be disclosed. Under rule 22.3(5), the court may direct the prosecutor to serve an application on the defendant or on any other person who the court considers would be directly affected by the disclosure. Rule 22.3(6) states that the court must then determine the application at a hearing in private, and which may take place in the absence of the defendant if the court so directs.

13.9   CLOSED MATERIAL PROCEDURES

Sections 6 to 14 of the Justice and Security Act 2013 provide for 'closed material procedures' in certain civil proceedings. These highly controversial provisions came into force on 25 June

---

70 Ibid. at [37].

2013. They permit a court to hear sensitive material in the absence of one or more of the parties to the proceedings. Such hearings take place in secret and contravene the principle of open justice. Under s. 6(1), a court hearing relevant civil proceedings[71] may make a declaration that the case is one in which a closed material application may be made to the court. The declaration may be made if two conditions are met. The conditions are:

1. a party to the proceedings would be required to disclose sensitive material in the course of the proceedings to another person, or would be required to make such a disclosure were it not for the availability of a claim for public interest immunity and other immunity rules (s. 6(4)); and
2. it is in the interests of the fair and effective administration of justice in the proceedings to make a declaration (s. 6(5)).

According to s. 6(11), 'sensitive material' means 'material the disclosure of which would be damaging to the interests of national security'. Where such a declaration has been made, the court has an obligation to keep the declaration under review and must undertake a formal review of the declaration once pre-trial disclosure has taken place, and it may revoke the declaration if it considers that the declaration is no longer in the interests of the fair and effective administration of justice.[72] In doing so, the court must consider all of the material that has been put before it in the proceedings.[73] An application under s. 6 must be made in the absence of every other party to the proceedings and their legal representatives.[74] Under s. 9, the Attorney General may appoint a special advocate to represent the interests of a party in a s. 6 application. However, while special advocates may be appointed to represent the absent party, they may not pass the details of the hearing on to the party, leaving the party without vital information. The courts have been critical of the closed material procedure. In *Al Rawi* v. *Security Service*,[75] Lord Dyson stated that 'a closed procedure is the very antithesis of a PII procedure'.[76] In the first ruling on the use of these provisions, *CF* v. *The Security Service and others* and *Mohamed* v. *Foreign and Commonwealth Office and others*,[77] Irwin J compared PII applications to closed material procedure and highlighted some of the objections to closed material procedure:

> A PII ruling ... has a stark result. The relevant documents are either in the open, or withheld and thus not brought to bear on the issues. Subject to some rather specific potential orders, anything which is brought into evidence is known to all the parties and to the public. The process of justice is visible. Evidence relied on is heard. Of course, evidence withheld is never heard or examined: it may be so because the PII application was successful, or because the State withheld the evidence anyway, in the

---

71 According to s. 6(11), this applies to the High Court, the Court of Appeal, the Court of Session or the Supreme Court.
72 Section 7(2) and (3), Justice and Security Act 2013.
73 Section 7(5), Justice and Security Act 2013.
74 Section 8(1)(b), Justice and Security Act 2013.
75 [2011] UKSC 34.
76 Ibid. at [41].
77 [2013] EWHC 3402 (QB).

face of an unsuccessful PII application, rendering that step proper by abandoning the case, or abandoning the issue to which that evidence relates … The Act permits the State to establish a regime, if the relevant criteria are established in the case in hand, allowing evidence to be adduced in private, under strict conditions which do not threaten national security. This can avoid the need for a concession which threatens or carries injustice for the State. It imports a corresponding risk of injustice to the Claimant acting against the State, whose case will now be met by evidence he never hears and cannot answer … One imperfection of closed material procedures that cannot be cured is the offence against the famous maxim of Lord Hewart CJ: in a closed material procedure, justice is not seen to be done, even when it is done … It is obvious that the lack of visibility is likely to diminish respect for the system, whatever the quality of justice actually delivered.[78]

Closed material procedures are objectionable and run the risk of diminishing public confidence in the justice system. They provide protection for government departments at the price of open justice and serve to cement an inequality in arms between the parties to the proceedings.

13.10 CONCLUSION

The law on disclosure and public interest immunity is controversial and often the subject of academic debate. In relation to prosecution disclosure, the problem facing the law is that of striking the right balance between protecting the defendant's right to a fair trial under Article 6 of the European Convention on Human Rights by ensuring openness and transparency through the disclosure of material held by the prosecution, such that the defendant is made aware of the evidence against him before trial, against the public interest in non-disclosure of certain sensitive material held by the prosecution. In relation to the issue of defence disclosure, the law must again balance the interest in ensuring an efficient and cost-effective trial through eliminating so-called 'ambush defences' by requiring defence disclosure, against the interest of the defendant in not assisting the prosecution case against him. Furthermore, the sanctions that the Criminal Procedure and Investigations Act 1996 lays down for defence non-disclosure has implications for the defendant in the sense that the jury may be permitted to draw adverse inferences from the defendant's disclosure failure. When compared with the sanctions for prosecution failures in disclosure, these defence sanctions are also troublesome. The public interest immunity procedure is particularly controversial because it allows for the use of *ex parte* applications without notice and the law must seek to ensure that this procedure does not infringe the defendant's right to a fair trial under Article 6 of the European Convention on Human Rights.

---

78 Ibid. at [16]–[21].

Summary

- Advance information under Part 21, Criminal Procedure Rules 2011 applies only in summary only and either way matters and is designed to provide the defence with any used material which supports the allegation against the defendant.
- In indictable only cases, the prosecution will serve both used material, including details of the charges against the defendant, the witness statements of witnesses the prosecution intends to rely on, and a schedule of unused material, alongside the material which should be disclosed as part of initial prosecution disclosure under s. 3, Criminal Procedure and Investigations Act 1996.
- Under s. 3, Criminal Procedure and Investigations Act 1996, the prosecution must disclose to the defence any unused material which 'might reasonably be considered capable of undermining the case for the prosecution against the accused or of assisting the case for the accused'.
- In a summary case, s. 6 of the Act applies which provides that the defence *may* serve a defence statement on the prosecution.
- In a case which is to be tried on indictment, s. 5 of the 1996 Act applies which provides that the defence *must* serve a defence statement on the prosecution.
- Under s. 6A(1), Criminal Procedure and Investigations Act 1996, the defence statement requires the defence to set out the nature of the defence, including any particular defences; indicate the matters of fact on which the accused takes issue with the prosecution and set out why; and indicate any point of law which the accused wishes to take and any authorities he intends to rely upon.
- Under s. 6A(2), Criminal Procedure and Investigations Act 1996, where the defence is alibi, the accused must provide particulars of any alibi witnesses, including the name, address and date of birth of the witness, or any information that the defendant has which might be of material assistance in finding the witness.
- Under s. 6C, Criminal Procedure and Investigations Act 1996, the defence must notify the prosecution of any witnesses the defence intends to call.
- The prosecution has a continuing duty of disclosure of unused material under s. 7A, Criminal Procedure and Investigations Act 1996.
- Where the defence believes that the prosecution has further material in its possession which should have been disclosed to the defence under the 1996 Act and it has failed to do so, the defence may make an application to the court for an order that the prosecution should comply with the disclosure under s. 8, Criminal Procedure and Investigations Act 1996.
- Under s. 11 of the Criminal Procedure and Investigations Act 1996, a defendant may be subject to sanctions for failing to comply with the provisions relating to defence disclosure.
- While the prosecution is subject to initial duties of disclosure, non-disclosure may be justified on grounds of public interest immunity where, for instance, the material is of a sensitive nature.

For discussion . . .

1. Identify the circumstances under which the defence is obliged to serve a defence statement.
2. To what extent do you agree with Professor Zander that defence disclosure is 'contrary to principle'? Give reasons for your answer.
3. Compare and contrast the sanctions for prosecution and defence failures to comply with the requirements of disclosure.
4. What criticisms might be made of the current system of disclosure?
5. Critically evaluate the current procedure governing public interest immunity applications.

Further reading

D. Corker, 'Disclosure stripped bare' (2004) 9 Archbold News 6.
This is a brief commentary on the reasons behind the reforms to the disclosure regime introduced by the Criminal Justice Act 2003 and the problems with the Criminal Procedure and Investigations Act 1996. The author also provides a summary of some cases from 2003 and 2004.

S. Forster, 'Disclosure of evidence in criminal trials' (2012) 176 JPN 85.
This article provides a brief up-to-date narrative of recent case law relating to disclosure.

R. Leng, 'Defence strategies for information deficit: negotiating the CPIA' (1997) 1 E&P 215.
This pre-Criminal Justice Act 2003 paper focuses on the effect of the disclosure rules on the defence and explores three concerns: (1) the requirement that defendants disclose their defences pre-trial, (2) the possibility that adverse evidential inferences may be drawn where the defendant fails to fulfil his disclosure obligations, and (3) the extent to which restrictions on the prosecution duty to disclose prejudice the defendant's right to a fair trial. The article considers the strategies that might be employed by the defence to overcome information deficit.

H. Quirk, 'The significance of culture in criminal procedure reform: why the revised disclosure scheme cannot work' (2006) 10(1) E&P 42.
This paper considers the effect of the reforms to the disclosure rules made by the Criminal Justice Act 2003 and argues that the legislation has prioritised the alleged problems suffered by the prosecution, rather than focusing on the importance of disclosure as a safeguard to the defendant against miscarriages of justice.

M. Redmayne, 'Criminal Justice Act 2003 (1): disclosure and its discontents' [2004] Crim LR 441.
This article considers the effect of the amendments made by the Criminal Justice Act 2003 on the disclosure regime. It considers the common law developments in relation to the procedure governing public interest immunity applications in the light of recent European Court of Human Rights jurisprudence.

S. Sharpe, 'The Human Rights Act 1998: Article 6 and the disclosure of evidence in criminal trials' [1999] Crim LR 273.

This article explores the effect that the enactment of the Human Rights Act 1998 might have on the law relating to disclosure and concludes that Article 6 is unlikely to undermine the statutory scheme of disclosure under the Criminal Procedure and Investigations Act 1996.

J. Sprack, 'The Criminal Procedure and Investigations Act 1996: (1) the duty of disclosure' [1997] Crim LR 308.

This paper provides a comprehensive summary of the disclosure regime under the Criminal Procedure and Investigations Act 1996 and explores the changes brought in by the Act.

14 Privilege and public interest immunity

14.1   INTRODUCTION

When a witness is called to give evidence and answers questions in examination-in-chief, he opens himself up to cross-examination by other parties in the case, and, as a general rule, he must answer any question put to him. However, the law acknowledges that there may be circumstances in which a witness should be permitted to refuse to answer certain questions: for instance, a lawyer should not be required to answer questions about the details of conversations he had with his client, a witness should not be required to answer questions if he might incriminate himself, and the prosecution should not be required to disclose information which might jeopardise national security or police operations. Thus, the law provides privileges for witnesses which protect the witness against such questioning. The circumstances mentioned above and many others are protected by the law of privilege. This chapter explores the law of privilege. It begins with an examination of legal professional privilege, and more specifically, the two categories of legal professional privilege, namely, legal advice privilege and litigation privilege. Other forms of privilege are then considered, including 'without prejudice' communications, the privilege against self-incrimination and public interest immunity.

14.2   LEGAL PROFESSIONAL PRIVILEGE

The relationship between a lawyer and his client is a protected one. The law provides that communications between a lawyer and his client are confidential and they are protected by legal professional privilege. Thus, a lawyer cannot be compelled to testify about the details of communications with his client. Legal professional privilege has been held to be an absolute privilege; there are no exceptions to the privilege and the court should not conduct a balancing exercise to weigh up the interests of the client in keeping the communications confidential and the interests of the public in disclosing the communications to the other party.[1]

Legal professional privilege has been traced as far back as the sixteenth century,[2] but it developed more fully through the eighteenth century and cases from the late eighteenth century established the fundamental principles of the privilege. In *Wilson* v. *Rastall*, it was held that legal professional privilege belongs to the client, not the lawyer.[3] This means that only the client can waive the privilege, and the court cannot allow or order a lawyer to reveal confidential client communications.[4] In *R* v. *Derby Magistrates' Court, ex parte B*, Lord Taylor CJ acknowledged the existence of the 'long established rule that a document protected by privilege continues to be so protected so long as the privilege is not waived by the client: once privileged, always privileged'.[5] Thus, legal professional privilege does not come to an end naturally through the progression of time: 'the mouth of such a person is shut forever'.[6]

The law protects the communications between lawyer and client in order to ensure that clients are able to make full and frank disclosure to their lawyers without fear that the information will be divulged in court and used against them. The rationale for the privilege was explored in the case of *Greenough* v. *Gaskell*,[7] in which Lord Brougham LC explained that the foundation for the privilege was grounded in the interests of justice. His Lordship stated that the administration of justice required skilled lawyers and considered that if the privilege did not exist, then citizens would rely upon their own judgement and would be deprived of the assistance of professional lawyers in their defence: 'a man would not venture to consult any skilful person, or would only dare to tell his counsellor half the case'.[8] It was thought that without the law of privilege, clients might fear that their communications might be revealed and used against them in proceedings, thus a client would have no confidence in his relationship with his lawyer.[9] In *Bolton* v. *Liverpool Corporation*, Lord Brougham LC stated that 'No man will dare to consult a professional adviser with a view to his defence or to the enforcement of his rights'.[10] Without confidence that what he says to his lawyer will remain confidential, a client might not feel comfortable divulging all of the details of his case, thus his lawyer

1 See Lord Taylor CJ in *R* v. *Derby Magistrates' Court, ex parte B* [1996] AC 487 at 508–9.
2 In *R* v. *Derby Magistrates' Court, ex parte B* [1996] AC 487 at 504, Lord Taylor CJ traces legal professional privilege back to the case of *Berd* v. *Lovelace* (1577) Cary 62.
3 (1792) 4 Durn & E 753 at 759.
4 Above (n. 1) at 504–5.
5 Ibid. at 503G; and see *Calcraft* v. *Guest* [1898] 1 QB 759 at 761.
6 *Wilson* v. *Rastall* (1792) 4 Durn & E 753 at 759.
7 (1833) 1 M & K 98.
8 Ibid. at 103. As Lord Taylor CJ points out in *R* v. *Derby Magistrates' Court, ex parte B* [1996] AC 487, this rationale was reiterated in several cases throughout the eighteenth century, such as *Anderson* v. *Bank of British Columbia* (1876) 2 Ch D 644, *Southwark and Vauxhall Water Co.* v. *Quick* (1878) 3 QBD 315 and *Pearce* v. *Foster* (1885) 15 QBD 114.
9 *Holmes* v. *Baddeley* (1844) 1 Ph 476 at 480–1.
10 (1833) 1 M & K 88 at 94.

may only end up with half the facts and may not be fully equipped to offer the client the full benefit of legal advice. Thus, the interests of justice require the protection of communications between lawyers and their clients. More recently, this rationale was repeated by Lord Taylor CJ in *Balabel and another* v. *Air India*:

BALABEL AND ANOTHER V. AIR INDIA [1988] CH 317
Lord Taylor CJ

[at 324]

It is common ground that the basic principle justifying legal professional privilege arises from the public interest requiring full and frank exchange of confidence between solicitor and client to enable the latter to receive necessary legal advice. Originally it related only to communications where legal proceedings were in being or in contemplation. This was the rationale which distinguished the solicitor and client relationship from that between any other professional man and his client. There is no doubt that legal professional privilege now extends beyond legal advice in regard to litigation. But how far?

In *Balabel and another* v. *Air India*, Lord Taylor CJ acknowledged the existence of two categories of legal professional privilege, namely legal advice privilege and litigation privilege. The leading case on legal professional privilege is now *Three Rivers District Council and others* v. *Governor and Company of the Bank of England*.[11] This case involved the collapse of the Bank of Credit and Commerce International SA (BCCI). An inquiry was conducted by Lord Bingham into the collapse of BCCI. The liquidators and creditors of BCCI brought an action against the Governor of the Bank of England for misfeasance in public office for failure to properly supervise BCCI. The claimants sought disclosure of documents held by the respondent, Bank of England, which had been created by the respondent's employees in order to pass on to the respondent's solicitors. The respondent claimed that the documents were subject to legal advice privilege. The Court of Appeal held that for legal advice privilege to apply, the advice being sought by the client had to be advice relating to legal rights or liabilities, and, as such, it did not extend to advice as to how the client should present its case to the inquiry. On appeal to the House of Lords the House held that legal advice privilege did attach to communications relating to advice as to how to present evidence to the Bingham inquiry. Lord Carswell in the House of Lords described legal professional privilege as 'a single integral privilege, whose sub-heads are legal advice privilege and litigation privilege'.[12] Lord Scott also confirmed that there are two distinct categories of legal professional privilege. His Lordship explains the difference between legal advice privilege and litigation privilege in the following extract:

---

11 [2004] UKHL 48.
12 Ibid. at [105].

THREE RIVERS DISTRICT COUNCIL AND OTHERS V. GOVERNOR AND COMPANY OF THE BANK OF ENGLAND [2004] UKHL 48
Lord Scott

10. The modern case law on legal professional privilege has divided the privilege into two categories, legal advice privilege and litigation privilege. Litigation privilege covers all documents brought into being for the purposes of litigation. Legal advice privilege covers communications between lawyers and their clients whereby legal advice is sought or given. In *re L* [1997] AC 16 Lord Jauncey of Tullichettle described litigation privilege as 'essentially a creature of adversarial proceedings' and held that the privilege could not be claimed in order to protect from disclosure a report prepared for use in non-adversarial proceedings (see p. 26). Lord Lloyd of Berwick and Lord Steyn expressed their agreement. The Bingham Inquiry could not have been described as adversarial. It was, as inquiries invariably are, an inquisitorial proceeding.

Lord Scott describes legal advice privilege as those communications which take place between lawyers and their clients where the lawyer provides legal advice or the client seeks legal advice. His Lordship describes litigation privilege as covering all documents which are created for the purposes of litigation. These two categories of legal professional privilege are discussed in the following paragraphs (see Figure 14.1).

14.2.1 Legal advice privilege

Legal advice privilege applies to 'all communications passing between a client and its lawyers, acting in their professional capacity, in connection with the provision of legal advice'.[13] In *Three Rivers District Council and others* v. *Governor and Company of the Bank of England*, Lord Scott reviewed the features of legal advice privilege.

THREE RIVERS DISTRICT COUNCIL AND OTHERS V. GOVERNOR AND COMPANY OF THE BANK OF ENGLAND [2004] UKHL 48
Lord Scott

24. First, legal advice privilege arises out of a relationship of confidence between lawyer and client. Unless the communication or document for which privilege is sought is a confidential one, there can be no question of legal advice privilege arising. The confidential character of the communication or document is not by itself enough to enable privilege to be claimed but is an essential requirement.

25. Second, if a communication or document qualifies for legal professional privilege, the privilege is absolute. It cannot be overridden by some supposedly greater public interest. It can be waived by the person, the client, entitled to it and it can be overridden by statute (c/f *R (Morgan Grenfell Ltd) v Special Commissioner of Income Tax* [2003] 1 AC 563), but it is otherwise absolute. There is no balancing exercise

---

13 *R (on the application of Prudential plc and another)* v. *Special Commissioner of Income Tax and another* [2013] 2 WLR 325, SC at [19].

that has to be carried out (see *B v Auckland District Law Society* [2003] 2 AC 736 paras. 46 to 54). The Supreme Court of Canada has held that legal professional privilege although of great importance is not absolute and can be set aside if a sufficiently compelling public interest for doing so, such as public safety, can be shown (see *Jones v Smith* [1999] 1 SCR 455). But no other common law jurisdiction has, so far as I am aware, developed the law of privilege in this way. Certainly in this country legal professional privilege, if it is attracted by a particular communication between lawyer and client or attaches to a particular document, cannot be set aside on the ground that some other higher public interest requires that to be done.

26. Third, legal advice privilege gives the person entitled to it the right to decline to disclose or to allow to be disclosed the confidential communication or document in question. There has been some debate as to whether this right is a procedural right or a substantive right. In my respectful opinion the debate is sterile. Legal advice privilege is both. It may be used in legal proceedings to justify the refusal to answer certain questions or to produce for inspection certain documents. Its characterisation as procedural or substantive neither adds to nor detracts from its features.

27. Fourth, legal advice privilege has an undoubted relationship with litigation privilege. Legal advice is frequently sought or given in connection with current or contemplated litigation. But it may equally well be sought or given in circumstances and for purposes that have nothing to do with litigation. If it is sought or given in connection with litigation, then the advice would fall into both of the two categories. But it is long settled that a connection with litigation is not a necessary condition for privilege to be attracted (see e.g. *Greenough v Gaskell* (1833) 1 My & K 98 per Lord Brougham at 102/3 and *Minet v Morgan* (1873) 8 Ch. App. 361). On the other hand it has been held that litigation privilege can extend to communications between a lawyer or the lawyer's client and a third party or to any document brought into existence for the dominant purpose of being used in litigation. The connection between legal advice sought or given and the affording of privilege to the communication has thereby been cut.

Thus, Lord Scott identified four features of legal advice privilege:

1. there must be a relationship of *confidence* between lawyer and client (a confidential communication or document alone is not sufficient);
2. legal advice privilege is absolute – it cannot be overridden by public interest. It can be waived by the client entitled to it and it can be overridden by statute;
3. legal advice privilege gives the person entitled to it the right to decline to disclose or to allow to be disclosed the confidential communication or document in question; and
4. legal advice privilege may overlap with litigation privilege.

The Supreme Court recently revisited the issue of legal advice privilege in *R (on the application of Prudential plc and another)* v. *Special Commissioner of Income Tax and another.*[14] Lord Neuberger held that legal professional privilege grants the client the right to object to a third party seeing any communications between the client and his lawyer unless:

- the client has agreed to the disclosure or waived his privilege,
- a statute overrides the privilege,

---

14 Ibid.

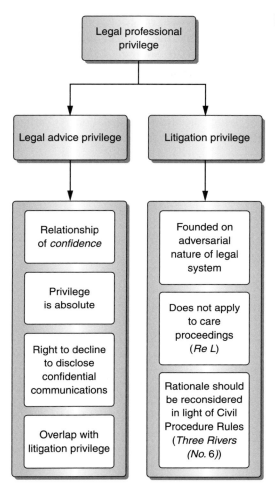

Figure 14.1 Overview of legal professional privilege

- the document was prepared for, or in connection with, a nefarious purpose, or
- another exception applies.[15]

In this case, the Supreme Court explored the scope of legal advice privilege. The question which the Court was asked to consider was whether legal advice privilege applied to professionals other than members of the legal profession who provided legal advice in the course of their profession. For instance, the particular facts of this case involved accountants who gave legal advice in respect of tax matters. The Special Inspector of Income Tax requested certain documents from Prudential (Gibraltar) Ltd and Prudential plc relating to its tax affairs. The Prudential claimed that the documents which contained legal advice given to them by their accountants, PricewaterhouseCoopers, should be subject to legal advice privilege. As stated above, the origins of legal advice privilege date back to the sixteenth century when only lawyers

---

15 Ibid. at [17].

dispensed legal advice; however, in modern society, a wider range of professionals might offer legal advice. Nevertheless, the Supreme Court held that the privilege did not extend beyond lawyers, and thus, it did not apply to accountants. The Supreme Court acknowledged the attractive argument in favour of extending the scope of the privilege, but were concerned that any such extension would render the privilege unclear and uncertain. The Court held that if the law should be amended to encompass other professionals within the remit of legal advice privilege, then it should be for Parliament to change the law with legislation. As Parliament had not seen fit to extend the law in this way, the Supreme Court would not interfere with the law as it stands.

In *Three Rivers District Council and others* v. *Governor and Company of the Bank of England*, Lord Scott considered the policy reasons which underpin the law relating to legal advice privilege.

THREE RIVERS DISTRICT COUNCIL AND OTHERS V. GOVERNOR AND COMPANY OF THE BANK OF ENGLAND [2004] UKHL 48
Lord Scott

28. So I must now come to policy. Why is it that the law has afforded this special privilege to communications between lawyers and their clients that it has denied to all other confidential communications? In relation to all other confidential communications, whether between doctor and patient, accountant and client, husband and wife, parent and child, priest and penitent, the common law recognises the confidentiality of the communication, will protect the confidentiality up to a point, but declines to allow the communication the absolute protection allowed to communications between lawyer and client giving or seeking legal advice. In relation to all these other confidential communications the law requires the public interest in the preservation of confidences and the private interest of the parties in maintaining the confidentiality of their communications to be balanced against the administration of justice reasons for requiring disclosure of the confidential material. There is a strong public interest that in criminal cases the innocent should be acquitted and the guilty convicted, that in civil cases the claimant should succeed if he is entitled to do so and should fail if he is not, that every trial should be a fair trial and that to provide the best chance of these desiderata being achieved all relevant material should be available to be taken into account. These are the administration of justice reasons to be placed in the balance. They will usually prevail.

Lord Scott distinguished the lawyer–client relationship, which involves the giving or receiving of legal advice, from other types of relationship in which communications are deemed to be confidential, such as doctor–patient, husband–wife and priest and penitent. While it is both in the public interest and the private interest of the individual to maintain the confidentiality of communications in all of these relationships, the administration of justice must be weighed against these interests. Thus, where the communications should be disclosed in the interests of justice, then the privilege afforded to the confidential communications is overridden. However, in the case of a lawyer–client relationship, the confidential nature of communications regarding legal advice is absolute. It is not outweighed by the interests of justice because the right of a person to seek and receive legal advice from a professional lawyer is paramount. In *R* v. *Derby Magistrates' Court, ex parte B*, Lord Taylor CJ held that:

> The principle which runs through all these cases, and the many other cases which were cited, is that a man must be able to consult his lawyer in confidence, since otherwise he might hold back half the truth. The client must be sure that what he tells his lawyer in confidence will never be revealed without his consent. Legal professional privilege is thus much more than an ordinary rule of evidence, limited in its application to the facts of a particular case. It is a fundamental condition on which the administration of justice as a whole rests.[16]

In *R (on the application of Prudential plc and another)* v. *Special Commissioner of Income Tax and another*,[17] Lord Neuberger made three important points about legal advice privilege and the rationale for the privilege.

R (ON THE APPLICATION OF PRUDENTIAL PLC AND ANOTHER) V. SPECIAL COMMISSIONER OF INCOME TAX AND ANOTHER [2013] UKSC 1
Lord Neuberger, PSC

21. First, LAP [legal advice privilege] exists to ensure that there is what Justice Rehnquist referred to in the Supreme Court of the United States as 'full and frank communication between attorneys and their clients', which 'promote[s] broader public interests in the observance of law and administration of justice' – *Upjohn Co v United States* (1981) 449 US 383, 389, quoted by Lord Scott in *Three Rivers (No 6)* at para 31. As Lord Scott went on to explain at para 34, the principle 'that communications between clients and lawyers, whereby the clients are hoping for the assistance of the lawyers' legal skills . . ., should be secure against the possibility of any scrutiny from others, whether the police, the executive, business competitors, inquisitive busybodies or anyone else' is founded upon 'the rule of law'.

22. Secondly, LAP exists solely for the benefit of the client. As Bingham LJ said in *Ventouris v Mountain* [1991] 1 WLR 607, 611, the expression 'legal professional privilege' is 'unhappy' in so far as it suggests that the privilege is that of the legal profession, when it is 'the client who enjoys the privilege'. Thus, as Lord Hoffmann pointed out in Morgan Grenfell at para 37, '[i]f the client chooses to divulge the information, there is nothing the lawyer can do about it'.

23. Thirdly, LAP is a common law principle, which was developed by the judges in cases going back at least to the 16th century . . . (Litigation privilege seems to have developed rather later . . .).

Lord Neuberger agreed with Justice Rehnquist in the US Supreme Court case *Upjohn Co.* v. *United States* that the rationale for legal advice privilege is to encourage full and frank communications between a client and his lawyer, and that this in turn promotes public interests through the observance of law and administration of justice. Finally, Lord Neuberger notes that while legal advice privilege dates back to the sixteenth century, litigation privilege (the other

---

16 Above (n. 1) at 507.
17 [2013] UKSC 1.

category of legal professional privilege) developed rather later. Litigation privilege will be considered in the next paragraph.

14.2.2 Litigation privilege

Litigation privilege applies to all documents which are created for the purposes of litigation.[18] Litigation privilege extends to documents prepared by third parties on the instructions of the client, but it only applies to documents which are prepared for anticipated litigation. Thus, a party to litigation cannot be compelled to disclose a report which they have instructed a third party to prepare for anticipated litigation. The rationale for this form of legal professional privilege seems to stem from the adversarial nature of our legal system. In *Re L (A minor) (Police investigation: privilege)*, Lord Jauncey described litigation privilege as 'an essential component of adversarial procedure'.[19] Lord Denning MR stated in *Re Saxton (deceased)* that, 'it is one of our notions of a fair trial that, except by agreement, you are not entitled to see the proofs of the other side's witnesses'.[20] In *Waugh* v. *British Railways Board*, Lord Simon said:

> This system of adversary forensic procedure with legal professional advice and represen-
> tation demands that communications between lawyer and client should be confidential,
> since the lawyer is for the purpose of litigation merely the client's alter ego. So too
> material which is to go into the lawyer's (i.e. the client's) brief or file for litigation. This
> is the basis for the privilege against disclosure of material collected by or on behalf of a
> client for the use of his lawyer in pending or anticipated litigation . . .[21]

This case involved a man who worked for British Rail. He was killed in an accident on the railway. The British Railways Board prepared a report in respect of the accident. Mrs Waugh, the widow, brought an action for negligence against the British Railways Board and sought disclosure of the report. However, the Board claimed that the report was subject to legal professional privilege. The Court of Appeal upheld the claim of the British Railways Board, but the House of Lords allowed the appeal by the claimant and held that the report should be disclosed in the interests of justice. The House held that the report was likely to contain the best evidence about the cause of the accident, that it would only be subject to legal professional privilege if the dominant purpose of preparing the report was anticipated litigation. The purpose of preparing the report here was both to ensure safety on the railways and the anticipated litigation, and these two purposes were of equal weight. As such, litigation was not the 'dominant purpose' and thus the document was not subject to litigation privilege. However, this case was not applied by the Court of Appeal in *BBC* v. *Sugar*,[22] in which the Court cast doubt on the 'dominant purpose' test and held that it could lead to uncertainty because of its subjective nature.

---

18 *Waugh* v. *British Railways Board* [1980] AC 521.
19 [1997] AC 16 at 25.
20 [1962] 1 WLR 968 at 972.
21 Above (n. 18) at 536.
22 [2010] EWCA Civ 715.

In light of the fact that litigation privilege is founded upon the adversarial nature of our legal system, in *Re L (A minor) (Police investigation: privilege)* the House of Lords had to consider whether litigation privilege applied to care proceedings under the Children Act 1989. Lord Jauncey regarded care proceedings as 'essentially non-adversarial' and held that 'litigation privilege never arose' in relation to such proceedings.[23] His Lordship disapproved of the approach taken by Sir Stephen Brown P in the earlier case of *Oxfordshire City Council* v. *M*,[24] in which it was held that litigation privilege did exist in care proceedings, but that the court had the power to override the privilege. Lord Jauncey stated that 'The better view is that litigation privilege never arose in the first place rather than the court has the power to override it. It is excluded by necessary implication from the terms and overall purpose of the [Children Act 1989]. This does not of course affect privilege arising between solicitor and client.' However, this approach in respect of non-adversarial proceedings was questioned by the House of Lords in *Three Rivers District Council and others* v. *Governor and Company of the Bank of England*. Lord Scott commented *obiter* that since the reforms to civil procedure in 1998, civil proceedings are 'in many respects no longer adversarial', and, as such, His Lordship considered that the decision in *Re L (A minor) (Police investigation: privilege)* and the justification for litigation privilege should be reconsidered. However, since litigation privilege was not the issue of the appeal in *Three Rivers District Council and others* v. *Governor and Company of the Bank of England*, Lord Scott declined to review the issue in this case.

14.2.3 Police powers

Where the police make an application for a warrant under s. 8 of the Police and Criminal Evidence Act 1984 to enter and search premises, in considering the application one of the factors that the magistrates must consider is whether the material reasonably believed to be on the premises is or includes items subject to legal privilege. Section 10(1) of the Police and Criminal Evidence Act 1984 defines 'items subject to legal privilege' as:

(a) communications between lawyer and client made in connection with the giving of legal advice to the client;

(b) communications between lawyer and client or between lawyer or client and any other person made in connection with or in contemplation of legal proceedings and for the purposes of such proceedings; and

(c) items enclosed with or referred to in such communications and made in connection with the giving of legal advice, or in connection with or in contemplation of legal proceedings and for the purposes of such proceedings, when they are in the possession of a person who is entitled to possession of them.

Under s. 10(2), any items held with the intention of furthering a criminal purpose are not subject to legal privilege.

---

23 Above (n. 19) at 27.
24 [1994] Fam 151.

14.3   'WITHOUT PREJUDICE' COMMUNICATIONS

'Without prejudice' communications are communications which take place between opposing parties in a case during negotiations to reach a settlement out of court. Where one party writes to the other party seeking to settle the case, he will usually preface his communication with the other party with the words 'without prejudice'. This means that in the event that the parties do not reach a settlement and the case does go to court, the party receiving the 'without prejudice' communication may not rely upon that communication in court. 'Without prejudice' communications are privileged. In *Oceanbulk Shipping and Trading SA* v. *TMT Asia Ltd and others*, the Supreme Court held that:

> . . . the without prejudice rule, initially focused on the case where the negotiations between two parties were regarded as without prejudice to the position of each of the parties in the event that the negotiations failed. The essential purpose of the original rule was that, if the negotiations failed and the dispute proceeded, neither party should be able to rely upon admissions made by the other in the course of the negotiations. The underlying rationale of the rule was that the parties would be more likely to speak frankly if nothing they said could subsequently be relied upon and that, as a result, they would be more likely to settle their dispute.[25]

The rationale for 'without prejudice' communications is to encourage parties to try to settle their disputes out of court. The privilege afforded to such communications ensures that parties who do make admissions in the course of the communications will be protected from the admission being revealed in court. In *Bill* v. *Simes*, the High Court held that 'This head of privilege is not confined to admissions, but applies to all bona fide without prejudice statements which touch upon the strength or weaknesses of parties' cases or which placed a valuation on a party's rights forming part of the attempt to compromise the litigation.'[26]

14.4   PRIVILEGE AGAINST SELF-INCRIMINATION

The privilege against self-incrimination is the right of a witness not to answer questions which might incriminate him in an offence. It is derived from the Latin maxim *nemo debet prodere se ipsum* which is translated to mean that 'no one can be, or ought to be, compelled or required to betray himself'. In criminal proceedings, an accused may refuse to answer questions put to him in police interview and he may refuse to testify at his trial, although there are implications for a defendant who refuses to testify at trial and a defendant who fails to mention a fact when questioned which he then relies upon as part of his defence at trial.

25 [2010] UKSC 44 at [19].
26 [2013] EWHC 2613 (QB) at [11].

Cross-reference

Refer back to Chapter 4 on Silence for further discussion of the privilege against self-incrimination and the adverse inferences provisions under ss. 34 to 37 of the Criminal Justice and Public Order Act 1994.

In civil proceedings, the privilege against self-incrimination means that a witness may refuse to answer questions in the witness box if it may expose him to a criminal charge.[27]

14.5 PUBLIC INTEREST IMMUNITY

While not really a privilege as such, public interest immunity is similar to the operation of privilege since it also involves the law's regulation of a refusal to disclose material in court proceedings. The key difference between the forms of privilege discussed above and public interest immunity is that privilege generally applies in order to protect the interests of an individual, whereas public interest immunity applies in order to protect much wider interests of the public.

In deciding whether certain evidence should be disclosed by a party in criminal or civil proceedings, there are three competing interests which fall to be considered: the first is that the parties should have access to all relevant evidence; secondly, there is the opposing interest of secrecy – one party may wish to avoid disclosing evidence in order to maintain their privacy; and, thirdly, there is the wider public interest in non-disclosure. Where it is not in the public interest to disclose evidence to the other party or for material to be disclosed in open court, that material may be held to be subject to public interest immunity. The operation of public interest immunity can be compared to exclusionary rules of evidence and the discretion to exclude. As Lord Edmund-Davies stated in *D* v. *National Society for the Prevention of Cruelty to Children*:

> To be received in evidence, facts must be both relevant and admissible, and under our law relevant facts may nevertheless be inadmissible. It is a serious step to exclude evidence relevant to an issue, for it is in the public interest that the search for truth should, in general, be unfettered. Accordingly, any hindrance to its seeker needs to be justified by a convincing demonstration that an even higher public interest requires that only part of the truth should be told.[28]

Consideration of questions of public interest immunity involves balancing competing interests, namely the right of the defendant to have a fair trial, which generally requires full disclosure of relevant evidence, against the wider public interest in non-disclosure of sensitive information if its disclosure might have an adverse effect on matters such as the administration of justice, national security, government policy, the national economy, international relations, the safety of individuals, or the identity of informants.

---

27 See s. 14(1), Civil Evidence Act 1968 and *Blunt* v. *Park Land Hotel Ltd* [1942] 2 KB 253 at 257.
28 [1978] AC 171 at 242.

14.5.1 Civil proceedings

In civil proceedings, a claim for public interest immunity is made at the stage of discovery of documents and is made under rule 31.19, Civil Procedure Rules. The party claiming public interest immunity may make an application without notice to the court for an order permitting him to withhold documents from inspection by other parties.[29] In considering the application, the court may require the party to produce the document to the court, and may invite any person to make representations to the court.[30]

The question of who should decide whether material is subject to public interest immunity in civil proceedings plagued the courts in the mid-twentieth century. In *Duncan* v. *Cammell, Laird & Co. Ltd*,[31] the House of Lords held that 'Crown privilege' (as public interest immunity was referred to then) could be decided by government ministers. The respondents in this case built a submarine for the Admiralty, but it sank in a trial dive killing almost all of the men on board. The plaintiffs sued the respondents for negligence on behalf of some of the deceased men. The respondents (under instruction from the Admiralty) objected to the disclosure of a number of documents relating to the construction of the submarine and the salvage reports on the ground of Crown privilege. Since this case took place during the Second World War, the claim to Crown privilege sought to protect national security. The House of Lords held that the certificate which had been provided by the First Lord of the Admiralty was conclusive and could not be questioned by the court. Viscount Simon LC considered Crown privilege more generally and held that where the Crown is a party in proceedings, the Crown is not obliged by law to make disclosure of documents. While the Crown would generally make disclosure in practice in the interests of justice, the Crown cannot be forced to do so by the courts. Viscount Simon LC stated *obiter* that:

> The principle to be applied in every case is that documents otherwise relevant and liable to production must not be produced if the public interest requires that they should be withheld. This test may be found to be satisfied either (a) by having regard to the contents of the particular document, or (b) by the fact that the document belongs to a class which, on grounds of public interest, must as a class be withheld from production.[32]

Thus, the House held that there are two possible claims to 'Crown privilege':

- contents claims – where the contents of the documents are sensitive and disclosure would damage the public interest; and
- class claims – this is a wider claim which applies where the documents belong to a class of documents that ought not to be disclosed in the public interest (e.g. minutes of government department meetings).

The decision in *Duncan* v. *Cammell, Laird & Co. Ltd* was criticised for many years until the issue of who should decide upon issues of public interest immunity came before the House of Lords again in the landmark case of *Conway* v. *Rimmer*.[33] In this case, the plaintiff was a former

---

29 Rule 31.19(1), Civil Procedure Rules.
30 Rule 31.19(6), Civil Procedure Rules.
31 [1942] AC 624, HL.
32 Ibid. at 636.
33 [1968] UKHL 2, [1968] AC 910, HL.

probationary police officer who brought an action against his former superintendent for malicious prosecution after the officer was prosecuted for, and acquitted of, theft. The defendant was in possession of five confidential reports made about the officer, four of which had been made by the defendant. The Secretary of State for Home Affairs objected to the production of the reports on the ground that they were of a class of documents, the production of which would be damaging to the public interest. The House of Lords overruled the *obiter* statements in *Duncan* v. *Cammell, Laird & Co. Ltd* and ordered that the reports be produced. The House of Lords held that public interest immunity is a question of law for the courts to decide, rather than a question for the executive.

CONWAY V. *RIMMER* [1968] UKHL 2
Lord Reid

[at 10–11]

. . . the courts should balance the public interest in the proper administration of justice against the public interest in withholding any evidence which a Minister considers ought to be withheld.

I would therefore propose that the House ought now to decide that courts have and are entitled to exercise a power and duty to hold a balance between the public interest, as expressed by a Minister, to withhold certain documents or other evidence, and interest in ensuring the proper administration of justice. That does not mean that a court would reject a Minister's view: full weight must be given to it in every case, and if the Minister's reasons are of a character which judicial experience is not competent to weigh, then the Minister's view must prevail. But experience has shown that reasons given for withholding whole classes of documents are often not of that character. For example a court is perfectly well able to assess the likelihood that, if the writer of a certain class of document knew that there was a chance that his report might be produced in legal proceedings, he would make a less full and candid report than he would otherwise have done.

I do not doubt that there are certain classes of documents which ought not to be disclosed whatever their content may be. Virtually everyone agrees that Cabinet minutes and the like ought not to be disclosed until such time as they are only of historical interest. But I do not think that many people would give as the reason that premature disclosure would prevent candour in the Cabinet. To my mind the most important reason is that such disclosure would create or fan ill-informed or captious public or political criticism. The business of government is difficult enough as it is, and no government could contemplate with equanimity the inner workings of the government machine being exposed to the gaze of those ready to criticise without adequate knowledge of the background and perhaps with some axe to grind. And that must, in my view, also apply to all documents concerned with policy making within departments including, it may be, minutes and the like by quite junior officials and correspondence with outside bodies. Further it may be that deliberations about a particular case require protection as much as deliberations about policy. I do not think that it is possible to limit such documents by any definition. But there seems to me to be a wide difference between such documents and routine reports. There may be special reasons for withholding some kinds of routine documents, but I think that the proper test to be applied is to ask, in the language of Lord Simon in *Duncan's* case, whether the withholding of a document because it belongs to a particular class is really 'necessary for the proper functioning of the public service'.

Thus, the House held that public interest immunity is a question of law for the courts (not ministers) to decide. Lord Reid pointed out that some classes of documents might require absolute protection, such as documents concerned with policy making within departments, minutes of government department meetings, other communications by junior officials, and correspondence with outside bodies. However, His Lordship held that such documents should not be limited by definition; rather, the test which should be applied is whether withholding the document is 'necessary for the proper functioning of the public service'. Thus, the courts will conduct a balancing exercise of competing interests: namely, the public interest in providing access to all relevant materials, and the public interest in preventing harm to the proper functioning of the relevant public service.

Public interest immunity does not only apply to government departments, but also extends to any other person or organisation. In *Rogers* v. *Lewes Justices, ex parte Secretary of State for the Home Department*[34] it was held that public interest immunity may be raised by any person and need not be raised by a minister (although Lord Reid acknowledged that a minister is often the most appropriate person).[35] This case concerned the disclosure of information passed to the Gaming Board about the plaintiff who had applied to the Board for certificates of consent in respect of a number of bingo halls. The plaintiff argued for disclosure of the identity of the supplier of the information. The Gaming Board received the information for the purpose of exercising its statutory powers under the Gaming Act 1968 and refused to disclose it, claiming public interest immunity. The function of the Board was to ensure that gaming is kept clean and it claimed that disclosure of the identity of the informant would prevent people supplying such information in the future. The House of Lords held that the public interest required that the information should not be produced, as such disclosure would hamper the Gaming Board in discharging its statutory duty. In *D* v. *National Society for the Prevention of Cruelty to Children*,[36] the defendant charity could also invoke public interest immunity in order to avoid disclosing the name of an informant who reported suspected child abuse. The public interest in excluding the evidence in this case is in ensuring that informants do come forward to report suspected child abuse, and if the charity was forced to disclose the identity of such informants this would deter people from coming forward, making it more difficult for the charity to operate.

Public interest immunity has also been held to apply to the identity of police informants.[37] In *D* v. *National Society for the Prevention of Cruelty to Children*, Lord Diplock explained that the rationale for this rule is to ensure that people are willing to act as police informants and to protect informants from reprisals:

> If their identity were liable to be disclosed in a court of law, these sources of information would dry up and the police would be hindered in their duty of preventing and detecting crime. So the public interest in preserving the anonymity of police informers had to be weighed against the public interest that information which might assist a judicial tribunal

---

34 [1973] AC 388, HL.
35 Ibid. at 400.
36 [1978] AC 171, HL.
37 *Marks* v. *Beyfus* (1890) 25 QBD 494.

to ascertain facts relevant to an issue upon which it is required to adjudicate should be withheld from that tribunal.[38]

While there used to be blanket immunity for certain types of cases, such as in cases involving informants, today the courts prefer to conduct a balancing exercise between the public interest in protecting informants and that of the right to a fair trial under Article 6 of the European Convention on Human Rights.[39] The courts have shown a reluctance to recognise class-based claims to public interest immunity: for instance, the House of Lords has refused to impose a general class of public interest immunity on documents created in the course of a police investigation into police misconduct.[40]

14.5.2 Criminal proceedings

While public interest immunity can be applied in both civil and criminal proceedings, there are very significant differences between the two types of proceedings. The civil and criminal justice systems have very distinct aims and consequences: civil proceedings aim to compensate a party, and the losing party suffers only financial loss; whereas criminal proceedings aim to punish offenders, and the guilty party suffers in far more serious terms through the potential loss of liberty. Thus, in criminal proceedings the public interest in withholding the document must be weighed against the interests of justice, which may include the loss of a person's liberty.[41]

Prior to the Criminal Procedure and Investigations Act 1996, the test for disclosure was much wider and was based upon the relevance of the information; thus, if the document in question might prove the defendant's innocence or avoid a miscarriage of justice, then the courts would rule that it should be disclosed.[42] In *R* v. *Ward*,[43] it was held that it was for the court, not the prosecution, to decide whether material should be withheld in the public interest. In *R* v. *H and C*,[44] the House of Lords held that the court should consider whether or not non-disclosure might lead to the defendant's right to a fair trial being compromised. Further guidance on the process of making a public interest immunity application was set out by the Court of Appeal in *R* v. *Davis*.[45] The prosecution may make an application to withhold material on grounds of public interest immunity in one of three ways:

- as an *inter partes* application,
- as an *ex parte* application with notice, or
- as an *ex parte* application without notice.

The common law position on public interest immunity was preserved by s. 21(2) of the Criminal Procedure and Investigations Act 1996 and the procedure is now contained within rule 22.3 of

---

38 Above (n. 36) at 218.
39 *Chief Constable of Greater Manchester* v. *McNally* [2002] EWCA Civ 14.
40 *R* v. *Chief Constable of the West Midlands, ex parte Wiley* [1995] 1 AC 274.
41 *R* v. *Governor of Brixton Prison, ex parte Osman* [1991] 1 WLR 281.
42 See Lord Taylor CJ in *R* v. *Keane* [1994] 1 WLR 746 at 751–2.
43 [1993] 1 WLR 619.
44 [2004] UKHL 3.
45 [1993] 1 WLR 613.

the Criminal Procedure Rules which provides that an application to withhold material on grounds of public interest immunity should be made initially in writing to the court, any other person who the prosecutor thinks would be directly affected by disclosure of the material, and the defendant, but only to the extent that serving it on the defendant would not disclose what the prosecutor thinks ought not to be disclosed.[46] The court may direct the prosecutor to serve an application on the defendant (if it has not already been done), or on any other person who the court considers would be directly affected by the disclosure.[47] The court must then determine the application at a hearing in private, and which may take place in the absence of the defendant if the court so directs.[48]

> **Cross-reference**
> Refer back to Chapter 13 on Disclosure for further discussion of public interest immunity in the context of criminal proceedings and the three types of application that may be made by the prosecution.

14.6 CONCLUSION

While both the criminal and civil justice systems operate on a system of open justice and full disclosure, the law imposes some limitations on the material which it can demand to be disclosed by a witness. The rationale for imposing these privileges varies from the need to encourage clients to be honest with their lawyers, to encourage parties to try to reach a settlement out of court, to protect a party from incriminating himself, and to protect other wider public interests such as national security, international relations, the identity of informants, etc. Legal professional privilege protects parties from having to disclose material which contains details of communications between client and lawyer regarding legal advice (legal advice privilege), and material which was created by either party or a third party in contemplation of litigation (litigation privilege). Here the law seeks to protect the relationship between a lawyer and his client with a view to encouraging full and frank discussions between them in order that the lawyer can offer accurate and useful legal advice to his client. 'Without prejudice' communications are also privileged since these encourage parties to try to settle out of court. The privilege against self-incrimination protects a witness from incriminating himself by providing him with a privilege not to answer questions which might amount to the admission of a criminal offence. This privilege goes hand-in-hand with the defendant's right to silence, but this is limited by the adverse inferences which may be drawn under ss. 34 to 37 of the Criminal Justice and Public Order Act 1994. Finally, public interest immunity operates to prevent the disclosure of materials in criminal and civil proceedings which it would not be in the public interest to disclose. Public

---

46 Rule 22.3(2)(b), Criminal Procedure Rules.
47 Rule 22.3(5), ibid.
48 Rule 22.3(6), ibid.

interest immunity is a question of law to be decided by the courts, which must weigh up the interests inherent in full disclosure, such as the right to a fair trial in criminal proceedings, against competing interests, such as the protection of informants or the details of police operations.

Summary

- There are two categories of legal professional privilege, namely legal advice privilege and litigation privilege: *Three Rivers District Council and others* v. *Governor and Company of the Bank of England (No. 6)*.
- Legal advice privilege applies to communications between lawyers and their clients where the lawyer provides legal advice or the client seeks legal advice. This privilege is absolute.
- Litigation privilege applies to all documents which are created for the purposes of litigation. It is founded on the adversarial nature of our legal system.
- 'Without prejudice' communications are communications which take place between opposing parties in a case during negotiations to reach a settlement out of court. In the event that the parties do not reach a settlement, the party receiving 'without prejudice' communications may not rely upon that communication in court.
- The privilege against self-incrimination is the right of a witness not to answer questions which might incriminate him in an offence. It is derived from the Latin maxim *nemo debet prodere se ipsum* which is translated to mean that 'no one can be, or ought to be, compelled or required to betray himself'.
- Questions of public interest immunity involve balancing competing interests, namely the full disclosure of relevant evidence against the wider public interest in non-disclosure of sensitive information.
- In civil proceedings, public interest immunity is a question of law for the courts to decide, it is not a question for a minister to decide: *Conway* v. *Rimmer*.
- In criminal proceedings, public interest immunity is a question of law for the courts to decide, it is not a question for a prosecutor to decide: *R* v. *Ward*.

For discussion . . .

1. Explain the rationale for legal professional privilege.
2. Explain the significance of the House of Lords decision in *Three Rivers District Council and others* v. *Governor and Company of the Bank of England* [2004] UKHL 48.
3. Critically evaluate the decision of the Supreme Court in *R (on the application of Prudential plc and another)* v. *Special Commissioner of Income Tax and another* [2013] 2 WLR 325, SC. In your opinion, was the decision rightly decided?
4. Should litigation privilege be extended to cover non-adversarial proceedings?
5. To what extent can principles of public interest immunity applied in civil proceedings also be applied in criminal proceedings?

Further reading

C. Carpenter, 'The scope of legal professional privilege' (2013) PN 132.

> This is a case commentary which examines the decision of the Supreme Court in *R (on the application of Prudential plc)* v. *Special Commissioner of Income Tax.*

H. L. Ho, 'Legal professional privilege and the integrity of legal representation' (2006) 9(2) *Legal Ethics* 163–86.

> In this article, the author explores the concept of legal professional privilege from the standpoints of the lawyer: he considers the privilege as a means of protecting the lawyer's honour and his professional self-interest as well as exploring the criticisms of the conventional argument relating to the promotion of candour. He also examines the privilege from the standpoint of the administration of justice, exploring the privilege as a means of protecting the integrity of legal representation.

C. Passmore, 'The future of legal professional privilege' (1999) 3(2) E&P 71.

> This article considers the case of *R* v. *Derby Magistrates' Court, ex parte B* as well as other cases and examines the extent to which legal professional privilege is under threat.

C. Tapper, 'Prosecution and privilege' (1996–7) 1 E&P 5.

> In this article, the author uses the case of *R* v. *Derby Magistrates' Court, ex parte B* to illustrate competing rules in the criminal justice system, such as the rules of admissibility and rules of procedure, and the different values protected by the procedural rules. He explores the rationale for the rule of privilege and the flaws in the rationale.

B. Thanki QC et al., *The Law of Privilege*, 2nd edn (Oxford University Press, 2011).

> This is a leading practitioner's text on the law of privilege. This text is extremely comprehensive. It covers the fundamental principles of legal professional privilege (both legal advice privilege and litigation privilege), without prejudice privilege and the privilege against self-incrimination.

A. Zuckerman, 'Without prejudice interpretation – with prejudice negotiations: *Oceanbulk Shipping and Trading SA v TMT Asia Ltd*' (2011) E&P 232.

> This article provides a detailed and highly analytical commentary on the decision of the Supreme Court in *Oceanbulk Shipping and Trading SA* v. *TMT Asia Ltd.*

Index

485